KOREA
BUSINESS

World Trade Press
Country Business Guides

CHINA Business
HONG KONG Business
JAPAN Business
KOREA Business
MEXICO Business
SINGAPORE Business
TAIWAN Business

KOREA
BUSINESS

The Portable Encyclopedia
For Doing Business With Korea

Christine A. Genzberger   Edward G. Hinkelman
David E. Horovitz   William T. LeGro
Jonathan W. Libbey   Charles Smithson Mills
James L. Nolan   Stacey S. Padrick
Karla C. Shippey, J.D.   Kelly X. Wang
Chansonette Buck Wedemeyer   Alexandra Woznick

Auerbach International • Baker & McKenzie
CIGNA Property and Casualty • Ernst & Young
Far Eastern Economic Review • Foreign Trade
Korea Trade Promotion Corporation (KOTRA)
Reed Publishing (USA) Inc.

Series Editor: Edward G. Hinkelman

WORLD
TRADE
PRESS ®

Resources for International Trade

1505 Fifth Avenue
San Rafael, California 94901
USA

Published by World Trade Press
1505 Fifth Avenue
San Rafael, CA 94901
USA

Cover and book design: Brad Greene
Illustrations: Eli Africa
Color Maps: Gracie Artemis
B&W maps: David Baker
Desktop Publishing: Kelly R. Krill and Gail R. Weisman
Charts and Graphs: David Baker and Kelly R. Krill
Prepublication Review: Aanel Victoria

Library of Congress Cataloging-in-Publication Data
S. Korea business : the portable encyclopedia for doing business with
    S. Korea / Christine Genzberger . . . [et al.].
        p. cm. – (World Trade Press country business guides)
    Includes bibliographical references and index.
    ISBN 0-9631864-4-2 : $24.95
        1. Korea (South)—Economic conditions—1960-   2. Korea (South)—
    Economic policy—1960-   3. Investments, Foreign—Government policy—
    Korea (South) 4. International business enterprises—Korea (South)
    I. Genzberger, Christine. II. Title: South Korea business.
    III. Series.
    HC467.S216 1994   93-45975
    658.8'48'095195–dc20   CIP

Printed in the United States of America

ACKNOWLEDGMENTS

Contributions of hundreds of trade and reference experts have made possible the extensive coverage of this book.

We are indebted to numerous international business consultants, reference librarians, travel advisors, consulate, embassy, and trade mission officers, bank officers, attorneys, global shippers and insurers, and multinational investment brokers who answered our incessant inquiries and volunteered facts, figures, and expert opinions.

A special note of gratitude is due to those at the U.S. Department of Commerce, the Korea Trade Promotion Corporation (KOTRA), and the Singapore Trade Development Board.

We relied heavily on the reference librarians and resources available at the Marin County Civic Center Library, Marin County Law Library, San Rafael Public Library, San Francisco Public Library, University of California at Berkeley libraries, and U.S. Department of Commerce Library in San Francisco.

Thank you to attorneys Robert T. Yahng and Anne M. Kelleher, with Baker & McKenzie, San Francisco, Ross Meador, with Morrison & Foerster, San Francisco, and Kim & Chang, Seoul, and Dennis Kim, Law Offices of Dennis Paul Kim, Santa Clara, who spent precious time in assisting us with the law section. We also extend our sincere appreciation to Barry Tarnef, with CIGNA Property and Casualty Co., who graciously supplied information on world ports, and to John Robb, who offered his resources on Korea.

We also acknowledge the valuable contributions of Philip B. Auerbach of Auerbach International, San Francisco, for translations; all the patient folks at Desktop Publishing of Larkspur, California; and Sun June Bae, Leslie Endicott, and Susan August for reviewing, proofing, and correcting down to the smallest details.

Thanks go to Elizabeth Karolczak for establishing the World Trade Press Intern Program, and to the Monterey Institute of International Studies for its assistance.

To Jerry and Kathleen Fletcher, we express our deep appreciation for their immeasurable support during this project.

Very special thanks to Mela Hinkelman whose patience, understanding, generosity, and support made this project possible.

DISCLAIMER

We have diligently tried to ensure the accuracy of all of the information in this publication and to present as comprehensive a reference work as space would permit. In determining the contents, we were guided by many experts in the field, extensive hours of research, and our own experience. We did have to make choices in coverage, however, because the inclusion of everything one could ever want to know about international trade would be impossible. The fluidity and fast pace of today's business world makes the task of keeping data current and accurate an extremely difficult one. This publication is intended to give you the information that you need in order to discover the information that is most useful for your particular business. As you contact the resources within this book, you will no doubt learn of new and exciting business opportunities and of additional international trading requirements that have arisen even within the short time since we published this edition. If errors are found, we will strive to correct them in preparing future editions. The publishers take no responsibility for inaccurate or incomplete information that may have been submitted to them in the course of research for this publication. The facts published indicate the result of those inquiries and no warranty as to their accuracy is given.

Contents

Introduction

South Korea, officially known as the Republic of Korea (ROK), is one of the world's most dynamic economies. An agricultural backwater with relatively few natural resources, it was dominated by its much-larger neighbors, China and Japan, throughout much of its turbulent history. Between 1950 and 1953 the Korean Peninsula was the scene of a devastating war between the north and the south and subsequently served as a focal point of East-West tensions throughout the Cold War.

Since the 1950s South Korea has built a modern, internationally oriented industrial economy largely from scratch. This economy, the third-largest in Asia, is based on low-cost, high-quality export production. It has grown at an average rate of more than 17.5 percent per year between 1962 and 1992. South Korea is also the thirteenth-largest trading economy in the world. Its trade has quadrupled since 1980, growing at an annual rate of more than 12 percent.

Ranked sixth in the world among newly industrialized countries in the 1993 *World Competitiveness Report*, South Korea is a market well worth investigating from a number of perspectives. For buyers, South Korea can provide a wide range of competitive goods at virtually any level of sophistication. It is a leading producer of automobiles and parts; ships; electronics, including consumer, imaging, and computer equipment and components, particularly semiconductors; machinery and advanced machine tools; steel products; chemicals; textiles, apparel, and footwear; and toys and sporting goods, among many other items. Its businesses can handle anything from the smallest to the largest orders.

For sellers, South Korea needs a wide range of agricultural and industrial raw materials, intermediate components, and specialty items to feed its active industries. Both the upgrading of its industrial base and its large public- and private-sector development projects require materials, capital goods, and services. And the rising demands of South Korea's newly unleashed consumers offer opportunities to place goods in the country's rapidly developing consumer market. South Korea has relied on Japan for many goods, but the strength of the yen has made Japanese products less competitive, opening up opportunities for new suppliers.

For manufacturers South Korea has a pool of well-educated semi-skilled to highly skilled labor experienced in the areas already noted as well as in many others. In addition to its generally advanced industrial plant, South Korea has built a variety of special production facilities, including free-export zones and high-technology science towns. This infrastructure offers a competitive base for a variety of outsourcing needs.

For investors South Korea is in the process of opening up additional areas of its economy that had previously been off-limits to foreigners, including its growing service and financial sectors. It particularly encourages foreign participation in its emerging high-technology industries and in the development of key technologies and targeted product groups, offering substantial tax breaks, operating exemptions, and other incentives.

The South Korean miracle is beginning to show signs of both maturity and age. South Korea is changing the focus of its economy to high- and mid-level technologies, and high-value-added, clean, capital-intensive products as it gives up some of its edge in low-cost, low-technology production. The power of its large business organizations, the *chaebol*, and the adaptability of its small- and medium-sized businesses argue that it will successfully make the transition to a new economy. South Koreans are notable for being among the hardest workers in the world.

South Korea is also making the transition to a more open and democratic political system after years of authoritarian rule, although it maintains a core of stability within its pro-business government. The overall pace and level of change are expected to accelerate over the near term, making South Korea one of the most complex and challenging—as well as one of the most compelling—places on the globe to do business.

SOUTH KOREA Business was designed by businesspeople experienced in international markets to give you an overview of how things actually work and what current conditions are in South Korea. It will give you the head start you need as a buyer, seller, manufacturer, or investor to be able to evaluate and operate in South Korean markets. Further, it tells you where to go to get more specific information in greater depth.

The first chapter discusses the main elements of the country's **Economy,** including its development, present situation, and the forces determining its future prospects. **Current Issues** explains the top four concerns affecting the country and its next stage of development. The **Opportunities** chapter presents 16 major areas of interest to importers and 19 major areas for exporters plus 10 additional hot prospects. Discussions of nine major sectoral growth areas and a section on special trade zones and other specialized facilities follow. The chapter also clarifies the nature of the government procurement that will drive South Korea's Five-Year Development Plan with its focus on multibillion dollar telecommunications, transportation, construction, environmental, energy, and aerospace programs. **Foreign Investment** details policies, incentives, regulations, procedures, and restrictions, with particular reference to South Korea's drive to develop its emerging high-technology sector.

Although South Korea is banking on high-technology as the wave of the future, it remains a highly diversified export-oriented economy with many thriving low- and medium-technology operations. The **Foreign Trade, Import Policy & Procedures**, and **Export Policy & Procedures** chapters delineate the nature of South Korea's trade: what and with whom it trades, trade policy, and the practical information, including nuts-and-bolts procedural requirements, necessary to trade with it. The **Industry Reviews** chapter outlines South Korea's 17 most prominent industries and their competitive position from the standpoint of a businessperson interested in taking advantage of these industries' strengths or in exploiting their competitive weaknesses. **Trade Fairs** provides a comprehensive listing of trade fairs in South Korea, complete with contact information, and spells out the best ways to maximize the benefits offered by these chances to see and be seen.

Business Travel offers practical information on how to travel in South Korea, including travel requirements, resources, internal travel, local customs, and ambience, as well as comparative information on accommodations and dining in Seoul and Pusan, the country's two main business markets. **Business Culture** provides a user-friendly primer on local business style, mind-set, negotiating practices, and numerous other tips designed to improve your effectiveness, avoid inadvertent gaffes, and generally smooth the way in doing business with South Koreans. **Demographics** presents the basic statistical data needed to assess the South Korean market, while **Marketing** outlines resources, approaches, and specific markets on the island, including five ways to build a good business relationship and five ways to help your local agent.

Business Entities & Formation discusses recognized business entities and registration procedures for setting up operations in South Korea. **Labor** assembles information on the availability, capabilities, and costs of labor in South Korea, as well as terms of employment and business-labor relations. **Business Law** interprets the structure of the South Korean legal system, giving a digest of substantive points of commercial law prepared from Martindale-Hubbell with additional material from the international law firm of Baker & McKenzie. **Financial Institutions** outlines the workings of the financial system, including banking and financial markets, and the availability of financing and services needed by foreign businesses. **Currency & Foreign Exchange** explains the workings of South Korea's complicated foreign exchange system. **International Payments** is an illustrated step-by-step guide to using documentary collections and letters of credit in trade with South Korea. Ernst & Young's **Corporate Taxation** and **Personal Taxation** provide the information on tax rates, provisions, and status of foreign operations and individuals needed to evaluate a venture in the country.

Ports & Airports, prepared with the help of CIGNA Property and Casualty Company, gives current information on how to physically access the country. The **Business Dictionary,** a unique resource prepared especially for this volume in conjunction with Auerbach International, consists of more than 425 entries focusing specifically on South Korean business and idiomatic usages to provide the businessperson with the basic means for conducting business in South Korea. **Important Addresses** lists more than 700 South Korean government agencies and international and foreign official representatives; local and international business associations; trade and industry associations; financial, professional, and service firms; transportation and shipping agencies; media outlets; and sources of additional information to enable businesspeople to locate the offices and the help they need to operate in South Korea. Full-color, detailed, up-to-date **Maps** aid the business traveler in getting around the major business venues in South Korea.

SOUTH KOREA Business gives you the information you need both to evaluate the prospect of doing business in South Korea and to actually begin doing it. It is your invitation to this fascinating society and market. Welcome.

Economy

South Korea, a proud nation with a long history, has existed as an industrial modernizing economy only since the early 1960s. Since then, it has achieved a developmental miracle through hard work and government encouragement of its export-oriented economy.

South Korea—The Republic of Korea (ROK)—is located between China and Japan on the southern half of the irregularly shaped Korean peninsula, which projects south from the Chinese mainland. North Korea, officially the Democratic People's Republic of Korea (DPRK) occupies the northern half. South Korea covers 45 percent of the peninsula, and it is slightly larger in size than Hungary or Portugal, slightly smaller than Iceland, and about the size of the US state of Kentucky. A north-south trending ridge of high mountains on its east coast grades into relatively flat coastal plains in the west and south. Some 70 percent of South Korea's territory consists of mountainous or broken, upland terrain. About 67 percent of South Korea is forested, 21 percent is arable, and 1 percent is grasslands. The remaining 11 percent is divided among developed urban areas, inland waters, and bare ground. Relatively poor in natural resources, the country does have exploitable reserves of coal, tungsten, graphite, molybdenum, and lead as well as hydropower from its many streams.

In 1992 South Korea's 99,237 square km (38,305 square miles) of territory supported a population exceeding 43.7 million. With an average population density of nearly 440 per square km (about 1,140 per square mile)—greater than that of either Japan or India—South Korea is the fourth most densely populated nation in the world. More than 70 percent of South Korea's citizens live in urban areas, and this percentage is expected to increase to nearly 80 percent by decade's end. Urban overpopulation and rural depopulation, with economic marginality of the rural areas, will be the inevitable result. Some 25 percent of the country's people already live in or around the capital of Seoul, and nearly half reside in the

country's six largest cities, each of which has a population of greater than 1 million.

Korea is extremely homogeneous ethnically, and the highly developed national identity of its people separates them from neighboring Asian peoples. The only sizable minorities in Korea are resident Chinese, variously estimated to number between 20,000 and 50,000; a shifting contingent of United States military personnel, numbering around 40,000; and several thousand foreign business and technical people centered in Seoul. The total foreign minority population is estimated at around 100,000, about 0.2 percent of the total.

Korea has historically been an exporter of high value goods. From the start of its existence as a modern nation state, South Korea has relied on the export of contemporary high-value-added manufactures to secure its place in the world.

HISTORY OF THE ECONOMY

Premodern Korea

Korea's beginnings date to the legendary culture hero, Tangun, who established a kingdom in 2333 BC. Korea received its first exposure to the outside world when it fell at least partially under the influence of China during the Han dynasty's expansion around the beginning of the Christian era. After the collapse of the Han dynasty, local kingdoms flourished in Korea, trading and serving as middlemen between China and Japan. During this period, Korea introduced to Japan many of the arts and crafts that would later become hallmarks of Japanese culture.

Near the end of this period, the smallest of the Korean Three Kingdoms, Shilla, allied itself with the Chinese Tang dynasty to gain ascendancy over its neighbors. However, the Koreans subsequently had to fight off the expansionist Tangs. After repelling the Chinese, the Three Kingdoms were unified in AD 676. The Koryo Kingdom (918-1392), which followed and from which the name Korea is derived, was disrupted by the Mongols, and replaced by the reform-oriented Choson dynasty, also known as the Yi dynasty (1392-1910). The Choson replaced Buddhism with Confucianism and codified Korean language and culture. Yi leaders fought off invasions by the Japanese in the late 1500s and by the Manchus in the early 1600s, maintaining a tenuous independence under Chinese protection throughout the 18th and 19th centuries. Korea's conservative rulers kept the country isolated despite increasingly importunate overtures from the West, and it was during this period that Korea became known as the Hermit Kingdom.

The Japanese Period

During the late 19th century, China struggled to maintain its sovereignty against Western inroads, while nearby Japan was involved in rapid industrialization. Korea was caught in the middle, falling victim to maneuvering among the Chinese, the Japanese, and the Russians. Japan bested China in the Sino-Japanese War of 1894 and established its dominance in the Far East by defeating Russia in 1895. Japan began to interfere more in Korean affairs, and finally annexed Korea as a colony in 1910.

Although the Japanese developed Korea's economy, educational system, and infrastructure, their rule was harsh and their motives were far from altruistic, because the economy that they constructed was designed to benefit Japan, not the Koreans, who were treated as inferiors and in many cases displaced by Japanese immigrants fleeing the overcrowding at home. As Japan became increasingly embroiled in the Pacific War (1931-1945), it exploited Korea relentlessly. By the time of Japan's defeat in 1945, Korea's economy was in a shambles.

Partition and Conflict

After World War II the USSR administered Korea's northern half and the United States administered its southern half. As the Cold War developed, the two superpowers jockeyed for position, and Korea became a pawn. United Nations-mandated elections became a sticking point. It was not until 1948 that such elections were held in the south under United States auspices. The southern half of the country was subsequently granted independence as the Republic of Korea (ROK). The Soviets simultaneously set up the Communist Democratic People's Republic of Korea (DPRK) in the north.

The DPRK attacked the ROK in 1950, precipitating the Korean War (1950-1953). When United States-led UN forces drove back the invaders, China entered to prevent the defeat of the Communist North, a move that prolonged the conflict until a cease-fire was finally arranged in 1953. The resulting standoff has lasted since 1953. Hostility between the two Koreas periodically ebbs and flows, and currently appears to be entering a period of heightened tension. The continued large United States military presence and, in recent years, the restraint that the North's Chinese and Soviet patrons have urged on it as they began to open up their own societies have prevented major blowups. There has been little progress toward resolution, although successive South Korean governments have made unification at least nominally a key element of their policies.

The DPRK, under Kim Il Sung, its only leader since the immediate post-World War II period, has stagnated socially and economically. It is now perhaps the most intransigent, closed, unreconstructed Stalinist society in the world. Its rigid centrally-planned economy has deteriorated substantially in recent years. Meanwhile, the south has grown and prospered until it has twice the population and its economy is ten times the size of that of its backward neighbor to the north.

Postwar Political Developments

Korea was devastated by the war fought over most of the peninsula. Seoul changed hands four times, and it was essentially destroyed in the fighting, while much of the country was denuded as Koreans tried to keep warm and scrounge a living during three years of combat, uncertainty, and economic disruption. The social and infrastructural destruction caused by the war and subsequent tensions—the two Koreas have remained at war since 1953—forestalled major development, and Korea's economy remained basically agricultural until the late 1950s. The situation was exacerbated by the presence in the south of a weak and corrupt civilian government headed by Syngman Rhee.

The military pressured Rhee to resign in 1960, and a short-lived successor civilian government was overthrown by a coup in 1961. A military junta ruled by fiat until a new constitution was promulgated in 1963, allowing coup leader Park Chung Hee officially to take over as president. Park held the position for 16 years, although it required the imposition of martial law in 1972 to keep him in power. He was assassinated by disgruntled associates in 1979.

After another, very brief attempt by a civilian government to rule, another military coup brought Chun Doo-Hwan to power in 1980. Unrest spread during the 1980s as increasingly broad segments of South Korea's population became disenchanted with Chun's heavy-handed rule. A series of bloody riots and the government's decision—later rescinded—to execute prominent members of the opposition on trumped-up charges of treason increased internal tensions and attracted international disapproval.

By 1988 the government had realized that it would have to allow some liberalization, although it was unprepared for the degree of change that the

Korea's Gross National Product (GNP)

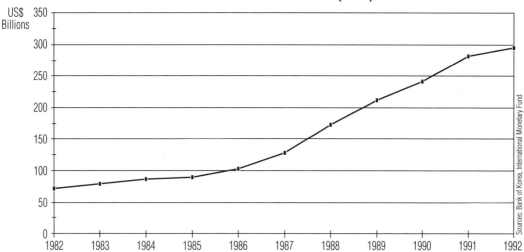

Sources: Bank of Korea, International Monetary Fund

public forced on it once the floodgates were opened. Chun's hand-picked successor, Roh Tae Woo, was elected by a bare plurality amid charges of electoral fraud. However, the opposition also fielded competing candidates, splitting the vote and preventing a united effort to defeat the official candidate.

With the new government less able to rule by decree, negotiations began in earnest to restructure the Korean political landscape. In 1990 the ruling Democratic Justice Party merged with the opposition Reunification Democratic Party and New Democratic Republican Party to form the Democratic Liberal Party (DLP). The remaining parties cried foul, but merged themselves to form the opposition Democratic Party (DP).

Local elections were held in 1991 for the first time since the military had deposed the civilian government 30 years before. The results firmly established the DLP in the lead. The DLP lost its majority in the legislative elections in 1992, which analysts regarded as a wake up call, the result of popular concern over the worsening economic situation. By the time the DLP was preparing for the first free presidential election to be held since 1961, the party was ready to try something different to regain its position. Kim Young Sam, a dissident and former opposition party member, was elected by a comfortable margin as an outsider promising political and economic reform. Kim took office in February 1993 with a populist agenda to clean up corruption and stimulate the lagging economy.

Postwar Economic Development

Park Chung Hee is widely credited as the author of South Korea's economic miracle. He instituted a de facto police state, implementing a series of economic and social development plans within a repressive framework that guaranteed the control and stability necessary to carry them through without serious opposition. The government's assessment in the early 1960s was that South Korea's population and economy was too small and too poor to support a consumption-driven economy, and so it encouraged the development of an export-oriented, manufacturing based economy. These policies, largely underwritten by United States government aid and US private investment, have driven the development of South Korea's economy.

As several other Asian countries have done, South Korea pursued its economic development through a series of Five-Year Plans. The first such plan was instituted in 1962. Although it paid some attention to agriculture and infrastructure, especially power generation, it set the pattern for subsequent development by decreeing an industrially-focused, export-led economy.

During the initial phase in the 1960s development focused on exports of low-tech light manufactures, such as textiles, toys, and footwear, and industrial commodities, such as cement and mining products. Once South Korea had an industrial base, the country shifted its focus to heavy industries, such as steel, shipbuilding, petrochemicals, and heavy equipment, in the 1970s. The progress toward increasingly value-added industries continued during the 1980s as South Korea became a significant player in world markets in the areas of automobiles, electronics, and semiconductors. In the mid-1980s South Korea also recognized the need to improve its social infrastructure.

As South Korea moves into the 1990s its emphasis is on becoming more competitive in world markets where low-tech, labor-intensive production is flowing to less-developed, lower cost locations. After flirting with the idea of trying to become a high-tech powerhouse, Korea's new administration has decided to focus on doing better what it already does well. Priorities include improved quality control, which has suffered recently, and the development of mid-level technologies.

SIZE OF THE ECONOMY

Known variously as one of the newly industrialized countries (NICs), Asian Tigers, and Little Dragons, South Korea boasts an economy that is the third largest in Asia after Japan and China. The absolute dollar value of its economy makes South Korea the 15th largest economy in the world, placing it in the company of Mexico, which is much larger, and of Australia, which is much wealthier. The country is the fifth largest exporter in Asia, after Japan, Hong Kong, China, and Taiwan. Korea's gross domestic product (GDP) in 1992 was US$296.3 billion, up from US$283 billion in 1991. The South Korean economy is also highly centralized geographically: in 1992 the Seoul metropolitan area accounted for 40 percent of total gross national product (GNP).

South Korea's economy grew at an average annual rate of greater than 17.5 percent in nominal terms from US$2.3 billion in 1962 to US$237.9 billion in 1990. However, the rate of increase in the GDP fell from 9.2 percent in 1990, to 8.4 percent in 1991, and to 4.7 percent in 1992, its worst performance since 1980. For the first six months of 1993, GDP increased at an annual rate of 3.9 percent, below the government's already modest target of 5.7 percent. Preliminary figures for 1993 suggest that growth was about 4.5 to 4.75 percent, about even with that experienced in 1992. Analysts estimate that the South Korean economy will grow at a 6 to 7 percent rate in 1994.

Korea's per capita gross national product (GNP), a paltry US$87 in 1962, had grown to US$6,811 in 1992, which places it ahead of most struggling Eastern European nations and on a par with such modest competitors as Guam, Macao, and New Caledonia, far lower than one would expect for an industrialized, exporting giant. Boosting this income figure is an unstated goal of the administration.

CONTEXT OF THE ECONOMY

Government Involvement

The transformation of South Korea from a war-torn backwater with a subsistence economy to a largely industrialized nation in less than 40 years has been accomplished through substantial direction from Korea's authoritarian government. In South Korea's so-called *command-capitalist system*, enterprises are privately owned, but government agencies give them detailed *administrative guidance*. One illustration of the government's involvement on the micro-level: until

1993 Finance Ministry bureaucrats appointed the senior officers of private banks. Although the political and economic process is slowly opening up, the government continues to exercise a high degree of control through a multitude of bureaucracies.

Despite the government's heavy-handed role in the economy, South Korea does not have a heavy roster of state-run enterprises. Although there are about 30 state-run companies dominating such important industries as steel, oil refining, chemicals, and utilities, the state sector is not considered to be of major importance in the functioning of South Korea's economy. The focal point is instead the *chaebol*.

Korean Big Business

Similar to the large Japanese trading companies that they are loosely modeled after, the *chaebol* are huge, big-name, highly diversified, often vertically-integrated conglomerates with a distinctly Korean flavor. Having originated as family businesses founded by charismatic patriarchs following World War II, these businesses often remain family owned and operated. There were officially 61 of these behemoths in 1991, up from 53 in 1990, as defined by total revenues, capital, profits, and credit lines. Hyundai, Samsung, Lucky-Goldstar, and Daewoo are the largest and best known. Each group usually has a minimum of 20 subsidiaries and operates in all major industries across the economy. In fact, the *chaebol* have come under fire for overdiversification, unfair trade practices, violation of restrictions on direct involvement in the financial sector, and such harmful activities as real estate speculation. Revenues of the top 30 *chaebol* were equal to 80 percent of South Korea's GDP in 1992, and the *chaebol* account for about one-third of all industrial production, which forms the core of the Korean economy.

Critics say that the *chaebol* regularly use profits from their more successful operations to subsidize their less successful units, thus keeping a finger in every pie and freezing out would-be competitors and smaller rivals. Such critics also accuse the *chaebol* of acting collusively, dividing up projects, businesses, and territories among themselves in back room deals between each other and the bureaucracy in which they get their way due to the amount of money and pressure they can bring to bear. It is further argued that such oligopolistic manipulation, which helped direct a developing economy in the past, ill serves Korea's current maturing economy.

The *chaebol* historically have provided much of the impetus for Korea's economic success. Their investment decisions continue to drive the economy, and this fact concerns the government. With capital investment increasing by only 1 percent in 1992 and an estimated 3 percent in 1993, after levels as high as 18 percent during the late 1980s and early 1990s,

Korea's economy could slow even more without the accustomed investments of the *chaebol*. However, the *chaebol* essentially have completed their near-term investment plans, and they seem to be taking a wait-and-see attitude regarding the new government and the economy in general before undertaking any new spending.

The *chaebol* are politically as well as economically powerful, and they have a vested interest in maintaining the status quo. Because of their size and pivotal position, they effectively exercise veto power over government plans and reforms. According to its critics the government caved in to the *chaebol* in early 1994 on a major telecomminications upgrade program, effectively allowing the *chaebol* to allocate the contracts instead of pursuing open bidding. Disappointed observers noted that despite good intentions, the reform government's clout seems to have been undermined by the relatively weak economy in its efforts to tame the *chaebol* and has conceded this round to the *chaebol*.

However, even the *chaebol* are recognizing that they cannot conduct business as usual if they want to compete in the new economic environment in which simply having the longest average workweek in the world is no longer enough to pile up profits. Nor can they continue to insulate themselves from an increasingly global market system that requires a level of responsiveness to which they are unaccustomed. The *chaebol* have become ponderously large, hierarchical, and inefficient. They were founded and run by authoritarian, hands-on tycoons, many of whom are aging and passing from the scene. Many *chaebol* must address issues of management succession, and they must also figure out how to inject new blood into an overblown structure that has rewarded loyalty rather than innovation.

Small Business

The government and the *chaebol* dominate the Korean economy so completely that they overshadow the numerous small business operations that make up the majority of its businesses. While the *chaebol* account for one-third of South Korea's industrial production and one-third of its exports, the bulk of the remaining two-thirds is produced by small- to medium-sized businesses.

The Confucian emphasis on hierarchy and hard work is rooted in Korea's rural past, when small, family-oriented operations were the dominant economic unit. Although the emergence of large companies has resulted in the rise of both a company-oriented worker and a professional middle class, most business is very hands-on. The level of entrepreneurialism may not reach that found in some other Asian societies and economies, but the level of labor inputs is challenged by none.

THE UNDERGROUND ECONOMY

While government intervention has allowed South Korea's economy to develop remarkably, it also has resulted in a great deal of complex and often rather arbitrary regulation. At least partially because of the level of government control on the micro-level, Korea has relatively little in the way of a parallel underground economy per se. Nevertheless, bureaucratic overregulation offers numerous ways in which to operate extralegally, and such measures have traditionally been necessary to do business effectively. In 1992 some observers estimated the underground economy at nearly US$40 billion, equal to nearly 14 percent of GNP.

Bribery, graft, kickbacks, and gift giving are highly developed and as yet an essential part of business in South Korea, which has been notorious for the level and pervasiveness of corruption. There are many regulations, they are often unpublished, and they are selectively enforced. As a result, there are opportunities for corruption at all levels. Rules, even those with statutory standing, have usually been considered open to interpretation, and the degree of interpretive leeway increases the higher up one is within the hierarchy and the greater one's political clout.

The new administration of President Kim Young Sam has made the attack on corruption the centerpiece of its program, going so far as to arrest and jail several highly placed business and political figures. Others have fled the country to avoid indictment. In August 1993 Kim also decreed an end to the use of fictitious, so-called *false name* financial accounts, a widespread means of hiding ownership and concealing cash of questionable origin. The move could backfire because in addition to providing the wherewithal for questionable dealings, the false name market is heavily used by small firms that either cannot obtain or cannot afford scarce conventional financing. Estimates place the value of the false name market as high as 10 percent of all money market funds and 30 percent of the total market value of listed equities on South Korea's stock exchange.

The entrenched bureaucrats and powers that be are resisting wholesale change in the traditional ways of doing business, and even President Kim acknowledges that real change will be very slow. Nevertheless, observers say that Kim's anti-corruption campaign is already beginning to make a difference, with greater efforts at transparency being noted in the operation of some agencies, along with a general increase in adherence to certain rules that had been allowed to go unenforced. And the removal of the shield provided by the false name accounts has also had an immediate and salutary effect in making it more difficult to conceal improper dealings. However, because the situation is in flux, it is difficult, especially for outsiders, to know whether to follow the old rules or the new rules when operating in Korea.

Intellectual Property Rights

Intellectual property rights are an issue in South Korea, which nominally protects most patents, copyrights, trademarks, and similar rights, although it hedges in some areas, such as pharmaceuticals, citing the greater good and the need to have affordable access to medicines for its failure to provide protection. Enforcement has increased over the last two years, largely due to the strenuous protests of Korea's major trading partners, and has received an added boost from Kim's campaign, but it is still considered somewhat lax. Penalties are light and do not serve as much of a deterrent. Infringements include counterfeiting, failure to pay royalties, and failure to hold trade secrets confidential. Although the United States decided in April 1993 not to name Korea a repeat offender on intellectual property rights, the move is seen more as a political gesture of goodwill toward President Kim and his new reform administration rather than an indication that conditions have improved to the point where they are no longer a concern.

Many observers see South Korea's poor history in the area of intellectual property rights protection as a roadblock to its future development because many foreign firms are leery of agreeing to transfer technology to Korean firms for fear that such technology will be unprotected. Hence South Korea has run into problems in gaining access to the types of advanced technology that it needs to carry out its development programs.

INFLATION

Despite the virtually uninterrupted headlong growth that the South Korean economy has experienced over the last quarter century, inflation has been a relatively minor concern. Inflation surged during the 1970s, averaging more than 19 percent annually, but it had shrunk to 1.7 percent in 1984. Rising wages—increases averaged 18 percent a year between 1988 and 1992—have served to drive inflation higher recently. The official inflation rate peaked at 9.3 percent in 1991, fell to 6.8 percent in 1992, and dropped to an annualized rate of 4.6 percent during the first six months of 1993. Forecasters are predicting a rate of increase of 5.6 percent in 1994.

Given the facts that wages have doubled since 1987 and that the depreciation of the Korean won has made goods more expensive, the government's statistics are rather suspect. Real costs seem to be rising much faster than the statistics indicate. As recently as January 1993 Korea's equivalent of the prime rate stood at 14 percent. By June 1993 it had dropped to 9.4 percent. But because the government, not the markets, sets interest rates, the drop does not mean that inflation has in fact abated.

LABOR

South Korea's work force is generally well trained and highly industrious. School attendance is mandatory for six years. Further attendance is encouraged, and a variety of educational options are available.

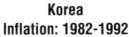

Korea
Inflation: 1982-1992

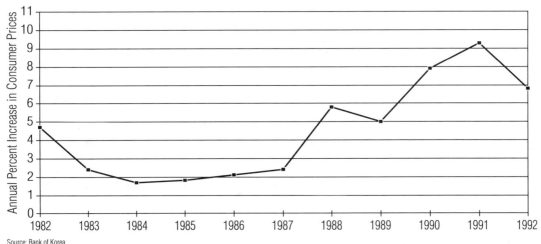

Source: Bank of Korea

Unemployment

Unemployment remained stable in the late 1980s and early 1990s at an average rate of 2.75 percent. In 1992 it stood at 2.4 percent. By June 1993 it had increased to 3 percent, and there were indications that it could go as high as 3.5 percent in 1994, a level it has not reached since 1986. South Korea currently has a shortage of unskilled and semi-skilled personnel, but there are few plans to recruit outside labor, at least partially because of worries about how guest workers would fit into the homogeneous Korean society. Illegal labor is a relatively minor but growing factor.

Unions

Until recently unionization has been a relatively minor factor in South Korea. Military governments had prohibited free union activity and tightly controlled the unions that were allowed to exist since the 1960s. That situation changed in 1987 when union activity was allowed and strikes were legalized as part of the lifting of martial law and the institution of democratic reforms. There were 3,749 labor disputes in 1987. By 1992 the number of disputes, which includes strikes, had dropped to 235, and in 1993 there had been only about 100 registered by midyear. Union membership, which surged to a high of 14 percent of the work force in 1989, had slipped to 12 percent by 1992, although as traditional industrial unions fade, new service industry unions are beginning to flex their muscles.

The government still wields substantial power over labor. For example, in July 1993 it pressured workers at Hyundai to settle for a 4.7 percent wage increase after they had gone out on strike demanding a 16.5 percent raise. The government has frozen

wages for civil servants, and it is jawboning the private sector to remain within a 9 percent guideline for 1993 and 1994, arguing that Korea's cost structure is making it uncompetitive. The government has recently set up a new panel to deal with labor disputes, especially those involving foreign employers, designed to mediate problems before they become major. However, if voluntary restraint doesn't do the trick, the government is capable of mandatory unilateral action. Unions are not as powerful a force as they might seem to be given the highly publicized labor unrest and the sharp wage increases that they have obtained in recent years, although they are firmly established and have been responsible for a significant portion of rising costs.

Labor Costs

In 1992 the average weekly wage in South Korea was US$254.44, plus mandated benefits of 19.9 percent or US$50.63, roughly 20 percent higher than the average weekly wage in Taiwan (US$244) and 15 percent higher than in Singapore (US$261). By contrast, the average weekly wage, including basic benefits, was US$705 in Japan and US$7.37 in China. The figure used for Korea leaves out additional compensation, such as bonuses, allowances, and overtime, which are customary, although not legally required, and which routinely account for 40 percent of the total compensation package, making Korea even less competitive.

Between 1987 and 1992 wages rose at an average annual rate of 18 percent and a total of 109 percent. Some employers report that because of benefits and work rules, actual costs went up by more than 500 percent during the period. Meanwhile productivity rose by only about 50 percent. In 1992 wage hikes

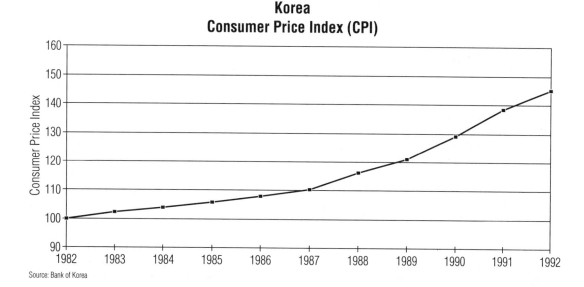

Korea
Consumer Price Index (CPI)

Source: Bank of Korea

Structure of the Korean Economy - 1992

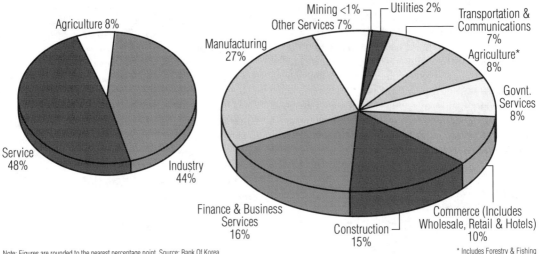

Agriculture 8%

Service 48%

Industry 44%

Manufacturing 27%

Mining <1%

Other Services 7%

Utilities 2%

Transportation & Communications 7%

Agriculture* 8%

Govnt. Services 8%

Commerce (Includes Wholesale, Retail & Hotels) 10%

Construction 15%

Finance & Business Services 16%

Note: Figures are rounded to the nearest percentage point. Source: Bank Of Korea

* Includes Forestry & Fishing

fell slightly to 15 percent and the government was hoping to hold overall wages to a 9 percent rise in 1993 and beyond.

As the Koreans watch their traditionally labor-intensive jobs move offshore, they are beginning to acknowledge that labor costs have gotten out of hand. It remains to be seen whether they can stomach the austerity necessary to make the country competitive on a cost basis again, especially if they don't see comparable sacrifices on the part of business and government.

Workweek

South Korean workers have the longest workweek in Asia: 47.9 hours on average. Korean factory workers rack up an even longer 54-hour average workweek; however, this is down from the 56- and 57-hour weeks that were common a few years ago. The workweek can still reach 60 hours, but it must be specified in the labor contract, and excess hours must be compensated at premium pay rates. The nominal manufacturing workweek is 48 hours, with a 44-hour week for clerical and retail personnel. Staff at small businesses, especially family-run operations, may put in 18-hour days six or even seven days per week.

By comparison, the workweek averages 46.7 hours in Singapore, 46.1 hours in Japan—although Japanese factory workers are down to an average 41 hours— 46 hours in Hong Kong, and 45.5 hours in Taiwan. Among Western industrialized countries, the average workweek is 43.6 hours in the United Kingdom, 39.9 hours in Germany, 39 hours in France, and 34.3 hours in the United States. Koreans are beginning to wonder why their standard of living isn't higher despite the fact that they work the longest hours in Asia. Wages have remained the major issue in labor dis-

putes, but observers expect that hours and other work rules may soon become the sticking point.

SECTORS OF THE ECONOMY

South Korea's economy relies heavily on its manufacturing sector, which in 1992 accounted for 26.8 percent of its GDP. Industry contributes an additional 17.3 percent, agriculture 7.5 percent, and services 48.1 percent. The proportions were very different 30 years ago. In 1962 agriculture accounted for 36.6 percent of GDP, the underdeveloped manufacturing and industrial sector contributed a paltry 14.3 percent, and the service sector, including government, produced the remaining 50.9 percent. As recently as 1986 agriculture contributed 11.7 percent of GDP, manufacturing and industry 42.9 percent, and services 45.4 percent of the total.

The role of agriculture has dropped sharply, and the trend is expected to continue; forecasts place agriculture as contributing less than 5 percent of GDP by decade's end. Although the role of manufacturing and industry has grown mightily since the early 1960s, its share of GDP seems to have stabilized in recent years. Given South Korea's problems with relatively high-priced labor and the lag time needed to substitute higher-value-added manufactures for its traditional lower-end products, observers expect the service sector to grow at the expense of both agriculture and manufacturing and industry, reaching close to a 60 percent share by the year 2000.

Although private consumption is growing—up 220 percent and more than three times in nominal dollar terms between 1984 and 1992—Korea is not a consumer-oriented society. As long as per capita income continues to remain at relatively low levels, consumer spending cannot be expected to drive overall growth in the economy, although it is becoming a more important factor.

In 1990 private consumption in Korea accounted for roughly 57 percent of GDP, with government consumption amounting to 10 percent, and gross domestic fixed capital formation 33 percent—evidence that Korea funded a high percentage of its growth from internal savings. Between 1988 and 1992 average annual fixed investment in South Korea was around 30 percent of GDP, compared to almost 33 percent for Japan and 15 percent for the United States. The government wants to boost such fixed investment to 35 percent.

External debt stood at US$44.5 billion in 1985 and remained, coincidentally, US$44.5 billion as of August 1993. However, in 1985 this figure represented almost 50 percent of GNP, while in 1993 it accounted for a far more manageable 15 percent of GNP. The Korean government has traditionally acted to restrain consumer spending, particularly spending on imports and luxuries, and it has used much of the resulting savings, which have exceeded investment needs, to pay down the foreign debt that it incurred during the early 1980s due to soaring oil prices. The government cannot expect to follow this policy indefinitely, although even at current rates, growth in the economy should allow the government to easily cover its obligations.

AGRICULTURE

Prior to the mid-1950s South Korea's economy was based on subsistence agriculture. Korea is now largely self-sufficient in food production, the major exception being wheat. However, agriculture has played a very small role in the country's modern development. The agricultural sector, which includes forestry and fisheries, accounted for only 7.5 percent of South Korea's GDP in 1992, but it employed 16.7 percent of the work force, primarily on tiny family farms. Agricultural production has remained fairly steady over the last several years, as has the farm population. However, most young people already have left the farm for urban jobs, and the farm population is aging rapidly. Tradition gives the agricultural sector a degree of influence far out of proportion to its importance in the economy. The government has supported land reform, but it heavily subsidizes and protects the outmoded agricultural sector. It has grudgingly agreed to open up certain areas of the agricultural sector to foreign investment, most recently agreeing to allow in foreign rice. However, it has not encouraged such investment.

South Korea's major crops are rice, barley, soybeans, and potatoes. Fruits and vegetables, silk, tobacco, and ginseng are also produced. Cattle, swine, and poultry are the major livestock products. Korea is a major buyer of such commodities as wheat, cotton, livestock feed, and raw hides. It imports few high-value, processed agricultural items, although the government, under pressure primarily from the United States, is slowly liberalizing import restrictions on agricultural products.

Forestry is of minor importance in Korea. Exploitable timber that had not been logged prior to 1945 fell victim to overcutting during and after the Korean War. Reforestation has not been a priority, and the lumbering industry cannot meet domestic demand. Korea is a major supplier of plywood in Asian markets, but it depends on imports of logs rather than domestic timber to feed its plants.

In 1990 South Korea was the world's seventh largest fishing nation, with its fisheries exports reaching US$1 billion. However, the sector is of small importance to the overall economy, and its share is likely to drop as overfishing and international competition slow production worldwide. In contrast to agriculture, the fisheries industry has relatively little political clout.

MANUFACTURING AND INDUSTRY

The manufacturing and industrial sector, which includes mining, utilities, and construction, has driven the growth of South Korea's economy. In 1992 this sector accounted for 44.1 percent of GDP, with manufacturing alone contributing 26.8 percent. At the same time the industrial sector employed about 27 percent of the workforce.

Korea's manufacturing and industrial sector has been in the process of change for some time. In 1970 low-end heavy industrial commodity products, such as bulk chemicals, accounted for 27.3 percent of the sector's production. Mid-range products, such as textiles, contributed 21.2 percent, and high-end, high-value-added products, such as electrical goods and components, produced the remaining 51.5 percent. By 1990 the contribution of low-end commodities had fallen to 9.6 percent, while mid-range items had moved up to 29.4 percent, and sophisticated upper-end items accounted for 61 percent of the sector's output. One reason for this shift lies in South Korea's lost competitiveness in low-end commodity products. Another reason is Korea's massive economies of scale in the production of mid-range and selected high-end items. The numbers also underscore the maturing of Korea's economy and its shift toward increasingly sophisticated manufacturing.

Future Directions

Manufacturing is expected to remain Korea's premier focus. Although still important exports items— Korea produces 9 percent of the world's textiles—

its lower-end, light industrial manufactures, such as textiles, footwear, and toys, are being threatened by lower-cost labor in China and Southeast Asia. Because its traditional strength has been as a manufacturer of low-cost commodity items, Korea is trying to compensate by upgrading the type of articles that it produces and expanding to do business in less sophisticated markets.

South Korea has had some success with high-tech products. However, its real strength is not in innovation but rather in following the leader, especially in mid-range technologies. And although the huge, vertically integrated *chaebol* that dominate the economy don't move rapidly or efficiently, they remain forces to be reckoned with because of their size and power.

Currently the electronics industry is at the forefront of development, shifting from assembly of lower-end consumer and commercial electronics to assembly of higher-end items and production of components and component subassemblies. Parts are also important, particularly semiconductors and integrated circuits. Auto parts and machinery, along with specialty chemicals and specialty steel, are other dynamic areas of the economy.

The Construction Sector

The construction sector, including shipbuilding and ship repair, is important in Korea. South Korea became a major exporter of heavy construction contracts during the 1970s and 1980s, primarily to the Middle East. The construction industry has since lost some of its luster, due mainly to its surging cost structure. However, Korean firms have recently won contracts in Southeast Asia and the Middle East. South Korea is marketing its construction expertise to Russia and China, and it has obtained contracts in Japan, Taiwan, Singapore, and the United States. Domestic construction helped pull Korea out of its recession in 1989-1991, but the government's attempts to cool off the economy by limiting growth in construction to 10 percent a year will probably keep construction from making a major contribution in the near term.

South Korea is the world's second largest shipbuilder, surpassed only by Japan. Despite heavy government subsidies, the industry is in trouble as a result of increasing costs, outmoded technology, and low financial returns. Other nations are pressuring Korea to reduce its subsidies and protectionism. South Korea's shipbuilders will probably lose market share as they struggle to adjust to an increasingly competitive environment. (Refer to "Opportunities" and "Industry Reviews" chapters.)

SERVICES

South Korea's service sector, which includes trade and commerce, transportation, communications, finance, health care, and business and government services, contributed 48.1 percent of GDP in 1992, far surpassing the contribution of manufacturing and industry. Services, which already employ about 56.3 percent of the workforce, are expected to take on an even greater role in the economy in coming years. The service sector is generally considered to be underdeveloped for such a major economy.

Finance

Finance, which represents 16.3 percent of GDP, is the largest single subsector within services, and the government is pushing to upgrade Korea's financial capabilities and make it an international financial center by the end of the decade. Progress to date has been halting. A business-as-usual attitude and restrictive regulations have prevented Korea from opening its financial system to the degree necessary to attract major foreign accounts away from their regular venues.

Korea's stock exchange, which in mid-1993 had a market value of US$118.8 billion, was tied with Malaysia's for the position of the seventh largest equity securities market in the world. Returns have outpaced those in the developed world, but lag behind those in other emerging markets. Share prices have fallen by about 12 percent since the market's speculative high point in 1989.

President Kim further roiled the market with his emergency declaration requiring the closing of all so-called false name accounts, which are commonly used in South Korea to conceal ownership, sources of funds, and taxable income. The market immediately fell by 8 percent, an indication of the less than open way in which financial affairs had been conducted in South Korea. Direct foreign ownership of shares is still hampered by restrictive limits and regulations; the proposed sale of shares in the 30 government enterprises is expected to be restricted to domestic investors. Foreign investors suspect that manipulation by closely affiliated firms and a core of traders is common.

Trade and Commerce

International trade is important to Korea, and it is relatively well developed and sophisticated. Domestic commerce is less developed. Large domestic wholesalers control most domestic markets. These wholesalers are often in a position to dictate terms to manufacturers and retailers alike, and in many cases they operate through exclusive relationships that prohibit competitors from gaining shelf space for their goods. Although the concepts of supermarket, department, and discount stores are gaining

Korea's Foreign Trade

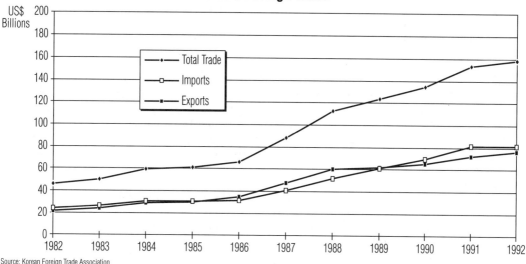

Source: Korean Foreign Trade Association

ground, especially in urban areas, the vast majority of goods and services are distributed through small mom-and-pop stores. And outside the largest centers, the market for upscale consumer goods is poorly developed.

TRADE

In 1991 South Korea was 13th among the world's trading nations, down from 11th the previous year, but still a signal achievement for a country that ranks 26th in the world in population and 103rd in land area and that was destitute in 1953. The government's stated goal is to reach the top ten by the year 2000. In 1992 Korea racked up total trade of US$158.4 billion, up 3.3 percent from the US$153.4 billion recorded in 1991. In June 1993 year-to-year figures suggested that 1993 would see total trade rise by 2.9 percent to US$163 billion. Official projections are for growth in total trade of 6.7 percent to US$169 billion in 1993. Trade has more than tripled during the last 12 years, growing by an average annual rate of 10.6 percent. Only in one of those years—1982— was it less than the previous year's total, and then it slipped by only 2.7 percent.

However, growth is slowing, and it can be expected to stay relatively low by past standards, although even the more sedate rate of expansion is higher than that averaged by economies in the developed world. In the meantime, the weakness of the Korean won against the Japanese yen is adding at least a temporary boost to Korea's export competitiveness. South Korean exports of semiconductors and consumer goods were up by about 50 percent during the first half of 1993, largely due to the strong yen. The problem is that because Japan is still South

Korea's primary supplier, imports purchased from Japan cost more as well.

Exports have grown by an annual 11.3 percent rate over the last 12 years. Growth slowed to an annual average of 4.75 percent during the last five years and reached a high in absolute terms of US$76.6 billion in 1992. Preliminary figures for 1993 put growth in exports at 7.6 percent for the year to about US$82 billion, and authorities believe that 1994 growth will be sustained at around 8 percent. Imports grew by 10 percent a year on average over the last 12 years, and at an average annual rate of 9.6 percent—double that of exports—during the last five years, reaching US$81.8 billion in 1992. The disparity in growth shows both that Korea is gearing up for a shift to more high-tech production, and that its economy is beginning to mature.

Balance of Trade

South Korea's balance of trade was negative from 1953 until 1986, but it showed surpluses between 1986 and 1989, reaching a surplus position high of US$8.9 billion in 1988. In 1990 the balance of trade again turned negative and registered a deficit of US$9.6 billion in 1991. The deficit eased to US$5.2 billion in 1992, and figures for the first six months of 1993 showed it to be US$2.2 billion. Preliminary figures for 1993 indicate that South Korea had a small current account surplus for the year, a result of renewed strong exports.

Over the past 12 years, exports have averaged 49.4 percent of total trade, and imports have averaged 50.6 percent, although these figures mask the seesaw between surplus and deficit. The proportions have fluctuated by as much as 9 percent during the period, ranging from one year in which exports were as low as 44.9 percent of the total to another in which they topped out at 53.9 percent.

South Korea's international reserves stood at US$18.9 billion in June 1993, up from US$14.6 billion a year earlier. Despite these healthy and growing foreign currency reserves, Korea's current account was in a deficit position of US$1.15 billion in June 1993, down from US$4.5 billion the year before and poised to reach surplus territory by year end.

Korea's trade imbalance results largely from the fact that many of its exports have been priced out of the market. Moreover, simply to maintain its exporting operations it must import both raw materials and high value equipment—much of it from Japan, where the strength of the yen hurt it. The bright spot for South Korea may lie in its growing exports to Southeast Asia, China, and Latin America, markets where the current strength of the yen has opened a window of opportunity.

EXPORTS

In 1991 South Korea's main exports were apparel, semiconductors, ships, imaging equipment, synthetic textiles, iron and steel products, footwear, computers, automobiles, and audio equipment, which together accounted for 48 percent of its total exports. Remaining miscellaneous categories each contributed less than 2.5 percent of the total value. In 1992 semiconductors and related electrical components replaced apparel as South Korea's leading export.

Between 1986 and 1990 manufactures of such export products as consumer and office electronics grew by an average rate in excess of 11 percent. Production of videocassette recorders increased by 17.8 percent, of photocopiers by 17.2 percent, and of color television sets by 15.8 percent. The only major cat-

egory to show a decline was telephones, down by an average 8.7 percent. Production of integrated circuits rose by 8.9 percent annually. The automotive industry has also been strong, with an average annual growth of 19.7 percent. Passenger cars were up by 16 percent, and buses and trucks by more than 21 percent, albeit from a low base.

Targeted export categories, such as autos, electronics, metal products, and chemicals, grew between 10 percent and 40 percent in 1992, but even these numbers can't hide a weakening from South Korea's past strength. Traditional light industrial exports have fallen, with footwear dropping in 1991 by 18.6 percent and toys by 28.3 percent. Textiles and apparel eked out a slim 1.9 percent gain. Most other categories, with the exception of high-end synthetic fabrics, either fell or barely held steady.

Although South Korea's export production of labor-intensive commodity manufactures is still strong, its high labor costs are expected to hurt it as lower-cost sources come on line, and the government is trying to focus on higher-value-added heavy industry and technological production to take up the slack. Overall labor-intensive exports have been falling, from 24 percent of the total in 1990 to 17 percent in 1992. The government has targeted semiconductors, cars, specialty steel, and advanced petrochemicals for development as major export products. Internal production of components and assembly of more sophisticated electronic products are also envisioned.

IMPORTS

In 1991 South Korea's main imports were crude oil, semiconductors, petrochemicals, iron and steel, computers, lumber, animal products, engines and

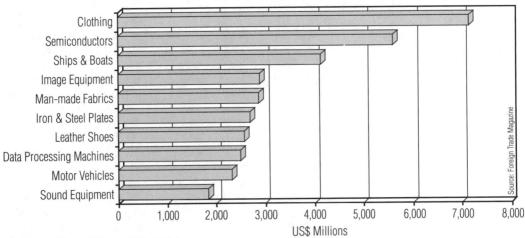

South Korea's Leading Exports By Commodity - 1991

Source: Foreign Trade Magazine

All others: US$37.4 Billion or 52% of total
Total 1991 Exports: US$71.9 Billion

generators, grain, and coal and coke, which together accounted for 35.4 percent of its imports. Other miscellaneous categories represented less than 2 percent of the total. Although the largest individual categories were dominated by raw materials, led by oil with a 9.9 percent share of total imports, imports of machinery made up the largest composite category, reflecting the emphasis that the government has placed on upgrading Korea's industrial capacity, especially in the high-tech area.

TRADING PARTNERS

South Korea's trade is in a process of flux at present, as it adjusts to internal and external changes and seeks new markets that can compensate for its deteriorating competitive position vis-a-vis its traditional markets. In 1991 the United States was still Korea's principal trading partner, taking 25.8 percent of its exports and providing 23.2 percent of its imports. Trade with Japan is increasing, and Japan has surpassed the US as a source of imports.

Together, the United States and Japan took 43 percent of Korea's exports, with other Asian countries—Hong Kong, Singapore, Taiwan, Indonesia, and Malaysia—receiving another 16.4 percent, and developed Western countries took 9.2 percent, while the remaining 31.4 percent was parceled out among other countries, each of which took less than 2 percent of the total. Among import sources, the United States and Japan accounted for 49.1 percent of Korea's purchases. Asian countries—China, Indonesia, Malaysia, and Taiwan—contributed another 10.9 percent, and developed Western nations provided 8.7 percent. Saudi Arabia alone sold 4 percent of South Korea's total imports, a figure that underlines its dependence on foreign energy sources. The re-

maining 27.3 percent of imports came from other sources, each of which represented less than 2 percent of the total.

The United States and South Korea's other trading partners have increasingly pressured it to open its relatively closed economy up to outside businesses and investors. One of Korea's main trade-related goals during the 1990s is to become less reliant on its major trading partners and to find new markets for its products as well as new sources of supply. Although, as already noted, the United States and Japan together account for 43 percent of its total exports and 49 percent of its total imports, South Korea already trades with much of the rest of the world, although its relationships with individual countries account for relatively small percentages of the total. Petroleum imports give Korea strong ties with Middle Eastern nations, and it is developing closer ties with European countries, Canada, Australia, Taiwan, Hong Kong, and Southeast Asian nations. Korea's developing trade relationship with China is a special case, as are its incipient relations with North Korea, Vietnam, and Russia. In fact, the government's economic plan calls for targeting the so-called Northern Countries—socialist or formally socialist countries—as trading partners.

TRADE WITH CHINA

Relations between South Korea and China have traditionally been hostile, the result of China's historically threatening role, its more recent ideological stance, and its support for North Korea during and after the Korean War. Nevertheless, the two countries established indirect trading ties in 1985, and formal diplomatic relations were opened in September 1992. Since 1985 trade has increased rapidly to a

South Korea's Leading Imports By Commodity - 1991

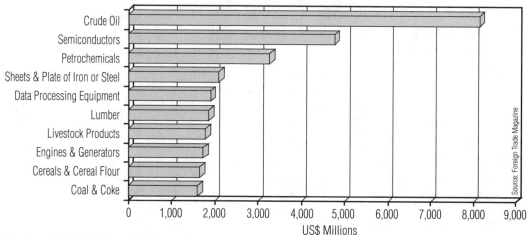

Source: Foreign Trade Magazine

US$ Millions

All others: US$52.7 Billion or 64.7% of total
Total 1991 Imports: US$81.5 Billion

level that should soon make China Korea's third largest trading partner behind the United States and Japan, although China hardly even appears on most lists of South Korea's trade partners.

China is an avid consumer of Korean goods, although until 1993 Korea was importing more than it was been able to export in return. Trade has grown from an estimated US$2.75 billion in 1988 to what some observers estimate to be US$8.2 billion in 1992, up 41 percent from 1991. According to some sources, total trade between the two nations was US$5 billion for the first six months of 1993, and it is expected to hit US$10 billion for all of 1993. Korea's main exports to China are steel and petrochemicals.

South Korean investors also have begun to establish factories in China to take advantage of cheap labor, and Korean investments in China account for 30 percent of total Korean overseas investment. Investment during the first half of 1993 totaled US$630 million. Some observers suggest that the China trade may be Korea's key to regaining its economic position, although they warn that Korea must act both carefully and quickly while the strength of the Japanese yen gives it an opportunity to consolidate its position.

FOREIGN PARTICIPATION IN THE ECONOMY

South Korea's trade-oriented economy depends heavily on foreign participation, although the country still prefers to keep foreigners at arm's length. Many barriers to foreign investment have been removed or scaled back, and by January 1992 about 80 percent of the sectors in Korea's standard industrial classification system were open to direct foreign investment, including 98 percent of industrial and 62 percent of service areas. There is still a negative list of 56 prohibited and 168 restricted categories. Participation in a restricted category requires government approval and the meeting of stringent organizational and local participation requirements when it is allowed at all.

All in all, Korea still is not fully user-friendly for foreign investors. Regulation is a very high hurdle and it often seems to have an anti-foreign bias. Corruption is rampant, and the us-versus-them tone of operations in a homogeneous culture are often difficult for foreigners to overcome. Even when investments are legal and doable, excessive red tape, secret rules, and silent as well as not so silent requests for bribes can slow down the process and make it more costly than it needs to be. The new administration has made major strides in altering this situation, reducing the nature of approvals and cracking down on corruption.

Size of Foreign Participation

By the middle of 1992 cumulative private foreign investment in South Korea since 1962 totaled US$9.9 billion, representing 3,947 separate investments. Japan is the top cumulative foreign investor in Korea with US$4.2 billion or 42 percent of the total, which is invested in some 2,200 projects. The United States is second with cumulative investment of US$2.8 billion—28 percent of the total—in more than 900 businesses. European countries collectively are third, with US$2.3 billion, representing 23 percent of the total in around 500 projects. Other international investors account for the remaining 7 percent—US$700 million, invested in fewer than 300 projects.

The increasing costs of doing business in Korea, development of lower-cost investment alternatives elsewhere in Asia, and the worldwide economic slowdown cut foreign investment in Korea from the high of US$1.4 billion recorded in 1991 to just under US$900 million in 1992. New Japanese investment fell by 31 percent to US$154 million, while European countries cut their year-over-year investments by 65 percent to US$282 million. The United States, Korea's number two investor, did increase its Korean investment by about two-thirds to US$380 million, but even this substantial increase was unable to stem the generally negative tide. The reduction in new investment is exacerbated by actual disinvestment as existing foreign operations have begun to close down and pull out at an increased rate.

Alarmed by this dwindling flow of external capital, South Korea announced revisions in its foreign investment regulations in November 1993. Slated to go into effect in March 1994, these would allow foreigners to buy land for office space and employee housing. Previously foreign entities were only allowed to own manufacturing facilities, and then only under highly restrictive rules. Other provisions, scheduled to go into effect on July 1, 1994, involve a cut in the waiting period for investment approvals, the elimination of limits on high-technology capital investments, and additional tax breaks for foreign investors.

Areas of Investment

Most foreign investment in South Korea has been in the manufacturing and foreign trade sector. The government is trying to direct new investment into high-tech, capital-intensive manufacturing activities via incentives. However, Korea still lacks the technical and infrastructural base needed to support investment in most areas of high-technology. The government will have a hard time selling South Korea to outsiders as a high-tech center until a minimum threshold has been reached and the country can demonstrate that it has the momentum needed to carry the plan forward.

In the services sector, foreign commercial banks

may operate under roughly the same rules as local banks as far as most commercial transactions are concerned. Many firms in Korea have a house bank and require all business to be channeled through it, which limits the options for foreign investors, both as service providers and service consumers. Foreign securities firms, insurance companies, and advertising firms are beginning to make some limited inroads. However legal, accounting, financial services, retailing, transportation, telecommunications, and many areas of consulting and business services are still on the negative list.

Wholesale distribution is limited to 26 sectors, and retail distribution is largely controlled by franchisees who handle only the brands produced by their franchisers. It is difficult for foreigners to break into this closed chain, because they must deal with established distributors who often have existing exclusive commitments. Even when imported goods are available, they are extremely expensive and uncompetitive, and their purchase can subject Koreans to taxation and sanctions for conspicuous consumption. The government also continues to promote localization, whereby it provides domestic businesses with funds and technological support to develop onshore sources that preempt imported products. (Refer to "Foreign Investment" chapter.)

South Korean Overseas Investment

As the global economy becomes a firmly established fact, countries that do not develop their own overseas investment presence will be at a growing disadvantage. Traditionally, Korea has looked abroad only for export markets and import sources and focused its resources internally. In fact, currency restrictions and other government controls discouraged virtually all overseas investment until very recently. Most of Korea's foreign investment has been in the form of trading companies and marketing entities designed to support and sell chaebol products abroad. As its leadership in low-cost production fades, Korea has been forced to deal with some of the countries where costs are lower.

Korea's primary foreign presence is in China, where Koreans are now operating factories that produce the low-end goods that used to be made at home. Operations have not been a total success because the Chinese have been reluctant to allow most products to be sold in China, and reexport of these products has put them in direct competition with Korean goods. Korean investment has tended to center in a few nearby Chinese provinces, and it has put the Koreans in the position of competing with each other for the few resources available in these relatively undeveloped areas.

Korea's Northern Countries strategy of market penetration in formerly socialist economies is off to a good start in China and, to a lesser extent, in Vietnam and Russia, although it has stalled in North Korea for political reasons.

GOVERNMENT ECONOMIC DEVELOPMENT STRATEGY

South Korea is recognizing that it will have to update its traditional command-capitalist economic structure, in which government sets goals and internal parameters that are usually set by markets in freer economies. Although the Korean system has been highly successful for 30 years, it is proving to be less adaptable to the needs of the emerging global economy. Korea has built its modern economy by imitating market leaders, succeeding through plain hard work and authoritarian control that has allowed the trains to run on time. However, Korea must now work not merely harder but also smarter if it wants to keep up, and the old structure is hindering its attempts to realize new goals.

At one point, South Korea considered jumping on the high-tech bandwagon, but it has since backed off, realizing that it lacks the basic social and physical infrastructure that it needs if it wants to become a dominant player in this area over the near-term. The government's strategy is still oriented towards moving upmarket in the areas in which Korea has had an advantage in hopes of reaping the benefits of the learning curve, but it is wary that skipping steps during the process could lead to a nasty tumble. Areas that the government has targeted include semiconductors, cars, specialty steel, and advanced petrochemicals, and has increased its focus on internal production of components and assembly of increasingly sophisticated electronic products.

THE NEW FIVE-YEAR DEVELOPMENT PLAN

In April 1993 President Kim issued a draft outline of what would become South Korea's seventh Five-Year Development Plan, the latest in the series of government documents that have directed Korea's economy since it began its climb to modern industrial status. The proposals presented to date have been weak on specifics and timetables, but they do serve to set the tone for Kim's administrative goals. The plan called for reforms to reduce the role of government in the economy through changes in financial, monetary, tax, and administrative procedures and regulations. The easing of heavy-handed bureaucratic controls over business and finance was singled out for special attention in the reform program.

Although the plan was billed as a get-the-government-off-our-backs measure, it still set fairly detailed prescriptions for enterprises at all levels. It did, however, promise near-term deregulation of many financial rates and procedures as well as customs reform. In the area of finance, the plan proposed to reduce controls over interest rates, with full deregulation to be accomplished by 1997. The banking system was to be restructured. Limits on *chaebol* ownership and control of financial institutions were to be tightened. Political control over monetary policy was to be reduced. And the false name system was to be replaced by a real name system of asset holdings, a goal that has been largely accomplished.

In the area of fiscal reform, the plan proposed new taxes on speculative property transactions and levied a new tax on capital gains. Tax administration is to be computerized to speed reporting and to catch evaders and cheats. In the area of business reform, the plan strengthened the Fair Trade Act to rein in *chaebol*. The government will strongly urge *chaebol* to specialize rather than compete on all fronts. Small business can expect technical and financial support, including soft loans. Spending on research and development was to increase to a 3 to 4 percent share of GDP.

The plan's targets included average growth in GDP of 7 percent a year and an annual expansion in exports of 9.9 percent. Domestic consumption is expected to increase, although it will be controlled so that continued high savings rates offset inflationary pressures and any slowing in the level of domestic investment. There are also plans to open domestic and imported credit up to foreign firms, give foreign investors more leeway in the purchase of land, and increase protection for intellectual property rights.

POLITICAL OUTLOOK FOR THE ECONOMY

South Korea is in the middle of massive political and economic change. Direct military rule ended in 1987 after a decade of increasingly violent student and civilian protest. The military's candidate was elected in a direct but less than pristine election. In February 1993 Kim Young Sam, a former dissident, became the first chief executive of South Korea to be popularly elected in an open election in at least 30 years. Supporters argue that Kim has a better chance of carrying out the Mister Clean reform platform that got him elected than any previous administration because former administrations always had to go along with the status quo.

Attacking Corruption

Kim moved boldly by arresting high-ranking business and political figures on corruption charges, publishing a list of 670 regulations to be dropped that have restricted the ability of businesses to operate freely, and abolishing false name accounts. The

new president has instituted austerity measures in the executive branch—he has symbolically sworn off golf and closed the presidential driving range—and pressured government officials to disclose personal finances as part of compliance with the new policy of real name accounts. The embarrassingly high net worth that has been revealed in the upper reaches of government has prompted several resignations, including those of the chief justice of the supreme court and the prosecutor general. So far the merely suspiciously wealthy far outnumber those who can be proved to have engaged in criminal misconduct. Although the resignations seem to have been demanded primarily from opponents rather than supporters of the new administration, even supporters are becoming nervous. They fear that Kim's focus on the political front could divert him from acting effectively on the economic front, and that he could turn on those who disagree with him or try to refocus him on economic issues, on which he has been relatively weak.

Kim also moved quickly to purge the military of the most reactionary generals and those with the coziest ties to former administrations and made it stick. In the process, he exposed rampant corruption in military weapons procurement deals that has sent the military running for cover and brought virtually all procurement activity to a halt, leaving some wondering about preparedness. Kim also reorganized the secret service, reining in some of its excesses and installing his own man, a progressive. The heads of the *chaebol* fear that they are next on Kim's hit list. Kim's government has already made an example of Hyundai's founder, Chung Ju Yung, who announced an independent political bid during the last elections. Hyundai units were cut off from routine government financing and approvals, and the elderly Chung was convicted of embezzlement and received a three year jail term. Clearly Kim is capable of playing hard ball.

Although bashing the rich has played well to the masses—Kim's approval rating was 86 percent in October 1993—the president must eventually deal with the demands of labor, which supported him in a liberalization platform that called for greater union freedom and participation. However, Korean labor is part of an overpriced cost structure, and economic recovery can only be achieved by austerity, which labor will have difficulty buying for long, especially if it doesn't see business and government making similar sacrifices.

Observers have noted that Kim is better at politics than he is at economics. His stated mandate is to rein in big business, the bureaucracy, and the military, but he must also deal with the worst economic slowdown in more 10 years—bankruptcies exceeded 10,000 in 1992, an all-time high—and how he deals with political issues will affect his success with economic problems, especially when the *chaebol* effectively have the power to veto presidential actions simply by failing to cooperate. *Chaebol* heads have already indicated their displeasure with the president by failing to get behind him in very public if so far largely symbolic ways as well as by scaling back their investment plans, which serves to hamstring the economy.

The *chaebol* argue that they are being prevented from making necessary external forays at a time when the strength of the Japanese yen gives them a window of opportunity. Although the argument is somewhat self-serving, the underlying concern is real. South Korea's government got the nation into its current fix by micromanaging the economy instead of relying on the play of market forces and seems to be holding true to form in its response to current challenges. More recently Kim has been seen as back-pedaling somewhat and becoming more conciliatory toward business at the cost of some of his labor support.

Politicians and Bureaucrat

Kim's reforms are also in trouble with the legislature and with the hordes of entrenched bureaucrats who run the economy on a day-to-day basis. Although the president can rule by fiat to a large extent, as he did when he ordered the reduction in regulations, instituted real name accounts, and called for the monitoring or outright control of consumer prices, Kim must convince the legislature to ratify the reform package. This he must do quickly or risk the loss of perceived legitimacy. Many in the legislature are concerned that the president's anticorruption campaign is largely a matter of settling old scores, noting that rule by fiat fails to alter the old way of doing things and continues to exclude the legislative branch from any meaningful role in the process.

Having lost one of its main issues when Kim took up the outsider anticorruption banner, the opposition Democratic Party is pressing the president to up the ante by dredging up old military misdeeds and corporate collusion. Such a move would put Kim directly at odds with the army and the *chaebol*, which historically have colluded to a greater or lesser extent. The bureaucracy, which Kim has tarred as the source of red tape, corruption, and inefficiency, is less than eager to cooperate after having been scapegoated, however well-deserved the charges. The military is also restive, arguing that the unaccustomed focus on misdeeds in its ranks has harmed morale, deflected its attention from important matters, and diminished combat readiness just when North Korea seems to be entering an unstable period.

Uncertainty over how far-reaching and real Kim's reforms will be and how vigorously and for how long they will be pursued has brought a great deal of economic activity in South Korea to an effective standstill. The necessity of getting around government meddling and strictures led to many of the alternate pathways that have developed and much of the corruption that is now endemic. Businesses do not know how much the government will continue to second-guess them through administrative guidance. They also do not know whether to play by the old rules and risk being caught by the new moralistic zealots or to play by the new rules and risk staying blocked due to failure to play the game.

The Situation with the North

Since South Korea began to open up its own political process after years of military leadership, it has made renewed overtures to North Korea about developing closer relationships between the two nations. The rhetoric on both sides remains rigid and inflammatory, although the two sides have undertaken some joint humanitarian and economic interactions. Although total trade between the two countries is still insignificant to the south's developed economy, it reached US$210 million in 1992, up 9.4 percent from 1991. Imports from North Korea, mostly of raw materials, increased by 19.8 percent to US$198.8 million, while exports—chemicals, steel products, textiles, machinery, and foodstuffs—fell by 56.6 percent to US$11.4 million. Trade was off significantly in early 1993, as tension increased over North Korea's withdrawal from the nuclear nonproliferation agreement and its refusal to allow international inspection of suspected nuclear sites.

International concern has focused on North Korea's nuclear potential, but the country has also been engaged in a conventional military buildup since 1991 with most of this activity occurring near the border with the south. Some observers in the intelligence community attribute the buildup to Kim Jong Il, the son and designated successor of the authoritarian ruler, Kim Il Sung. They suggest that the buildup is designed to curry favor among the officer corps and cement the otherwise somewhat lightweight younger Kim's position as successor. Other analysts paint a more alarming picture of a nearly bankrupt state eating its seed corn, isolated from the world community and from its Communist patrons as well. They suggest that such a state might consider a desperate assault on its fraternal enemy. Whether the military activity reflects an actual threat or represents saber rattling primarily for domestic consumption, the consensus is that North-South relations cannot improve until Kim Il Sung is out of the way and chances for an improvement in the near term are slim even if he is removed from the scene.

SOUTH KOREA'S
INTERNATIONAL ROLE

South Korea is a member of 53 international organizations, 17 of which are United Nations agencies. As part of its effort to expand its international contacts, Korea has participated in the General Agreement on Tariffs and Trade (GATT), the Asia Pacific Economic Cooperation group (APEC), the European Bank for Reconstruction and Development (EBRD), and the Dynamic Asian Economies section of the Organization for Economic Cooperation and Development (OECD). South Korea also has established the Economic Development Cooperation Fund (EDCF) to provide loans and technical assistance to Third World countries, primarily in Southeast Asia, Latin America, and Africa.

Current Issues

A NEW PRESIDENT!
A NEW KOREA?

December 1992: South Korea holds its first democratic election in more than thirty years. The result? A leader from the old ruling Democratic Liberal Party (DLP) is chosen. Yet Kim Young Sam is anything but "one of the old boys." President Kim is fiercely opposed by party veterans and hard-liners, as he has fiercely opposed them. In fact, he only joined the party in 1990 when it was created from the merger of the dominant party and several former opposition parties. And now he is Korea's first democratically elected civilian leader since 1960.

A Typhoon Hits the Korean Peninsula

Before Kim's election South Koreans had been kept on a short leash by authoritarian military leaders. Although a military man himself, former President Roh Tae Woo had made some conciliatory efforts to bridge the gap between authoritarian and democratic rule and pave the way for more popular input. However, the mechanisms leading to true democracy have yet to be put in place. The completion of such necessary economic, political, and diplomatic reforms is exactly what the new president has pledged to undertake.

President Kim, already in high gear from his electoral competition, hit the floor running. Although an outsider, Kim has had long experience in Korean politics. In 1979 he was forced to give up the seat to which he had been elected and was kept under house arrest for two years after criticizing the ham-handed antidemocratic tendencies of President Park Chung Hee, a general who had come to power via military coup. Kim seemingly has developed the savvy and the calluses necessary to deal with sharp attacks from the DLP's fat cats.

The Korean Disease

During the first one hundred days following his February 25, 1993 inauguration, President Kim relentlessly pursued a "New Korea" policy aimed at eradicating what he termed the "Korean disease." He claimed that contemporary Korea has lost touch with many of its traditional values and is exhibiting the symptoms—moral laxity, rampant corruption, growing crime rates, and a weakening work ethic—which lead to cultural and national decline, not to mention economic weakness.

Kim's main reforms were aimed at expanding and strengthening democracy, deregulating the labyrinthine financial and business system, and improving relations with the black sheep of the family, North Korea. Above all, he came to power with a mandate to clean house and get rid of the corruption that had become endemic in Korean politics and business.

Target One: Politics

President Kim has ruffled feathers in the DLP in more ways than one. On taking office he appointed academics and other technocrats to key cabinet jobs, ignoring some of the old politicos who assumed that their lengthy careers and long party service gave them the right to key posts. He also surprised and dismayed many in this traditionally patriarchal society by appointing women to three of the twenty-seven cabinet level positions.

In the name of democracy Kim drew the sting out of the Agency for National Security Planning, the feared and detested secret police, banning it from conducting domestic political surveillance. Moreover, he demoted the former head of the agency directly to a jail cell and replaced him with a "clean" progressive academic with no links to the generals and bureaucrats who had controlled the agency in the past.

Target Two: Economics

One of East Asia's economic miracles, South Korea's economic growth rate averaged 17.5 percent annually from 1962 to 1990. However, in 1992 the growth rate declined to 4.7 percent, the lowest in 11 years. For Koreans, accustomed to double-digit growth, this amounted to an omen of doom. Although most Western industrialized nations would be delighted with South Korea's current GNP, Koreans, who base their modern identity on their economic growth rates, have lost considerable face over this decline.

With these economic figures in mind, President Kim has outlined plans for a "New Economy." To date, even a year into his term, his actual economic plans are more in the nature of a posture rather than a program. However, Kim's goal is to further economic development by moving away from past authoritarian practices in which the so-called command-capitalist economy grew according to centrally determined policy and under the watchful eye of powerful and intrusive bureaucrats, and move toward more "voluntary participation of the people," code words for a more open, free market oriented system. Recognizing both the need to reform Korea's authoritarian economic regime and the fact that the country has priced itself out of many of its traditional markets due to rapidly increasing costs, Kim is calling on the Korean people to sacrifice and endure the pain while South Korea undergoes economic and political surgery.

Kim's high ranking in the opinion polls, which show consistently that more than 70 percent of Koreans believe he is doing well as a leader, has helped ease some of the pain. Another poll showed that 90 percent of the Korean people strongly endorse Kim's reform program and have a high regard for his character. Koreans have called him "resolute and credible," impressive words to describe a leader in Korea's society. However, as Kim approached the first anniversary of his inauguration, there were signs that his popular support was receding around the margins as he still had not only failed to come to grips with the intransigent problems of the economy but

also had seemed to give in somewhat to the established big business interests.

Target Three: New Diplomacy

President Kim is also determined to position South Korea among at least the second tier global powers. In his inauguration speech Kim stated, "The 'New Korea' will stand tall and proud on the center stage of a new and civilized world, making a vital contribution to global peace and progress." Under Kim's "New Diplomacy" plan, Seoul is committed to placing a new emphasis on values such as democracy, liberty, and human rights. South Korea also plans to be increasingly involved in global affairs such as United Nations peace-keeping operations, arms control negotiations, technical assistance to less-developed countries, and environmental protection. Politically and economically, Kim wants his nation to play a more active international role and gain more recognition, particularly in the Asia-Pacific region. And, as has every administration before him, he speaks of accommodation and reunification with belligerent North Korea. And although some have criticized Kim for ignoring a growing threat from the north, he does seem more pragmatic and willing to actually reach such accommodations than have some of his predecessors.

SPRING CLEANING: ROOTING OUT CORRUPTION FROM THE KOREAN LEADERSHIP

"Deep in my heart I have a vision of a New Korea. The New Korea will be a freer and more mature democratic society. Justice will flow like a river through-

out this land." These words were spoken with passion and power by President Kim Young Sam at his inauguration. However, for many Koreans, true justice seemed quite remote in a land where many government and leading officials have traditionally risen through a notoriously corrupt system to reach the top. Of Kim's three essential tasks, his number one priority was to root out "misconduct and corruption." By making the attack on corruption his top priority, he indicated both the severity of the problem in Korean society and that he was staking his reputation on his ability to handle it. Kim spoke as if growth could not again become strong, and the nation could not renew itself unless corruption was immediately addressed. How did South Korea dig itself into such a hole?

The Confucian Past

Although Confucianism was a relatively late and foreign transplant to the country, Korea is the most zealously Confucian society in all of Asian. Confucius's teachings prescribed a harmonious society to be achieved through submission to authority. Confucius, of course, had in mind that enlightened, benevolent superiors would take wise and altruistic care of their subordinates in the natural order, avoiding the temptations to use power in less than honorable ways for less than honorable ends. This ideal is challenged by the more cynical Western view expressed in the adage that absolute power corrupts absolutely.

Filial piety, one of the foremost tenets of Confucianism, sees loyalty and obligation to one's family group as the highest of all virtues. With this in mind, a Korean who attained political or other power was obliged, according to Confucian teachings, to provide the family with the benefits of special privilege derived from his position. Indeed, denying a favor that is within your power to grant to a family member—or friend or colleague representing an extension of the family—regardless of the issues of ethics, public policy or trust, or fiduciary or other responsibility involved is regarded as contemptible in Confucian society. Using relationships to one's advantage developed into a national sport.

The Corrupt Present

Although politicians in the West are not generally depicted as wearing halos, most Western societies have not experienced the degree of corruption prevalent in the Korean government, business, and other sectors of its contemporary society. Millions of dollars of hidden assets are now being revealed among Korea's top politicians. What began with Confucius as paternalism in the best sense of the word has evolved into a complicated web of obligation and opportunism that reaches into all sectors of Korean society. It is not a pretty sight, especially to outsiders, and Koreans as well have become uncomfortable with some of its more extreme manifestations.

Gift giving, for example, has evolved from a means of showing respect and confirming reciprocal relationships into a means of obtaining business, political election, favors, and so on, degenerating into bribery and graft. Although the problem exists throughout all levels of society, it has been exacerbated by the Confucian emphasis on submission to authority that has drawn many lower level functionaries to go along with bribery and other legal violations at the behest of their superiors.

In Korea's corporate world, large businesses bribed government officials to avoid paying substantial taxes that were due or to gain lucrative contracts that could in turn be milked. Companies bribed bank officials to get loans. Sons of officials obtained positions in schools and then jobs in companies denied to other more-qualified but less well-connected candidates. In the military, promotion kickback scandals have been uncovered, and a number of senior military officers have been removed from their posts. No sector or group seems to be untainted by this endemic disease.

South Korea's unprecedented success and rapid economic growth during the last thirty years has also contributed the funds to fuel an increasingly corrupt system and a certain diminished sense of ethics. Whereas the dirty secret could be ignored when it involved small amounts around the edges of society, it became less deniable and more important when it involved huge amounts that became central to operating in both the public and private spheres.

Slowed Economic Growth
Quickens the Pace of Reform

Although these forms of corruption had been prevalent in Korea prior to the forming of the Republic of South Korea, they did not cause national concern. For most of Korea's history, these acts were not viewed as "corruption" in the Western sense of the word. Rather, gift giving and seeking favors from family members and acquaintances in power was simply a cultural norm. In the late 1980s the waning economic growth rate shamed Koreans and curtailed their expanding wallets. And, under the influence of such stress, corruption began to be seen as economically counterproductive, as well, adding costs to an already inflated expense structure. Suddenly, corruption became a great evil to be rooted out at all costs. Hence, President Kim made the anticorruption campaign as his number one priority.

To follow through with his stated reforms, Kim acted quickly and harshly, depending to some extent on the shock value of such actions to gain public attention and support. As part of this radical sur-

gery, he early on disqualified three of his new appointees who were found to have unclean hands. The cabinet ministers of health, justice, and construction were asked to step down almost as soon as they were appointed due to allegations of ethical violations.

To expose corrupt campaign contributions, Kim ordered members of the National Assembly and high-ranking officials in the judicial and executive branches, including himself, to publicly disclose not merely personal but family assets. Kim's order quickly revealed the enormity of the political fat cats' financial accumulation: Parliamentary Speaker Park Jun Kyu, for instance, disclosed assets of US$14 million and was forced to resign. Kim also changed rules governing inheritance tax, another loophole customarily exploited to hide financial assets. His changes should prevent future instances such as the one involving an eight year old (the grandson of a DLP lawmaker) who was the registered owner of a US$1.2 million dollar mansion.

Targeting Korea's
Financial Establishment

Knowing that government leaders were not the only ones involved, Kim next focused on the financial establishment in his efforts to weed out corruption. During his election, Kim had pledged to immediately enforce the "real name policy," to stem the practice of conducting financial transactions under false names—a common Korean way of avoiding taxes, funding corrupt practices, making illegal political contributions, and concealing the proceeds of illicit activities.

When Kim temporized on this pledge after the election and "temporarily shelved" the proposal,

critics were quick to label him as just another politician who promised much but failed to deliver. They also questioned his resolve to undertake other difficult and highly symbolic reforms, effectively daring Kim to put up or shut up. Kim surprised virtually everybody by actually putting up and launching the real name program by executive decree. The importance of this real name financial reform program is amply illustrated by the subsequent disclosure of the amassed assets of Korean politicians, who are assumed to be among the wealthiest in the world.

While his critics were still saying I-told-you-so, Kim took many by surprise when, in August 1993, he issued a Presidential Emergency Order banning all financial transactions using false names immediately. This decree further required all Koreans holding accounts under false names to close them and transfer the funds to real names by October 12, 1993. This step made South Korea the first country in Asia to implement such a system. Kim hopes that by banning false name transactions, he will bring an end to the age-old backroom collusion between the ruling party and big business. Thus, enterprises should be able to better promote their own business by investing more funds in research and development instead of in bribes and other forms of corruption. By sealing off the funds that fuel such underground economic activity (estimated by some observers to be nearly 15 percent of the total economy) and coincidentally blocking speculative activity, especially in the stock market and real estate through this policy, Kim aims to address some of the distortions in South Korea's economic structure.

Kim's anticorruption reforms are also sweeping like a scythe through the banking sector, where he ordered audits of all Korean banks. Already the presidents of two of Korea's largest banks have been fired for involvement in deals providing loans for kickbacks. This cleanup is expected to reduce the cost of borrowing by 2 to 3 percent by eliminating the add-ons for "commissions" and to facilitate smaller firms' ability to borrow.

Kim's ban on false name transactions coupled with tighter controls over bank deposits sent shock waves through the markets and the financial system. South Korea's stock index plunged nearly 8 percent in the two days following the announcement, reflecting the fears of the financial community. Yet these fears subsided within a week when the stock market and other general economic indicators recovered to previous levels with only minimal disintermediation from financial institutions.

Finding Mr. Clean

As Kim tries to forge ahead successfully with his anticorruption campaign, one of his biggest problems is finding a sufficiently clean ally to lead the reform. Kim's right-hand man, Choi Hyung-Woo, the secretary-general of the DLP, and one of his oldest and closest political allies whom he designated to spearhead his anticorruption campaign, is a case in point. As Choi cast his net to pull in corrupt party officials, he ended up caught in it himself. Choi's wife was exposed for using political influence and bending rules to obtain a university position for their child, a relatively minor infraction compared to some, but one that was still enough to trip up an otherwise stalwart ally under the new rules.

Also, because of fallout from Choi's ruling that party lawmakers disclose their assets, six party lawmakers were implicated in real estate scandals and resigned within three months after Kim took office.

In a society where almost by definition no one has clean hands, it will become increasingly difficult to find capable people to manage the ambitious reforms.

Can Korean Society Ever Be Cleansed of Corruption?

Regardless of how far President Kim is able to continue his reforms, one thing is clear: corruption is and has long been a way of life in South Korea. The country has watched in astonished unease as the pervasiveness of corrupt practices has been brought into the light of day in politics, the press, universities, business, the military, and virtually every other sphere of Korean national life. As Kim turned the spotlight on such practices, it exposed more dirt than the Korean people had ever imagined or are comfortable with. Although certainly Kim's attempts are laudable (his public approval rating soared to 87 percent after he initiated the real name policy), considering the depth and breadth of such practices and the entrenched role they play in society, one must question how far his reforms can go and how successful they will be. Will the Korean mindset, in which influence peddling is an acknowledged daily routine, really change? And even more importantly, how far can Kim push forward with reform before too many officials, fearing exposure, effectively call a halt? Finally, how far will the public back the campaign?

Many Koreans seem to have faith that Kim's reforms will bring an end to the large-scale corporate and political corruption occurring today. And that is fine with the populace at large, who like to see the mighty brought low. But his ability to root out corruption from smaller scale, daily interactions—which after all is the point of origin for the higher level corruption—is unlikely. In the words of one Korean describing the role of such activities in his country's society, "That is our culture. It will not change."

CUTTING THE RED TAPE: KIM'S FINANCIAL REFORM PROGRAM

Deteriorating economic growth, flailing small- and medium-sized businesses strangling from a lack of investment capital, a weakened work ethic, and declining international competitiveness: is South Korea really falling off the cutting edge? President Kim Young Sam seems to think so, and many foreigners are also questioning Korea Inc.'s capacity to stay ahead of the pack. Korea's slowed economic growth is especially alarming to the powers-that-be as other emerging Asian economies are manifestly starting to eat Korea's lunch.

Moreover, South Korea's bureaucracy, with its anti-foreign regulations, has been thwarting foreign investors. For instance, critics argue that tax authorities blatantly single out foreign subsidiaries for audits, and numerous tariff and nontariff barriers discourage imports, some of which come to light as "unpublished" regulations only after the foreign entity has already stuck its neck out and been assured that it has permission to undertake the activity. And despite Korea's panting desire for high technology, it has to date failed to provide adequate protection for such intellectual property, so that few foreign firms are willing to entrust the Koreans with the crown jewels. Consequently, foreign investment has begun declining, especially in the high technology industries that Korea needs in its drive to become competitive again. Not only is new investment falling off, but existing enterprises are calling it quits, adding insult to injury from the Korean perspective. In 1992 Korea had to kiss good-bye more than US$369 million redeemed from joint venture terminations and watch from the sidelines with a great gnashing of teeth as a large portion of that money was redeployed to the People's Republic of China and various Southeast Asian competitors.

Kim Uses the Scissors

Immediately after his inauguration, President Kim announced a hundred-day plan to stimulate economic growth and ease administrative restrictions. His "three-phase financial market liberalization" plan intends to fully open Korea's business and financial system to foreign competition by 1996. Kim resolutely stated, "The 'New Economy' must be driven by initiative and involvement rather than by commands and controls."

Kim's sharp scissors are poised to excise or at least edit 670 regulations imposed on business activities, including those related to finance and taxation. Yet these are the easy ones and some 400 additional known regulations will remain intact (Korea has a habit of finding "unpublished" regulations that emerge when they are least expected). The Economic Planning Board claims that proposed reforms to distribute the existing tax burden in a more equitable fashion and improve tax distribution should lower effective tax rates and simplify the system. The Finance Ministry has disclosed plans to reduce interest rates in a bid to deemphasize stringent anti-inflation measures and concentrate on economic growth policies. To reduce private sector borrowing costs, the Bank of Korea plans to lower its interbank lending rate. In a coordinated step, Korea's commercial banks plan to cut their lending rates two percentage points to approximately 9 percent. By reducing debt financing costs, corporate debt service should ease, thereby raising business profits and funds available for capital spending.

If all goes according to plan, these actions will generate new jobs and expand the national economy. To dampen inflation as the money supply expands, Kim has called upon the "voluntary participation" of labor to sacrifice increased wages and incomes. In a country whose secret of success has been its well-educated and low-wage labor force, such sacrifice might be just the medicine that is needed. But will Koreans swallow it now that they have tasted the sweetness of economic prosperity?

The overall economic plan also calls for reviving small- and medium-sized companies that are gasping for air in a "stagnant economy." Such small- and medium-sized companies have been crowded out with respect to access to official lending by the heavyweight *chaebol* which have monopolized what little funding has been available, many contend through bribery. Kim now plans to double the government financial support available for these smaller firms and simplify the procedures for establishing them.

Many observers are nervous about a reform that uses the same old directive methods of thou shalt and

father knows best. On one hand, Kim has called for economic liberalization and deregulation. On the other hand, he plans to undertake his Five-Year Plan by government fiat (sounding a bit like his northern kin, not to mention his discredited predecessors). Although the message is now one of freeing up the markets and preventing the bureaucracy from overregulating the private sector, the means are still the same: government dictating to business what and how to reform.

Additionally, many question Kim's lack of solid direction for rebuilding the economy and his ability to actually push through the proposed reforms.

Effect on the Foreign Business

Regardless of how far Kim's reforms go, foreigners are anxious to benefit from the "new economy." The long-term focus of the economic plan—to further international competitiveness of Korean industries—should open South Korea's markets to foreign competition. Kim has also introduced measures he claims will eliminate virtually all restrictions on foreign investment in Korea, including those restricting participation in the financial services industry and access to the retail distribution system. One example is the proposed removal of barriers to foreign investment in 132 business sectors within the next five years. These sectors include hospital administration, film production and distribution, credit card services, and transportation.

The government also plans to revise laws that hinder the ability of foreign businesses to buy land and build plants. Beginning in 1994 foreign investors will be allowed to purchase Korean land for any line of business operations. Moreover, on July 1, 1993 the allowable floor space of foreign retail owners increased from a 1,000- to a 3,000-square meter limit. Foreign retailers can now open up to twenty outlets nationwide, resulting in a three-fold increase in the number of such stores that can be operated by foreigners.

Prior to Kim's election, the Korean government restricted foreign ownership of real estate by requiring approval on a case-by-case basis. As of March 1993 foreigners can invest in wholesale business and small- and medium-sized firms' projects simply by reporting to the Korean government; however, some projects including the tourist hotel businesses, remain subject to the approval system. However, the approval system itself is to be liberalized considerably, allowing the bulk of foreign investments to proceed on a notification basis and reducing the paperwork and time needed to reach a determination on those proposals still requiring approval.

How have foreigners responded to these moves toward openness? If the stock market is any indication, very positively. Liberalization in Korea's stock market has led to a record amount of overseas investment in the Seoul stock exchange. By the end of April 1993 foreign investment totaled US$1.76 billion, more than double the amount for all of 1992. Leading the pack was the United States with a net investment of US$460 million, representing 37 percent of the total. By year-end the Korean stock market was up about 45 percent, led largely by foreign investors, who, however, are near their authorized limit for holding Korean stocks. Yes, amid all this new economic freedom there are still stringent limits on how much Korean stock foreigners can buy and hold and how they can do so.

The Bottom Line

Kim closed his economic policy speech by saying, "When all of us share the sacrifices and pain, we will succeed in making a new leap forward." In many other nations, words like these would represent glib rhetoric and roll off people's backs as such. However, in Korea listeners know the meaning of sacrifice and, historically, have been willing to pay the price. Kim is betting that although there have been changes in society, the ability to make the necessary sacrifices remains deeply engrained in the Korean people.

SIBLING RIVALRY: RELATIONS WITH NORTH KOREA

Though glaring differences exist between the two Koreas, they do agree on one thing: a desire for reunification. The problems start when they get down to such issues as under whose terms it should take place.

Historical Efforts

However, wanting a thing and working for it are two very different matters. Although the governments of North and South Korea have repeatedly affirmed their desire to reunite throughout the postwar period, they had no official contact between 1953 and 1971. By 1972 the leaders finally reached an agreement to work toward peaceful reunification and to end the hostile atmosphere prevailing on the Korean peninsula. However, only one year later talks had reached an impasse. This breakdown reflected basic differences in approach: Pyongyang insisted on immediate steps toward reunification before discussing specific issues, while Seoul maintained that, given the long history of mutual distrust, reunification required a gradual step-by-step process with each incremental step being hashed out well in advance.

This pattern of anticlimactic ebb and flow continued in talks throughout the 1970s and 1980s. In a major initiative in July 1988, South Korean President Roh Tae Woo called for new efforts to promote exchanges, family reunification, inter-Korean trade, and contact in international forums. Over the following months the two sides met several times, even forming a joint North-South Korean team for the 1990 Asian Games in Beijing.

However, by February of 1989 North Korea once again suspended such talks following the annual joint US-ROK military exercises, labeling them as a provocation. The North and South were able to reconcile more quickly, and by 1990 they were again ready for talks on the ministerial level. Still they had little progress to show from the three meetings held by the delegations. When the annual joint US military exercises rolled around again the following February, the North canceled the planned fourth meeting, citing the exercises as a threat from the South. Hopes for a future presidential summit were dashed again with Kim Il Sung and Roh Tae Woo were unable to agree on a protocol.

Although diplomatic relations fell two steps back, trade relations moved one step ahead. Following South Korea's decision to allow trade with the North, South Korean firms began to import North Korean goods via the fig leaf of third-country contracts. North Korea has denounced and denied this trade, yet did not refrain from publicizing a visit by the founder of Hyundai and proposed plans to develop projects and tourism in the North.

More Recently

Most recently the tension between North and South Korea (and the rest of the world, for that matter) has been mounting over nuclear weapons. In 1985 North Korea signed the Nuclear Non-Proliferation Treaty (NPT) agreeing to abide by international regulations designed to curtail the spread of nuclear weapons. However, the North refused to allow inspectors from the International Atomic Energy Agency (IAEA) to visit designated sites in order to allay suspicions that it had accumulated a supply of weapons grade plutonium and was capable of putting together a bomb. If US analysts are correct, Pyongyang may already have the materials for at least one nuclear device ready for assembly.

On March 12, 1993 North Korea withdrew from the treaty, sparking a major crisis in relations with the rest of the world, save its old ally, China. When threatened with sanctions from the United Nations, North Korea (bearing in mind that China holds veto power in the UN Security Council) seemed undaunted.

Nevertheless, priorities change, and China has to some extent turned its back on North Korea while rubbing shoulders with its once despised capitalist enemies. North Korea can no longer assume that China can be counted on to tip the scales in its favor should the Security Council vote to enforce sanctions. There is also the little matter of China's own 1993 violations of nuclear testing bans which complicates matters and could make China less eager to point the finger at others. Even North Korea's old friends in Russia have voiced condemnation of its actions: Foreign Minister Sergei Yastrzhembski stated, "Russia will not remain silent. It is necessary for North Korea to reach a complete agreement with the IAEA." However, China has continued to argue that it is better able to exercise restraint over the North by using the carrot rather than the stick.

Although previous sanctions have been enforced against such countries as Iraq with mediocre results, they can be expected to deal a much heavier blow to the already frail North Korean economy. This economy—a fraction of that of the South—is rapidly deteriorating, particularly since the cessation of barter trade with Russia and China. Some analysts argue that Kim Il Sung underestimated the gravity of his withdrawal from the Nuclear Non-Proliferation Treaty and subsequent refusal to allow IAEA inspections. At a time when international peace and security is the rallying cry of the global community, leaders in the UN have little tolerance for even a hint of nuclear arms proliferation. The members of the nuclear club want to set a precedent for the many other nations aspiring to build nuclear weapons.

Their Side of the Story

North Korea claims that suspected sites designated for inspections are military areas and exempt from the treaty. True, neither the NPT nor the IAEA agreement signed by North Korea have provisions for "special inspections." However, since the Persian Gulf War which revealed Iraq's shockingly well advanced nuclear weapons program, IAEA inspectors have become jumpy. The North argues that the IAEA's revision infringes upon its national sovereignty by subjecting it to the IAEA's additional new rules. North Korea also claims that South Korea has not been inspected for nuclear bases and that the United States maintains nuclear weapons there.

So much for the official position. North Korea has not helped its situation by continuing to insist on its position as an international renegade and a law unto itself. It has also been involved in a massive conventional arms buildup centered along its border with the South at a time when it has no visible means of supporting such an investment or justifiable rationale for doing so.

Time for Concessions

While not treating all this lightly, South Korean officials have so far viewed the whole situation with relatively little concern. This could change now that there has been more publicity over military procurement scandals in the South, scandals that call into question the South's overall equipment strength and combat readiness. On the other hand the military is on the run politically and is playing the preparedness and the threat-from-the-North cards in an ef-

fort to shield itself from even greater unwelcome attention, so it is difficult for outsiders to assess the real danger in the situation.

In response to immediate nuclear concerns, South Korea and the US have agreed to tone down and even to cancel their "Team Spirit" military exercises, a perennial bone of contention. The South has also stated its willingness to hold reciprocal IAEA inspections. President Kim, after initially seeking to sweeten the deal with promises of economic cooperation and aid, has ended current economic exchanges and called a halt to future ones until the North reverses its decision to withdraw from the NPT and allows IAEA inspections. These issues have served to heighten tensions between the Korean siblings to levels equivalent to the 1970s cold war standoff.

In June 1993 the United States attempted to persuade North Korea to cancel its withdrawal from the NPT and allow entry to IAEA inspectors. One day before its withdrawal would have taken effect, North Korea agreed to "suspend as long as it considers necessary" its determination to withdraw from the NPT. In mid-February 1994 the North Koreans pulled back from the brink by agreeing to allow international inspection of seven installations. However, they continued to deny the existence of and verification by inspection of two additional suspected nuclear sites. Observers caution that this agreement could prove illusory—on a previous inspection, personnel were only allowed to examine the facilities at night in the dark by flashlight—and the North has been known to renege on deals at the last minute. Even if the proposed inspection goes off without a hitch, analysts caution that it will simply show whether additional fissionable material has been drawn off for potential weapons use, not whether such material was diverted in the past. The DPRK could still have nuclear weapons that the much-touted inspections have no way of finding.

Still Unpredictable

What does North Korea have to lose by conceding to UN demands to allow inspections? Face and possible exposure of its bluff. What it has to gain appears to be far more, including possible diplomatic recognition from the United States, aid and trade from South Korea and Japan, and a few new (and old) friends in the world. Its leadership apparently wants to use its nuclear wild card to gain material concessions, particularly from the US and Japan. But even more than this, North Korea wants to be acknowledged as a real and important player on the world scene, despite its bankrupt social and economic system. When dealing with a nation that indoctrinates its people with slogans such as "Let us become guns and bombs for safeguarding the Party," this is one guessing game South Korea and rest of the world do not want to lose.

Opportunities

OPPORTUNITIES FOR IMPORTING FROM KOREA

After adhering to a policy of export-led growth for more than a decade and a half, South Korea has emerged as one of the world's leading newly industrialized countries (NICs). One indicator of success: South Korea's manufacturing output experienced double-digit annual growth between 1962 and 1991. Now, as the world's thirteenth-largest trading nation, South Korea is focusing on upgrading its industrial competitiveness in international markets. Traditional exports such as toys, textiles, sporting goods, and footwear continue to contribute to Korea's economic growth, and industries such as machinery, electronics, specialty chemicals, and automobiles have been targeted for increased investment and intensive technological upgrading. The following section describes Korea's most important industries and the opportunities they offer to foreign importers.

AUTOMOBILES

South Korea is the tenth-largest automobile producer in the world. The range of Korean-made vehicles has also diversified, and now includes passenger cars, buses, trucks, jeeps, and other special-purpose vehicles. These are sold locally and exported to leading international markets in China, the United States, Canada, Germany, and Taiwan.

Korea's automobile industry is closely tied to developments in the steel, nonferrous metals, machinery, petrochemical, and electronics industries. The auto industry is pursuing various technical development strategies through large-scale investments in the production of automobile engines and R&D involving new materials. Other projects aim at making vehicles lighter and incorporating a greater array of modern electronic components.

Through such ongoing efforts, the South Korean auto market will continue to grow steadily. As of mid-1993 auto exports totaled US$1.4 billion. Projections for the year 2000 are for the production of 3.2 million vehicles, with 1.2 million being exported.

Some of the HOT items:
- auto parts and accessories
- auto spark-ignition engines
- buses
- passenger cars
- radial tires
- trucks

SHIPS

South Korea's shipbuilding industry, which has solidified its position as the second-largest producer in the world, has benefited from rising global demand and increasing orders for high-value-added container ships in the late 1980s. The Korea Shipbuilders' Association estimates that domestic shipbuilders received orders for 3.2 million gross tons in the first half of 1993, constituting a phenomenal increase of almost 700 percent over the same period in 1992.

Tankers and bulk carriers comprise the majority of the ships on order or under construction. The remainder includes container ships and other types of commercial vessels.

Korea's share of the world shipbuilding market is expected to decline slightly as foreign competitors undercut Korea's prices, but the country will continue to be a major player in this market. Meanwhile, in order to compete more effectively in the international market, Korean shipbuilders have been developing more economical models of tankers and bulk carriers as well as constructing such high-value-added vessels as LNG and LPG carriers.

Some of the HOT items:

- container ships
- crude oil tankers
- floating structures
- tankers and bulk carriers

ELECTRONICS

Electronics have been designated by the Korean government as a strategic export, and the electronics industry plays an important role in driving the country's economic expansion. Stimulated by dramatic increases in domestic and foreign demand, projected growth for electronics products remains high. Consumer electronics, home appliances, and electronic components are the three primary exports.

Consumer Electronics

In response to rising world demand for state-of-the-art products, South Korea's manufacturers are making continual advances in producing sophisticated consumer electronics. Boosted by growing local production of parts and components, this export-oriented sector is expected to expand steadily throughout the 1990s. Product opportunities include radio receivers, television receivers, video cassette recorders, musical instruments, electronic watches, microwave ovens, speaker systems, computers, and peripherals, electronic calculators, data communications systems, and photocopying machines.

Home Appliances

Home electrical appliances have been a strategic export and a mainstay of South Korea's economic development since the 1970s. Such exports account for a significant percentage of total exports in the electronics industry. Korea exports refrigerators, air conditioners, washing machines, dryers, microwave ovens, vacuum cleaners, dishwasher, and ovens and ranges.

Electronic Parts and Components

As South Korea's economy becomes increasingly dependent on information-based technology, the electronic components industry will continue to expand. At present, about 300 companies in Korea produce a wide range of electronic components and parts, including integrated circuits (ICs), cathode ray tubes (CRTs,) resistors, capacitors, speakers, magnetic tapes, magnetic heads, printed circuit boards, and TV tuners. Of these, ICs account for the highest revenues, and magnetic tapes constitute the fastest-growing area.

Some of the HOT items:

- air conditioner compressors
- laser disc players
- color TVs
- digital audio tape recorders
- electronic copiers
- 4 mm camcorders
- integrated circuits
- magnetic tapes
- microwave ovens
- radio broadcast receivers
- refrigerators
- video cassette recorders (VCRs)
- washing machines

SEMICONDUCTORS

Exports of semiconductors bring South Korea more revenue than any other single product. The market, estimated at US$6.1 billion in 1992, is projected to grow at an average annual rate of 10 percent through 1995.

Direct random access memory chips (DRAMs) experienced particularly rapid growth due to both local sales and exports. Other products manufactured locally in significant quantities include monolithic ICs, memory devices, silicon transistors and silicon diodes, photosensitive semiconductor devices (photovoltaic cells, light-emitting diodes), crystal vibrators, and lead frames. Of the six major manufacturers of semiconductors in Korea, Samsung Electronics, Hyundai Electronics, and Goldstar Electron produce 4MB DRAM chips, mostly for export.

Some of the HOT items:

- diodes
- direct random access memory chips (DRAMs)
- memory devices
- monolithic ICs
- photosensitive transistors
- VSLI chips

COMPUTERS AND PERIPHERALS

Computers and peripherals will lead the growth of the South Korean electronics industry. At present, 16-bit personal computers (PCs) are the focus of local production and are manufactured by some 20 local manufacturers, including Samsung Electronics, Goldstar Co., Hyundai Electronics, Daewoo Electronics, and Trigem Computer. Some of these firms also produce 32-bit 386 and laptop computers.

Peripherals produced locally include auxiliary memory devices (floppy hard disk drives), printers, CRT terminals, and monitors. Most of the CRT terminals and monitors are exported, while a large portion of the other peripherals are for the domestic market.

Some of the HOT items:
- CRT terminals and monitors
- laptop computers
- laser printers
- 16-bit PCs

MACHINERY AND EQUIPMENT

South Korea's machine industry has grown quickly as a result of increased investment in equipment and the rapid expansion of the electrical, electronics, and automobile industries. From 1975 to 1988, machinery exports expanded at an impressive rate of 40 percent.

Korea is capable of producing a full range of machinery—turbines, generators, earthmoving equipment, and numerically controlled machinery centers—but remains dependent on imports for technology and design assistance. Manufacturers are beginning to focus on producing industrial machinery, environmental equipment, measuring tools, chemical equipment, and precision machine parts. Other opportunities should develop for durable precision parts used in robotics, flexible assembly operations, and heat treatment technologies. All of these are now in the initial stages of development.

Some of the HOT items:
- electrical machinery and parts
- heavy machinery
- machine parts
- mechanical handling equipment and parts
- turbo propellers (a/c engines)
- turbojet parts

MACHINE TOOLS AND RELATED EQUIPMENT

Import substitution and increased R&D have enabled major machine tool manufacturers to make the transition from standard types of machine tools to more sophisticated, higher value-added products. The latter include computer numerically controlled (CNC) machine tools such as copy milling machines, lathes, machining centers, horizontal machining centers, and wire cutters.

The United States has already adopted import restrictions on certain categories of South Korean-made machine tools. So Korean machine tool manufacturers are now concentrating on competing against higher-priced Japanese products. If the United States does not impose a total ban on Korean machine tools, and if Korea is able to continue making inroads into European markets, exports will steadily increase.

Some of the HOT items:
- CNC copy milling machines
- CNC lathes
- CNC machining centers
- CNC horizontal machining centers
- CNC wire cutters

IRON AND STEEL

The outlook for South Korea's steel industry is optimistic. Analysts foresee reduced steel inventories, increased export competitiveness, increased supply of steel bar, continued healthy performance of the construction and shipbuilding industries, and improved automobile and electronics industries. As a result, crude steel production is expected to increase in step with steel exports. Primary markets for Korean iron and steel include India, China, Southeast Asia, and the United States.

Some of the HOT items:
- cold-rolled sheets
- iron and steel tubes, pipes, and fittings
- nails, screws, and nuts
- reinforced steel bars
- wire ropes

CHEMICAL PRODUCTS

Chemical products are one of South Korea's major export items. Exports of chemical products used in heavy industry represented more than 60 percent of total chemical exports in early 1993. Exports of chemical products should also benefit from continued worldwide growth in light industry.

Some of the HOT items:
- ethylene
- naphtha
- polyvinyl chloride (PVC)
- propylene

SPORTING GOODS AND RECREATIONAL EQUIPMENT

Korea's 350 sporting goods makers began to expand their local and overseas market share to capture the excitement of the 1986 Asian Games and the 1988 Olympics. Although some sectors of the South Korean sporting goods industry are still in the early stages of development, the industry has already demonstrated its ability to supply many high-quality products. Balls, gloves, mountaineering equipment, fishing tackle, reels, tennis and badminton rackets, and camping equipment are the major export items.

Some of the HOT items:

- balls
- fishing rods
- gloves
- mountaineering equipment
- tennis rackets
- tents

TEXTILES AND APPAREL

South Korea ambitiously hopes to become the world's largest supplier of textile products, with US$30 billion in annual exports by the year 2000. The textile industry is attempting to reduce labor costs in the spinning stage by adopting modern automated equipment for handling raw materials. Apparel, synthetic filaments, and silk are the primary exports.

Shifting from the traditional production of apparel, Korea's textile makers are establishing quick response systems in order to meet rapid changes in world demand. Textile plants are being relocated to countries with lower labor costs. Korea has also been stepping up production of textile machinery, with increased exports of machinery to the Philippines, Indonesia, Saudi Arabia, and the United Arab Emirates.

Some of the HOT items:

- apparel
- headgear
- silk
- synthetic filaments
- textile arts (needlecraft kits)
- textile machinery
- water-resistant garments
- woven fabrics
- yarns

TOYS

South Korea's toy industry got its start in the production of stuffed toys for export. But many of the labor-intensive activities, including hand sewing, have been transferred to countries with lower labor costs. In the last five years, some 60 factories making stuffed toys have been moved to China, Thailand, Indonesia, and other Asian countries.

Sensing an urgent need to raise the quality of their products, Korean producers are now focusing on domestic production of higher value-added toys. Domestic production of metal and plastic toys is expected to grow by 3 to 5 percent annually.

Some of the HOT items:

- dolls
- games
- metal toys
- plastic toys
- stuffed toys

FOOTWEAR

Footwear is South Korea's sixth-largest export industry in terms of value. After experiencing a slump in the late 1980s, the Korean footwear industry is now enjoying improved sales abroad. The new pump feature shoes are extremely popular in overseas markets. Another popular item is leather sport shoes, which account for more than half of Korea's total footwear exports. Other items include boots, slippers, sandals, and dress shoes. Major export markets are the United States, Japan, Canada, Germany, and Russia and the other former Soviet republics.

However, rising wages are forcing Korean footwear producers to move manufacturing facilities to other countries, mostly in Southeast Asia. Korea's footwear industry is now actively seeking to meet more diversified demand by replacing outdated machinery, promoting automation of production facilities, and aggressively introducing new patterns, designs, and materials. Even so, the industry as a whole is in decline, with just over 80,000 workers employed in the footwear industry in 1993, down nearly 40 percent from about 130,000 in 1990.

Some of the HOT items:

- athletic shoes
- boots
- leather shoe parts
- pump shoes
- sandals
- slippers

AGRICULTURAL PRODUCTS

South Korea's agricultural policy objectives have shifted: The long standing emphasis on attaining basic self-sufficiency in the production of food has yielded to a policy of restructuring the rural economy to make it more efficient. Although rising incomes have caused many Koreans to leave the agricultural sector, improvements in infrastructure and farming techniques have brought impressive increases in domestic agricultural output. Leather, seafood, chestnuts, leaf tobacco, and ginseng are among Korea's primary agricultural exports.

Some of the HOT items:

- ginseng
- leaf tobacco
- leather and associated products
- processed seafood and meat products
- seafood
- tubers and root vegetables

MUSICAL INSTRUMENTS

In the early 1990s South Korea's musical instruments industry began to focus on breaking into the overseas market for higher-end products. A key area of growth has been the manufacture of pianos, and Korea's acoustic piano industry is now the third largest in the world. Electronic musical instruments are also gaining a competitive position in the international market.

Some of the HOT items:

- acoustic pianos
- electronic keyboards
- guitars

COOKWARE

The total size of the South Korean market for cookware is estimated at US$170 million and is expected to grow at an average annual rate of 20 percent for the next three years. Production of cookware for export has been the primary focus, but recent production has also been directed toward the domestic market. Local firms are very strong in this industry, both in domestic and export sales. One of the best established Korean manufacturers is Kyung-dong Industrial Co., Ltd., which began exporting flatware in 1963. Since the mid-1970s, many other local firms have been manufacturing cookware for export.

Some of the HOT items:

- ceramic dinnerware
- containers
- flatware
- glassware
- kitchen tools
- stemware
- stoneware
- tableware

OPPORTUNITIES FOR EXPORTING TO KOREA

Many foreign products are widely known in the South Korean market. Foreign firms offering competitive pricing and quality service can take advantage of lucrative prospects, ranging from automotive parts and communications products to videos and cosmetics. Demand is particularly strong for advanced machinery and electronics equipment. The following section describes the most attractive opportunities for exporting to Korea.

COMPUTERS AND PERIPHERALS

Competition among US, Japanese, and European suppliers over the computerization of South Korea's government agencies and private commercial organizations is anticipated in the years to come. Sales of terminals should be particularly brisk due to increasing demand for on-line and real-time computerization as well as increasing reliance on decentralized data processing systems. Computer hardware, storage units, and input-output devices will continue to provide additional opportunities for foreign exporters. The import market for many of these items is expected to increase at an annual average rate of 15 percent through at least 1995.

Some of the HOT items:
Computers
- digital mainframes and minicomputers
- engineering workstations
- high-end and midrange computers
- local area networks/file servers
- special-purpose microcomputers
- value-added networks/file servers

Storage Units
- main storage units
- peripheral storage units

Input-Output Units
- digitizers
- high-speed special-purpose printers
- graphic displays and plotters

Computer Terminals
- display terminals (CRT modeling)
- special-purpose terminals

COMPUTER SOFTWARE

As computerization progresses in almost all sectors of the economy, the demand for software is rising. Annual growth of imported computer software is projected to average 20 percent through 1995.

Although South Korea is capable of developing its own applications software, much of the systems software is imported. A foreign supplier's willingness to modify software slightly to meet the specific needs of Korean consumers will greatly enhance sales prospects.

Some of the HOT items:
- application development tools
- applications systems software
- business software
- computer-aided design (CAD) systems
- database management systems
- military simulation systems
- networking systems
- operating systems
- programming languages
- systems and utility software

CAD/CAM SYSTEMS

Widespread growth of computer-aided design and computer-aided manufacturing (CAD/CAM) systems is expected in South Korea's electronics, aerospace, automotive, shipbuilding, and machinery industries. CAD/CAM systems have already become a critical element in automated design and manufacturing. Foreign sales of CAD/CAM equipment in Korea are likely to expand, with projected imports reaching US$230 million in 1995.

The CAD/CAM systems supplied to Korea have generally used IBM, VAX, or Hewlett-Packard central processing units (CPUs). Recently, systems based on such engineering workstations as Micro Vax, Sun Micro, and HP/Apollo platforms have become available. Technological developments in both computer hardware and software have substantially reduced the price of CAD/CAM systems and increased user friendliness. The CAD/CAM market in personal computers has far surpassed that for the mid-range and large CAD/CAM systems. However, the general trend is now shifting away from microcomputer-based CAD systems (first introduced to Korea in 1987) toward systems based on engineering workstations. Demand for three-dimensional CAD systems in the architecture, shipbuilding, and automobile industries has been increasing rapidly.

Some of the HOT items:
- architectural, engineering, and construction systems
- cartography systems
- electrical and electronic PCB design systems
- mechanical design systems

REFRIGERATION EQUIPMENT

Applications for commercial refrigeration equipment include the food, medical, and pharmaceutical industries. South Korea's imports of air conditioners and refrigerators have continued to rise sharply.

The domestic market for refrigeration equipment is also likely to grow due to an increased demand for processed food. Korean consumers are showing a preference for large refrigerators with energy-saving features. Rotary compressors, room air conditioners, and heat pumps present additional opportunities for foreign exporters.

Some of the HOT items:
- air conditioners (with temperature cycle valve)
- air and other gas compressors
- air and vacuum pumps
- blood storage refrigerators
- ice cream making machines
- ice-cube units
- refrigeration show cases
- refrigerators and freezers (greater than 400 liter capacity)

AUTOMOTIVE PARTS AND SERVICE EQUIPMENT

Over the past two and a half decades, South Korea's automotive parts and service industries have grown rapidly. Imported products for which there is a high demand include a large variety of engines, electronic control systems, catalytic converters, and automobile servicing equipment. Korea's import market reached US$1.5 billion in 1992 and is expected to grow by 12 percent a year through 1995.

Some of the HOT items:
- automatic antenna motors
- automobile servicing equipment
- brakes
- catalytic converters
- clutches
- electrical control units
- engines
- fan motors
- power window motors
- starters
- sunroof motors
- washer and wiper motors

ELECTRONICS INDUSTRY PRODUCTION AND TEST EQUIPMENT

Expansion of the electronics industry is one of the main objectives of South Korea's economic development strategy. Thus there are various government and private sector initiatives to modernize this industry. In particular, efforts by Korean electronics manufacturers to maximize the local content of finished industrial and consumer goods have brought significant new capital investment. While a large portion of lower-end equipment can be acquired locally, most large electronics firms depend on imports of such items as PCB testers, integrated circuit (IC) testers and handlers, burn-in systems, sputtering systems, ion implantation systems, and other automatic equipment.

Some of the HOT items:
- assembly machines and systems
- automatic component sorters
- automatic DIP handlers
- chemical vapor deposition equipment
- chip mounters and PCB auto inserters
- component inserting machines
- component sequencing machines
- component soldering
- components coating machines
- dicing machines
- discrete testers
- dryers (PCB)
- high-current and high-voltage ion implanters
- IC and LSI/VLSI device testers
- IC, diode, and transistor handling equipment
- labeling and marking machines
- linear device testers
- memory testers
- PCB etching, scrubbing, developing, and stripping machines
- PCB testers
- physical vapor deposition equipment (sputtering equipment)
- semiconductor (reactive ion) etchers

FILMS, VIDEOS, AND AUDIO RECORDINGS

The South Korean market for films and video recordings totaled US$550 million in 1992. Fostered by a 10-year trend of rising incomes and five years of exports and direct operation by foreign video distributors, growth is expected to continue for several years to come. The home video market in particular has been showing remarkable growth, primarily due to the increased use of VCR equipment and rising demand for videotape recordings. The US$90 million import market in films, videos, and audio recordings is expected to expand at an average annual rate of 10 percent through at least 1995.

Some of the HOT items:
- cartoons for children
- documentaries

- English-language instruction programs
- entertainment movies
- hobbies and travel
- music videos

ELECTRONIC COMPONENTS

South Korea's production of electronic components and equipment is growing at an annual rate of 15 percent. But despite developments in local production capabilities, Korean manufacturers still must import a variety of electronic components and equipment. Korean purchases of foreign-made components and parts are spurred by the local electronic industry's increasing needs for advanced components. Principal imports include microcircuits, semiconductor parts, fixed capacitors, cathode ray tubes, micromotors, instrument transformers and inductors, relays and switches, magnetic heads, and computer parts.

Some of the HOT items:

- computer parts
- CRT tubes
- electrolytic and ceramic capacitors and parts
- inductors
- large-scale integrated circuits (LSIs)
- magnetic heads
- motors and parts
- electronic microcircuits and parts
- parts for transistors and diodes
- relays, fuses, and switches
- semiconductor lead frames
- silicon, germanium, and other diodes
- very-large-scale integrated circuits (VLSIs)

TELECOMMUNICATIONS EQUIPMENT

With a projected annual growth exceeding 10 percent, South Korea is one of the fastest-growing telecommunications markets in the world. The Korean government has recently lifted barriers to imports of equipment to be attached to the public telecommunications network. The government is now in the process of replacing existing mechanical analog telephone switching systems and semi-electronic switching systems with fully digital, time-division switching systems. Government plans also call for improving telegraph services, data communication, and other new types of communication services.

Some of the HOT items:

- coaxial cable and other coaxial electronic conductors
- communication cables

- electronic switching parts
- facsimile, printing, and phototelegraphic apparatus
- line systems
- optical-fiber carriers
- radar apparatus and parts
- radio remote control apparatus
- radio telephone and telegraph reception parts
- radio-broadcast receivers
- radio-broadcasting and television equipment
- signal converters (modems)
- TDM-type multiplexers
- telephone set parts
- transmission apparatus

FOOD PROCESSING AND PACKAGING EQUIPMENT

The South Korean market for modern food processing and packaging equipment is relatively new. But increased local demand for processed food makes for favorable prospects. Significant investments in labor-saving machinery have recently been made to increase food processing capacity. Korean firms that specialize in food processing are enhancing their production technologies by affiliating with foreign firms through licensing agreements or joint ventures. The most significant imports include cooling and heating machinery, confectionery machinery, line equipment for food containers, and automatic wrapping machines.

Some of the HOT Items:

- automatic wrapping machines
- bakery equipment
- confectionery equipment
- filling and sealing packaging machines
- food and beverage processing machines
- fruit and juice processing machines
- heating and cooling machinery
- meat processing equipment
- seafood processing equipment

HOUSEHOLD CONSUMER GOODS

In 1989 the South Korean electrical appliance market was first opened to foreign competition. Since then, foreign exports of home appliances to Korea have been increasing, and some foreign name-brand washing machines, dryers, dishwashers, ranges, and refrigerators have acquired a strong market position. Given Korea's growing demand for products that utilize advanced technologies, the market for foreign exporters of home appliances is expected to remain attractive.

Some of the HOT items:

- dishwashers
- dryers
- electric ovens and ranges
- fully automated washing machines
- refrigerators
- vacuum cleaners

LABORATORY INSTRUMENTS

Demand for laboratory instruments in South Korea is likely to be high in the next several years due to the planned expansion of many research laboratories and hospitals. Private research facilities are also being established by companies that wish to develop and produce their own products locally. All of these facilities require advanced instruments and equipment, much of which can be obtained only from other countries. Opportunities exist for foreign exporters of sterilizers, centrifuges, laser instruments, and various testing apparatus. Korea's import market is expected to expand at an average annual rate of 10 to 15 percent for the next three years.

Some of the HOT items:

- calorie meters
- cathode-ray oscilloscopes
- chromatography and electrophoresis instruments
- fault and crack detecting instruments
- frequency measuring apparatus
- gas and smoke analysis apparatuses
- laboratory centrifuges
- laboratory sterilizers and autoclaves
- laser apparatus (other than diodes)
- pH meters
- radiation measuring instruments
- radiography apparatus for physical and chemical testing
- spectrometers
- spectrophotometers
- universal-type testing machines
- viscometers

AIRPORT AND GROUND SUPPORT EQUIPMENT

Increased air traffic has placed a strain on South Korea's airports. To relieve congestion and increase air service, many facilities are undergoing expansion and new ones are being constructed. New airport construction projects will provide multi-million-dollar sales opportunities for advanced foreign-made ground support equipment.

Some of the HOT items:

- air traffic control systems
- automated message switching systems
- automated shuttle systems
- baggage handling equipment
- instrument landing systems
- magnetic levitation trains
- passenger information systems
- radio-controlled trucking network systems
- snow blowers

MEDICAL EQUIPMENT

Motivated by increasing domestic demand, South Korean firms have begun to manufacture high-tech medical equipment. But most firms are able to do so only through technical licensing agreements with foreign firms. Even so, few of the items produced in Korea are considered equal in quality to foreign products. Thus Korea is likely to continue relying on foreign suppliers to meet its medical equipment needs for many years to come. Cardiological equipment, surgical and orthopedic instruments, respiratory equipment, and diagnostic apparatus are among the primary imports.

Some of the HOT items:

- anesthesia apparatus and oxygen tents
- cardiac pacemakers
- cobalt therapy units
- CAT scanners
- defibrillators
- diagnostic apparatus
- electrocardiograph (EKG) equipment
- electroencephalograph (EEG) equipment
- gamma ray equipment
- heart-lung machines
- incubators and respirators for infants
- linear accelerators
- medical x-ray film
- MRI equipment
- nebrilizers
- orthopedic instruments and implants
- oxygenators
- patient monitoring systems
- pulmonary function analyzers
- sterile surgical sutures
- surgical instruments
- ultrasonic diagnostic and therapeutic equipment

MACHINE TOOLS AND METAL-WORKING EQUIPMENT

Demand for advanced machine tools and metal-working equipment has increased remarkably. Although local machine tool manufacturers are focusing on domestic research and development, the import demand for numerically controlled machine tools is anticipated to increase in the next few years. South Korea's import market for machine tools and metal-working equipment is expected to increase at an average annual rate of 12 to 15 percent through 1995.

Some of the HOT items:

- automatic lathes
- bending machines
- broaches
- cylindrical grinders
- drilling machines
- drilling tools
- forming machines
- gear cutters
- hydraulic and other presses (greater than 300 mt)
- lathes
- machining centers
- milling cutters
- multispindle drilling machines
- planing machines
- punching machines
- reamers
- surface grinders
- tapping machines
- tool grinders
- universal milling machines

INDUSTRIAL PROCESS CONTROL EQUIPMENT

Many of South Korea's oil refineries, steel mills, electrical power companies, and petrochemical plants require new process control equipment, much of which must be imported. Although the quality and quantity of domestic equipment are expected to improve, imports should increase at an average annual rate of 11 percent through 1995.

Some of the HOT items:

- automatic regulators
- chronometric systems
- electrical quantity-measuring instruments
- electronic automatic regulators
- electronic radiation-measuring instruments and apparatus
- flow meters
- level indicators
- liquid- and gas-pressured measuring instruments
- non-electrical quantity-measuring instruments

POLLUTION CONTROL EQUIPMENT

South Korea's rapid industrialization has resulted in severe pollution, especially in large urban centers and industrial areas. Water pollution, caused by local manufacturing industries, is the most serious problem. Korea is heavily dependent on landfills for disposal of solid waste (93 percent); only 1.8 percent is incinerated. Citing the lack of landfill sites and the increasing amount of garbage, the Korean government intends to increase the rate of incineration and recycling. This policy will create a huge demand for incineration and recycling equipment, most of which will need to be imported. The US$282 million import market for pollution control equipment is expected to expand at an annual average rate 17 percent through 1995.

Some of the HOT items:

- atomic absorption spectrometers
- bag filters
- BOD incubators
- chemical balancers
- dissolved oxygen meters
- gas chromatographs
- liquid chromatographs
- multi-cyclone separators
- packed towers
- submersible aerators
- surface aerators

PULP AND PAPER PROCESSING EQUIPMENT

The South Korean paper manufacturing industry has grown steadily over the past three decades, and domestic demand for paper products has risen rapidly since the mid-1980s. The import market is expected to continue expanding at an average annual rate of 16 percent over the next three years. Demand is particularly strong for equipment used in the production of printing paper, toilet paper, and newsprint. Rising exports of liner board and corrugated medium paper will, in turn, increase import demand for production equipment.

Some of the HOT items:

- manufacturing equipment for printing paper
- paper production equipment for corrugated medium
- production equipment for liner board
- production equipment for newsprint
- production equipment for toilet paper

COSMETICS AND TOILETRIES

Foreign investment in South Korea's cosmetics industry was opened to foreign wholesalers in July 1991 and is expected to be opened to foreign retailers in 1994. Although foreign suppliers are still trying to establish themselves in this market, continued import liberalization and diversification of sales channels will be the most important factors affecting future sales opportunities. Foreign imports are expected to increase by at least 30 percent a year over the next few years.

Some of the HOT items:

- baby care preparations
- bath products
- hair fixatives
- lipstick
- makeup products
- perfume
- shampoo and conditioners
- skin care preparations

TEN EXTRA PROSPECTS FOR EXPORTING TO KOREA

- advanced materials
- aircraft and parts
- building products
- business equipment (non-computer)
- chemical production machinery
- drugs and pharmaceuticals
- electrical power systems
- furniture
- printing and graphic equipment
- pumps, valves, and compressors

OPPORTUNITIES FOR GROWTH

TRAVEL AND TOURISM

In January 1989 the South Korean government relaxed almost all restrictions on the issuance of passports to its citizens. Since then, overseas travel by Koreans has tripled, and the travel industry estimates that the total number of outbound travelers will easily pass 3 million by 1996. At least three market segments in Korea's travel and tourism industry remain underdeveloped: individual foreign travel, honeymoon travel, and transportation services.

Koreans' former reliance on group travel was more a reflection of their inexperience as international travelers than of any desire to travel in a group. Since the liberalization of international travel, many more Koreans are traveling alone, either for business or pleasure. Nearly 60 percent of all individual Korean travelers are repeat travelers.

Only 4 percent (approximately 16,000) of Korean newlyweds go abroad on their honeymoon. International airlines are keenly interested in this market, and travel agents are encouraged to promote honeymoon packages. Guam, Honolulu, Bangkok, and Taipei are popular destinations.

The loosening of travel restrictions has given a boost to providers of transportation services, especially airlines. The recent opening of Asiana Airlines' international service is an indication of the growing market for transportation services. Moreover, in April 1992 Korea opened the market to foreign suppliers of computerized reservation systems. This change will create numerous opportunities for foreign firms, technicians, and consultants.

INFORMATION SERVICES

Development of South Korea's information services is a cornerstone of the country's overall development strategy. The Ministry of Information has taken an aggressive stance toward improving access to information by individuals and businesses on both the national and regional levels. The markets for on-line databases and data communications look especially promising for foreign firms and specialists.

Foreign suppliers of on-line database services will find a relatively small but growing market in Korea. The government encourages them to step up their marketing efforts in order to establish a presence in Korea. The development of close contacts between foreign suppliers and local database operators will be critical in this emerging market.

Korea's data communications industry is divided into three sectors: communications equipment, electronic parts for information equipment, and software. According to a report from the Electronics and Tele-

communications Research Institute (ETRI) of Korea, the three sectors exported more than US$12 billion and imported more than US$9 billion in 1992.

The ETRI expects local production and export of communications equipment to grow at an average annual rate of 13.5 percent into the next decade. Imports in the software sector are expected to grow by 12 percent for the next several years.

TELECOMMUNICATIONS SERVICES

The South Korean government is loosening its monopoly over telecommunications. As economic restructuring and deregulation in the telecommunications services industry accelerate, opportunities will unfold for foreign suppliers. Overseas service providers will find they have a competitive advantage because few Korean firms have ventured into this industry. The establishment of joint ventures and technology licensing arrangements are two ways for foreign suppliers to enter the market.

The Korean government's plans call for improving telegraph services, data communications, and other types of communication services. The expansion of telephone systems and other communications networks are creating increased demand for a wide variety of equipment, including data transmission and facsimile machines.

CABLE TELEVISION

South Korea recently enacted a cable television law that splits cable broadcasting into three sectors: network providers, program providers, and system operators. Korea Telecom (KT) has built and currently operates the country's first complete cable television broadcasting system.

The major Korean electronics firms now involved in developing cable television are mostly working in collaboration with foreign suppliers of programs and systems. However, the Korean government is committed to fostering a local cable equipment manufacturing industry. It is projected that Korean-made cable TV equipment and systems will become common in the near future, making it more difficult for overseas suppliers of finished cable products to enter and remain in the market.

But foreign suppliers should still benefit from Korean investment in this rapidly growing sector, because the Korean market cannot support the internal development of a cable TV industry equal to that of other countries. Thus opportunities exist for foreign suppliers to conclude technology licensing and second sourcing agreements with local operators. Demand for video equipment used in studios is also expected to grow as requirements for modernization and variety in programming increase.

ADVERTISING SERVICES

South Korea's market for advertising services was liberalized in January 1991, and since then many foreign firms have entered the market. However, industry analysts point out that cultural differences and preferences in advertising methods give an inherent advantage to Korean agencies. Foreign advertisers may be able to reach only a 20 percent share of the country's total advertising market.

Foreign advertising services must receive approval from the Foreign Investment Information Center of the Economic Cooperation Bureau at the Ministry of Finance in order to operate in Korea. Most foreign firms find it beneficial to establish a joint venture or other business arrangement with local firms.

The market for foreign public relations firms appears to be more promising. Until recently, firms that specialize in public relations were largely unknown in Korea. Now public relations is considered one of the most promising sectors of the country's advertising industry. During the 1990s foreign firms, agricultural associations, and tourist agencies have been some of the best clients for public relations firms. In this sector, multinational firms such as Burson Marsteller Korea, Communications Korea, Hans PR, Merit Communication, and KPR are estimated to control some 40 percent of the market.

SECURITIES MARKET

The South Korean government is commitment to institutional reform for the securities market. Proposals include prohibiting individuals from conducting stock market transactions under fictitious names. Although some observers are skeptical about how long the new rules will be enforced, reform is part of President Kim's national campaign to make Korea "an attractive level playing field for foreign investors."

Active investment by foreigners in Korea's securities market is based upon the expectation of keeping their *net-purchaser* status, in which purchased securities may exceed sales. In the first half of 1993, overall purchases of Korean shares and net purchases by foreign investors amounted to W2.6 trillion (about US$3.2 million) and W1.7 trillion (about US$2.1 million) respectively, far surpassing 1992 figures.

By law, no more than 10 percent of a company's outstanding shares may be in foreign hands. Individual foreigners may purchase no more than 3 percent of a company's shares. Accordingly, some foreign investors have favored the stock issues of the largest listed companies, the *chaebol*, which are ac-

tually loose conglomerations of companies in several industries. Despite cries to raise the level of allowable foreign investment in listed securities, the Bank of Korea affirmed its existing limits on foreign participation in early 1994.

RETAIL DISTRIBUTION

In July 1993 the South Korean Ministry of Trade and Industry (MTI) announced the third phase in the opening of the retail distribution market: foreign companies are allowed to open up to 20 outlets with a maximum floor space of 3,000 square meters per outlet. (These figures represent a doubling in the number of outlets and a tripling of floor space.) Furthermore, foreign firms are permitted to run street stalls as well as to deliver products to customers on a contract basis.

Beginning in 1996 MTI will fully open the retail distribution market to foreigners, without any limits on the number or size of outlets. Nonetheless, restrictions on the ownership of land by foreigners and the difficulty and expense of finding appropriate sites are still major obstacles for foreign retailers.

REAL ESTATE

In order to promote economic liberalization and attract further foreign investment in South Korea, the government has announced a plan to open the domestic real estate market to foreign investors. The plan allows foreign companies to freely buy offices, factory sites, and sales outlets. A revision of the Alien Land Ownership Law is also expected to permit foreigners to purchase real estate for personal or business use only.

Revised guidelines issued during 1992 enabled foreign high-tech and insurance firms to buy real estate related to their business operations. But the government intends to continue to prohibit foreign investors from buying real estate for speculative purposes.

BUILDING PROJECTS

The size of the South Korean construction market was US$34 billion in 1990, with about 40 to 45 percent of the total accounted for by the cost of materials. The market for lumber products, in particular, is large and growing, due to Korea's lack of natural resources. There is also a developing interest in wood construction for residential housing in a market than traditionally has been dominated by concrete.

PUBLIC PROCUREMENT OPPORTUNITIES

South Korea's economic policies in the early and mid-1980s emphasized rapid export-led development, protection of domestic industries, and reduction of the country's large external debt. Throughout the 1980s government intervention in the economy to promote these objectives was pervasive, and restrictions on foreign trade and investment were common.

But Korea is now undergoing a fundamental transition. A new generation of leaders is intent on introducing political reform to turn the low-wage, low-skill economy into one based on high technology and advanced skills. Policymakers are also trying to strike a balance between export-driven growth and growth based on local demand. Foreign firms can thus expect to encounter a much more receptive market for their goods and services.

New liberalization measures will also open market sectors that have until now been off limits to foreigners. In particular foreign firms will have access to various public procurement projects. Although trade and investment in many procurement areas will probably remain tightly regulated for the foreseeable future, foreign suppliers of high-tech products and services related to infrastructure development will be welcome.

South Korea's Economic Planning Board has proposed incentives to encourage domestic and some foreign participation in public works projects such as roads. The new rules offer tax breaks and the possibility of partial ownership, and would allow companies to charge tolls and rents on projects they have participated in. They could also profit by building leisure and tourist facilities in conjunction with infrastructure. Participants would also be allowed to borrow abroad for such projects, which they are currently usually prevented from doing. The new rules require legislative approval.

FIVE-YEAR PLANS

In theory Korea is a free market economy based on private ownership of the means of production and distribution. However, the government has traditionally managed the economy through central economic development plans, specific industry expansion plans, price controls, and other special economic measures to achieve stabilization and growth.

Korea's seventh Five-Year Development Plan (1992-1996) sets forth the government's goals for expediting the development of technological capabilities and liberalizing the market. The proposed eighth Five-Year Development Plan (1993-1997) provides for the implementation of tax, financial, monetary, and administrative reforms that would significantly reduce the government's role in the economy.

A list of all major projects under the Five-Year Plan that are open to foreign competition is available from the Office of Supply of the Republic of Korea. The list may also be obtained at Korean embassies and consulates, or at the Office of Major International Projects, US Department of Commerce.

TRANSPORTATION

Major projects include the upgrading and extension of South Korea's road network, a new international airport near Seoul, a high-speed rail system, and expansion of port facilities in Pusan, Inchon, and Kwangyang. Seoul's metropolitan government hopes to alleviate the city's massive traffic congestion by expanding the current subway system and implementing a new underground express system. With the commission of the new Seoul Airport near Inchon city, Korea expects to become a Northeast Asian international air transport hub that can accommodate supersonic aircraft.

TELECOMMUNICATIONS

The Ministry of Government Administration has formulated a plan for a nationwide digital network that will integrate all computer systems and networks by the end of this decade. The national computer networking project has five components: the administrative network, the education and research network, the national defense network, the public security network, and the banking and financial network.

ENVIRONMENT

South Korea's rapid industrialization, urbanization, and population growth have compelled policymakers to focus on environmental issues. This promises to expand the opportunities for foreign producers of environmental technologies and pollution control equipment.

A plan by the Ministry of the Environment calls for a combined investment by government and private industry of US$11.7 billion over the next five years. The government is also drafting a "green plan," which will place environmental requirements on development projects. Eventually, antipollution measures will become compulsory for all industries.

Projects associated with the plan include the construction of 60 wastewater treatment plants, 55 incineration facilities, 157 sewage plants, and 34 sanitary landfill sites throughout the country. Waste disposal and collection systems will also be revised to minimize waste discharge and to separate recyclable waste.

ENERGY

South Korea's enormous economic successes have dramatically boosted its energy needs. Power generation facilities are straining to meet the increased demand. Thus the Korea Electric Power Company (currently the only power company in Korea) has embarked on an ambitious plan to construct up to 85 power plants during the next 15 years. This initiative will generate a continued demand for power generation systems and engineering services.

The Ministry of Energy and Resources is conducting a feasibility study to look into the possibility of electric power generation by private companies. The MOTIE is also considering opening participation in these types of projects to foreign firms.

Finally, the Atomic Energy Commission has approved a 10 year R&D plan for nuclear energy, which provides for a US$2.65 billion investment in 34 projects.

CONSTRUCTION AND LAND DEVELOPMENT

The Ministry of Construction recently formulated South Korea's third national land development plan, which outlines a long-term comprehensive policy for land use, development, and conservation. Over the next 10 years, the plan calls for the creation of three new industrial zones in the southwestern and central regions of the country, where industrial development has lagged behind that in the north and the east. Half of the factories located in and around Seoul are to be relocated to the three new industrial belts. By 2001 the new industrial regions are expected to account for 25 percent of the nation's industrial production, up from the present 15 percent.

The Ministry of Construction also intends to create high-tech industrial complexes in nine provincial cities, including Taejon, Kwangju, and Taegu. Office parks will be constructed in other major cities, and new towns will be developed in rural areas to ease the concentration of people in and around Seoul.

Finally, the Ministry of Construction has put forth a 10-year plan under which Pusan will become a center for international trade and finance, Taegu will become a center for business and the fashion industry, Kwangju will become a center for high technology and culture, and Taejon a center for R&D and public administration.

AEROSPACE

Much of South Korea's economic success has come from a strategy of export-led growth. But the government hopes to build the aircraft industry through public procurement contracts as well as through revenue derived from allowing the expansion of international carriers and a planned commuter air service. Both military and private sector orders are expected provide the necessary demand to greatly expand the aerospace industry.

In 1993 military demand from procurement programs helped push gross production in Korea's aircraft industry to an estimated US$600 million. Imports of aircraft and parts are estimated to top US$2.5 billion due to increased purchasing of military and civilian aircraft and parts.

US companies have traditionally dominated this market, but other countries are now entering it. Spain has recently made its first sale to the Korean military, England is becoming more aggressive, and Russia is believed to be testing the waters. The Russians have contacted major Korean aircraft companies about working together on Russia-based manufacturing that would blend Russian technology with Korean capital and marketing skills.

The civilian aircraft market is also expected to profit due to increased business by Korea's two national carriers, Korean Airlines (KAL) and Asiana Airlines. Asiana plans to procure 51 aircraft worth US$6 billion between 1993 and 1998. KAL will acquire 63 aircraft by the year 2000, including 14 in 1993 alone.

PUBLIC PROCUREMENT PROCESS

The Office of Supply of the Republic of Korea (OSROK) is responsible for supervising procurement by government agencies and government-owned enterprises in which the government holds a majority share. Formal public invitations to bid are issued for all procurement, although occasionally OSROK is obligated to make direct purchases, as in the case of spare parts for specialized equipment. Purchases are financed either through government-held foreign exchange or through loan and credit funds from foreign aid programs and international financial organizations. The invitation to bid specifies the source of financing.

Generally, bidding is worldwide and the deadline for receiving bids is 40 calendar days after the invitation is issued. By law the award must be made to the lowest qualified bidder who conforms to the terms and conditions of the bid invitation, taking into account the total cost, delivery time, quantity, specifications, and financial terms.

After various ministries and agencies determine their procurement needs, the Ministry of Trade and Industry reviews them to see whether the requirements can be met by local sources. If not, the Ministry of Finance must allocate the necessary foreign exchange. Specifications are normally drawn up by the government agency requesting the goods and services, and these agencies frequently call upon representatives of foreign suppliers for information and assistance. Foreign suppliers who wish to participate in Korean government business therefore find it helpful to have a local representative. Having a local representative also facilitates keeping abreast of developments in procurement plans and invitations to bid.

If a bid is made by a supplier's agent in Korea, the agent must be registered with OSROK as authorized to make offers on the supplier's behalf. If a supplier or manufacturer submits a tender directly to OSROK, the bid must be certified by a Korean embassy, consulate, or local chamber of commerce.

Korea is not a signatory to the GATT Government Procurement Code but has applied for accession. Accession to the code would expand opportunities for foreign firms bidding on OSROK-procured projects and would also qualify Korean firms to bid on the projects of foreign governments.

For further information contact:

Office of Supply of the Republic of Korea (OSROK)
520-3, Banpo-dong, Kangnam-gu
Seoul, Rep. of Korea
Tel: [82] (2) 533-9656 Tlx: OSROK K23244, 23703

OSROK procurement representatives can be reached at Korean embassies and consulates (Refer to the "Important Addresses" chapter for Korean embassies, consulates, and other procurement contacts.)

SPECIAL TRADE ZONES

FREE EXPORT ZONES

Location

South Korea's free export zones are special industrial areas in which foreign invested enterprises (FIEs) can manufacture, assemble, or process products for export using freely imported, tax-free raw materials or semi-finished goods. The government has designated two such free export zones for the bonded processing of imported materials into finished goods for export. The Masan Free Export Zone, located near Pusan in the south, was established in 1971. The Iri Free Export Zone, located on the western coast near Gunsan, was established in March 1975.

Incentives

Among the incentives offered to FIEs are various types of tax breaks and exemptions. No taxes or other duties are levied on foreign materials imported into the zones. Many facilities in the free export zones, including factories and warehouses, are for sale or lease at below market rates.

Facilities and Services

The Masan Free Export Zone has a port with a 20,000-ton capacity berth. The Iri Free Export Zone is 20 km from Kunsan port. Both zones have water and power supplies. Other facilities include on-site employee dormitories as well as apartments for foreigners which are located outside the zone.

Authority

The two zones are managed by the Free Export Zone Administration Office. Because there are no duties or taxes on foreign materials entering the zones, only limited regulation is needed. Therefore, in matters concerning customs in the free export zones, much of the authority over matters normally handled by the Ministries of Economic Planning, Trade and Industry, and Finance has been delegated to the Free Export Zone Administration Office and the customs house.

For further information, contact:

Director, Regional Industry Division
Ministry of Trade and Industry
Unified Goverent Building
1, Jungang-dong, Gwachon City
Kyonggi Province, Rep. of Korea
Tel: [82] (2) 503-9405 Fax: [82] (2) 503-9496
Tlx: 24478

WAREHOUSING

Storage

Adequate bonded storage facilities are available, and all are under the direct supervision of the Collector of Customs. Korea has two kinds of bonded areas: *designated bonded areas* consist of storage sites and customs inspection sites, and *licensed bonded areas* consist of storage, factory, exhibition, and sales sites.

Goods may be stored in bonded warehouses for up to two years, and duties are payable only when the goods are cleared through customs. Storage fees are high, however, and the use of bonded warehouses to maintain inventories is uneconomical.

Regulations

There are 171 licensed commercial bonded warehouses in Korea. In addition, some 517 manufacturing enterprises operate as licensed private bonded facilities. With the permission of the Collector of Customs, owners of goods stored in bonded facilities may repackage, divide and combine, or repair the goods, as long as the nature and quality of the goods are not changed as a result of these activities.

In principle, bonded warehouses are the only warehouse facilities available in Korea to foreign companies that wish to store shipped goods and still maintain title until they are cleared through customs by normal import procedures. Customs law states that privately owned and operated bonded warehouses may be established with the approval of the Collector of Customs. An application must include the name of the bonded warehouse, location, structure, numbers and sizes of buildings, storage capacity and types of products to be stored. Relevant articles of incorporation and corporate register must accompany the application.

For further information, contact:

Director, Surveillance Division
Office of Customs Administration
71, Nonhyun-dong, Kangnam-gu
Seoul, Rep. of Korea
Tel: [82] (2) 542-7141 Tlx: 24346, 24716

SCIENCE TOWNS

Location

The primary purpose of science towns is to encourage new innovations in science and technology. Taedok Science Town, located in Taejon City, was completed in 1992. Kwangju Science Town and two or three other zones are also being targeted for such use.

Facilities and Services

As of mid-1993, Taedok Science Town was home to 37 organizations, including government-supported institutions, industry labs, and university research institutes. Housing and recreational facilities are also available to employees and their families. Korea's first exposition, the Taejon International Exposition, is slated to take place in Taedok Science Town under the slogan, Challenge of a New Road to Development.

Regulations

On-site management is handled by the Taedok Science Town Administration. But overall authority rests with the Ministry of Science and Technology, which is responsible for the promotion and support of government-funded research institutes, private institutes, and universities. Only research organizations are permitted to locate in the science towns.

For further information, contact:

Taedok Science Town Administration Office
386-3, Toryong-dong, Yusung-gu
Taejon 305-340, Rep. of Korea
Tel: [82] (42) 861-5005/6 Fax: [82] (42) 861-1276

Foreign Investment

INVESTMENT CLIMATE AND TRENDS

Since the late 1980s South Korea's economy has struggled under the weight of slowed growth and declining foreign investment. In 1992 gross domestic product (GDP) grew by only about one-third the nominal average annual rate sustained during the 1980s. Preliminary estimates for 1993 suggest that GDP grew at about 4.5 percent, slightly behind 1992's 4.7 percent rate and anemic by Korean standards. Even more worrisome is the fact that foreign investment has fallen steadily since 1990. In fact, not only is new investment growing at a much reduced rate, but some foreign businesses are also actually divesting themselves of their Korean operations. If this trend continues, Korea will be deprived of critical capital and, more importantly, of the technology needed to enhance its industrial base. Korea's decline in foreign investment can be attributed to overregulation, rising labor costs, poor protection for intellectual property rights that causes foreigners to be unwilling to bring in advanced technology, and widespread corruption in business and government.

Overregulation By most accounts the overabundance of regulation and its enforcement by unsympathetic bureaucrats more than bloated cost structures is the main reason that investors are packing up and moving to other Southeast Asian countries or staying away in the first place. Many complain that regulations tend to be biased against foreigners and that key rules are unpublished or selectively enforced to the detriment of foreigners.

Rising Labor Costs Since martial law ended and trade union activity became legal in 1987, workers' compensation has doubled on average and the cost of benefits has risen dramatically, while productivity has increased by at most 60 percent. Korean factory wages are now the third highest in Asia, after Japan and Taiwan. In 1992 the government attempted to limit wage hikes to 5.7 percent, but most firms and trade unions settled on wage increases of around 15.5 percent. However, a realization that Korea is pricing itself out of the market and unprecedented cooperation between the main labor and employer federations in 1993 is expected to restrict wage increases to between less than 9 percent. However, South Korea has largely lost its edge in many areas of production due to its rapidly rising cost structure.

Corruption Bribery and other forms of corruption have been commonplace in Korea. On the one hand, gifts, favors, and kickbacks are simply a part of doing business in Korea, as they are in much of Asia. On the other hand, the burden of strict regulation and government bureaucracy has turned many "irregular" business practices into a necessity beyond what is simply a difference in cultural norms. For example, the applicant for a loan can often speed up or assure the approval process by paying the loan officer a percentage of the amount loaned, and traditional practice has factored such costs into the rates charged by banks for scarce credit. Naturally, these practices are a burden to investors, especially those with limited financial resources. While it is difficult to identify specific practices that are particularly detrimental to investment, the overall climate of corruption in Korea has definitely had a negative impact.

Lack of Access to the Domestic Market Since the early 1960s, when Korea began its phenomenal economic climb, autocratic officials, powerful civil servants, and domestic business leaders have adhered to a policy of export-led growth. High tariffs and other barriers have effectively shut out imported goods. And until very recently consumption of imported goods has been actively and officially discouraged. With little hope of producing for the domestic market, fewer foreign enterprises have been willing to brave Korea's high-costs, unfavorable regulatory environment, and often corrupt system.

Major Reforms In the face of the gloomy outlook for continued foreign investment, South Korea's first freely elected civilian president in 30 years has pledged to restore the country's economic prowess. President Kim Young Sam, who took office in February 1993, has made a public commitment to stamp out such corruption, institute market-oriented reforms, and open the economy to freer foreign participation. Two of the most significant measures specifically designed to boost such investment are the shift to a notification system for new foreign investments to replace the old prior approval system, and the easing of restrictions on foreigners operating in the real estate market.

Since taking office, President Kim has made enemies among powerful industrialists, bureaucrats, politicians, and the military who have found themselves the targets of corruption investigations and, adding insult to injury, public ridicule. Some of these individuals have already ended up in jail and others have fled the country to avoid the prospect of jail. These moves have generally played well with the public. However, Kim is risking his popularity among that public by focusing on a series of austerity measures, including wage freezes. Such measures will be combined with expansionary steps to jump-start the economy. These steps include a cut in central bank lending rates, an easing of the money supply, and a loosening of commercial regulations aimed at attract-

ing investment, especially in the area of high technology. Other planned reforms include a long overdue overhaul of the country's tax and banking systems.

The Challenge of Reform While many of President Kim's recent and intended reforms should help make the business climate more attractive to investors, the entrenched practices of politicians, bureaucrats, and businesspeople that have become institutionalized over time make the prospect of lasting change less certain. Of greatest concern are the under-the-table methods of getting around red tape, regulations, and other barriers to efficient business operation. More often than not, these methods involve bribery in one or another form.

As part of the reform plans, Kim intends to put an end to irregular practices not only by rooting out corruption but also by eliminating some of the red tape and regulations that have allowed it to flourish in the first place. If these reforms are successful—and early indications are that they have been to a greater degree than was initially anticipated—many familiar business practices will no longer be valid. Many businesspeople fear that they could be the next in line to be scapegoated in the rush to become noticeably purer. As it is, the system has been thrown into disarray while the players sit back to see what will happen. Reports are that much business activity in Korea has come to a halt because of this uncertainty.

LEADING FOREIGN INVESTORS

As of 1992 cumulative direct foreign investment in South Korea since 1962 had reached US$9.9 billion in 3,947 separate approved investments. Japan, Korea's former colonial master, is the top modern foreign participant in the Korean economy with US$4.2 billion, or 42 percent of the total since 1962. This includes investment in about 2,200 separate projects. However, in 1992 new Japanese investment fell by 31 percent from its 1991 level to US$154 million. Although this reflects disillusion with the situation in Korea, it is also indicative of a general pullback abroad by Japanese investors in the face of Japan's continuing severe recession.

The United States, a patron of Korea since the late 1940s, is the second largest foreign investor with total investments of US$2.8 billion in more than 900 separate projects, or about 28 percent of cumulative direct foreign investment since 1962. During 1992 the United States was the only major foreign investor to raise its stake in South Korea. In that year US investment rose by nearly two-thirds to US$380 million.

European countries represent 23 percent of investment since 1962, with interests in about 500 projects. In 1992 new European investment fell by 65 percent to US$282 million. The remaining 7 percent of direct foreign investment—US$700 million

Imported Goods Taboo for Korean Consumers

To sell a product or service, there must be a market. But in Korea, imported goods traditionally have not had one. Even as President Kim Young Sam now seeks to lure foreign investors into the country, the Korean government is doing little to encourage consumers to buy imported goods.

Most Koreans have been taught that imports are by definition luxury goods. Government-funded consumer groups routinely conduct "frugality campaigns" against overconsumption. Such campaigns are particularly detrimental to the sale of imported goods. Another tactic is to have consumer groups claim, usually without foundation, that imported foods are unsafe or that they cause mysterious illnesses or have unpleasant side effects.

The government has also been known to monitor (or at least it has threatened to monitor) Koreans' credit card purchases abroad and blacklist those who spend excessively. Periodic reports in the press caution Korean consumers against filling their suitcases with foreign goods.

in about 300 projects—has come from other countries, most of which have minor stakes in Korea.

In 1992 new direct foreign investment totaled US$894.6 million, down 36 percent from its record high of US$1.4 billion in 1991. And while foreign investment in most Asian countries is growing, with each year's new amount representing an increasing proportion of the cumulative total, in Korea 1992's roughly US$900 million represented only about 9 percent of that total, down from 1991's 14 percent of the total.

More than two-thirds of all foreign investment has been in manufacturing (68.2 percent). Within this category, the chemical industry has received the greatest amount, 15.1 percent of total investment, followed by electronics (14.4 percent), transportation (8.6 percent), and machinery (6.6 percent). Services account for most of the rest—31.2 percent—with hotels (15.4 percent) and banking (7.8 percent) representing the largest areas of foreign service investment. Foreign investment in such restricted areas as agriculture and mining accounted for only about 0.5 percent of total cumulative investment.

INVESTMENT POLICY CHANGES

Early in 1993 Korean authorities introduced changes designed to simplify the foreign investment process and lure back foreign capital. Several previously restricted areas were opened to new foreign investment, including the operation of harbor and port facilities, forestry nurseries, the logging business, wholesaling of alcoholic beverages and foodstuffs, foreign trade brokerage, and the leasing of air transport equipment. In addition, in early 1994 the government announced that it intended to allow foreign investors to participate in public works projects. Foreigners would not be allowed to own majority stakes or lead the development groups in these projects, but would be allowed to join domestic groups and take minority positions in such ventures. The proposal also includes tax and nontax incentives designed to guarantee a return on investment in such infrastructure projects that are to form a significant part of Korea's industrial upgrade plans. This measure is part of a broader attempt to attract more private capital to public works and infrastructural development projects that have been closed to foreigners and unattractive to domestic firms in the past.

Of even greater importance is the new system governing direct foreign investment. In the past foreign investments valued at more than US$5 million required review and prior approval by the Foreign Investment Review Committee (FIRC). Since 1993 only investments valued at US$20 million or more require such extended policy review. But the true heart of the recent reforms is the adoption of a notification system for most new investments to replace the cumbersome prior approval system.

Since March 1, 1993, foreign investors have been allowed to proceed with an investment within 30 days of formally notifying the Korean government of their intent to do so unless the investment is specifically denied within that period. That is, an investment proposal can be considered as having been approved if the investor had received no adverse response within 30 days.

In early 1994 the government announced additional changes that would allow foreign investments on the approved list below the US$20 million level to proceed concurrent with formal notification and without additional government approval. For larger investments and those in areas requiring confirmation, final approval is supposed to come within five days rather than the 30 established in the preceding round of liberalizations. These changes are slated to go into effect on July 1, 1994. Certain activities will remain off limits or restricted to foreigners, and there are considerable differences of opinion on the margins that require negotiation and could result in roadblocks for foreigners, but the system is rapidly becoming more transparent and user-friendly.

As part of the same round of reforms, the government also announced that beginning March 1, 1994 the Korea Development Bank and the Industrial Bank of Korea would be allowed to accept foreign investment proposals in addition to the Bank of Korea (BOK). Beginning July 1, 1994 other foreign exchange authorized banks will also be allowed to accept such proposals, further opening the investment process.

Prior to these reforms foreign investors needed explicit prior government approval. Such approval could take several months to receive. Now foreign investors need only notify Korea's Ministry of Finance (MOF), the BOK, or in some cases a local authority acting on behalf of these entities of their investment plans. Moreover, foreign nationals may now invest in manufacturing and service industries by means of the notification procedure provided their equity share is under 50 percent.

This amendment to the Foreign Capital Inducement Act is aimed not only at reversing the decline in foreign investment but also at bringing the Korean system into greater conformity with international standards and practices. Such standards are endorsed in the Trade-Related Investment Measures Agreement of the General Agreement on Tariffs and Trade (GATT).

Negative List Korea maintains a negative list of industries and activities in which foreign investment is prohibited or restricted. Of 1,148 sectors recognized under Korea's standard industrial classification codes, 56 (about 5 percent) are listed as prohibited to foreign investment, and 168 (about 15 percent) are restricted.

Restricted activities are those in which the Korean government allows foreign investment only under certain conditions. To be considered to operate in restricted business areas, a foreign applicant usually must participate in a joint venture with a Korean national company, with the domestic entity maintaining majority control over the venture. For the most part, restricted activities are those that require specific government assistance, produce pollution, depend heavily on energy and other imported materials, or involve investment in undeveloped targeted sectors of the economy—so-called infant industries—that the Korean government feels need protection from predatory foreign firms.

The restricted list is slated to be reduced as of July 1, 1994, allowing foreigners more leeway to invest in areas that had previously been restricted because of heavy use of energy and imported raw materials or because of infant industry protections. The exact industries to be included in the eligible category have yet to be determined and restrictions will still apply to industries placed on the negative list due to environmental concerns and "incompatibility with national tradition," a catch-all category.

Automatic Investment Approval The BOK was recently granted the authority to approve foreign investments automatically, that is without prior consultation with the MOF or other ministries. As noted, this authority is to be expanded to official and other foreign exchange authorized banks. Since 1989 the Korean government has gradually expanded the list of investments eligible for the automatic approval process.

At first only firms with less than 50 percent foreign equity investment were eligible for automatic approval. Now, the 49.9 percent limit for automatic approval may be waived if the enterprise exports 60 percent or more of its output, although the upper limit of foreign ownership allowed is still open to interpretation. Moreover, if a joint venture produces an item for domestic consumption deemed to be of such significance that it constitutes a material import substitution, it may be exempt from import licensing restrictions on most other items.

Repatriation of Capital and Profits As stated in the Foreign Capital Inducement Act, foreign investors may repatriate or otherwise remit abroad capital and profits derived from approved investments and activities. The investor must file an application with the president of a foreign exchange bank for approval of the specific transfer, which is usually granted after a review of the requested remittance, the status of tax payments, and other such matters.

Reinvestment of Dividends Foreign investors can reinvest earnings in their own enterprise or in new business ventures. To reinvest in their own enterprise, they are required only to report the reinvestment and the increase of capital that will be eligible for subsequent repatriation to the MOF. To invest such profits in a separate new venture, they must obtain formal approval from the MOF to the extent that would be required of a new foreign investment. In the past, the MOF was somewhat more lenient in approving new investment made with earnings generated by foreign operations in Korea, because such investments kept the funds working inside Korea instead of resulting in their loss through repatriation. Now that approval has become somewhat less of an issue, such reinvestment may represent less of an end-run around barriers to foreigners.

Access to the Stock Market The Korean government allows foreign investors to acquire a cumulative maximum of 10 percent of a listed national company's outstanding shares. No single foreign entity or individual may purchase more than 3 percent of a company's shares. Such limitations effectively prevent foreigners from gaining a controlling position in Korean listed firms, making stock market acquisition of limited significance in overall foreign investment in Korea.

Korean Investment Partners As recently as 1992 it was difficult for foreign investors to operate a business in Korea without a Korean partner. At the very least, the partner assisted in obtaining permits, dealing with government agencies, and interpreting regulations. The reforms of 1993 have made foreign direct investment without a partner more feasible.

While direct investment appears to be the trend of the future, having an investment partner still has its advantages, especially in dealing with labor unions and negotiating with government officials. Korean nationals have a certain edge in dealing with the system and its nuances that are unlikely to be easily penetrated and understood by a foreigner. At least one business analyst in Korea believes that the optimal arrangement is to form a joint venture in which a Korean partner has a relatively small 10 percent to 15 percent stake. The primary role of such a partner is to run interference with labor and officialdom and certify the enterprise as not fully foreign in the eyes of consumers and regulators in this homogeneous and highly ethnocentric country.

INVESTMENT INCENTIVES

For tax purposes, foreign invested enterprises are considered equal to Korean enterprises and therefore eligible for tax exemptions and reductions in accordance with the Income Tax Law, the Corporation Tax Law, and the Tax Exemption and Reduction Control Law. (Refer to "Taxation" chapters for more information.) However, special tax allowances are available to foreign invested enterprises in both the service and manufacturing sectors that bring advanced technology into the country and to small- and medium-sized foreign-invested firms regardless of industry or technology.

Foreign invested enterprises eligible for tax concessions are:

- Enterprises that use high technology
- Enterprises located in free trade areas
- Enterprises that have been granted tax concessions by presidential decree

TAX CONCESSIONS AVAILABLE TO FOREIGN-INVESTED ENTERPRISES

Income and Corporate Taxes Foreign invested enterprises are exempt from income and corporation taxes during the first four years of operation. During the fifth and sixth years, they pay 50 percent of the normal income and corporation taxes.

Acquisition, Property, and Aggregate Land Taxes Foreign invested enterprises that acquire commercial property after starting operations are eligible for a 50 percent reduction for the first six years of operation. Enterprises that acquire commercial property before beginning operations are eligible for the 50 percent reduction for the first five years.

Dividends Foreign invested enterprises that earn dividend income from shares of stock are eligible for a 50 percent reduction in income or corporate taxes during the first six years of operation.

Customs Duty, Value-Added Tax, and Special Excise Taxes Foreign invested enterprises that bring capital goods into Korea are eligible for a 50 percent reduction from these levies.

Royalties Suppliers of technology who operate under a government-authorized technology inducement contract are exempt from income or corporation taxes on resulting royalties for five years.

Tax Deductions Enterprises that provide technology-related services (for example, computer support services) can receive a 50 percent deduction on taxable income during the first six years of operation.

Local Tax Exemptions or Reductions Foreign invested enterprises located in industrial estates or designated rural areas can receive local tax concessions.

AVAILABILITY OF LOANS AND CREDIT

Foreign investors in Korea are eligible to obtain various types of financing. However, the funds available are generally limited. As a result, it can be difficult to acquire adequate funding from Korean sources. Typically borrowers pay bank lenders so-called commissions of 2 to 3 percent of the loan amount, essentially a kickback to the lending and

other senior offices of the bank. Under President Kim Young Sam's anticorruption campaign, this kind of practice is heavily discouraged, but it is as yet uncertain to what extent such common operating procedures are being altered in actual practice. (Refer to Financial Institutions for more information.) If successful, the banking cleanup is expected to make it much easier for small- and medium-size firms to receive loans without the usual under-the-table payments. It remains to be seen whether President Kim's reforms will produce lasting change.

General Loans Foreign invested enterprises may receive loans from commercial and specialized banks in the form of overdrafts, discounted notes, and general operating loans. Because funds are so limited financial institutions often provide funds by discounting notes. The major lending institutions in Korea are the Korean Exchange Bank, The Commercial Bank of Korea, The Korea First Bank, Hanil Bank, Cho Hung Bank, Bank of Seoul, Shinhan Bank, The Daegu Bank, The Bank of Pusan, Kyungki Bank, and the Korea Development Bank. (Refer to "Important Addresses" chapter for contact information on financial institutions.)

Trade Loans Commercial banks lend to exporters and manufacturers of materials and products that will be exported under the terms of letters of credit (L/Cs), documents against payment (D/Ps) or documents against acceptance (D/As).

Swap Loans Branches of foreign banks that borrow foreign currency from their headquarters or affiliates can exchange it for Korean currency under a repurchase agreement with a spread guaranteed by the BOK. Foreign banks can then use the resulting won for loans (swap loans) to foreign-invested businesses or to purchase monetary stabilization securities issued by the BOK to control the amount of currency in circulation. This foreign bank funding avenue is being reduced by the BOK which due to increased trade now has access to additional sources of foreign exchange and no longer feels that it needs to cater to foreign banks to ensure a ready supply.

Foreign Loans Korea-based enterprises can obtain a loan directly from a foreign investor to finance the purchase of locally made materials and equipment. However, the MOF must approve such loans, and has shown a preference for onshore financing to better control foreign exchange.

Direct Financing Enterprises can theoretically raise money directly by issuing bonds or selling stocks; however, few foreign invested enterprises have tried to do so.

COMMERCIAL AND INDUSTRIAL SPACE

Foreign Ownership As of July 1993 foreign nationals with business operations in Korea were only permitted to buy real estate and buildings directly linked to the operation of their enterprises. Such real estate included offices, factories, and sales outlets. Foreign personnel were also allowed to own residential property for personal use provided they complied with a host of rules. Korea continues to bar foreign investors from buying real estate for speculative purposes.

In revising the Alien Land Ownership Law, Korea has taken a substantive step toward opening its economy. Before this revision, foreign investors faced numerous restrictions, regulations, and other barriers when they tried to acquire real estate, including high financing costs and a general lack of funding sources. These impediments effectively shut foreign nationals out of the Korean real estate market. In fact, two large US-based banks were the only financial service firms that owned office buildings and residences for expatriate employees.

Property Guarantee All property of foreign invested enterprises is guaranteed and protected from requisition or expropriation. The same rights, privileges, and protection enjoyed by Korean nationals are extended to foreign nationals and enterprises, except in cases specifically prescribed by law.

Selecting or Building a Factory Korean law permits the building of new factories only in designated industrial areas. The government's policy of decentralization, aimed at relieving congestion in Seoul, prohibits new factory construction in the district. However, there is little problem in finding sites in more outlying industrial estates. The Korean government is building many industrial estates and providing the necessary infrastructure facilities in coastal and inland areas.

The government is particularly interested in attracting foreign investment to these areas. The 24 industrial estates have been classified in four groups: six specialized industrial estates, 14 local industrial estates, two private industrial estates, and the Iri and Masan Free Export Zones (although there are currently no available spaces in the free export zones). All offer low land costs, developed power and water supplies, transportation and support facilities, and special administrative assistance. All the industrial estates are open to foreign as well as local enterprises.

Notable among the industrial estates are the Gumi Electronics Zone, established for the assembly of electronic items and the manufacture of electronic components, materials, and related industrial products; the Changwon Industrial Complex, designed as an integrated machinery manufacturing base; and the Yochun Petrochemical Industrial Estate, which has been designated a petrochemical products manufacturing base. Additional information on industrial estates can be obtained from the director of the MTI's Regional Industry Division.

INVESTMENT ASSISTANCE

Special offices of the MOF are set up to assist potential investors with their initial investigations and provide help in carrying out the investment process. Other sources of investment advice include public organizations, commercial banks, and merchant banks, as well as local foreign firms. In seeking the latest information on Korean government rulings for specific cases, it will be necessary to refer to special laws, separate regulations, and announcements. Legal counsel should be obtained at an early stage.

Foreign Investment Promotion Division
International Finance Bureau
Ministry of Finance
Unified Government Bldg.
1, Jungang-dong
Gwachon City, Kyonggi Province, Rep. of Korea
Tel: [82] (2) 503-9276

Foreign Investment Information Center
Ministry of Finance
Unified Government Bldg.
1, Jungang-dong
Gwachon City, Kyonggi Province, Rep. of Korea
Tel: [82] (2) 503-9259

One-Stop Service Office
Ministry of Finance
1, Jungang-dong
Gwachon City, Kyonggi Province, Rep. of Korea
Tel: [82] (2) 503-9258

Foreign Investment Advice Office
Bureau of Economic Cooperation
1, Jungang-dong
Gwachon City, Kyonggi Province, Rep. of Korea
Tel: [82] (2) 503-7171

Center for Foreign Investment Services
Small and Medium Industry Promotion Corporation
24-3, Youido-dong, Yongdungpo-gu
Seoul, Rep. of Korea
Tel: [82] (2) 783-9611 Fax: [82] (2) 784-9230

Korea Chamber of Commerce and Industry
Investment Consultation Division
111, Sokong-dong, Chung-ku
Seoul, Rep. of Korea
Tel: [82] (2) 777-8048

Korea Development Bank
10-2, Kwanchul-dong, Chongno-ku
Seoul 110-111, Rep. of Korea
Tel: [82] (2) 733-2121 Fax: [82] (2) 731-8115
Tlx: 27463

Foreign Trade

South Korea is a relatively small country only marginally endowed with natural resources. Although it is largely self-sufficient in food production, it lacks many raw materials and must import a large percentage of its energy needs and many of the other inputs necessary to run its economy. During the past four decades South Korea has evolved from a predominantly agricultural, subsistence economy into an industrialized, internationally prominent economic power, based on its efforts to become an export power.

Because of the limited size and purchasing power of South Korea's domestic market in the early 1960s, national economic planners adopted a strategy that relied on exports to propel the rapid industrialization of the economy. Government initiatives included customs procedures designed to allow exporters to import necessary inputs cheaply and easily. Officials also encouraged foreign investment in such export-oriented activities, while at the same time protecting nascent national producers by discouraging competing imports through a host of restrictions, tariffs, and non-tariff barriers. By the mid-1980s South Korea's industries had become firmly established. Its increased attempts to produce high-technology, high-value-added items and growing investment in research and development have helped put to rest doubts about its ability to become more than the low-technology, low-quality commodity exporter it was in past years.

A significant shift in the structure of South Korea's economy has occurred over the years. Largely influenced by export production, the manufacturing sector's share of gross national product (GNP) increased steadily from 16.2 percent in 1962 to a high of 32.3 percent in 1988, while that of agriculture, forestry, and fisheries declined from 36.6 percent to 10.8 percent during the same period. By 1992 the agricultural sector had dropped even further, accounting for only 7.5 percent of the economy, a share that is expected to continue to fall in the future. Although Korean plans call for the manufacturing sector to continue to lead the economy, by 1992 it had dropped to a 26.8 percent share of that economy, 5.5 percentage points below its high point only five years earlier. Instead, the surging services sector has taken the lead in growth, an indication of economic maturation and the increasing importance of the domestic economy.

By design, South Korea's economic growth was led by its export industries. In 1992 26 percent of its gross domestic product (GDP) was generated by exports, although this was down from 37.5 percent in 1985. By comparison, exports represent only about 9 percent of Japan's total economy and 8 percent of that of the United States. (In contrast, the total value of exports is equal to 121 percent of Hong Kong's GDP, an indication of the colony's true dependence on trade.) Exports now play only a slightly greater role in South Korea than they do in Great Britain, where they accounted for 21.6 percent of GDP.

Exports grew by an average annual rate of 36.1 percent from 1962 through 1982, by 16.7 percent from 1982 through 1988, and by 6 percent from 1988 through 1992. Although preliminary figures for 1993 indicate growth in exports of 7.6 percent for the year, the overall declining rate reflects the increasing role of the maturing domestic economy as well as South Korea's loss of international competitiveness in recent years.

By contrast imports grew by an average 10 percent annual rate from 1981 through 1992. However, this figure masks the fact that between 1981 and 1986 they grew at only a 3.2 percent rate, while from 1986 through 1992 they surged at a 17.2 percent rate. Some of this growth in imports can be accounted for by heavy expenditures on energy, although oil prices have been either quiescent or trending downward during much of this period. And some import growth is attributable to investment in capital equipment designed to further South Korea's program of increasing high technology production, but the majority seems to be due to increased domestic consumption. In 1985 growth in GDP was 13 percent, roughly half of which was attributable to foreign demand and half to domestic demand. In 1992 out of a total change in GDP of 4.7 percent, almost three-quarters was due to domestic demand, while only somewhat more than one-quarter was due to foreign demand.

In the early 1990s South Korea was thirteenth among the world's trading powers. In 1992 exports reached a high of US$76.6 billion, while imports also set a record at US$81.8 billion. The country has posted a trade deficit in eight of the last 12 years, amounting to a net deficit of US$11.7 billion or just over 1 percent of total trade during the period. Although South Korea has been able to meet most of its investment needs with its substantial domestic savings, this apparent structural deficit is causing international borrowings to rise. External debt has been rising at an annual rate of about 8.5 percent in recent years, reaching US$44.5 billion in August 1993.

EXPORTS AND IMPORTS

In 1991 South Korea's exports were led by apparel (9.9 percent), semiconductors (7.8 percent), ships (5.7 percent), imaging equipment (4 percent), synthetic textiles (4 percent), iron and steel products (3.8 percent), footwear (3.6 percent), computers (3.5 percent), automobiles (3.2 percent), and audio equipment (2.5 percent). Together these top ten export categories accounted for slightly less than half of all exports, with all other categories representing less than 2.5 percent of total exports.

South Korea's main imports included crude oil (9.9 percent), semiconductors (5.9 percent), petrochemicals (4 percent), iron and steel (2.6 percent), computers (2.3 percent), lumber (2.3 percent), animal products (2.2 percent), engines and generators (2.1 percent), grain (2.1 percent), and coal and coke (2 percent). Together these top ten import catego-

ries accounted for slightly more than one-third of total imports, and virtually all of them can be classed as raw materials with capital goods representing a small portion. Remaining import categories accounted for less than 2 percent of the total.

TRADE PARTNERS

The United States has been the major customer for South Korean goods, taking 25.8 percent of its exports in 1991 followed by Japan with 17.2 percent. Hong Kong, Germany, Singapore, Liberia, and the United Kingdom collectively took an additional 20.4 percent of exports. Canada, Taiwan, Indonesia, Thailand, the Netherlands, France, Malaysia, China, Australia, Saudi Arabia, Italy, and Mexico, in rank order, are important as buyers of Korean products, although all of these countries took less than 2 percent of South Korea's exports. South Korea, in turn, buys most of its imports from Japan (26 percent) and the United States (23.2 percent). Germany, China, Saudi Arabia, Australia, and Indonesia sell it an additional 19.3 percent of its goods. Canada, Malaysia, the United Kingdom, Taiwan, Italy, France, Oman, the United Arab Emirates, Singapore, Iran, Brazil, and Hong Kong are other notable trading partners, but none supplies more than 2.5 percent of South Korea's total imports.

South Korea is seeking to diversify its trade so as not to depend so heavily on the United States and Japan. Its trade with China has been growing astronomically, such that according to some estimates China will soon be South Korea's third largest trading partner. South Korea is making a major effort to attract business from Eastern Europe and among the former Soviet states and has also made attempts to strengthen its ties and deepen its business relationships with nations in Southeast Asia, Latin America,

Korea's Top 10 Imports by % Increase

Commodity	% Increase from 1990
Steel angles for construction	141%
Ceramic products	109
Aircraft	99
Naptha	84
Prime movers	53
Iron ores	48
Agricultural food products	45
Frozen marine products	45
Pigs & steel bars	45
Wireless telecommunications equipment	37

Source: Foreign Trade Magazine

Korea's Top 10 Exports by % Increase

Commodity	% Increase from 1990
Ships & boats	47%
Petrochemical products	40
Semiconductors	25
Man-made fabrics	23
Motor vehicles	21
Domestic appliances	20
Electronic tubes & parts	20
Engines & generators	20
Leather & leather articles	19
ADP machines	14

Source: Foreign Trade Magazine

South Korea's Leading Trade Partners

Exports - 1991

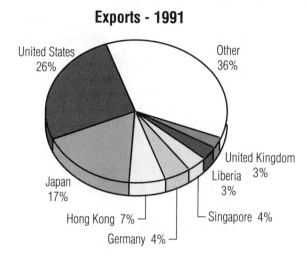

United States 26%

Other 36%

Japan 17%

United Kingdom 3%

Liberia 3%

Hong Kong 7%

Singapore 4%

Germany 4%

Total 1991 Exports: US$ 71.9 Billion

Imports - 1991

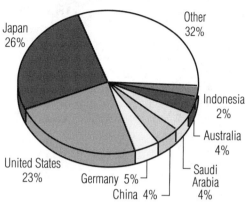

Japan 26%

Other 32%

Indonesia 2%

Australia 4%

United States 23%

Germany 5%

China 4%

Saudi Arabia 4%

Total 1991 Imports: US$ 81.5 Billion

Source: Foreign Trade Magazine
Note: Figures rounded to the nearest whole percent.

and Africa. The strength of the yen during 1993 has given it the opportunity to penetrate some markets that had previously been conceded to Japan.

The problem is that South Korea has run a chronic and growing trade deficit with Japan and a chronic and growing trade surplus with the United States, causing the US in particular to push for a greater opening of Korean markets while threatening to reduce South Korean access to its own all-important markets. South Korea has been struggling to get out of this bind, so far with only limited success. As its imports grow, and it moves closer toward open markets, South Korea has reduced the magnitude of the problem but has been unable to defuse it. Its decision to open its markets to foreign rice in late 1993 after a year of drought and domestic underproduction may enable it to win some respite on this front as it attempts to broaden its trade and become less dependent on its major partners.

GOVERNMENT DEVELOPMENT POLICY

South Korea's overall economic policy has been undergoing a major review in recent years to reflect its changing economic situation and international trends. Economic policy in the early and mid-1980s clearly reflected South Korea's outdated and disingenuous self-image as an underdeveloped and deficit-ridden underdog. Policy focused on rapid export-led development, protection of domestic production and markets, and the reduction of external debt, amounting to modern-day mercantilism. Government intervention was pervasive in virtually every aspect of the economy, and restrictions on foreign partici-

pation, both in trade and investment, were common and exclusionary in nature.

In recent years the government has announced a number of actions designed to open the economy to greater foreign participation, reduce its current account surplus, and limit its direct involvement in the economy. Policies include cutting tariffs, allowing the currency to appreciate, eliminating the import surveillance system, placing substantially more manufactured items on the automatic approval list, eliminating a number of restrictions on foreign direct investment, and taking a more active role in attempting to resolve trade disputes with key trading partners.

The sixth Five-Year Development Plan, covering the period from 1987 through 1991, outlined South Korea's development strategy for foreign trade and the economy in general and specified the major domestic infrastructure development projects to be undertaken. The plan's major objectives included continued economic growth, enhanced standard of living, greater technological autonomy, and improved industrial infrastructure. The government emphasized market principles—reliance on greater competition between both large and small companies and domestic and imported products—arguing that only through competition could Korean industry achieve world-class status. However, much of this supposedly unfettered competition has continued to be tempered by protectionism and government intervention. The plan also called for the government to encourage the development of high-value-added and high-technology industries to drive future export growth.

Underscoring these directives, the official sev-

Top 50 Korean Imports by Commodity (in $US millions)

Commodity	1991	% Change from 1990	Commodity	1991	% Change from 1990
Crude oil	$8,134	27%	Paper printing machines	679	19
Semiconductors	4,757	14	Inorganic chemicals	634	31
Petrochemicals	3,264	-1	Naphtha	616	84
Sheets & plate of iron or steel	2,098	26	Pigs & steel bars	596	45
ADP equipment	1,899	14	Articles or leather and furskin products	570	-8
Lumber	1,855	16	Ceramic products	569	109
Livestock products	1,781	3	Articles of paper & paperboard	538	30
Engines & generators	1,736	53	Motor vehicles	524	33
Cereals & cereal flour	1,650	0	Wireless telecommunications equipment	522	37
Coal & coke	1,600	24	Electronic application equipment	506	18
Natural vegetable materials	1,580	5	Balloon parts	478	12
Aircraft	1,568	99	Liquefied gases	449	15
Measuring equipment & parts	1,449	13	Steel angles for construction	432	141
Machinery parts	1,286	28	Optical instruments	424	23
Aluminum & aluminum products	1,142	-13	Sound equipment	403	7
Textile & leather machines	1,092	2	Fabrics of man-made staple fibers	379	20
Metal processing machines	1,052	12	Precious or semi-precious stones, precious metals	376	15
Copper & copper products	1,058	14	Testing and measuring equipment	365	20
Essential oils, perfumery	998	20	Agricultural food products	359	45
Static apparatus	923	23	Yarn of man-made fibers	338	21
Paper stock	890	-12	Frozen marine products	336	45
Motor vehicle parts	857	27	Gas oils	328	-36
Iron ores	828	48	Iron or steel pipes	309	20
Tobacco products	817	2	Total, including others	$56,500	17%
Nonferrous metals	709	-4			
Plastic products	697	21			
Electronic tubes & parts	691	32			

Source: Foreign Trade Magazine

enth Five-Year Plan governing economic activity from 1991 through 1996, emphasizes the following:

- Improvement of South Korea's international competitiveness. The government proposes to bolster the private sector by encouraging technological and managerial innovation. By 1996 investment and research in high-technology industries is expected to increase to between 3 and 4 percent of GNP from the 2.1 percent target set in 1988. Most of this growth is supposed to come from investment by the private sector. The government also plans to increase expenditures for education and other social services, expand available industrial sites, and ease chronic labor shortages.

- Coordination of economic policies in line with South Korea's rapid internationalization and promotion of a greater role in the global economy. This primarily involves adjusting regulations to comply with the dictates of the General Agreement on Tariffs and Trade (GATT), while actively courting potential partners to take advantage of the growing trend toward regional trade blocs.

- Realignment of social and economic systems according to free-market principles in order to strengthen the nation's economic structure. The roles of the public and private sectors are expected to be readjusted to promote greater competition and innovation among businesses. This goal has particular reference to the reining in of the *chaebol*, which the government considers to be too powerful and too diffuse. Planners will accordingly devise schemes to reduce economic concentration, while also removing administrative controls on smaller competitors. The functions of the central and local governments will also be more clearly delineated, allowing for greater autonomy and responsiveness at the local level.

The government projects average annual economic growth of 7 percent during the plan period. Its goal is to pass the per capita GNP threshold of US$10,000 by 1996, although Korean per capita income has stagnated at around the US$6,500 level, and the Korean cost structure has grown to where it is uncompetitive, which militates against increasing incomes. With increases in trade with so-called Northern—socialist and formerly socialist—Countries and in the international competitiveness of Korean industries, exports are expected to increase

at a 9.9 percent annual rate. Unless the world economy comes roaring back over the next couple of years, such an increase will be a stretch. A trade surplus of US$5.5 billion is projected for 1996.

Consumption is expected to increase at a rate more or less equivalent to that of GNP growth. At the same time, the government anticipates a gross savings ratio of at least 35 percent. Increased investment for industrial restructuring is expected to result in a gross investment ratio approximately equivalent to the gross savings ratio. Those managing the economy will have their work cut out for them in getting all of these often mutually exclusive factors to fall into line to support the overall program.

INDUSTRIAL FOCUS

South Korea made its reputation on commodity exports but has experienced difficulty in moving along the curve to the manufacture of more sophisticated products. Although it has considerable power, largely due to its huge *chaebol,* and pockets of highly sophisticated production, South Korea has lacked the openness, infrastructure, and skill to bring its industry along across a broad front. Hence, most observers take Korean official grand designs for the development of a high-technology industrial base with a grain of salt and predict that South Korea's competitive advantage will continue to rest with the incremental improvement of its large-scale heavy industry.

Korean industry has also experienced a surge in its cost structure, primarily due to the demands of labor since the late 1980s. Two of the reasons for the success of Korean industry were its low wage scale and the longest workweek in Asia or anywhere else. South Korea is losing much of its labor intensive mid-range production to cheaper offshore competitors, although the acute domestic labor shortage is likely to keep this phenomenon from resulting in a lowering of wages.

The government is currently working on the implementation of its 1991 policy document "Measures to Strengthen the Competitiveness of Manufacturing Industries." The goal of this program is to support the efforts of private enterprises to improve their individual competitiveness through research and development investment and rationalized management. Within this general framework, the government plays a supportive role in resolving problems that private businesses are ill equipped to solve by themselves, such as developing so-called bottleneck technologies that are holding back across-the-board development, providing better-quality education, expanding social service capital investment, and preparing additional industrial site capacity.

Technology-intensive fields—automobiles, machinery, specialty chemicals, electronics, and semi-

Top 20 Korean Exports by Commodity (in $US millions)

Commodity	1991	% Change from 1990
Clothing	$7,141	-6%
Semiconductors	5,586	25
Ships & boats	4,124	47
Image equipment	2,890	10
Man-made fabrics	2,874	23
Iron & steel plates	2,700	9
Leather shoes	2,564	-15
ADP machines	2,486	14
Motor vehicles	2,315	21
Sound equipment	1,832	-5
Petrochemical products	1,641	40
Domestic appliances	1,142	20
Electronic tubes & parts	1,032	20
Leather & leather articles	976	19
Containers	937	-9
Tires & tubes	898	3
Engines & generators	748	20
Canvas shoes	731	-1
Fabrics of man-made staple fibers	711	10
Radio communications equipment	624	13
Total, including others	$43,700	11%

Source: Foreign Trade Magazine

Korean Imports by Country (in $US billions)			
Country	1991	1990	% change
Japan	$21.2	$18.6	14%
United States	18.9	16.0	18
EC	9.9	8.4	18
Germany	3.7	3.3	12
China	3.4	2.3	48
Saudi Arabia	3.4	1.7	100
Australia	3.2	2.6	23
Indonesia	2.0	1.6	25
Canada	1.9	1.5	27
Malaysia	1.9	1.6	19
United Kingdom	1.7	1.2	42
Taiwan	1.5	1.5	0
Italy	1.5	1.2	25
France	1.4	1.2	17
Oman	1.2	1.4	-14
United Arab Emirates	1.1	1.1	0
Singapore	1.0	0.9	11
Iran	1.0	0.7	43
Brazil	0.9	0.7	29
Hong Kong	0.8	0.6	33

Source: Foreign Trade Magazine

Korean Exports by Country (in US$ billions)			
Country	1991	1990	% Change
United States	$18.6	$19.4	-4%
Japan	12.4	12.6	-2
EC	9.7	8.9	9
Hong Kong	4.8	3.8	26
Germany	3.2	2.9	11
Singapore	2.7	1.8	50
Liberia	2.1	.6	250
United Kingdom	1.8	1.8	0
Canada	1.7	1.7	0
Taiwan	1.6	1.2	29
Indonesia	1.3	1.1	25
Thailand	1.3	1.0	38
Netherlands	1.2	1.0	21
France	1.1	1.1	0
Malaysia	1.0	0.7	13
China	1.0	0.6	67
Australia	1.0	1.0	0
Saudi Arabia	0.9	0.7	29
Italy	0.8	0.8	0
Mexico	0.8	0.6	33

Source: Foreign Trade Magazine

conductors—have been targeted to become the nation's leading industries. This development has been accompanied by growing expertise in the areas of telecommunications equipment, computers, biotechnology, materials science, and aerospace. The development of high-quality downstream parts and components suppliers has also been targeted as key to the improvement of heavy industries.

REDUCING IMPORT RESTRICTIONS

Korea has been liberalizing its import regulations since 1980. The percentage of products decontrolled has increased from 68.6 percent in 1980 to 96.4 percent in 1990. In October 1989 the government agreed to either eliminate remaining import controls or otherwise make them conform with GATT provisions by 1997. South Korea plans additional cuts in its tariff rates between 1991 and 1994. According to the new tariff reduction schedule, the average overall tariff rate will be lowered from 11.4 percent in 1991 to 7.9 percent by the end of 1994. By then, average tariff

rates are expected to be on a par with those in the industrialized countries.

Foreign business people report that despite this lowering of official trade barriers, South Korea remains a difficult place to do business. High-status bureaucrats have come to wield despotic control over day-to-day activities, often using labyrinthine regulations and numerous "unpublished" and selectively enforced rules. A bias against foreigners and foreign goods continues to exist, making it difficult to capitalize on the increased nominal openness in the system and the growing demand for imported goods and services.

INTERNATIONAL ORGANIZATION MEMBERSHIPS

South Korea participates in many international forums. As of 1990 it was a member of 53 official international bodies, including 17 United Nations agencies, and a variety of nongovernmental international organizations, including GATT, the International Monetary Fund, and the Asia Pacific Economic Cooperation group. South Korea joined the European Development Bank in March 1990 and has committed itself to support development programs in Eastern Europe. The government has also begun an informal dialogue with the Organization for Economic Cooperation and Development concerning membership and has held OECD Dynamic Asian Economies workshops.

In 1987 South Korea established the Economic Development Cooperation Fund to provide bilateral official loans to developing countries. As of 1990 it had lent on seven projects in seven developing nations. South Korea also promotes private overseas investment and the transfer of technology. As of 1991 the government had approved overseas investment of US$4.59 billion in 81 countries. The principal recipients of this private Korean investment were China and developing countries in Southeast Asia, Latin America, and Africa. Because of South Korea's successful economic development over the past quarter century, trainees from other developing countries frequently visit South Korea to study its development. The country also sends development experts to work with foreign governments and businesses overseas.

Leading Exporters to South Korea (in $US billions)

Country	1990	% Increase
Japan		
Electric & other machinery	$8.7	4
Chemicals	2.4	7
Iron & steel	1.3	-11
Scientific instruments	1.0	-10
Textile yarn, cloth & manufactures	.6	5
United States		
Electric & other machinery	$4.0	8
Chemicals	1.7	3
Aircraft & parts	1.0	-21
Cereals & products	0.8	-13
Hides & skins, undressed	0.7	11
European Community		
General Machinery	$2.6	48
Organic chemicals	0.8	1
Pharmaceutical raw materials	0.5	7
Base metal products	0.5	-4
Agriculture, forestry & fishery products	0.4	15

Source: Foreign Trade Magazine

Import Policy & Procedures

INTRODUCTION

With the arrival of a new administration in South Korea at the beginning of 1993, the country's leaders signaled their intention to speed up reforms of the import regime. Of particular importance to South Korean-based importers and foreign exporters are the recent reductions in tariff rates on most commodities to standard international levels and the planned elimination of nearly all import restrictions by 1997. (Many restrictions have already been removed.)

To a certain extent importing into South Korea can still be a complicated and time-consuming process. An import licenses must be obtained for all goods brought into the country, and all foreign suppliers must work through local agents and distributors licensed by the Association of Foreign Trading Agents of Korea. Korean branches of a foreign company may now serve as local agents and distributors, but only licensed traders are permitted to import directly and take title to goods under their own name.

REGULATORY AUTHORITY

The Ministry of Trade and Industry (MTI) governs most aspects of Korea's foreign trade. It sets trade policy, issues trading and import licenses, and regulates import restrictions, among its other functions.

Ministry of Trade and Industry
1 Jungang-dong
Gwachon City, Kyonggi Province, Rep. of Korea
Tel: [82] (2) 503-9405, Fax: [82] (2) 503-9496
Tlx: 24478

The Association of Foreign Trading Agents of Korea registers local sales agents and distributors. These local representatives may be Korean branches of foreign firms. Only licensed traders are permitted to import and export directly.

Association of Foreign Trading Agents of Korea (AFTAK)
Dongjin Bldg.
218, Hangangno 2-ga,
Yonsan-gu
Seoul, Rep. of Korea
Tel: [82] (2) 792-1581/4, Fax: [82] (2) 785-4373

IMPORT POLICY

Import Authorization

Those who wish to engage in foreign trade in Korea must first register with and obtain a license from the MTI. Only traders who have registered in this way are authorized to import and export goods in their own name. Many Korean licensed traders also act as agents for foreign suppliers.

Trading Licenses

Traders are classified into two groups: Class A traders are specialized traders whose activities are not restricted while Class B traders are small- and medium-sized manufacturing enterprises whose activities are restricted. Class A trading companies may import any product to supplement their own products and, with certain exceptions spelled out later in this chapter, may import products unrelated to their manufacturing business in Korea. Both Class A and Class B trading companies may import an entire line of products from their parent company.

Class A Trading License Foreign-invested Class A traders may export and import all products except grains, meats, fruits and vegetables, alcoholic beverages, fertilizers, pesticides, books and newspapers, coal briquettes, fuel oil, bottled gas, food and beverages, antiques, and artwork. Both domestic and foreign applicants for a new Class A trading license must meet two criteria: First, they must have paid-in capital of not less than W50 million (about US$62,000), or they must have maintained a minimum W50 million bank deposit balance during every day of the preceding month. Second, they must have manufactured and supplied export goods valued at more than US$100,000 through the use of local letters of credit or procurement authorizations during the six months before they apply for the license. In order to renew its trading license, a Class A trader must have done a minimum of US$500,000 in export sales between January 1 and December 31 during the two years preceding its application for renewal.

Class B Trading License Class B traders may export products that a foreign-invested manufacturing company produces and import the raw materials, equipment, and components that the company needs for manufacturing. For companies with no foreign investment, the Class B trader may import goods that the parent or affiliated company has manufactured, but it may not export products.

Both domestic and foreign-invested applicants for a new Class B trading license must meet one of the following criteria: they must either be engaged in the manufacturing or mining sectors or they must have been licensed and approved under Articles 8, 11, 12, and 23 of the Marine Products Industry Law, Article 7 of the coastal Fisheries Law, or Article 4 of the Military Supply Law and they are exporting products that they have manufactured or importing products for their own use. They may also have been designated by the MTI as a special trader under restricted conditions and have obtained membership in a trade association; or they are a corporation established under other laws; or they are a special corporation dealing with energy or tourism; or they are a Korean branch of a foreign enterprise approved under Ministry of Finance procedures.

A branch office must meet two criteria. First, it must have paid-in capital of not less than W50 million (about US$62,000). Second, it must have received export letters of credit totaling at least US$50,000. To renew its trading license, a branch office must have exported a minimum of US$500,000 worth of goods between January 1 and December 31 during the two years preceding its application for renewal.

General Trading Companies

Korean general trading companies (GTCs), known in Korean as *chaebol*, are modeled after the highly successful large-scale Japanese trading firms. GTCs are eligible for preferential measures regarding importation of major raw materials, participation in international tenders, and so forth. Under revised criteria for recognition as a GTC that went into effect on June 30, 1988 the firm must be public, and its annual export sales must be equal to at least 2 percent of the value of all Korean exports.

Eight firms met these requirements as of June 30,

1988: Hyundai Corporation, Daewoo Industrial, Samsung, Sangyong Corporation, Lucky-Goldstar, Hyosung Company, Sunkyong, and Korea Trading International (Koryo Trading). Such firms must meet the criteria just outlined every year in order to maintain their designation, except for Korea Trading International, which the government established specifically to help small, independent manufacturers market their products abroad.

Offer Agents

Foreign suppliers must submit their agency agreements to the MTI for registration through the Association of Foreign Trading Agents of Korea. The agents in this association act as representatives of foreign manufacturing suppliers and make offers on behalf of their principals. However, unless they are also registered traders, they may not import for their own account. In many cases offer agents who also act as distributors pay a small fee to registered trading firms that import for them. A new applicant for offer agent status must either be a local branch of a foreign company or represent at least two suppliers from two different countries, one of which is located outside Asia. To remain qualified, a registered offer agent must earn a minimum of US$50,000 in sales commissions annually.

The Korean government does not prescribe any particular form or period of validity for such agency agreements, nor has it established ceilings for markups. An agency agreement executed on the foreign company's letterhead does not need to be notarized by a notary public or approved by any other official body. An agreement not on the foreign company's letterhead must be notarized by the Korean consulate or by a notary public stationed in the country of export. The foreign supplier generally extends exclusive sales right to the agent, who is then obligated not to represent or handle competitive products, usually for a period of two years. A temporary nonexclusive agreement is possible, but Korean agents do not favor such agreements. Standard provisions for a recommended agency or distributorship agreement can be obtained by contacting the AFTAK.

Import Licensing

In addition to a trader's license, an importer must have a specific license for every import transaction, and he must obtain the license before a letter of credit can be opened for the foreign supplier. Licenses for unrestricted commodities are issued automatically on application to the Korea Exchange Bank or any Class A foreign exchange bank or branch. The documents required vary with the nature of the applicant's business and the type and origin of the product. Licenses are valid for up to 12 months. Applications for licenses to import restricted items on the government's negative list are approved on a case-by-case basis after screening by relevant government agencies or manufacturing associations. Neither consular legalization nor certification by a chamber of commerce is required. Before a license is issued, the pro forma invoice is checked to see whether the offer price exceeds the maximum import price established by the government for the commodity.

Restrictions

The government establishes criteria for the contents and safety of products in Korea, especially consumer goods. The penalty for violations is severe. The MTI publishes a negative list, the Export and Import Notice, as part of its annual trade plan. The negative list remains in effect until its next revision, usually in July of each year. In general, goods are classified into three categories: automatically approved, restricted, and prohibited. Most raw materials, capital goods basic to economic development, and consumer goods not domestically produced fall into the automatically approved category. Restricted items are limited by the government. They can be allowed into Korea on a case-by-case basis. The importation of some luxury items, protected domestically produced goods, and goods considered harmful to public health and morals is prohibited.

The Korean government is taking steps toward the gradual liberalization of imports, and it has significantly reduced the number of restricted items. In 1989 the Korean government reviewed many individual laws to eliminate or amend the provisions that restrict imports. As part of a bilateral agreement that Korea reached with the United States in May 1989 Korea agreed to internationalize standards affecting such commodities as cosmetics, pharmaceuticals, and food products. Further liberalization is anticipated. At the beginning of 1991 some 376 items were classified as restricted. All such import restrictions are scheduled to be phased out by July 1, 1997 in accordance with the General Agreement on Tariffs and Trade (GATT). On January 1, 1991 import restrictions were lifted on 102 additional items including 37 seafoods, such as crab, carp, octopus, perch, and frozen sea cucumber; 29 farm products, such as pineapples, corn, walnuts, bananas, and melons; 10 livestock products, such as venison, mutton, frozen pork, and live honey bees; 17 miscellaneous items, such as art paintings, diamonds, rubies, and two kinds of Taiwanese liquor; and nine agricultural products, including sorghum, millet, and green peas.

Under an approved foreign investment, foreign investors can generally import anything needed to set up a manufacturing plant. If the plant's products are intended for export, there are very few limits on what can be imported as long as the imports contribute directly to the exports.

Duty Exemptions

Certain types of imports are encouraged through reduction of or exemption from duties. Import duties are not assessed on capital goods or raw materials imported in connection with approved foreign investment projects. Raw materials used in the production of goods for reexport are often exempt from duty. Finally, certain machinery, materials, and parts used in designated industries may enter Korea either duty free or at reduced rates.

Tariffs and Valuation

Korea adheres to the GATT Customs Valuation Agreement, which details rules for a fair, uniform, and neutral system of valuation and precludes the use of arbitrary or fictitious value. These rules stipulate a primary method of valuation and list acceptable alternative methods to be applied in a prescribed sequence under specified conditions. Korea maintains a three-column import tariff schedule comprised of general rates, temporary rates, and GATT rates. Most Korean duties are assessed on an ad valorem basis. Some items are assessed at specific rates or a combination of ad valorem and specific rates. The dutiable value of imported goods is the normal CIF price at the time when the import was declared. Tariffs must be paid in Korean won before goods can clear customs.

Tariff Reduction Plan

In 1989 to reduce trade friction, manage its current account, and improve its competitiveness, the South Korean government implemented a Five-Year Plan to reduce tariff rates on imported raw materials and manufactured goods to levels equivalent to those that prevail in the world's developed economies. Levels were to be reduced from an average 13 percent in 1988 to 7.9 percent in 1993. The plan proceeded on schedule until August 1990 when the Korean government announced that the implementation schedule would be delayed by one year to counteract reduced revenues. Completion of the tariff reduction package is scheduled for January 1, 1994.

Despite these scheduled reductions, the Korean government has announced plans to raise tariffs on 14 farm and marine products from the current rates of between 9 and 50 percent to as much as 100 percent. These adjustments include a rise to 60 percent from the current 13 to 30 percent rate on dry radishes, soybean malt, and carrots, and to 100 percent from the current 9 to 50 percent rate on oak mushrooms, bracken, dried persimmons, acorns, toothpicks and raw materials for toothpick making, tropical fish, sea bream, mudfish, and canned bai top shell.

Customs Classification

Korea's tariff classification is based on the internationally recognized Harmonized Commodity Description and Coding System.

Preshipment Classification

A ruling regarding the customs classification of items not shown in the tariff schedules or the dutiable status of goods on which there is some question can be obtained in advance of shipment. Firms needing preshipment determination should write to the Collector of Customs in Seoul.

Customs Administration
71, Nonhyun-dong, Kangnam-gu
Seoul 135-00, Rep. of Korea
Tel: [82] (2) 542-7141 Tlx: 24346, 24716

If feasible, submit samples. If this is not possible, include photographs, specifications, and descriptive literature with the application.

Taxes Applicable to Imports

A value-added tax of 10 percent is levied on the CIF value of the import plus the amount of customs duty paid. Exempt goods include various unprocessed foodstuffs, certain services, and minor items like books and newspapers. A special excise tax is levied on certain luxury items (such as jewelry, furs, and golf equipment), durable consumer goods (such as air conditioners, refrigerators, automobiles, and pianos), and other items whose use the government wishes to control (such as gasoline, coffee, and soft drinks). The tax, which ranges from 15 to 100 percent, is levied when such commodities are sold, carried out of the factory, or imported.

Antidumping Duties, Subsidies, and Countervailing Duties

Korea is an adherent to the GATT conventions covering antidumping, subsidies, and countervailing duties.

Countertrade

The Korean government has established guidelines for countertrade transactions. Each transaction must follow established export-import procedures, and the Korean export must precede the imports. The transactions must be covered either by a single contract or by two separate contracts—one for import, one for export, each of which refers to the other. Guarantees of payment or performance should be used only under the most extenuating circumstances. In such cases, letters of credit should be used for reciprocal payments between the trading parties. Price differentials between the commodities exported and imported must be reconciled according to Korea's foreign exchange control law. Approval from the MTI is required for transactions involving foreign governments or state-owned enterprises and goods valued at US$5 million or more. Such transactions are subject to international bidding procedures. No restrictions are imposed on countertrade exports for which Korea does not anticipate a domestic shortage.

The following import items are generally eligible for countertrade: raw materials imported by necessity, items not produced or not available locally, items that can readily be supplied to a third country, and items imported due to policy considerations. The Korean government limits countertrade to firms that can directly handle both the export and import involved. If a government ruling is required to determine the exporters or importers, the Korean government will name Korea Trading International or another GTC. Finally, countertrade transactions must be economically balanced. The importer-exporter bears any financial loss that occurs and the government accepts no liability for such financial losses.

ATA Carnet

Korea is a signatory to the ATA Carnet Convention and accepts carnets under the ATA carnet scheme established by the Customs Cooperation Council in conjunction with the International Bureau of Chambers of Commerce. Under the ATA convention, a single customs document allows expeditious, duty-free entry of articles having commercial value that are intended for display at trade fairs, exhibitions, seminars, or similar events. Travelers may bring such goods into Korea or have them shipped by air or sea, and they may remain in Korea up to six months. Customs officials at the port of entry use information provided by the shipper to set the time limit.

Samples

Careful documentation and handling of samples are essential to minimize problems with customs clearance. Merchandise samples and advertising material used solely for promotional purposes are exempt from customs duties at the discretion of port-of-entry customs officials. Valuable samples can be admitted temporarily on a duty free basis if the value of the duty is deposited with customs officials. With prior approval from the Korea Trade Promotion Corporation, foreign salesmen may bring in samples intended for demonstration without paying duty. There are specific additional regulations for pharmaceutical samples.

Personal Use

Goods carried in by a foreign businessperson for use while in Korea can enter duty free. In this case, the customs official makes a note on the passport indicating that the traveler may not leave the country without the item in question.

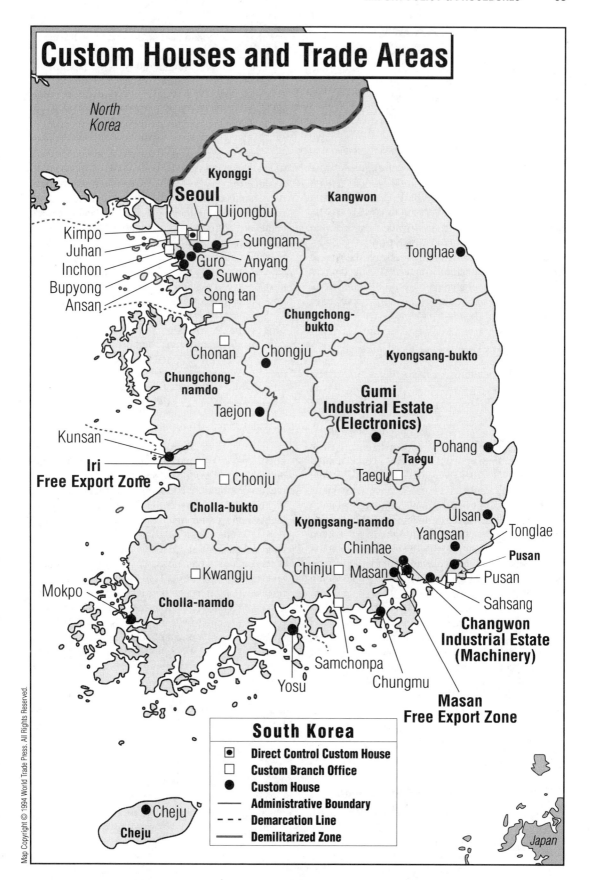

Custom Houses and Trade Areas

North
Korea

Kyonggi

Seoul

Kangwon

Uijongbu

Kimpo
Juhan
Inchon
Bupyong
Ansan

Sungnam

Tonghae

Guro
Anyang
Suwon
Song tan

Chungchong-
bukto

Chonan

Chongju

Kyongsang-bukto

Chungchong-
namdo

Taejon

**Gumi
Industrial Estate
(Electronics)**

Kunsan

Pohang

**Iri
Free Export Zone**

Chonju

Taegu

Taegu

Cholla-bukto

Kyongsang-namdo

Ulsan

Yangsan

Tonglae

Pusan

Chinhae

Mokpo

Kwangju

Chinju

Masan

Pusan

Sahsang

Cholla-namdo

**Changwon
Industrial Estate
(Machinery)**

Samchonpa

Yosu

Chungmu

**Masan
Free Export Zone**

South Korea

- ⊡ **Direct Control Custom House**
- ☐ **Custom Branch Office**
- ● **Custom House**
- — **Administrative Boundary**
- --- **Demarcation Line**
- — **Demilitarized Zone**

Cheju

Cheju

Japan

Warranty Parts

Spare or other parts shipped to Korea under warranty will normally be subject to tariffs unless it can be shown that the part to be replaced was sent out of the country for repair. In the case of repaired parts, duty is based on the value of the repairs plus round-trip freight costs.

Exhibition Materials

Goods entering Korea for exhibition purposes must be stored in a bonded area, such as the US Trade Center at the US embassy in Seoul or the Korea Exhibition Center (KOEX). Exhibit goods may be kept without charge at the US Trade Center during the exhibition period, after which they must be reshipped directly out of Korea; presented at customs for payment of regular duty on the value declared at time of entry; or transferred to the Seoul customhouse bonded storage area for no more than 90 days from the date of their entry into Korea.

IMPORT PROCEDURES

General procedures for importing into Korea include the following steps. First, conclude an import contract. Second, secure permission to import. For restricted items, approval must also be obtained from the relevant government or industrial authority before applying for the import license. Third, apply for an import license. Fourth, establish a letter of credit. (The licensed party must do this within the time period indicated by the license. Extensions can be obtained by making application to the bank.) Fifth, receive the transport documents. (The foreign exporter sends them when the goods have been shipped. If the freight arrives before the transport documents, the importer may present a letter of guarantee to the shipping company in order to procure the goods.) Sixth, clear customs.

Clearing customs involves the submission of a report of import to customs after the shipment has been unloaded and stored in a bonded warehouse. The customs clearance report must be prepared by the consignee, who has employed a certified customs specialist or a certified customs clearance corporation for this purpose. The customs inspector verifies that the shipment conforms to the documents, calculates and levies the tariff, and issues an import approval notice to the consignee. At this point, the merchandise can be removed, and customs clearance is completed.

Marking and Labeling Requirements

Country-of-origin marking in Korean or English is required on all goods imported into South Korea. For goods processed or manufactured in more than one country, the country where the most substantial change was made is considered to be the country of origin.

There are also commodity-specific labeling requirements. For example, electricity consumption data must appear on all electrical home appliances. When the name of a pesticide is in a foreign language, the Korean name is also required. Pharmaceuticals, medical instruments, sanitary materials, and cosmetics must be accompanied by certificates of inspection for each item and by statements of authority to manufacture issued by the government of the country of manufacture. For pharmaceuticals, the certificate of inspection must include the manufacturer's name and address; date of manufacture; lot, batch, and control numbers; and, when applicable, expiration date. Ideally, the importer submits the certificate of inspection with the application for the import license. It may not be submitted later than the time of customs clearance.

For imports of food, product labels must show product name; the name, address, and telephone number of the importer; the business report number; manufacture and sell-by dates; weight or volume; the names and characteristics of five or more ingredients; methods of preservation; and places where the product can be returned or exchanged.

Documentation

Extreme care should be taken when shipping documents are prepared. Errors can result in costly delays in customs clearance, in reshipment to correct an unintentional undershipment, and in double payment of customs duties. In general, the documents required for nearly all surface shipments to Korea include a signed commercial invoice, a certificate of insurance endorsed in blank for 110 percent of the invoice value, and a bill of lading made out to an exchange bank designated by the importer. A certificate of origin issued by a Korean consulate is required for some goods from selected countries. Such a certificate must be issued by a Korean consulate and show the marks, numbers, commodity descriptions, quantities, prices, and country of origin. With very few exceptions, all imported goods must be new, not having been used previously. Multiple copies of documents are required. The number depends on the nature of the shipment. The following nine sections describe the documents that Korean customs requires for imports.

Import License

Every import requires a license. For most imports, the license is issued automatically upon application. The applicant must be a registered trader (contact the Ministry of Trade and Industry).

Pro Forma Invoice

The pro forma invoice is required for obtaining an import license and opening a letter of credit, and it must contain at least a full description of the goods in question, their FOB value, and insurance and freight, individually and as a total figure. At least two copies should be issued and certified by a chamber of commerce, which makes and retains a copy for its files. Two copies are then presented to a Korean consulate for "legalization" (certification). The consulate retains the copy and returns the legalized original.

Commercial Invoice

The commercial invoice must be issued at least in triplicate (three copies) and signed by the seller. It should include the place and date of shipment, port of arrival, unit cost of each item, and cost of freight, insurance, and all other charges. All three copies must be certified by a chamber of commerce, which retains one of the copies for its files. After certification, two copies must be legalized by a Korean consulate, which retains the copy and returns the original.

Bill of Lading

There are no special requirements regarding the form of a bill of lading, but all markings and case numbers appearing on the packages in the shipment must appear on it. The grouping of marks or numbers on shipments of mixed commodities is not permitted. For shipments coming by air, air waybills replace bills of lading. Bills of lading and air waybills must conform strictly to the conditions and terms of the buyer's letter of credit.

Packing lists

Packing lists are required, and they must include a full and concise description of the items in the shipment. They should be issued at least in duplicate. One copy should be enclosed in the relevant package, and one should be sent with the other documents.

Certificates of Origin

A special form supplied free of charge by Korean consular offices is required for certificates of origin. Such certificates must show method of payment (for example, letter of credit, sight draft). If payment is by letter of credit, the letter number must appear on the certificate, and a copy of the L/C must be attached. If not, this fact must be stated on the certificate of origin. Other data required on the origin certificate include description of goods, quantities, value, name and address of importer, name and address of exporter, marks and numbers, and name of carrier. A certificate of origin must be certified by a chamber of commerce and then presented to the Korean consulate along with the other documents required for legalization. The consulate retains one copy of the legalized certificate and returns the original and two copies. Certificates of origin are not required for shipments consigned to government agencies of the Republic of Korea, shipments consigned to members of the diplomatic corps and related international organizations, personal effects, and shipments valued at less than US$100 FOB, unless a letter of credit specifically requests it.

Insurance Certificate

When the exporter arranges insurance, an insurance certificate must accompany the other documents. Normal commercial practices generally apply, but requirements for CIF shipments are somewhat complicated. Firms should follow the insurance company's advice regarding this document.

Steamship Company Certificate

Korean regulations pertaining to the steamship company certificate are subject to change without notice. A waiver certificate may be required for goods not shipped on a Korean flag vessel. Follow the advice of the importer and the shipping line that you have selected.

Other Documents

A letter of correction is required when corrections are necessary on the certificate of origin. The Korean consulate supplies the requisite form free of charge. It must be filled out, signed, and notarized. Three copies must be presented together with the certificate of origin that it is correcting. When the documents to be corrected have already been sent to Korea, the consulate will forward the legalized letter of correction there.

Certificates of inspection and statements of authority to manufacture are issued by appropriate government officials in the country of manufacture and are required for each item in shipments of pharmaceuticals, medical instruments, sanitary materials, and cosmetics.

Prohibited plants and plant products can be imported for experimental or research purposes with a special import permit from the Ministry of Agriculture, Forests, and Fisheries. Such permits must accompany the goods to their destination.

Appropriate quarantine certificates issued by the relevant government agencies in the country of export are required for shipments of live animals. Without these certificates, imports of livestock can suffer significant delays. When the livestock shipment arrives in Korea, an application for a Korean quarantine certificate must be filed with the National Veterinary Quarantine Station. The shipment cannot clear customs until the certificate is issued. There are special regulations for dogs, cats, and other pets.

Regulatory Requirements

A number of regulations require inspection and approval of domestic and foreign industrial and agricultural goods prior to sale.

Under the Food Sanitation Law, all importers of foodstuffs, food additives, and similar items destined for domestic sale must file a report on import with the Ministry of Health and Social Affairs through the head of the quarantine office at the port of entry. The report must be accompanied by copies of the import license, a detailed description of ingredients, and shipping documents. Where required, materials collected for inspection are reviewed by the health institute under the administrative jurisdiction of the quarantine office at the port of entry.

In March 1989 the Korean government took numerous measures to simplify import approval procedures for pharmaceutical, food, chemical, and industrial products. As part of a bilateral agreement reached with the United States in May 1989 the Korean government committed to further simplify its standards and approval procedures for additional categories of food products, cosmetics, and other industrial products designed to bring it into greater conformance with international practice. In many cases, marks of international standards and inspection certification should serve to meet the Korean requirements.

Dispute Settlement and Arbitration

South Korean government regulations stipulate that any commercial dispute or difference of opinion in international trade be settled amicably by the immediate parties to the transaction without delay. Korea is a member of the International Commercial Arbitration Association. Several leading local law firms handle the legal affairs of international companies. However, Korea is not a litigious society, and Korean business practice emphasizes compromise. The only action available short of litigation is to submit a complaint or dispute to the Korean Commercial Arbitration Board (KCAB). Besides arbitrating the disputes brought to its attention, the KCAB conducts informal investigations to assure that Korean companies do not renege on international contracts to the detriment of Korea's business reputation.

Free Zones

The government has designated two free export zones for the bonded processing of imported materials into finished goods for export. The free export zones are special industrial areas where foreign-invested firms can use raw materials or semi-finished goods imported tax free to manufacture, assemble, or process export products. The Masan Free Export Zone, established in 1971, is located near Pusan in the southern part of the country. The Iri Free Export Zone, opened in March 1975, is located near Gunsan on the western coast of Korea. The Free Export Zone Administration Office (FEZAO) manages both zones and shares customs authority with the customhouse located inside the zone. No factory buildings are currently available in either of the free export zones. Information on free export zones can be obtained from:

Director, Regional Industry Division
Ministry of Trade and Industry, Unified
Government Building
1, Jungang-dong
Gwachon City, Kyonggi Province, Rep. of Korea
Tel: [82] (2) 503-9405 Fax: [82] (2) 503-9496
Tlx: 24478

Reexports

Customs duties paid are rebated on all goods exported within 18 months from the date of import. This rule applies to raw materials and semi-finished components that are used in the production of goods for reexport. Where applicable these goods are also exempt from such local taxes as value-added tax, special consumption tax, and liquor tax. The duty rebate also applies to goods originally imported for local consumption but subsequently exported as long as export occurs within 12 months of the import date. Traders should note that in all cases importers and end users are required to post a bond in the amount of the estimated duties and taxes until they can provide proof of the reexport.

Warehousing

Adequate bonded storage facilities are available in Korea. All are under direct supervision of the Collector of Customs. Korea has two kinds of bonded areas: designated bonded areas (designated storage sites and customs inspection sites) and licensed bonded areas (bonded storage sites, bonded warehouses, bonded factories, bonded exhibit sites, bonded construction sites, and bonded sales sites). Goods can be stored in bonded warehouses for up to two years, and duties are payable only when the goods are cleared through customs. With the permission of the Collector of Customs, goods stored in bonded facilities can be repackaged, stored, divided and combined, or repaired, provided that the nature and quality of the goods are not materially altered in the process. Storage fees are high, and the use of bonded warehouses to maintain inventories is limited by the costs and lack of space. Inquiries regarding bonded facilities in Korea can be addressed to:

Commissioner, Customs Administration
71 Nonhyun-dong, Kangnam-ku
Seoul 135-00, Rep. of Korea
Tel: [82] (2) 543-7441 Fax: [82] (2) 503-9324

The two-year storage period does not apply to the storage of live animals or plants, perishable merchandise, or other commodities that can cause damage to other merchandise or the warehouse facility. The Collector of Customs bears no responsibility for goods stored in customs facilities.

Technical Standards and Requirements

The principal agency establishing industrial standards in Korea is the Bureau of Standards of the Industrial Advancement Administration (IAA), an agency of the Ministry of Trade and Industry. Metric weights and measures are in common use in Korea, but the current domestic system combines metric, pound, yard, and *chockkwan* (a traditional Oriental system) weights and measures.

Electric Current

The electric current used in Korea is AC, 60 cycles, 100/200, 105/210, 220/380 volts, single- and three-phase, (3), (2, 4), (2, 3, 4) wires. All household appliances must be designed to operate at 220 volts without the addition of transformers or other modifications. The Korean government plans to shift to a standard system of 220/380 volts by the year 2000.

The Industrial Standardization Law of September 1961 established the Bureau of Standards and the Council for Industrial Standardization. The bureau establishes and publishes standards and urges voluntary adherence. Thus far, 7,000 standards have been published for mechanical, electrical, civil, and metallurgical engineering; mining; construction; the textile and chemical industries; foodstuffs; and ceramics; and 802 items have been approved for certification to carry the Korean Standard (KS) marks. Because past and pending standardization legislation has been patterned on US models, equipment acceptable in the United States usually meets Korean standards.

On December 31, 1982 the Ministry of Trade and Industry revised the KS system to allow the KS mark to be awarded to foreign products after product inspections. However, the KS system has been applied primarily to items manufactured in Korea. As yet there are no provisions for inspecting overseas production facilities. All applications for the use of KS marks on products must be submitted on the prescribed forms to:

Bureau of Standards, Industrial Advancement Administration
2, Jungang-dong
Gwachon City, Kyonggi Province, Rep. of Korea
Tel: [82] (2) 503-7928

Foreign Goods Subject to Quality Inspection

The Korean government requires quality testing for about 70 products, including such diverse items as electric shavers, rice cookers, baby carriages, tricycles, pencil sharpeners, roller skates, umbrellas, and toys.

Quality Guarantee

Importers are required to supply detailed information on quality for 820 products, including detergents, soaps, furniture wax, shoe polish, paints, toilet tissue, and ready-made men's and women's suits, purses, shoes, shirts, and ties.

Methods of Payment for Imports and Deposit Requirements

Deposits must accompany the application for the required import license. The balance is due when the bank releases the shipping documents. All import transactions except those conducted directly by the government are subject to the following deposits: for small- and medium-sized industries, 10 percent of the total value of the shipment; for large industries, 15 percent of the total value of the shipment.

There are three principal methods of importing using Korean foreign exchange: letters of credit (L/Cs), documents against acceptance (D/As), and documents against payment (D/Ps). All follow universal commercial practice. (Refer to the "International Payments" chapter.)

Imports on deferred payment terms (for example, D/As and L/Cs) are allowed only for commodities not subject to specific commercial duties on which the tariff rate is 20 percent or less; commodities for incorporation into export production; and crude, light, and heavy oil. Deferred payment terms are valid only up to 60 days with two exceptions. Terms are 30 days for procurement from nearby sources (such as Japan, Hong Kong, Taiwan, and the Philippines) where sailing time does not exceed 10 days, and 90 days for crude oil and liquefied petroleum gas (propane and butane), which usually come from farther away and require longer shipping times.

Import Facilitators

Local representation in the Korean market is crucial for successful sales promotion. Alternatives for a foreign firm include establishing a branch sales office in Korea managed by home office personnel, appointing one of the foreign trading firms in Korea as its representative, selecting a licensed trader to act as its agent, or authorizing a registered offer agent to represent it in Korea. (Refer to the "Business Formation" chapter for additional information.)

Export Policy & Procedures

INTRODUCTION

Under the leadership of President Kim Young Sam, who took office in early 1993, Korea is pushing ahead with efforts to liberalize its export process. Korea now allows many more agents and distributors to serve as local buyers and sellers of products made in Korea. Korean branches of foreign firms are now also permitted to act as agents and distributors. However, only licensed trading companies are authorized to export directly. This development has opened up many more distribution channels for foreign importers and for foreign companies operating in Korea.

The formal export procedure remains somewhat arduous. In addition to having to work through licensed trading companies, exporters must obtain approval for all products exported. Many categories of goods must also be inspected. Inspection of the materials used in a product may also be required during the manufacturing process.

REGULATORY AUTHORITY

The Ministry of Trade and Industry (MTI) governs most aspects of Korea's foreign trade. It sets trade policy, issues trading and import licenses, and regulates import restrictions, among other functions.

Ministry of Trade and Industry
1, Jungang-dong
Gwachon City, Kyonggi Province, Rep. of Korea
Tel: [82] (2) 503-9405 Fax: [82] (2) 503-9496
Tlx: 24478

The Association of Foreign Trading Agents of Korea registers locals sales agents and distributors. These local representatives may be Korean branches of foreign firms. Only licensed traders are permitted to import and export directly.

Association of Foreign Trading Agents of Korea (AFTAK)
Dongjin Bldg.
218, Hangangno 2-ga Yongsan-gu
Seoul, Rep. of Korea
Tel: [82] (2) 792-1581/4 Fax: [82] (2) 785-4373

EXPORT POLICY

Export Authorization

Korea's trading system consists primarily of licensed traders and offer agents. All persons desiring to engage in foreign trade in Korea must first register with and obtain a license from the MTI. Only traders who have registered in this way are authorized to import and export goods in their own name. Many Korean licensed traders also act as agents for foreign suppliers.

Trading Licenses

Traders are classified into two groups: Class A traders are specialized traders whose activities are not restricted. Class B traders are small- and medium-sized manufacturing enterprises whose activities are restricted.

Class A Trading License Foreign-invested Class A traders may export and import all products except grains, meats, fruits and vegetables, alcoholic beverages, fertilizers, pesticides, books and newspapers, coal briquettes, fuel oil, bottled gas, food and beverages, antiques, and artwork. Both domestic and foreign applicants for a new Class A trading license must meet two criteria: First, they must have paid-in capital of not less than W50 million (about US$62,000), or have maintained a minimum W50 million bank deposit balance during every day of the preceding month. Second, they must have manufactured and supplied export goods valued at more than US$100,000 through the use of local letters of credit or procurement authorizations during the six months before they apply for the license. In order to renew its trading license, a Class A trader must have done a minimum of US$500,000 in export sales between January 1 and December 31 during the two years preceding its application for renewal.

Class B Trading License Class B traders may export products that a foreign-invested manufacturing company produces and import the raw materials, equipment, and components that the company needs for manufacturing. For companies with no foreign investment, the Class B trader may import goods that the parent or affiliated company has manufactured, but it may not export products.

Both domestic and foreign-invested applicants for a new Class B trading license must meet one of the following criteria: they must either be engaged in the manufacturing or mining sectors or have been licensed and approved under Articles 8, 11, 12, and 23 of the Marine Products Industry Law, Article 7 of the coastal Fisheries Law, or Article 4 of the Military Supply Law and they must be engaged in exporting products that they have manufactured or importing products for their own use. They may also have been designated by the MTI as a special trader under restricted conditions and have membership in a recognized trade association; or they are a corporation established under other laws; or they are a special corporation dealing with energy or tourism; or they are a Korean branch of a foreign enterprise approved under Ministry of Finance procedures.

A branch office must meet two criteria. First, it must have paid-in capital of not less than W50 million (about US$62,000). Second, it must have received export letters of credit totaling at least US$50,000. To renew its trading license, a branch office must have exported a minimum of US$500,000 worth of products between January 1 and December 31 during the two years preceding its application for renewal.

General Trading Companies

Korean general trading companies (GTCs), known in Korea as *chaebol*, are modeled after the highly successful large-scale Japanese trading firms. GTCs are eligible for preferential measures regarding importation of major raw materials, participation in international tenders, and so forth. Under the revised criteria for recognition as a GTC that went into effect on June 30, 1988, the firm must be public, and its annual export sales must be equal to at least 2 percent of the value of all Korean exports. Eight firms met these requirements as of June 30, 1988: Hyundai Corporation, Daewoo Industrial, Samsung, Sangyong Corporation, Lucky-Goldstar, Hyosung Company, Sunkyong, and Korea Trading International (Koryo Trading). Such firms must meet the criteria just outlined every year in order to maintain their designation, except for Korea Trading International, which the government established specifically to help small, independent manufacturers market their products abroad.

Export Inspection

In order to maintain and enhance the viability of Korean products in the international market, the Korean government requires that certain designated products intended for export be inspected for compliance with minimum standards in four areas: quality (structure, function, performance, external appearance), packaging, materials, and design and manufacturing. The quality inspection is required for nearly all items subject to inspection. The materials inspection must be performed during the manufacturing process to assess the quality of the materials from which the product is made. The design and manufacturing inspection is conducted for products in which design and manufacturing methods are particularly crucial to the determination of quality.

Goods can be inspected either by a private agency or by the Korea Institution of Trade Inspection (KITI). When the buyer contracts with a private inspection agency, the inspection certificate that it issues takes the place of the government export inspection certificate. Under certain conditions—for example, the export agreement designates inspection as the buyer's responsibility—the government requirement may be waived. Some products—for example, those bearing the KS mark of the Korean Bureau of Standards—are automatically exempted from inspection because the designation itself implies a quality inspection.

Korean Bureau of Standards, Industrial
Advancement Administration
2 Chungang-dong
Gwachon City, Kyonggi Province, Rep. of Korea
Tel: [82] (2) 503-7928, Fax: [82] (2) 503-7941
Tlx: 28456 FINCEN K.

Goods that fail the mandatory quality inspection may not leave the country. Goods that pass are issued an inspection certificate, which is required for customs clearance.

Voluntary Inspections

The KITI offers a variety of fee-based voluntary inspection services, both to buyers of Korean products who wish to have a final check on the goods before they leave Korea (preshipment inspection) and to manufacturers who want help with quality control. Foreign buyers of Korean goods are advised to contract for preshipment inspection by writing an inspection clause into the letter of credit and to stipulate that shipping documents must include an inspection certificate. The KITI will make sure that the products conform exactly to the buyer's specifications and to any international standards specified and forward its report to the buyer by fax, letter, or telex. The KITI inspects the shipment as many times as it takes to satisfy the buyer that the specifications have been met. It issues an export certificate only after the buyer confirms that the findings are satisfactory. Preshipment inspection may involve verification of materials; verification of manufacture when production begins; assessment of workmanship after one-quarter of the order has been produced; assessment of the function of the materials after one-quarter of the order has been produced; and post-production inspection for construction, appearance, workmanship, function, packaging, marking, and conformity to samples. Visual tests and chemical tests are also available.

The cost of inspection is assessed on the total invoice value of each shipment. Applications for preshipment inspection can be made by fax, letter, or telex to the KITI and should provide such details as the supplier's address, a description of the products, the quantity ordered, and specific quality and inspection requirements. Forwarding a copy of the letter of credit to the KITI together with the application will ensure that the supplier complies with the inspection clause. The KITI's involvement with the transaction ends when the buyer indicates that the test results are satisfactory. Any dissatisfaction on receipt of the goods must be negotiated between buyer and exporter without KITI involvement.

Export Inspection Centers

A number of commodities on the Korean tariff schedule are subject to compulsory government export inspection, and they must receive a government-issued export inspection certificate before they are permitted to leave the country. The number of commodities subject to mandatory inspection has dropped as the general quality of Korean manufactures has risen to meet the standards required for sale on international markets. The products that required export inspection in 1990 included:

- adhesive tapes
- cigarette lighters
- dolls
- electronic parts
- fishing gear
- handbags and luggage
- jewelry
- leather products (garments, gloves, footwear)
- lighting and other electric products
- metal arts and crafts
- packaging materials
- photo albums
- plastic ware
- roller skates
- sports balls
- toys
- zippers

The supplier is responsible for complying with mandatory export inspection. He or she obtains the application forms from KITI. The supplier pays the export inspection charges, which are assessed at 0.1 percent of the shipment's FOB invoice value. If testing reveals that the goods are deficient in quality, the exporter has 20 days in which to bring the shipment up to standard and a second test is administered. If the products fail the second test, the goods must undergo remanufacture and retesting in order for the export contract to be fulfilled.

EXPORT PROCEDURES

General procedures for exporting from Korea include the following steps. First, conclude an export contract. Second, secure approval to export. Third, produce the export goods. Fourth, clear customs. Fifth, ship the goods. Sixth, collect payment.

The nature of the transaction and the type of goods to be exported may require any of the following additional procedures: obtaining letters of credit, obtaining an export recommendation; purchasing raw materials in Korea or importing raw materials into Korea; obtaining loans; having the export goods inspected; and applying for refunds of tariffs paid.

Export Approval

Official approval is required for all exports from Korea. For unrestricted items, the exporter must simply obtain approval from a foreign exchange bank. For items on the MTI's negative list, which is published annually as the Export and Import Notice, a recommendation by the appropriate government ministry or trade association is required. Some items restricted under special laws may require additional, more formal approval, including actual export permits. The Import and Export Notice lists specific export requirements for individual restricted commodities.

Applying for Export Approval

When applying to a foreign exchange bank for export approval, the exporter must provide the following information: the exporter's name, a documentary letter of credit (the original plus a duplicate), export terms, a description of the goods, the port of lading and the transport route, and the settlement method and period of validity.

Export permits are valid for one year, but an extension can be granted if there is an unavoidable delay in meeting the order.

Customs Clearance

Commodities for export must be stored in a bonded area pending customs clearance. After the goods have been deposited, the exporter submits the requisite documents to customs officials. Customs checks the goods to be sure that they conform to the paperwork and issues an export declaration authorizing customs clearance. The export declaration procedure requires the following documents: five copies of the application for export declaration, one copy of the export license, one copy of the invoice, one copy of the packing list, and one copy of the bill of lading. Additional documentation may be required by customs in specific cases.

Export Shipment

Once customs has issued the export permit, shipping can be contracted for, marine insurance can be purchased, and the goods can be shipped out. The exporter then issues a bill of exchange for the export proceeds and submits the shipping document, letter of credit, and any other required documents to the foreign bank.

Bill of Lading

The bill of lading is considered the most important document in a transaction involving transport by sea or by air. (It is called an air waybill if the goods are transported by air.) It is the document used to take title to the merchandise, and as such, it must conform to the terms in the letter of credit in every particular. When shipping under cost, insurance, and freight (CIF), cost, freight/carriage, and insurance paid (CIP), or other related methods, the supplier contracts and pays for the freight.

However, many buyers prefer to arrange for the shipment themselves in cooperation with a local freight forwarder, consolidator, or shipping line. In this case, payment is made under such terms as free alongside ship (FAS), free on board (FOB), free on board airport (FOA), or other related methods. Make certain that the shipping agent is aware of the correct terms and how the freight charges will be paid. This will help to ensure that the carrier prepares the bill of lading in accordance with the conditions of the letter of credit, purchase contract, and other documents.

The bill of lading lists the port of departure, port of discharge, name of the carrying vessel, and date of issue. The date of issue is very important because it indicates whether goods have been shipped within the time period required in the letter of credit. The supplier must be careful to submit all required documents on time to receive payment under the terms of the credit.

Bills of lading can be either negotiable or nonnegotiable. A negotiable bill of lading is made to the order of the shipper, who makes either a blank endorsement on the back or endorses it to the order of the bank issuing the letter of credit. A nonnegotiable bill of lading is consigned to a specific party (the buyer or the buyer's representative), and endorse-

ment by the shipper is not required. In this case, the consignee must produce the original bill of lading in order to take delivery.

Certificates of Origin

Certificates of origin verifying country of manufacture for an export shipment may be required either by the terms of a bilateral trade agreement between the countries involved or for reasons specific to the individual transaction. Unless a letter of credit stipulates otherwise, any manufacturer or trader can issue certificates of origin without government or other official authorization. When an international trade agreement or a buyer requires a certificate of origin, the supplier is responsible for providing it. Three types of certificates of origin are available for Korean export goods: Form CCI-1, which is issued by the Korea Chamber of Commerce and Industry (KCCI); GSP Form A, which is available from the Korea Foreign Trade Association (KFTA); and forms issued by foreign consulates in Korea.

Methods of Settlement

Most of Korea's export transactions are made under irrevocable letters of credit (L/Cs) in the form of either on-sight drafts or usance drafts. Exports on documents against payment (D/Ps) and documents against acceptance (D/As) terms are also permissible. Settlement should be by normally accepted international methods in designated currencies obtained through authorized foreign exchange banks. The settlement period should conform to standard international financial and commercial practices.

Within this framework, methods of payment are classified as standard and nonstandard. Standard methods are those that occur by normal international procedures. These include transactions to be completed within 360 days and handled through a bill of exchange under an irrevocable L/C or D/A; those completed within 60 days under a D/P; those that are prepaid within 120 days of shipment; or those that are completed within 60 days on COD terms. Nonstandard methods, such as revocable letters of credit, can be used if the transaction is valued at less than US$10,000 and the settlement date is within one year of the date of shipment. Nonstandard settlement methods must be authorized by the head of a foreign exchange bank or in some special cases by the governor of the Bank of Korea.

Free Trade Zones

The government has designated two free export zones for the bonded processing of imported materials into finished goods for export. The free export zones are special industrial areas where foreign-invested firms can use raw materials or semi-finished goods imported tax free to manufacture, assemble, or process products exclusively for export. The Masan Free Export Zone, established in 1971, is located near Pusan at the southern part of the country. The Iri Free Export Zone, located near Gunsan on the western coast of Korea, opened in March 1975. The Free Export Zone Administration Office (FEZAO) manages both zones and shares customs authority with the customhouse located inside the zone. No factory buildings are currently available in either of the free export zones. Information on operations in the free export zones can be obtained from the director:

Ministry of Trade and Industry, Regional Industry Division
1 Jungang-dong
Gwachon City, Kyonggi Province, Rep. of Korea
Tel: [82] (2) 503-9462

Reexports

Customs duties collected are rebated on all goods exported within 18 months from the date of import. This rule applies to raw materials and semi-finished components that are used in the production of goods for reexport. Such goods are also exempt from local taxes, such as value-added tax, special consumption tax, and liquor tax where applicable. The duty rebate also applies to goods originally imported for local consumption but subsequently exported as long as export occurs within 12 months of the import date. Traders should note that in all cases, importers and end-users are required to post a bond in the amount of the estimated duties and taxes until they can provide proof of the reexport.

Warehousing

Adequate bonded storage facilities are available in Korea. All are under the direct supervision of the Collector of Customs. Korea has two kinds of bonded areas: designated bonded areas (designated storage sites and customs inspection sites) and licensed bonded areas (bonded storage sites, bonded warehouses, bonded factories, bonded exhibit sites, bonded construction sites, and bonded sales sites). Goods may be stored in bonded warehouses for up to two years, and duties are payable only when the goods are cleared through customs. With the permission of the Collector of Customs, goods stored in bonded facilities can be repackaged, stored, divided and combined, or repaired, provided that the nature and quality of the goods are not materially altered in the process. Storage fees are high, and the use of bonded warehouses to maintain inventories is limited by the cost and lack of space. Inquiries regarding bonded facilities in Korea can be addressed to the director:

Surveillance Division, Office of Customs Administration
71, Nonhyun-dong, Kangnam-ku
Seoul, Rep. of Korea
Tel: [82] (2) 542-8242

The two-year storage period does not apply to the storage of live animals or plants, perishable merchandise, or other commodities that can cause damage to other merchandise or the warehouse facility. The Collector of Customs bears no responsibility for goods stored in customs facilities.

Korea Export Buying Offices Association

The MTI created the Korea Export Buying Offices Association in 1978 in response to the proliferation of buying offices that foreign companies were establishing in Korea. The association acts as liaison with foreign buying offices in Korea and controls their number, activities, and expansion. Membership in the association is mandatory for all foreign buying offices. Members receive a number of benefits, including exemption from the regular processes of export inspection (the buyer or his agent has control over the process); relatively informal treatment on customs clearance of samples; support for applications to extend the visas of foreign representatives in buying offices under certain conditions; assistance in reconciling trade complaints; assistance in advertising for and employing workers at newly established offices; and access to informative publications, such as newsletters, bulletins, and a trade directory.

Countertrade

The Korean government has established guidelines for countertrade transactions. Each transaction must follow established export-import procedures, and the Korean export must precede the imports. The transactions must be covered either by a single contract or by two separate contracts—one for import, one for export—each of which refers to the other. Guarantees of payment or performance should be used only under the most extenuating circumstances. In such cases, letters of credit should be used for reciprocal payments between the trading parties. Price differentials between the commodities exported and imported must be reconciled according to Korea's foreign exchange control law. Approval from the MTI is required for transactions involving foreign governments or state-owned enterprises and export goods valued at US$5 million or more. Such transactions are subject to international bidding procedures. No restrictions are imposed on countertrade exports for which Korea does not anticipate a domestic shortage.

The following import items are generally eligible for countertrade: raw materials imported by necessity, items not produced or not available locally, items that can readily be supplied to a third country, and items imported due to policy considerations. The Korean government limits countertrade to firms that can directly handle both the export and import involved. If a government ruling is required to determine exporters or importers, the Korean government will name Korea Trading International or another GTC. Finally, countertrade transactions must be economically balanced. The importer-exporter must bear any financial losses that occur, with the government accepting no contingent liability for such losses.

Industry Reviews

This chapter describes the status of and trends in major South Korean industries. It also lists key contacts for finding sources of supply, developing sales leads and conducting economic research. We have grouped industries into 17 categories, which are listed below. Some smaller sectors of commerce are not detailed here, while others may overlap into more than one area. If your business even remotely fits into a category don't hesitate to contact several of the organizations listed; they should be able to assist you further in gathering the information you need. We have included industry-specific contacts only. General trade organizations, which may also be very helpful, particularly if your business is in an industry not covered here, are listed in the "Important Addresses" chapter.

Each section has two segments: an industry summary and a list of useful contacts. The summary gives an overview of the range of products available in the industry and that industry's ability to compete in worldwide markets. The contacts listed are government departments, trade associations, publications, and trade fairs which can provide information specific to the industry. An entire volume could likely be devoted to each area, but such in-depth coverage is beyond the scope of this book. Our intent is to provide you with a solid foundation for your own research.

All addresses and telephone numbers given are located in the Republic of Korea, unless otherwise noted. The telephone country code for South Korea is [82]; other telephone country codes are shown in square brackets where appropriate. Telephone city codes, if needed, appear in parentheses.

We highly recommend that you also peruse the chapters on "Trade Fairs" and "Important Addresses," where you will find additional resources including a variety of trade promotion organizations, chambers of commerce, business services, and media.

AIRCRAFT & AIRCRAFT PARTS

Aircraft and aircraft parts manufacturing is one of South Korea's fastest growing export industries. Most of these products are shipped to major aircraft companies in the United States. Other countries that buy substantial amounts of Korean-made aircraft parts include England, Germany, and Japan.

Korea's aircraft manufacturers are mainly assemblers of aircraft and aircraft parts. Korea exports only used planes as finished aircraft. However, exports currently account for more than half of Korea's production of aircraft parts.

Aircraft Korea's three aircraft factories assemble primarily fuselages and engines. They have little experience in the design of aircraft systems or in the production of critical composite materials, precision components, or avionics equipment. Aircraft under assembly include military helicopters and fighters, civilian commercial passenger jets, and multipurpose light planes. All Korean firms are currently assembling aircraft through joint production contracts with foreign aircraft companies. Korean-assembled planes are used domestically and sold to foreign countries as second-hand aircraft.

Aircraft Parts Korea's three major aircraft companies specialize in the manufacture of various parts in collaboration with overseas aircraft firms. Through technology and licensing agreements with foreign firms, Korean manufacturers are now producing several exportable aircraft parts. In particular, Korean aircraft companies are manufacturing stringers, fuselages, engines, tail assemblies, main wings, and lightweight wing spoilers from special composite materials. Aircraft parts available for export vary because parts are made to order. Approximately 20 Korean firms manufacture aircraft-related products, including brake discs, carbon fiber brake discs, precision bearings, fuel tanks and pylons, and platinum alumina-coated turbine blades. Some firms are also producing high-tech materials for use by aircraft part manufacturing companies, including specialty steel for fuselage structures, landing gear materials, glass fiber and carbon fiber reinforced composite materials, aluminum materials, and Nomex and aluminum honeycomb structural materials.

Competitive Situation

Increasing export orders and growing domestic demand for military and civilian aircraft are contributing to a dramatic rise in Korea's production of aircraft and parts. With increased domestic demands from its military, the world's fifth largest armed force, and from two new civilian airport projects, Korea's aircraft industry more than doubled its gross production in 1992. In that same year, exports accelerated by 14 percent. Korea's aircraft parts industry is also benefiting from the relatively high value of the Japanese yen, which has motivated United States military authorities to shift an increasing number of orders to Korea from Japan. In addition, an increasing number of major foreign aircraft companies have turned to Korea as an attractive industrial base for aircraft and parts assembly.

To promote Korea's aircraft industry authorities have selected it as a priority industry for receipt of government support, and they have established several research programs with large R&D investments in aerospace design technologies. Korea's three major aircraft companies have also invested heavily in construction of new facilities to expand production and test flight capabilities and to increase R&D with the intent of beginning to produce aircraft of Korean design. To diversify their export markets, Korean aircraft manufacturers are negotiating joint production arrangements with Italy, France, and the Russian Republic. Many projects currently under development are for lightweight, small- to medium-size military and civilian craft that seat two to six persons. At least one Korean aircraft firm is working on remote-controlled craft for agricultural, fishery, military, and other uses. Korean aircraft part manufacturers are concentrating on using special composite materials to remain technologically competitive in international markets.

In addition to a lack of technology and production capability, Korea's aircraft manufacturers are facing such problems as positive protectionism for this industry, the continued appreciation of the Korean won, and increased competition from aircraft industries in other developing countries, particularly Brazil, Taiwan, and Indonesia. Korean aircraft manufacturers are also taking a major risk in making substantial investments to expand production facilities, which could be underutilized if world demand for aircraft should drop. Finally, domestic competition among Korea's aircraft companies is rising as they shift from specialized products to integrated aircraft manufacture.

Government Agencies

Ministry of Transportation
168, 2-ka, Bongnae-dong, Chung-ku
Seoul
Tel: (2) 392-9801, 392-7606 Fax: (2) 392-9809
Tlx: 24778

Directories/Publications

Asian Aviation
(Monthly)
Asian Aviation Publications
2 Leng Kee Rd., #04-01 Thye Hong Centre
Singapore 0315
Tel: [65] 4747088 Fax: [65] 4796668

Trade Fairs

Refer to the Trade Fair chapter for complete listings, including contact information, dates, and venues. The following trade fair is of particular relevance to this industry and is listed in that chapter under the heading given below:

Aerospace & Oceanic
- International Aerospace Symposium & Exhibition (AEROSPACE)

For other trade fairs that may be of interest, we recommend that you also consult the headings Computer & Information Industries; Electronic & Electric Equipment; and Factory Automation.

COMPUTERS AND OTHER INFORMATION PRODUCTS

Computers and peripherals still rank among South Korea's top exports, but growth in this industry has slowed in recent years. The major export markets for Korean computer equipment are Japan and the United States.

Approximately 600 computer-related companies are now operating in Korea, of which only about 60 are major companies. A majority of firms are small to medium in size with fewer than 50 employees. Most Korean computer firms offer both hardware and software products. Only about 21 percent specialize in software development. Korean computer manufacturers generally operate under licensing agreements with overseas companies and merely assemble components that are imported mainly from US and Japanese firms.

Hardware Products South Korea's leading exports of computer hardware are color monitors. Other significant exports include personal computers (PCs), microcomputers, color graphics terminals, and disk drives. Approximately 80 percent of the floppy disk drives assembled in Korea (3.5- and 5.25-inch drives ranging in capacity from 160KB to 1.6MB) are incorporated into Korean-assembled PCs and then exported. Hard drive production in Korea is limited to low-capacity drives (20MB to 40MB) used primarily for exported microcomputers and PCs. Production of floppy and hard disk drives is mostly on an original equipment manufacturer (OEM) basis for domestic or foreign computer companies. A few major computer producers in Korea are making optical disk drives under license to foreign companies.

Peripherals South Korean computer manufacturers are producing a few computer peripherals, including printers, cathode-ray tube (CRT) terminals, and auxiliary floppy and hard disk drives.

Korea's printer-manufacturing industry is one of the slowest growing sectors of Korea's computer industry. About 20 Korean manufacturers are producing nearly 80 different models of printers, including band, serial, and inkjet models. About 90 percent of the units produced are dot matrix printers, the only type of printer exported. Korean printer manufacturers have a fairly advanced technology for the design and production of electronic circuits, cases and frames, 9-pin head assemblies, color components, printer heads, stepper motors, and digital circuits.

In anticipation of growing international demand, Korean printer manufacturers are trying to develop color dot matrix models and laser printers for export. Although its toner production and font technology are considered fairly advanced, Korea's computer printer industry lacks technology in such crucial areas as printer engine design, processing, and manufacturing; optics design; laser diode and light-emitting diode (LED) design; development/exposer (sensitive material) production; and polygon mirror precision processing. Most upgrade efforts are being undertaken through licensing arrangements with foreign manufacturers.

Software South Korea imports most of its computer software, and exports of Korean-made software are minimal because Korean computer firms lack technology and funds for software development. Korea's limited software exports consist primarily of applications software packages. There is an acute shortage of qualified software engineers, and most Korean firms prefer to import software, which is less costly than developing it. Exports of Korean-made software are further inhibited by language barriers and inadequate maintenance and support for consumers.

As Korean manufacturers have begun to install an increasing amount of computer-aided design (CAD) hardware to improve their production capabilities, a few Korean firms have actively undertaken development of CAD software designed specifically for local application, such as for use in designing semiconductor circuits and in mechanical, electronic, construction, and interior design. Several government programs have been created to promote Korea's software industry, and Korean law now provides some copyright protection for software. However, development is still far behind the levels found in Japan and the United States, particularly in systems software.

Competitive Situation

In addition to inadequate technology and lack of skilled labor, South Korea's computer firms have been adversely affected by declining demand for low-end products in US markets and by increasing competition from foreign manufacturers, particularly Taiwanese manufacturers. Korean computer firms are attempting to upgrade their technology, to produce all components required for assembly of computers and peripherals domestically, and to shift production to high-end products. Some firms are capable of producing low-tech items, such as printer heads, logic boards, computer cases, and power supplies. A few firms are also using their own technology to produce printer controllers and engines. Major Korean computer manufacturers are concentrating on creating faster, higher-capacity hard disks, erasable optical disk drives, and laptop computers. Korean authorities have designated computers as an area for export growth, and the government is currently providing substantial financing for software and hardware development, particularly of engineering workstations and superminicomputers.

Government Agencies

Ministry of Science and Technology
1, Jungang-dong
Gwachon City, Kyonggi Province
Tel: (2) 503-7609 Fax: (2) 503-7673
Tlx: 24230

Trade Associations

Korea Advanced Institute of Science & Technology
373-1, Kusong-dong, Yusong-gu
Taejon
Tel: (42) 869-2114 Fax: (42) 869-2210

Korea Data Processing Cooperative
14-8, Youido-dong, Yongdungpo-gu
Seoul
Tel: (2) 780-0511/3

Korea Institute of Science & Technology
39-1, Hawolgok-dong, Songbuk-gu
Seoul
Tel: (2) 982-8801 Fax: (2) 963-4013

The Korea Invention and Patent Association
143-19, Samsung-dong, Kangnam-gu
Seoul
Tel: (2) 557-1077/8 Fax: (2) 554-1532

Directories/Publications

Asian Computer Directory
(Monthly)
Washington Plaza
1/F., 230 Wanchai Rd.
Wanchai, Hong Kong
Tel: [852] 8327123 Fax: [852] 8329208

Asian Computer Monthly
(Monthly)
Computer Publications Ltd.
Washington Plaza, 1st Fl.
230 Wanchai Road
Wanchai, Hong Kong
Tel: [852] 9327123 Fax: [852] 8329208

Asia Computer Weekly
(Bimonthly)
Asian Business Press Pte., Ltd.
100 Beach Rd., #26-00 Shaw Towers
Singapore 0718
Tel: [65] 2943366 Fax: [65] 2985534

Asian Sources: Computer Products
(Monthly)
Asian Sources Media Group
22/F., Vita Tower
29 Wong Chuk Hang Rd.
Wong Chuk Hang, Hong Kong
Tel: [852] 5554777 Fax: [852] 8730488

Computer-Asia Software Guide
(Annual)
Syme Media Enterprises
6-12 Wing Kut St.
Central, Hong Kong

Computer Journal
(Monthly)
Miraesidae Corp.
12-20, Daeheung-dong, Mapo-ku
Seoul
Tel. (2) 716-7291

Computer World
(Monthly)
Computer Engineering Co., Ltd.
63-1, 3-ka, Choongjung-ro,
Seoul
Tel: (2) 587-0211

Computerworld Hong Kong
(Weekly)
Asia Computerworld Communications, Ltd.
701-4 Kam Chung Bldg.
54 Jaffe Rd.
Wanchai, Hong Kong
Tel: [852] 86132258 Fax: [852] 8610953

Information Age
(Monthly)
Information Age Co.
1575-8, Suhcho-dong, Suhcho-ku
Seoul
Tel: (2) 587-7291

Management & Computer
(Monthly)
Mincom Ltd.
393-4, Seokyo-dong, Mapo-ku
Seoul
Tel: (2) 333-4101

What's New in Computing
(Monthly)
Asian Business Press Pte., Ltd.
100 Beach Rd., #26-00 Shaw Towers
Singapore 0718
Tel: [65] 2943366 Fax: [65] 2985534

Trade Fairs

Refer to the Trade Fair chapter for complete listings, including contact information, dates, and venues. Trade fairs with particular relevance to this industry include the following, which are listed in that chapter under the heading given below:

Computer & Information Industries
- Communication Networks Korea (CN KOREA)
- Computer Software Exhibition of Korea (SEK)
- Korea International CAD/CAM & Graphics Exhibition (CAD/CAM)
- Korea International Exhibition for Computers, Office Automation & Related Equipment (KIECO)
- SCAN-TECH KOREA
- Seoul International Information Technology Show (INFORTEC)
- Seoul International Personal Computer Show (PC SHOW)

For other trade fairs that may be of interest, we recommend that you also consult the headings Electronic & Electric Equipment; and Factory Automation for other trade fairs that may be of interest.

ELECTRONICS PRODUCTS

South Korea's electronics industry accounts for more than one-quarter of the nation's total exports. Following a slowdown in sales beginning in 1989, Korea's electronics industry has been growing more moderately except in the sector that produces and exports semiconductors. Korea's major export markets are Japan and the United States. Exports to Southeast Asian, Eastern European, and Middle Eastern countries are rising.

Industrial and home electronics products are manufactured in Korea. Major exports can be divided into consumer electronics and electronic parts and components.

Consumer Electronics Exports of South Korean-made consumer electronics include compact disc (CD) players, videocassette recorders (VCRs), liquid crystal color television sets, 4-millimeter camcorders, digital audio tape recorders, and various types of audio equipment. Sales of Korean-made consumer electronics have slowed in recent years, although they continue to account for a substantial share of the nation's electronics exports.

Electronic Parts and Components About 300 companies in South Korea produce electronic parts and components, including display and electronic tubes, such as cathode-ray tubes and liquid crystal displays; semiconductors, such as integrated circuits, memory devices, and logical elements; and passive components, such as resistors, capacitors, and most important, printed circuit boards. Other products include components for consumer electronics and computers, such as speakers, magnetic tapes, magnetic heads, and television tuners. Of these electronic parts and components, semiconductors have accounted for the largest production, and magnetic tapes have had the fastest growth.

Semiconductors South Korea is a major world producer and exporter of semiconductors. In recent years, semiconductors have accounted for nearly 10 percent of Korea's total exports. Six major manufacturers produce almost all Korean-made semiconductors for export. Korea's other semiconductor firms are primarily assembly or simple manufacturing operations. Most Korean electronics companies operate under licenses from manufacturers in the United States.

A wide range of very-large-scale-integration (VLSI) level semiconductors are available from Korean electronic firms, including integrated circuits (ICs), transistors, diodes, memory devices, and logic elements. Memory devices made in Korea include random access memory (RAM) chips, dynamic RAMs (DRAMs), and static RAMs (SRAMs); and read only memory (ROM) chips, erasable programmable ROMs (EPROMs), and extended EPROMs (EEPROMS). Most significant among the exports of Korean-made logic

elements are transistor-transistor logic (TTL) devices and gate arrays. Other important exports are crystal vibrators, lead frames, and photosensitive semiconductor devices, such as photovoltaic cells and light-emitting diodes (LEDs).

To remain competitive and to meet increased domestic and overseas consumer demand for high-tech semiconductors, Korean electronic firms are focusing on production of more sophisticated products, including mega-DRAM chips and flash memory devices. Several manufacturers have increased their capital investments substantially to expand their production and R&D capabilities. As further incentive, Korean authorities have implemented programs to encourage construction of new plants, modernization and expansion of existing production facilities, and increased R&D outlays. In an effort to promote investment in production of logic elements, the Ministry of Trade and Industry has limited production of memory devices to the three existing manufacturers.

Printed Circuit Boards More than 100 Korean electronic firms manufacture printed circuit boards (PCBs). Seven major firms account for 70 percent of Korea's production of PCBs, while small firms account for the remaining 30 percent. Korean-made PCBs include bare boards, single-sided and double-sided boards, 3-16 multilayer boards, single- to 8-layer flexible boards, and silver-through-hole boards. Technologically advanced products include 4- to 10-layer characteristic-controlled impedence boards of a microstrip type, a stripline type, and an embedded microstrip type.

South Korea's export-oriented PCB industry continues to expand in response to rising world demand for sophisticated electronic consumer and industrial products. Innovations in Korean PCB equipment are aimed at automating and improving manufacturing processes, thereby cutting labor and production costs. Moreover, Korean electronics firms are integrating an increasing number of multilayer PCBs into computers and communications systems. Korea's PCB firms are making substantial capital investments to increase their processing capacity, keep pace with technological advances, and acquire machinery with labor-saving and cost-efficient features. To expand and modernize this industry, Korean electronic firms are focusing on producing more high-tech products, such as 42-layer PCBs, and on maximizing the use of Korean-made PCBs in industrial and consumer electronic goods produced domestically. Korea's PCB industry urgently needs wider adoption of clean-room technology during production so as to improve product quality and lower defect rates, which currently can average as much as 50 percent of output. Korea is also seeking to develop its own production capabilities for sophisticated PCB-making equipment, most of which is now imported.

Competitive Situation

South Korean electronics firms are increasing their R&D investments to improve their technology for electronic products. Manufacturers are concentrating on multifunctional, high-value-added products, including high-capacity DRAM chips and high-resolution television sets. Korea's government is strongly supporting growth and technological development in Korea's electronic sector, which it has designated a strategic export industry.

Government Agencies

Ministry of Science and Technology
1, Jungang-dong
Gwachon City, Kyonggi Province
Tel: (2) 503-7609 Fax: (2) 503-7673 Tlx: 24230

Trade Associations

Korea Electric Power Corporation
167, Samsung-dong, Kangnam-gu
Seoul
Tel: (2) 550-3114 Fax: (2) 550-5982

Korea Electrical Manufacturer's Cooperative
103-10, Shingil 2-dong, Yongdungpo-gu
Seoul
Tel: (2) 849-2811/9 Fax: (2) 848-8337

Electronic Industries Association of Korea
5/F., Danwoo Bdlg.
850-22, Pangbae-dong, Sochu-gu
Seoul
Tel: (2) 553-0941/7, 553-8725 Fax: (2) 555-6195

Korea Electronic Industries Cooperative
813-5, Pangbae-dong, Sochu-gu
Seoul
Tel: (2) 533-2309 Fax: (2) 553-0949

Korea Illuminating Industry Cooperative
94-357, Yongdungpo-dong, Yongdungpo-gu
Seoul
Tel: (2) 676-9391/3, 633-4590 Fax: (2) 675-2482

Directories/Publications

Asian Electricity
(11 per year)
Reed Business Publishing Ltd.
5001 Beach Rd., #06-12 Golden Mile Complex
Singapore 0719
Tel: [65] 2913188 Fax: [65] 2913180

Asian Electronics Engineer
(Monthly)
Trade Media Ltd.
29 Wong Chuck Hang Rd.
Hong Kong
Tel: [852] 5554777 Fax: [852] 8700816

Asian Sources: Electronic Components
(Monthly)
Asian Sources Media Group
22/F., Vita Tower
29 Wong Chuk Hang Rd.
Wong Chuk Hang, Hong Kong
Tel: [852] 5554777 Fax: [852] 8730488

Directory of Korean Electronics Exporters
(English and Korean)
Korea World Trade Center
159-1, Samsung-dong, Kangnam-ku
Seoul
Tel: (2) 551-5251/2 Fax: (2) 551-5181 Tlx: 24265

Electric Power in Korea
(Annual)
Korea Electric Power Corporation
167, Samsung-dong, Kangnam-gu
Seoul
Tel: (2) 550-3114 Fax: (2) 550-5982

Electronic Business Asia
(Monthly)
Cahners Publishing Company
249 West 17th St.
New York, NY 10011-5301, USA.

Electronic Times
(Daily)
14-11, Yoido-dong, Yungdungpo-ku
Seoul
Tel. (2) 784-3091/7

Journal of Korean Electronics
(Annual)
EIAK
648, Yuksam-Dong, Kangnam-Ku
Seoul
Tel. (2) 553-0940

Journal of Korean Electronics
Electronic Industries Association of Korea
5/F., Danwoo Bldg.
850-22, Pangbae-dong, Sochu-gu
Seoul
Tel: (2) 553-0941/7, 553-8725
Fax: (2) 555-6195

Korea Electronics Buyer's Guide
(Biennial)
Korea Electronic Industries Cooperative
813-5 Pangbae-dong, Sochu-gu
Seoul
Tel: (2) 533-2309 Fax: (2) 553-0949

Korea Electronics Directory and Catalog
(Annual)
Electronic Industries Association of Korea
5/F., Danwoo Bldg.
850-22, Pangbae-dong, Sochu-gu
Seoul
Tel: (2) 553-0941/7, 553-8725 Fax: (2) 555-6195

Trade Fairs

Refer to the Trade Fair chapter for complete listings, including contact information, dates, and venues. Trade fairs with particular relevance to this industry include the following, which are listed in that chapter under the heading given below:

Electronic & Electric Equipment
• Asia Pacific Conference & Exhibition on the Electronic Data Interchange (EDICOM)

- Exhibition for Electronics Manufacturing, Processing, Assembly & Testing (INTERNEPCON / SEMICONDUCTOR KOREA)
- Government Supply Electronic Products Show (GOSEPS)
- Korea Electronics Show (KES)
- Korea International Electronic Parts & Equipment Show (KEPES)
- SEMICON/KOREA
- Seoul International OEM Parts & Components Show

For other trade fairs that may be of interest, we recommend that you also consult the headings Computer & Information Industries; Factory Automation; Furniture & Housewares; and Multimedia & Audiovisual Equipment.

FOOD PRODUCTS

South Korea's food industry is domestic-oriented, with exports accounting for only a small percentage of total production. Korea has a large fishing industry, but it is weak in agricultural products. Only about 21 percent of Korea can be cultivated, and all available land is farmed intensively. Most Korean food producers are small family operations.

Products Korean food products include bakery and confectionery items, refined sugars, artificial sweeteners, instant noodles, dairy products, meat products, health drinks, rice wines and other traditional alcohols, beer, wine, and such alcohols as whisky. Major exports include beer, various types of frozen fish, and canned traditional Korean food, such as kimchi.

Competitive Situation

Except in flour milling, sugar refining, and condiment making, the technology in Korean food-manufacturing facilities lags behind the levels in other advanced nations. Korean food producers generally have inadequate funds to invest in efforts to improve quality or develop new products.

Government Agencies

Fisheries Administration
541, 5-ga Namdaemun-no, Chung-ku
Seoul
Tel: (2) 777-8271 Tlx: 24719

Ministry of Agriculture, Forestry and Fisheries
1, Jungang-dong
Gwachon City, Kyonggi Province
Tel: (2) 503-7209, 503-7208 Tlx: 24759

Ministry of Health & Social Affairs
1, Jungang-dong
Gwachon City, Kyonggi Province
Tel: (2) 503-7524, 503-7504 Fax: (2) 503-7505
Tlx: 23230

Trade Associations

Agriculture & Fishery Marketing Cooperation
191, Hangangno 2-ga, Yongsan-gu
Seoul
Tel: (2) 795-8201/5
Fax: (2) 790-5265, 798-7513

Korea Agriculture & Fisheries Food Trade Association
Rm. 1905, KWTC Bldg.
159, Samsung-dong, Kangnam-gu
Seoul
Tel: (2) 551-1936/9 Fax: (2) 551-1940

Korea Alcohol & Liquor Industry Association
10, Youido-dong, Yongdungpo-gu
Seoul
Tel: (2) 780-6411/5, 780-6661/4
Fax: (2) 783-8787

Korea Assorted Feed Industry Cooperative
1581-13, Socho-dong, Socho-gu
Seoul
Tel: (2) 586-8720 Fax: (2) 521-5508

Korea Bakers Association
120-3, Chungmuro 4-ga, Chung-gu
Seoul 100-014
Tel: (2) 273-1830 Fax: (2) 271-1822

Korea Center Cooks Association
Union Bldg.
69-75, Kalwol-dong, Yongsan-gu
Seoul 140-150
Tel: (2) 712-2183 Fax: (2) 713-7148

Korea Deep Sea Fisheries Association
6/F., Samhomulsan Bldg.
Yangjae-dong, Socho-gu
Seoul
Tel: (2) 589-1621/4 Fax: (2) 589-1030/1

Korea Fishery Exporters Association
Rm. 1904, KWTC Bldg.
159, Samsung-dong, Kangnam-gu
Seoul
Tel: (2) 551-1925 Fax: (2) 551-1931

Korea Foods Industry Association
1002-6, Pangbae-dong, Socho-gu
Seoul
Tel: (2) 585-7062 Fax: (2) 586-4906

Korea Ginseng Products Manufacturers Association
30-6, Chamwon-dong, Socho-gu
Seoul
Tel: (2) 549-4330 Fax: (2) 511-4533

Korea Poultry Association
1516-5, Socho 3-dong, Socho-gu
Seoul 137-073
Tel: (2) 588-7651 Fax: (2) 588-7655

Korea Seed Association
1358-6, Socho-dong, Socho-gu
Seoul
Tel: (2) 568-2034 Fax: (2) 563-6711

Korea Sugar Manufacturers Association
Rm. 501, Choyang Bldg.
49-17, Chungmuro 2-ga, Chung-gu
Seoul
Tel: (2) 275-6071/3 Fax: (2) 277-5858

Directories/Publications

Asia Pacific Food Industry
(Monthly)
Asia Pacific Food Industry Publications
24 Peck Sea St., #03-00 Nehsons Bldg.
Singapore 0207
Tel: [65] 2223422 Fax: [65] 2225587

Asia Pacific Food Industry Business Report
(Monthly)
Asia Pacific Food Industry Publications
24 Peck Sea St., #03-00 Nehsons Bldg.
Singapore 0207
Tel: [65] 2223422 Fax: [65] 2225587

Trade Fairs

Refer to the Trade Fair chapter for complete listings, including contact information, dates, and venues. Trade fairs with particular relevance to this industry include the following, which are listed in that chapter under the headings given below:

Agriculture, Forestry & Fisheries
- International Exhibition of Machinery, Science & Technology for Agriculture, Forestry, Fisheries & Livestock (SIEMSTA)
- Korea Poultry Expo

Food, Beverages & Food Processing
- Korea International Food & Health Equipment Fair (INTERHEALTH)
- Korea International Food Festival
- International Culinary Show
- Seoul International Bakery Fair (SIBA)
- Seoul International Food Technology Exhibition (SEOUL FOOD)
- Seoul International Hotel Equipment Show (SIHOTES)
- Seoul International Wines, Beers, Spirits & Beverages Exhibition (WINEKOREA)

For other trade fairs that may be of interest, we recommend that you also consult the heading Packaging; and Printing & Papers.

FOOTWEAR

Footwear is one of South Korea's top ten exports, although sales have been slowing since 1989. Major export markets are European countries and the United States. Five major Korean companies produce almost all exported footwear.

Products Korea's international reputation for low-cost quality footwear has arisen primarily from its production of athletic shoes. Most athletic shoes are made in Korea on an original equipment manufacturer (OEM) basis for such foreign companies as Nike, Reebok, and Adidas. Other Korean-made footwear includes an array of boots, slippers, sandals, and casual and dress shoes. Korea's footwear manufacturers offer products in a variety of materials, ranging from leather and canvas to plastic and rubber. Of these items, leather sandals and dress shoes are Korea's most significant exports.

Competitive Situation

South Korea's footwear industry is facing rising labor costs and international demand for higher-quality products. Many smaller manufacturers have closed because they were unable to lower prices while improving quality to the point that would have allowed them to compete in world markets. Exports of Korean-made footwear are slowing as foreign buyers shift to imports from Southeast Asia, China, and other developing countries where labor is cheaper.

To become more competitive in world markets, Korea's major footwear manufacturers are updating factory machinery, automating production facilities, and incorporating new patterns, designs, and materials into their products. In an effort to modernize this industry, Korean authorities have established a footwear laboratory to train Korean footwear makers in such areas as computer-aided design (CAD) and quality control systems. Manufacturers of Korean footwear are shifting away from OEM production, and some companies have moved their labor-intensive operations to factories in Southeast Asia. Footwear production within Korea is concentrated on high-end products, and major manufacturers are now establishing their own brand names and direct marketing channels.

Trade Associations

Korean Footwear Exporters Association
Rm. 1001, KWTC Bldg.
159, Samsung-dong, Kangnam-gu
Seoul
Tel: (2) 551-1411/29 Fax: (2) 551-1430

Korea Tanners Association
Rm. 805, Samhwa Bldg.
204-4, Nonhyon-dong, Kangnam-gu
Seoul
Tel: (2) 549-5432/3 Fax: (2) 549-6733

Directories/Publications

Asia Pacific Leather Directory
(Annual)
Asia Pacific Leather Yearbook
(Annual)
Asia Pacific Directories, Ltd.
6/F. Wah Hen Commercial Centre
381 Hennessy Rd.
Hong Kong
Tel: [852] 8936377 Fax: [852] 8935752

Fashion Accessories
(Monthly)
Asian Sources Media Group
22nd Fl., Vita Tower
29 Wong Chuk Hang Road
Wong Chuk Hang, Hong Kong
Tel: [852] 5554777 Fax: [852] 8730488

Trade Fairs

Refer to the Trade Fair chapter for complete listings, including contact information, dates, and venues. Trade fairs with particular relevance to this industry include the following, which are listed in that chapter under the heading given below:

Textiles & Apparel

• Korea International Exhibition of Footwear Industry (KORSHOETECH)
• Seoul International Fashion Fair (SIFF)

For other trade fairs that may be of interest, we recommend that you also consult the headings Industrial Materials & Chemicals; and Sporting Goods.

HOUSEWARES AND HOUSEHOLD APPLIANCES

South Korea's houseware and household appliance industry has developed rapidly, primarily through government programs that have targeted it as a major export industry. Japan and the United States are Korea's major export markets for housewares and household appliances. Other significant export markets are in China, Mexico, the Middle East, and the Russian Republic.

Five Korean companies supply more than 75 percent of Korea's total production of housewares and household appliances, more than half of which is exported. Some of these firms operate as joint ventures or under licenses with foreign companies.

Housewares Of Korea's total production of housewares, more than 50 percent is exported. Korean manufacturers of housewares also supply more than 80 percent of the domestic market. Korean-made flatware and hollowware are top exports. Other major exports include stainless and aluminum pans, metal and plastic cookware, scissors, glassware, stemware, bar accessories, and plastic, ceramic, and stoneware dishes.

Household Appliances Microwave ovens are among Korea's top exports, and Korean-made microwave ovens account for nearly one-quarter of the microwave ovens sold in the world. Korean manufacturers also supply nearly all microwave ovens sold on Korea's domestic market. Other Korean-made appliances that are exported include refrigerators, washing machines, gas ovens and ranges, and air conditioners. Smaller appliances available from Korean firms include vacuum cleaners, irons, toasters, Dutch ovens, rice cookers, bread makers, food processors, electric frying pans, coffee makers, and pressure cookers. Many of these Korean-manufactured products are of medium quality and price.

Competitive Situation

Consumer demand for high-quality goods has affected Korean production and exports of housewares and household appliances adversely. Another reason for the decline in exports of Korean-made household appliances in recent years is that manufacturers are promoting their products aggressively on Korea's domestic market, which has risen substantially.

South Korean firms are attempting to become more competitive in international and domestic markets by improving their technological capabilities, expanding production capacity, and manufacturing high-quality housewares and appliances at competitive prices—a task made even more difficult by dramatic increases in labor costs. To meet consumer demand, many Korean manufacturers have switched product lines away from aluminum goods to stainless steel items. A few major Korean firms are trying to develop industrial-size appliances, such as large-capacity refrigerators and air conditioners.

Trade Associations

Korea Bedding Goods Industry Cooperative
159-1, Samsung-dong, Kangnam-gu
Seoul
Tel: (2) 551-1919 Fax: (2) 551-1918

Korea Earthenware Industry Cooperative
1423, Sung-in-dong, Chongno-gu
Seoul
Tel: (2) 252-0663 Fax: (2) 235-8327

Korea Federation of Furniture Industry Cooperatives
374-2, Changan-dong, Tongdaemun-gu
Seoul
Tel: (2) 215-8838/9 Fax: (2) 215-9729

Korea Illuminating Industry Cooperative
94-357, Yongdungpo-dong, Yongdungpo-gu
Seoul
Tel: (2) 676-9391/3, 633-4590
Fax: (2) 675-2482

Korea Kitchen Furniture Cooperative
910-14, Pangbae-dong, Socho-gu
Seoul
Tel: (2) 586-2451/3 Fax: (2) 586-2454

Korea Lighting Fixtures Industry Cooperative
Rm. 308, KFS Bldg.
16-2, Youido-dong, Yongdungpo-gu
Seoul
Tel: (2) 786-9876 Fax: (2) 701-0944

Korea Refrigeration and Air-Conditioning
Industries Association
13-31, Youido-dong, Yongdungpo-gu
Seoul
Tel: (2) 780-9038 Fax: (2) 785-1195

Korea Towel Industry Cooperative
20-20, Chungmuro 5-ga, Chung-gu
Seoul
Tel: (2) 275-7288/9 Fax: (2) 277-0896

Directories/Publications

Asian Sources: Gifts & Home Products
(Monthly)
Asian Sources Media Group
22/F., Vita Tower
29 Wong Chuk Hang Rd.
Wong Chuk Hang, Hong Kong
Tel: [852] 5554777 Fax: [852] 8730488

Trade Fairs

Refer to the Trade Fair chapter for complete listings, including contact information, dates, and venues. Trade fairs with particular relevance to this industry include the following, which are listed in that chapter under the headings given below:

Construction & Housing
- Heating, Air Conditioning, Refrigerating & Fluid Exhibition (HARFKO)

Furniture & Housewares
- Kyung Hyang Housing Fair
- Seoul International Kitchen Show (SIKITCHEN)
- Seoul International Lighting Show (SLIGHT)
- Seoul International Total Interior Show (SINTEX)

For other trade fairs that may be of interest, we recommend that you also consult the headings Electronic & Electric Equipment; Gifts, Jewelry & Stationery; and Health & Safety.

INDUSTRIAL MACHINERY

Most industrial machinery made in South Korea is used domestically to support Korea's manufacturing industries, the most significant of which are producers of vehicles, aircraft, electronics products, industrial chemicals, and textiles. Exports of Korean-produced industrial machinery account for less than 15 percent of production, but this percentage is growing slowly as Korean firms become more technologically advanced and expand their production facilities.

Diamond Machinery Exports of Korean-manufactured diamond machinery, which is used primarily in refining marbles and stones, are rising gradually. Diamond machinery available from Korean firms includes grinding wheels, saw blades, polishing disks, cutters, core and turning bits, dressers, and electroplated machines. Korea's major export markets for diamond machinery are European countries.

Electronic Plants Korea's industrial machinery manufacturers have entered into technology exchange agreements with overseas companies, resulting in a gradual increase in electronic plant exports. Korean-produced electronic plants include manufacturing equipment for television sets, electronic television guns, air conditioner compressors, and refrigerator compressors. Korea has found export markets for electronic plants in China, Southeast Asia, the Middle East, Eastern Europe, and Latin America.

Environment-Related Equipment Korean manufacturers of water pollution control equipment are mostly small- to medium-sized firms. They produce nearly all types of water pollution control equipment, including agitators, aerators, mixers, screening machines, filtering machinery, and purifiers. These products are fairly advanced in technology. Korean users of this equipment generally prefer Korean-manufactured items because the price is often 30 percent below the level of comparable foreign-made equipment.

Although exports of Korean-made water pollution equipment account for less than 1 percent of total sales, exports are expected to increase because a number of major South Korean environmental protection engineering firms are now installing water pollution control facilities overseas. These engineering firms manufacture some of their own equipment, and they can adequately fund development of high-quality products that use the latest technology. In addition, Korean-made water pollution control equipment has considerably improved through technology transfer arrangements with foreign countries. To remain competitive in this industry, several Korean companies have been steadily increasing their investments in R&D.

Food-Processing and Packaging Equipment The South Korean food-processing and packaging equipment industry supplies for plants for homogenizing, irradiating, sterilizing, condensing, and drying milk; rice and barley polishing machinery; flour mills; bakery machinery; bottling and milling machinery; and machinery for beverage production. Exports of this type of machinery are minimal, and they have declined slightly each year because manufacturers are concentrating on domestic sales. Although production of Korean food-processing and packaging equipment has gradually increased as Korean manufacturers have expanded their facilities, it still does not meet the demands of Korea's domestic market.

Metalworking Machinery More than 750 South Korean firms manufacture metalworking machinery. Most are small- to medium-size fewer than operations with less than 300 employees. Less than 1 percent of total production is exported—mainly to Japan and other Asian countries. Other major export markets are Germany, the Netherlands, Italy, and the United States.

Metalworking equipment produced in Korea consists primarily of conventional and general-use machinery, such as lathes, shapers, gear cutters, and planing, grinding, milling, sawing, boring, and drilling machines. Some companies are also making metalforming machinery, including presses, forges, rolling mills, punches, and notching, bending, wire-drawing, and shearing machinery.

Korea's metalworking equipment industry is confronting such problems as a lack of qualified design engineers, relatively undeveloped technology, low quality, and inadequate supplies of parts and components. To produce increasingly sophisticated products, Korea's major manufacturers of metalworking equipment have been improving their heat treatment technology with the intent of diversifying into new product lines, such as spindles, bearings, gears, pumps, and chucks. A few larger companies have developed numerically controlled machine tools and machining centers to meet increasing market demands for automated machines. Most Korean manufacturers of metalworking machinery have negotiated licensing and technology transfer agreements to acquire the technology needed to produce machinery with improved precision, thickness, and durability.

Plastics-Processing Machinery Of South Korea's 12 major manufacturers of plastics-processing machinery, more than half have fewer than 100 employees. Korea's makers of plastics-processing machinery cannot meet domestic demand, largely because of inadequate investment in production, which is primarily on an order-received basis. Korean-made plastics-processing machinery includes injection and automatic molding machines, extruders, and rubber-processing and molding machines. Exports have grown steadily in recent years, but they still account for less than 20 percent of Korea's total production in this area. More than half of the exports go to Southeast Asia. Other major export markets are Japan, Indonesia, and the Philippines.

Textile Machinery South Korea has more than 450 manufacturers of textile machinery. All but two are small- to medium-sized operations. Korea's two major textile machinery manufacturers produce machinery that requires sophisticated technology, such as rapier looms and airjet weavers. The other firms mainly supply low-end machines, such as spinners, twisters, dyeing machines, and leather-processing machines. A small percentage of Korea's output of textile machinery, led by dyeing and leather-processing machinery, is exported. The major export markets are Indonesia, Japan, Taiwan, and the United States.

Competitive Situation

South Korea's substantial imports of industrial machinery are a major cause of its trade imbalance. Korean firms that produce industrial machinery have been unable to invest adequate funds in efforts to upgrade facilities, expand production, and improve technology fast enough to meet the rapidly growing domestic need in such industries as electronics and automobile manufacturing. In an attempt to meet market demands, most Korean producers of machinery are diversifying their product lines into increasingly high-end machinery, such as numerically controlled machine tools, environmental equipment, precision measuring tools, chemical equipment, precision machine parts, and industrial robots. To stimulate exports, several major Korean producers of industrial machinery have established overseas offices to market their products.

Government Agencies

Ministry of Science and Technology
1, Jungang-dong
Gwachon City, Kyonggi Province
Tel: (2) 503-7609 Fax: (2) 503-7673
Tlx: 24230

Ministry of the Environment
7-16, Sincheon-dong, Songpa-ku
Seoul
Tel: (2) 421-0217, 422-0282, 423-0282
Fax: (2) 421-0280

Trade Associations

Korea Academy of Industrial Technology
790-2, Yoksam-dong, Kangnam-gu
Seoul
Tel: (2) 563-6891 Fax: (2) 554-8016/8

Korea Association of Machinery Industry (KOAMI)
13-31, Youido-dong, Yongdungpo-gu
Seoul
Tel: (2) 780-3611/4
Fax: (2) 784-6749, 784-1032

Korea Boiler Industry Cooperative
288-1, Dohwa-dong, Mapo-gu
Seoul
Tel: (2) 719-4151/3 Fax: (2) 719-4154

Korea Die & Mold Industry Cooperative
KOAMI Bldg.
13-31, Youido-dong, Yongdungpo-gu
Seoul 150-010
Tel: (2) 783-1711/3 Fax: (2) 784-5937

Korea Farm Machinery & Tool Industry Cooperative
11-11, Tongja-dong, Yongsan-gu
Seoul
Tel: (2) 757-1451/6 Fax: (2) 757-1430

Korea Fastener Industry Cooperative
221, Hyoje-dong, Chongno-gu
Seoul
Tel: (2) 743-1219, 763-7442 Fax: (2) 743-1219

Korea Federation of Machinery Industry
Cooperative
172-11, Yomni-dong, Mapo-gu
Seoul
Tel: (2) 715-7172 Fax: (2) 702-6974

Korea Fire-Fighting Equipment Industry
Cooperative
16-2, Yoido-dong, Yongdungpo-gu
Seoul
Tel: (2) 785-4121/4 Fax: (2) 785-4125

Korea Industrial Safety Corp.
Kookje Bldg.
191, Han-gangno 1-ga, Yongsan-gu
Seoul 140-702
Tel: (2) 797-5996 Fax: (2) 795-4872

Korea Institute of Machinery & Metals
66, Sangnam-dong
Changwon-shi, Kyongnam
Tel: (551) 80-3000 Fax: (551) 80-3333

Korea Machine Tool Manufacturers' Association
35-4, Youido-dong, Yongdungpo-gu
Seoul
Tel: (2) 780-3521 Fax: (2) 784-8023

Korea Plastic Industry Cooperative
146-2, Ssangnim-dong, Chung-gu
Seoul
Tel: (2) 275-7991/4 Fax: (2) 277-5150

Korea Plating Industry Cooperative
KOAMI Bldg.
13-31, Youido-dong, Yongdungpo-gu
Seoul 150-010
Tel: (2) 784-0721/2 Fax: (2) 784-0723

Korea Valve Industry Cooperative
16-2, Youido-dong, Yongdungpo-gu
Seoul
Tel: (2) 783-5611/2 Fax: (2) 783-5613

Directories/Publications

Asiamac Journal: The Machine-Building and Metal
Working Journal for the Asia Pacific Region
(Quarterly; English, Chinese)
Adsale Publishing Company
21/F., Tung Wai Commercial Bdlg.
109-111 Gloucester Rd.
Hong Kong
Tel: [852] 8920511
Fax: [852] 8384119, 8345014

Asian Manufacturing
Far East Trade Press Ltd.
2/F., Kai Tak Commercial Building
317 Des Voeux Rd.
Central, Hong Kong
Tel: [852] 5453028 Fax: [852] 5446979

Korean Machinery
(Annual)
Korea Association of Machinery Industry
13-31, Youido-dong, Yongdungpo-gu
Seoul
Tel: (2) 780-3611/4
Fax: (2) 784-6749, 784-1032
Catalogue of Korean machinery.

Trade Fairs

Refer to the Trade Fair chapter for complete listings, including contact information, dates, and venues. Trade fairs with particular relevance to this industry include the following, which are listed in that chapter under the headings given below:

Factory Automation
- International Automation System Exhibition in Korea (AUTO KOREA)
- International Factory Automation System Show Korea (KOFAPS)
- Korea International Factory Automation System Exhibition (KOFA)
- Korean International Robot and Automation System Show
- Seoul International Shop System & Shop Automation Show (KOREASHOP)

Machines & Instruments
- Exhibition of Powder, Fluid & Air Regulation Machinery (IPAMA)
- Korea Machinery Fair (KOMAF)
- Korean International Stone & Machine Industry Exhibition (KOSTONE)
- Seoul International Machine Tool Show (SIMTOS)
- Seoul International Sewing Machinery Exhibition (SIMEX)
- Seoul International Vending Machine Show (SIVENDING)

Metal & Metal Finishing
- International Fastener, Cable & Wire Finished Products, Production Machinery & Technology Exhibition for Korea (FASTENER, CABLE & WIRE KOREA)
- International Foundry, Forging & Heat-Treatment Technology Exhibition (FOUNDRY & FORGING KOREA)
- Pusan International Die & Mold Machining Equipment Show
- Seoul International Die, Mold & Machining Equipment Exhibition (SEOUL INTERMOLD)

Packaging, Printing & Paper
- International Exhibition of Machinery & Materials for Package Processing & Production (IPP)
- International Printing Machinery & Equipment Show (KIPES)
- Seoul International Packaging Exhibition (SEOUL PACK)

For other trade fairs that may be of interest, we recommend that you also consult the headings Aerospace & Oceanic; Agriculture, Forestry & Fisheries; Computer & Information Industries; Construction & Housing; Electronic & Electric Equipment; Environmental & Energy Industries; Food, Beverages & Food Processing; and Textiles & Apparel.

INDUSTRIAL CHEMICALS AND MATERIALS

Industrial chemicals and materials rank as one of South Korea's top 15 exports. The major exports of this industry are steel and oil products. Exports of industrial chemicals and materials tend to fluctuate with domestic demand from such related domestic industries as shipbuilding, construction, and automobile, textile, and plastics manufacturing.

Ceramics Korean-made fine ceramics include electromagnetic materials, insulating materials, hydroelectric materials, semiconductor ceramics, structural ceramics, and compressive-electric materials. Although production is still quite low compared to market demand, it is being stimulated by dramatic growth in domestic and international electronics industries. However, Korean manufacturers lag behind more advanced nations in fine ceramic development, primarily because they have not invested in R&D.

Composite Materials The composite materials manufactured in South Korea are a combination of glass fibers and unsaturated polyesters. Korean manufacturers of composite materials are now producing carbon fabrics largely for use in sports and leisure equipment. To diversify into high-tech products, Korean manufacturers are concentrating R&D funds on the development of carbon-resin composites for use in aircraft, on improving composite structures to reduce weight and increase performance, and on upgrading molding technology.

Nonferrous Metals Korea's metal producers are investing in the creation of new metal products, particularly those made of aluminum, such as high-tension aluminum alloys and high-purity aluminum sheets for electrolytic condensers. Also under development are such metals as sand-dust thin film, shape-memory alloys, and optical-magnetic memory materials.

Petrochemicals China has become a major customer for ethylene and propylene produced in Korea. To boost their exports to China, Korean producers are considering joint ventures with Chinese firms to build tank terminals in China.

Polymeric Materials South Korea's polymeric industry is still in an initial phase of development. The polymeric materials now produced in Korea include general-purpose and special-purpose engineering plastics, photo registers, polymer-separating membranes, and medical-purpose polymers. Demand from domestic vehicle and electronic industries has motivated Korea's manufacturers of polymers to focus on developing general-purpose engineering plastics

Steel Korea's steel manufacturers produce and export steel structures, reinforced bars, cold-rolled sheets, and wire ropes. Korea's largest export market for steel is the United States, although these exports have slowed in recent years. Exports of Korean steel to Japan continue to rise, and Korean steel manufacturers have diversified their export markets to India and China as well. Korea's steel industry has implemented an expansion program to improve its technology, produce high-value-added steel products, and increase production in existing plants. A joint venture between Korean and Vietnamese companies to construct a steel pipe plant and an electric furnace minimill in Vietnam has been announced.

Competitive Situation

South Korea's industrial chemical and materials industry has been inhibited by a lack of modern technology. Despite technology transfer agreements with foreign countries, Korea's firms still lag behind other more advanced nations because technological development has not matched the rapidly changing requirements of domestic and world markets. To promote these industries, Korean authorities have established government-funded research programs.

Government Agencies

Ministry of Energy and Resources
1, Jungang-dong
Gwachon City, Kyonggi Province
Tel: (2) 503-9611, 503-9605 Tlx: 23472

Ministry of the Environment
7-16, Sincheon-dong, Songpa-ku
Seoul
Tel: (2) 421-0217, 422-0282, 423-0282
Fax: (2) 421-0280

Trade Associations

Korea Abrasives Industry Cooperative
7, Pongnae-dong 1-ga, Chung-gu
Seoul
Tel: (2) 752-6545 Fax: (2) 754-6057

Korea As-Con (Asphalt-Concrete) Industry Cooperative
1599-11, Socho-dong, Socho-gu
Seoul
Tel: (2) 583-5241/3 Fax: (2) 583-5244

Korea Battery Industry Cooperative
1304-4, Socho-dong, Socho-gu
Seoul
Tel: (2) 553-2401/3 Fax: (2) 556-1290

Korea Cement Industrial Association
539-11, Shinsa-dong, Kangnam-gu
Seoul
Tel: (2) 546-3861 Fax: (2) 546-7398

Korea Ceramic Industry Association
53-20, Taehyon-dong, Sodaemun-gu
Seoul
Tel: (2) 363-0361/3 Fax: (2) 392-8149

Korea Chaff Charcoal Industry Cooperative
Rm. 304, Chungyou Bldg.
910-14, Pangbae-dong, Socho-gu
Seoul
Tel: (2) 522-9802 Fax: (2) 522-9803

Korea Coal Association
80-6, Susong-dong, Chongno-gu
Seoul
Tel: (2) 734-8891/4 Fax: (2) 734-7959

Korea Coal Mining Industry Cooperative
10-2, Youido-dong, Yongdungpo-gu
Seoul
Tel: (2) 784-7821/7

Korea Federation of Non-Ferrous Metal Industry
Cooperatives
Rm. 715, Backsang Bldg.
35-2, Youido-dong, Yongdungpo-gu
Seoul
Tel: (2) 780-8551/4 Fax: (2) 784-9473

Korea Glass Industry Cooperative
53-20, Taehyon-dong, Sodaemun-gu
Seoul
Tel: (2) 364-7799 Fax: (2) 312-8838

Korea Iron and Steel Association
51-8, Susong-dong, Chongno-gu
Seoul
Tel: (2) 732-9231/5 Fax: (2) 739-1090

Korea Institute of Machinery & Metals
66, Sangnam-dong
Changwon-shi, Kyongnam
Tel: (551) 80-3000 Fax: (551) 80-3333

Korea Petrochemical Industry Association
1-1, Yonji-dong, Chongno-gu
Seoul
Tel: (2) 744-0116 Fax: (2) 743-1887

Korea Plywood Industries Association
Rm. 203, Wonchang Bldg.
26-3, Youido-dong, Yongdungpo-gu
Seoul
Tel: (2) 780-3631 Fax: (2) 780-3634

Korea Rubber Industry Cooperative
7, Shinmunno 1-ga, Chongno-gu
Seoul
Tel: (2) 733-8584/6 Fax: (2) 730-3355

Korea Stainless Steel Pipe Industry Cooperative
4/F., Cheil Bldg.
58-85, Mullae-dong 3-ga, Yongdungpo-gu
Seoul
Tel: (2) 679-1932 Fax: (2) 633-0379

Korea Steel Industry Cooperative
16-2, Youido-dong, Yongdungpo-gu
Seoul
Tel: (2) 785-4127/9

Korea Steel Pipe Association
35-6, Youido-dong, Yongdungpo-gu
Seoul
Tel: (2) 782-8211/3 Fax: (2) 784-0971

Korea Stone Products Industry Cooperative
741-11, Yoksam-dong, Kangnam-gu
Seoul
Tel: (2) 565-0631 Fax: (2) 558-3430

Mining Association of Korea
35-24, Tongui-dong, Chongno-gu
Seoul
Tel: (2) 736-2501 Fax: (2) 720-5592

Directories/Publications

Asian Oil & Gas
(Monthly)
Intercontinental Marketing Corp.
P.O. Box 5056
Tokyo 100-31, Japan
Fax: [81] (3) 3667-9646

Asian Plastic News
(Quarterly)
Reed Asian Publishing Pte., Ltd.
5001 Beach Rd.
#06-12 Golden Mile Complex
Singapore 0719
Tel: [65] 2913188 Fax: [65] 2913180

Oil & Gas News
(Weekly)
Al Hilal Publishing (FE) Ltd.
50 Jalan Sultan, #20-06, Jalan Sultan Centre
Singapore 0719
Tel: [65] 2939233 Fax: [65] 2970862

Petroleum News, Asia's Energy Journal
(Monthly)
Petroleum News Southeast Asia, Ltd.
6/F., 146 Prince Edward Rd. West
Kowloon, Hong Kong
Tel: [852] 3805294 Fax: [852] 3970959

Trade Fairs

Refer to the Trade Fair chapter for complete listings, including contact information, dates, and venues. Trade fairs with particular relevance to this industry include the following, which are listed in that chapter under the heading given below:

Industrial Materials & Chemicals
- International Basic Materials & Stuff Show in Seoul (IMASS)
- International Glass Industry Technology Exhibition for Korea (GLASS KOREA)
- Korea International Ceramics Industry Show (CERAKOR)
- Korea International Clean, Wash & Laundry Technology Exhibition (CLEANTEC)
- Korea International Nonwovens & Machinery Show (NONWOVEN KOREA)
- Korea International Plant Piping Material Show (PLANT PIPING)
- Korean International Plastics and Rubber Show (KOPLAS)
- Seoul International Chemical Plant Exhibition (SICHEM)

For other trade fairs that may be of interest, we recommend that you also consult the headings Aerospace & Oceanic; Agriculture, Forestry & Fisheries; Construction & Housing; Environmental & Energy Industries; and Metal & Metal Finishing.

JEWELRY AND TIMEPIECES

Jewelry is an important export item and South Korea is one of the world's top five suppliers of watches. Its major export markets are Southeast Asia, Europe, the United States, and the Middle East.

Jewelry

Products South Korea's approximately 3,700 jewelry manufacturers can be divided into four categories: small handicraft manufacturers with fewer than 10 employees, medium to large casting firms, chain manufacturers, and gold metal jewelry manufacturers. Korea's jewelry industry produces precious stone, semiprecious stone, precious metal, and costume jewelry. Precious and semiprecious stones used in Korean-made jewelry include diamonds, rubies, sapphires, emeralds, chrysoberyls, agates, amethysts, alexandrites, jades, topazes, pearls, opals, and zircons. Most items produced are exported, with diamond jewelry accounting for more than 40 percent of these exports.

Competitive Situation

In 1976 Korea's government opened a jewelry export compound in Eri, Chungbuk, to promote jewelry as a strategic export item. All local jewelry makers were directed to move into the compound, and only firms in the compound were allowed to export jewelry and import raw materials needed for production. By 1990 these restrictions had been largely removed, although imports of certain precious stones must still be recommended by the Eri Jewelry Industry Cooperative.

South Korea's government has failed to give steady support to its jewelry industry, and Korea's jewelry manufacturers have been slow to adopt to domestic or international market trends. Most of Korea's jewelry manufacturers are in the initial stages of developing their design and stone-setting skills. Although imports were liberalized in 1990 the jewelry industry is still in an abnormal situation, and Korea's tax structure forces manufacturers to rely heavily on smuggling. Imports of stones are subject to extremely high taxes, while Korean jewelry producers struggle to keep their reportable income small so as to retain their tax-exempt status—annual sales must be kept below W36 million (about US$45,000). For the same reason, most imports are loose stones that must be set or mounted in Korea.

Timepieces

Products A wide variety of South Korean watches are exported, including analog and digital models, analog-digital combinations, and chronographs. Production has been mostly on an original equipment manufacturer (OEM) basis.

In terms of volume, analog watches are Korea's largest export. Models are available with numerous features, including ultrathin quartz movements, luminous hands, scratch-resistant sapphire crystals, winding stems, 18-karat gold-plated cases, coin-edged crowns, and deep-knurled timing bezels. Watch bands range from lizard leather or precious metal straps to expansion or folding-buckle metal bands. Korea produces dials in even greater variety.

Exports of Korean-made chronographs are rising. Moonphase chronographs are top-selling items, particularly to Europe and the United States. International markets for Korean-made digital watches have declined, and Korean watchmakers are shifting to high-value-added models with liquid crystal displays (LCDs) to try to become more competitive. Models available from Korean producers include picture watches for children, fancy and ultrathin LCD models, and specialty digitals for divers, military personnel, and athletes. Multifunctional digitals that include such devices as compasses and biorhythm graphs are becoming popular exports.

Competitive Situation

South Korea's watch exports are threatened by low-end competition from developing countries, particularly China. To boost exports, Korean watchmakers are focusing on upgrading the quality of their products and improving local technology. Most Korean watchmakers have diversified their product lines to include products that appeal to youth and high-value-added products, such as 18-karat solid gold, zirconium, and titanium watches. Many exports are now being offered with multiple functions and special features, including stopwatches, calendars, sweep-second hands, chime alarms, black chrome-plated stainless steel backs, 18-karat gold dials and hands, and rectangular crystal faces. Korean watchmakers have also improved water resistance and have developed a revolutionary glass cutting method to produce geometrically shaped watch crystals.

In an effort to remain competitive in international markets, Korean watchmakers are attempting to localize production of core watch parts and thus cut their dependence on imports. To this end, major Korean watchmakers have increased the funds allocated to R&D and have made joint technology and financial agreements with foreign investors. Some Korean watchmakers have moved their labor-intensive operations to countries where wages are lower. A few major Korean watch manufacturers are shifting their marketing strategies by developing their own brands and diversifying their export markets.

Trade Associations

Iri Jewelry Industry Cooperative
215-2, Yongdung-dong
Iri City, Chonbuk
Tel: (653) 855-0363/4 Fax: (653) 856-7275

Korea Federation of Handicrafts Cooperatives
Rm. 202, Bosung Bldg.
163-3, Ulchiro 2-ga, Chung-gu
Seoul 100-192
Tel: (2) 757-1678 Fax: (2) 757-8582

Korea Glass Industry Cooperative
53-20, Taehyon-dong, Sodaemun-gu
Seoul
Tel: (2) 364-7799 Fax: (2) 312-8838

Directories/Publications

Asian Sources: Timepieces
(Monthly)
Asian Sources Media Group
22/F., Vita Tower
29 Wong Chuk Hang Rd.
Wong Chuk Hang, Hong Kong
Tel: [852] 5554777 Fax: [852] 8730488

Jewellery News Asia
(Monthly)
Jewellery News Asia Ltd.
Rooms 601-603, Guardian House
32 Oi Kwan Rd.
Wanchai, Hong Kong
Tel: [852] 8322011 Fax: [852] 8329208

World Jewelogue
(Annual)
Headway International Publications Co.
907 Great Eagle Center
23 Harbour Rd.
Hong Kong
Tel: [852] 8275121 Fax: [852] 8277064

Trade Fairs

Refer to the Trade Fair chapter for complete listings, including contact information, dates, and venues. Trade fairs with particular relevance to this industry include the following, which are listed in that chapter under the heading given below:

Gifts, Jewelry & Stationery Includes timepieces
- Exhibition for Wedding Goods Korea (WEDDEX KOREA)
- Korea International Jewelry & Watch Fair (JEWELEX)
- Seoul International Gift Fair / Seoul International Fashion Jewelry & Accessories Fair (SIGIFT/ACCESS)
- Seoul International Premium Show (SIPREMIUM)
- Seoul International Stationery Fair (SISFAIR)

MUSICAL INSTRUMENTS

South Korea is a top supplier of pianos and middle- and lower-end musical instruments in international markets. Korea exports instruments to more than 70 countries, with the largest share going to Canada, Europe, and the United States. Most Korean musical instrument manufacturers are small- to medium-sized firms.

Pianos In terms of number of units, pianos account for more than half of Korea's exports of musical instruments. Korean piano firms produce acoustic concert grand and upright models in a variety of woods and finishes. Major Korean piano manufacturers have established well-known brand names, such as Samick and Young Chang.

Other Instruments Korea's other significant exports of musical instruments include electronic organs and keyboards, woodwinds, drums and related percussion instruments, and such stringed instruments as zithers, banjos, and violins.

Competitive Situation

To remain competitive, Korean manufacturers of musical instruments have established stringent quality control systems and have automated their production lines and testing equipment. Many manufacturers are focusing on production of high-end instruments and electronic keyboards, areas in which demand is growing worldwide. Piano makers in Korea are continuously developing new designs and production processes to improve both the appearance and sound of their products. Moreover, they are trying new marketing strategies. For example, they are participating in international trade fairs and sending sales promotion teams to targeted countries. South Korean authorities have designated the piano industry as a recipient for government assistance in marketing and exporting.

Trade Associations

Korea Musical Instrument Industry Association
51-1, Tohwa-dong, Mapo-gu
Seoul
Tel: (2) 719-5037/8 Fax: (2) 718-0493

Directories/Publications

Asian Sources: Gifts & Home Products
(Monthly)
Asian Sources Media Group
22/F., Vita Tower
29 Wong Chuk Hang Rd.
Wong Chuk Hang, Hong Kong
Tel: [852] 5554777 Fax: [852] 8730488

Trade Fairs

Refer to the Trade Fair chapter for complete listings, including contact information, dates, and venues. The following trade fair is of particular relevance to this industry and is listed in that chapter under the heading given below:

Hobbies, Recreation & Travel
- Seoul International Audio & Musical Instruments Show (SIAM)

For other trade fairs that may be of interest, we recommend that you also consult the heading Furniture & Housewares.

SHIPS AND OTHER VESSELS

South Korea is the world's second largest producer of ships. Shipbuilding in Korea relies heavily on contracts with foreign shipping companies, because Korea's domestic shipping industry is small.

Products In general, the gross tonnage of vessels produced each year by Korean shipbuilders exceeds 4.5 million. Tankers and bulk carriers account for more than 80 percent of the tonnage of ships produced in Korean shipyards. The remaining production consists of container ships, car and truck carriers, and other vessels, such as cruisers, ferries, and barges.

Competitive Situation

In recent years, South Korea's shipbuilding industry has faced increasing competition, particularly from China, and decreasing financial support from Korea's government. Nevertheless, Korea's shipbuilders have maintained a competitive edge by cutting prices to gain orders and by concentrating on ships in high global demand, such as high-value-added container ships. As market demand has risen with the recent upturn in global trade, vessel prices have also increased, returning Korea's shipyards to profitable operations. To remain competitive internationally, Korean shipbuilders are intensifying their efforts to produce high-value-added vessels, such as liquid natural gas and liquid petroleum gas carriers.

Government Agencies

Inchon Port Authority
1-17, 7-ga, Hangdong, Chung-ku
Inchon

Ministry of Transportation
168, 2-ka, Bongnae-dong, Chung-ku
Seoul
Tel: (2) 392-9801, 392-7606 Fax: (2) 392-9809
Tlx: 24778

Ministry of Transportation
Maritime and Port Administration
112-2, Inui-dong, Chongno-ku
Seoul
Tel: (2) 774-4030 Tlx: 26528 HANGMAN

Pusan Port Authority
No. 5, Container Terminal
Pusan Port
Tel: (51) 65-0708 Tlx: 3371

Trade Associations

Korea Marine Equipment Association
12-5, Youido-dong, Yongdungpo-gu
Seoul
Tel: (2) 783-6952/4 Fax: (2) 785-7647

Korea Register of Shipping
1465-10, Socho 3-dong, Socho-gu
Seoul
Tel: (2) 582-6601

Korea Shipbuilders Association
65-1, Unni-dong, Chongno-gu
Seoul
Tel: (2) 766-4631/5
Fax: (2) 766-4307, 739-4306

Korea Shipbuilding Industry Cooperative
915-14, Pangbae-dong, Socho-gu
Seoul
Tel: (2) 587-3121/3 Fax: (2) 583-2922

Korea Shipowners' Association
10/F., Sejong Bldg.
100, Tangju-dong, Chongno-gu
Seoul
Tel: (2) 739-1551/7 Fax: (2) 739-1558

Korean Shippers Council
Rm. 4404, KWTC Bldg.
159, Samsung-dong, Kangnam-gu
Seoul
Tel: (2) 551-5383/5 Fax: (2) 551-5231

Korea Shipping Agency Association
Rm. 901, Hyundae Bldg.
80, Chockson-dong, Chongno-gu
Seoul
Tel: (2) 734-1531/3 Fax: (2) 738-3760

Korea Shipping Association
3, Yangpyong 2-dong 6-ga, Yongdungpo-gu
Seoul
Tel: (2) 675-2711 Fax: (2) 675-2714

Directories/Publications

Asian Shipping
(Monthly)
Asia Trade Journals Ltd.
7/F., Sincere Insurance Bldg.
4 Hennessy Rd.
Wanchai, Hong Kong
Tel: [852] 5278532 Fax: [852] 5278753

Korea Shippers News
(Quarterly)
Korea Foreign Trade Association
159-1, Samsung-dong, Kangnam-gu
Seoul
Tel: (2) 551-5114 Fax: (2) 551-5100

Shipping & Transport News
(Monthly)
Al Hilal Publishing (FE) Ltd.
50 Jalan Sultan, #20-06, Jalan Sultan Centre
Singapore 0719
Tel: [65] 2939233 Fax: [65] 2970862

Trade Fairs

Refer to the Trade Fair chapter for complete listings, including contact information, dates, and venues. Trade fairs with particular relevance to this industry include the following, which are listed in that chapter under the heading given below:

Aerospace & Oceanic
- International Shipbuilding, Marine, Port & Shipping, Intermodal, Small Ships & Fishing Exhibition (KORMARINE)

- International Underground & Sea Resources Exploitative Equipment Exhibition in Korea (UNDERSYSTEM)

For other trade fairs that may be of interest, we recommend that you also consult the headings Environmental & Energy Industries; and Sporting Goods.

SPORTING GOODS AND OUTDOOR EQUIPMENT

South Korea's sporting goods have a substantial share of world markets. In some product lines, Korea is one of the world's top five producers. More than 40 percent of the sporting goods produced in Korea are exported. This industry is supported by well-developed domestic industries, particularly in petrochemicals, textiles, chemicals, and sewing.

At least 350 sporting good manufacturers are operating in Korea. Only a few are large-scale companies. Small- and medium-sized Korean sporting good companies produce specialized, labor-intensive equipment for foreign firms on an original equipment manufacturer (OEM) basis and for local firms on a contract basis, while large-scale companies produce a broad range of sport and leisure goods and have their own domestic and foreign marketing structures. In general, Korea's sporting goods can be divided into bowling, fishing, golf, tennis, and outdoor equipment; recreational boats; and sports balls.

Bowling Equipment

Exports of Korean-produced bowling equipment are rising rapidly, particularly since Korean authorities have targeted this industry to expand its export levels. Korea's sporting goods firms make pinsetters, ball return lift systems, and automatic scoring systems as well as balls, bags, shoes, and other equipment for bowlers. The major markets for these products include China, Indonesia, Sri Lanka, England, Germany, and the United States. To remain competitive worldwide, Korea's bowling equipment manufacturers are concentrating on domestication of all part production, development of new designs, and establishment of their own brand names.

Fishing Equipment

Products South Korea is now supplying nearly 40 percent of the fishing equipment sold in world markets. Exports of fishing rods have a 60 percent share of international markets, and fishing reels have a 30 percent share. Other notable Korean fishing exports are nets, ropes, floats, hooks, swivels, and fish finders. Most of Korea's fishing equipment is produced by 11 firms on an original manufacturer equipment (OEM) basis, although a number of major firms are developing brand names of their own and are marketing actively through international trade fairs

and branch offices in foreign countries. Korea's primary markets for fishing equipment are Japan, the United States, Germany, France, and Italy.

Competitive Situation In recent years, Korea's fishing equipment manufacturers have faced increasing competition from developing countries, particularly China, and rising domestic labor costs. To remain competitive in international markets, Korea's firms have invested heavily in R&D, resulting in the manufacture of lightweight, flexible, and durable fishing tackle from such high-tech materials as carbon graphite and compounds of Kevlar, boron, and wisker. A number of firms have automated their production facilities in Korea and have moved their labor-intensive operations to countries where wages are lower. Most firms have shifted away from fiberglass fishing rods to high-end products with multiple features, such as telescoping and adjustable-length rods.

Golf and Tennis Equipment

Golf and tennis equipment rank second and third respectively among Korea's exports of sporting goods. Korean companies offer a wide variety of irons, metal and wood drivers, golf bags, gloves, and other golfing accessories. Most Korean golf clubs are assembled from imported parts on an original equipment manufacturer (OEM) basis. Korean manufacturers are producing tennis rackets from high-tech metals, with a special emphasis on durability and tensile strength.

Outdoor Equipment

Products Korean-made outdoor goods are rapidly developing a reputation worldwide for quality at reasonable prices. South Korea exports a wide array of products, including cooking sets, knives, burners, tents, and backpacks. Most Korean-made outdoor equipment is produced on an original equipment manufacturer (OEM) basis. Korean manufacturers of tents and backpacks have been targeted for support from the government-backed Korea Trade Promotion Corporation (KOTRA).

Tents Korea is the world's top supplier of tents, which it distributes to more than 50 nations. Approximately 20 Korean tent manufacturers using computer-aided design (CAD) systems to develop innovative structures. A wide variety of tent models are available, including dome, bungalow, cabin, pup, pop-up, cycling, and dining tents. Much research has been devoted to the development of high-tech tents that are easy to erect, waterproof, lightweight, safe, comfortable, and durable. Technological advances in Korean-made tents include the use of one-touch erection apparatus, nylon-blended fabrics, and fiber glass, carbon fiber, and duraluminum poles. Most Korean tent manufacturers have eliminated labor-intensive operations by installing computer-automated equipment. To remain competitive, some Korean firms have moved their labor-intensive operations to countries where wages are lower, particularly Indonesia. Eight Korean tent manufacturers are suppliers to such well-known foreign companies as Sears, Wal-Mart, and K-Mart. Some manufacturers are now establishing their own brand names in international markets.

Recreational Boats The manufacture of Korean sporting boats is relatively undeveloped. Only about 120 small South Korean firms produce sporting boats on an order basis, and their products are primarily limited to inflatables and fabricated rubber boats, although one firm also manufactures and exports outboard motors. Approximately 60 percent of all Korean-made recreational boats are exported. Korean authorities have designated recreational boats as an item for promotion and development of local manufacturing, but domestic production and exports continue to decline. Large shipbuilders recently attempted to produce recreational motor boats, but this field remains unpromising for them.

Sports Balls Korea's leading sporting goods export is sports balls. Korean sporting good manufacturers produce balls for nearly every sport, including basketball, baseball, soccer, pool and billiards, golf, tennis, squash, and table tennis. Golf balls are the most significant of these exports; most carry the brand names of Korean companies, such as Fantom, Far Max, and Choice. Most production is on an original equipment manufacturer (OEM) basis, but several Korean firms have established their own brand names.

Government Agencies

Fisheries Administration
541, 5-ga Namdaemun-no, Chung-ku
Seoul
Tel: (2) 777-8271 Tlx: 24719

Ministry of Agriculture, Forestry and Fisheries
1, Jungang-dong
Gwachon City, Kyonggi Province
Tel: (2) 503-7209, 503-7208 Tlx: 24759

Ministry of Sports and Youth
77, Sejong-no, Chongno-ku
Seoul
Tel: (2) 734-5283, 720-2181 Tlx: 22926

Trade Associations

Agriculture & Fishery Marketing Cooperation
191, Hangangno 2-ga, Yongsan-gu
Seoul
Tel: (2) 795-8201/5
Fax: (2) 790-5265, 798-7513

Korea Agriculture & Fisheries Food Trade Association
Rm. 1905, KWTC Bldg.
159, Samsung-dong, Kangnam-gu
Seoul
Tel: (2) 551-1936/9 Fax: (2) 551-1940

Korea Bicycle Industry Association
Rm. 604, Sanjung Bldg.
15-16, Youido-dong, Yongdungpo-gu
Seoul
Tel: (2) 784-2582/3 Fax: (2) 785-7270

Korea Deep Sea Fisheries Association
6/F., Samhomulsan Bldg.
Yangjae-dong, Socho-gu
Seoul
Tel: (2) 589-1621/4 Fax: (2) 589-1030/1

Korea Sporting Goods Industry Cooperative
Rm. 814, Life Officetel
61-3, Youido-dong, Yongdungpo-gu
Seoul
Tel: (2) 786-7761 Fax: (2) 786-7764

Directories/Publications

Asian Sources: Gifts & Home Products (Monthly)
Asian Sources Media Group
22/F., Vita Tower
29 Wong Chuk Hang Rd.
Wong Chuk Hang, Hong Kong
Tel: [852] 5554777 Fax: [852] 8730488

Trade Fairs

Refer to the Trade Fair chapter for complete listings, including contact information, dates, and venues. Trade fairs with particular relevance to this industry include the following, which are listed in that chapter under the heading given below:

Sporting Goods
- Korea International Fishing Tackle Show (KOFISH)
- Korea International Golf Show (KOGOLF)
- Korea International Mountaineering Show (KOMOUNT)
- Korea International Sports, Leisure & Boat Show (SPOKOR BOAT SHOW)

For other trade fairs that may be of interest, we recommend that you also consult the headings Gifts, Jewelry & Stationery; and Hobbies, Recreation & Travel.

TELECOMMUNICATIONS EQUIPMENT

Fewer than 50 manufacturers are producing telecommunications equipment in South Korea. Most firms use components, subassemblies, and assemblies imported from abroad. Many Korean telecommunications companies operate as joint ventures or under technology transfer arrangements with foreign companies. A small but growing percentage of Korean-produced telecommunications products is shipped overseas.

Premises Customer Equipment Korean telecommunications firms produce cellular phones, corded and cordless phones, teleprinters, and facsimile machines. In recent years, export sales of Korea's portable phones have declined, primarily as the result of low quality and poor after-sales service. However, exports of telephone sets are substantial, representing at least 60 percent of Korea's total production. Exports are high in part because of the wide variety of features offered, including party lines, coin options, originating call barring, call restriction, absentee service, wake-up, and priority services, conference calling, abbreviated dialing, call tracing, hot and warm line services, call waiting and call transfer, and circuit-switched data services. Multiple features, such as automatic paper feeding, abbreviated dialing, tone or pulse dialing options, redialing, and security devices are available on facsimile machines assembled in Korea. These machines are offered for both office and home use.

Key Telephone Systems and Private Branch Exchanges About 10 South Korean manufacturers are making key telephone systems (KTSs), and only 5 are producing private branch exchanges (PBXs). These companies offer large, mid-size, and small models. Only about 9 percent of Korea's production of keyphone systems and PBXs are exported.

Competition in Korean markets for KTSs and PBXs is so severe that Korean suppliers have had to reduce their profit margins to maintain their market share, and they are now negotiating price levels to sell their products. To become more competitive, some of Korea's firms are shifting to production of Integrated Service Digital Networks (ISDNs) and other electronic digital systems that can transmit through multiple media, including personal computers, facsimiles, and word processors. They are also trying to diversify into additional export markets, and they have been successful with some products in Britain and Spain.

Network Equipment Most Korean manufacturers of telecommunications equipment produce basic telecommunications terminals, such as low-cost general-purpose internal dial-up modems used primarily in personal computer communications. A few firms have started producing dial-up modems of a data-compression type and multiport-type modems for leased lines. Although these products are advanced in technology, most Korean firms currently lack the technology needed to produce sophisticated network equipment, and after-sales service is still limited.

Competitive Situation

Korea's telecommunications industry has been spurred by increased demand from the private and public sectors, especially since Korean authorities relaxed restrictions on this industry and encouraged the development of network systems. Several local firms are promoting localization of network-ing technology, but they have technical problems with critical components, such as protocol transistors and routers.

With a general trend in consumer demand away from modems to digital service units (DSUs), major Korean manufacturers of telecommunications equipment are increasing capital investment to develop high-end DSU products. Korean firms that produce modems are upgrading to high-end products, such as T1 MUX modems, modems for satellite communications, and leased-line modems that incorporate a network management system (NMS) card. Major telecommunication producers in Korea are producing high-tech and experimental packet-switching products to meet growing market demands, and some firms are already offering packet concentrators and packet assemblers/disassemblers (PADs) on domestic markets. A number of Korean manufacturers of transmission devices are developing NMS products that provide quick identification of network failures and extensive troubleshooting operations. To gain access to knowledge in these technologies, Korean manufacturers are negotiating technical licensing and distribution agreements with foreign companies. Korean firms are also investing in R&D to develop high-tech equipment for satellite communications.

Government Agencies

Ministry of Communications
100, Sejong-no, Chongno-ku
Seoul 110-777
Tel: (2) 750-2811, 750-2800 Tlx: 24819

Trade Associations

Korea Tele-Communication Industry Cooperative
KCE Bldg.
16-6, Hangango 3-ga, Yongsan-gu
Seoul
Tel: (2) 711-2266 Fax: (2) 711-2272

Directories/Publications

Asia Pacific Broadcasting & Telecommunications
(Monthly)
Asian Business Press Pte., Ltd.
100 Beach Rd.
#26-00 Shaw Towers
Singapore 0718
Tel: [65] 2943366 Fax: [65] 2985534

Telecom Asia
(Bimonthly)
CCI Asia-Pacific (HK)
Suite 905, Guardian House
32 Oi Kwan Rd.
Wanchai, Hong Kong
Tel: [852] 8332181 Fax: [852] 8345620

Trade Fairs

Refer to the Trade Fair chapter for complete listings, including contact information, dates, and venues. Trade fairs with particular relevance to this industry include the following, which are listed in that chapter under the heading given below:

Multimedia & A/V Equipment
- Korea International Broadcast & Audio Equipment Show (KOBA)
- Seoul International Audio & Musical Instruments Show (SIAM)
- Seoul International CATV Show (CATV SEOUL)
- Seoul International Photo, Video & Optical Industry Show (PHOTO SHOW SEOUL)

For other trade fairs that may be of interest, we recommend that you also consult the headings Computer & Information Industries; and Electronic & Electric Equipment.

TEXTILES AND GARMENTS

Garments and textiles are South Korea's second and third largest exports respectively, although exports have declined in recent years. Major export markets for Korean textiles are Japan and the United States, and fiber exports to China are rising dramatically.

South Korean textile manufacturers produce man-made fibers, natural fibers, various fabrics, leather, garments, and carpets.

Man-Made Fibers Korea's man-made fiber (MMF) industry is led by 13 firms with facilities that are considered highly developed. Approximately 70 percent of Korea's total production of MMFs is currently exported. MMF fibers include ethylene glycol, terephthalic acid, dimethyl terephthalate, acrylonitrile, caprolactam, chemical wood pulp, and acetate-flake. Demand in textile and nontextile industries for caprolactam and polyester fiber has increased worldwide, but demand for acrylonitrile remains sluggish. Korea's production of MMFs is expected to increase with the installation or expansion of several MMF plants in Korea, but it is still not expected to meet anticipated local demand, and Korean manufacturers will need to continue importing much of their MMF fibers.

Carpets and Rugs Four major firms account for approximately 53 percent of Korea's production of carpets and rugs. About 10 small- to medium-sized firms produce the rest. These firms produce primarily rugs, wall-to-wall carpeting, and roll carpets in various materials, including acrylic, nylon, polypropylene, and wool. Approximately one-third of the total production is exported. The major markets are Japan, the United Arab Emirates, and the United States.

However, Korean carpet and rug exports have declined in recent years, reflecting substantial increases in domestic demand. In addition, Korean products lag behind others in selection, quality, and price. Most parent companies of Korean rug manufacturers have not supported their carpet divisions with the investments needed for improving machinery and design.

Korean consumer trends suggest that carpet tiles will become extremely popular, and most local companies are now planning carpet tile operations. A few firms are already manufacturing carpet tiles in cooperation with Japanese and Dutch companies. Most Korean carpet manufacturers distribute through sales agents. A few major firms also have their own retail shops and chain stores.

Competitive Situation

South Korean textile manufactures have been affected adversely by rising costs for labor and raw materials and by intense competition from other textile-producing regions, particularly Southeast Asia. In an attempt to reduce labor costs, Korea's spinners are installing automated equipment to handle raw materials between each process. Korean textile producers are modernizing their fashion designs and installing quick-response systems to change designs in accordance with international trends. Some spinners and knitters have moved nearly all labor-intensive operations to countries where wages are lower. To improve their profits, many Korean textile makers are concentrating on synthetic fibers, which are in high demand in domestic industries, and they have shifted their production of fiber to high-end products, including spin-draw, preoriented, and polyester filament yarns.

Trade Associations

Korea Apparel Sub-Material Association
2A-1, KOEX Bldg.
159, Samsung-dong, Kangnam-gu
Seoul
Tel: (2) 551-6000/2 Fax: (2) 551-6006

Korea Canvas Products Industry Cooperative
19-1, Namdaemunno 5-ga, Chung-gu
Seoul
Tel: (2) 755-9033/6

Korea Chemical Fibers Association
80, Chokson-dong, Chongno-gu
Seoul
Tel: (2) 734-1191/4 Fax: (2) 738-0111

Korea Dyestuff & Pigment Industry Cooperative
17-1, Youido-dong, Yongdungpo-gu
Seoul
Tel: (2) 783-0721 Fax: (2) 786-1888

Korea Export Association of Textiles
Rm. 1803/4, KWTC Bldg.
159, Samsung-dong, Kangnam-gu
Seoul
Tel: (2) 551-1876, 551-1895 Fax: (2) 551-1896

Korea Fastener Industry Cooperative
221, Hyoje-dong, Chongno-gu
Seoul
Tel: (2) 743-1219, 763-7442 Fax: (2) 743-1219

Korea Federation of Knitting Industry Cooperatives
48, Shinmunno 1-ga, Chongno-gu
Seoul
Tel: (2) 735-5951/3 Fax: (2) 735-1447

Korea Federation of Textile Industries
944-31 Daechi-dong, Kangnam-gu
Seoul
Tel: (2) 528-4005 Fax: (2) 528-4069

Korea Federation of Weaving Industry
Cooperatives
169-2, Namchang-dong, Chung-gu
Seoul
Tel: (2) 778-4295, 752-8098 Fax: (2) 755-6994

Korea Garment Industry Cooperative
105-238, Kongdok-dong, Mapo-gu
Seoul
Tel: (2) 717-3191, 715-8998 Fax: (2) 718-3192

Korea Garments & Knitwear Export Association
Rm. 801, KWTC Bldg.
159, Samsung-dong, Kangnam-gu
Seoul
Tel: (2) 551-1456 Fax: (2) 551-1519

Korea Nonwoven Industry Cooperative
Rm. 1513, Yoowon Office
164-11, Chungjongno 2-ga, Sodaemun-gu
Seoul
Tel: (2) 365-2332 Fax: (2) 393-5098

Korea PP Textile Industrial Cooperative
1-1, Yonji-dong, Chongno-gu
Seoul
Tel: (2) 741-7801/5 Fax: (2) 741-7851

Korea Tanners Association
Rm. 805, Samhwa Bldg.
204-4, Nonhyon-dong, Kangnam-gu
Seoul
Tel: (2) 549-5432/3 Fax: (2) 549-6733

Korea Textile Inspection & Testing Institute
819-5, Yoksam-dong, Kangnam-gu
Seoul
Tel: (2) 567-7591 Fax: (2) 557-3739

Korea Wadding Industry Cooperative
51-1, Tohwa-dong, Mapo-gu
Seoul
Tel: (2) 702-6678/9 Fax: (2) 702-6612

Korea Woolen Spinners & Weavers Industry
Cooperative
120-3, Chungmuro 4-ga, Chung-gu
Seoul
Tel: (2) 273-0677/9 Fax: (2) 277-9789

Raw Silk Exporters Association
17-9, Youido-dong, Yongdungpo-gu
Seoul
Tel: (2) 785-5911/4 Fax: (2) 785-5915

Spinners & Weavers Association of Korea
43-8, Kwanchol-dong, Chongno-gu
Seoul
Tel: (2) 735-5741/8 Fax: (2) 735-5749

Directories/Publications

Asia Pacific Leather Directory
(Annual)
Asia Pacific Leather Yearbook
(Annual)
Asia Pacific Directories, Ltd.
6/F. Wah Hen Commercial Centre
381 Hennessy Rd.
Hong Kong
Tel: [852] 8936377 Fax: [852] 8935752

ATA Journal: Journal for Asia on Textile & Apparel
(Bimonthly)
Adsale Publishing Company
21/F., Tung Wai Commercial Bldg.
109-111 Gloucester Rd.
Wanchai, Hong Kong
Subscriptions: PO Box 20032, Hennessy Rd., Hong Kong
Tel: [852] 8920511 Fax: [852] 8384119

Fashion Accessories
(Monthly)
Asian Sources Media Group
22nd Fl., Vita Tower
29 Wong Chuk Hang Road
Wong Chuk Hang, Hong Kong
Tel: [852] 5554777 Fax: [852] 8730488

Korea Apparel Sub-Material Directory
(Biennial)
Korea Apparel Sub-Material Association
2A-1, KOEX Bldg.
159, Samsung-dong, Kangnam-gu
Seoul
Tel: (2) 551-6000/2 Fax: (2) 551-6006

Textile Asia Index
(Annual)
Business Press Ltd.
30-32 d'Aguilar St.
11/F., Tak Yan Commercial Bldg.
Central, Hong Kong
Tel: [852] 5247441 Tlx: 60275

Textile Asia: The Asian Textile and Apparel
Monthly
(Monthly)
Business Press Ltd.
1l/F., California Tower
30-32 d'Aguilar St.
Central, Hong Kong
Tel: [852] 5247467 Fax: [852] 8106966

Trade Fairs

Refer to the Trade Fair chapter for complete listings, including contact information, dates, and venues. Trade fairs with particular relevance to this industry include the following, which are listed in that chapter under the heading given below:

Textiles & Apparel
- Exhibition for wedding goods korea (WEDDEX KOREA)
- Korea International Nonwovens & Machinery Show (NONWOVEN KOREA)
- Seoul International Fashion Fair (SIFF)
- Seoul International Gift Fair / Seoul International Fashion Jewelry & Accessories Fair (SIGIFT/ACCESS)
- Seoul International Textile Fair (SEOUL STUFF)
- SFA Seoul Collection (SFA)
- Taegu International Textile Fair

For other trade fairs that may be of interest, we recommend that you also consult the headings Furniture & Housewares; Industrial Materials & Chemicals; and Sporting Goods.

TOOLS AND INSTRUMENTS

South Korea's tool and instruments industry has developed rapidly in recent years, and it now exports approximately half of all the tools and instruments that it produces. This industry is being stimulated by Korea's focus on the development of high-tech industries, such as computer manufacturing, mechatronics, industrial material manufacturing, genetic engineering, fine chemistry, energy production, aerospace, maritime, and medicines. Major export markets are in other Asian countries and the United States.

Korean-produced tools and instruments include hand and power tools as well as precision and scientific instruments. With the exception of a few firms, most Korean makers of hand tools and instruments are small, and nearly all production is on an original equipment manufacturer (OEM) basis. In contrast, more than half of Korea's power tool manufacturers are large firms that operate under technology transfer agreements with foreign companies.

Hand and Power Tools Korean companies still produce primarily hand and do-it-yourself (DIY) power tools. Major exports include tape measures and other measuring tools, screwdrivers, wrenches, work bench sets, grinding wheels, and power drills, sanders, and planers.

Laboratory and Scientific Instruments Korean-produced laboratory and scientific instruments include high-precision tensile strength testers, compression testers, automatic balances, pendulum balances, digital electronic thermometers, and hydrometers. Other less sophisticated instruments are also available.

Competitive Situation

Korea's tool and instrument industry lacks the high-technology capability required for production of sophisticated instruments. A number of larger firms are expanding their production facilities significantly and investing in R&D to develop high-tech products. To become more competitive in world markets, Korean power tool makers are focusing on production of computer numerically controlled (CNC) tools.

Government Agencies

Ministry of Science and Technology
1, Jungang-dong
Gwachon City, Kyonggi Province
Tel: (2) 503-7609 Fax: (2) 503-7673
Tlx: 24230

Trade Associations

Korea Advanced Institute of Science & Technology
373-1, Kusong-dong, Yusong-gu
Taejon
Tel: (42) 869-2114 Fax: (42) 869-2210

Korea Farm Machinery & Tool Industry Cooperative
11-11, Tongja-dong, Yongsan-gu
Seoul
Tel: (2) 757-1451/6 Fax: (2) 757-1430

Korea Gauge & Meter Industry Cooperative
13-31, Youido-dong, Yongdungpo-gu
Seoul
Tel: (2) 783-5686

Korea Institute of Science & Technology
39-1, Hawolgok-dong, Songbuk-gu
Seoul
Tel: (2) 982-8801 Fax: (2) 963-4013

Korea Machine Tool Manufacturers' Association
35-4, Youido-dong, Yongdungpo-gu
Seoul
Tel: (2) 780-3521 Fax: (2) 784-8023

Korea Medical Instrument Industry Cooperative
284-6, Nagwon-dong, Chongno-gu
Seoul
Tel: (2) 764-3815, 762-3814 Fax: (2) 744-6567

Korea Scientific Instruments Industry Cooperative
60, Myo-dong, Chongno-gu
Seoul
Tel: (2) 742-6083 Fax: (2) 744-4934

Korea Tools Industry Cooperative
Rm. 401, Bohun Bldg.
12-5, Youido-dong, Yongdungpo-gu
Seoul 150-010
Tel: (2) 780-0731 Fax: (2) 785-2457

Directories/Publications

Asian Sources: Hardware
(Monthly)
Asian Sources Media Group
22/F., Vita Tower
29 Wong Chuk Hang Rd.
Wong Chuk Hang, Hong Kong
Tel: [852] 5554777 Fax: [852] 8730488

Korea Medical Instrument Directory
(Annual)
Korea Medical Instrument Industry Cooperative
284-6, Nagwon-dong, Chongno-gu
Seoul
Tel: (2) 764-3815, 762-3814 Fax: (2) 744-6567

Korea Tools Magazine
Korea Tools Industry Cooperative
Rm. 401, Bohun Bldg.
12-5, Youido-dong, Yongdungpo-gu
Seoul 150-010
Tel: (2) 780-0731 Fax: (2) 785-2457

Trade Fairs

Refer to the Trade Fair chapter for complete listings, including contact information, dates, and venues. Trade fairs with particular relevance to this industry include the following, which are listed in that chapter under the heading given below:

Tools: Precision & Measuring
- Changwon Tool Tech Show
- Korea International Medical Equipment Show (KIMES)
- Seoul International Instrumentation Exhibition (SEOUL INSTRUMENT)
- Seoul International Machine Tool Show (SIMTOS)
- Seoul International Photo, Video & Optical Industry Show (PHOTO SHOW SEOUL)
- Seoul International Scientific Instrument Show (INTERSIS)

For other trade fairs that may be of interest, we recommend that you also consult the headings Electronic & Electric Equipment; Construction & Housing; Factory Automation; Health & Safety; Machines & Instruments; and Metal & Metal Finishing.

TOYS

South Korea was a leading toy exporter in the early 1980s, but production and export of Korean toys have declined continuously since 1987. Between 1989 and 1991 an average 15 percent of local production was lost every year, and exports suffered about a 25 percent annual reduction. This decline primarily reflects the dramatic drop in global demand for Korean stuffed toys, formerly a mainstay of Korea's toy industry.

About 400 Korean companies are now manufacturing toys, including ride-on toys, dolls, stuffed toys, and metallic and plastic toys. Most producers are small companies that employ about 30 persons. Korea's largest export markets are in European countries and the United States.

Metallic and Plastic Toys Nearly one-half of Korea's toy manufacturers produce metallic and plastic toys, which account for half of Korea's toy market. Exports of Korean-made metallic and plastic toys grew slowly until 1992, when they plunged to a level 20.6 percent below that of the preceding year.

Dolls and Stuffed Toys Since 1987 the market for Korean-made dolls and stuffed toys has declined about 3 percent every year. In particular, exports of stuffed toys have dropped by between 20 and 30 percent annually, a trend that is expected to continue for several years, because Korean producers are only in the initial stage of expanding their R&D efforts to create innovative, high-quality products. Korean toy makers are shifting product lines to high-end toys in an effort to compete against low-end products now being exported from developing countries with lower labor costs, particularly China.

Competitive Situation

Korean toy manufacturers have suffered from rising wages, increasing costs for raw materials, and declining export markets. Many US buyers now prefer to deal with other Asian countries where prices and production costs are lower. European countries are importing more electronic video games than metallic and plastic toys. In 1992 exports to Europe and the United States fell by 41.2 percent and 33 percent respectively below the levels for the preceding year.

In an effort to turn Korea's declining toy exports around, many Korean toy makers are moving from production of low-cost labor-intensive products to high-tech high-value-added goods. About 60 factories for stuffed toys have transferred production of labor-intensive products to developing countries, particularly China, Thailand, and Indonesia; high-tech toys continue to be produced in Korea. Major Korean toy makers have begun to create innovative designs and use high-quality, expensive materials in their products.

Trade Associations

Electronic Industries Association of Korea
5/F., Danwoo Bdlg.
850-22, Pangbae-dong, Sochu-gu
Seoul
Tel: (2) 553-0941/7, 553-8725
Fax: (2) 555-6195

Korea Electronic Industries Cooperative
813-5, Pangbae-dong, Sochu-gu
Seoul
Tel: (2) 533-2309 Fax: (2) 553-0949

Korea Plastic Industry Cooperative
146-2, Ssangnim-dong, Chung-gu
Seoul
Tel: (2) 275-7991/4 Fax: (2) 277-5150

Korea Rubber Industry Cooperative
7, Shinmunno 1-ga, Chongno-gu
Seoul
Tel: (2) 733-8584/6 Fax: (2) 730-3355

Korea Toy Industry Cooperative
361-1, Hangangno 2-ga, Yongsan-gu
Seoul
Tel: (2) 795-9505, 795-9818 Fax: (2) 795-0401

Directories/Publications

Asian Plastic News
(Quarterly)
Reed Asian Publishing Pte., Ltd.
5001 Beach Rd.
#06-12 Golden Mile Complex
Singapore 0719
Tel: [65] 2913188 Fax: [65] 2913180

Asian Sources: Gifts & Home Products
(Monthly)
Asian Sources Media Group
22/F., Vita Tower
29 Wong Chuk Hang Rd.
Wong Chuk Hang, Hong Kong
Tel: [852] 5554777 Fax: [852] 8730488

Trade Fairs

Refer to the Trade Fair chapter for complete listings, including contact information, dates, and venues. Trade fairs with particular relevance to this industry include the following, which are listed in that chapter under the heading given below:

Hobbies, Recreation & Travel
- Phila Korea World Stamp Exhibition (PHILA KOREA)
- Seoul Book Fair
- Seoul International Audio & Musical Instruments Show (SIAM)
- Seoul International Toy Fair (SITOY)

For other trade fairs that may be of interest, we recommend that you also consult the headings Computer & Information Industries; Electronic & Electric Equipment; Gifts, Jewelry & Stationery; and Sporting Goods.

VEHICLES AND VEHICLE PARTS

South Korea is one of the world's top 10 automobile makers. Leading export markets for Korean-made vehicles are Canada, the United States, Europe, and Southeast Asia.

Korea's vehicle industry exports finished vehicles and vehicle parts. Most Korean firms are still assemblers of imported parts.

Vehicles Korea has seven major vehicle manufacturers, most of whom have financial and technical cooperation agreements with Japanese or American vehicle companies. Approximately 80 percent of Korea's total production represents passenger cars, and 20 percent are commercial vehicles. A wide array of Korean-made vehicles is available, including passenger cars, buses, trucks, jeeps, and special-purpose vehicles.

Vehicle Parts In terms of growth, Korea's vehicle parts industry has followed Korea's automobile industry, and all parts and accessories manufacturers maintain a relationship with one or more Korean vehicle factories. Major accessories available include car-cleaning products, safety belt clips, and car deodorants. More than 1,200 Korean firms produce vehicle parts, primarily on an original manufacturer equipment (OEM) basis. Most producers are small- to medium-sized companies with fewer than 100 employees. Korean vehicle parts makers lack the technology needed to produce high-end products, the funds needed to invest in R&D and capital improvements, and quality control systems. Major Korean vehicle parts manufacturers have joint investment or technology transfer agreements with United States, Japanese, and German vehicle makers, an arrangement that has stimulated technological and production growth for the Korean partners. All parts and accessories are delivered to Korean vehicle assemblers, who in turn allocate approximately 7 percent for export.

Competitive Situation

Vehicle makers in South Korea remain dependent on foreign technology—their largest obstacle to expansion and competitiveness in world markets. An average 10 percent of their production costs are royalties paid to foreign companies for use of their technology. Another adverse factor has been Korea's inability to localize parts and accessories manufacture without foreign technology transfer arrangements. In an effort to improve this situation, vehicle parts producers in Korea have established comprehensive research institutions and laboratories to develop advanced technology and production processes. In particular, they are focusing on improvements in design, testing, assembly, processing, and inspection of vehicle parts. About 60 percent of the R&D funds are being provided by the Korean government.

Despite a decrease in international demand, Korea's vehicle exports continue to rise gradually. Japanese models are becoming more price competitive with Korean vehicles, a development that is affecting Korea's volume exports to markets that it shares with Japanese firms. Since stabilizing labor relations in 1991, Korean vehicle manufacturers again face labor shortages. They are also affected by developments in several closely related industries, primarily those producing petrochemicals, electronic parts and components, nonferrous metals, steel, and machinery. Several manufacturers are also experiencing cash flow problems that are slowing production.

The increases seen in recent years can be ascribed to Korea's diversification of overseas markets and the development of new models. In an effort to improve their technology, Korean vehicle manufacturers have invested heavily in the local production of automobile engines and the development of new materials. They are also undertaking intensive research to produce lighter vehicles and subcompacts with more electronic components. Net profits on 1992 sales of Korean-made cars declined primarily because of increased sales of passenger cars on an interest-free, installment basis. Korea's vehicle makers have expanded sales by stepping up promotion activities and stabilizing labor-management relationships. Exports in 1993 rose slightly as a result of the weak Korean won, manufacturers' market diversification efforts, and economic recovery in the United States, Korea's primary export market.

Government Agencies

Ministry of Transportation
168, 2-ka, Bongnae-dong, Chung-ku
Seoul
Tel: (2) 392-9801, 392-7606 Fax: (2) 392-9809
Tlx: 24778

Trade Associations

Korea Auto Industries Cooperative Association
1683-3, Socho-dong, Socho-gu
Seoul
Tel: (2) 587-3416 Fax: (2) 583-7340

Korea Automobile Manufacturers Association
8/F., 63 Bldg.
Youido-dong, Yongdungpo-gu
Seoul
Tel: (2) 782-1360/1 Fax: (2) 782-0464

Korea Battery Industry Cooperative
1304-4, Socho-dong, Socho-gu
Seoul
Tel: (2) 553-2401/3 Fax: (2) 556-1290

Korea Tire Manufacturers Association
Rm. 1910, KWTC Bldg.
159, Samsung-dong, Kangnam-gu
Seoul
Tel: (2) 551-1903/7 Fax: (2) 551-1910

Directories/Publications

Korea Automobile & Auto Parts Catalogue
(Biennial)
Korea Auto Industries Cooperative Association
1683-3, Socho-dong, Socho-gu
Seoul
Tel: (2) 587-3416 Fax: (2) 583-7340

Trade Fairs

Refer to the Trade Fair chapter for complete listings, including contact information, dates, and venues. The following trade fair is of particular relevance to this industry and is listed in that chapter under the heading given below:

Automobiles & Automotive Parts
• Korea international auto parts & Accessories Show (KAPAS)

For other trade fairs that may be of interest, we recommend that you also consult the headings Electronic & Electric Equipment; Environmental & Energy Industries; Factory Automation; and Industrial Materials & Chemicals.

Trade Fairs

South Korea hosts a wide range of trade fairs and expositions that should interest anyone who seeks to do business in this dynamic and expanding economy. Whether you want to buy Korean goods or exhibit your own goods and services for sale in the Korean market, you will almost undoubtedly find one or more trade fairs to suit your purposes.

The listing of trade fairs in this section is designed to acquaint you with the scope, size, frequency, and length of the events held in Korea and to give you contact information for the organizers. While every effort has been made to ensure that this information is correct and complete as of press time, the scheduling of such events is in constant flux. Announced exhibitions can be canceled and dates and venues are often shifted. If you're interested in attending or exhibiting at a show listed here, we urge you to contact the organizer well in advance to confirm the venue and dates and to ascertain whether it is appropriate for you. (Refer to Tips for Attending a Trade Fair, following this introduction, for further suggestions on selecting, attending, and exhibiting at trade fairs.) The information in this volume will give a significant head start over others who have considered participating in a trade fair as an exhibitor or attendee.

In order to make access to this information as easy as possible, fairs have been grouped alphabetically by product category and within product category, alphabetically by name. Product categories, with cross references, are given following this introduction in a table of contents. Note that the first and last headings listed are out of alphabetical order. Trade fairs listed under Comprehensive do not focus on a single type of product but instead show a broad range of goods that may be from one geographic area or centered around a particular theme. The final category, Others, is a miscellaneous listing of fairs that do not fit easily into one of the other categories. When appropriate, fairs have been listed in more than one category. The breadth of products on display at a given fair means that you may want to investigate categories that are not immediately obvious. Many exhibits include the machinery, tools, and raw materials used to produce the products associated with the central theme of a fair; anyone interested in such items should consider a wide range of the listings.

The list gives the names and dates of both recent and upcoming events, together with site and contact information. Attendance information, including figures on the number of countries attending, the number of Korean attendees, and the number of overseas attendees, is provided for some events. Many shows take place on a regular basis. Annual or biennial schedules are common. When we were able to confirm the frequency of a show through independent sources, it has been indicated. Many others on the list may also be regular events. Some are onetime events. Because specifics on frequency are sometimes difficult to come by and because schedules for some 1994 and many 1995 shows were not available at press time, we have given both recent and future dates. It is quite possible that a fair listed for 1993 will be held again in 1994 or 1995, so it would be worthwhile getting in touch with the contact listed for any show that looks interesting. Even if we were not able to confirm the frequency, you can infer a likely time cycle if several dates are given for a fair.

As you gather further information on fairs that appeal to you, do not be surprised if the names are slightly different from those listed here. Some large trade fairs include several smaller exhibits, some use short names or acronyms, and Korean names can be translated in a variety of ways. Dates and venues, of course, are always subject to change.

For further information The Korea National Tourism Corporation (KNTC) publishes an annual calendar of conventions and exhibitions in Korea. Listings are arranged by date. For each event, the calendar includes the name, venue, organizer, and expected attendance. For a copy of the calendar, contact the main office of KNTC or one of its 18 offices worldwide. Another excellent source of information is the Korea Trade Promotion Corporation

(KOTRA), which also provides calendars. They are somewhat less complete, but they are updated more often. Contact KOTRA's main office or one of its many offices worldwide for information. A third source is the Korea Exhibition Center (KOEX) in Seoul, the venue where most international trade fairs in Korea are held. (Refer to "Important Addresses" chapter for KNTC offices and KOTRA offices.)

Korea National Tourism Corporation (KNTC)
C.P.O. Box 903
Seoul 100-609
Tel: [82] (2) 757-6030 Fax: [82] (2) 757-5997

Korea Trade Promotion Corporation (KOTRA)
Trade Center PO Box 123
Seoul
Tel: [82] (2) 551-4181 Fax: [82] (2) 551-4477
Tlx: KOTRA K23659, K27326

Korea Exhibition Center (KOEX)
159 Samsung-dong, Kangnam-ku
Seoul
Tel: [82] (2) 551-1117, 551-1124
Fax: [82] (2) 551-1311 Tlx: KOEXCEN K24594

Other valuable resources for trade fair information include the commercial sections of Korean diplomatic missions, chambers of commerce and other business organizations dedicated to trade between your country and Korea, and the embassy and consulate of your own country located in Korea. Professional and trade organizations in Korea involved in your area of interest may also be worth contacting. (Refer to "Important Addresses" chapter for Korean embassies and consulates, Korean chambers of commerce and business organizations, diplomatic missions located in Korea, and trade organizations.)

While the annual directory *Trade Shows Worldwide* (Gale Research Inc., Detroit, Michigan) is far from comprehensive, it may provide further information on some trade fairs in South Korea, and it is worth seeking out at your local business library.

TRADE FAIRS
TABLE OF CONTENTS

TRADE FAIRS
TABLE OF CONTENTS

Tips for Attending a Trade Fair

Overseas trade fairs can be extremely effective for making face-to-face contacts and sales or purchases, identifying suppliers, checking out competitors, and finding out how business really works in the host country. However, the cost of attending such fairs can be high. To maximize the return on your investment of time and money, you should be very clear about your goals for the trip and give yourself plenty of time for advance research and preparation. You should also make sure that you are aware of the limitations of trade fairs. The products on display probably do not represent the full range of goods available on the market. In fact, some of the latest product designs may still be under wraps. And while trade fairs give you an opportunity to make face-to-face contact with many people, both exhibitors and buyers are rushed, which makes meaningful discussions and negotiations difficult. These drawbacks can easily be minimized if you have sufficient preparation and background information. Allow at least three months for preparation—more if you also need to identify the fair that you will attend. Under ideal circumstances, you should begin laying the groundwork nine to 12 months in advance.

Tips for Attending a Trade Fair

Selecting an appropriate trade fair

Consult the listings of trade fairs here to find some that interest you. Note the suggestions for finding the most current calendars of upcoming fairs. Once you have identified some fairs, contact their organizers for literature, including show prospectus, attendee list, and exhibitor list. Ask plenty of questions. Do not neglect trade organizations in the host country, independent show-auditing firms, and recent attendees. Find out whether there are "must attend" fairs for your particular product group. Fairs that concentrate on other but related commodities might also be a good match. Be aware that there may be preferred seasons for trade in certain products. Your research needs to consider a number of points.

Audience • Who is the intended audience? Is the fair open to the public or only to trade professionals? Are the exhibitors primarily foreigners looking for local buyers or locals looking for foreign buyers? Many trade fairs are heavily weighted to one or the other. Decide whether you are looking for an exposition of general merchandise produced in one region, a commodity-specific trade show, or both.

Statistics • How many people attended the fair the last time it was held? What were the demographics? What volume of business was done? How many exhibitors were there? How big is the exhibition space? What was the ratio of foreign to domestic attendees and exhibitors?

Specifics • Who are the major exhibitors? Are particular publications or organizations associated with the fair? On what categories of products does the fair focus? Are there any special programs, and do they require additional fees? Does the fair have particular themes that change each time? How long has the fair been in existence? How often is it held? Is it always in the same location, or does it move each time? How much does it cost to attend? To rent space?

Before you go

- If you have not already spoken with someone who attended the fair in the past, make sure to seek someone out for advice, tips, and general information.
- Make your reservations and travel arrangements well in advance, and figure out how you are going to get around once you get there. Even if the fair takes place in a large city, do not assume that getting around will be easy during a major trade fair. If the site is a small city or less-developed area, the transportation and accommodation systems are likely to be saturated even sooner than they can be in metropolitan areas.
- Will you need an interpreter for face-to-face business negotiations? A translation service to handle documents? Try to line up providers well in advance of your need for their services.
- Do you need hospitality suites and/or conference rooms? Reserve them as soon as you can.
- Contact people you'd like to meet before you go. Organize your appointments around the fair.
- Familiarize yourself with the show hours, locations (if exhibits and events are staged at several different venues), and schedule of events. Then prioritize.

While you are there

- Wear businesslike clothes that are comfortable.
- Immediately after each contact, write down as much information as you can. Do not depend on remembering it.

After the fair

- Within a week after the conclusion of the fair, write letters to new contacts and follow up on requests for literature. If you have press releases and questionnaires, send them out quickly as well.
- Write a report evaluating the experience while it is still fresh in your mind. Even if you don't have to prepare a formal report, spend some time organizing your thoughts on paper for future reference and to quantify the results. Did you meet your goals? Why or why not? What would you do differently? What unforeseen costs arose?
- With your new contacts and your experience in mind, start preparing for your next trade fair.

If you are selling

- Set specific goals for sales leads, developing product awareness, selling and positioning current customers, and gathering industry information; for example, number of contacts made, orders written, leads converted into sales, visitors at presentations, brochures or samples distributed, customers entertained, seminars attended. You can also set goals for total revenue from sales, cost-to-return benefit ratio, amount of media coverage, and amount of competitor information obtained.

- Review your exhibitor kit, paying particular attention to show hours and regulations, payment policies, shipping instructions and dates, telephone installation, security, fire regulations, union regulations, and extra-cost services. Is there a show theme that you can tie into?

- Gear your advertising and product demonstrations to the audience. Should you stress certain aspects of your product line? Will you need brochures and banners in different languages? Even if you do not need to translate the materials currently in use into another language, do you need to re-write them for a different culture? Consider advertising in publications that will be distributed at the fair.

- Plan the display in your booth carefully; you will have only a few seconds to grab the viewer's attention. Secure a location in a high-traffic area—for example, near a door, restroom, refreshment area, or major exhibitor. Use banner copy that is brief and effective. Focus on the product and its benefits. Place promotional materials and giveaways near the back wall so that people have to enter your area, but make sure that they do not feel trapped. If you plan to use videotapes or other multimedia, make sure that you have enough space. Such presentations are often better suited to hospitality suites, because lights are bright and noise levels high in exhibition halls.

- Do not forget about the details. Order office supplies and printed materials that you will need for the booth. If you ordered a telephone line, bring your own telephone or arrange to rent one. Have all your paperwork—order forms, business cards, exhibitor kit and contract, copies of advance orders and checks, travel documents, and so on—in order and at hand. Draw up a schedule for staffing the booth.

- Plan and rehearse your sales pitch in advance, preferably in a space similar to the size of your booth.

- Do not sit, eat, drink, or smoke while you are in the booth.

- If you plan to return to the next show, reserve space while you're still at the fair.

- Familiarize yourself with import regulations for products that you wish to exhibit at the fair.

If you are buying

- Set specific goals for supplier leads and for gathering industry information; for example, number of contacts made, leads converted to purchases, seminars and presentations attended, booths visited. Other goals might be cost-to-return benefit ratio, amount of competitor information gathered, and percentage of projected purchases actually made.

- List all the products that you seek to purchase, their specifications, and the number of units you plan to purchase of each.

- Know the retail and wholesale market prices for the goods in your home country and in the country where you will be buying. List the highest price you can afford to pay for each item and still get a worthwhile return.

- List the established and probable suppliers for each of the products or product lines that you plan to import. Include their addresses and telephone numbers and your source for the information. Contact suppliers before you go to confirm who will attend and to make appointments.

- Familiarize yourself with customs regulations on the products that you seek to purchase and import into your own country or elsewhere. Be sure to include any products that you might be interested in.

Trade Fair	Site		Contact

COMPREHENSIVE Trade fairs exhibiting a wide range of goods

Trade Fair	Site		Contact
China Economic & Trade Exhibition (CETC) Last held: August 19-23, 1993	Seoul KOEX		China Economic & Trade Consultants Cooperative (in China) Tel: [86] (1) 5051569, 5052255 Fax: [86] (1) 5051571/2
China Trade Exhibition (CCOIC) Last held: May 20-26, 1993	Seoul KOEX		China Chamber of Int'l Commerce Tel: (2) 755-2001 Fax: (2) 755-1589
Chinese Science & Technology Exhibition (CATPE) Last held: July 1-8, 1993	Seoul KOEX		Best Travel Service 11F, Royal B/D,5, Dangju-dong, Chongno-gu, Seoul Tel: (2) 732-8008 Fax: (2) 732-3220
Seoul International Chain Store Show (CHAIN STORE) October 20-24, 1993 October 24-28, 1994	Seoul KOEX	C: 9 O: 300 K: 30,000	Korea Super Chain Stores Assn. Jinsuk Bldg., 1536-6, Socho-dong, Socho-gu, Seoul 137-070 Tel: (2) 522-1271 x119 Fax: (2) 522-1275 Contact: Lee Kwang-lim
Seoul International Trade Fair (SITRA) September 26-October 2, 1994	Seoul KOEX		Korea Trade Promotion Corp. 159 Samsung-dong, Kangnam-gu Seoul 135-729 Tel: (2) 551-4181 Fax: (2) 551-4477 Tlx: KOTRA K23659 K27326
Taejon International Exposition Last held: August 7-Nov. 7, 1993	Taejon Taedok Science Town	C: 106 O: 1/2 mil. K: 10 mil.	Taejon International Organizing Committee 277-3, Toryong-dong, Yusong-gu, Taejon 305-340 Tel: (42) 862-1993 Fax: (42) 861-9757

AEROSPACE & OCEANIC

Trade Fair	Site		Contact
International Aerospace Symposium & Exhibition (AEROSPACE) September 30-October 3, 1994	Seoul KOEX		Korea Exhibition Center (KOEX) 159 Samsung-dong, Kangnam-gu, Seoul Tel: (2) 551-1116 Fax: (2) 551-1311 Tlx: KOEXCEN K24594
International Shipbuilding, Marine, Port & Shipping, Intermodal, Small Ships & Fishing Exhibition (KORMARINE) Last held: October 19-22, 1993	Pusan Yachting Center	C: 16 O: 800 K: 9,000	Kyun Yon Exhibition Corp. Rm. 501, Kumsan Bldg., 17-1, Youido-dong, Yongdungpo-gu Seoul 150-010 Tel: (2) 785-4771 Fax: (2) 785-6118 Contact: Kim Kyong-ki
International Underground & Sea Resources Exploitative Equipment Exhibition in Korea (UNDERSYSTEM) Last held: May 11-15, 1993	Seoul KOEX	C: 15 O: 4,500 K: 100,000	Korea Productivity Center 122-1, Chokson-dong, Chongno-gu Seoul 110-052 Tel: (2) 739-5868 Fax: (2) 722-0089 Contact: Chung Shi-hyon

AGRICULTURE, FORESTRY & FISHERIES
See also Food, Beverages & Food Processing

Trade Fair	Site		Contact
International Exhibition of Machinery, Science & Technology for Agriculture, Forestry, Fisheries & Livestock (SIEMSTA) November 7-13, 1994	Seoul KOEX		Korea Exhibition Center (KOEX) 159 Samsung-dong, Kangnam-gu, Seoul Tel: (2) 551-1144 Fax: (2) 551-1311 Tlx: KOEXCEN K24594

Trade Fair	Site		Contact
International Shipbuilding, Marine, Port & Shipping, Intermodal, Small Ships & Fishing Exhibition (KORMARINE) Last held: October 19-22, 1993	Pusan Yachting Center	C: 16 O: 800 K: 9,000	Kyun Yon Exhibition Corp. Rm. 501, Kumsan Bldg., 17-1, Youido-dong, Yongdungpo-gu Seoul 150-010 Tel: (2) 785-4771 Fax: (2) 785-6118 Contact: Kim Kyong-ki
International Woodworking, Forestry, Sawmilling Machinery & Wood Products Supply Show (WOOD WORKING KOREA) Every 2 years Last held: December 4-8, 1993	Seoul KOEX		Korea Exhibition Center (KOEX) 159 Samsung-gu, Kangnam-gu, Seoul Tel: (2) 551-1117/1124 Fax: (2) 551-1311 Tlx: KOEXCEN K24594
Korea Poultry Expo Last held: August 19-21, 1993	Seoul KOEX	C: 20 O: 1,000 K: 100,000	Korea Poultry Assn. 1516-5, Socho 3-dong, Socho-gu Seoul 137-073 Tel: (2) 588-7651 Fax: (2) 588-7655 Contact: Cho Jong-soo

AUTOMOBILES & AUTOMOTIVE PARTS

Trade Fair	Site		Contact
Korea International Auto Parts & Accessories Show (KAPAS) November 16-20, 1993 November 9-13, 1994	Seoul KOEX	C: 21 O: 600 K: 30,000	Korea Trade Promotion Corp. 159 Samsung-dong, Kangnam-gu Seoul 135-729 Tel: (2) 551-4181 Fax: (2) 551-4477 Tlx: KOTRA K23659 K27326 Contact: Lee Du-young

COMPUTER & INFORMATION INDUSTRIES Includes communications
See also Electronic & Electric Equipment, Multimedia & Audiovisual Equipment

Trade Fair	Site		Contact
Communication Networks Korea (CN KOREA) September 22-25, 1993 September 12-15, 1994	Seoul KOEX	C: 8 O: 500 K: 20,000	Korea Exhibition Center (KOEX) 159 Samsung-dong, Kangnam-gu, Seoul Tel: (2) 551-1144 Fax: (2) 551-1311 Tlx: KOEXCEN K24594
Computer Software Exhibition of Korea (SEK) Annual June 24-28, 1993 June 24-29, 1994	Seoul KOEX	C: 9 O: 1,000 K: 80,000	Electronic Times Daeha Bldg. 9F., 14-11, Youido-dong, Yongdungpo-gu, Seoul 150-715 Tel: (2) 784-3091 x 120 Fax: (2) 784-5145 Contact: Kyon Sang-rok
Korea International CAD/CAM & Graphics Exhibition (CAD/CAM) September 10-14, 1993 November 1-5, 1994	Seoul KOEX	C: 5 O: 3,000 K: 12,000	Korea Exhibition Center (KOEX) 159 Samsung-dong, Kangnam-gu, Seoul Tel: (2) 551-1122 Fax: (2) 551-1311 Tlx: KOEXCEN K24594
Korea International Exhibition for Computers, Office Automation & Related Equipment (KIECO) April 21-27, 1993 May 17-22, 1994	Seoul KOEX	C: 3 O: 2,000 K: 300,000	Korea Economic Daily 441, Chungnim-dong, Chung-gu Seoul 100-791 Tel: (2) 392-0107 Fax: (2) 360-4503 Contact: Park Yong-keun
SCAN-TECH KOREA September 28-October 1, 1994	Seoul KOEX		Kyungyon Exhibition Co. Rm. 501, Kumsan Bldg., 17-1, Youido-dong, Yongdungpo-gu Seoul 150-010 Tel: (2) 785-6166 Fax: (2) 785-6118

Note: Country codes for telephone and fax numbers are not displayed unless they are *outside* of Korea.
All country codes have square brackets around them, while city codes have parentheses.
The country code for Korea is [82].

Trade Fair	Site		Contact
Seoul International Information Technology Show (INFORTEC) September 22-26, 1993 September 12-15, 1994	Seoul KOEX	C: 15 O: N/A K: 50,000	Korea Exhibition Center (KOEX) 159 Samsung-dong, Kangnam-gu, Seoul Tel: (2) 551-1602 Fax: (2) 551-1311 Tlx: KOEXCEN K24594
Seoul International Personal Computer Show (P.C. SHOW) September 22-25, 1993 September 12-15, 1994	Seoul KOEX	C: 5 O: 300 K: 45,000	Korea Exhibition Center (KOEX) 159 Samsung-dong, Kangnam-gu, Seoul Tel: (2) 551-1145 Fax: (2) 551-1311 Tlx: KOEXCEN K24594 Contact: Lee Kyong-gu

CONSTRUCTION & HOUSING
See also Furniture & Housewares

Trade Fair	Site		Contact
Heating, Air Conditioning, Refrigerating & Fluid Exhibition (HARFKO) Last held: March 18-22, 1993	Seoul KOEX	C: 17 O: 180 K: 20,000	Korea Refrigeration & Air Conditioning Industry Assn. 13-31 Youido-dong, Yongdungpo-gu Seoul 150-010 Tel: (2) 780-9038 Fax: (2) 785-1195 Contact: Kim Yong-sik
Korea International Building Show (KOBUILD) March 18-22, 1993 March 24-28, 1994	Seoul KOEX	C: 4 O: 400 K: 40,000	Korea Exhibition Center (KOEX) 159 Samsung-dong, Kangnam-gu, Seoul Tel: (2) 551-1116 Fax: (2) 551-1311 Tlx: KOEXCEN K24594
Kyung Hyang Housing Fair March 4-11, 1993 March 2-7, 1994	Seoul KOEX	C: 6 O: 2,000 K: 200,000	Kyung Hyang Daily News 22, Chong-dong, Chung-gu, Seoul 100-702 Tel: (2) 730-5151 Fax: (2) 722-1161 Contact: Lee Chong-yong
Seoul International Building & Construction Exhibition (SIBEX) Last held: November 1-5, 1993	Seoul KOEX	C: 21 O: 250 K: 15,000	Korea Trade Promotion Corp. 159 Samsung-dong, Kangnam-gu Seoul 135-729 Tel: (2) 551-4181 Fax: (2) 551-4477 Tlx: KOTRA K23659 K27326 Contact: Oh Tae-young
Seoul International Building Industry (SIBUILD) November 29-December 3, 1993 December 2-6, 1994	Seoul KOEX	C: 7 O: 500 K: 30,000	Joong-Ang Daily News 7, Sunhwa-dong, Chung-gu, Seoul 100-759 Tel: (2) 751-5033 Fax: (2) 778-2038 Contact: Park Ki-bok
Seoul International Kitchen Show (SIKITCHEN) Annual June 25-29, 1993 May 6-10, 1994	Seoul KOEX	C: 15 O: 1,500 K: 50,000	Korea Exhibition Center (KOEX) 159 Samsung-dong, Kangnam-gu, Seoul Tel: (2) 551-1118 Fax: (2) 551-1311 Tlx: KOEXCEN K24594
Seoul International Lighting Show (SILIGHT) Annual July 8-12, 1993 May 6-10, 1994	Seoul KOEX	C: 3 O: 1,000 K: 25,000	Korea Exhibition Center (KOEX) 159 Samsung-dong, Kangnam-gu, Seoul Tel: (2) 551-1159 Fax: (2) 551-1311 Tlx: KOEXCEN K24594 Contact: Lim Hyon-hwan
Seoul International Total Interior Show (SINTEX) Annual July 8-12, 1993 May 6-10, 1994	Seoul KOEX	C: 4 O: 100 K: 27,000	Korea Exhibition Center (KOEX) 159 Samsung-dong, Kangnam-gu, Seoul Tel: (2) 551-1159 Fax: (2) 551-1311 Tlx: KOEXCEN K24594

Trade Fair	Site		Contact

ELECTRONIC & ELECTRIC EQUIPMENT
See also Computer & Information Industries, Multimedia & Audiovisual Equipment

Trade Fair	Site		Contact
Asia Pacific Conference & Exhibition on the Electronic Data Interchange (EDICOM) Last held: October 28-30, 1993	Seoul KOEX	C: 20 O: 150 K: 400	Korea Exhibition Center (KOEX) 159 Samsung-dong, Kangnam-gu, Seoul Tel: (2) 551-1118 Fax: (2) 551-1311 Tlx: KOEXCEN K24594
Exhibition for Electronics Manufacturing, Processing, Assembly & Testing (INTERNEPCON / SEMICONDUCTOR KOREA) March 30-April 2, 1993 March 7-10, 1994	Seoul KOEX	C: 15 O: 800 K: 12,000	Kyungyon Exhibition Co. Rm. 501, Kumsan Bldg., 17-1, Youido-dong, Yongdungpo-gu Seoul 150-010 Tel: (2) 785-6166 Fax: (2) 785-6118 Contact: Park Je-woo
Government Supply Electronic Products Show (GOSEPS) May 29-June 2, 1994	Seoul KOEX		Korea Electronic Industries Cooperative 813-5 Pangbae-dong, Sochu-gu, Seoul Tel: (2) 533-2309 Fax: (2) 553-0949
Korea Electronics Show (KES) October 9-14, 1993 October 12-17, 1994	Seoul KOEX	C: 18 O: 500 K: 255,000	Electronic Industries Assn. of Korea Electronic Bldg., 648, Yoksam-dong, Kangnam-gu, Seoul 135-080 Tel: (2) 553-0940/1 Fax: (2) 555-6195 Contact: Ahn Jun-il
Korea International Electronic Parts & Equipment Show (KEPES) April 29-May 3, 1993 May 29-June 2, 1994	Seoul KOEX	C: 17 O: 600 K: 80,000	Korea Trade Promotion Corp. 159 Samsung-dong, Kangnam-gu Seoul 135-729 Tel: (2) 551-4181 Fax: (2) 551-4477 Tlx: KOTRA K23659 K27326 Contact: Kim Jae-pyung
SEMICON/KOREA Last held: November 8-10, 1993	Seoul KOEX	C: 15 O: 500 K: 10,000	SEMI Rm. 401, Changhakhoekwan Bldg., 945-15, Taechi-dong, Kangnam-gu, Seoul 135-280 Tel: (2) 556-5755 Fax: (2) 556-5756 Contact: Lee Jeong-hak
Seoul International OEM Parts & Components Show October 27-29, 1993 November 7-9, 1994	Seoul KOEX	C: 9 O: 50 K: 450	Korea Trade Promotion Corp. 159 Samsung-dong, Kangnam-gu Seoul 135-729 Tel: (2) 551-4181 Fax: (2) 551-4477 Tlx: KOTRA K23659 K27326 Contact: Lim Taek

ENVIRONMENTAL & ENERGY INDUSTRIES

Trade Fair	Site		Contact
Energy Conservation Exhibition Last held: November 13-19, 1993	Seoul KOEX	C: 15 O: 5,000 K: 75,000	Korea Energy Management Corp. 1467-3, Socho 3-dong, Socho-gu Seoul 137-073 Tel: (2) 520-0095 Fax: (2) 582-5057 Contact: Lee Byeong-yong
International Exhibition for Environmental Pollution Control, Measuring and Testing Equipment (INPOCO) April 19-23, 1993 April 25-29, 1994	Seoul KOEX	C: 11 O: 300 K: 16,000	Korea Environmental Preservation Assn. 45, Namdaemunno 4-ga, Chung-gu Seoul 100-743 Tel: (2) 753-7640 Fax: (2) 756-6141 Contact: Ok Sam-bok

Note: Country codes for telephone and fax numbers are not displayed unless they are *outside* of Korea.
All country codes have square brackets around them, while city codes have parentheses.
The country code for Korea is [82].

Trade Fair	Site		Contact
International Underground & Sea Resources Exploitative Equipment Exhibition in Korea (UNDERSYSTEM) Last held: May 11-15, 1993	Seoul KOEX	C: 15 O: 4,500 K: 100,000	Korea Productivity Center 122-1, Chokson-dong, Chongno-gu Seoul 110-052 Tel: (2) 739-5868 Fax: (2) 722-0089 Contact: Chung Shi-hyon
Korea International Recycling Industry Exhibition Last held: August, 1993	Seoul KOEX	C: 11 O: 1,500 K: 15,000	Korea Resources Recovery & Reutilization Corp. 24-5, Youido-dong, Yongdungpo-gu Seoul 150-010 Tel: (2) 780-4610 Fax: (2) 780-4620
Korea International Waste Disposal & Recycling Industry Exhibition (RECYCLING) June 16-20, 1993 June 19-23, 1994	Seoul KOEX	C: 16 O: 5,000 K: 45,000	Korea Int'l Exhibitions & Conferences Assn. Rm. 804, Century II Bldg., 1595-2, Socho-dong, Socho-gu, Seoul 137-070 Tel: (2) 588-3484 Fax: (2) 522-1102 Contact: Kang Cheol-gyun
Seoul International Environmental Industry Fair Last held: September 22-26, 1993	Seoul KOEX	C: 12 O: 700 K: 50,000	Joong-Ang Daily News 7, Sunhwa-dong, Chung-gu, Seoul 100-759 Tel: (2) 751-5033 Fax: (2) 778-2038 Contact: Park Ki-bok

FACTORY AUTOMATION
See also Computer & Information Industries, Machines & Instruments

Trade Fair	Site		Contact
International Automation System Exhibition in Korea (AUTO KOREA) Last held: May 25-29, 1993	Changwon Industrial Complex Exhibition Hall		Korean Management Corporation for South-East Industrial Estates 851-1 Woe-Dong Changwon, Kyungsangnam-Do Tel: (551) 60-1381/2 Fax: (551) 60-1421 Korea Productivity Center 122-1, Chokson-dong, Chongno-gu Seoul 110-052 Tel: (2) 739-5868 Fax: (2) 722-0089
International Automation System Exhibition in Korea (AUTO KOREA) Last held: December 7-11, 1993	Seoul KOEX		Korea Productivity Center 122-1, Chokson-dong, Chongno-gu Seoul 110-052 Tel: (2) 739-5868 Fax: (2) 722-0089
International Factory Automation System Show Korea (KOFAPS) October 26-30, 1994	Seoul KOEX		Korea Assn. of Machinery Industry 13-31 Youido-dong, Yongdungpo-gu, Seoul Tel: (2) 780-3611/4 Fax: (2) 784-6749
Korea International Factory Automation System Exhibition (KOFA) Annual March 29-April 2, 1993 March 14-18, 1994	Seoul KOEX	C: 7 O: 2,000 K: 70,000	Korea Exhibition Center (KOEX) 159 Samsung-dong, Kangnam-gu, Seoul Tel: (2) 551-1126 Fax: (2) 551-1311 Tlx: KOEXCEN K24594
Korean International Robot and Automation System Show Last held: April 8-12, 1993	Changwon Industrial Complex Exhibition Hall	C: 10 O: 150 K: 45,000	Korean Machine Tool Manufacturers' Assn. 35-4, Youido-dong, Yongdungpo-gu, Seoul Tel: (2) 780-3521 Fax: (2) 784-8023 Contact: Yeun Bo-kee
Seoul International Shop System & Shop Automation Show (KOREASHOP) November 29-December 3, 1993 December, 1994	Seoul KOEX	C: 7 O: 500 K: 30,000	Joong-Ang Daily News 7, Sunhwa-dong, Chung-gu, Seoul 100-759 Tel: (2) 751-5033 Fax: (2) 778-2038 Contact: Park Ki-bok

Trade Fair	Site		Contact

FOOD, BEVERAGES & FOOD PROCESSING
See also Agriculture, Forestry & Fisheries

Trade Fair	Site	Codes	Contact
Korea International Food & Health Equipment Fair (INTERHEALTH) April 8-12, 1993 May 19-23, 1994	Seoul KOEX	C: 11 O: 15,000 K: 80,000	Korea Int'l Exhibitions & Conferences Assn. Rm. 804, Century II Bldg., 1595-2, Socho-dong, Socho-gu, Seoul 137-070 Tel: (2) 588-3484 Fax: (2) 522-1102 Contact: Yang Chun-hee
Korea International Food Festival June 26-29, 1993 June, 1994	Seoul KOEX		Korean Center Cooks Assn. Union Bldg., 69-75 Kalwol-dong, Yongsan-gu, Seoul 140-150 Tel: (2) 712-2183 Fax: (2) 713-7148 Contact: Baek In-soo
International Culinary Show June 10-12, 1994	Seoul		Glahe International, Inc. 1700 K Street, N.W. Washington, D.C. 20006 USA Tel: [1] (202) 659-4557 Fax: [1] (202) 457-0776
Seoul International Bakery Fair (SIBA) Last held: November 9-12, 1993	Seoul KOEX	C: 5 O: 400 K: 100,000	Korean Bakers Assn. 120-3, Chungmuro 4-ga, Chung-gu Seoul 100-014 Tel: (2) 273-1830 Fax: (2) 271-1822 Contact: Lee Sun-woo
Seoul International Food Technology Exhibition (SEOUL FOOD) April 9-13, 1993 April 26-30, 1994	Seoul KOEX	C: 22 O: 500 K: 25,000	Korea Trade Promotion Corp. 159 Samsung-dong, Kangnam-gu Seoul 135-729 Tel: (2) 551-4181 Fax: (2) 551-4477 Tlx: KOTRA K23659 K27326 Contact: Lee Jong-sup
Seoul International Hotel Equipment Show (SIHOTES) May 6-10, 1994	Seoul KOEX		Korea Exhibition Center (KOEX) 159 Samsung-dong, Kangnam-gu, Seoul Tel: (2) 551-1119 Fax: (2) 551-1311 Tlx: KOEXCEN K24594
Seoul International Wines, Beers, Spirits & Beverages Exhibition (WINEKOREA) December 11-15, 1993 December 7-11, 1994	Seoul KOEX	C: 16 O: 5,000 K: 20,000	Korea Int'l Exhibitions & Conferences Assn. Rm. 804, Century II Bldg., 1595-2, Socho-dong, Socho-gu, Seoul 137-070 Tel: (2) 588-3484 Fax: (2) 522-1102 Contact: Kang Cheol-gyun

FURNITURE & HOUSEWARES
See also Construction & Housing

Trade Fair	Site	Codes	Contact
Exhibition for Wedding Goods Korea (WEDDEX KOREA) February 25-28, 1993 February 24-27, 1994	Seoul KOEX	C: 13 O: 3,000 K: 22,000	Seoul Fairs Co. Rm. 803, Samho Bldg., 17-1, Yangjae-dong, Sochu-gu, Seoul 137-130 Tel: (2) 589-1225 Fax: (2) 589-1228 Contact: Kim Min-Soo
International Furniture & Woodworking Machinery Fair Seoul (KOFURN) November 19-25, 1994	Seoul KOEX		Korea Federation of Furniture Industry Cooperatives 127, Nonhyon-dong, Kangnam-gu, Seoul Tel: (2) 215-8838 Fax: (2) 215-9729

Note: Country codes for telephone and fax numbers are not displayed unless they are *outside* of Korea.
All country codes have square brackets around them, while city codes have parentheses.
The country code for Korea is [82].

Trade Fair	Site		Contact
International Office Furniture & Faculty Fair (IOFFA) October 21-25, 1993 November 5-9, 1994	Seoul KOEX	C: 5 O: 2,000 K: 70,000	Korea Exhibition Center (KOEX) 159 Samsung-dong, Kangnam-gu, Seoul Tel: (2) 551-1602 Fax: (2) 551-1311 Tlx: KOEXCEN K24594
Kyung Hyang Housing Fair March 4-11, 1993 March 2-7, 1994	Seoul KOEX	C: 6 O: 2,000 K: 200,000	Kyung Hyang Daily News 22, Chong-dong, Chung-gu, Seoul 100-702 Tel: (2) 730-5151 Fax: (2) 722-1161 Contact: Lee Chong-yong
Seoul International Kitchen Show (SIKITCHEN) Annual June 25-29, 1993 May 6-10, 1994	Seoul KOEX	C: 15 O: 1,500 K: 50,000	Korea Exhibition Center (KOEX) 159 Samsung-dong, Kangnam-gu, Seoul Tel: (2) 551-1118 Fax: (2) 551-1311 Tlx: KOEXCEN K24594
Seoul International Lighting Show (SLIGHT) Annual July 8-12, 1993 May 6-10, 1994	Seoul KOEX	C: 3 O: 1,000 K: 25,000	Korea Exhibition Center (KOEX) 159 Samsung-dong, Kangnam-gu, Seoul Tel: (2) 551-1159 Fax: (2) 551-1311 Tlx: KOEXCEN K24594 Contact: Lim Hyon-hwan
Seoul International Total Interior Show (SINTEX) Annual July 8-12, 1993 May 6-10, 1994	Seoul KOEX	C: 4 O: 100 K: 27,000	Korea Exhibition Center (KOEX) 159 Samsung-dong, Kangnam-gu, Seoul Tel: (2) 551-1159 Fax: (2) 551-1311 Tlx: KOEXCEN K24594

GIFTS, JEWELRY & STATIONERY Includes timepieces

Trade Fair	Site		Contact
Exhibition for Wedding Goods Korea (WEDDEX KOREA) February 25-28, 1993 February 24-27, 1994	Seoul KOEX	C: 13 O: 3,000 K: 22,000	Seoul Fairs Co. Rm. 803, Samho Bldg., 17-1, Yangjae-dong, Sochu-gu, Seoul 137-130 Tel: (2) 589-1225 Fax: (2) 589-1228 Contact: Kim Min-Soo
Korea International Jewelry & Watch Fair (JEWELEX) October 20-24, 1993 September 1-5, 1994	Seoul KOEX	C: 13 O: 215 K: 17,800	Korea Exhibition Center (KOEX) 159 Samsung-dong, Kangnam-gu, Seoul Tel: (2) 551-1127 Fax: (2) 551-1311 Tlx: KOEXCEN K24594
Seoul International Gift Fair / Seoul International Fashion Jewelry & Accessories Fair (SIGIFT/ACCESS) October 30-November 2, 1993 October 23-27, 1994	Seoul KOEX	C: 10 O: 1,200 K: 30,000	Korea Fed. of Handicrafts Cooperatives 163-3, Ulchiro 2-ga, Chung-gu Seoul 100-192 Tel: (2) 757-1678 Fax: (2) 757-8582 Contact: Lee Dong-ick
Seoul International Premium Show (SIPREMIUM) August 27-September 1, 1993 February 24-27, 1994	Seoul KOEX	C: 5 O: 100 K: 30,000	Korea Exhibition Center (KOEX) 159 Samsung-dong, Kangnam-gu, Seoul Tel: (2) 551-1143 Fax: (2) 551-1311 Tlx: KOEXCEN K24594 Contact: Lee Byong-tae
Seoul International Stationery Fair (SISFAIR) October 30-November 2, 1993 November 1-4, 1994	Seoul KOEX	C: 17 O: 800 K: 30,000	Korea Trade Promotion Corp. 159 Samsung-dong, Kangnam-gu Seoul 135-729 Tel: (2) 551-4181 Fax: (2) 551-4477 Tlx: KOTRA K23659 K27326 Contact: Kim Jae-pyung Korea Stationery Industry Cooperative 36-3, Chungmuro 5-ga, Chung-gu, Seoul Tel: (2) 278-7891 Fax: (2) 275-1065

Trade Fair	Site		Contact

HEALTH & SAFETY Includes medicine

Trade Fair	Site		Contact
Korea International Food & Health Equipment Fair (INTERHEALTH) April 8-12, 1993 May 19-23, 1994	Seoul KOEX	C: 11 O: 15,000 K: 80,000	Korea Int'l Exhibitions & Conferences Assn. Rm. 804, Century II Bldg., 1595-2, Socho-dong, Socho-gu, Seoul 137-070 Tel: (2) 588-3484 Fax: (2) 522-1102 Contact: Yang Chun-hee
Korea International Medical Equipment Show (KIMES) March 18-22, 1993 March 17-20, 1994	Seoul KOEX	C: 14 O: 100 K: 25,000	Hankook Ilbo 14, Chunghak-dong, Chongno-gu Seoul 110-150 Tel: (2) 739-5272 Fax: (2) 738-1048 Tlx: K23644 Contact: Kim Jeong-jo
Korea International Prevention of Fire & Disaster Exhibition (KOFIRE) October 8-12, 1993 August 23-26, 1994	Seoul KOEX	C: 11 O: 5,000 K: 35,000	Korea Int'l Exhibitions & Conferences Assn. Rm. 804, Century II Bldg., 1595-2, Socho-dong, Socho-gu, Seoul 137-070 Tel: (2) 588-3484 Fax: (2) 522-1102 Contact: Jeon Young-heon
Korea International Safety & Security Exhibition (KISS) Last held: July 1-5, 1993	Seoul KOEX	C: 10 O: 100 K: 7,000	Korea Industrial Safety Corp. Kookje Bldg., 191, Han-gangno 1-ga, Yongsan-gu, Seoul 140-702 Tel: (2) 797-5996 Fax: (2) 795-4872 Contact: Hwang Soon-dong
Seoul International Beauty Salon (SISALON) Last held: December 2-5, 1993	Seoul KOEX		Seoul Fairs Co. Rm. 803, Samho Bldg., 17-1, Yangjae-dong, Sochu-gu, Seoul 137-130 Tel: (2) 589-1225 Fax: (2) 589-1228 Contact: Kim Min-Soo
Seoul International Rehabilitation Assistance Exhibition (SIREX) Last held: November 6-10, 1993	Seoul KOEX	C: 16 O: 5,000 K: 30,000	Korea Sports Assn. for the Disabled 11-7, Shinchon-dong, Songpa-gu Seoul 138-742 Tel: (2) 416-7802 Fax: (2) 412-0463 Contact: Chung Ho-yong

HOBBIES, RECREATION & TRAVEL Includes books, photography, toys
See also Sporting Goods

Trade Fair	Site	Contact
Korea World Travel Fair (KOTFA) September 13-16, 1994	Seoul KOEX	Travel Trading Inc. 10F, Sisa B/D, 70-27, Yeaguan-dong, Chongno-gu, Seoul Tel: (2) 268-7171/6 Fax: (2) 268-7177
Overseas Travel Fair (OTF) Last held: June 10-13, 1993	Seoul Interconti nental Hotel	Travel Trading Inc. 10F, Sisa B/D, 70-27, Yeaguan-dong, Chongno-gu, Seoul Tel: (2) 268-7171/6 Fax: (2) 268-7177 Korea Assn. of General Travel Agents Hanil Bldg., 132-4, 1-ga, Pongnae-dong, Chung-gu, Seoul 100-161 Tel: (2) 752-8692 Fax: (2) 752-8694 Contact: Han Mung-suk
PATA Travel Mart April 9-13, 1994	Seoul KOEX	Korea National Tourism Corp. 10, Ta-dong, Chung-gu, Seoul 100-180 Tel: (2) 757-6030, 757-5124 Fax: (2) 757-5997, 771-1994 Contact: Lee Sang-oh

Note: Country codes for telephone and fax numbers are not displayed unless they are *outside* of Korea.
All country codes have square brackets around them, while city codes have parentheses.
The country code for Korea is [82].

Trade Fair	Site		Contact
Phila Korea World Stamp Exhibition (PHILA KOREA) August 16-25, 1994	Seoul KOEX	C: 150 O: 1,000 K: 50,000	Ministry of Communications 100, Sejongno, Chongno-gu, Seoul 110-777 Tel: (2) 750-2243 Fax: (2) 750-2236 Contact: Lim Ho-yong
Seoul Book Fair May 7-13, 1993 July 8-17, 1994	Seoul KOEX	C: 7 O: 100 K: 230,000	Korean Publishers Assn. 105-2, Sagan-dong, Chongno-gu Seoul 110-190 Tel: (2) 735-2702 Fax: (2) 738-5414 Contact: Kwon Se-hyun
Seoul International Audio & Musical Instruments Show (SIAM) Last held: June 1-5, 1993 June 8-12, 1994	Seoul KOEX		Korea Exhibition Center (KOEX) 159 Samsung-dong, Kangnam-gu, Seoul Tel: (2) 551-1147 Fax: (2) 551-1311 Tlx: KOEXCEN K24594
Seoul International Photo, Video & Optical Industry Show (PHOTO SHOW SEOUL) June 8-12, 1994	Seoul KOEX		Korea Exhibition Center (KOEX) 159 Samsung-dong, Kangnam-gu, Seoul Tel: (2) 551-1124 Fax: (2) 551-1311 Tlx: KOEXCEN K24594
Seoul International Toy Fair (SITOY) September 22-25, 1993 September 29-October 3, 1994	Seoul KOEX	C: 4 O: 500 K: 20,000	Korea Toy Industry Cooperative 361-1, Han-gango 2-ga, Yongsan-gu Seoul 140-012 Tel: (2) 795-9505 Fax: (2) 795-0401 Contact: Kim Moon-Silk

INDUSTRIAL MATERIALS & CHEMICALS
See also Metal & Metal Finishing

Trade Fair	Site		Contact
International Basic Materials & Stuff Show in Seoul (IMASS) March 16-20, 1994	Seoul KOEX		Korea Productivity Center 122-1, Chokson-dong, Chongno-gu Seoul 110-052 Tel: (2) 739-5868 Fax: (2) 722-0089
International Glass Industry Technology Exhibition for Korea (GLASS KOREA) Last held: February 19-21, 1993	Seoul KOEX	C: 14 O: 600 K: 15,000	Korea Trade Fairs Ltd. 17-1, Youido-dong, Yongdungpo-gu Seoul 150-010 Tel: (2) 783-8261 Fax: (2) 784-6810 Contact: Yu Seo-jin
Korea International Ceramics Industry Show (CERAKOR) June 2-6, 1993 June 11-15, 1994	Seoul KOEX		Hankook Ilbo 14, Chunghak-dong, Chongno-gu Seoul 110-150 Tel: (2) 739-5272 Fax: (2) 738-1048 Tlx: K23644
Korea International Clean, Wash & Laundry Technology Exhibition (CLEANTEC) August 23-26, 1994	Seoul KOEX		Korea Int'l Exhibitions & Conferences Assn. Rm. 804, Century II Bldg., 1595-2, Socho-dong, Socho-gu, Seoul 137-070 Tel: (2) 588-3484 Fax: (2) 522-1102
Korea International Nonwovens & Machinery Show (NONWOVEN KOREA) Last held: September 14-17, 1993	Seoul KOEX		Korea Nonwoven Industry Cooperative 36-2, Youido-dong, Yongdungpo-gu, Seoul Tel: (2) 365-2332 Fax: (2) 393-5098
Korea International Plant Piping Material Show (PLANT PIPING) Last held: March 29-April 2, 1993	Seoul KOEX	C: 7 O: 2,000 K: 25, 000	Korea Exhibition Center (KOEX) 159 Samsung-dong, Kangnam-gu, Seoul Tel: (2) 551-1160 Fax: (2) 551-1311 Tlx: KOEXCEN K24594
Korean International Plastics and Rubber Show (KOPLAS) Annual June 2-6, 1993 June 11-15, 1994	Seoul KOEX		Hankook Ilbo 14, Chunghak-dong, Chongno-gu Seoul 110-150 Tel: (2) 739-5272 Fax: (2) 738-1048 Tlx: K23644

Trade Fair	Site		Contact
Seoul International Chemical Plant Exhibition (SICHEM) April 26-30, 1994	Seoul KOEX		Korea Exhibition Center (KOEX) 159 Samsung-dong, Kangnam-gu, Seoul Tel: (2) 551-1602 Fax: (2) 551-1311 Tlx: KOEXCEN K24594

MACHINES & INSTRUMENTS
See also Tools: Precision & Measuring, other categories which may include exhibitions with machines specific to those industries

Trade Fair	Site		Contact
Exhibition of Powder, Fluid & Air Regulation Machinery (IPAMA) October 24-28, 1994	Seoul KOEX		Korea Federation of Machinery Industry Cooperative 172-11, Yomni-dong, Mapo-gu, Seoul Tel: (2) 715-7172 Fax: (2) 702-6974 Korea Exhibition Center (KOEX) 159 Samsung-dong, Kangnam-gu, Seoul Tel: (2) 551-1118 Fax: (2) 551-1311 Tlx: KOEXCEN K24594
Korea Machinery Fair (KOMAF) Last held: September 10-15, 1993	Seoul KOEX	C: 30 O: 25,000 K: 275,000	Korea Assn. of Machinery Industry 13-31, Youido-dong, Yongdungpo-gu, Seoul Tel: (2) 780-3611/4 Fax: (2) 784-1032 Contact: Lee Sang-un
Korean International Stone & Machine Industry Exhibition (KOSTONE) December 10-14, 1993 December 7-11, 1994	Seoul KOEX	C: 26 O: 10,000 K: 30,000	Korea Int'l Exhibitions & Conferences Assn. Rm. 804, Century II Bldg., 1595-2, Socho-dong, Socho-gu, Seoul 137-070 Tel: (2) 588-3484 Fax: (2) 522-1102 Contact: Shin Yong-won
Seoul International Instrumentation Exhibition (SEOUL INSTRUMENT) September 21-25, 1993 June 21-25, 1994	Seoul KOEX	C: 22 O: 350 K: 20,000	Korea Trade Promotion Corp. 159 Samsung-dong, Kangnam-gu Seoul 135-729 Tel: (2) 551-4181 Fax: (2) 551-4477 Tlx: KOTRA K23659 K27326 Contact: Kang Young-jin
Seoul International Machine Tool Show (SIMTOS) April 12-18, 1994	Seoul KOEX		Korea Machine Tool Manufacturers' Assn. 35-4 Youido-dong, Yongdungpo-gu, Seoul Tel: (2) 780-3521 Fax: (2) 784-8023
Seoul International Sewing Machinery Exhibition (SIMEX) Last held: October 29-November 1, 1993	Seoul KOEX	C: 16 O: 750 K: 25,000	Korea Exhibition Center (KOEX) 159 Samsung-dong, Kangnam-gu, Seoul Tel: (2) 551-1122 Fax: (2) 551-1311 Tlx: KOEXCEN K24594
Seoul International Vending Machine Show (SIVENDING) Last held: October 19-22, 1993	Seoul KOEX		Korea Exhibition Center (KOEX) 159 Samsung-dong, Kangnam-gu, Seoul Tel: (2) 551-1117/1124 Fax: (2) 551-1311 Tlx: KOEXCEN K24594

METAL & METAL FINISHING
See also Industrial Materials & Chemicals

Trade Fair	Site		Contact
International Fastener, Cable & Wire Finished Products, Production Machinery & Technology Exhibition for Korea (FASTENER, CABLE & WIRE KOREA) Last held: October 20-23, 1993	Seoul KOEX	C: 12 O: 350 K: 10,000	Korea Trade Fairs Ltd. 17-1, Youido-dong, Yongdungpo-gu, Seoul 150-010 Tel: (2) 783-8261 Fax: (2) 784-6810 Contact: Cho Min-jae

Note: Country codes for telephone and fax numbers are not displayed unless they are *outside* of Korea.
All country codes have square brackets around them, while city codes have parentheses.
The country code for Korea is [82].

Trade Fair	Site		Contact
International Foundry, Forging & Heat -Treatment Technology Exhibition (FOUNDRY & FORGING KOREA) Last held: December 8-14, 1993	Seoul KOEX		Korea Trade Fairs Ltd. 17-1, Youido-dong, Yongdungpo-gu, Seoul 150-010 Tel: (2) 783-8261 Fax: (2) 784-6810
Korea International Welding Show (WELDING KOREA) October 17-25, 1993 October 24-27, 1994	Seoul KOEX	C: 9 O: 2,000 K: 22,000	Korea Exhibition Center (KOEX) 159 Samsung-dong, Kangnam-gu, Seoul Tel: (2) 551-1122 Fax: (2) 551-1311 Tlx: KOEXCEN K24594
Pusan International Die & Mold Machining Equipment Show Last held: October 21-25, 1993	Pusan	C: 11 O: 500 K: 35,000	Korea Die & Mold Industry Cooperative KOAMI Bldg., 13-31, Youido-dong, Yongdungpo-gu, Seoul 150-010 Tel: (2) 783-1711/3 Fax: (2) 784-5937 Contact: Oh Suck-jun
Seoul International Die, Mold & Machining Equipment Exhibition (SEOUL INTERMOLD) Last held: April 30-May 5, 1993	Seoul KOEX	C: 16 O: 3,000 K: 92,000	Korea Die & Mold Industry Cooperative KOAMI Bldg., 13-31, Youido-dong, Yongdungpo-gu, Seoul 150-010 Tel: (2) 783-1711/3 Fax: (2) 784-5937 Contact: Oh Suck-jun
Seoul International Finishing Show (FINISHING) April 17-21, 1993 April 14-18, 1994	Seoul KOEX	C: 6 O: 500 K: 6,500	Korea Exhibition Center (KOEX) 159 Samsung-dong, Kangnam-gu, Seoul Tel: (2) 551-1160 Fax: (2) 551-1311 Tlx: KOEXCEN K24594
Seoul International Surface Finishing Show (IPLEM) October 23-27, 1994	Seoul KOEX		Korea Plating Industry Cooperative KOAMI Bldg., 13-31, Youido-dong, Yongdungpo-gu, Seoul 150-010 Tel: (2) 784-0721/2 Fax: (2) 784-0723

MULTIMEDIA & AUDIOVISUAL EQUIPMENT
See also Computer & Information Industries; Electronic & Electric Equipment

Trade Fair	Site		Contact
Korea International Broadcast & Audio Equipment Show (KOBA) August 18-21, 1993 May 25-28, 1994	Seoul KOEX	C: 15 O: 500 K: 35,000	Hankook Ilbo 14, Chunghak-dong, Chongno-gu Seoul 110-150 Tel: (2) 739-5272 Fax: (2) 738-1048 Tlx: K23644 Contact: Kim Jeong-jo
Seoul International Audio & Musical Instruments Show (SIAM) June 1-5, 1993 June 8-12, 1994	Seoul KOEX		Korea Exhibition Center (KOEX) 159 Samsung-dong, Kangnam-gu, Seoul Tel: (2) 551-1147 Fax: (2) 551-1311 Tlx: KOEXCEN K24594
Seoul International CATV Show (CATV SEOUL) June 1-5, 1993 September 12-15, 1994	Seoul KOEX		Korea Exhibition Center (KOEX) 159 Samsung-dong, Kangnam-gu, Seoul Tel: (2) 551-1147 Fax: (2) 551-1311 Tlx: KOEXCEN K24594
Seoul International Photo, Video & Optical Industry Show (PHOTO SHOW SEOUL) June 8-12, 1994	Seoul KOEX		Korea Exhibition Center (KOEX) 159 Samsung-dong, Kangnam-gu, Seoul Tel: (2) 551-1124 Fax: (2) 551-1311 Tlx: KOEXCEN K24594

OFFICE PRODUCTS & EQUIPMENT

Trade Fair	Site		Contact
International Office Furniture & Faculty Fair (IOFFA) October 21-25, 1993 November 5-9, 1994	Seoul KOEX	C: 5 O: 2,000 K: 70,000	Korea Exhibition Center (KOEX) 159 Samsung-dong, Kangnam-gu, Seoul Tel: (2) 551-1602 Fax: (2) 551-1311 Tlx: KOEXCEN K24594

Trade Fair	Site		Contact
Korea International Exhibition for Computers, Office Automation & Related Equipment (KIECO) April 21-27, 1993 May 17-22, 1994	Seoul KOEX	C: 3 O: 2,000 K: 300,000	Korea Economic Daily 441, Chungnim-dong, Chung-gu Seoul 100-791 Tel: (2) 392-0107 Fax: (2) 360-4503 Contact: Park Yong-keun

PACKAGING, PRINTING & PAPER Includes handling

Trade Fair	Site		Contact
International Exhibition of Machinery & Materials for Package Processing & Production (IPP) April 26-29, 1994	Seoul KOEX		Kyungyon Exhibition Co. Rm. 501, Kumsan Bldg., 17-1, Youido-dong, Yongdungpo-gu Seoul 150-010 Tel: (2) 785-6166 Fax: (2) 785-6118
International Material Handling & Distribution Show in Korea (LOGIS-TECH) October 21-25, 1993 May 31-June 4, 1994	Seoul KOEX		Korea Exhibition Center (KOEX) 159 Samsung-dong, Kangnam-gu, Seoul Tel: (2) 551-1114 Fax: (2) 551-1311 Tlx: KOEXCEN K24594
International Material Handling & Distribution Show in Korea (LOGIS-TECH) October 21-25, 1993 May 31-June 4, 1994	Seoul KOEX		Korea Exhibition Center (KOEX) 159 Samsung-dong, Kangnam-gu, Seoul Tel: (2) 551-1114 Fax: (2) 551-1311 Tlx: KOEXCEN K24594
International Printing Machinery & Equipment Show (KIPES) September 2-6, 1994	Seoul KOEX		Hankook Ilbo 14, Chunghak-dong, Chongno-gu Seoul 110-150 Tel: (2) 739-5272 Fax: (2) 738-1048 Tlx: K23644
International Pulp & Paper Exhibition & Conference for Korea (PULP & PAPER KOREA) June 23-26, 1994	Seoul KOEX		Korea Trade Fairs Ltd. 17-1, Youido-dong, Yongdungpo-gu Seoul 150-010 Tel: (2) 783-8261 Fax: (2) 784-6810
Seoul International Packaging Exhibition (SEOUL PACK) Last held: April 9-13, 1993	Seoul KOEX	C: 22 O: 300 K: 25,000	Korea Trade Promotion Corp. 159 Samsung-dong, Kangnam-gu Seoul 135-729 Tel: (2) 551-4181 Fax: (2) 551-4477 Tlx: KOTRA K23659 K27326 Contact: Lee Jong-sup

SPORTING GOODS
See also Hobbies, Recreation & Travel

Trade Fair	Site		Contact
Korea International Fishing Tackle Show (KOFISH) March 5-8, 1993 March 4-7, 1994	Seoul KOEX	C: 6 O: 3,000 K: 100,000	Korea Exhibition Center (KOEX) 159 Samsung-dong, Kangnam-gu, Seoul Tel: (2) 551-1148 Fax: (2) 551-1311 Tlx: KOEXCEN K24594
Korea International Golf Show (KOGOLF) March 5-8, 1993 March 4-7, 1994	Seoul KOEX	C: 10 O: 1,500 K: 70,000	Korea Exhibition Center (KOEX) 159 Samsung-dong, Kangnam-gu, Seoul Tel: (2) 551-1148 Fax: (2) 551-1311 Tlx: KOEXCEN K24594
Korea International Mountaineering Show (KOMOUNT) March 5-8, 1993 March 4-7, 1994	Seoul KOEX	C: 5 O: 900 K: 50,000	Korea Exhibition Center (KOEX) 159 Samsung-dong, Kangnam-gu, Seoul Tel: (2) 551-1117/1124 Fax: (2) 551-1311 Tlx: KOEXCEN K24594

Note: Country codes for telephone and fax numbers are not displayed unless they are *outside* of Korea.
All country codes have square brackets around them, while city codes have parentheses.
The country code for Korea is [82].

Trade Fair	Site		Contact
Korea International Sports, Leisure & Boat Show (SPOKOR BOAT SHOW) Annual June 8-12, 1993 March 4-7, 1994	Seoul KOEX		Korea Exhibition Center (KOEX) 159 Samsung-dong, Kangnam-gu, Seoul Tel: (2) 551-1146 Fax: (2) 551-1311 Tlx: KOEXCEN K24594

TEXTILES & APPAREL

Trade Fair	Site		Contact
Exhibition for Wedding Goods Korea (WEDDEX KOREA) February 25-28, 1993 February 24-27, 1994	Seoul KOEX	C: 13 O: 3,000 K: 22,000	Seoul Fairs Co. Rm. 803, Samho Bldg., 17-1, Yangjae-dong, Sochu-gu, Seoul 137-130 Tel: (2) 589-1225 Fax: (2) 589-1228 Contact: Kim Min-Soo
Korea International Exhibition of Footwear Industry (KORSHOETECH) Every 2 years Last held: June 17-20, 1993	Seoul KOEX	C: 14 O: 800 K: 10,000	Kyungyon Exhibition Co. Rm. 501, Kumsan Bldg., 17-1, Youido-dong, Yongdungpo-gu Seoul 150-010 Tel: (2) 785-6166 Fax: (2) 785-6118 Contact: Oh Jun-seok
Korea International Nonwovens & Machinery Show (NONWOVEN KOREA) Last held: September 14-17, 1993	Seoul KOEX		Korea Nonwoven Industry Cooperative 36-2, Youido-dong, Yongdungpo-gu, Seoul Tel: (2) 365-2332 Fax: (2) 393-5098
Korea International Textile Machinery Exhibition (KORTEX) May 7-11, 1994	Seoul KOEX		Korea Federation of Textile Industries Rm. 705, KWTC Bldg., 159, Samsung-dong, Socho-gu, Seoul Tel: (2) 551-1474 Fax: (2) 551-1496
Seoul International Fashion Fair (SIFF) November 17-20, 1994	Seoul KOEX		Korea Fashion Association Tel: (2) 528-4741 Fax: (2) 528-4746
Seoul International Gift Fair / Seoul International Fashion Jewelry & Accessories Fair (SIGIFT/ACCESS) October 30-November 2, 1993 October 23-27, 1994	Seoul KOEX	C: 10 O: 1,200 K: 30,000	Korea Fed. of Handicrafts Cooperatives 163-3, Ulchiro 2-ga, Chung-gu Seoul 100-192 Tel: (2) 757-1678 Fax: (2) 757-8582 Contact: Lee Dong-ick
Seoul International Sewing Machinery Exhibition (SIMEX) Last held: October 29-Nov. 1, 1993	Seoul KOEX	C: 16 O: 750 K: 25,000	Korea Exhibition Center (KOEX) 159 Samsung-dong, Kangnam-gu, Seoul Tel: (2) 551-1122 Fax: (2) 551-1311 Tlx: KOEXCEN K24594
Seoul International Textile Fair (SEOUL STUFF) November 17-20, 1994	Seoul KOEX		Korea Federation of Textile Industries Rm. 705, KWTC Bldg., 159, Samsung-dong, Socho-gu, Seoul Tel: (2) 551-1474 Fax: (2) 551-1496
SFA Seoul Collection (SFA) Twice a year (Spring and Autumn) May 2-4, 1993; Nov. 18-22, 1993 May 14-18, 1994; Nov. 17-21, 1994	Seoul KOEX		Korea Exhibition Center (KOEX) 159 Samsung-dong, Kangnam-gu, Seoul Tel: (2) 551-1117/1124 Fax: (2) 551-1311 Tlx: KOEXCEN K24594
Taegu International Textile Fair Last held: October, 1993	Taegu	C: 31 O: 250 K: 50,000	Korea Trade Promotion Corp., Trade Center Taegu-Gyongbuk 109, Shinchon 3-dong, Tong-gu, Taegu 701-023 Tel: (53) 756-2341/3 Fax: (53) 751-0449 Contact: Koh Weon-cheol

Trade Fair	Site		Contact

TOOLS: PRECISION & MEASURING
See also Machines & Instruments; other categories which may include exhibitions with tools specific to those industries

Trade Fair	Site		Contact
Changwon Tool Tech Show Last held: October 20-24, 1993	Changwon Industrial Complex Exhibition Hall	C: 12 O: 200 K: 20,000	Korea Tools Industry Cooperative Rm. 401, Bohun Bldg., 12-5, Youido-dong, Yongdungpo-gu, Seoul 150-010 Tel: (2) 780-0731 Fax: (2) 785-2457 Contact: Kim Mi-ae
Korea International Medical Equipment Show (KIMES) March 18-22, 1993 March 17-20, 1994	Seoul KOEX	C: 14 O: 100 K: 25,000	Hankook Ilbo 14, Chunghak-dong, Chongno-gu Seoul 110-150 Tel: (2) 739-5272 Fax: (2) 738-1048 Tlx: K23644 Contact: Kim Jeong-jo
Seoul International Instrumentation Exhibition (SEOUL INSTRUMENT) September 21-25, 1993 June 21-25, 1994	Seoul KOEX	C: 22 O: 350 K: 20,000	Korea Trade Promotion Corp. 159 Samsung-dong, Kangnam-gu Seoul 135-729 Tel: (2) 551-4181 Fax: (2) 551-4477 Tlx: KOTRA K23659 K27326 Contact: Kang Young-jin
Seoul International Machine Tool Show (SIMTOS) April 12-18, 1994	Seoul KOEX		Korea Machine Tool Manufacturers' Association 35-4 Youido-dong, Yongdungpo-gu, Seoul Tel: (2) 780-3521 Fax: (2) 784-8023
Seoul International Photo, Video & Optical Industry Show (PHOTO SHOW SEOUL) June 8-12, 1994	Seoul KOEX		Korea Exhibition Center (KOEX) 159 Samsung-dong, Kangnam-gu, Seoul Tel: (2) 551-1124 Fax: (2) 551-1311 Tlx: KOEXCEN K24594
Seoul International Scientific Instrument Show (INTERSIS) April 7-10, 1993 September 12-15, 1994	Seoul KOEX	C: 9 O: 1,200 K: 35,000	Korea Exhibition Center (KOEX) 159 Samsung-dong, Kangnam-gu, Seoul Tel: (2) 551-1148 Fax: (2) 551-1311 Tlx: KOEXCEN K24594

OTHERS Miscellaneous trade fairs

Trade Fair	Site		Contact
Invest in Europe Last held: March 29-31, 1993	Seoul KOEX	C: 9 O: 130 K: 20,000	Korea Exhibition Center (KOEX) 159 Samsung-dong, Kangnam-gu, Seoul Tel: (2) 551-1126 Fax: (2) 551-1311 Tlx: KOEXCEN K24594 Contact: Kim Myong-skin
Korea International Clean, Wash & Laundry Technology Exhibition (CLEANTEC) August 23-26, 1994	Seoul KOEX		Korea Int'l Exhibitions & Conferences Assn. Rm. 804, Century II Bldg., 1595-2, Socho-dong, Socho-gu, Seoul 137-070 Tel: (2) 588-3484 Fax: (2) 522-1102
International Education & Language Fair for Korea (LANGUAGE & EDUCATION FAIR KOREA) February 26-28, 1993 April 1-3, 1994	Seoul KOEX	C: 15 O: 600 K: 15,000	Korea Trade Fairs Ltd. 17-1, Youido-dong, Yongdungpo-gu Seoul 150-010 Tel: (2) 783-8261 Fax: (2) 784-6810 Contact: Song Myong-chol

Note: Country codes for telephone and fax numbers are not displayed unless they are *outside* of Korea. All country codes have square brackets around them, while city codes have parentheses. The country code for Korea is [82].

Trade Fair	Site		Contact
National Inventions Exhibition **(NIEX)** November 16-22, 1993 November 3-13, 1994	Seoul KOEX		The Korea Industrial Property Office 823-1, Yoksam-dong, Kangnam-gu, Seoul Tel: (2) 568-6073 Fax: (2) 553-9584
Promising Small Industries **Exhibition** **(PROMISON)** Last held: October 29-Nov. 4, 1993	Seoul KOEX		The Citizens National Bank 9-1, 2-ka, Namdaemun-no, Chung-ku Seoul 100 Tel: (2) 754-1211 Fax: (2) 757-3679, 777-4239 Tlx: 23481
Seoul International Sanitary **Show** **(SANI)** June 25-29, 1993 May 6-10, 1994	Seoul KOEX	C: 15 O: 1,500 K: 50,000	Korea Exhibition Center (KOEX) 159 Samsung-dong, Kangnam-gu, Seoul Tel: (2) 551-1602 Fax: (2) 551-1311 Tlx: KOEXCEN K24594
Seoul International Vending **Machine Show** **(SIVENDING)** Last held: October 19-22, 1993	Seoul KOEX		Korea Exhibition Center (KOEX) 159 Samsung-dong, Kangnam-gu, Seoul Tel: (2) 551-1117/1124 Fax: (2) 551-1311 Tlx: KOEXCEN K24594
TRADEMARK EXHIBITION Last held: November 13-18, 1993	Seoul KOEX		The Korea Industrial Property Office 823-1, Yoksam-dong, Kangnam-gu, Seoul Tel: (2) 568-6073 Fax: (2) 553-9584

Business Travel

Korea is not a simple place. Its history is violent and its culture and people are richly complex and contradictory. It is more modern than neighboring China. It is also more nationalistic and even more bureaucratic than neighboring Japan. It is very pro-Western in some ways, yet so highly suspicious of foreigners in general that its Hermit Kingdom sobriquet sometimes seems to describe it perfectly. But it is also possessed of a bureaucracy whose single-minded goal is to run an extraordinary tourism effort that really responds to the traveler's every concern.

Travel in Korea is about as easy as you will find anywhere in the Far East. Seoul has a subway system second to none, world-class hotels, cutting-edge business services, and a high degree of public health and safety. Koreans are typically Confucian—rude if they don't know you and warm if they do. They are extraordinarily hard-working, driven to succeed for the good of all (all Koreans, that is). Korea bristles with energy, yet this is also "The Land of the Morning Calm," where islands of peace float in misty mountains and seas and tranquillity beckons to the weary, over-stimulated traveler.

NATIONAL TRAVEL OFFICES WORLDWIDE

The Korea National Tourism Corporation (KNTC) is a source of books, brochures, maps, and advice. Some of the publications are quite beautiful and highly informative. The KNTC has offices worldwide.

Asia

Bangkok CCT Building, 11th Floor, 109, Surawongse Road, Bangkok 10500, Thailand; Tel: (2) 238-9021, 233-1399 Fax: (2) 236-2800

Hong Kong Bank of America Tower, Suite 506, 12 Harcourt Road C, Hong Kong; Tel: 523-8065/7 Fax: 845-0765

Singapore Clifford Centre, #20-03, 24 Raffles Place, Singapore 0104; Tel: 533-0441/2 Fax: 534-3427 Tlx: KOTOURS RS 21673

Taipei International Trade Center, Room 1813, 333 Keelung Road, Section 1, Taipei, 10548, Republic of China; Tel: (2) 720-8049/8281 Fax: (2) 757-6514

Australia

Sydney Tower Building, 7th Floor, Australia Square, George Street, Sydney, NSW 2000, Australia; Tel: (2) 252-4147/8 Fax: (2) 251-2104

Europe

Budapest ALAG Center Buda, Room 139, 1016, Budapest, Hegyalja ut 7-13, Hungary; Tel: (1) 202-2219/2373 Fax: (1) 202-2325

Frankfurt Mainzer Landstrasse 71, 6000 Frankfurt am Main 1, Germany; Tel: (69) 233226 Fax: (69) 253519

London Vogue House, 2nd floor, 1 Hanover Square, London W1R 9RD, UK; Tel: (71) 409-2100, 408-1591 Fax: (71) 491-2302

Paris Tour Maine Montparnasse, 33, avenue du Maine, B.P. 169, 75755 Paris Cedex 15, France; Tel: (45) 38-71-23 Fax: (45) 38-74-71

Japan

Fukuoka Asahi Building, 6th Floor, 1-1, 2-Chome, Hakata-ekimae, Hakata-ku, Fukuoka, Japan; Tel: (92) 471-7174/5 Fax: (92) 474-8015

Osaka KAL Building, 8th Floor, 1-9, 3-Chome, Hon-machi, Chuo-ku, Osaka, Japan; Tel: (6) 266-0847/8 Fax: (6) 266-0803

Sapporo Sapporo MN building, 7th Floor, Nishi 3-Chome, Kita 1-jo, Chuo-ku, Sapporo, Japan; Tel: (11) 210-8081/2 Fax: (11) 210-8083

Tokyo Sanshin Building, Room 124, 4-1, 1-Chome, Yuraku-cho, Chiyoda-ku, Tokyo, Japan; Tel: (3) 3580-3941/2 Fax: (3) 3591-4601

North America

Chicago 205 North Michigan Avenue, Suite 2212, Chicago, IL 60601, USA; Tel: (312) 819-2560/2 Fax: (312) 819-2563

Honolulu Korea Travel Service, 1188 Bishop Street, Century Square Penthouse 1, Honolulu, HI

96813, USA; Tel: (808) 521-8066 Fax: (808) 521-5233

Los Angeles 3435 Wilshire Boulevard, Suite 350, Los Angeles, CA 90010, USA; Tel: (213) 382-3435 Fax: (213) 480-0483

New York 2 Executive Drive, 7th Floor, Fort Lee, NJ 07024, USA; Tel: (201) 585-0909 Fax: (201) 585-9041

Seattle Evance Public Relations, 190 Queen Anne North, Seattle, WA 98109, USA; Tel: (206) 285-5522 Fax: (206) 285-2551

Toronto 480 University Avenue, Suite 406, Toronto, Ontario, M5G 1V2 Canada; Tel: (416) 348-9056 Fax: (416) 348-9058.

KNTC OFFICES IN KOREA

The main office is at 10, Ta-dong, Chung-gu, Seoul 100-180; the mailing address is CPO Box 903, Seoul 100-609, Rep. of Korea; Tel: [82] (2) 757-6030 Fax: [82] (2) 757-5997. A visit to this office is time well-spent. Its basement level tourist information hall has an interactive computer system, videos, and large topographic displays of the city and the nation, along with a huge supply of printed matter. The KNTC also has centers at Seoul's Kimpo and Pusan's Kimhae airports, and branches scattered all over Seoul: in the It'aewon shopping district, Tongdaemun and Namdaemun markets, Pagoda Park, Seoul Express Bus Terminal, and Toksugung Palace.

VISA AND PASSPORT REQUIREMENTS

All foreigners need valid passports to enter South Korea. Citizens of all Western European countries (except Ireland) and several Asian, American (excluding the United States), and African nations can enter Korea as tourists for from 30 to 90 days without visas. Most other foreigners with confirmed onward tickets can stay for 14 days without visas. Those wishing to stay 15 days or longer must first get visas from a Korean consulate or embassy abroad or, for US citizens, on arrival.

A tourist visa application requires your passport and one photo. And if you want to extend your visa, you'll need to apply at the Korean immigration office before your visa expires. The authorities might ask for a letter of recommendation or proof of a sponsor.

A business visa requires a letter or telex of invitation from your Korean business contact. Korean consulates and embassies worldwide can help with business travel. (Refer to "Important Addresses" chapter for a list of Korean embassies and consulates worldwide.)

IMMUNIZATION

You need proof of vaccinations only if you're arriving from an infected area, such as South America (cholera), or tropical South America or Africa (yellow fever).

CLIMATE

South Korea has a typical northern hemisphere continental climate—four seasons and wide extremes of temperature and humidity similar to those of Europe and the Middle Atlantic states of the US. Spring is sunny and mild with little rain, while summer brings heat—Seoul's high temperatures match those of Rome or Washington, DC—humidity and rain, with the occasional typhoon thrown in for good measure. July alone gets 38 cm (15 inches) of rain, so raincoats or umbrellas are a must. Doubly so because pollution fills the raindrops with sooty particulates that can stain your best suit.

Fall is gorgeous, with warm days and cool nights, but you'll have to bundle up for winter, when snow blankets the north and frigid winds sweep the country, keeping temperatures right around freezing. Yet even then there's a saving grace—Koreans say their winter weeks have "three cold and four warm" days that seem to come as a package deal.

BUSINESS ATTIRE

The Confucian concept and social system of face is strong in Korea. Dignity, status, and formality are the order of the day, and this extends to dress. Koreans favor conservative three-piece business suits and expect foreigners to wear the best attire possible. This includes fine fabrics, dark colors, and white shirts or blouses. Conservative fashion is especially important to foreign businesswomen: hemlines, necklines, sleeves, and makeup. Pantsuits are out. Koreans also appreciate fine gold accessories and jewelry, although gaudiness and excess can result in loss of face.

Matching your attire to the climate is simple: Dress as warmly for winter and as coolly for summer as you would in northern Europe or the United States. Get yourself a fur hat with earflaps for bitter winter winds. Tropical-weight attire is necessary for summer survival. You can buy your much-needed summertime raingear right outside your hotel.

AIRLINES

Seoul (Kimpo International Airport) Korea's immense capital city (population: 10.6 million) is the nation's political, cultural, industrial, commercial, and financial center. It is served by nearly 30 international carriers, including Air France, Alitalia, All Nippon, British Airways, Cathay Pacific, China Airlines, Continental, Delta, Garuda Indonesia, Japan Airlines, Japan Air System, KLM, Korean Airlines, Lufthansa, Malaysia Airlines, Northwest, Philippine Airlines, Qantas, Singapore Airlines, Swissair, Thai Airways, and United.

Pusan (Kimhae International Airport) While most foreigners enter Korea through Seoul, some, especially if they are coming from Japan, may want to fly into Pusan, Korea's second largest city, principal seaport, and a prominent industrial center. The city is served by Korea's Asiana Airlines as well as Korean Airlines and Japan Airlines.

AIR TRAVEL TIME TO SEOUL

This is a small sampling of the flights available from cities around the world to Seoul. In airline-speak, direct means that you have to stop over in another city along the way, but you don't have to change planes. The direct flight times below include time on the ground in the stopover cities.

Air Travel Time

- From Auckland nonstop on Qantas to Sydney: 3 hours; from Sydney to Seoul nonstop on Korean Airlines: 10 hours 15 minutes[1]
- From Bangkok nonstop on Thai Airways: 7 hours
- From Beijing direct to Osaka via Shanghai: 6 hours; from Osaka nonstop to Seoul on Korean Airlines: 1 hour 30 minutes[2]
- From Frankfurt nonstop on Lufthansa: 11 hours 45 minutes
- From Hong Kong nonstop on British Airways: 3 hours 15 minutes
- From Jakarta nonstop on Garuda Indonesia: 7 hours
- From Kuala Lumpur nonstop on Malaysia Airlines: 6 hours 15 minutes
- From London direct on British Airways via Hong Kong: 17 hours 25 minutes
- From Manila nonstop on Philippine Airlines: 4 hours
- From New York City on United: 18 hours 25 minutes[3]
- From San Francisco nonstop on United: 12 hours
- From Singapore nonstop on Singapore Airlines: 6 hours
- From Sydney nonstop on Qantas: 10 hours 15 minutes
- From Tokyo nonstop on Japan Airlines: 2 hours 15 minutes

1. The only same-day flight from Auckland to Seoul, available only on Tuesdays; plus changeover time in Sydney.
2. The only same-day flight from Beijing to Seoul; plus changeover time in Osaka.
3. Plus changeover time in San Francisco or Chicago

TIME CHANGES

Korea shares its time zone, nine hours ahead of Greenwich Mean Time, only with Japan and the western half of the island of New Guinea. When you're in Korea, you can determine what time it is in any of the cities listed here by adding or subtracting the number shown to or from Korean time.

Auckland	+3
Bangkok	-2
Beijing	-1
Frankfurt	-8
Hong Kong	-1
Jakarta	-2
Kuala Lumpur	-1
London	-9
Manila	-1
New York	-14
SanFrancisco	-17
Singapore	-1
Sydney	+1
Taipei	-1
Tokyo	0

CUSTOMS ENTRY (PERSONAL)

Customs can be easy at Seoul's Kimpo Airport: If you're carrying less than 20 kg (44 pounds) of duty-free items and not carrying restricted or prohibited items, you can choose the green channel for customs inspections. It's faster because officials inspect bags only at random. Keep in mind, though, that Korean Customs officials are exacting and thorough. Woe be unto those who are caught in the green line with dutiable, restricted, or prohibited items! They "may be severely punished," the government says, without elaboration.

Duty free

- Personal clothing and toiletries
- Equipment and tools needed for work
- ATA carnet items: professional equipment, commercial samples, and advertising material that you plan to take with you when you leave

Declarable

- Cameras, valuable watches, jewelry, electronic items, or furs. They will be recorded on your passport. If you leave Korea without them, or without having declared them, you'll be charged duties.
- Gifts valued up to 300,000 won (Korea's official currency) total (about US$375).
- No more than 1,520 cc (two fifths) of liquor
- Nor more than 56 grams of perfume
- No more than 500 grams of tobacco—any combination of 400 cigarettes, 50 cigars, or 200 grams of pipe tobacco

Cash

Foreigners bringing in more than US$5,000 or a foreign equivalent must declare it at Customs. If you bring in more than the equivalent of US$5,000 without declaring it, you won't be allowed to take the excess with you when you leave. This includes funds in excess of the declared amount that may have been transferred to you during your stay. Keep all your money-exchange receipts if you want to be able to reconvert your unused won when you leave. Without the receipts, you'll be allowed to convert only the won equivalent of US$500 back to your country's currency.

Restricted

- Firearms, narcotics, radio equipment, and commercial items

Prohibited

- Publications and other articles that the government thinks are pornographic or could jeopardize national security

(Refer to "Import Policy & Procedures" chapter for information about commercial imports.)

FOREIGN EXCHANGE

The Korean won (W) comes in coin denominations of W1, W5, W10, W100, and W500, although the smaller coins are not in common use because of their lack of purchasing power. Bills are issued in denominations of W1,000, W5,000, and W10,000. The won is subject to fluctuation, mostly of the inflationary type. At the end of 1993 the exchange rate was US$1=W808.1, making the W10,000 note worth about US$12.40. The won's low value and the absence of large-denomination bills mean that Koreans and visitors alike have to carry around large amounts of cash.

Foreigners and nationals can legally carry up to W2 million (about US$2,475) into or out of the country, but it is illegal to buy won outside the country and there is no international market in this not freely convertible currency. It is easy enough to exchange cash or traveler's checks in Korea, beginning at the

24-hour-a-day currency exchange counters at Kimpo Airport. Banks and major hotels also sell won, although the hotels offer a less favorable rate.

There is a relatively small black market for foreign currencies, which are usually in ample supply. It tends to operate out of electronics stores near the central post office in Seoul. Those willing to risk potential penalties can get about a 6 to 8 percent premium over the official exchange rate on small transactions. Major department stores, restaurants and electronics stores may give you change in won for US dollars and other desirable foreign currencies at a rate that amounts to a premium. Although it is technically illegal to use foreign currencies, there are so many dollars floating around because of the US military presence that they are accepted in many places, especially in the It'aewon shopping, entertainment, brothel, and embassy district.

Most major hotels, restaurants and stores accept major credit cards.

When you convert foreign currency to won, you'll get a receipt. Save it if you want to be able to convert your wads of won back when you leave Korea. Otherwise, you will be able to convert only the equivalent of US$500.

TIPPING

Korea is one of those all-too-rare advanced societies in which tipping is uncommon. Hotels and restaurants add a service charge to their bills, and it is proper to tip porters (W100 per bag, about US$0.12), taxi drivers (W700, about US$0.85, provided they help with your bags), and guides who go out of their way to be helpful. Beyond that, a smile, a slight bow, and a sincere thank you (especially in Korean— *kamsa hamnida*) will suffice.

ACCESS TO CITY FROM AIRPORT

Seoul Kimpo Airport is about 18 km (16 miles) west of downtown. The airport express buses run every eight to 20 minutes, and, depending on the particular route, stops at major hotels, the city center, the Seoul Sports Complex, the Korea Exhibition center, and other major destinations. The fare is usually about W580 (about US$0.75). Warning: There is very little luggage space.

If you've got lots of luggage, the most convenient way to get from the airport to the city is on the nonstop limousine bus, which leaves every 10 to 15 minutes and takes you to the Korea City Air Terminal just south of downtown next to the Korea World Trade Center, Korea Trade Promotion Corporation, and the Inter-Continental Hotel. This service costs W2,000 (about US$2.50) one way and takes about one hour. If you've made prior arrangements, your hotel can usually provide a bus or shuttle for a fee.

Taxis are metered and cost from W5,000 to W8,000 (about US$6.25 to US$10) from the airport. The more expensive rate is for "call" taxis, ordered by telephone. However, some drivers try to add surcharges to the meter fare, keep the meter running between passengers, or refuse to use the meter at all. Keep your eyes open, and report the drivers if they try to cheat you. In Korea some taxi drivers pose more of a threat to visitors' wallets than do pickpockets.

Pusan Kimhae Airport is 29 km (18 miles) northwest of the city. The bus fare to downtown is W320 (about US$0.40) for the one-hour trip, while a taxi should cost W5,000 to W6,000 (about US$6.25 to US$7.50).

ACCOMMODATIONS

South Korea fits right in with the rest of the world when it comes to hotels: high-rises so internationally homogenized that, during an especially hectic swing through the region, you may not be able to tell what country you're in from the architecture and decor of the hotel. That's unless you are either particularly alert or have reserved a Korean-style room with a mattress, quilt, and headrest on the floor. Incidentally, going native often costs less.

Korea's highrise hotels can match the high prices of lodging anywhere on the international circuit. And because the local Confucian mind-set puts a lot of emphasis on status there is a severe lack of more affordable places to stay in Seoul. The truly frightening highest room rates listed here are for truly elaborate suites. Most of the hotels listed have restaurants, bars, air conditioning, and television, while many also have business centers and health clubs.

Seoul–Top-end

Inter-continental 159-8, Samsong-dong, Kangnam-gu; in Korea World Trade Center complex. Business center, meeting rooms, health club. Rates: W135,000 to W200,000 (about US$167 to US$250). Tel: [82] (2) 555-5656 Fax: [82] (2) 559-7990; Tlx: 34254.

Koreana 61-1, T'aep'yongno 1-ga, Chung-gu; city center, two blocks from Capitol, on subway line, airport express shuttle stop, near museums, palaces, and British Embassy. Business center, meeting rooms, conference facilities. Rates: W103,500 to W253,000 (about US$128 to US$313). Tel: [82] (2) 730-9911 Fax: [82] (2)734-0665; Tlx: 26241.

Lotte 1, Sokong-dong, Chung-gu; in city center, on subway line, near Seoul Station. Huge, most prestigious hotel for foreign businesspeople. Business center, convention facilities, meeting rooms, health club, 12 restaurants, shops. Rates: if you have to ask, you can't afford it (W135,000 to W3,000,000, about US$167 to US$3,715). Tel: [82] (2) 771-1000 Fax: [82] (2) 752-3758; Tlx: 23533.

Moderate

While not as elaborate as the top-end hotels, these "moderately-priced" hotels are still classed as deluxe or first-class and often have all the amenities you might want for somewhat less money.

Garden Hotel 169-1, Tohwa-dong, Map'o-gu; near Han River, Seoul Station, and city center; airport express shuttle stop. Business center, meeting rooms. Rates: W84,000 to W440,000 (about US$105 to US$545). Tel: [82] (2) 741-7811 Fax: [82] (2) 715-9441; Tlx: 24742.

King Sejong 61-3, Ch'ungmuro 2-ga, Chung-gu; in business district, on subway line. Secretarial services, meeting rooms, health club, shops. Rates: W79,000 to W240,000 (about US$98 to US$297). Tel: [82] (2) 776-1811 Fax: [82] (2) 755-4009; Tlx: 27265.

New Seoul Hotel 29-1, T'aep'yong-no 1-ga, Chung-gu; in city center, near Palace, City Hall, British and Canadian embassies, on subway line. Business center, meeting rooms. Rates: W58,000 to W130,000 (about US$72 to US$161). Tel: [82] (2) 735-9071 Fax: [82] (2) 735-6212.

Budget

Seoul Hotel 92, Ch'ongjin-dong, Chongno-gu; near city center, Capitol, subway line, and Canadian, Japanese and United States embassies. Restaurants, banquet facilities, sauna. Rates: W40,000 to W61,000 (about US$50 to US$76). Tel: [82] (2) 735-9001 Fax: [82] (2) 733-0101.

Seoul Prince Hotel 1-1, Namsan-Dong 2-ga, Chung-gu; in business district, near Taiwanese Embassy, on subway line. Business center, meeting rooms, conference facilities. Rates: W27,000 to W70,000 (about US$33.50 to US$87). Tel: [82] (2) 752-7111/8 Fax: [82] (2) 752-7119. Tlx: 25918.

Sunshine Hotel 587-1, Shinsa-dong, Kangnam-gu; south of Han River, near Kangnam Express Bus Terminal and subway line. Business center, restaurant, coffee shop. Rates: W33,000 to W65,000 (about US$41 to US$80). Tel: [82] (2) 541-1818 Fax: [82] (2) 547-0777; Tlx: 25289.

Yogwan

The best alternative to Seoul's high prices is the *yogwan*, or traditional Korean inn. Even a first-class *yogwan* room averages only one-fourth the cost of a deluxe homogenized hotel room. Expect to pay W20,000 to W30,000 (about US$25 to US$37) for a room with private bath at a first-class *yogwan*. Many experienced travelers say the *yogwan* is the best way to go. Most are convenient to business areas, although located on alleys instead of main streets. They are usually busy places full of interesting, well-traveled people of all types. The following *yogwan* are recommended for foreigners. For more complete information, call the KNTC Tourist Information Center in Seoul at [82] (2) 757-0086.

Dae Won Dangju-dong, Chongno-gu; near Sejong Cultural Center, city center, subway, United States and Japanese embassies, Wendy's and Kentucky Fried Chicken. Very popular, so plan ahead. Shared baths, courtyard, clean. Tel: [82] (2) 738-4308.

Emerald Near T'apkol (Pagoda) Park and subway lines. Tel: [82] (2) 743-2001.

Kwang Pyung 123-1 Dadong, Chung-gu; in city center, near subway. Very popular. Courtyard, clean, private and shared baths. Tel: [82] (2) 778-0104.

Sung Do 120 Nae Su-dong, Chongno-gu; near Sejong Cultural Center, Seoul Police Bureau, United States Embassy. Private and shared baths. Tel: [82] (2) 737-1056.

Pusan

This city of 3.8 million has a large selection of hotels. Most of the best ones are at Haeundae Beach, 17 km (11 miles) northeast of city center but easily accessible by bus or local train. Keep in mind, however, that the beach is thoroughly packed during the summer. Visitors will be relieved to learn that the starting rates at many top-end Pusan hotels are much lower than at comparable hotels in Seoul, and there are also more moderate and budget hotels to choose from.

Top-end

Commodore Deluxe. 743-80, Yongju-dong, Chung-gu; near city center. Extraordinary harbor view. Conference facilities, meeting rooms, health club. Rates: W57,000 to W350,000 (about US$71 to US$433). Tel: [82] (51) 466-9102 Fax: [82] (51) 462-9101; Tlx: 53717.

Hyatt Regency Superdeluxe. 1406-16, Chung-dong, Haeundae-gu; at beach. Conference facilities, meeting rooms, health club, casino. Rates: W92,000 to W880,000 (about US$114 to US$1,090). Tel: [82] (51) 743-1234 Fax: [82] (51) 743-1250; Tlx: 52668.

Sorabol Deluxe. 37-1, 1-ga, Taech'ong-dong, Chung-gu; in city center, near Post Office, US Information Service, Bank of Korea. Business center, conference facilities, meeting rooms. Rates: W35,000 to W275,000 (about US$44 to US$340). Tel: [82] (51) 463-3511 Fax: [82] (51) 463-3510; Tlx: 53827.

Moderate

Phoenix First-class. 8-1, 5-ga, Namp'o-dong, Chung-gu; in city center, near subway stations. Restaurant, shops. Rates: W40,000 to W90,000 (about US$50 to US$111). Tel: [82] (51) 245-8061 Fax: [82] (51) 245-1523; Tlx: 53704.

Pusan Tourist Hotel First-class. 12, 2-ga, Tonggwang-dong, Chung-gu; in center of business and shopping district, near subway line. Restaurants, barber and beauty shops, nightclub, sauna. Rates: W33,000 to W77,000 (about US$41 to US$95). Tel: [82] (51) 241-4301 Fax: [82] (51) 241-1153; Tlx: 53657.

Royal First-class. 2-72, Kwangbok-dong 2-ga, Chung-gu; in city center, near Pusan Tower Park and subway station. Restaurant, shops. Rates: W45,000 to W82,000 (about US$56 to US$102). Tel: [82] (51) 241-1(51) 5 Fax: [82] (51) 241-1161; Tlx: 53824.

Budget

Bando Second-class. 36, Chung-ang-dong, 4-ga, Chung-gu; in city center, near Customs and Chungang-dong Subway Station. Restaurant, shops. Rates: W27,000 to W32,000 (about US$33 to US$40). Tel: [82] (51) 469-0561/7 Fax: [82] (51) 464-0553.

Moon Hwa Second-class. 517-65, Pujon 2-dong, Pusanjin-gu; 6 km (4 miles) north of city center, near subway station. Restaurant, coffee shop, banquet facilities, sauna. Rates: W18,000 to W29,000 (about US$22 to US$36). Tel: [82] (51) 806-8001/7.

Tong-Yang Third-class. 27, 1-ga, Kwangbok-dong, Chung-gu; in city center, near subway station. Banquet facilities, shops. Rates: W17,000 to W46,000 (about US$21 to US$57). Tel: [82] (51) 245-1205 Fax: [82] (51) 242-1001.

EATING

If you're the observant type of visitor to Korea, one thing you'll notice is the number of clay pots scattered or stacked around Korean dwellings. These are *kimch'i* pots. You'll find *kimch'i* served with every Korean meal. This healthy Korean staple is a mixture of Chinese cabbage, garlic, ginger, chili peppers, carrots, radishes, and other vegetables fermented below ground in the pots for days or weeks at a time. Did we mention the chilis? Well, anyway, you'll discover them on your own. And if the chilis don't get you, the ginger will. The degree of spiciness ranges from hot, to very hot, to call-the-fire-department hot. It's an acquired taste, to say the least, and one that can leave you craving for *kimch'i* long after your trip is over.

Korean cuisine beyond *kimch'i* is unlike anything else you'll find in East Asia. It's varied, nutritionally superior, and lower in fat than either Chinese and Japanese food. It's also much spicier—Koreans love their ginger, chilis and garlic—although you can find or specify milder dishes. Most Korean dishes are totally or predominately vegetarian because meat is so expensive, so there is an enormous variety of rice-and-vegetable dishes. But also try *pulgogi* ("fire beef"— Korean barbecue fired up at your table), *kalbi* (beef or pork short ribs, also grilled at the table), *shinsollo* (a mixture of meat, fish, vegetables, and bean curd), *kalbit'ang* (a broth of beef, sesame seeds, spices, and sesame oil), and *mandukuk* (an extraordinary meat dumpling soup). It's proper in Korea to eat with gusto, so there's always plenty of appreciative slurping to be heard, even appreciative belching, and diners can make quite a mess. One thing they never do, however, is blow their noses at the table. No matter how spicy the food, it's just not done.

With the ocean lapping along three of its four sides, Korea also loves fish, and you can find it prepared in ways you never even dreamed of. There are also many Japanese, Chinese, and Western restaurants in Korea, especially in the hotels and in the It'aewon district near the Yongsan US Army Base, but you would be lax if you failed to try some of the Korean restaurants listed below. Also recommended: the Korean restaurants in the Lotte and Shilla hotels in Seoul. Feel free, too, to wander the alleys of Ta-dong and Mugyo-dong (between Seoul City Hall and the main street Namdaemun-ro), where there are dozens of good, cheap restaurants.

Seoul

Daewon 89-10, Nonhyon-dong, Kangnam-gu. Tel: [82] (2) 548-0323/7.

Han Il-Hoe Kwan 1-4, Ulchiro 1-ga, Chung-gu. Tel: [82] (2) 753-0537.

Korea House 80-2, P'il-dong, 2-ga, Chung-gu. Tel: [82] (2) 752-2734.

Myong Woul 34, Ikson-dong, Chongno-gu. Tel: [82] (2) 762-4071.

River Garden 261-4, Yomch'ang-dong, Kangso-gu. Tel: [82] (2) 696-4180.

Sogyang Garden 267-14, Nonhyon-dong, Kangnam-gu. Tel: [82] (2) 549-5995.

Pusan

Bu Kwang Garden 1489-10, Chung 2-dong, Haeundae-gu. Tel: [82] (51) 743-0041/3.

Ever Spring Park 187-7, Onch'ong 1-dong, Tongnae-gu. Tel: [82] (51) 53-1800.

Geo Goo Jang 8, 1-ga, Shinch'ang-dong, Chung-gu. Tel: [82] (51) 245-5858.

Hyangwon Shamketang 24, 2-ga, Nam'o-dong, Chung-gu. Tel: [82] (51) 246-1674.

Moon Viewing House 1489-1, Chung 2-dong, Haeundae-gu. Tel: [82] (51) 742-3386/8.

LOCAL CUSTOMS OVERVIEW

Korea's culture in many respects is similar to that of Japan and China, but there are also some marked differences. To understand and accept both the similarities and the differences is to endow your business venture in Korea with the greatest chance of success.

- Korea is Confucian. That means face—courtesy, status, dignity, respect for authority. To lose face is anathema, while to have it or gain it is what life is all about. Face is part of every human relationship. Western harsh directness, sarcasm, readiness to criticize, and impatience are counterproductive in the extreme.

- As part of their continuing quest to save face, Koreans place a high value on maintaining harmony—*kibun*. *Kibun* makes Koreans helpful, friendly, and polite on a personal level. It also makes them extreme conformists who avoid making individual decisions and abhor having to utter the word "no." These traits leaves Westerners frustrated and confused, wondering why middle management Koreans always say yes, never seem to give a straight answer, and never assume personal responsibility for anything. In Korea the buck never stops here—it always floats around over there somewhere. As a Westerner, you can handle these situations by not demanding yes or no answers, by learning to read between the lines, and by patiently accepting the Korean need for consensus decision making.

- Confucian society is male-dominated and rigid; women are second-class citizens. In business the boss is all-powerful; his employees honor and respect him as if he were their own father. The boss is involved in every phase of his subordinates' lives, from cradle to grave, and he honors their devotion by trying to do his best for them. Add to this a nationalism even more extreme than Japan's, and you can appreciate the difficulties that face a foreigner trying to do business in Korea. It's a cross between inviting yourself to become a member of someone else's family and invading his country. You are manifestly not part of the family. You are probably either not important to them or you are viewed as a threat to them.

- Thus you absolutely will need intermediaries who will help you to get a foot in the door by formally introducing you to business contacts. Personal relationships are more important to Koreans than paper contracts or rational Western-style economic mutual interest.

- You'll need all the patience, flexibility, and respect you can muster to negotiate business deals.

- Business cards are crucial. Carry plenty of them, always. When you meet someone, shake hands and exchange cards, using both hands to present and accept cards. When you receive a card, study it carefully and respectfully, then place it in a pocket above the waist. Make sure your foreign-language card has a Korean translation on the reverse.

- Be prepared to attend banquets, and to reciprocate. If you can carry it off with any degree of aplomb and self-respect, be prepared to drink any challenger under the table.

- Although Koreans are personally polite, crowds

of Koreans are not, by Western standards. It's not impolite to push and shove your way onto a bus or train or to bump somebody off the sidewalk. When face meets crowded conditions, it must often wear a mask.

(Refer to "Business Culture" chapter for an in-depth discussion.)

DOMESTIC TRANSPORTATION

Air Korean Airlines and Asiana Airlines provide efficient, reasonably priced domestic service to 13 major cities. No on-time flight takes more than an hour. There is a free shuttle bus between the Korean Airlines international and domestic terminals at Kimpo Airport in Seoul. Foreigners need to present their passports before boarding domestic flights. The Seoul-to-Pusan flight (26 daily) takes 50 minutes and costs about W36,000 (about US$45).

Train Korea's excellent train system has four levels. The fastest, most luxurious, and most expensive is the superexpress, *Saemaul*. It will haul you from Seoul to Pusan nonstop in less than five hours for about W26,000 first-class (about US$32) and W20,000 second-class (about US$25). The express line, *Mugunghwa*, makes very few and very brief stops, the T'ong-il somewhat more and longer stops, while the *Pidulgi* trains stop everywhere but still run on time.

Trains are popular, especially on weekends, so reserve your seat on the express trains at least two weeks in advance at a train station, a travel agency, or the Korea Travel Bureau's Tourist Information Center in Seoul (Tel: [82] (2) 753-9870). You can't reserve seats on the slower trains.

Subway The Seoul and Pusan subways are among the world's fastest, most modern, most comfortable, and least expensive. Seoul's is the world's seventh largest. Its four lines are color-coded, and have stops at or near every possible major destination point in the city, connecting with each other and with the Korean National Railroad. Outside city center, the trains run above ground. They leave about every six minutes and the most expensive ticket is only W300 (about US$0.40). Four more lines are under construction, including a line to Kimpo Airport, due to open in 1994.

Pusan's subway has only one line, but it also is cheap and easy to use, with the most expensive ticket priced at W250 (about US$0.30).

Bus Korean bus travel is fast, smooth, safe, inexpensive, and on time. The reserved-seat express *kosok* buses speed along major expressways nonstop except for the longest routes. The Seoul-to-Pusan bus leaves every five to 10 minutes and takes five hours 20 minutes for a fare of about W8,000 (about US$10). The *chikheng* buses have limited stops, while

wanheng buses are strictly local, but they often are parked side by side at the terminals, so be sure to get on the right one. Schedules for express and limited buses are now printed in both Korean and English, while the local bus schedules are available only in Korean.

The express bus terminals in Seoul are the Kangnam (also called Seoul) on the south side of the Han River—take the subway line 3—and the Tongseoul on Koo Eui-dong in Songdong-gu, east of city center.

Korean cities have very good bus service. Buses run frequently and they're cheap—in Seoul a token costs W210 (about US$0.25), no matter the distance—but they can get incredibly crowded at rush hour. Seoul city express buses are green, more comfortable, and airconditioned; you're guaranteed a seat, and they stop less frequently—and they cost W500 (about US$0.60). However, city bus schedules and stops are marked only in Korean. It's best to have your hotel write down your bus number and desti-

Korean Holidays

New Year's Day*–January 1-3

Folklore Day (lunar New Year)*–
    End of January to early March

Independence Movement Day*–March 1

Labor Day*–March 10

Hansik Day (lunar)[1]–Early April

Arbor Day–April 5

Buddha's Birthday (lunar)*–April or May

Children's Day–May 5

Memorial Day*–June 6

Farmers' Day–June 15

Tano Day (lunar)[2]–Late June

Constitution Day*–July 17

Liberation Day*–August 15

Thanksgiving Day (lunar)*–
    Late September to early October

Armed Forces Day–October 1

National Foundation Day*–October 3

Hangul Day[3]–October 9

Christmas Day*–December 25

1. A day of visits to graves of ancestors with offerings of food and wine.
2. A major festival day of visits to ancestral shrines with food offerings and prayers for good harvests.
3. Celebrates adoption of written Korean language (Hangul) by King Sejong in 1448.

nation for you, or travel with a Korean-speaking acquaintance, although you can usually find someone at the bus stop who speaks English.

Taxi Although taxis are plentiful and relatively cheap, there's a growing problem with crooked drivers, which is why the KNTC wants you to call if you meet one—(2) 735-0101 or (2) 777-5000. Usually, it's a driver who doesn't want to take you where you want to go because it isn't costly enough; who tries to charge an excessive fare; or who tries to get away with not using the meter at all or not resetting it after the previous passenger.

Korea has several types of taxis, color-coded for identification. The cheapest is yellow or green—the kind you can hail on the street. The call taxi is beige and costs more, while the biggest and most expensive cabs are white with a blue stripe. Whatever the class of taxi, the fare goes up W100 (about US$0.12) for every 92 seconds that the taxi is traveling at less than 15 kph. In Seoul, that can be much of the time. Don't even bother with a taxi during rush hour; take the subway. The streets are jammed, and the meter just keeps clicking away as you sit there fuming in gridlock.

It is common practice for the driver to pick up two or three passengers along the way who are going the same direction—a custom called *hapsung*. Each passenger pays the fare on the meter less the amount showing when he got in. It's believed that cab drivers originated this custom.

HOLIDAYS/BANK HOLIDAYS

Korea uses the Gregorian (Western) calendar, but three of the 13 official holidays are based on the traditional Oriental lunar calendar and so fall on different dates from one year to the next. There are also some unofficial holidays when some or many businesses close but government offices remain open. If a holiday falls on a weekend, it is observed the following Monday. Holidays are not a good time for foreigners to try to travel or do business, especially lunar New Year, when Koreans jam the highways, trains, and buses in pilgrimages to the place of their birth. An asterisk (*) in the list to the left signifies a bank holiday.

BUSINESS HOURS

Government agencies are open from 9 am to 6 pm Monday through Friday from March through October, but close at 5 pm from November through February. On Saturdays they are open from 9 am to 1 pm. Foreign diplomatic missions are open from 9 am to 5 pm Monday through Friday. Some main Post Office branches are open every day until late.

Most businesses are open from 8:30 am until 7

Korean Area Codes		Country Codes of Major Countries	
Seoul:	2	Australia	61
Chongjiu:	431	Brazil	55
Chonju:	652	Canada	1
Inchon:	32	China	86
Iri:	653	France	33
Kwangju:	62	Germany	49
Kyongju:	561	Hong Kong	852
Masan:	551	India	91
Mokpo:	631	Indonesia	62
Pohang:	562	Italy	39
Pusan:	51	Japan	81
Sogwipo/Cheju:	64	Malaysia	60
Taegu:	53	Mexico	52
Taejon:	42	New Zealand	64
Ulsan:	522	Pakistan	92
Yosu:	662	Philippines	63

Korea's country code is 82. If you are dialing within Korea, add a "0" before the city code.

Russia	7
Singapore	65
South Africa	27
Spain	34
Taiwan	886
Thailand	66
United Kingdom	44
United States	1

pm or later. Department stores are generally open from 10:30 am to 7:30 pm six days a week, closing one weekday. Smaller shops are usually open from 9 am to 9 pm, but many open and close later.

Banking hours are 9:30 am to 4:30 pm Monday through Friday, and 9:30 am to 1:30 pm Saturday.

COMMUNICATIONS

Korea's communications systems are first-rate and continually improving.

Telephones Telephone service in Korea is very good, and the Korean Telecommunications Authority is digitalizing rapidly. Public telephones, like taxis and subways, in Korea are color-coded. The orange pay phones are for local calls only; calls cost W20 (about US$0.03) and cut off after three minutes. You can use the blue phones and gray phones for local and long-distance calls; they take W10, W50 and W100 coins, which you keep depositing for more time—unused money is returned when you hang up. You can make local, long-distance, or international calls on card phones, which take cards of W3,000, W5,000 and W10,000. You can buy the cards at banks, telephone offices and post offices and at shops near the phone booths.

To direct dial internationally from Korea, first dial the international access code—001—then the country code, area code (if there is one) and the local phone number. For example, to call World Trade Press direct, dial 001-1-415-454-9934. Long-distance and international calls are 30 percent cheaper on weekends and between 9 pm and 8 am.

USEFUL TELEPHONE NUMBERS

- KNTC Kimpo Airport Information Center .... (2) 665-0088/0988
- KNTC Kimhae Airport Information Center .... (51) 98-1100
- Seoul Tourist Information Center .... (2) 731-6337, 735-8688
- Tourist Complaint Center .... (2) 735-0101
- Traffic Complaint Center .... (2) 777-5000
- Domestic collect calls 114
- International operator 0077
- International collect calls 007
- International call information 0074
- Overseas telegraph 115
- Country Direct* 009-11

*Country Direct enables you to bypass the local telephone system (in this case, Korea) and reach the US or another country directly. A recording or an operator will offer you the option of using your home country calling card, a credit card, or waiting for an operator to make a collect call.

Fax and telex Fax machines are in wide use because they are the fastest way to transmit messages written in Korean characters. Most major hotels have both fax and telex services.

Computer communications Korea's Data Communications Corporation (DACOM) has developed a computer data packet network that connects 52 foreign countries with 3,000 domestic end users and provides e-mail, databases, videotex, and value-added networks. The number of local area networks (LANs) has been doubling every year since 1980. DACOM's Customer Support Center numbers are (2) 220-0220 or 080-023-0220 (toll-free).

Post Office Korea's postal service is first-rate. Airmail to or from Korea generally arrives within a week. Most major hotels and the larger post offices have packing and wrapping services. Domestic letters cost W100 (about US$0.12) for up to 50 grams, and are delivered within a day in Seoul and two to three days elsewhere in Korea. Airmail letters to the Far East cost W370 (about US$0.46); to Southeast Asia, W400 (about US$0.50); to Europe, North America, and the Middle East, W440 (about US$0.55);

to Africa and Latin America, W470 (about US$0.58).

English-language media The two Korean English-language newspapers are the *Korea Herald* and the *Korea Times*, published daily except Monday. *The Korea Economic Journal* is published weekly, as is the newsmagazine *Korea Herald.* Monthly magazines include *Korea Business World, Business Korea*, and *Korea Economic Report.*

The state-run Korea Broadcasting System airs foreign broadcasts in 12 languages.

COURIER SERVICES

Most of the big international courier services operate in Korea.

Federal Express PRI-EX, Inc., 158-11, Dongkyo-dong, Mapo-gu, Seoul (at Hapchong Subway Station); Tel: [82] (02) 333-8000.

TNT 687-8, Konghang-dong, Kangseo-ku, Seoul; Tel: [82] (2) 666-6660/4865 Fax: [82] (02) 666-9001; Tlx: K23977 TNTSEL.

TNT 1194-11, Choryang 3 Dong, Dong-ku, Pusan; Tel: [82] (51) 465-6677 Fax: [82] (51) 465-0198; Tlx: K23977 TNTSEL.

UPS Korea Air Freight Limited, 111-1, Whakok-dong, Kangseo-ku, Seoul; Tel: [82] (2) 601-3300/5500 Fax: [82] (2) 690-2489; Tlx: 26374 KAFAIRS K.

LOCAL SERVICES

Korea can provide every kind of business service you need. Government trade agencies, business organizations, lawyers, advertising and marketing agencies, shipping companies, accountants, telecommunications and computer services—all are available and easy to find. Here is a short listing of the services you're likely to need soon after you arrive in Korea.

Business centers

Major hotels often have business centers equipped with secretarial and delivery services, computers, telephones, telexes, and fax machines. Among them are:

Seoul Capital, Garden, Inter-Continental, Koreana, Lotte, Lotte World, New Seoul, Palace, President, Prince, Ramada Renaissance, Riviera, Sunshine, Swiss Grand.

Inchon New Star.

Kyongju Chosun.

Pusan Sorabol.

Taegu Kumho, Prince, Taegu.

Korea also has companies that specialize in providing offices and accompanying services. One such is Offitel 2000. It provides several classes of rooms, a conference service, secretarial services, telecommunications, personnel services, and an international network answering service. The address is:

Offitel 2000
Pumyang Building
750-14, Ban Bae-dong, Socho-gu
Seoul
Tel: (2) 599-7131/9, 591-7536/9
Fax: (2) 533-8089, 532-0875
Tlx: K22223 SELKOR, K22023 PUMKOR

Printers

You'll need business cards right away, and Korean printers can place the Korean translation on the reverse of each card. Service is fast and inexpensive— you can expect to pick the cards up in a few days. The concierge at the better hotels can refer you to a printer, or you might try one of the following:

Dong Sung Printing Company 3-63, Yangpyung-dong, Yongdungpo-gu, Seoul; Tel: [82] (2) 675-5151 Fax: [82] (2) 678-5157.

Shing Poong Company 27-1 1-ga, Inhyun-dong, Chung-gu, Seoul; Tel: [82] (2) 273-4581.

Translation and Secretarial Agencies

Several firms combine translation and secretarial services. Among them are:

International Translation Company, Ltd. More than 16 languages; interpretation services. 69-3, 2-ga, Taepyung-ro, Chung-gu, Seoul; Mailing Address: CPO Box 3070; Tel: [82] (2) 779-2222, 752-2244, 778-3344 Fax: [82] (2) 755-2757; Tlx: K25806.

Korea Translation-Interpretation Service 22 languages. Also provides conference and exhibition services, copywriting and proofreading, placement in trade media, company publications, foreign firm representation and liaison. Hyundai Department 7F, Korea World Trade Center, 159-2 Samsung-dong, Kangnam-gu, Seoul 135-090; Mailing Address: CPO Box 6699; Tel: [82] (2) 555-5373/4, 555-5594/5, 535-2000 Fax: [82] (2)557-5533; Tlx: K29165 SSTARS; CABLE: KOTICORP.

Star Communications, Inc. #306, Westin Chosun Hotel, 87, Sokong-dong, Chung-gu, Seoul; Mailing Address: CPO Box 8541; Tel: [82] (2) 756-0761/3, 753-0760, 752-5948 Fax: [82] (2) 756-0755; Tlx: K23256, K23745; CABLE: BUMARST AR.

STAYING SAFE AND HEALTHY

Korea is, by and large, a safe, sane, and healthy society. Its doctors and nurses are well trained, hospitals are well equipped, prescription and over-the-counter medicines are available, public health standards are generally high, and roads are modern and well maintained. Once you get used to the food, the large amounts of garlic, ginger, chilis, and vegetables you'll be eating will keep you strong and healthy. There are, of course, some commonsense precautions you must take.

Bronchitis This inflammation of the bronchial tubes is probably the most disabling ailment a traveler faces in Korea. The air in Seoul and other major cities is terrible. Air pollution plus a flu virus often adds up to bronchitis, which in turn can lead to pneumonia, so get a flu shot before you leave for Korea. If you get the flu, you can help prevent bronchitis and pneumonia by getting plenty of rest in your hotel room. Avoid cigarette smoke, eat a balanced and varied diet, and drink plenty of liquids.

You'll know you've developed bronchitis by the persistent cough, the phlegm, chest congestion, fever, and wheezing. If the phlegm is greenish, the cause is bacterial, and you should see a doctor for antibiotics, usually erythromycin, penicillin, or tetracycline. If the phlegm is clear, the cause is viral and antibiotics won't help. In either case, inhale steam and take Robitussin to loosen the phlegm, and drink plenty of liquids. Your hotel staff will help you make arrangements to see a doctor.

Diarrhea Your digestive system won't be used to the intestinal flora it will pick up in Korea, or to the food. The same problems afflict travelers all over the world, no matter how advanced the country. You can try to prevent it by not eating fresh fruits and vegetables that you can't wash in bottled water and peel yourself. Drink only bottled water and beverages. Tap water in the big cities is treated, but it's still not totally reliable. Hotels provide bottled water and their ice is made from purified water. Brush your teeth with bottled water.

Despite all precautions, it's still likely you'll have at least one bout of traveler's diarrhea. You're best off to ride it out; let your system adapt to or expel the invaders. In the meantime, drink plenty of bottled water, fruit juice, herbal tea, and clear broth to keep yourself hydrated. If nausea or vomiting accompanies the diarrhea, drink as much fluid as you can in small frequent sips. If the vomiting doesn't stop within six to 12 hours—or the diarrhea in a few days—have your hotel staff arrange a visit to a doctor.

Always drink a couple of glasses of water after each trip to the bathroom. Avoid greasy food, highly spiced food (difficult in Korea), raw fruits (except bananas) and vegetables, and dairy products. Eat only bland foods—bananas, rice, crackers, potatoes, fish, lean meats, beans, and lentils. Avoid caffeine and alcohol—both are diuretics (they cause your body to lose water).

If you have to plug yourself up—to travel, or attend a banquet or meeting—take Pepto-Bismol for a mild or moderate case, or Immodium or Lomotil for a severe case. (These are good items to bring with you on your travels anywhere). A doctor can furnish the antibiotics doxycycline and trimethoprim/sulfamethoxazole, which kill the offending flora—and all the good flora, too. Keep in mind, however, that these drugs will keep your system from adjusting for as long as you take them.

Traffic Why end your life under a bus in Seoul? While drivers in the cities obey traffic signals and let pedestrians cross at signals, they don't let them cross where there is no signal. Drivers don't often use turn signals, and they throw bottles and food out of their windows, so beware of flying objects. And experienced travelers have learned to be wary of Korean bus drivers who often seem to make up their own rules.

Crime Koreans are a law-abiding people. Most of the really serious crime is of the white-collar variety. There is very little street crime, especially against travelers. Be on the lookout for pickpockets in crowded open markets, but you're much more likely to encounter a crooked taxi driver. Still, it's wise to take precautions.

- Check in with your embassy or consulate when you arrive in Korea. Ask them about street crime.
- Avoid flashy displays of wealth—gold, jewelry, clothes.
- Carry cash—won comes in huge wads—in a money belt.
- Always act as if you know where you are and where you're going.

Personal-care products Bring your own prescription medicines, vitamins, women's sanitary products, deodorant, shaving lotion, and the like. The kinds of products you're used to are in short supply and very expensive, if they're available at all. Film is readily available, but foreign film is very expensive.

EMERGENCY INFORMATION

Dial 112 for a police emergency or 119 for fire. Your hotel front desk can arrange for a doctor or ambulance, or ask a policeman on the street. Most police officers in the major cities are college graduates and speak at least some English. Every major street has a police call box.

Asia Emergency Assistance, for a fee, provides 24-hour emergency service for foreigners, linking them with hospitals: Call [82] (2) 790-7561.

HOSPITALS

Seoul

Ewha Women's Hospital, 70, Chongno 6-ga, Chongno-gu; Tel: [82] (2) 760-5114.

Korea National Medical Center, 18-79, Ulchiro 6-ga, chung-gu; Tel: [82] (2) 265-9131.

Seoul National University Hospital, 28, Yongon-dong, Chongno-gu; Tel: [82] (2)760-2114.

Severance Hospital, 134, Shinch'on-dong, Sodaemun-gu; Tel: [82] (2) 361-5114.

St. Mary's Hospital, 62, Youido-dong, Yongdungp'o-gu; Tel: [82] (2) 789-1114.

Inchon

Chung-ang Gil General Hospital, 172, Kuwol-dong, Nam-gu; Tel: [82] (32) 432-9011.

Pusan

Pusan National University Hospital, 10, Ami-dong 1-ga, So-gu; Tel: [82] (51) 256-0171.

Taegu

Kyungpook National University Hospital, 335, Samdok-dong 2-ga, Chung-gu; Tel: [82] (53) 422-1141.

DEPARTURE FORMALITIES

If you want to be able to leave with everything you brought into Korea, be sure to make a full declaration of restricted and dutiable items when you enter the country—especially foreign currency and things like cameras, jewelry, watches, precious metals, and furs. Otherwise, your foreign currency in excess of US$5,000 or the equivalent will be confiscated, and you will have to pay duties on the rest. If you haven't kept your receipts for exchanging foreign currency for won, you won't be able to reconvert more than the won equivalent of US$500.

Korea doesn't allow the export of important cultural properties—paintings, sculpture, crafts, antiques, and the like. If you have any doubts about whether you'll be able to take a purchase home with you, take it to the Art and Antiques Assessment Office (Tel: [82] (2) 662-0106, 664-8997) for evaluation and permission (or rejection).

BEST TRAVEL BOOKS

A good travel book can acquaint you with the country and people you're about to visit, enough to help you absorb as much culture shock as possible. Especially for those from a different major cultural tradition, travel in the Orient takes a goodly amount of openness, tolerance and objectivity—even more so if you're there on business.

Korea itself publishes some of the best travel books about Korea—somewhat sugar-coated, yes, but often very attractive, and so informative as to anticipate every question a traveler might have. Just call any of the KNTC offices listed in the beginning of this chapter. Two of the choice offerings are Travel Manual Korea and Travelers' Korea; the business traveler should get *Facts About Korea* for background.

When it comes to hotel prices, train schedules, and the like, even the best travel books will be somewhat out of date—it's the nature of the beast. Not even the KNTC can keep up with all the changes.

Among other good books:

Fodor's 93 Korea, edited by Julie Tomazs. New York: Fodor's Travel Publications, 1993. ISBN 0-679-023-100. 275 pages, US$15.00. Up-to-date; oriented towards the tourist and tour group, and towards having fun. Worth buying just for its information on hotels and restaurants. Excellent maps.

Korea, by Geoff Crowther and Choe Hyung Pun. Hawthorn, Victoria, Australia: Lonely Planet Publications, 1991. ISBN 0-86442-099-4. 265 pages, US$11.95. Another in Lonely Planet's "travel survival kit" series, and it does its job well. Informal, an easy read, packed with information, though geared more to the budget-minded independent traveler. Good

insights into the culture, the people, and the places, not to mention the daily hassles of travel. It suffers from the typical Lonely Planet weakness in indexing —it contains only place names. Things are changing so fast in Korea that this book needs updating, but it is still an invaluable source.

The Korea Guidebook, by Kyung Cho Chung, Phyllis Haffner, and Fredric M. Kaplan. Boston: Houghton Mifflin Company, 1991. ISBN 0-395-58580-5. 608 pages, US$18.95. One of the publisher's Eurasia Travel Guides series; fat, detailed, insightful, matter-of-fact. Three of its strong points are a 100-page "Doing Business with Korea" section, which includes Korea's foreign trade structure, strategies for success, and a "Ten Commandments" section; a detailed table of contents; and a good index. This book also needs updating.

Typical Daily Expenses in Korea

All prices are in won (W) unless otherwise noted. At press time, the exchange rate was US$1 = W809

Expense	LOW		MODERATE		HIGH	
	Seoul	Pusan	Seoul	Pusan	Seoul	Pusan
Hotel	36,000	30,000	120,000	85,000	180,000	145,000
Local transportation *	600	500	3,000	3,000	8,000	8,000
Food	15,000	12,000	45,000	30,000	75,000	50,000
Local telephone †	100	100	500	500	1,000	1,000
Tips	200	200	200	200	2,000	2,000
Personal entertainment **	4,000	3,000	12,000	9,000	65,000	50,000
TOTAL	**55,900**	**45,800**	**180,700**	**127,700**	**331,000**	**256,000**
One-way airport trans.	580	320	2,000	6,000	6,000	6,000

US Government per diem allowance as of December, 1993

	Lodging (US$)	Food & Incidentals (US$)	Total (US$ and W)
Seoul	$127	$77	$204 = W165,000
Pusan	$151	$71	$222 = W179,600

10% service charge has been included in the hotel and restaurant figures, and an additional 10% tax is included for hotel charges. Tipping is uncommon in Korea, except for porterage in airports or train stations and for extra service in top-end hotels.

* Based on 2 subway rides for low cost, 2 medium length taxi rides for moderate cost and 4 longer taxi rides for high cost.
† Based on 2 telephone calls from pay phones for low cost, 4 calls from hotel for moderate cost and 6 calls from hotel for high cost
** Based on a visit to a cultural site and coffee shop for low cost, a visit to a disco with 1-2 drinks for moderate cost and a tour of city nightspots (including a floor show and dinner) for high cost.

Business Culture

Business in Korea is unlike business in any other country. The forces that have shaped modern Korean society have formed a wholly indigenous value system and world view. While Koreans share many cultural traditions with other peoples in the Far East, it would be a mistake to presume what is true of Japanese or Chinese is also true of Koreans. Korea's past was molded by a strictly hierarchical society, and in more recent times the country has been scarred by colonialism, partition, and the ravages of civil war.

Emerging from centuries of isolated feudalism, the Japanese empire made Korea a vassal state and subjected it to harsh rule. The invading Japanese forces did everything possible to erase Korean nationalism. The Japanese banned Korean in schools and replaced it with Japanese. Japan ruled Korea from 1895 to 1945.

When the Japanese empire collapsed at the end of World War II, the Korean peninsula was divided in two: Communist North Korea was dominated by Russia and China, while the authoritarian capitalist South Korea was dominated by the United States. The invasion of South Korea by North Korean forces in 1950 began a bloody three-year civil war during which millions of lives were lost, and family members were divided forever. Korea at this time was a hot theater of conflict in the midst of the Cold War. Within a year or two, Korean forces were decimated, and from then on the war was fought by proxy as American and Chinese troops battled for a land that neither side claimed as a home. The entire country was essentially destroyed. The Korean people, North and South alike, suffered terribly.

The cease-fire of 1953 left the Korean peninsula divided, much as it had been before the war. The land is still divided today. The north remains ostensibly Communist under the totalitarian rule of Kim Il Sung and his family. North Korea is a backward, xenophobic country teetering on the brink of economic collapse.

The Republic of Korea (ROK) in the south is a very different story. After the Korean War, South Koreans,

aided heavily by the United States, began a reconstruction effort that has truly transformed the country. A combination of indigenous free market capitalism, extensive government promotion of export-oriented industry, and tight protectionist policies have accomplished this economic miracle. But the spirit of the Korean people has perhaps been more important. Discipline, hard work, nationalism, and the willingness to suffer hardship for the good of the country are hallmarks of the Korean mentality.

Foreign businesspeople working with Korea should recognize that it is the sheer toughness of the Korean people that has driven their rapid ascent to economic success. The discussion that follows examines aspect of the Korean mentality to help foreigners understand the cultural values that permeate the Korean business world.

UNDERSTANDING HAHN

The Korean language has a word for the pent-up energies and frustrations that develop in the human psyche under conditions of extreme oppression and hardship—*hahn*. *Hahn* is one of the forces that have led the Korean people to their present prosperity. Ossified dogma and brutal rulers repressed Koreans' natural desires and creative energies for centuries, but in the last few decades they found a degree of freedom and ability to choose that, although minimal by Western standards, has released a tidal wave of energy. Koreans of differing backgrounds have experienced many kinds of *hahn*, which stems from causes as varied as foreign occupation, social immobility, sexual discrimination, family vendettas and—most of all—crushing poverty.

Under the Japanese, the Korean people built up tremendous hatred for the Japanese and a sense of shame at their own subjugation. Today, the *hahn* of past foreign domination translates into extreme nationalism in every sphere of Korean life and mistrust of foreign endeavors on Korean soil. Koreans continue to debate how far to take cooperation with foreign business interests in Korea.

Because Korean society is strictly hierarchical and the upper, middle, and lower classes have been clearly defined, few people in Korea have an opportunity to rise above the social position into which they were born. Nevertheless, Koreans today can distinguish themselves through higher education, financial success, or military advancement and thereby ascend the social ladder. In reaction to the *hahn* of social immobility, common people aspire to higher rank. That is why students study so hard to get accepted to university and why businessmen of humble origin will work twelve or more hours a day.

Until a few decades ago, the vast majority of Koreans were among the poorest people in the world, and they had few opportunities to improve their standard of living. Then, beginning with massive economic growth plans in 1962, the average person could through hard work attain a degree of comfort that in the past had been unimaginable. The *hahn* energy that this opportunity released into the economy resembled a volcano erupting after centuries of pressure.

Two kinds of *hahn* present in the Korean psyche have yet to be fully released: one stems from authoritarian rule, and the other from male dominance. While the energies of *hahn* are apparent in massive street demonstrations against corruption and abuses of power in government, much of the road to true democracy remains to be traveled. Women continue to be second-class citizens with little economic independence or political representation. One wonders not whether, but when and in what form the *hahn* of women's rights will be released into society.

Despite their impressive economic advances, the Korean people still believe themselves to be relatively poor, especially in comparison with their great rival Japan. This inferiority complex is another aspect of *hahn*. By believing themselves to be poor, Koreans muster the energy and zeal that they will need to realize their dream of economic parity with Japan.

CONFUCIANISM

The mentality of modern Koreans is still shaped largely by the teachings of Confucius, who lived in China more than 2,500 years ago. In fact, Korea is more deeply imbued with Confucian habits than any other country, including China. Confucianism is so pervasive that Koreans unconsciously behave in a Confucian manner. To be Korean is essentially to be Confucian.

Confucianism is more of a social code for behavior than it is a religion. The basic tenets of Confucian thought are obedience to and respect for superiors and parents, duty to family, loyalty to friends, humility, sincerity, and courtesy. Confucius identi-

fied five types of relationships, each with very clear duties. They are: ruler to people, husband to wife, parent to child, older to younger, and friend to friend.

Ruler to People In the Confucian view, the ruler commands absolute loyalty and obedience from his people. They are never to question his directives or his motives. In return, the ruler is to be wise and work for the betterment of his people. He should always take their needs and desires into account.

Husband to Wife The Confucian husband rules over his wife as a lord rules over his people. The wife is to be obedient and faithful, and she has a duty to bear her husband sons. The husband has the duty of providing his wife with all the necessities of life.

Parent to Child Children must be loyal to their parents and obey their wishes without question. While the parents must raise and educate their children, the children must care for their parents in old age and always love and respect them.

Older to Younger Respect for age and obedience to all older family members is a key element of the Confucian ethic. Grandparents receive deferential treatment from grandchildren as well as from children.

Friend to Friend The relationship between two friends is the only equal relationship in Confucianism. Friends have a duty to be loyal, trustworthy, and willing to work for each other's benefit. Dishonesty between friends is a social crime and demands punishment.

The Confucian ethic transfers easily into Korea's business environment. In a company, the boss is a ruler and father to his subordinates. Workers have a duty to obey the boss and work diligently to help the company succeed. They are expected to make great self-sacrifices by working overtime without additional pay. In return, the boss must concern himself with the daily affairs of his workers and make sure that all their basic needs are met.

Among coworkers, those of greater status and age command the respect of their juniors. Younger people are expected to defer to their elders in speech and manner by opening doors, being polite, and so on. In return, elders are expected to reward their juniors for work well done and to assure that their subordinates benefit from any personal successes or promotions that they receive.

There is a strong bond among friends in the Korean business world. People who have established mutual trust and respect for each other will work hard to make each other successful. Favors and gifts between friends must constantly be reciprocated.

Confucianism places women in a distinctly inferior role, and Korean business observes the Confucian rule. Women of exceptional skill or talent may achieve some success in business, but not likely. They are usually relegated to subservient positions such as secretary. The result is that women with high levels of education and training are likely to be frustrated in their attempts to find challenging or creative positions in business. In old Korea, women were treated virtually as slaves. Women and men lived in separate quarters, and higher-class women were almost never allowed out of the family compound. While the situation has markedly improved, women are still second-class citizens in Korea.

The main effect of Confucianism on Korean business has been in the development of a strictly hierarchical working environment in which workers are dedicated and industrious. As in most Confucian societies in the Far East, productivity is high, and labor relations are mostly harmonious.

The negative side of Confucianism is that Koreans are extremely conformist and rather uncreative people. Workers fill roles that prohibit new ideas which could challenge the status quo. In this way, the positive and negative aspects of Korean society are perpetuated and strengthened from generation to generation.

KIBUN

Koreans function under an ethic that places the highest premium on harmony and the maintenance of good feelings—*kibun* (pronounced kee-boon) in Korean. *Kibun* is a sort of intuitive feeling for social balance and correct behavior. Koreans try to always maintain a harmonious environment in which a person's *kibun* can stay balanced. They also try never to do anything that could upset another person's *kibun*. Social etiquette and behavior are centered on respect for *kibun*.

Kibun plays an important role in the business environment. For this reason, Koreans are very formal in business relations. On the surface, polite Koreans will always appear to be good-natured and friendly. They will try hard not to say no or deliver bad news. Foreigners interacting with Koreans can have problems if a project runs into difficulty, because no one may want to confess that a problem exists. Instead, managers must learn to read between the lines or interpret subtle hints that a problem has developed.

The good-natured appearance can also be misleading. Koreans are a naturally hot-blooded people with strong convictions. These characteristics conflict with the social demand for harmonious relationships. As a result, personal grudges or dislikes can be kept beneath the surface. An unwitting foreigner could mistake everyday courtesy for true friendliness and work with or confide in someone who really wishes his downfall.

THE FACE FACTOR

The concept of face is closely related to *kibun*. Having face means having a high status in the eyes of one's peers, and it is a mark of personal dignity. Koreans are acutely sensitive to having and maintaining face in all aspects of social and business life. Face can be likened to a prized commodity: it can be given, lost, taken away, or earned. You should always be aware of the face factor in your dealings with Koreans and never do or say anything that could cause someone to lose face. Doing so could ruin business prospects and even invite recrimination.

The easiest way to cause someone to lose face is to insult the individual or to criticize him or her harshly in front of others. Westerners can offend Koreans unintentionally by making fun of them in the good-natured way that is common among friends in the West. Another way to cause someone to lose face is to treat him or her as an underling when his or her official status in an organization is high. People must always be treated with proper respect. Failure to do so makes them and the transgressor lose face for all others aware of the situation.

Just as face can be lost, it can also be given—by praising someone for good work in front of peers or superiors or by thanking someone for doing a good job. Giving someone face earns respect and loyalty, and it should be done whenever the situation warrants. However, it is not a good idea to praise others too much, as it can make you appear to be insincere.

You can also save someone's face by helping him to avoid an embarrassing situation. For example, in playing a game you can allow your opponent to win even if you are clearly the better player. The person whose face you save will not forget the favor, and he will be in your debt.

A person can lose face on his own by not living up to other's expectations, by failing to keep a promise, or by behaving disreputably. Remember in business interactions that a person's face is not only his own but that of the entire organization that he represents. Your relationship with the individual and the respect accorded him is probably the key to your business success in Korea.

IT'S NOT WHAT YOU KNOW . . .

Personal connections are the key element of doing business in Korea. As in other Asian countries, little or no distinction is made between business and personal relationships. This point cannot be overemphasized. To succeed in Korea, you must cultivate close personal ties with business associates and earn their respect and trust. Attempts to establish long-term businesses in the country have often failed because foreigners did not recognize that business relationships were also personal relationships.

Many Koreans reserve trust, respect, and honor only for those people whom they count as personal friends. Foreigners working in Korea tell stories of contracts broken and promises reneged on simply because the Koreans had no qualms about cheating someone foolish enough to enter into a business relationship without having first established a personal relationship. Westerners may have a hard time understanding this attitude.

At the same time, one businessman with extensive experience as the head of a major international business in Korea claims that the services or goods available to the Korean side take precedence over any personal allegiance. "If you've got something they really want," he says, "then you're in good shape."

Clans

The importance of personal connections has its roots in the traditional Korean concept of family. For the Koreans, individuals are parts of the collective family whole. The family is the source of identity, protection, and strength. In times of famine or war, the Korean family structure was a bastion against the outside world, where no one and nothing could be trusted. As a result, trust was reserved for family members and extremely close friends. Through arranged marriages or other means, heads of families could establish connections with other households, thereby strengthening the support system. New connections incorporated psychologically into the family, and they gained (and gave) unequivocal loyalty.

Today, Koreans are safe from the dangers that their ancestors faced, but the tradition of personal connections is as strong as ever. In the business world, the company plays the role of the clan. Those inside the clan work cooperatively and view those outside the clan either as inconsequential or as potential threats. Loyalty is demanded and given within the company, but those on the outside are fair game. What's more, outsiders have no place in the Confucian system of relationships, so the moral obligation of honesty does not apply when a Korean deals with strangers.

To be accepted into a network of personal or business relations in Korea is an honor for foreigners, but it entails responsibility and commitment to the members of the network. It is extremely difficult to be accepted as anything but an outsider unless you are first introduced by a third party and you have excellent business and social credentials.

Even if they have close relationships with the right Koreans, foreigners must never forget that they are foreigners. No amount of Koreafication or time spent in the country will change this. Koreans will almost always identify an expatriate first as a foreigner, second as a businessman, and only then—perhaps—as a friend.

Networking for profit

Korean executives work constantly to maintain and expand their networks of connections. Largely through classmates or family associations, networks extend to other companies and individuals. While the purpose of such contacts is mutual financial profit, the criteria are the same as those for personal networks. Cultivating friendships in business circles is an art learned through practice and close attention to the needs and expectations of others. You form such relationships by doing favors and exemplifying integrity and sincerity.

CULTIVATING RELATIONSHIPS

For the foreign businessman with little or no understanding of Korean behavior, cultivating solid relationships can be the biggest obstacle to success in the country. It is therefore important for a businessperson to spend several months learning the Korean language and culture before going to do business there. A Korean who does not already know a potential business associate will hesitate to do business until he has had time to get acquainted and size up the potential associate's character and intentions. As already mentioned, doing business with strangers in Korea is very dangerous.

Find a Matchmaker

The only good way to make contact with potential Korean business associates is to have a mutual friend serve as an intermediary and introducer. If the third party has close relationships with both sides, they alone may establish preliminary grounds for the conduct business. Anyone who has worked in Korea or who has cooperated with Koreans in the past could be a key source of business contacts. If personal contacts cannot be found, your last recourse may be to hire a consultant based in Seoul who specializes in bringing business interests together.

Meeting the Company

After finding someone to introduce you to a company in Korea, it is imperative that you meet people on the appropriate levels who can make important decisions. These people may well include the company boss, however Korean CEOs are often jealously cloistered by a host of vice presidents and junior executives.

Whomever you meet first, even if he is the head of the company, you will need to meet many more people on many different levels if you want to ensure good relations. Simply going to the top of a company and getting the boss's approval does not mean that everything is taken care of. Indeed, you must also establish good relations with middle- and junior-level managers. If you don't, they may resent you for having bypassed them and feel that their personal integrity has been insulted. Then you are sure to encounter numerous delays and have a vague feeling that someone is working against you.

Patience!

During your first several months in Korea, you may not accomplish more than getting to know several possible candidates for business relationships. Rushing into business before you have established a personal relationship is an invitation to failure. After drawing up a list of possible candidates, take time to evaluate each person carefully. Weigh his strengths and weaknesses before you decide who to follow up on. In future visits, you will learn more about these and other people and gain valuable first-hand experience in the country.

After making your first contacts with businessmen in Korea, be prepared to spend a lot of time deepening and strengthening relationships through visits, dinners, gift giving, and many small favors. While this process can be costly and time-consuming, Koreans appreciate all sincere efforts in this area, and no favor done goes unnoticed. Likewise, keep a running account of all favors done for you, all small gifts received, and the like. The odds are good that you will be expected to reciprocate in the future. Remember this aspect of Korean business culture whenever someone offers you a favor, dinner, or gift. If you absolutely do not want to be in the person's debt, be creative and find some polite excuse for declining the offer. And decline it only if you have no intention of having a relationship, because declining offers can be insulting to Koreans.

Maintain Your Perspective

Finally, foreign businesspeople will benefit from the process of cultivating personal connections by keeping in mind that it gives them an opportunity to learn about the people with whom they are dealing. Getting to know your business associates is practical regardless of your culture. Learning about the personality of an associate can make communication and understanding smoother, and the resulting knowledge can be critical when it comes time to decide how far to take the business relationship.

The Company Face

A foreign business should designate a personable member of the company to act as the face man for the organization in Korea, and that individual should continue to represent the business on a long-term basis—a minimum of three years. Whether they are dealing with a large foreign company or an individual, Koreans like to deal with the same individual, and they treat every interaction as a personal one. Over time, if the business relationship is a success, Ko-

rean associates may come to regard the face man as a close personal friend, and he may earn the personal allegiance of employees. Replacing that individual could jeopardize the business relationship, unless the current representative introduces the new representative and spends at least several months bringing him closer to the Koreans.

Foreign mangers should be older individuals with at least middle-level executive rank who have some experience working with Koreans or Japanese. They should be flexible, patient people who understand that the way to get things done in a foreign country is not always by the book. Before arriving in the country, managers should read up on Asian culture and Confucian ethics in particular. Ideally, they should have at least an elementary command of the Korean language.

Choosing a Partner

Foreign or multinational companies that wish to do business in Korea must establish a joint venture with a Korean company or find an agent to represent their interests. Expatriate executives with years of experience in Korea say that choosing the right people to work with is one of the keys to success in the country.

Although large conglomerates wield tremendous power and influence in the all-important government circles, government policy in recent years has at least nominally favored the growth and development of small and medium-sized companies. It may therefore be more conducive to work with one of these companies than to enter into a venture with a large Korean conglomerate. Smaller companies are more likely to be flexible about remittance of profits in joint ventures, and they may place a greater premium on success in a joint venture than a large conglomerate would. The smaller companies may also tend to be more creative in management techniques and more receptive to foreign input on key operational procedures. Of course, conglomerates can bring more capital and more experienced personnel to a joint venture.

Korean Advisers

Every foreign manager in Korea should have at least one trustworthy and loyal Korean adviser who is well rewarded for his service. Such an adviser will be invaluable from a cultural standpoint in negotiations, employee management, and public relations. Fluency in English and management skill are not the only criteria for a good adviser. The individual whom you hire must have both expertise and social credentials needed to move comfortably within the highest circles of business and government. Age, education, place of birth, and family background are all important to consider.

ASPECTS OF KOREAN BUSINESS

The foreigner who wants to do business in Korea must work diligently to understand many alien concepts related to Korea's business world. In international business, foreigners and Koreans quite often hold contrary views of the goals in a business relationship and the proper ways of attaining them. A foreigner with no appreciation for the Korean view is in for a rude awakening, because Koreans can be very different. This section reviews a few of the basic concepts that need to be grasped.

Corporate Structure Japan-Style

The industrial might of Japan has had a resounding effect on concepts of business in every Asian country, but in none more than it has in Korea. Korea is Japan's closest neighbor and biggest regional competitor. Because Japan dominated Korea for fifty years, older Koreans and many younger ones, too, hold a deep loathing for the Japanese. But at the same time, Korea's business establishment has carefully studied Japan's economic success and incorporated many business practices indigenous to Japan.

One of the most obvious Japanese imports has been the way in which corporations ally in tight coalitions called *chaebol* in Korean. A typical *chaebol* can include producers, distributors, suppliers of finished parts and raw materials, financial institutions, and even trade schools. Large megacorporations, such as Hyundai and Daewoo, are flagship corporations around which subsidiaries and smaller companies gather for security and profit. Quite often, parts suppliers and banks are locked in to such allegiances and work only with other member corporations. International and foreign businesses also often work into such groupings. If successful, these companies gain access to business relations with every other member of the coalition.

On the negative side, the smaller companies in a *chaebol* are likely to be held virtual prisoners to the demands of the larger companies. If they do not comply with their directives, they may encounter payment stoppages, decreased production orders, and any number of coercive measures. Any attempt to cross over and work with a rival *chaebol* invites recrimination and the loss of carefully cultivated relationships.

Contracts

The Korean view of contracts is closely related to the value that Koreans place on personal connections. Koreans rarely use written contracts with each other. Only a verbal agreement between associates who respect one another and who have a close relationship is sufficient. And if a contract is signed, it is no better than the personal relationship between the signatories. Essentially, the contract is a formal acknowledgment of what the parties have already agreed to. Foreigners should under no circumstances assume that a contract is binding, especially if it is not backed by face-to-face personal commitment.

Contracts generally have three distinct phases. First, through close personal interaction, foreign and Korean businessmen arrive at a mutual understanding of the goals and obligations entailed in the potential business endeavor. And at the same time they forge ties of mutual trust and respect. Second, the agreement should be put down on paper and signed by the individuals who will be working together and who have reached a verbal agreement. The written contract should anticipate all future possibilities and state how adjustments are to be made if they are needed. Third, the contract agreements must be monitored and reviewed during the life of the working relationship to make sure all agreements are free of snags and that the situation has not changed to such a degree that the Korean side finds the contract untenable.

If the associates who sign a contract have a long, strong relationship, then the contract is usually workable for as long as the two signatories remain in close cooperation. If a signatory is relocated or if he quits his job, then in all likelihood the Koreans will view the contract as null and void. It must then be renegotiated by new individuals.

In some situations, especially where the ROK government is involved, there is no guarantee that the Korean side will not renege on an agreement. This is one of the major pitfalls of doing business in Korea, which will be discussed further.

The Importance of Status

Koreans are an extremely class-conscious people, and the business world is dominated by members of the power elite. In fact, many movers and shakers in modern Korea are direct descendants of Korean nobles. Individuals lacking the proper social credentials to move in powerful circles are usually locked out forever, so foreign businesspeople must take a Korean's social status into account when they look for a partner or employee.

Businessmen in Korea are so concerned about status that they cannot be sure of how to behave at their first meeting until their relative status has been properly established. For this reason, they may enquire of one another's alma mater, parental lineage, place of birth, and age. Once status has been determined, they behave in a superior-subordinate relationship, with the junior person being exceptionally polite.

Education

In modern Korea, people born into the lower class have only a slim chance of ever rising in social status. The only way is through education, and for this reason young people live under tremendous pressure to perform well in school so that they can be accepted to the best universities. The top university in Korea is Seoul National University (SNU). Graduates of SNU are recruited into the best and biggest corporations in Korea as well as the government. The pressure to be accepted by a prestigious college is so great that, every year after college placement examinations, Korean high school students commit suicide because of poor marks.

Schools are not simply empty signals of status. They are in essence training grounds for the business world where young people develop close relationships that later in life will sustain the networks necessary for business success. When meeting a Korean businessman, be sure to find out his alma mater and year of graduation. The chances are good that former schoolmates will continue to have close relations and be more receptive to foreigners introduced by their classmates.

Nationalism

Korean business is the number one source of national pride in the country. For Korean businessmen, national interests come even before personal profit. It is therefore advantageous to engage in business that will have obvious benefit to the country as a whole. Koreans are very sensitive to the idea of being exploited by foreign interests—a direct result of the Japanese occupation—and business dealings can be ruined if the work is perceived as contrary to the national interest. Business ventures that involve national defense or increased export potential are most likely to be viewed positively, while endeavors to claim domestic market share at the expense of native companies are likely to be derailed either by private business or government intervention.

Militarism

Because Koreans live in constant threat of invasion by the Communist North, the military plays a preeminent role in society. The military heavily influences politics, business, and education. All males in Korea must register for the draft, undergo military training, and serve in the army reserves.

Military training has a direct effect on the structure and guiding philosophies of government and business entities. Businesses and government departments are in essence organized militarily, with clear-cut hierarchies of command. Subordinates are expected to receive and execute commands without question and with the self-sacrifice and commitment that a successful military operation demands.

The military is also a major customer of foreign businesses. Because it plays a very crucial role in the country's security, the military is constantly in need of the latest technology, which can only be found overseas. Six percent of Korea's GNP is devoted to military expenditures, so the army has the funds needed to purchase the very best equipment that money can buy. The arms business is highly lucrative, and companies with close connections to the military often bypass the red tape that can otherwise entangle foreign business efforts.

Sexism

As noted earlier, Korea is a male-dominated society in which women play supportive roles to men. Unfortunately for Western businesswomen, this male chauvinism is not confined to Korean nationals. Foreign women have a tough time being taken seriously in the Korean business environment, and only through hard work and lots of time spent proving herself can a woman hope to be treated as an equal.

There are exceptions to this rule. However, women preparing to do business in Korea must be ready to encounter many difficulties because of their sex. They will have to work harder than men and at the same time do everything they can not to upset male egos. They may even have to transfer credit for a job well done to their male colleagues, and take a back seat in negotiations even if they are in fact the most responsible person in their group. Staying calm and cool in the face of prejudice is of utmost importance.

Working for a Boss, Not a Company

Korean workers are loyal and willing to make extraordinary sacrifices for their employers, but foreigners should not confused these notions with the Western concept of company loyalty. Koreans have no concept of being loyal to a faceless entity but instead define their work relationship in personal terms. Their allegiance lies with the individual people who head the corporation or their particular unit, not the corporation as a whole.

This is true of Koreans working for foreign businesses, and foreign managers should pay close attention to their personal relationships with employees. If the manager quits or returns to the home country, employees will cease to feel any particular allegiance for the business, and they may quit or stop being effective in their work. This is another reason why foreign managers must operate in Korea over the long term if they want to accomplish substantive work.

Passing the Buck

In Korean offices, very few initiatives come from middle management. This may be a result of the conformist nature of Confucian society, but it is probably due as much to fear of punishment if a plan goes awry. For this reason, consensus among all parties involved is important before a certain plan of action is implemented. Consensus is achieved by passing written suggestions around the office place to receive approval from everyone. In this way, if something goes wrong, no individual can be blamed for having made a poor plan.

Foreign managers must take this method of consensus making into account when they want to implement new policies or management techniques. It is a good idea to circulate a new plan as a suggestion and win people's enthusiasm first, then to allow the plan to be directed down the hierarchy from top to bottom. In this way, employees will feel a unity in decision making and at the same time be free from personal responsibility. Attempts to impose individual responsibility on Korean employees are likely to meet with resistance.

Cooking the Books

Accounting practices are highly irregular in Korean businesses. It is common for companies to juggle financial figures so that they always show a profit at year's end. Government-related businesses cook the books to avoid being investigated by ministries; investigations could result in a company's collapse or the replacement of top-level personnel. Private businesses may falsify records to make the company appear to be in good shape and maintain investor and consumer confidence. Foreign businesses looking for a joint venture partner or agent should be extremely careful when checking on a potential associate's financial viability.

"GIFTS"

Gift giving is an honored tradition in all Asian cultures, but in Korea the tradition has transformed into what can only be called bribery. Corruption and graft are the modus operandi of getting things done in Korea, and most foreign businesspeople in the country are likely to have to play the game or quit.

While presenting a legitimate gift to a company is standard operating practice, substantive "gifts" of money given to individuals in the company are what really grease the wheels for many business agreements. Because bribery is a sensitive subject, there is very little authoritative material in print on how to give a bribe and how much to give. Knowledgeable foreigners are understandably reticent to provide details that might be self-incriminating.

Bribes may be solicited by company executives, government officials, or military officers. However, most likely the need for a bribe will be inferred in conversation. Amounts are up to the discretion of the giver and depend on the value of the impending business deal. Normally, foreign businesspeople do not give the "gift" directly, but rely instead on Korean intermediaries, such as consultants or joint venture partners, to carry out the delicate process.

Bribery is so ingrained in Korean business that few offenders are ever caught, and if they are punishment is very light. However, many countries have laws prohibiting their nationals from such behavior. The US Foreign Corrupt Practices Law, which prohibits payments or gifts in excess of US$50, is a prime example. It is worthy of note that the American law pertains only to payments made to get someone to do something that he otherwise would not do. It does not pertain to payments made to speed up or facilitate movement which in absence of such payment would only be delayed.

Since 1980, the Korean government has stepped up campaigns to curb corruption, but its success has been limited. The new Kim Young Sam government has vowed to end official corruption. Only time will tell whether its efforts prove successful.

BIG BROTHER

The ROK government has for decades been closely allied with the business community, and foreign businesspeople operating in the country are bound to come into close contact with one or more government entities. Government policies are designed to protect and nurture national companies, often at the expense of free trade principles. For this reason, foreign companies are effectively excluded from many areas of the Korean economy, including consumer marketing of foreign products and decisive control over joint venture operations. In order to eliminate foreign competition in Korea, the government may impose import or export restrictions even after goods are on the dock, deny licensing applications, stop payments for goods or services already rendered, or invalidate contracts deemed contrary to the national interest.

The Korean government's red tape is legendary. The number of documents that one needs for government approval to do business can be ten times the number necessary in Western countries, and even after you have them there is no guarantee that anything can be accomplished. Usually several ministries and subdepartments with very little lateral interaction will be drawn into a proposed foreign business operation. For example, on a single construction project, a foreign company may need to get approval from the Ministry of Construction, the Ministry of Finance (for the transfer of foreign exchange), the Ministry of Science and Technology (if there is a technology transfer), and the Ministry of Trade and Industry (if imports are to be involved). In addition, any signed contract is open to review and veto by one or more persons within each ministry. Individual officials can sometimes have drastically different ideas of how and to what extent Korea should work with foreign businesses, and bureaucrats will try to revise draft agreements to maximize the benefit to the Korean side.

These obstacles to fair trade can be difficult to deal with, but they are not insurmountable for a savvy person with the right relationships. Nothing is handled by blanket policies. Instead, everything is handled on a highly individual and personal basis. It is therefore of paramount importance to maintain good relations with every person involved in a business deal, ranging from top business executives to middle-level managers and government officials. Business is bound to be much smoother if all those involved already have a working relationship and if they have proved mutually beneficial to one another in the past. Significant "gifts" may well be called for.

The MOF and Other Ministries

Korea's Ministry of Finance (MOF) is the most powerful ministry dealing with foreign business concerns in the country. Among other areas, the MOF controls taxation, import and export tariffs, foreign exchange regulations, and government accounting. It behooves the foreign businessperson in Korea to become familiar with the MOF's functions and its various subdepartments. It is also a good idea to work with Korean businesspeople who are in good standing with the MOF and who have good relations with MOF officials on a personal basis. Likewise, close relations with the Ministry of Trade and Industry (MTI) and the Bank of Korea can expedite government approval of a foreign enterprise.

Reform and Intransigence

Korea's political winds recently changed course when Kim Young Sam was elected president on a platform advocating clean government and fairness in business. In conjunction with significant pressure from foreign governments, such as the United States, Korea is lowering import tariffs, dropping bans on certain foreign goods, and making repatriation of profits easier.

But although the highest levels of government seem committed to reform, the bureaucracy is filled with conservative-minded officials who care not a whit for Kim's efforts. They see freer trade as a threat to the national interest, and they will go to great lengths to prevent the implementation of open-door policies. Customs officials often reclassify products coming into the country and thereby raise tariffs to unacceptable levels, or they slow paperwork to a crawl to make costly delays.

Mr. Kim Goes to the Blue House

For three decades, South Korea was ruled by a string of general/politicians known for their paternalistic attitudes, intolerance to opposition, and entrenched interests in the military and big business. These nominally retired military men fostered economic growth while stifling meaningful progress towards full democracy.

But in early 1993, Kim Young Sam, a former opposition leader with no military background, became President of Korea. Though elected on the long-ruling Liberal Democratic Party's ticket, Kim promises to bring a new attitude to government, promoting greater democracy and cracking down on widespread bribery and corruption. Three ministers were forced to resign for influence-peddling, and notice has been served that huge conglomerates such as Hyundai and Daewoo must make room for small- and medium-sized competitors in the marketplace.

So far, Kim appears to have support among the working class, but he faces great opposition from fat-cats in the military and business who have grown rich off decades of doing things through the back door. In his own party, hard-liners who would prefer the old-style way of doing things work behind the scenes to discredit Kim's liberal policies and to secure decisive influence over his presidency. The military establishment is certainly upset with the new openness in the press, which reported that two high-ranking officers made over US $400,000 apiece by selling promotions to junior officers.

Kim has until the 1996 elections to prove he is earnest in cleaning up Korea's business environment, controlling inflation, and ushering in a stable age of pluralism in politics. And, most importantly, the country needs to maintain positive economic growth which is the measuring stick of political success. Otherwise, Kim's noble aspirations will be for naught, and in all likelihood the country will return to the system of corruption and elitism which has defined the Korean way of doing things.

MEETING THE KOREANS

Trade Delegations

There are a few important points to remember when you send a trade delegation to Korea. First, keep in mind that the Koreans are a group-oriented people and that they are more comfortable functioning as members of a group than as individuals. Generally, they assume that this is true of all people. They are confused when members of a visiting group speak as individuals and make statements that are contradictory or inconsistent with the stated views of the group as a whole. Individual opinions are not wanted. Therefore, every trade delegation should have a designated speaker, who is also its most senior member. Koreans will look to that member for all major communication and accept his words as the words of the entire organization.

Koreans are really concerned about the status that an individual holds in a company or organization. They will evaluate the seriousness of a trade delegation by the rank of its members, and a delegation is not likely to succeed if the Koreans know that its head is a junior executive. Likewise, they will wish to match your delegation with executives of similar status from their own organization. It is wise to send them a list of the delegates who will attend that gives their ranks in the company and to request that they do the same. If the Korean company sends someone to a meeting who is obviously of lower rank, the chances are that it is not particularly interested in you or that it is unaware of the status of the members of your delegation.

Arranging the Meeting

Business meetings in Korea are conducted formally, and Westerners should always arrange the time and place well in advance. Before the meeting, you should mail or fax a document outlining the matter to be discussed in as much detail as possible. This will give the Koreans time to discuss the matter among themselves and send an appropriate reply. While the Koreans are reticent to deny a meeting outright, their response may send signals indicating their degree of interest in your offer, and they may send no reply at all if they are not interested. Another way of arranging a meeting is to enlist the aid of a Korean agent in feeling out potential partners. An experienced agent with the right credentials will already have many contacts in the business world that may be of real use.

Shaking and Bowing

When meeting Korean businesspeople, foreigners should display sincerity and respect. Handshaking, imported from the West, is generally the accepted form of salutation, though in very formal situations bowing is still used. Westerners should bow to older Korean people unaccustomed to foreign ways. If you are not sure whether to bow or shake hands, allow the Korean side to take the initiative. Usually Koreans will shake hands firmly, sometimes with two hands as an expression of particularly warm feelings.

Among Koreans, the bow is still common. There are different grades of bows, as there are among the Japanese. Those of higher or more senior status bow less deeply, and subordinates bow quite deeply. Westerners may be able to determine the relative status of Korean associates by observing the depth of their bows.

Business Cards

The first time you meet, handshakes or bows are followed by a ritualistic exchange of business cards. Foreigners should always carry an ample supply of business cards, preferably with English text on one side and Korean on the other. A business card should include name, company, and a title that can give the Koreans some idea of the person's relative status within the company.

The proper procedure for exchanging business cards is to give and receive cards with both hands. hold the card by the corners between thumb and forefinger. On receiving a card, do not simply pocket it immediately, but take a few moments to study the card and what it says. The business card represents the person who is giving it, and it should be given respect accordingly.

When two Koreans are meet for the first time and are unsure of their relative status, they exchange cards before bowing. If the cards are too vague, they may first ask one another's age, company position, or alma mater. Only after determining who is superior and who is subordinate will they bow.

Letters of Introduction

Presenting letters of introduction from well-known business leaders, overseas Koreans, or former government officials who have dealt with Korea is an excellent way of showing both that you are a person of high standing and that you mean business. The Koreans are very concerned about social standing, and anything that you can do to enhance their regard for you is a plus. But be careful not to appear arrogant or haughty, as Confucian morality condemns such behavior.

Appropriate Dress

Koreans are very formal dressers and usually wear three-piece suits in business interactions. A Westerner may be judged by the quality of his suit, so you should wear the best clothes that you can. Although it may sound trite, it is a fact that your

Korean counterpart will notice your gold adornments, such as rings or watches, and will include them in his evaluation of your person. Excessively heavy or gaudy jewelry is, of course, to be avoided.

Names and Forms of Address

In Korean, an individual's family name precedes a generational name and his or her personal name. For example, Kim Young Sam's family name is Kim, his generational name is Young, and his personal name is Sam. All his male siblings will have the same generational name Young, and all his female siblings will have another generational middle name. Because Koreans formerly used Chinese characters in their writing, each syllable in a person's name is represented by a single Chinese character.

While there are hundreds of family names in Korea, more than half of all Koreans are named Kim, Lee, Park, or Choi. This can be extremely confusing for foreigners and Koreans alike, especially in large companies where there may be hundreds of people with the same family name. Knowing how to hail the right Mr. Lee is further complicated by the fact that people outside the family almost never address each other by their personal names, even if they are very close.

To minimize the confusion, Koreans in the workplace are referred to by positions and department. For example, a manager in the accounting office will be referred to as Manager Lee of Accounting. Another common form of address is to use a person's designated position in society. For example, a teacher with the last name Kim may be referred to as Teacher Kim. This form of address also applies to government officials.

Language Obstacles

It is fortunate for foreigners operating in Korea that English is widely used by upper-level managers and government officials. English is not only recognized as the lingua franca of international commerce, but fluency in the language is both a status symbol and a prerequisite for university education. Also, thousands of Koreans have been educated in English-speaking countries and returned to take up key positions in business.

However, workers and lower-level functionaries are not likely to possess more than a smattering of English. This is another reason why foreigners should have trusted bilingual Korean advisers, who can be valuable in fostering close relationships between managers and employees.

Being an extremely nationalistic people, Koreans have mixed feelings toward foreigners who speak their language. Nationals appreciate Westerners who speak rudimentary, polite Korean, but they may sometimes regard foreigners whose Korean is too good as intrusive. Quite often, Koreans speak to one another casually over a matter foreigners are meant not to understand, and they will feel embarrassed or uncomfortable if a foreigner overhears. Thus, while it is an asset to learn as much Korean as you can, it may not be advisable to let the Korean side know what you understand. Understanding without reacting can be important if information is being withheld from your side.

NEGOTIATING WITH KOREANS

Koreans have a reputation for being extremely difficult to negotiate with. As mentioned earlier, outsiders are considered fair game. Many experienced businesspeople comment that the Korean approach to negotiations is that the end result justifies any means necessary. Foreigners should therefore be extremely cautious when negotiating in Korea. They should be prepared for intimidation, unrealistic promises, and other negotiation strategies designed to get the best deal possible for the Korean side. Some observers have said that Koreans may also feel that they deserve the better side of the deal when they negotiate with foreigners from richer, more developed nations.

These are a few key points to remember when negotiating with Koreans:

Never let the Korean side know when you plan to leave the country. Koreans are notorious for delaying substantive negotiations until a delegation's last day in Korea and then pressing for unreasonable agreements. A foreign group should try to reserve several plane departure dates, and be willing to stay in the country longer than anticipated.

Know as much as you can about the Korean side. Know the individuals with whom you are negotiating and their relations within their company. In this way, you can gauge their degree of up-front decision-making ability. Try also to know whom they know in government circles to get an idea of how much big brother pressure they can bring to bear on your organization.

Know your own products or assets thoroughly. If you have something that the Koreans want badly and that they cannot get elsewhere, you are in a position of strength. Let the Koreans know what you have to offer and present it as invaluable to their interests.

Stay calm, and be patient. The Koreans will use any number of means to confuse your position and wear you down. They negotiate in teams, and they are prepared for long-drawn-out negotiations, knowing that when you are tired you will make mistakes. Stay alert.

Be willing to walk away. If the Koreans know that you are anxious to make a deal, they will increase their demands. Instead, let them know that no deal is far more acceptable than a bad deal.

Never give something away for nothing. On even the smallest points, the Koreans will view concessions that you mean as a sign of good faith as a sign of weakness. Every agreement must be reached by give and take.

Finally, be aware that even after you have cut a deal, the Koreans are likely to delay and maneuver for a better deal. Sometimes a Korean delegation will sign a contract knowing full well that they have no intention of honoring it. Further negotiations will probably be necessary.

A FINAL NOTE

The preceding discussion of Korean business ethics, practices, and etiquette is full of negative examples and warnings that Koreans can be hard people to work with. Nevertheless, very many foreign companies working in Korea have been extraordinarily successful. In general, the business environment in Korea is good. Of the newly industrialized countries of the Far East, Korea has the cheapest wages, a well-educated work force, and a burning national desire to progress. A well-prepared foreign business with open-minded personnel and high-demand products or services is likely to succeed in Korea.

This discussion is by no means complete, and interested persons will profit greatly by referring to two other publications on business customs in Korea.

The Business Climate in Korea, by the American Chamber of Commerce in Korea. $200. (Available from the American Chamber of Commerce in Korea, Document Sales Department, Room #307, Westin Chosun Hotel, Seoul 100.)

Although this book is quite pricey, it contains up-to-date information compiled by hundreds of expatriate businesspeople operating in Korea. Full of personal anecdotes, it examines most major aspects of working in Korea from a foreign business perspective and includes valuable information on banking, taxation, government controls, business formation, and culture.

Korean Etiquette and Ethics in Business, by Boye De Menthe. Lincolnwood, Ill.: NTC Business Books, 1988. ISBN #0-8442-8522-6 $14.95.

Demographics

AT A GLANCE

The figures given here are the best available, but sources vary in comprehensiveness, in definition of categories, and in reliability. Sources include the United Nations, the World Bank, the International Monetary Fund, and the Korean government. The value of demographics lies not just in raw numbers but in trends, and the trends illustrated here are accurate.

POPULATION GROWTH RATE AND PROJECTIONS

Average annual growth rate

1970-80	1980-91	1991-2000
1.8	1.1	0.8

Age structure of population (percent)

	1990	2025
Under 15 years old	26%	18.2%
15 - 64 years old	66%	66.6%
Over 64 years old	8%	15.2%

POPULATION

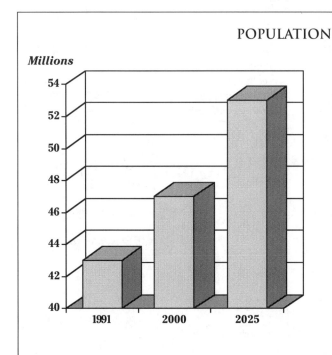

Millions

| | 1991 | 2000 | 2025 |

Male **(1990):**	21,782,154
Female **(1990):**	21,628,745
TOTAL:	**43,410,899**

Population density per square km

1992	439.7

Urban population (% of total)

	Urban	Rural
1960	28	72
1970	41	59
1980	57	43
1991	73	27

PRINCIPAL CITIES

(1990 census)

Seoul	10,612,577
Pusan	3,798,113
Taegu	2,229,040
Inchon	1,817,919
Kwangju	1,139,003
Taejon	1,049,578
Ulsan	682,411
Suwon	644,805
Songnam	540,754
Chonju	517,059
Masan	493,731
Chongju	477,783
Chinju	255,695
Mokpo	243,064
Cheju	232,643
Kunsan	218,205
Chunchon	174,224
Yosu	173,169

POPULATION BY AGE & SEX, 1990

Age	Total	Male	Female
All ages	42,793,000	21,564,000	21,229,000
birth - 1	684,000	355,000	329,000
1 - 4	2,632,000	1,374,000	1,259,000
5 - 9	3,803,000	1,978,000	1,825,000
10 - 14	3,950,000	2,036,000	1,913,000
15 - 19	4,468,000	2,303,000	2,166,000
20 - 24	4,368,000	2,251,000	2,117,000
25 - 29	4,224,000	2,160,000	2,064,000
30 - 34	4,056,000	2,069,000	1,987,000
35 - 39	3,057,000	1,607,000	1,450,000
40 - 44	2,511,000	1,288,000	1,223,000
45 - 49	2,208,000	1,128,000	1,080,000
50 - 54	2,048,000	1,023,000	1,024,000
55 - 59	1,601,000	754,000	847,000
60 - 64	1,156,000	494,000	662,000
65 - 69	872,000	356,000	516,000
70 - 74	559,000	212,000	347,000
75 - 79	345,000	113,000	232,000
80 +	249,000	60,000	189,000

VITAL STATISTICS

Live births	1991	671,000
Birth rate		
(per 1,000 persons)	1970	30
	1991	15.5
Child mortality rate		
(per 1,000 births)	1960	33.3
	1975	29
	1990	10
Deaths	1991	251,000
Death rate		
(per 1,000 persons)	1970	9
	1991	5.8
Life expectancy at birth	1960	53
	1970	63
	1980	66
	1990	72
	2000	74
Marriages	1989	309,872
Rate per 1,000		7.3
Divorces	1989	32,474
Rate per 1,000		0.8
Fertility rate	1970	4.3%
	1991	1.8%
	2000	1.8%
Women of childbearing age		
(% of all women)	1965	46%
	1991	57%

EDUCATION, 1992

Category	Institutions	Teachers	Enrollment
Kindergarten	8,498	21,107	450,882
Primary schools	6,122	138,880	4,560,128
Intermediate schools	2,539	95,330	2,336,284
High schools	1,735	96,342	2,125,573
Junior vocational colleges	125	8,518	404,996
Junior teachers' colleges	11	719	16,504
Universities, colleges	121	37,287	1,070,169
Graduate schools	335	N.A.	96,577

THE AGING POPULATION OF KOREA

Those 65 and over (in millions):

	Number	% of total
1970	1.04	3.0
1980	1.46	3.8
1985	1.75	4.3
1990	2.14	5.0
1995	2.54	5.7
2000	3.17	6.8

MANUFACTURING WAGES

Monthly, in thousands of won

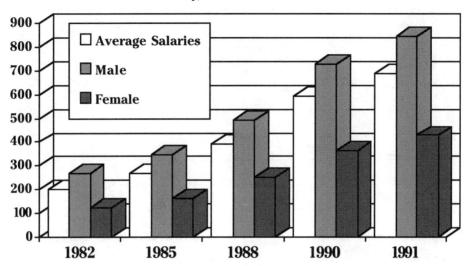

NATIONAL INCOME

GNP per capita, US$

1975	590
1987	3,098
1988	4,040
1989	4,994
1990	5,659
1991	6,498

Average annual growth rate 1980-91: 8.7 percent

SPENDING PATTERNS

(percentage of total household consumption)

Category	1989	1990	1991
Food, beverages and tobacco	7.6	6.8	6.2
Clothing and footwear	4.2	7.0	4.9
Rent, utilities, fuel	5.5	10.0	8.2
Household furnishings, equipment & maintenance	9.2	12.9	10.8
Medical care & health	14.9	14.4	11.9
Transport & communications	14.4	14.8	12.7
Education, recreation, entertainment	11.3	9.3	9.4
Other	15.8	11.9	11.2

AVERAGE HOUSEHOLD INCOME AND EXPENSES

in won (millions)

Category	1986	1987	1988	1989	1990
Income	687	833	1,008	1,348	1,608
Expenses	332	380	443	562	650
Food	34	35	37	38	41
Housing	16	17	19	23	30
Utilities	23	24	25	26	29
Household durable goods	17	21	25	33	38
Clothing	26	30	37	48	55
Medical care	19	20	24	31	34
Education, recreation	36	42	49	67	77
Transp., commun.	21	26	32	46	55
Other	53	65	78	105	121

Korea
Consumer Price Index (CPI)

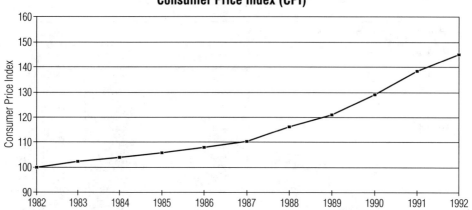

Consumer Price Increases

Average **1970-80**	20.1%
Average **1975-84**	14.6%
1985	1.8%
1986	2.1%
1987	2.4%
1988	5.8%
1989	5.0%
1990	7.9%
1991	9.3%
1992	6.8%

Price Index by Category (1985 = 100)

Category	1989	1990	1991
Food	124	137	151
Housing	122	135	152
Utilities and fuel	98	99	105
Furniture and utensils	118	125	136
Clothing and footwear	129	142	152
Medical care	117	126	131
Education and recreation	123	136	148
Transportation and communication	109	113	126
All categories	120	130	142

COMMUNICATION CHANNELS

Newspapers

	Circulation (millions)			Per 1,000 persons		
	1979	**1986**	**1988**	**1979**	**1986**	**1988**
	6.50	8.65	10.43	29	35	39

Televisions and radios

	Number (millions)			Per 1,000 Persons		
	1980	**1985**	**1989**	**1980**	**1985**	**1989**
TVs	6.30	7.72	8.80	165	189	207
Radios	20.00	38.60	42.57	525	946	1,003

Telephones

	Number (millions)			Per 100 Persons		
	1980	**1987**	**1990**	**1980**	**1987**	**1990**
	3.39	10.73	15.74	9	26	37

Books

	1987	1988	1989	1991*
Titles	44,288	42,842	39,267	22,770
Copies	170,814	178,522	193,138	134,616

* New and revised titles only; previous years include reprints

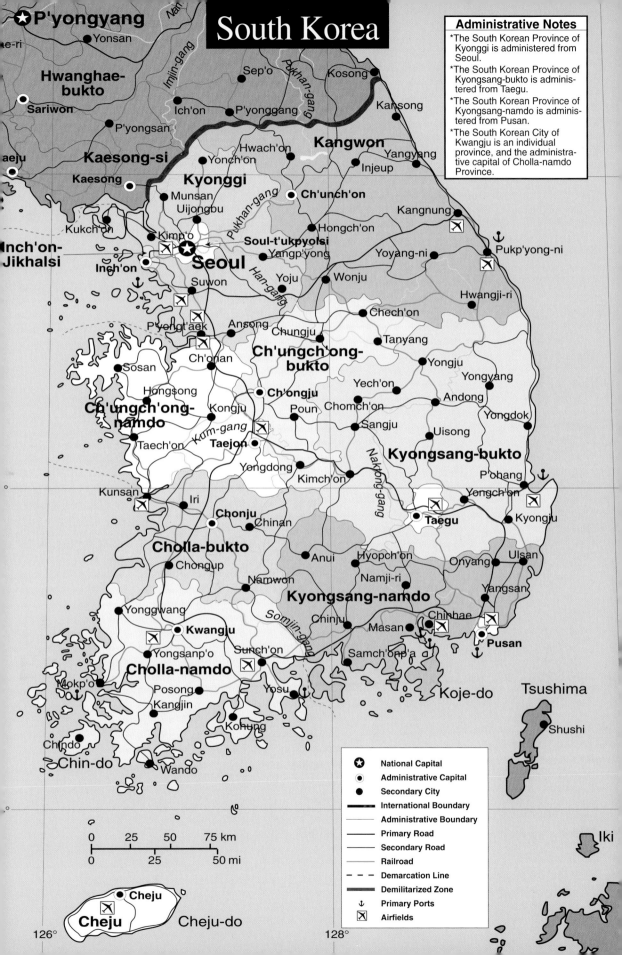

South Korea

P'yongyang
Yonsan
-ri

Hwanghae-
bukto
Sariwon
P'yongsan

Nan
Imjin-gang
Sep'o
Ich'on
P'yonggang
Kosong

Kansong

Kangwon

Pukhan-gang

-aeju
Kaesong-si
Kaesong

Hwach'on
Yonch'on
Yangyang
Injeup

Kyonggi
Ch'unch'on
Kangnung

Kukch'on
Munsan
Uijongbu
Hongch'on
Yoyang-ni
Pukp'yong-ni

Kimp'o
Soul-t'ukpyolsi
Inch'on-
Jikhalsi
Inch'on
Seoul
Yangp'yong
Wonju
Hwangji-ri

Suwon
Yoju
Chech'on

Pyongt'aek
Ansong
Chungju
Tanyang

Ch'onan
Ch'ungch'ong-
bukto
Yongju
Yongyang

Sosan
Yech'on
Andong

Hongsong
Ch'ongju
Chomch'on
Yongdok

Ch'ungch'ong-
namdo
Kongju
Poun
Sangju
Uisong

Taech'on
Kum-gang
Taejon
Kyongsang-bukto

Yongdong
Kimch'on
P'ohang
Yongch'on

Kunsan
Iri
Chinan
Nakdong-gang
Taegu
Kyongju

Chonju

Cholla-bukto
Anui
Hyopch'on
Onyang
Ulsan

Chongup
Namji-ri
Yangsan

Namwon
Kyongsang-namdo

Yonggwang
Chinju
Chinhae
Pusan

Kwangju
Masan

Yongsanp'o
Sunch'on
Somjin-gang
Samch'onp'a
Koje-do
Tsushima

Cholla-namdo
Shushi

Mokp'o
Posong
Yosu

Kangjin

Kohung

Ch'indo
Wando

Chin-do

Iki

0 25 50 75 km	
0 25 50 mi	

Cheju
Cheju
Cheju-do

126°
128°

Legend

⊛ National Capital
◉ Administrative Capital
● Secondary City
━━ International Boundary
── Administrative Boundary
── Primary Road
── Secondary Road
── Railroad
- - - Demarcation Line
▓▓▓ Demilitarized Zone
↓ Primary Ports
⊠ Airfields

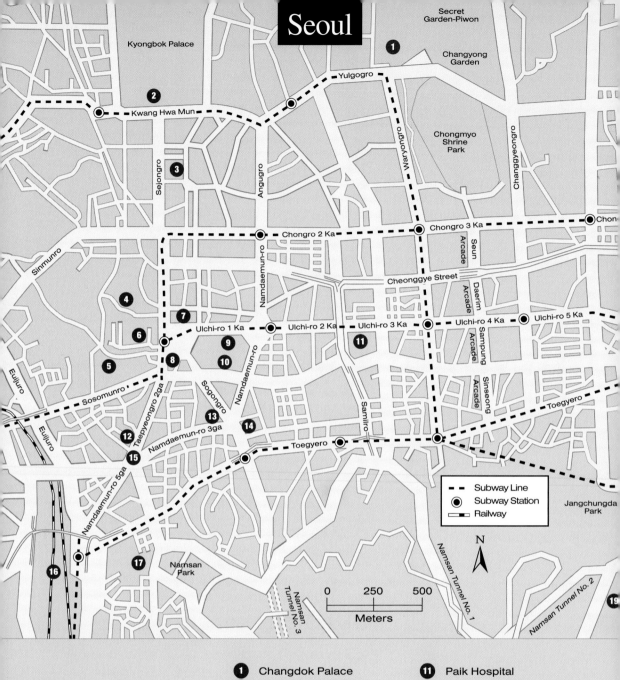

Seoul

Secret Garden-Piwon

Kyongbok Palace

Changyong Garden

Chongmyo Shrine Park

Yulgogro

Kwang Hwa Mun

Sejongro

Angugro

Waryongro

Changgyeongro

Chongro 3 Ka

Chon

Chongro 2 Ka

Namdaemun-ro

Cheonggye Street

Seun Arcade

Daerim Arcade

Sinmunro

Ulchi-ro 1 Ka

Ulchi-ro 2 Ka

Ulchi-ro 3 Ka

Ulchi-ro 4 Ka

Ulchi-ro 5 Ka

Sampung Arcade

Sinseong Arcade

Namdaemun-ro

Sosomunro

Eujiro

Eujiro

Taepyeongro 2ga

Sogongro

Namdaemun-ro 3ga

Samiro

Toegyero

Toegyero

Jangchungda Park

Namdaemun-ro 5ga

Namsan Park

Namsan Tunnel No. 3

Namsan Tunnel No. 1

Namsan Tunnel No. 2

N

- - -	Subway Line
⊙	Subway Station
▭	Railway

0   250   500
Meters

1. Changdok Palace
2. National Museum
3. American Embassy
4. British Embassy
5. Ministry of Justice Immigration Department
6. Toksu Palace
7. City Hall
8. Plaza Hotel
9. Hotel Lotte
10. Westin Chosun Hotel
11. Paik Hospital
12. Korea Chamber of Commerce and Industry
13. Bank of Korea
14. Central Post Office
15. South Gate (Namdaemun)
16. Seoul Railway Station
17. Hilton Hotel
18. Hotel Shilla
19. Seoul Club

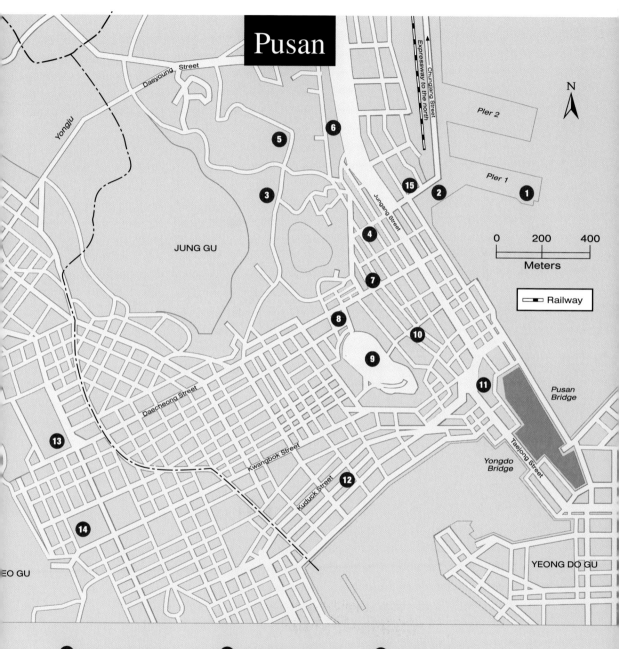

Pusan

JUNG GU

SEO GU

YEONG DO GU

Pier 2

Pier 1

Pusan Bridge

Yongdo Bridge

Daeyoung Street

Yongju

Chunjang Street

Expressway to the north

Jungang Street

Daecheong Street

Kwangbok Street

Kuduck Street

Taejong Street

N

0   200   400
Meters

Railway

1. Ferry Terminal
2. Customs House
3. Mary-Noll Hospital
4. Bando Hotel
5. Commodore Hotel
6. Police Bureau
7. Sorabul Hotel
8. Bank of Korea
9. Yongdoosan Park
10. Busan Hotel
11. City Hall
12. Phoenix Hotel
13. Court
14. Busan University Hospital
15. Busan Trade Center

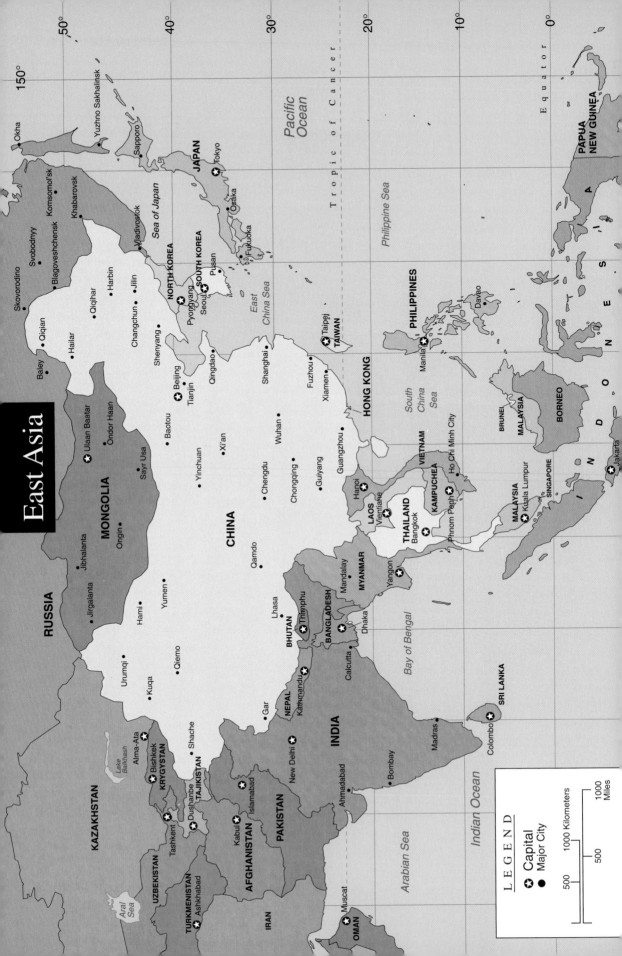

HEALTH

Health expenditures (**1990**):   US$16.1 billion
        Per capita: US$377.00

Health expenditures as a percentage of GDP (**1990**):

Total:	6.6
Public:	2.7
Private:	3.9

Population per doctor:

1970	**1990**
2,220	1,370

Tobacco consumption per year (kilograms per capita adult)

1974-76	**1990**	**2000**
2.4	2.9	3.5

Licensed medical personnel and pharmacists

Category	1988	1989	1990
Physicians	36,845	39,769	42,554
Dentists	7,657	8,630	9,619
Oriental medical doctors	4,932	5,435	5,792
Midwives	7,167	7,397	7,643
Nurses	76,143	82,657	89,032
Nursing aides	123,115	128,867	135,714
Technicians	37,889	43,725	57,224
Pharmacists	34,344	35,756	37,118
TOTAL	**328,092**	**352,236**	**384,696**

NUTRITION

Calories			% of Calorie Requirement			Protein (grams)		
1980	1986	1990	1967/70	1980	1984/6	1980	1986	1990
2,767	2,852	2,840	102	129	122	75	76	79

RELIGION (1989)

Religion or Belief	Number (in millions)	% of Total Religious Population
Buddhism	8.1	19.1
Protestantism	6.5	15.3
Catholicism	1.9	4.5
Confucianism	0.5	1.2
Others	0.3	0.7
Nonreligious	25.2	59.2
TOTAL	**42.5**	**100.0**

ENERGY CONSUMPTION

(kilograms per capita of coal equivalent)

1980	1988	1990
1,349	2,097	2,495

MOTOR VEHICLES IN USE

(in thousands)

	1982	1985	1988	1990	1991
Passenger	306	557	1,118	2,075	2,727
Commercial	294	541	895	1,308	1,505

Marketing

Selling to South Korea isn't as difficult as tales of woe from veterans might make it seem. True, Korea's fraudulently unscientific food inspection rules can keep a shipment of raisins drying up in customs for nine months. And when Korea let down its import barriers in 1991 it also expanded the list of imports that must have both factory and retail prices displayed on store shelves—a ridiculous rule that doesn't exactly inspire consumers to buy imported products.

Yes, selling to South Korea is easy in theory. However, there are import barriers, a huge language barrier, obstructive bureaucrats, nontransparent regulations (laws hidden from foreigners just in case they're thinking of violating them), and octopus-like conglomerate monopolies that can stop a less-than-obsessively-committed salesperson dead in their tracks. Nevertheless, all along the way, you'll find knowledgeable, experienced people whose job it is to help you wend your way through the mazes constructed by the knowledgeable, experienced people whose job it is to get you lost.

You don't need to spend a fortune on marketing to learn if there is a market. You can find that out in very little time at very low cost from a variety of sources. This book is one, and others include your own embassy, trade associations, and even Korea's own government trade agency, the Korea Trade Promotion Corporation (KOTRA). You don't need to learn a foreign language. You must, however, take into account the cultural nuances that make one country different from another.

You will need to keep your initial costs as low as possible—probably through direct sales—until you have established a toehold. You need to adapt your product to local requirements and laws; most of the time that adaptation will be minimal. You must go overboard to service your orders *immediately*, and you must answer your faxes *immediately*. Above all your company must make a genuine commitment to export, because otherwise your worst problems will come from within, not from abroad. Export sales generate a momentum of their own that is hard to stop, and once they get going they pull along repeat business, new accounts, and offers from people eager to be your agent or partner.

HOW TO ENTER THE KOREAN MARKET

Because South Korea is so poor in natural resources, it will always have a need for raw materials, its main import. It also continues to bring in large amounts of advanced machinery in an effort to upgrade its industry. But one of the fastest-growing segments of its import market is consumer goods. The wealthier Koreans get, the more consumer goods they demand. This is a demand that Korea itself can't meet. Korean's are eating more processed food, stocking up on reference and educational books, becoming more interested in health and fitness, and buying more cars, computers, software, color television sets, videocassette recorders, stereo systems, refrigerators, washing machines, and microwave ovens. Although small one-family stores and stalls in markets on narrow side streets still dominate retail trade in consumer goods, more Koreans are shopping at midrange and upscale department stores and boutiques; they're traveling more, and they're using credit cards more frequently both as payment instruments and to finance purchases. More of their consumer goods are being imported, and there is more travel to foreign countries—this despite the government's xenophobic reactions to foreign goods on store shelves and its threats of tax audits against Koreans traveling abroad who try to bring back too many foreign purchases.

Profitable export to Korea requires a well-laid marketing plan, and there are several marketing agencies in Korea that can help, including foreign affiliates, partners, and subsidiaries. But distribution is a different story. Although there are four major recognized ways for a foreign manufacturer to gain access to the Korean market—via the use of an agent, a branch office, a joint venture, and a subsidiary—only two major channels dominate distribution: registered traders and offer agents.

Registered traders are government-licensed importers and wholesalers who buy and sell for their own accounts. These traders handle all imported merchandise, with three exceptions: goods imported in connection with foreign private investment; goods imported by selected associations and organizations established under special laws; and goods purchased through official government procurement procedures.

A registered trading firm has an advantage over an offer agent because it can handle the paperwork of importing and can also import for its own account. A disadvantage is that trading firms import and export a wide range of goods from many firms in many countries, and they may not be able to give your product the import attention and market support it deserves and requires. This is especially true of the larger firms. On the other hand, the biggest traders, some affiliates of the *chaebol*, wield considerable influence in trading circles. Their size also allows them to extend credit to importers—which is very hard to get in Korea—or to vouch for you and your product. Another plus is that some firms are foreign based and somewhat more sympathetic. These include firms from Japan, the United States, and several European countries.

Offer agents act as representatives of foreign firms and make offers on their behalf. They can import in their own names only if they are also registered traders or if they pay a registered trader a fee for the privilege of using its authorization. Many of these agencies are branches or liaison offices of foreign firms, including US, Hong Kong, and Japanese companies. Most offer agencies are small enough to give sufficient time and attention to your needs. However, they don't often have the influence and connections on the scale found among the large trading firms.

The Korean distribution system is in a state of upheaval. Korea threw its doors open to imports only in 1991, and ever since foreign firms have been filling vacuums created by the monopolistic, inefficient systems built up by the Korean *chaebol*. The trading firms and offer agents still dominate distribution—except in the common instance in which Korean manufacturers exclusively franchise their products or operate their own retail stores—but, while the horror stories you may have heard about exporting to Korea may be real, they may also be dated. It is true that foreign companies, fed up with Korean obstructionism, cut their investment in Korea by one-third between 1991 and 1992. But reforms enacted that same year that should be fully in force by January 1, 1994, meaning that you should investigate

anew before you decide against exporting. You will likely find that Korean law is breaking the stranglehold of the *chaebol* and that foreign traders are gradually driving the antiquated Korean distribution system into either radical change or into distributor's oblivion.

Initial Strategies

Before you even consider which of these distribution systems or market access routes is best for you, you may want to use one of the best initial strategies for foreign companies that want to enter the Korean market:

Exhibit your products at trade fairs This is the preferred route for the promotion of existing products and the introduction of new ones, although it's available only if the trade fair includes your product. Trade fairs are popular in Korea, as they are throughout East Asia.

Advantages
- They foster contacts with large and small buyers,
- You get access at a single event to foreign and local industry contacts, and
- Hands-on demonstration techniques increase product awareness.

Disadvantages
- Your potential market is limited to attendees,
- Competition may be high because the fairs by their very nature showcase different companies' products targeted for the same industries and markets.

Other cost-effective strategies you can use:

Advertising in professional trade journals Use a local agent or distributor to circulate product literature among prospective end-users.

Make your embassy work for you Your embassy's commercial service has many programs designed by experts for exporters, including seminars, workshops, market analyses, and introductions to prospective agents and partners. Single-company exhibitions under the auspices of your embassy can be particularly effective.

The Four Major Access Routes

These early-on strategies open the door to the following four major access routes to the Korean market, which vary in their dependence on the two distribution systems. The first is the most dependent on the system as it exists with all its limitations. It is also the quickest and easiest way to gain a foothold.

1. Get a distributor or agent

Either a registered trading firm or an offer agent; preferred for consumer products that have well-established competitors, and for nonconsumer products (business and vertical applications software, industrial machinery, electronic parts) aimed at government or commercial institutions.

Advantages Easiest way to start exporting to Korea; simple contract; no need to create your own marketing structure; agent knows local needs and customs; often aware of opportunities before a bid is announced; knows ins and outs of bidding; monitors and promotes smaller sales which can add up over time; can handle importing, marketing, distribution, and wholesale and retail selling; foreign trading firms may be more attuned to foreign products and needs.

Disadvantages Middleman fees raise cost of product in market; marketing is limited by agent's knowledge, abilities, preferences, and biases; larger agencies may not give your product the attention it needs, while smaller agencies may lack resources; government prohibits manufacturing in Korea.

2. Establish a branch office

Preferred for products needing heavy after-sales service and cultivation of close relationships with clients—for example, software, computers, appliances, sophisticated or large-scale equipment.

Advantages Allows you to retain a competitive edge with prompt service, customer commitment, and consulting aspects of a sale; suggests to your buyers that you have a permanent presence in domestic markets, promoting image of stability and long-term availability; use of local agents and distributors adds expertise and clout.

Disadvantages Represents a heavier commitment and entails heavy exposure to red-tape, Korean-style; high cost of setting up office and hiring staff; ineligible for Foreign Capital Inducement Act tax incentives; cannot directly engage in manufacturing or financial service activities; still dependent on local agents or distributors.

3. Form a joint venture with a local company

Preferred for consumer items, foods (especially fast foods) and clothing, and for high-tech products that must be modified for sale in local market, that are in growing international demand, and that are protected by copyright, patent, or similar intellectual property laws (for example, software).

Advantages Direct resource for creating specialized products aimed at particular needs of consumers in domestic market; allows use of local company's marketing, distribution, and other contacts; government allows manufacturing in Korea; highly favored by Korean government as a way of keeping profits in the country; tax incentives.

Disadvantages Represents an even heavier commitment and entails heavy exposure to red-tape, Korean-style (one German firm had to meet 376 different regulations—many of them unpublished—to get government approval); allows for technology transfer, plus potential infringement on design,

patent, copyright, and technology rights, and resulting enforcement problems—a real problem in Korea (you may find someone has appropriated your own name and wants to sell it back to you); foreign partner often limited to less than 50-percent share of JV company (although 100 percent is sometimes permitted); no legal status except contractual, so no protection under foreign investment law; liable for Koreans partner's misdeeds and losses.

4. Establish a subsidiary

Allowed by recent reforms; preferred for products needing heavy after-sales service and cultivation of close relationships with clients—for example, software, computers, appliances, sophisticated or large-scale equipment; new rules open up prospect of foreign firms dumping inefficient, incompetent, take-the-money-and-run JV partners (for example, Proctor & Gamble, Unilever, Price Waterhouse, and United Distillers have all recently gotten JV divorces from their Korean partners).

Advantages Allows you to retain a competitive edge in prompt service, customer commitment, and consulting aspects of a sale; suggests to your buyers that you have a permanent commitment to maintaining a presence in domestic markets, promotes image of stability and long-term availability; eligible for Foreign Capital Inducement Act incentives; can engage in manufacturing and financial service activities; may be able to set up own distribution system, ultimately giving direct access to store shelves.

Disadvantages Represents truly heavy commitment and entails heavy exposure to red-tape, Korean-style; high cost of setting up office, hiring workforce, building or leasing facilities (foreigners are allowed to own land only in limited circumstances); not terribly popular with Korean government because seen as a threat to domestic firms and profits leave the country; lack of local partner makes dealing with government, labor unions, and *chaebol* problematic.

ADVERTISING

Koreans are beginning to love their ads and commercials, and respond to them in ways strikingly similar to those of Western consumers. In East Asia only Japan is a bigger market for advertising than Korea. Advertising spending rose to about US$3.5 billion in 1992, an increase of 15 percent over the previous year but rather low compared with the 25-30 percent annual increases racked up in previous years. This growth reflects the increasing wealth and sophistication of the Korean market, a level of sophistication that the advertising industry, still tightly controlled by the government, has yet to attain.

Newspapers, magazines, TV, and radio claim 80 percent of the advertising market.

Five Ways to Build a Good Overseas Relationship

1. Be careful in choosing overseas partners and distributors.

This is crucial. Whether you choose to go with a subsidiary, agent, export trading company, export management company, dealer, distributor, or your own setup, you must investigate the potential and pitfalls of each. Pay personal visits to potential partners to assure yourself of their long-term commitment to you and your product, and their experience, ability, reputation, and financial stability. Rather than relying on bank or credit sources for information on a prospective distributor's financial stability and resources, hire an independent expert to advise you.

The keys to McDonald's Corporation's success, says company spokesman Brad Trask, is a meticulous search for partners that focuses on "shared philosophies, past business conduct, and dedication. After all, we're asking a businessman to give up two years to be absorbed into the McDonald's way of business. We want to be sure we're right for each other."

2. Treat your overseas distributors as equals of their domestic counterparts.

Your overseas distributors aren't some poor family relations entitled only to crumbs and handouts. They are part of your company's future success, a division equal to any domestic division. Offer them advertising campaigns, discount programs, sales incentives, special credit terms, warranty deals, and service programs that are equivalent to those you offer your domestic distributors and tailored to meet the special needs of that country.

Also take into account the fact that distributors of export goods need to act more independently of manufacturers and marketers than do domestic distributors because of the differences in trade laws and practices, and the vagaries of international communications and transportation.

McDonald's partners in Korea adhere to the company's overall standards of consistency and quality, Trask says, but in all other ways, the McDonald's restaurants in Korea are thoroughly Korean—Korean owned, staffed and operated. "We're not operational police," Trask says. The company knows to leave well enough alone and trust its partners. "Those partners have purchased the rights to a formula for proven success. We've never found anyone foolish enough to fly in the face of success. Instead, they've adapted the formula to suit their needs." Kentucky Fried Chicken sees things the same way. "We mandate that our partners or licensees have the Colonel up on the logo, and they have to serve original recipe chicken and cole slaw," says Steve Provost, KFC's vice president of International Public Affairs. "Beyond that it's up to them."

3. Learn the do's and taboos.

Each country does business in its own way, a process developed over years to match the history, culture and precepts of the people. Ignore these practices and you lose. "McDonald's system has enough leeway in it to allow the local businessmen to do what they have to do to succeed," Trask says. Thus every new McDonald's in Thailand holds a "staff night" just before the grand opening. The families of the youthful employees descend en masse to be served McDonald's meals in an atmosphere that they can see for themselves is clean and wholesome. [Refer to "Business Culture" chapter for a detailed discussion.]

4. Be flexible in forming partnerships.

American companies in particular are notoriously obsessed with gaining a majority share of a joint venture, the type of partnership most favored by East Asian governments. One reason is accounting: Revenue can show up on the books at home only when the stake is more than 50 percent. Another reason is the US Foreign Corrupt Practices Act, which makes US citizens and companies liable for the conduct of their overseas partners; the idea, presumptuous at best, is that majority control translates into control of the minority partner.

Here, again, Japanese practices are illuminating. Ownership is yet another area where the Japanese have succeeded; they see a two-sided relationship where Americans see themselves as the superior partner in knowledge, finances, technology, and culture—in other

Five Ways to Build a Good Overseas Relationship (cont'd.)

words, know-it-alls. Westerners, and Americans in particular, have a lot to learn about flexibility in business relationships. McDonald's has chosen the 50-50 joint-venture route, with great profitability—more than half its income now comes from outside the US. KFC is another American company that has found enormous success by being flexible. "We have a philosophy of relying heavily on our joint venture or franchise partners to guide us," says KFC's Trask. "We'd never dream of trying to impose our attitudes on them."

Finally, keep in mind that there is more than one way to do business overseas and that changing laws or market conditions will often force you to consider other options. Where a distributorship may be best at first, a joint venture or a licensing agreement may be the way to go later.

5. Concentrate on the relationship.

We cannot emphasize this point too greatly. The Confucian culture of East Asia emphasizes personal relationships above all else. Building a good relationship takes time, patience, courtesy, reliability, dignity, honorable conduct, and farsightedness; a poorly developed relationship dooms even your best marketing efforts to failure. One US computer maker made a great mistake when it fired its Asian distributor after a falling-out. The dismissal, handled in a typically abrupt American way, caused the man to lose face, and ruined all the relationships the company had built through this man. For three years afterward, company executives couldn't find another distributor because no one would talk to them. Not only did the company lose untold millions of dollars in sales, but it took US$40 million in advertising to create enough consumer-driven demand for local distributors to even consider meeting with the firm.

So do your very best to build a sound, trusting and profitable relationship with your overseas partners. They are putting themselves on the line for you, spending time, money and energy in hopes of future rewards and a solid, long-term relationship.

And by all means, don't expect your foreign distributors to jump through hoops on a moment's notice. For example, they need price protection so they don't lose money on your price changes. If they buy your product for US$100 and a month later you cut your price to US$90, you have to give them credit so they don't get stuck with inventory at the higher price. If you raise your price, you have to honor your prior commitment while you give ample notice of the increase.

With their focus on long-term personal relationships, mutual respect and trust, East Asians, in particular, make honorable partners once you have gained their confidence by showing them they have yours.

Print media

South Korea has a highly literate population that loves to read, and so newspapers and magazines are the biggest recipients of advertising spending in the country—US$1.67 billion in 1992. Publishers and advertisers often make direct contact, bypassing the agency connection. When this happens, the agency simply prepares the ad for a flat fee, and the client does his own negotiating with the publisher.

Warning Korean publishers have been lying about their circulations for years, inflating their ad fees, and threatening advertisers with negative stories if they don't fork over the money. In fact, to cover their tracks, many publishers print thousands of extra copies that they know they can never sell—nearly one-fifth of all the newspaper copies printed daily go straight from the printer to the dump. That means even higher ad rates to cover the losses. Only since 1989 has there been an official Korea Audit Bureau of Circulation (KABC) to help advertisers learn what they're getting for their money, but so far, the audit has been a flop. Fewer than half the dailies had joined by the end of 1992, and those that haven't account for about 95 percent of total circulation. Joining the KABC would mean revealing to the public how dishonest they've been in the past. It would also mean lowering their ad rates to conform to reality and abandoning certain of their time-honored business practices.

The push for reform that is overtaking Korean business and politics, along with intense pressure from Korean and foreign advertisers, will eventually force the publishers to clean up their acts. Until then you and your ad agency should be prepared to bargain hard and challenge a newspaper's claims, which may have a substantial chance of being questionable.

Newspapers South Korea has dozens of dailies—including many new ones that have resulted from recent liberalizations in licensing procedures—and a total circulation of more than 10 million in a wide range of editions. Seoul alone has 13 dailies with national circulation, including four with alleged (unaudited) circulations of more than 500,000: *Dong-A Ilbo, Chosun Ilbo, Han Kook Ilbo,* and *Joong Ang Ilbo.* Each claims to have the largest circulation. Korean newspapers account for 40 percent of all advertising spending or US$1.49 billion in 1992, up 13 percent from 1991. Newspapers represented 56 percent of total ad spending during the first three months of 1993. The cost of a centimeter-wide single-column ad in the larger newspapers ranged from W50,000 to W160,000 (about US$62 to US$198) in 1993.

Magazines Koreans can choose from more than 6,955 magazines with circulations ranging from 10,000 to 240,000. Some are general interest, but more have target audiences, with the largest target being women. Advertisers spent US$179 million in Korean magazines in 1992, 5 percent more than in the preceding year. The rate in a leading magazine for a single-page color ad with an offset picture ranged from W1 to W2.2 million (about US$1,237 to US$2,725) in 1993.

Television and radio

Unlike the print media, radio and television are subject to a high degree of government control and ownership. The government-run Korean Broadcasting Advertising Corporation (KOBACO) wholly controls the broadcast advertising market. KOBACO designates official broadcast ad agencies every year—95 in 1992, including 14 newcomers—determines agency commissions, and pays the agencies. An advertiser can either take his agency-produced commercial directly to KOBACO, which then negotiates with the broadcaster for time and rates, or have the agency both produce a commercial and take it to KOBACO, which in turn deals with the broadcaster. All radio and television advertising must meet KOBACO's standards of fairness, truthfulness, dignity, public morality, and legality. The problem with this system is self-evident: The KOBACO bureaucracy is notoriously heavy-handed and autocratic, pleasing only itself and proving decidedly unimaginative in the field of advertising.

Television The number of televisions is increasing rapidly, and color TVs now account for more than half of all sets in use. Television commercials account for about 35 percent of all advertising spending, reaching about US$1 billion in 1992. Korean law limits television advertising to 8 percent of total program time, which has created a severe and contentious shortage of available commercial ad time (and in the process strengthened the lead of newspapers in ad spending): ads can be aired only between, not during, programs. To make matters worse, most stations air programs for only about 10 hours a day on weekdays.

There are four TV broadcasting companies. The largest is the state-run Korea Broadcasting System (KBS), which has three networks: KBS-TV I and II, and EBS, which is exclusively educational. KBS has 25 TV substations and 353 relay stations. KBS also owns 65 percent of the privately operated Munwha Broadcasting Company (MBC), which has one central station in Seoul and nine substations and 10 relay stations scattered around the country. The completely privately owned Seoul Broadcasting System (SBS) has one TV and one radio station, both on the air only since the end of 1991 but already reaching 43 percent of the nation's households; both may go nationwide in the near future. The Buddhist Broadcasting System (BBS) airs religious programming. The cost of a 15- to 20-second commercial in Seoul during prime time, which runs from 7:00 pm to 11:00 pm, ranged from W4 to W6.5 million (about US$4,950 to US$8,050) in 1993.

The recently approved cable TV system is slated to begin commercial broadcasting in April 1995 and is expected to have 28 channels by the turn of the century. Industry analysts predict that CATV will develop into an extremely important ad market, with more than 40 channels and more than US$6 billion worth of advertising by the turn of the century. Advertisers and agencies will be glad to hear that KOBACO won't control cable TV advertising.

Radio There are more radios in Korea than there are people, and radio is the third most popular advertising medium. There are seven radio broadcasting companies: KBS, MBC, Christian Broadcasting System (CBS), Pyonghwa Broadcasting Corporation (PBC), BBS, Traffic Broadcasting System (TBS), and SBS. These companies air their wares over 54 radio stations, including five FM stations, and 47 relay stations. KBS is the largest network with 20 affiliated stations, and it also owns 65 percent of MBC, which, with its 19 provincial affiliate stations, remains privately run. The other networks that accept advertising are SBS and CBS, which devotes its four provincial stations to religious programming and news. Prime time runs from 7 am to 1 pm. The price for a 20-second spot in Seoul during prime time ranged from W98,400 to W470,800 (about US$122 to US$583) in 1993.

Movie Theaters

All movie theaters in Korea project advertising stills or strips in black and white or color that range in length from 30 seconds to 1 or 2 minutes.

Advertising Agencies

Sophistication arrived in Korean advertising only in 1988 when two large foreign agencies broke into the market by forming joint ventures with local agencies. The government opened the market completely in 1991, and now the world's largest and most prominent agencies, including Ogilvy & Mather, J. Walter Thompson, McCann-Erickson, and Saatchi and Saatchi, have offices in Korea. Often these offices are joint ventures with Korean firms. However, most of the largest Korean *chaebol* companies use their own in-house agencies for import marketing—Samsung, for example, uses its Cheil Communications, Inc., the best Korean ad agency.

These agencies serve all arms of the conglomerate's subsidiaries—and, despite having clients outside the *chaebol*, lag far behind the foreign firms in market research, creativity, and general industry savvy. With guaranteed in-house accounts, a glaring absence of print media circulation audits, and assured commercial spots despite severely limited TV time, the *chaebol* agencies have had little incentive to adopt or adapt to international professional standards. If your product is being handled by one of the *chaebol*, you may want to insist as part of your agreement that your advertising account be given to one of the foreign firms or a foreign-local joint venture firm. (Refer to "Important Addresses" for a listing of advertising agencies.)

Public Relations

The same money put into a well-executed public relations effort will usually buy a lot more publicity and recognition value than will an ad or commercial. A good PR firm will have experts in your specific field of business and will help you understand the local market and communicate effectively with your target consumers as well as provide crisis management. On the other hand, bad PR is worse than none at all. It can create a crisis where none existed before, and then can't clean up its own mess.

Unfortunately the PR market in Korea is only four or five years old, and although it is growing at 20 to 30 percent a year, most Korean firms aren't yet convinced of the concept, value, or role of PR. This is the case despite Burson-Marsteller's stellar success in promoting the 1988 Seoul Olympics overseas, a drive that served to jump-start the Korean PR industry.

Indeed more than 90 percent of PR clients in Korea are foreign firms, and the most accomplished PR agencies are either foreign owned or divisions of foreign or joint venture ad agencies. The domestic agencies are usually undernourished divisions of in-house ad agencies. Besides their lack of experience, objectivity, and general professionalism, their people often lack the language skills needed to handle foreign

Five Ways to Help Your Local Agent

1. Make frequent visits to Korea to support your agent's efforts. They help to build the relationship, without which no amount of effort can succeed in Korea. Keep in mind that your competitors are also paying personal visits to their agents and customers. And invite your agent to your country to reciprocate his hospitality and familiarize him with your country and your company.

2. Hold many demonstrations and exhibits of your products. For suppliers to Korean manufacturers, the value of sales presentations at factories cannot be overemphasized. Factory engineers and managers are directly responsible for the equipment and machinery to be purchased, and they have much influence over the decision to buy. This is so highly effective—and so cheap—a sales booster that it's irresponsible for an exporter to ignore it.

3. Increase the distribution of promotional brochures and technical data to potential buyers, libraries and industry associations. When your agent makes personal sales calls, your potential customers won't be completely in the dark.

4. Improve follow-up on initial sales leads. Let your agent know you're backing him up with whatever it takes to pursue the lead. Make your agent proud to be associated with you. "All of our foreign partners know that they have the support of a large system behind them," McDonald's spokesman Brad Trask says. "The support system is available on request."

5. Deliver on time. If you don't, you can believe that someone else will. Failure to deliver on time not only makes your agent lose face and thereby undermines your relationship, but it jeopardizes your sales. There's not much you can do to make ships go faster or airlines schedule more flights, but you can stockpile your products in Korea to ensure that your agent has a steady supply. When you have to (and it's possible) forget the expense and airfreight the product for two-day delivery: The extra effort will go a long way in establishing and fortifying your reputation.

clients. They are thus unable to provide high-quality PR services. Even giant Daewoo first got into international PR by bypassing its in-house ad agency in favor of a relationship with Hill & Knowlton, which owns Communications Korea. Although this situation is changing, as Korean companies grow to recognize the value of PR, and in the long run the proportion of clients who are foreign will drop to 10 percent, you don't want a Korean agency to learn PR on your time or budget. If you've hooked up with a major foreign trader or *chaebol* firm to market your product, and you want a good PR effort, make sure your agreement allows you to go outside the in-house ad agency for PR services.

MAJOR MARKETS

Seoul

South Korea's capital, economic, industrial, political, financial, educational, communications, transportation, and cultural center, and its largest city (and with 10.6 million people, the tenth largest city in the world), Seoul is nothing less than the heart and soul of Korea. Skyscrapers dominate its downtown, where streets are packed with creeping traffic and sidewalks thronged with hurrying crowds. Because Seoul is no more than an hour by air (Seoul's Kimpo International Airport is the world's tenth-ranking cargo handling airport) or five hours by road or rail from every other major city in the nation, a market presence in Seoul represents a market presence in Korea. Foreign countries have their embassies here, and foreign firms establish their representative offices here. Citicorp, Chase Manhattan, Commercial Bank of Korea, Bank of Korea, Ernst & Young, Price Waterhouse, the Korea Stock Exchange—all are centered in Seoul, as is the World Trade Center, with its trade service associations, export firms, and trade fairs.

Seoul has factories making textiles, chemicals, electronics, pharmaceuticals, steel, automobiles, and engineering products. It has Seoul National University, Korea University, and Yonsei University and more than 80 other colleges, universities, and institutes. More than 80 percent of the nation's writers, artists, and musicians call Seoul home. Everywhere there are cultural treasures—palaces, shrines, temples, royal tombs, museums, galleries, pavilions, and fortresses. On manmade Yoi-do Island in the Han River, highrise office buildings and apartment complexes have made the area the "Manhattan of Seoul," a prestigious business address and exclusive residential center. Enriched by Seoul's economy and influenced by its large foreign community, the residents of Seoul are the nation's wealthiest and most cosmopolitan and sophisticated—and the most inclined to know about and buy imported products.

Pusan

South Korea's second largest city (population 3.8 million) is also its major port, the historic seagate to the nation. Half of the country's exports and imports flow through Pusan's modern harbor facilities on the south coast. Pusan also ranks second to Seoul in finance, trade, industry, transportation, and commerce. The region has Korea's major concentration of heavy industry: its iron and steel foundries, petroleum refineries, textile factories, shipyards, electronics factories, concrete plants, wood and food processors, and engineering products firms. Hyundai and Daewoo, among other chaebol, have major facilities here.

Pusan also has more than 25 colleges and universities, a highly skilled and educated labor force, and a outward-looking business elite.

Taegu

Korea's third largest city is Taegu. Located in the southeast region, sitting astride the railway and superhighway linking Pusan and Seoul, Taegu has become a major transportation and distribution center for the large industrial and agricultural area that surrounds it. For years, Taegu was called the apple capital of Korea, but textiles and other industries have taken over. Taegu is the site of the Taegu Dyeing Industry Complex, where more than 80 companies have their plants, and of the Panwol Dyeing and Finishing Industry Estate, where more than 50 factories are located. The industry is said to be Korea's most backward, so there are good opportunities for foreign technology imports. With several universities and colleges, Taegu, with a population of 2.2 million, has a well-educated and highly skilled labor force.

Inchon

This huge suburb of Seoul, located an hour west of the city and served by a Seoul subway line, is, at 1.8 million, not only Korea's fourth largest city but serves as the capital's port. It is a major center for oil and container shipping. Glass plants, oil refineries, petrochemical factories, and wood products plants are also located here. The port's new canal is 60 feet wide, has a 25-acre dock, and can accommodate five 5,000- to 6,000-ton ships at a time, and is capable of handling ships of up to 10,000 tons. Rail lines and expressways connect the city with Seoul and other major Korean cities.

HELPING YOUR COMPANY LEARN TO LOVE EXPORTING

Five In-House Rules

1. Eliminate as much guesswork as you can

Expert export consultation is usually time and money well spent. You need a well thought out marketing plan. You cannot get into successful exporting by accident. It's not a simple matter of saying, "Let's sell our product in Korea." You need to know that your product will, in fact, sell and how you're going to sell it. First, do you need to do anything obvious to your product? Who is your buyer? How are you going to find him? How is he going to find you? Do you need to advertise? Exhibit at a trade fair? How much can you expect to sell? Can you sell more than one product? A plan may be the only way you can begin to uncover hidden traps and costs before you get overly involved in a fiasco. While you may be able to see an opportunity, knowing how to exploit it isn't necessarily a simple matter. You must plot and plan and prepare.

2. Just go for it

We're not suggesting you throw caution to the winds, but sometimes your "plan" may be to use a shotgun approach—rather than the more tightly targeted rifle approach—and just blast away to see if you hit anything. You can narrow things down later. If your product is new to the market, there may be precious little marketing information, and you may have essentially no other choice. Two scenarios illustrate these points: Two companies decide to begin selling similar products in East Asia, which has never seen such products before. Company A hires a market research firm, which spends six months and US$50,000 to come up with a detailed plan. Company Z sends its president to a trade fair—not to exhibit but just to look around and meet people. He follows that trip up with two others. On the last one his new associates present him with his first order. Company Z also spent six months and US$50,000 investigating doing export business, but it has an order to show for it, while Company A only has an unproven plan.

3. Get your bosses to back you up and stick with the program

Whether your company consists of 10, 50, 500, or 5,000 people—or just you—and whether you're the head of the company, the chief financial officer, or the person leading the exporting charge, there must be an explicit commitment to sustain the initial setbacks and financial requirements of export marketing. You must be sure that the firm is committed to the long-term: Don't waste money by abandoning the project too early.

International marketing consultants report that because results don't show up in the first few months, the international marketing and advertising budget is *invariably* the first to be cut in any company that doesn't have money to burn. Such shortsighted budgetary decisions are responsible for innumerable premature failures in exporting.

The hard fact is that exports don't bring in money as quickly as domestic sales. It takes time and persistence for an international marketing effort to succeed. There are many hurdles to overcome—personal, political, cultural, and legal, among others. It will be at least 6 to 9 months before you and your overseas associates can even begin to expect to see glimmers of success. And it may be even longer. Be patient, keep a close but not a suffocating watch on your international marketing efforts, and give the venture a chance to develop.

4. Avoid an internal tug-of-war

Consultants report that one of the biggest obstacles to successful export marketing in larger companies is internal conflict between divisions within a company. Domestic marketing battles international marketing while each is also warring with engineering, and everybody fights with the bean counters. All the complex strategies, relationship building, and legal and cultural accommodations that export marketing requires mean that support and teamwork are crucial to the success of the venture.

5. Stick with export marketing even when business booms at home

Exporting isn't something to fall back on when your domestic market falters. Nor is it something to put on the back burner when business is booming at home. It is difficult to ease your way into exporting. All the complex strategies, relationship-building, legal and cultural accommodations, and financial and management investment, and blood, sweat, and tears that export marketing requires means that a clear commitment is necessary from the beginning. Any other attitude as good as dooms the venture from the start, and you may as well forget it. We can't overstress this aspect: take the long-range view or don't play at all. Decide that you're going to export and that you're in it for the long haul as a viable money-making full-fledged division within your company.

McDonald's Corporation spokesperson Brad Trask, commenting on his company's overwhelming international success, notes, "We're a very long-term focused company. We do things with patience; we're very deliberate. We're there to stay, not to take the money and run." And Texas Instruments, which has suffered recent losses in its semiconductor business, has made a considered move into long-term joint ventures in East Asia, banking that these investments will provide a big payoff five years down the road.

SEVEN RULES FOR SELLING YOUR PRODUCT

1. Respect the individuality of each market

The profit motive generally operates cross-culturally and the nationals of most countries, especially within a given region, will have much in common with one another. However, there will also be substantial differences, enough to cause a generic marketing program to fall flat on its face and even build ill-will in the process. You may have some success with this sort of one-size-fits-all approach, but you won't be able to build a solid operation or maximize profits this way. "Japan proves this point phenomenally," says Steve Provost, KFC's vice president of International Public Affairs. "Our first three restaurants in Tokyo were modeled after our American restaurants, and all three failed within six months. Then we listened to our Japanese partner, who suggested we open smaller restaurants. We've never looked back." However, what works in Japan doesn't necessarily work in Korea. Korean tastes may be more similar to US tastes than to Japanese or may differ in other ways.

2. Adapt your product to the foreign market

Markets are individual, and you may well need to tailor your products to suit individual needs. As the United States' Big Three automakers have yet to learn, it's hard to sell a left-hand-drive car in a right-hand-drive country. Black may be a popular color in your country, but may also be seen as the color of death in your foreign market. Dress, styles, and designs considered fashionably tasteful at home can cause offense abroad. One major US computer manufacturer endured years of costly marketing miscalculations before it realized that the US is only one-third of its market, and that the other two-thirds required somewhat different products as well as different approaches.

You can avoid this company's multi-million dollar mistakes by avoiding lazy and culturally-biased thinking. A foreign country has official regulations and cultural preferences that differ from those of your own. Learn about these differences, respect them, and adapt your product accordingly. Often it won't even take that much thought, money, or effort. Kentucky Fried Chicken offers a salmon sandwich in Japan, fried plantains in Mexico, and tabouleh in the Middle East—and 450 other locally specific menu items worldwide. And even the highly standardized McDonald's serves pineapple pie in Thailand, teriyaki burgers and tatsuda sandwiches (chicken with ginger and soy) in Japan, spicy sauces with burgers in Malaysia (prepared according to Muslim guidelines), and a seasonal durian fruit shake in Singapore.

3. Don't get greedy

Price your product to match the market you're entering. Don't try to take maximum profits in the first year. Take the long-term view. It's what your competitors are doing, and they're in it for the long haul. Koreans are very price-conscious. When you're pricing your product, include in your calculations the demand for spare parts, components, and auxiliary equipment. Add-on profits from these sources can help keep the primary product price down and therefore more competitive.

4. Demand quality

A poor-quality product can ambush the best-laid marketing plans. Koreans may look at price first, but they also want value and won't buy junk no matter how cheap. And there's just too much competition to make it worth your while to put this adage to the test. Whatever market you gain initially will rapidly fall apart if you have a casual attitude towards quality. And it is hard to come back from an initial quality-based flop. On then other hand, a product with a justified reputation for high quality and good value creates its own potential for market and price expansions.

5. Back up your sales with service

Some products demand more work than others—more sales effort, more after-sales service, more hand-holding of the distributor, and more contact with the end user. The channel you select is crucial here. Paradoxically in this age of ubiquitous and lightning-fast communications and saturation advertising, people rely more than ever on word of mouth to sort out the truth from hyperbole. Nothing will sink your product faster than a reputation for poor or nonexistent service and after-sales support. US firms in particular need to do some serious reputation building for such after-sales service. Although Koreans see US products as generally superior in quality and performance, they rate Japanese after-sales service as vastly better. And guess whose products they buy.

Consider setting up your own service facility. If you're looking for a Korean agent to handle your product, look for one who has qualified maintenance people already familiar with your type of product or who can handle your service needs with a little judicious training. And make sure that this partner understands how important service and support are to you and to your future relationship with him.

6. Notice that foreigners speak a different language

Your sales, service, and warranty information may contain a wealth of information but if it's not in their language, you leave the foreign distributors, sales and service personnel, and consumers out in the cold. It's expensive to translate everything into Korean, but it's absolutely necessary.

7. Focus on specific geographic
areas and markets

To avoid wasteful spending, focus your marketing efforts. A lack of focus means that you're wasting your money, time, and energies. A lack of specificity means that your foreign operations may get too big too fast. Not only does this cost more than the local business can justify or support, it also can translate into an impersonal attitude towards sales and service and the relationships you've working so hard to build. Instead concentrate your time, money, and efforts on a specific market or region, and work on building the all-important business relationships that will carry you over the many obstacles to successful export marketing.

Business Entities & Formation

FORMS OF BUSINESS ORGANIZATION

Commercial codes in the Republic of Korea (ROK) offer Koreans and foreign nationals a variety of recognized options for establishing a business. These include a variety of company, partnership, branch, and liaison office structures. Investors can also form agent or technical assistance agreements. The specific type of business entity selected will be determined by the objectives, circumstances, the degree of control desired, and the anticipated duration of the investment. However, the range of likely solutions to most business needs is fairly narrow.

Of particular interest to foreign investors are the joint stock company, the branch office, and the liaison office. Although it is legal to structure businesses in other ways, other forms are not generally recognized in Korea as appropriate vehicles for serious foreign investment, and electing one of these forms could cause the investor to have difficulties with authorities and in gaining acceptance in the local business community.

Companies

A company is an entity that has been organized and registered for profit-seeking purposes. Companies have legal status as a separate juridical person. The Korean commercial code recognizes four types of companies: unlimited partnership companies, limited partnership companies, joint stock companies, and limited liability companies. In practice, foreigners are not allowed to form or participate in partnership companies in Korea. Foreigners can use limited liability companies in certain circumstances, but more than 90 percent of all foreign and domestic operations in South Korea choose to structure their business as a joint stock company.

Joint Stock Companies The joint stock company, also known as a company limited by shares, or *chusik hoesa* in Korean, is not only the company structure that foreign and Korean firms use most often, but it is also the type most familiar to and preferred by Korean authorities. The legal concepts and regulatory frameworks governing Korean joint stock companies are similar to those for corporations under US, Japanese, and German law. Such a company can be 100 percent foreign owned, and both its initial capital and its annual net earnings can be repatriated. A joint stock company is eligible for tax incentives under the terms of the Foreign Capital Inducement Law (FCIL).

A joint stock company requires a minimum of seven founding shareholders or promoters. If all initial subscribers are classified as promoters, the local district court appoints an outside inspector to determine whether subscription procedures are fair. To avoid this additional step, joint stock companies usually arrange for at least one token outside subscriber. After incorporation, the total number of shareholders can be reduced to as few as one. However, the law states that shares cannot be withdrawn to disenfranchise existing shareholders without the approval of those shareholders. There is no legal upper limit on the number of shareholders. Shareholder liability is limited to the amount of capital invested in shares.

Remittances of dividends; proceeds of sales; principal, interest, and fees from loans; and royalties are guaranteed for approved companies. Companies must apply for approval and document the sources and amounts of funds in order to obtain foreign exchange under the terms of the Foreign Exchange Control Act (FECA). Inward remittances are generally allowed. However, to prevent the entry of funds to be used for speculation in domestic markets, the government has begun to restrict inward remittances to amounts justified by actual operating needs. Earnings may be reinvested in the business that generates the profits through the retention of earnings that are within the limits of authorized capital. Reinvestment in other existing Korean businesses or new ventures must receive the approval normally required by the Ministry of Finance (MOF) for new foreign investment. Companies can invest in the securities of new firms or in the new offerings of existing

GLOSSARY

Bank of Korea (BOK) Under the revised Foreign Capital Inducement Law (FCIL), the Bank of Korea, the nation's central bank, has the authority to approve foreign investments without prior consultation with other ministries. The BOK can grant such automatic approval if the foreign equity investment represents less than 50 percent of total equity.

Foreign Capital Inducement Deliberation Committee (FCIDC) The Foreign Capital Inducement Deliberation Committee must approve foreign investment proposals that involve special tax exemptions or reductions. If the FCIDC grants approval, the MOF then authorizes the proposed foreign investment project.

Foreign Capital Inducement Law (FCIL) The Foreign Capital Inducement Law is the statutory framework governing all foreign investment in Korea. It sets guidelines for the approval of foreign investment, repatriation of funds, and the granting of incentives.

Foreign Investment Review Committee (FIRC) An advisory body to the Ministry of Finance, the Foreign Investment Review Committee passes on foreign investments exceeding US$20 million.

Foreign Exchange Control Act (FECA) The Foreign Exchange Control Act is the statutory framework that governs all foreign exchange activity in Korea. The FECA requires an entity that wants to make foreign exchange transactions to obtain prior authorization. Approval of foreign investment carries the right to obtain foreign exchange for specified purposes. The entity must also obtain specific authorization for each transaction by documenting how it is eligible under the general authorization. The FECA is administered by the BOK, which delegates most operations to specified Korean banks.

Ministry of Finance (MOF) The Ministry of Finance exercises ultimate legal authority over essentially all areas and aspects of foreign business operations and foreign investment in Korea.

Ministry of Trade and Industry (MTI) The Ministry of Trade and Industry exercises jurisdiction over the manufacture and trade of goods, importing and exporting, and certain areas of technical cooperation in Korea.

Small and Medium Company Formation Support Law (SMCFSL) The Small and Medium Company Formation Support Law governs favored investment by smaller entities and the incentives offered to such entities.

firms. They may not purchase the existing shares of extant firms.

Limited Liability Companies A limited liability company or *yuhan hoesa* requires a minimum of two and can have a maximum of 50 participants. Liability is limited by the amount of each participant's capital contribution. Although this format is not common and it is not the preferred vehicle for foreign investment in Korea, it is favored by some foreign investors because legal provisions, which restrict the transfer of shares, enable them to maintain control over the enterprise.

Other company forms recognized by Korean law but not available to foreigners include two types of partnership companies. The general outlines of such entities are given for the benefit of those who may encounter such companies as they do business in Korea:

Unlimited Partnership Companies An unlimited partnership company or *hapmyung hoesa* requires two or more partners bearing both unlimited and joint and several liability for obligations beyond company assets. Individuals involved in legal, accounting, or other professional practices generally use this business format.

Because they are legal persons but not individuals, foreign companies are prohibited from forming or participating in existing unlimited partnership companies. Although they are not specifically prohibited by law from forming or participating in Korean unlimited partnership companies, foreign individuals are not allowed to do so in practice.

Limited Partnership Companies A limited partnership company or *hapja hoesa* is a variation on the partnership company and similar to a US limited partnership. It requires one or more partners with unlimited liability for company obligations and one or more partners whose liability is limited to the amount of their capital contribution. Those bearing limited liability cannot contribute personal services or credit as capital. Limited partners may not represent the company officially, but they can be directly involved in management and operations, and they have access to all business records.

Foreign companies are prohibited from forming or participating in existing Korean limited partnership companies. Although there are no specific legal restrictions to this effect, Korean authorities do not allow foreign individuals to form limited partnerships or participate in existing limited partnership companies.

Company Capital Requirements The minimum actual paid-in capital required to establish a joint stock company is W50 million (about US$62,000). The minimum capital for a limited company is W10 million (about US$12,400). A minimum of 25 percent of authorized shares must be issued on incorporation. All capital must be divided into shares of equal value.

However, companies can issue stock units representing a percentage of ownership in place of a specific number of shares. The shares of a joint stock company must be transferable, although the company can set fairly restrictive conditions for transfer in its articles of incorporation. The transfer of shares held by foreigners requires prior approval from the MOF. In limited companies, all shareholders must approve a transfer of ownership interest. This provision is attractive to some foreign investors who wish to retain control over their investment. ·

Issued shares must have a par value; the minimum such value allowed is W5,000 (about US$6.20). Companies can issue common, preferred, and various classes of shares with differential rights regarding voting or distribution of profits. Shares can be issued in either registered or bearer form. Common shares usually carry voting rights, and no more than 25 percent of all shares can be nonvoting shares. Preferred shares are usually nonvoting unless preference dividends are in arrears. Joint stock companies are also allowed to issue straight or convertible bonds in minimum denominations of W10,000 (about US$12.40) up to an amount equal to twice their issued capital.

Joint stock companies must establish legal reserves equal to 10 percent of their annual cash dividends until the reserves total 50 percent of issued capital. Share premiums are also credited to this reserve. There is no requirement that dividends be paid.

Capital may be increased by the sale of additional authorized stock; contributions by existing shareholders, such as through a rights offering; or capitalization of retained earnings. However, the sum of such additions may not exceed authorized capital unless the company obtains new approvals and reincorporates. Capital may be decreased only with the approval of shareholders. Securities can be purchased and retired, although shares may not be bought in and held as treasury stock except in narrowly defined instances in which they are used to fund employee stock purchase plans. Decreases can also be accomplished through redemptions, decreases in par value when par is greater than the minimum value allowed, and reverse stock splits.

Foreign capital investment must meet the minimum threshold level of W50 million (about US$62,000). Lower minimum investments are allowed for joint ventures involving approved technology transfer. There is no stated minimum for additional investments in the same entity. Since 1993 new foreign investments exceeding US$20 million and investments involving additional amounts greater than US$5 million are subject to review by the Foreign Investment Review Committee (FIRC). Investments below these threshold amounts in open—as opposed to restricted or prohibited—sectors no longer require advance approval.

To prohibit cross-holdings, subsidiaries that are more than 40 percent owned by a parent are barred from acquiring the stock of the parent firm.

Shareholders, Directors, Officers, and Corporate Governance A meeting of shareholders must be held at least once a year. To establish a legal quorum, holders of more than half the voting shares outstanding must be represented.

A joint stock company must have a board of directors consisting of at least three members elected by its shareholders. A limited company must have at least one but not more than three directors chosen by shareholders from among their number. Individuals must be formally elected by shareholders in order to represent a limited company legally.

Directors can serve a maximum term of three years, but they can be reelected for additional terms. There is no nationality requirement for board membership. Board members are responsible for hiring and firing corporate officers and for undertaking and monitoring company operations. Corporate officers and board members are barred from holding other employment in any similar business without specific authorization from the board.

The board is the ultimate authority for a company. However, it may call special shareholder meetings to decide issues of governance. A special meeting can also be called if shareholders representing 5 percent of the company's stock formally request it. Most issues are decided by a simple majority vote of shareholders. Some issues specified in the commercial code require a two-thirds majority, and companies may stipulate in their articles of incorporation that certain issues require unanimous approval.

The Korean civil code requires a stock company to elect at least one supervisor who is neither an officer nor a director to serve as an internal auditor for a maximum term of two years. This individual is charged with examining the business and financial condition of the company and inspecting the corporate books, records, and documents.

Outside audits by certified public accountants are not generally required. However, annual audits by a Korean certified public accountant are required for companies that are listed on the Korean Stock Exchange, foreign and domestic banks and their branches, entities representing foreign investment that remit profits abroad, other entities that remit royalties abroad, and companies with total assets exceeding W4 billion (about US$5 million).

Companies are governed by their articles of incorporation, and Korean law and practice allows considerable leeway in the provisions that can legally be written into these documents. Articles must state the following to be legal: business objective, total number of shares authorized, value of each share, total number of shares issued at the time of

Foreign Entities

In principle, foreign nationals are permitted to establish a joint stock corporation, a limited partnership, an unlimited partnership, a limited company, or a branch office, which can be structured as a liaison or representative office. In practice, virtually all foreign entities are structured as a company limited by shares or *chusik hoesa,* branch office, or liaison office.

Foreign enterprises may be established in any eligible industry sector. However, foreigners are often prevented in practice from making an investment unless they form a joint venture with a Korean company in which the foreign participation is limited to less than 50 percent. There are exceptions to this rule, usually in cases where a crucial domestic need has been identified, and exceptions are becoming more common.

Korean resistance to the operation of large foreign corporations in its domestic economy is evidenced by government policy that gives preference to small and medium-sized businesses. In addition to the negative list that applies to all foreign investors, a special list reserves certain areas for small and medium-sized businesses and excludes large foreign businesses from participation. Because total company holdings are taken into consideration when investment approval is considered, large corporations cannot sidestep this issue by setting up a small subsidiary.

Korea is becoming increasingly aware of its position as part of a global economy, and its restrictive policies are changing, albeit slowly. Government agencies, industry organizations, and individual companies are beginning to address the concept of complementary as opposed to exclusive roles for small and medium-size industries and large enterprises.

Dissolution A company can dissolve under any of the following circumstances: the criteria for dissolution are specified in the company's articles of incorporation; the company has achieved, or failed to achieve, the organizational objectives defined in its articles of incorporation; all those with an ownership interest in the company agree to dissolve it; the company has merged or been consolidated with another company; the company is bankrupt; or official permission to maintain incorporation has been withdrawn. In the case of dissolution, the courts oversee liquidation and distribution of assets. The MOF must approve the repatriation of any proceeds from liquidation.

Branch Offices

A branch office is any office that is registered and maintained in Korea for which ultimate responsibility is held by the company's principal office. Branch offices are allowed to earn income from direct operations, which may be remitted to the parent. However, branch offices are not eligible for tax incentives under the FCIL. As a unit of a recognized foreign company, a branch is accorded the status of a legal person which allows it to hold assets in its own name. However, branches may not own land or shares in Korean companies, nor may they engage directly in manufacturing or financial service activities. The MOF can allow foreign financial service firms to establish branches, but it usually requires such businesses to be organized as companies rather than as branches.

Although branches may be accorded a high degree of autonomy, they technically must remain under the direct official control of their parent firm. As resident legal persons, foreign branch offices are subject to the same laws and regulations that govern domestic companies. As income-earning entities, they are subject to income and value-added taxes. There are no additional withholding requirements on remitted profits.

Because all funds must be channeled through the parent company, there is no minimum working capital requirement for branches except for specially authorized financial services branches. These must have a minimum capital of W3 billion (about US$3.7 million) and they must be audited annually. All transfers must be registered to be eligible for repatriation, and prior approval from the Bank of Korea (BOK) is required for transfers of amounts in excess of US$1 million during any calendar year.

Ordinary income may be remitted immediately, although remittance of business gains cannot begin until three years after the date on which for the establishment of the branch was approved. Standard FECA approval procedures apply to branches wishing to obtain foreign exchange for remittance. No funds from business activities not specifically autho-

incorporation, address of the company's principal office, arrangements for publishing official and required public notices, names and addresses of all promoters, special benefits accorded to promoters, property to be acquired on incorporation, and duration of the company.

rized for the branch office may be remitted. Prior approval from the BOK is currently necessary for the remittance of amounts exceeding US$1 million. Officials are reviewing regulatory changes that would raise this amount to US$2 million. Branches desiring to remit amounts greater than 100 percent of authorized working capital or amounts of greater than W100 million (about US$124,000) must undergo an annual outside audit by a Korean certified public accountant.

As part of an independent foreign entity, a branch may be closed by its parent at any time, provided that such closure does not represent an attempt to evade legal obligations. If a branch office is closed, approval from the BOK must be obtained for the repatriation of any proceeds from liquidation, and the repatriation of such funds is limited to the cumulative amount of operating funds introduced, plus any earned surplus and other legally established reserves.

A branch office can be established solely to conduct activities that earn no income. If the parent company later expands the scope of branch business operations to encompass direct profit-making activities, the branch must obtain approval and register with tax authorities before beginning such income generating activities.

Liaison Offices

A liaison office is an entity involved in indirect business activities that do not generate profits for the office. It is allowed only to conduct activities on behalf of its parent company, and it is prohibited from acting on a cooperative basis for other entities, whether they are related or separate. Liaison office functions generally include such activities as advertising, conducting market research, gathering information, handling customer inquiries, providing product and business information, processing orders, inspecting products, and storing goods that are not to be distributed in the Korean market. There are no capital requirements because the head office covers expenses. Because liaison offices generate no funds, they are not eligible to obtain foreign exchange.

A liaison office is not recognized as a separate legal entity under Korean law, although it is well defined in practice. Because it lacks independent legal status, a liaison office need only register with the BOK and make quarterly flow-of-funds reports. The parent firm can also register it with the district court. Because the liaison office is not a legal person, its operating assets are held in the name of an individual representative, who in turn exercises complete control over the assets and business operations. Because the office is not a legal person, its bank accounts must in particular be held by the representative. However, its other assets can be registered to the office itself provided the office has been registered with the district court. These facts make the

choice of a representative especially important. If representatives are changed, assets must be formally and legally transferred from the old representative to the new one.

A liaison office is easier to set up than other types of entity. A liaison office also gives a foreign business flexibility and control if it wants to hedge its bets by establishing an immediate if limited market presence without either committing to increase its presence at a later date or foreclosing any options to expand its scope of activity in the future.

Because the office generates no income, no income tax is due. Some experts assert that it is possible to establish a liaison office that exploits loopholes in Korean law allowing it to earn income and avoid taxes legally. Nevertheless, if a liaison office begins to earn income, intentionally or not, it becomes liable for income taxes, and at the very least the authorities are likely to require the parent to close the liaison office and establish a taxable branch office. Even if income-producing operations continue undetected, it is not likely that they can be sustained on a very large or profitable scale, and difficulties can be expected if the office attempts to remit funds. However, such operations might be able to cover a significant portion of office expenses and thereby limit the parent firm's out-of-pocket expenses through such maneuvers.

Representative Offices

A representative office is an anomalous entity without legal standing that Korean authorities allow to exist but not to carry on business or earn income. In contrast to the liaison office, it is not acknowledged to be an official representative of a foreign entity, and it is seen as an independent local entity with no official backing or connection to any other entity, foreign or domestic. The functions of a representative office are unofficial and severely limited. Some investors set up informal presences that they refer to as representative offices to gather information that helps them to decide whether to make a commitment in Korea, but because such offices lack standing, they are not viewed as an appropriate vehicle for those interested in serious business.

Commercial Agents and Distributorships

Agents are individuals or firms that provide local representation for a foreign business in the buying of Korean products or in selling the business's own products in Korea. Domestic agents can be authorized to conclude contracts on behalf of foreign clients, and they are often responsible for day-to-day operations, information gathering and market research, and the purchase and delivery of goods. They cannot serve as a proxy office in Korea.

Ideally, foreign businesses would be able to

choose an individual or firm that had specific expertise in its area of interest. In practice, the business that wants to retain a Korean agent must select from among existing registered Korean agents. There is a wide range of established Korean agents from which to choose. Purchasing agents must be registered with the Korean Export Buying Offices Association. Selling agents must be members of the Association of Foreign Trading Agents of Korea.

Agency agreements offer the simplest means of establishing a business presence in Korea, because they involve a simple contract that can easily be terminated without additional liability if there is no breach of contract or outstanding liability involved. However, agents should be selected only after a thorough examination of their qualifications and experience. Most foreign entities that anticipate a steady and growing volume of business in Korea find that it is better to set up a branch office than to rely exclusively on agents. However, the use of an agent can give a foreign firm a way to gain information and recognition and exploit immediate opportunities in the market while it decides whether it wants to develop a larger presence in Korea.

Agency agreements place limits on income-earning activities and remittability of profits, and great care must be taken to assure the tax status of the relationship. Income earned for foreign entities by agents who have the authority to execute contracts that are binding on their foreign clients is generally taxable in Korea. However, an independent agency that acts for its own account without creating terms and conditions binding on the foreign entity produces sales the proceeds of which are tax exempt to the foreign entity.

Agency agreements can be made on the basis of a distributor arrangement, in which the agency holds inventories for its own account; on a consignment basis; or on a straight commission basis. It is possible to hire agents for a monthly salary or retainer. Another possibility is to appoint an exclusive agent or an agent who handles the accounts of several firms in the same industry.

Licensing and Technical Assistance Agreements

Licensing and technical assistance agreements are contractual agreements by foreign nationals to license or sell specific technologies to firms or individuals in the ROK. In exchange for the use of foreign-owned technical expertise or patent rights, the Korean entity agrees to pay fixed fees or negotiated royalties. Such technology transfers are exempt for five years from income and other corporate taxes on royalty and licensing fees. Foreign businesses are guaranteed the right to remit such royalties and fees, although they must follow the standard FECA procedures in order to obtain the foreign exchange needed for such remittances.

There is no specific legal framework for such agreements, nor is there any prior approval process. Technology agreements must be reported to the MOF. If no notification to the contrary is received within 20 days, the agreement can be assumed to have been approved. However, to prevent difficulties later on, foreign investors will wish to confirm approval. Licensing agreements often face bureaucratic delays as well as retroactive restrictions that can have a significant impact on profitability.

The MOF is likely to reject agreements involving low-grade or obsolete technologies, agreements that restrict exports generated by the technology, that heighten domestic competition, or that compete directly with existing domestic technology. In addition, agreements must conform to Korea's Fair Trade Act, that prohibits contracts which include provisions requiring the Korean partner to buy inputs exclusively from the licensing entity or its designee; that name the licensing party or its designee as the exclusive exporter of items produced; or that limit the Korean partner's access to export markets via exclusive territories, quotas, or other restrictions. Foreign technology that is part of a joint venture does not require separate authorization.

Joint Ventures

As in much of the rest of Asia, a joint venture in Korea is a vague description that refers to a wide range of mutual agreements between contracting parties, often—but not always—of different nationalities. It is not a specific type of business structure with legal standing, as it is in most Western legal theory and practice. South Korea's legal codes contain no legal definitions of or provisions for joint venture agreements, nor are joint ventures as such recognized as legal entities in Korea. For these reasons, unless a joint venture is carefully structured within the accepted framework of Korean law, it can cause difficulties for the foreign partner in such areas as obtaining foreign exchange, repatriating funds, paying taxes, and resolving disputes.

The vast majority of joint ventures in Korea are set up as a joint stock company under the provisions of the Foreign Capital Inducement Law (FCIL). Joint venture companies are subject to the normal requirements to obtain any required foreign investment authorization. There is no separate review process for the specific terms of joint venture agreements, but investors should remember that agreements can be nullified if they violate the provisions of Korea's Fair Trade Act. These provisions prohibit requirements that the Korean partner buy inputs exclusively from the foreign partner or its designee; that grant exclusive export rights of goods produced to the foreign partner or its designee; that limit the Korean partner's access to export markets via assignment of exclusive territories, quotas, or other restrictions; or that give the foreign partner undue control over the operation of the venture through conditions that give the foreign partner the right to appoint a disproportionate number of directors or exercise disproportionate control over voting shares.

The issues of control and finances can become points of conflict between foreign and Korean venture partners. Agendas other than strict profit making as it is understood in the West are common in Korean business. For example, Korean companies often elect not to declare dividends in order to reinvest all earnings in operations even if the foreign partner needs to realize income on current operations. Such a choice may reflect the financial needs of the Korean parent organization, which may wish to call on the financial resources of its downstream partners to bolster its own credit. Financial policy and other governance issues should be worked out before entering into a joint venture agreement, as should any government concessions, exemptions, or benefits on which the venture is counting. These benefits should be confirmed in writing by the appropriate governmental authority before the investment is made. Joint venture agreements should be prepared in both Korean and English.

Partnerships

Partnerships in South Korea are generally organized as specially incorporated companies. Although in theory it is possible to organize a partnership as a noncorporate entity, this is not done in practice and in any case the resulting entity would not be recognized as having separate legal standing. Foreigners are not allowed to form or participate in partnerships in Korea. Finally, partnerships are not seen as appropriate vehicles for serious foreign investment.

Sole Proprietorships

Sole proprietorships are not recognized as separate legal persons in South Korea, meaning that a business operated as a sole proprietorship has unlimited personal liability. Koreans, and in theory foreign nationals, may set up sole proprietorships in compliance with relevant Korean laws. In practice, a sole proprietorship is neither an accepted nor a feasible vehicle for a serious foreign investor.

REGISTERING A BUSINESS

Businesses in Korea must register with the appropriate authorities before commencing business operations. Moreover, no enterprise may conduct business in areas or activities beyond the scope allowed by the terms of its registration. This section outlines the procedures and documentation required to register a business in Korea. Most entities are formed under Korean commercial law, but foreign entities also need to comply with the provisions governing foreign investments.

Although it is theoretically possible for an investor to handle business formation and registration without professional assistance, the complex nature of the regulations governing such procedures, makes it highly advisable that, besides conferring with government authorities, individuals or firms wishing to do business in Korea obtain legal and accounting assistance to ensure that they are in compliance with the myriad of regulatory requirements and procedures. Individuals or companies doing business in Korea should continually monitor progress and status of agency approvals and follow-up registration procedures to ensure that the process does not become sidetracked and that additional requirements are clearly identified as such. (Refer to "Important Addresses" chapter for a partial listing of government agencies and legal and accounting firms.)

Licensing Foreign businesses operating in Korea require foreign investment approval and business licenses from the appropriate authorities. In order to operate legally, every business must be entered in the commercial register maintained by the district court that has jurisdiction in the area in which it is located.

Special Registration for Businesses In addition to the regulations that cover the particular form of entity selected, some areas of business require additional special authorization or licensing. Businesses can be approved and registered only after such permission has been granted. Businesses that require special authorization include food processing, travel agencies, hotels, restaurants, airlines, freight forwarding, shipping, insurance, financial services, and pharmaceuticals. This list is not exhaustive, and investors should consult the Bureau of Economic Cooperation in the Foreign Investment Office of the MOF and the Consultation Office for Overseas Companies of the Ministry of Trade and Industry (MTI) for specifics on the areas that require additional licensing.

Restrictions Korea's Foreign Capital Inducement Law (FCIL), which governs foreign investment, divides domestic economic sectors into three classes: Prohibited, restricted, and eligible for foreign investment. As of the end of 1993 some 56 sectors were prohibited, including projects judged to have a harmful effect on health or the environment and projects deemed contrary to morals and traditions. Sectors closed to foreign investment under Korea's negative list include public utilities, communications, broadcasting, publishing, and transportation; grain farming; the manufacture of tobacco products; and the operation of bars or gambling establishments.

Activities in which foreign participation was restricted and thus effectively disallowed unless special approval was obtained from the MOF included 168 sectors. Restricted activities include projects that require specific government assistance, are officially determined to produce pollution, depend heavily on energy and other imported materials, involve the production of luxury goods, endanger protected agricultural production, and compete with designated domestic infant industries. Specific activities that are currently restricted include dairying operations; livestock breeding; anthracite coal mining; wholesale and retail distribution of fruits, vegetables, meats, alcoholic beverages, bakery, and confectionery items; and wholesale and retail petroleum sales.

In early 1994 the government announced that it would reduce the number of restricted industries as of July 1, 1994. Specifics were not announced; however, the official statement indicated that industries that had been restricted because of heavy energy or imported raw materials use or because of infant industry protections would be made more available to foreign participation in accord with the provisions of the General Agreement on Tariffs and Trade (GATT).

In theory, all business areas not on either the prohibited or restricted lists—924 of 1,148 sectors as defined by Korea's standard industrial classification codes—are eligible for foreign participation. Under new foreign investment rules, investments in eligible industries valued at less than US$20 million can now use the notification procedure. Under this system, the foreign investor notifies the MOF of the intended investment and unless he receives a formal rejection within 30 days, he can proceed with implicit authorization. Despite this more user-friendly procedure, specific proposals can be rejected for what are often idiosyncratic policy reasons. The MOF exercises a high degree of discretion regarding specific projects, and it is suspected that the influence brought to bear by investors and their friends or by domestic firms seeking to block competitors plays a role in what is actually allowed.

In addition to obtaining a current copy of the negative list from the MOF, investors should contact the government offices responsible for specific industries for details and current rulings. Offices that can handle such inquiries include the Investment Promotion Division, Foreign Investment Information Center, and the One-Stop Service Office, all agencies of the MOF. The Consultation Office for Overseas Companies of the MTI also deals with these issues. The Center for Foreign Investment Services of the Small and Medium Industry Promotion Corp. handles inquiries from individuals or firms interested in smaller operations. (Refer to "Important Addresses" chapter for contact information for these agencies.)

Fees and Expenses Licensing fees vary with the industry, the size and complexity of the venture, and the type of entity involved. A registration tax of 2.4 percent of paid-in capital is required for joint stock companies registered in Seoul, Pusan, Taegu, and Inchon. Those registered elsewhere pay 0.48 percent, a rate designed to attract businesses to less developed areas. Registration fees and other associated costs are generally lower for other types of business entities. The estimated legal costs involved in establishing a basic joint stock company are between US$6,250 and US$12,500, excluding cost of facilities, equipment, inventory, and staffing. The cost of establishing a branch office is about US$10,000.

Basic Authorizations Needed and Applications Procedures

Specific provisions exist for the formation and registration of each type of entity. However, every entity must complete three basic steps. First, it must obtain foreign investment approval from the MOF or the BOK. Second, it must complete registration procedures in the jurisdiction where it plans to carry on activities. Third, it must register with local tax authorities in the jurisdiction where the business is to operate.

Summary of Approval and Registration Procedures by Type of Entity

Companies Joint stock companies involving foreign investment must notify or receive approval from the MOF, the BOK, or another designated entity, carry out required incorporation procedures, register and enroll in the commercial register maintained by the district court that has jurisdiction in their area of operations, and register with the appropriate local tax authorities.

Branch Offices Branch offices intending to make remittances to their head offices are required to obtain a license issued by the BOK. Branch offices must file quarterly reports on establishment with the BOK. They must also register with local tax authorities and the commercial registry office of the local district court.

Representative or Liaison Offices Representative and liaison offices do not have to register with the local district court, although they may register in order to allow the entities to hold certain assets that the appointed representative must otherwise hold individually. Such offices should file an establishment report with the BOK in order to be allowed to carry out any future foreign exchange transactions. They should also notify tax authorities that have jurisdiction over the location of the business although such offices are not allowed to earn income.

Licensing and Technical Assistance Agreements Licensing and technical assistance agreements must be submitted to the MOF or other authorized authorities and register with the BOK in order to obtain foreign exchange for the remittance of royalties.

Basic Procedures

Approval Procedures Every foreign entity that wants to do business in Korea and every agreement that involves foreign investment must obtain official approval from the Investment Promotion Division of the International Finance Bureau of the Ministry of Finance (MOF) or, if the investment is eligible for automatic approval, from the Department of Foreign Exchange of the Bank of Korea (BOK).

In March 1993 the government instituted a notification procedure for foreign investment approvals by which foreigners could notify the BOK on all investments in eligible industries valued at less than US$20 million and proceed unless their investment was formally rejected within 30 days. In early 1994 the government announced that it was eliminating the formal approval procedure for such investments and that they would be allowed to proceed concurrently with the filing of formal notification papers with the BOK. The approval period on foreign proposals requiring government approval—those valued at more than US$20 million and those operating in restricted and otherwise questionable areas would be approved or denied within five days.

It used to be necessary to begin investigations and preparations as far in advance of the date proposed for the beginning of operations as possible in order to allow adequate time for all necessary approvals and registrations. Although regulations stipulated specific periods for action on proposals, the actual time elapsed could extend to months before a business was finally allowed to operate. For small-to medium-sized investments the new notification system should serve to shorten or eliminate this period. However, there is still a significant chance that there will be snags and holdups in obtaining all necessary approvals.

New rules also allow most foreign investments to bypass the MOF and apply directly to the BOK. Beginning on March 1, 1994, foreign investors are to be allowed to submit the necessary paperwork to the Korea Development Bank and the Industrial Bank of Korea as well. On July 1, 1994, other authorized foreign exchange banks are also to be allowed to accept such paperwork. All notifications and applications for approval or registration must be submitted by Korean residents. Nonresidents must act through a resident Korean agent designated by proxy. A certified translation into Korean is required for all materials in another language.

As a general guideline, notifications and applications, where required, including the following certified documentation, should be submitted in quintuplicate (five copies) to the MOF or to the BOK in cases where automatic approval is sought:

- Application for approval
- Project plan, including the scope of business to be conducted within the ROK
- Certification of investor nationality
- Statement of capital requirements and sources of capital
- Location, size, and nature of the planned presence within the ROK
- Notarized copies of the proposed articles of incorporation for the Korean entity
- Proxy authorization for the entity's Korean agent, including executed power of attorney
- Contractual agreements, where appropriate
- Minutes of the parent company's shareholders meetings or directors meeting at which the resolution regarding the decision to authorize the entity to do business in Korea was adopted
- Minutes of the company's shareholders meetings or directors meeting at which the resolution regarding the election of a representative was approved
- Documentation and certification pertaining to stock shares

Registration Procedures Once notification has been filed or investment approval has been received from the MOF or the BOK if required, the entity must then register with the district court that has jurisdiction in the area where the operation is to be located, the Bank of Korea (BOK), or both, depending on the nature of the business being registered.

Joint Stock Companies Registration of a joint stock company involves the following procedures:

- After investment approval has been received, articles of incorporation for a joint stock must be approved and notarized.
- The company must register with the commercial registry office of the district court that has jurisdiction over the location of business and with the local tax authorities. Registration requires that the following documents be submitted: articles of incorporation, certification of actual receipt of payment for subscribed shares, receipt showing deposit of subscribed funds, report of first promoters meeting and minutes of meeting, company auditor's report, report on election of directors and auditor, minutes of shareholders meeting reporting election of a legal representative, certificate of power of attorney for the representative, and a copy of the investment approval granted by the MOF or the BOK.

Companies that want to set up a manufacturing facility must apply for a permit to construct a production facility from the Ministry of Home Affairs. When construction has been completed, the company must obtain a factory license. Companies conducting import or export operations must obtain a license from the Ministry of Trade and Industry.

Branch Offices A license issued by the BOK is required for the establishment of a branch office. In addition to filing a standard report on establishment, which states the purpose of the office, the foreign investor must supply the following documentation:

- A business plan and pro forma financial statements for three years
- Certified copies of the articles of incorporation of the head office in its home jurisdiction, licenses and registrations, or equivalent documentation
- Proxy authorization, including power of attorney, for agents submitting the applications
- The annual reports of the parent firm
- Lease agreement for office premises

Other significant points regarding the establishment of a branch office include:

- A branch office must register with the commercial registry of the district court that has jurisdiction over the location in which it will operate. This crucial step establishes the branch office as a legal entity. The branch must submit a certificate of incorporation; a copy of its articles of incorporation; a corporate inventory stating the assets to be registered; certification of the request for registration made by the board of directors for such registration; and a power of attorney executed in favor of a local attorney who will be responsible for dealings on the branch's behalf.
- A branch engaged in activities related to insurance services, investment management, securities trading, management consulting services, or other financial or business services activities other than banking, which is regulated separately, requires approval from the MOF not a license from the BOK.
- A branch that engages in commission sales of imported goods must register with the Association of Foreign Trading Agents of Korea. A branch involved in the export of Korean-made goods on a commission basis must register with the Korea Export Buying Offices Association before it can submit its branch office application to the BOK.
- A branch office must renew its license every three years, unless governing regulations specify a different—usually shorter—schedule.
- A branch office must designate an authorized foreign exchange bank to act as its agent in

foreign exchange transactions. This appointment must be registered with and confirmed by the BOK. To obtain such confirmation, the branch must submit an application, a copy of its BOK registration, and a copy of its commercial registry entry.

- Every branch office must submit quarterly reports detailing the flow of operating funds to the BOK. These reports must follow a prescribed format and include a copy of the branch's confirmed designation of a foreign exchange bank and a copy of the branch's value-added tax certificate.

Liaison Offices As a rule, the only registration required of a liaison office is to file an initial establishment report with the BOK. Liaison offices must also file quarterly flow-of-operating-funds reports with the BOK. A liaison office can register with the district court that has jurisdiction over its business location if it wants to register certain assets other than financial assets to the entity rather than in the name of its registered representative.

Technical Licensing Agreements A foreign firm must report its technical licensing agreements to the Ministry of Finance and the ministry that has jurisdiction over the industry in which it operates. Approval can usually be assumed to have been granted if the applicant has not been told otherwise within 20 days from the filing of the report. However, to assure subsequent approval for remittance of royalty payments, the firm should confirm that the agreement has been approved.

Registration with Local Tax Authorities A new business must file registration or notification of business establishment with local tax authorities within 20 days of beginning operations.

- Entities established to undertake profit-making activities must apply for a business license from local tax authorities, who will assign them identification numbers for tax purposes.
- Non-income-producing offices must also register. They receive a tax identification number and certification of their nontaxable status.
- Companies must submit a certificate of incorporation; copies of their articles of incorporation; the names, addresses, and shares held by promoters; opening balance sheets; a detailed inventory of property and assets; the company's registered seal; certification that payment for shares has been deposited in a bank; a roster of shareholders; a roster of directors; and any other documents that the local tax office may require of petitioners for business licenses and tax identification numbers.
- Branches must submit a copy of their district court registration, a copy of their articles of

incorporation, a copy of their office lease agreement, an opening balance sheet, a map showing the location of their office, and any other documents requested by the particular local tax office to obtain business licenses and tax identification numbers.

- To obtain a value-added taxpayers number, the branch submits a copy of its certificate of incorporation, a copy of any special business licenses, a copy of its lease agreement, and other documents requested by the local tax office.

TEN REMINDERS, RECOMMENDATIONS, AND RULES

1. The joint stock company and branch office are the most common types of business entity used by both local and foreign investors. These are also the business formats that Korean authorities prefer.
2. The importance of establishing and fostering personal relationships with individuals in Korean ministries, governmental agencies, and business organizations cannot be overemphasized.
3. Although South Korea allows 100 percent foreign ownership of businesses, the scrutiny that a foreign investment application receives increases with the percentage of foreign ownership, as does the likelihood that the application will be denied, modified, or delayed.
4. Korean regulators believe that the growth of Korea's economy as a whole should take precedence over the success of individual businesses or sectors within the economy, regardless of the efficiency, skill, or competitive advantage that a particular business or sector exhibits. Foreign investors can encounter invisible barriers that arbitrarily restrict or block their operations if bureaucrats decide that a proposed entity will be too successful— that is, that it will result in disproportionate growth on an individual or sectoral basis.
5. For purposes of registration, branches and any other Korean offices of foreign firms are considered to be resident entities even if the firm's main office is located abroad.
6. The Foreign Exchange Control Act (FECA) and the Foreign Capital Inducement Law (FCIL) define the legal status and operating regulations for foreign individuals or companies doing business in Korea. The Korean commercial code contains provisions that govern all business entities, foreign or domestic. Foreign entities are subject to both sets of regulations.
7. Under new regulations foreign investors should be able to begin most operations concurrent with filing a formal notification with the BOK or other designated authority. Those that require official approval should receive it, or official notification of delay or denial within 30 days of the formal application. According to new rules scheduled to go into effect on July 1, 1994, this review period is to be shortened to five days. No response within the stated time period can be taken as a sign of approval, although investors should seek positive confirmation. Despite a speeded-up approval procedure, the necessary registration procedures that follow can still take up to six months or more, depending on the complexity of the specific business and the policy issues raised.
8. Foreign entities with less than 50 percent foreign equity investment are generally eligible to apply directly to the BOK for foreign investment approval under Korea's automatic approval system. This procedure is shorter than the MOF's. Waivers of the 50 percent rule are available for investments that are more than 50 percent foreign owned and that export at least 60 percent of their production. Waivers allow automatic BOK approval.
9. Companies with 50 percent or more foreign ownership can purchase and hold land with advance approval from the Ministry of Home Affairs (MHA), the Ministry of Trade and Industry (MTI), or provincial or municipal authorities. Land can only be purchased for uses directly connected with business operations. Branches, liaison offices, and other forms of business entities set up by foreign investors are barred from owning land.
10. The Ministry of Trade and Industry (MTI) regulates the manufacturing and trading of commodities. It sets import and export controls and reviews certain programs involving technical cooperation. The fact that the MOF also claims authority over policy and regulation in these areas introduces a level of regulatory double jeopardy and produces bureaucratic turf battles. Investors can find themselves caught in the middle.

USEFUL ADDRESSES

In addition to the government agencies listed here, individuals or firms should contact chambers of commerce, embassies, banks and other financial service firms, local consultants, legal and accounting firms, and resident foreign businesses for assistance and information. (Refer to "Important Addresses" chapter for a more complete listing.)

Association of Foreign Trading Agents of Korea
45-20, Youido-dong, Yongdungpo-ku
Seoul, Rep. of Korea
Tel: [82] (2) 782-4411 Fax: [82] (2) 785-4373

Bureau of Economic Cooperation
Foreign Investment Advice Office
Ministry of Finance (MOF)
1, Jungang-dong
Gwachon City , Kyonggi Province, Rep. of Korea
Tel: [82] (2) 503-7171

Center for Foreign Investment Services (CFIS)
Small and Medium Industry Promotion
Corporation
24-3, Yoido-dong, Yongdeungpo-gu
Seoul, Rep. of Korea
Tel: [82] (2) 783-9611/9466 Fax: [82] (2) 782-9702
Tlx: SMCKO K25542

Consultation Office for Overseas Companies
(COOC)
Ministry of Trade and Industry
1st Floor, KOEX Main Building.
159, Samsung-dong, Kangnam-gu
Seoul, Rep. of Korea
Tel: [82] (2) 551-6781 Fax: [82] (2) 551-6784

Department of Foreign Exchange
Bank of Korea (BOK)
110, 3-Ga, Namdeamun-ro, Jung-ku
Seoul, Rep. of Korea
Tel: [82] (2) 752-9151/9 Fax: [82] (2) 752-0620

Foreign Investment Information Center
Ministry of Finance (MOF)
1 Jungang-dong
Gwachon City, Kyonggi Province, Rep. of Korea
Tel: [82] (2) 503-9259

Investment Promotion Division
International Finance Bureau
Ministry of Finance (MOF)
1, Jungang-dong
Gwachon City, Kyonggi Province, Rep. of Korea
Tel: [82] (2) 503-9276

Korea Export Buying Offices Association
Korea World Trade Center
159, Samsung-Dong, Kangnam-ku
Seoul, Rep. of Korea
CPO Box 8148
Tel: [82] (2) 551-3195 Fax: [82] (2) 551-3199

Korea Trade Promotion Corporation (KOTRA)
159, Samsung-dong, Kangnam-gu
Seoul, Rep. of Korea
Tel: [82] (2) 551-4181 Fax: [82] (2) 551-4477
Tlx: KOTRA K23659, K27326, K28819

One-Stop Service Office
Ministry of Finance (MOF)
1, Jungang-dong
Gwachon City, Kyonggi Province, Rep. of Korea
Tel: [82] (2) 503-9258

FURTHER READING

The preceding discussion is provided as a basic guide for those interested in doing business in South Korea. The resources described in this section provide additional information on company law, investment, taxation and accounting requirements, and procedural requirements.

Doing Business in Korea, Ernst & Young. New York: Ernst & Young International, 1991. Available in the United States from Ernst & Young, 787 Seventh Avenue, New York, NY, Tel: (212) 773-3000. Available in Korea from Young Wha Accounting Corporation, Dae Uy Building, Floors 11-14, 25-15, Yoido-dong, Youngdeungpo-ku, GPO Box 428, Seoul 150-010, Korea, Tel: [82] (2) 784-6991. Provides an overview of the investment environment in Korea together with information about taxation, business organizational structures, business practices, and accounting requirements.

Doing Business in Korea, Price Waterhouse. Los Angeles: Price Waterhouse World Firm Limited, 1992. Available in the United States from Price Waterhouse, 400 South Hope Street, Los Angeles, CA 90071-2889, Tel: (213) 236-3000. Available in Korea from Seihwa Accounting Corporation, Samwhan Building, 9th Floor, 98-5 Unni-dong, Chongro-ku, Seoul 110-350, Tel: [82] (2) 745-8500, or Price Waterhouse Associates, Inc., International Business Development Center, Royal Building, 8th Floor, 5, Dangju-dong, Chongro-ku, Seoul 110-071, Tel: [82] (2) 723-3015/3016. Covers the investment and business environment in Korea and audit, accounting, and taxation requirements.

How to Market in Korea, Washington, DC: US-DOC Overseas Business Reports, International Trade Administration, US Department of Commerce, 1990. Available from the United States Government Printing Office, Washington, DC 20402. Further information: US-DOC Office of the Pacific Basin, Tel: (202) 482-3877/2522, or US-DOC Korea Desk, Tel: (202) 482-4390. An annual overseas business report with general information and brief overviews of foreign trade, economic and industry trends, marketing, transportation, trade regulations, and investment in Korea.

Trade With Korea, Korea Trade Promotion Corporation. Seoul, ROK: Korea Trade Publications Department, Doc. 91-61-4-68, 1991-1992. Available in Korea from Korea Trade Promotion Corporation, 159, Samsung-dong, Kangnam-gu, Trade Center PO Box 123, Seoul, Korea, Tel: [82] (2) 551-4181. Available in the United States from Korea Trade Promotion Corporation, 460 Park Avenue, New York, NY 10022, Tel: (212) 826-0900, or Korea Trade Promotion Corporation, 1129 20th Street NW, Suite 410, Washington, DC. An informative guidebook for foreign traders and companies interested in establishing business relations in Korea.

Labor

THE LABOR ECONOMY

Just as South Korea's overall economy underwent dramatic changes in the late 1980s and early 1990s, so, too, did Korea's labor economy. The lifting of martial law in 1987 made union organization and the right to strike legal again. Unions took to the streets and won a series of unprecedented concessions from corporate entities and the government. Wages doubled between 1988 and 1992—some foreign companies report that overall wages and benefits rose by more than 500 percent during the period—and the average workweek decreased to 47.9 hours in 1991, down from 56 hours a week in some manufacturing industries.

Against this backdrop, Korea's first civilian leader in 30 years, President Kim Young Sam, took office in February 1993 with bold plans to reinvigorate a sluggish economy. On taking power, he froze wages in the civil service and instituted voluntary price and wage restraints (which could be made mandatory if necessary) in the private sector. Surprisingly, the leading labor and employer federations reached an agreement to hold down wages except in state enterprises. And they did this without any overt intervention by the government. There is a general consensus that high labor and financing costs, declining product quality and declining productivity, and aggressive competition from Southeast Asia and China threaten the livelihood of all Koreans. But it remains to be seen whether this labor-management-government truce will last long enough to put Korea's economy back on track.

Population

The population of Korea was 43.7 million in 1992, an increase of 0.8 percent over the preceding year. The country is ethnically homogeneous, and non-Koreans comprise less than 1 percent of the population. More than 70 percent of the country's inhabitants live in urban areas, compared to only 41 percent in 1970 and 57 percent in 1980, and this is expected to rise to 80 percent by decade's end.

Labor Force Population

The civilian labor force totaled 19 million in 1991—11.3 million men and 7.7 million women. The labor force is growing at a rate of 2.7 percent annually, more than three times as fast as Korea's population. This growth can be attributed to an increase in the number of women entering the work force, an increase in the retirement age, and increasing numbers of foreign workers, including illegal ones.

Labor Availability and Distribution by Sector

In the early 1990s the South Korean government, business, and the press expressed concern about labor shortages in the manufacturing sector, particularly among small- and medium-size companies. In 1991 the Labor Ministry estimated a nationwide shortage of 250,000 workers—220,000 production workers and 30,000 technical workers.

As of 1993 foreign investors were allowed to bring into the country as many foreign personnel as they wish, and there was no limit on the number of foreign workers in a given company. But all foreigners must obtain a visa and work permit if they wish to stay and work for more than 90 days. The Korean government currently does not recruit foreign workers.

Foreign nationals doing business in Korea are encouraged to draw from the local work force whenever possible. In general the Korean work force is well educated, motivated, and extremely hardworking. In addition the number of skilled workers in Korea is increasing steadily due to rising participation in vocational and technical training programs.

As of 1991 27 percent of Korea's work force was employed in industry, 16.7 percent in agriculture, and 56.3 percent in services. As the country's economy continues to mature, the proportion of workers who find employment in the service sector is expected to grow. Currently, the percentage of the work force employed in that sector is growing at an annual rate of 7 percent, while industry is expanding by only 2 percent, and the agricultural sector is shrinking by more than 6 percent a year.

Foreign Workers

Despite periodic labor shortages, Korea generally has not recruited foreign workers. Because Korea is such an ethnically homogeneous country, the prospect of increased diversity is much more controversial than it is in multiethnic countries. Many Korean companies do employ Western workers in their domestic offices and factories, but the workers tend to be highly skilled specialists or professionals, whose expertise the Koreans judge to be especially valuable. However, as part of President Kim's plans to liberalize the economy, he may call for some type of foreign labor recruitment program to import semi-skilled and unskilled workers.

Even without an official labor program, the number of illegal foreign workers is likely to increase, as it did recently. In late 1992 the government attributed a sudden drop in wages of laborers at construction sites and in garment factories to an influx of foreign workers. At the time, the Justice Ministry estimated that there were more than 60,000 illegal foreigners in Korea, while other labor analysts estimated the number to be as high as 100,000.

Unemployment Trends

During the late 1980s and early 1990s the unemployment rate remained fairly stable at about 2.75 percent, fluctuating by only one- or two-tenths of a percentage point. However, as declining exports and foreign investment slowed growth, unemployment climbed to 3 percent by mid-1993. By Korean standards, such a figure is cause for concern, and it served as a catalyst in getting organized labor and employers to temper their demands during the 1993 wage negotiations.

Even with the prospect of slow growth rates for the next several years, there is little chance that unemployment will rise above 3.5 percent. Merely the threat of such an occurrence would mobilize government, industry, and labor to cooperate until unemployment dropped to a tolerable level.

HUMAN RESOURCES

As do other Asian countries, South Korea considers its human resources to be one of its most valuable assets. Great amounts of time, energy, and money are spent every year on education and training. Even long after finishing their formal studies, Koreans seek to enhance their knowledge and skills through self-education, in company-sponsored programs, or at night school. One indicator of the country's high regard for education is the claim that the Korean government employs more people with doctoral degrees than any other country in the world.

Education and Attitudes Toward Learning

Koreans place a high value on education and heavy demands are placed on students at all levels. The adult literacy rate is estimated at more than 96 percent. Expenditures on education represent more than 19 percent of all government spending.

Primary education is free and compulsory for children ages 6 to 12. Afterward, students enter secondary schools, where they stay for up to six years (two cycles of three years each). In 1991 there were 115 university-level institutions and 316 graduate schools with a combined student enrollment of more than one million. There are also numerous vocational

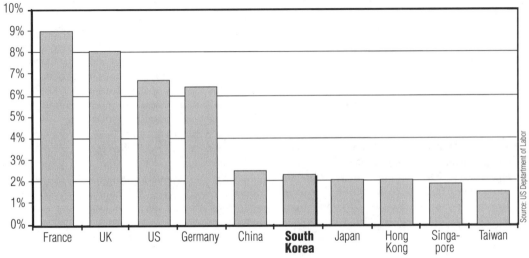

Comparative Unemployment 1990-1991

Source: US Department of Labor

training schools. Korea boasts one of the world's highest enrollment rates for post secondary education—more than 90 percent of the relevant age group.

Competition for entry into the best Korean high schools and universities is fierce. The Seoul National University (SNU) is the most prestigious institution of higher education, and virtually every high school graduate takes that university's examination. A degree from SNU all but guarantees a desirable starting position in government or business.

The ties that Koreans establish during high school and college last throughout their lives. These contacts form the basis of the network through which individuals conduct many of their private and professional affairs.

Training

Vocational and technical training is regarded as essential to the continued growth of the Korean economy in the 1990s. Thus, Korea's intended shift to increasingly high-tech production will undoubtedly involve extensive training and retraining to generate more technically proficient workers.

Workers typically receive a great deal of training immediately after being hired. In particular larger companies conduct rigorous training programs lasting two to five months. The purpose of the programs goes beyond the knowledge and skills that enable the new employee to make a contribution to the company. They tend to emphasize the importance of dedication, loyalty, and team spirit. But such programs also include more practical aspects, such as intensive foreign language courses (particularly English). Workers also receive considerable informal on-the-job training.

Companies are not obligated by law to offer formal or informal training to their workers, but the vast majority of firms spend significant amounts of time and money to upgrade workers' skills.

Women in the Work Force

Traditionally, women (mostly young women) have been concentrated in the labor-intensive manufacturing industries, such as textiles, apparel, footwear, and electronics. However, over the last five years, increasing numbers of women have taken jobs in the growing service sector.

At the end of 1991 women accounted for 40.5 percent of Korea's economically active population. Despite the Equal Rights Law that went into effect in 1988, Korean women still do not enjoy true equal rights in the workplace. Normally, women stop working after marriage or, at the latest, after the birth of a child.

This pattern is slowly changing due to economic necessity, a general labor shortage, and a very gradual erosion of traditional, patriarchal Confucian social values. Even so, the average female worker's wage is 53 percent of the average male worker's wage. The Labor Ministry also reports that starting pay for female university graduates is 40 percent less than the pay of their male counterparts.

Many Korean women have found challenging opportunities with foreign companies located there. But foreign businessmen with extensive experience in Korea warn that firms should exercise caution when using female employees as interpreters or negotiators with government officials and other Korean businessmen. Although attitudes are changing gradually, traditional attitudes toward the sexes in Korea dictate that the face that a company presents to the outside world in Korea should be male if the company wants to ensure cooperation and acceptance.

CONDITIONS OF EMPLOYMENT

Working conditions in Korea are regulated by the Labor Standards Law and the Industrial Safety and Health Law. Labor inspectors from the Ministry of Labor are responsible for enforcing these laws. The laws prescribe basic standards for working hours, overtime, employment of minors, vacations, special leave, and dismissal procedures. They also cover wages, health insurance, and labor insurance.

Working Hours, Overtime, and Vacations

According to the Labor Standards Law, working hours may not exceed eight hours per day and 44 hours per week in firms employing more than 300 people. But a workweek of up to 56 hours is possible if provided for in a labor-management contract. A workweek of more than 56 hours, which has become common in some manufacturing industries, requires prior approval from the Ministry of Labor.

Ministry of Labor
1 Jungang-dong
Gwachon City, Kyonggi Province, Rep. of Korea
Tel: [82] (2) 503-9700 Fax [82] (2) 503-9771
Tlx: 24718

The Korean government reports that Koreans now work a much shorter week than in the past, when the International Labor Organization listed Koreans as having the longest working hours in the world. In 1991 Koreans worked an average of 47.9 hours per week, down from 48.3 hours in 1990. In the 1980s the average was well over 50 hours. Workers are entitled to one hour off per eight-hour period and one day off per week. Employers are required to pay one-and-a-half times the normal wage for overtime hours in excess of the standard eight hours per day.

An employee in Korea is entitled to one vacation day with pay per month, and these days can be accumulated. In addition, employees receive 10 days

Comparative Average Weekly Wages - 1991

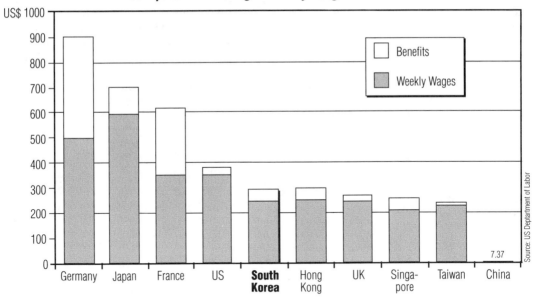

Source: US Deptartment of Labor

of vacation with pay after one full year with perfect attendance but only eight days for 90 percent attendance. It is common for employees to use one or more of the monthly days for sick leave and thus leave the 10 full days of annual vacation intact.

Special Leave

The Labor Standards Law includes broad guidelines for special leave, allowing labor and management at a given company to work out an appropriate policy. Maternity leave of up to 60 days for women and sick leave for all employees are normally granted to employees. Whether such time away from work is paid and at what rate depends on the individual company's policy.

Employment of Minors

Minors are defined as those less than 18 years of age. The Labor Standards Law prohibits the employment of persons under 13 years of age without a special employment certificate. In addition, children under 18 must have written approval from a parent or guardian as a condition for employment. Officially, minors and female workers are prohibited from working as many overtime hours as men, and they may not work at night without special permission from the Ministry of Labor. However, many employers consider teenage and female workers to be "regular" workers and do not observe such regulations. Nevertheless, foreign employers should seek legal counsel or the advice of Korean business partners and contacts before hiring minors.

Termination of Employment

Korean companies generally try to avoid dismissing employees. However, it is possible to fire a worker for just cause, if that worker has been notified 30 days in advance or given a month's wages. A Labor Dispute Mediation Committee exists for the purpose of conciliation, mediation, and arbitration of labor grievances. The committee has the authority to examine whether an employee has been dismissed for just cause. It can order a dismissed worker to be reinstated.

If a worker who has been employed continuously for one year or more is fired for any reason, the employer must pay him severance pay of at least one month's average pay for every year of employment. Average pay is computed on the basis of compensation for the three months immediately preceding the termination. Foreign nationals should consult qualified legal counsel for explanations regarding dismissal procedures and other labor practices.

WAGES AND BENEFITS

Most Korean companies offer generous pay and benefit packages, so it is essential for foreign-owned companies to do the same if they want to attract qualified workers and prevent them from going to the competition. Base wages account for only about 60 percent of the total compensation package, with overtime, allowances, and bonuses making up the rest.

Another factor working against the foreign business owner is that Koreans tend to perceive employment at a foreign company as less than permanent, because foreign-owned firms are not expected to have the same staying power or to adopt the same paternalistic practices as a Korean firms. Thus, foreign enterprises should expect to provide such benefits as health care plans, retirement plans, stock options, and unemployment insurance in order to be competitive employers.

Wages, Salaries, Allowances, and Bonuses

The Labor Standards Law (LSL) provides guidelines for employee compensation, but they are not binding, and most companies frankly ignore them. The Korean system of compensation is a mixture of the Japanese seniority system, the American merit system, and the official LSL provisions. Although the Korean compensation system can be divided into three broad categories—basic wages, allowances, and bonuses—it is notorious for its complexity. It is said that no two companies, even in the same industry, use the same pay structure.

Most unskilled and semi-skilled workers in manufacturing industries are paid on a piecework basis, although daily wage rates are also common. Workers are usually paid on a fixed date once a month. In 1991 the average weekly base pay (excluding benefits) in manufacturing was 160,145.22 Korean won (W) or US$223 at the January 1991 exchange rate. At the time, hourly compensation for production workers in manufacturing was W3,102.36 (US$4.32). Clerical workers in all industries received an average W6,635 (US$9.24) per hour. Although wages increased by an annual 15 to 21 percent between 1988 and 1991, wage negotiations since then have kept the rates of increase much lower.

Salaries for middle managers and professionals vary widely by industry, company, individual performance, and seniority. Typically, managerial employees in manufacturing receive W1 to W1.2 million per month (US$1,392-US$1,671).

Senior managers and executives usually receive between W3 and W4 million per month (US$4,177-US$5,570) in addition to other perquisites, such as a car and driver, club memberships, and "confidential expenses" (freedom to spend certain amounts of company money without having to provide an itemized account).

Korean companies typically pay a number of allowances, including late-hour work, holiday, monthly rest, and annual leave; women also receive menstruation and maternity leave allowances. Officially, each of the allowances just mentioned is required under the LSL. Many firms also provide allowances for such things as special skills, housing, transportation, large families, and perfect attendance.

It is common practice in Korea to pay employees bonuses during the year. The amount and frequency vary, but usually the total is equal to two to six times the monthly pay, divided into four equal installments, which are paid during the year.

Foreign managers are often surprised to learn that Koreans do not consider wage and salary information confidential. Since everyone generally knows what everyone else is earning, any instance of over- or underpayment is likely to come to light and can easily become a major issue among the staff of an entire company.

Average Monthly Earnings by Industry - 1992

Industry	W(000)	US$*	% Change from 1991
All Industry	869.3	1,099	15.2
Manufacturing	798.5	1,010	15.7
Utilities	1,216.1	1,537	8.3
Construction	1,020.2	1,290	15.3
Commerce	884.3	1,118	14.4
Transportation	777.7	983	11.3
Finance	1,053.8	1,332	13.3
Other Services	11,079.4	1,365	14.9

Source: National Statistical Office, ROK
* US$1.00 = W790.9

Average Hourly Earnings by Occupation - 1991

Occupation	Won	US$	Change from 1990
Clerical	6,635	9.24	3.6
Mechanical	7,065	9.84	4.3
Commercial	17,554	24.44	3.7

Source: US Department of Labor
* US$1.00 = W718.1

Minimum Wage

A legal minimum wage was first introduced in 1988. In January 1992 it was W222,000 per month, not including overtime pay and benefits (US$290.58 per month, US$1.65 per hour). Very few workers would accept such low pay, especially since the average hourly pay for production workers in manufacturing is more than two-and-a-half times the minimum wage. (Manufacturing workers are paid the least among Korea's major industries.)

Labor Insurance

All business establishments are required to have labor insurance. According to the Industrial Accident Compensation Insurance Law, workers who suffer job-related accidents receive full medical coverage from their employer and 70 percent of their wages during the time they are out of work. For job-related fatalities, the employer must pay the worker's family funeral expenses and the equivalent of 300 days of wages.

Health Insurance

Since July 1989 companies with five or more employees have been required to participate in the government's health insurance program. A total premium cost of 3 percent of gross wages is shared equally by employer and employee. Under the program, employers must provide a complete medical examination for every employee at the time of hiring and at least once a year thereafter.

It is also possible for employees in companies with fewer than five people to participate in the government's health insurance program. But such firms must work through local authorities rather than the central government.

Retirement Plan

In January 1988 the National Pension System was enacted under the National Pension Law. All residents of Korea between the ages of 18 and 60 are eligible for this program. In fact, participation in the government's retirement plan is mandatory for workers in companies with 10 or more people. A temporary worker with more than three months' service is also eligible, as are self-employed individuals who obtain approval from the Ministry of Health and Social Affairs.

Ministry of Health and Social Affairs
1 Junggang-dong
Gwachon City, Kyonggi Province, Rep. of Korea
Tel: [82] (2) 503-7524, Fax: [82] (2) 503-7505

In 1993 the total premium rate was increased to 6 percent of an employee's gross compensation; 2 percent is contributed by the employer, 2 percent by the employee, and 2 percent by the government. In 1998 the premium is scheduled to increase to 9 percent, to be shared equally.

Legal retirement age was recently raised from 55 to 58 years (61 years for civil servants). Senior executives and employees of small family-owned businesses often work beyond the official retirement age.

LABOR RELATIONS

Labor-management relations have undergone radical changes since 1987. In that year, martial law was lifted, and the government of Roh Tae Woo began to introduce democratic reforms. When strikes were legalized, organized labor went on the offensive, winning a series of major concessions from government and business. During the next several years, wages skyrocketed, working hours decreased, and labor-management relations remained in a constant state of discord.

By late 1990 union activity had subsided somewhat as economic growth slowed, Korea's international competitiveness had perceptively declined, and the Korean government had taken an increas-

ingly tough stand against radical unions. Nevertheless, labor continued to win huge wage increases: 18.8 percent in 1990, 17.5 percent in 1991, and 15.5 percent in 1992.

Labor-management relations entered yet another phase with the election of President Kim Young Sam in early 1993. An increasingly weak economy and the drying up of foreign investment prompted a series of liberalization measures, the success of which depends in no small part on voluntary wage and price restraints. Without government mediation and to the surprise of many, labor and management reached an agreement in mid-1993 to limit wage increases in 1994 to 9 percent. In the coming years, President Kim wants to limit wage increases to the annual rate of inflation—between 4 and 5 percent.

Unions and the Labor Movement

Traditionally organized labor in Korea has been heavily controlled by the government. But the situation changed dramatically in 1987 when President Roh Tae Woo ushered in a series of modest democratic reforms. Since then organized labor has grown in size, diversity, and independence. However, Korea's rate of unionization remains relatively low. Unionized workers as a percentage of the work force grew from just 9 percent in 1986 to a high of 14 percent in 1989. By 1991 the proportion of workers who belonged to a union had dropped to 12 percent of the work force.

Most Korean unions are organized on an enterprise basis, although there are trade unions in some well-established industries, such as textiles, railroads, and utilities. Some 21 different labor federations claim to represent the interests of enterprise unions at annual negotiations, but workers in enterprise unions also negotiate (or strike) to improve their own conditions.

The largest and most established federation is the Federation of Korean Trade Unions (FKTU), with roughly 8,000 affiliated unions. Many affiliates do not pay FKTU dues. The FKTU is basically an umbrella organization for 20 smaller federations and serves as the main labor representative at annual labor-employer negotiations in the spring and summer. In this sense, the FKTU attempts to set a benchmark for all workers, but actual labor conditions vary widely from enterprise to enterprise.

Federation of Korean Trade Unions (FKTU)
35 Yoido-dong, Yongdeungpo-ku
Seoul, Rep. of Korea
Tel: [82] (2) 782-3884; Fax: [82] (2) 784-6396

Aside from the FKTU, a so-called democratic union movement emerged from the massive wave of strikes that took place in late 1987. It was founded by labor activists who rejected the FKTU as too closely tied to the government. The first national body of democratic unions, the National Trade Union Council, was formed in early 1990; it represented about 700 unions. Since then, the number of member unions has shrunk to about 350.

Strikes and Disputes

Labor unrest reached a high point in 1987, when a total of 3,749 disputes (including strikes) occurred. Since then, the number of labor disputes has decreased sharply, to 235 in 1992. Although labor was still able to secure significant wage increases between 1987 and 1992, labor-employer relations have become less adversarial. Both sides seem to recognize that Korea's slower economic growth threatens the county's international competitiveness and thus the welfare of all.

Some foreign banks have reported that labor has made an issue of government guidelines for employee welfare funds. Such accounts are to be funded from a percentage of gross earnings. While most larger foreign firms have set up employee welfare funds, the foreign companies claim that strict compliance with the official guidelines would be very costly and would result in giving up management prerogatives to labor. They also note that only an estimated 5 percent of affected domestic firms comply with the terms of the guidelines. Some foreign firms feel that they are increasingly being singled out as test cases by labor in an effort to extend worker rights and employer-paid benefits beyond what workers can expect to win from domestic firms.

Chaebol *and Employer Organizations*

The *chaebol*, South Korea's giant business conglomerates, are a unique and critical aspect of the Korean economy. The term *chaebol* refers both to the individual tycoon and to far-reaching business groups he heads. The former is someone who has established a large, diversified, family-owned business, and the latter is the parent company that controls a number of subsidiaries.

Korea's Fair Trade Commission designated 61 conglomerates as *chaebol* in 1991, up from 53 in 1990. Some indicators used to define *chaebol* are combined total revenue, paid-in capital, profits, and bank credit lines. *Chaebol* have played a pivotal role in Korea's industrialization over the past four decades and in successfully transforming an agrarian society into a modern, industrialized economy. The *chaebol*, which account for about one-third of the country's total production in the mining and manufacturing sectors, dominate Korea's economy.

A single *chaebol* can have anywhere from 20 to 58 subsidiaries in virtually all major industries, including electronics, automobiles, textiles, shipbuilding, construction, and finance, although *chaebol* are legally barred from direct ownership of financial institutions. The Lucky-Goldstar Group has the most subsidiaries with 58, followed by Samsung with 52, Hyundai with 43, and Sunkyong with 31.

The principal employer organization is the Korea Employers' Federation (KEF). It comprises 10 regional employers associations that in 1992 had a membership of 1,503 companies. The KEF represents employers in wage and other labor-related negotiations.

Korea Employers' Federation (KEF)
538, Tohwa-dong, Mapo-gu
Seoul 121-743, Rep. of Korea
Tel: [82] (2) 706-1058 Fax: [82] (2) 705-1059

The Future of Organized Labor in Korea

There are essentially three possible scenarios for organized labor in coming years. The first is for labor to stand up to business and the government, as it has done more or less since 1987. That there are now fewer strikes than there were seven years ago and that wage increases have shrunk are simply reflections of Korea's current economic slump. Once the economy picks up again, labor will demand and win higher wage increases, shorter hours, a greater voice in management decisions, and so forth.

The second scenario is for President Kim to clamp down on labor and reassert the government's traditional control, perhaps even outlawing strikes. In doing so, he would remove organized labor as a major player and, together with economic liberalization, make Korea a more desirable investment location. Despite boasting that he can deliver high growth without resorting to authoritarian measures, President Kim used strong-arm tactics when he sent riot police to end a strike at Hyundai Motor in late July 1993.

The third and most likely scenario involves a gradual decrease in labor's power and influence as the result of changing economic realities. During the 1980s Korean business leaders, labor unions, and government officials became complacent while riding a wave of economic growth that averaged 9.7 percent a year. The *chaebol* grew, and their work forces became increasingly militant. While growth has slowed in the 1990s for various domestic reasons, the real threat comes from low-cost China and other developing countries of Southeast Asia; Thai, Chinese, Vietnamese, and Indonesian production workers earn a fraction of what their Korean counterparts make. One remedy is to switch over to high-tech industries, as Japan has done. Although President Kim plans to lead the country in this direction, Korea currently lacks the infrastructure needed to support a highly advanced economy. The alternative is for labor to temper its demands in exchange for commitments by government and business to begin retraining workers for a more prosperous high-tech future.

Business Law

INTRODUCTION

South Korea is reforming its business laws, particularly as they relate to the activities of foreign businesses. Changes are frequent, and the trend is to improve the climate for foreign investment. In addition, many rules and regulations that significantly affect foreign businesses are in unpublished government advisories and internal policy statements, rather than in the statutes. You should investigate the status of the legal requirements that may affect your particular business activities. The information in this chapter is intended to emphasize the important issues in commercial law, but it should not replace legal advice or council. You should be certain to review your business activities with an attorney familiar with international transactions, the laws of the Republic of Korea (ROK), and the laws of your own country. Refer to "Important Addresses" chapter for a list of attorneys in Korea.

BASIS OF KOREA'S LEGAL SYSTEM

Korea is a civil code country, which means that the legal system is based on codified laws. Trials are held before judges only, and judicial decisions are based directly on code provisions, not necessarily on judicial precedent.

Historically, Korea was a monarchy governed by traditional Confucian doctrine. After a period of annexation by the Japanese, the country assumed its modern democratic form in 1948. With rapidly increasing industrialization, Korea has borrowed extensively from Western laws to regulate commercial relationships.

STRUCTURE OF KOREA'S GOVERNMENT AND LAWS

Under the 1948 constitution, as amended, South Korea is a democratic republic (Constitution 1). The government has three branches: the National Assembly exercises legislative powers (Constitution 40), the President administers executive powers (Constitution 66), and the Supreme Court holds judicial authority (Constitution 103). Korea's constitution sets forth the rights of citizens and the basic organization and powers of the government.

Korea's constitution is the country's supreme law, controlling when in conflict with domestic statutes. In addition to the Civil Code and Code of Civil Procedure, numerous special laws regulate specific entities, events, and relationships. Korean courts consider ratified treaties and other recognized rules of international law as having the same effect as domestic statutes (Constitution 6). (*See* Treaties section for a list of international treaties and conventions recognized in Korea.)

LAWS GOVERNING BUSINESS IN KOREA

Commercial transactions must comply with provisions of the Commercial Code and the Commercial Registration Regulations. (*See* Commercial Register.) General contract requirements, sales transactions, and principal-agency relationships are governed by the Civil Code, and requirements for standard commercial contracts and commission agents are found in the Commercial Code. (*See* Contracts; Sales; and Principal and Agent.) Contracting parties may also have to comply with specific laws, such as the Interest Limitation Law, which prohibits usury, and the National Accounting Law, which regulates government contracts and bidding. (*See* Contracts; and Interest.) Financial and shipping documents are regulated under provisions of the Commercial Code, Bills and Notes Act, and Checks Act. (*See* Bills and Notes.) Foreign exchange controls are imposed pursuant to the Foreign Exchange Control Act. (*See* Foreign Exchange.) Acknowledgment of articles of incorporation and commercial documents is covered

Based on interviews with Dennis Kim, of Dennis Paul Kim Law Office, in Santa Clara, California; and Ross Meador, associated with Morrison & Foerster, San Francisco, California and working since 1989 as a foreign legal consultant with Kim & Chang, in Seoul, Republic of Korea.

BUSINESS LAW
TABLE OF CONTENTS

under Korea's Commercial Code, and requirements for seals and signatures of foreigners are set forth in the Foreigner's Signature and Seal Act. (*See* Acknowledgments.)

Formation and operation of legal entities in Korea are governed by the Civil Code, Commercial Code, and special legislative acts or charters. (*See* Corporations; and Partnership.) Certain industries may be subject to further regulation under special acts, such as Korea's Mining Law. (*See* Corporations.) Foreign investment must be government-approved and in compliance with the Foreign Capital Inducement Law. (*See* Foreign Investment.) Korean-based exporters and importers are subject to the Foreign Trade Law. (*See* Foreign Trade Regulations.) Environmental protection is provided by the Basic Environmental Policy Law, Air Environment Preservation Law, Water Quality Preservation Law, and Waste Treatment Law.

Intellectual property and trademark rights are protected under the Copyright Act, Patent Act, Design Act, and Trademark Act. (*See* Copyright; Patents; and Trademarks and Trade Names.) Separate protection for trade names is provided under the Commercial Code, and for trade secrets under the Unfair Competition Prevention Law. (Refer to Monopolies and Restraint of Trade.) Employers with five or more employees are regulated by the Labor Standards Law. Certain businesses must also comply with the Industrial Injury Compensation Insurance Act. (*See* Labor Relations.) Some employees enjoy rights and protections under the Labor Union Law, Labor Disputes Adjustment Law, and Labor Management Council Law. (*See* Labor Relations.) Monopolies, unfair competition, and unreasonable restrictive trade practices are prohibited under Korea's Unfair Competition Prevention Law and Monopoly Regulation and Fair Trade Act. (*See* Monopolies and Restraint of Trade.)

GEOGRAPHICAL SCOPE
OF KOREAN LAWS

Laws digested in this section are in effect throughout areas under the control of Korea's national government. Regional governments, however, are gaining more autonomy and have authority to levy and collect certain taxes and fees. A business owner may therefore need to comply with local requirements when transacting business within a particular region.

PRACTICAL APPLICATION
OF KOREAN LAWS

Contract Negotiation Traditionally, Korean companies have preferred short contracts containing statements of the broad principles that will guide long-term planning between the contracting parties.

Lengthy contracts were thought to be a sign of bad faith and unnecessary between parties who should trust each other. Today, however, Koreans experienced in international transactions will expect detailed agreements and will negotiate explicit terms and conditions aggressively.

Most international agreements are subject to government approval and, accordingly, the government may object to certain terms and conditions. Certain terms common in international commercial contracts may be inadvisable or unenforceable in Korea. For example, certain territorial restrictions limiting the area in which a Korean company can sell products are prohibited. (*See* Contracts.)

During business negotiations, social contact is a central concern. The presence of a Korean attorney representing the foreign business may facilitate negotiating sessions, but may also occasionally be perceived as a sign of bad faith. Parties who desire the presence of an attorney should give prior notice to the other contracting parties. Traditional Korean business owners tend to view attorneys as neutral parties, and thus asking advice from another party's attorney is not unusual.

Use of Attorneys In recent years, the legal profession in Korea has grown in response to increasingly complex commercial laws and transactions. Foreign law firms are barred from practice in Korea, but the leading Korean law firms employ foreign lawyers as legal consultants. Foreign lawyers may not, however, appear as counsel in courtroom litigation. A few domestic law firms have substantial experience representing foreign companies and can provide assistance in securing government approval and tax exemptions.

Use of Notaries Notaries primarily legalize signatures. Notary fees are comparatively high because compensation is based on a percentage of the transaction. (*See* Notaries Public.)

Dispute Resolution Contracting parties usually negotiate settlements of contract disputes; traditionally, lawsuits are rare because they are deemed to disrupt social harmony. Litigation should not be threatened or used unless there is no hope for an amicable settlement.

If a foreign judicial award is granted, it may be difficult to enforce in Korea. Inclusion of an arbitration clause in the contract is therefore often advisable. (*See* Arbitration and Award.) However, the rules of the Korean Commercial Arbitration Board are restrictive and arbitration before this Board should generally be avoided. Arbitration through an overseas association such as the American Arbitration Association or, a more expensive alternative, the International Chamber of Commerce may be preferable. Korea is a party to the Convention on the Recognition and Enforcement of Foreign Arbitral Awards of 1958, and accordingly foreign arbitral awards are enforceable by the Korean courts, as long as the awards do not violate Korean public policy.

Intellectual Property Rights Protection of intellectual property rights both the securing and enforcing of such rights is increasing in Korea. In 1991 the National Assembly extended protection to trade secrets, and in 1992 it passed a semiconductor mask works law. Copyright and computer program protection laws are under revision. (*See* Copyright.) The desire to license technology, especially from the United States, has prompted vigorous government enforcement of laws protecting intellectual property rights, with the result that piracy has largely been eradicated, particularly for large commercial sales and exports. Registration and certification of some intellectual property rights is burdensome for foreigners, often requiring submission of detailed product information, including formulas or blueprints.

Registration of trademarks is on a "first in time, first in right" basis; that is, whoever files first for trademark protection is granted ownership rights. However, several ways to invalidate or cancel a previously registered trademark exist. Further, infringement of unregistered marks and designs can be challenged using the Unfair Competition Prevention Act if the plaintiff can prove that its product is trademark or design are well-known. However, costs and delays should be avoided if possible by filing for ownership registration first. (*See* Trademarks and Trade Names.)

Unfair Trade Practices Large domestic conglomerates, such as Samsung, Daewoo, Hyundai, and Lucky Goldstar, continue to be the major business players in Korea. The Fair Trade Law and the Small and Medium-Sized Business Promotion Law are designed to further competition among manufacturers. As a result, the role of smaller companies is expected to increase, although this process is likely to be slow. (*See* Monopolies and Restraint of Trade.)

RELATED CHAPTERS

Refer to "Corporate Taxation" and "Personal Taxation" chapters for a discussion of tax issues, and "Business Travel" chapter for details on immigration and visa requirements.

Foreign Corrupt Practices Act

United States business owners are subject to the Foreign Corrupt Practices Act (FCPA). The FCPA makes it unlawful for any United States citizen or firm (or any person who acts on behalf of a US citizen or firm) to use a means of US interstate commerce (examples: mail, telephone, telegram, or electronic mail) to offer, pay, transfer, promise to pay or transfer, or authorize a payment, transfer, or promise of money or anything of value to any foreign appointed or elected government official, foreign political party, or candidate for a foreign political office for a corrupt purpose (that is, to influence a discretionary act or decision of the official) and for the purpose of obtaining or retaining business.

It is also unlawful for a US business owner to make such an offer, promise, payment, or transfer to any person if the US business owner knows, or has reason to know, that the person will offer, give, or promise directly or indirectly all or any part of the payment to a foreign government official, political party, or candidate. For purposes of the FCPA, the term *knowledge* means *actual knowledge*—the business owner in fact knew that the offer, payment, or transfer was included in the transaction—and *implied knowledge*—the business owner should have known from the facts and circumstances of a transaction that the agent paid a bribe but failed to carry out a reasonable investigation into the transaction. A business owner should make a reasonable investigation into a transaction if, for example, the sales representative requests a higher commission on a particular sale for no apparent reason, the buyer is a foreign government, the product has a military use, or the buyer's country is one in which bribes are considered customary in business relationships.

The FCPA also contains provisions applicable to US publicly held companies concerning financial record keeping and internal accounting controls.

Legal Payments

The provisions of the FCPA do not prohibit payments made to *facilitate* a routine government action. A facilitating payment is one made in connection with an action that a foreign official must perform as part of the job. In comparison, a corrupt payment is made to influence an official's discretionary decision. For example, payments are not generally considered corrupt if made to cover an official's overtime required to expedite the processing of export documentation for a legal shipment of merchandise or to cover the expense of additional crew to handle a shipment.

A person charged with violating FCPA provisions may assert as a defense that the payment was lawful under the written laws and regulations of the foreign country and therefore was not for a corrupt purpose. Alternatively, a person may contend that the payment was associated with demonstrating a product or performing a preexisting contractual obligation and therefore was not for obtaining or retaining business.

Enforcing Agencies and Penalties

Criminal Proceedings The Department of Justice prosecutes criminal proceedings for FCPA violations. Firms are subject to a fine of up to US$2 million. Officers, directors, employees, agents, and stockholders are subject to fines of up to US$100,000, imprisonment for up to five years, or both.

A US business owner may also be charged under other federal criminal laws, and on conviction may be liable for fines of up to US$250,000 or up to twice the amount of the gross gain or gross loss, provided the defendant derived pecuniary gain from the offense or caused pecuniary loss to another person.

Civil Proceedings Two agencies are responsible for enforcing civil provisions of the FCPA: The Department of Justice handles actions against domestic concerns, and the Securities and Exchange Commission (SEC) files actions against issuers. Civil fines of up to US$100,000 may be imposed on a firm; any officer, director, employee, or agent of a firm; or any stockholder acting for a firm. In addition, the appropriate government agency may seek an injunction against a person or firm that has violated or is about to violate FCPA provisions.

Conduct that constitutes a violation of FCPA provisions may also give rise to a cause of action under the federal Racketeer-Influenced and Corrupt Organizations Act (RICO), as well as under a similar state statute if enacted in the state with jurisdiction over the US business owner.

Administrative Penalties A person or firm that is held to have violated any FCPA provisions may be barred from doing business with the US government. Indictment alone may result in suspension of the right to do business with the government.

Department of Justice Opinion Procedure

Any person may request the Department of Justice to issue a statement of opinion on whether specific proposed business conduct would be considered a violation of the FCPA. The opinion procedure is detailed in 28 C.F.R. Part 77. If the Department of Justice issues an opinion stating that certain conduct conforms with current enforcement policy, conduct in accordance with that opinion is presumed to comply with FCPA provisions.

Legal Glossary

Accrual of obligation The time at which an obligation matures or vests, requiring the obligor to perform. Example: In a contract between a buyer and a seller, the seller's obligation to deliver goods may accrue when the buyer tenders payment in full. However, if the contract terms require delivery of goods by a particular date, the seller's obligation will accrue only at that time, even if the buyer has already tendered payment.

Agent The person authorized to act on behalf of another person (the principal). Example: A sales representative is an agent of the seller.

Appurtenance An accessory connected with a primary item. Example: Appurtenances to ships may include movable equipment used for loading and unloading cargo.

Attachment The legal process for seizing property before execution of a judgment to ensure a successful execution. Provisional attachment may also be allowed before a judgment is granted to secure payment of damages if they are awarded later. Example: A party who claims damages for breach of contract may request a court to issue an order freezing all transfers of specific property owned by the breaching party pending resolution of the dispute.

Authentication The act of conferring legal authenticity on a written document, typically made by a notary public who attests and certifies that the document is in proper legal form and that it is executed by a person identified as having authority to do so.

Bill of exchange A written instrument signed by a person (the drawer) and addressed to another person (the drawee), typically a bank, ordering the drawee to pay unconditionally a stated sum of money to yet another person (the payee) on demand or at a future time.

Chattel An item of personal property.

Composition with creditors An agreement between an insolvent debtor and one or more creditors under which the creditors consent to accept less than the total amount of their claims in order to secure immediate payment.

Crossed check A check that is stamped with the name of a specific bank to which the check must be presented.

Execution The legal process for enforcing a judgment for damages, usually by seizure and sale of the debtor's personal property. Example: If a court awards damages in a breach of contract action and the breaching party has failed to remit the sum due, the party awarded damages may request the court to order seizure and sale of the breaching party's inventory to the extent necessary to satisfy the award.

Fieri facias writ A court writ to "cause to be done," which orders an officer of the law or other authorized person to satisfy a judgment by seizing and selling a debtor's property.

Fungibles Goods that are identical with other goods of the same nature. Example: A merchant who is unable to deliver a specific load of grain may negotiate to replace that grain with fungibles, that is another load of grain that is of the same nature and quality.

Ipso jure By operation of law.

Joint and several liability The liability of two or more persons who are responsible together and individually, allowing the person harmed to sue all or any of the wrongdoers.

Juridical person An individual or entity recognized under law as having legal rights and obligations. Example: Stock companies, associations, foundations, and corporations are entities that are recognized as juridical persons.

Mutatis mutandis Generally the same, but with necessary changes for details. Example: If two different transactions are governed by similar rules, and the transactions vary only in such minor details as the name of a document or the parties involved, the rules apply mutatis mutandis.

Negotiable instrument A written document that can be transferred merely by endorsement or delivery. Example: A check or bill of exchange is a negotiable instrument.

Legal Glossary (cont'd.)

Pari passu On an equal basis without preference. Example: Creditors who receive payment pari passu are paid in proportion to their interests without regard to whether the claims of some would have taken priority over others.

Prima facie Presumption of fact as true unless contradicted by other evidence. Example: A debtor's failure to pay a debt is prima facie evidence of the debtor's inability to do so, establishing a ground for bankruptcy.

Principal A person who authorizes another party (the agent) to act on the principal's behalf.

Promoter of corporation The individual or entity that organizes a corporation.

Real rights Rights in real estate or in items attached to real estate.

Rescind A contracting party's right to cancel the contract. Example: A contract may give one party a right to rescind if the other party fails to perform within a reasonable time.

Rescission See Rescind.

Servitude A charge against or burden on property that benefits other property. Example: An owner of property may grant another person a right to travel over that property for a particular purpose, in which case the owner has created a servitude against the property.

Sight draft An instrument payable on demand. Example: A bill of exchange may be made payable at sight (that is, payable on demand) or after sight (that is, within a particular period after demand is made).

Statute of Frauds A law that requires designated documents to be in writing in order to be enforced by a court. Example: Articles of incorporation must be written for a court to recognize the resulting corporation as a legal entity.

Superficies Rights to build on the surface of real property. Example: A landowner may transfer to a developer the right to build on the property in exchange for an annual rent, in which case the property becomes subject to superficies.

Ultra vires An act performed without the authority to do so. Example: A corporate representative who is authorized to enter into a particular contract commits an ultra vires act by agreeing to a different contract.

Vis major A major force or disturbance, usually a natural cause, that a person cannot prevent despite the exercise of due care.

International Sales Contract Provisions

When dealing internationally, you must consider the business practices and legal requirements of the country where the buyer or seller is located. For a small, one-time sale, an invoice may be commonly accepted. For a more involved business transaction, a formal written contract may be preferable to define clearly the rights, responsibilities, and remedies of all parties. The laws of your country or the foreign country may require a written contract and may even specify all or some of the contract terms. Refer to Contracts and to Sales for specific laws on contracts and the sale of goods.

Parties generally have freedom to agree to any contract terms that they desire. Whether a contract term is valid in a particular country is of concern only if you have to seek enforcement. Thus, you have fairly broad flexibility in negotiating contract terms. However, you should always be certain to come to a definite understanding on four issues: the goods (quantity, type, and quality), the time of delivery, the price, and the time of payment.

You need to consider the following clauses when you negotiate an international sales contract.

Contract date

State the date when the contract is signed. This date is particularly important if payment or delivery times are fixed in reference to it—for example, "shipment within 30 days of the contract date."

Identification of parties

Designate the names of the parties, and describe their relation to each other.

Goods

Description Describe the type and quality of the goods. You may simply indicate a model number, or you may have to attach detailed lists, plans, or drawings. This clause should be clear enough that both parties fully understand the specifications and have no discretion in interpreting them.

Quantity Specify the number of units, or other measure of quantity, of the goods. If the goods are measured by weight, you should specify net weight, dry weight, or drained weight. If the goods are prepack-aged and are subject to weight restrictions in the end market, you may want to provide that the seller will ensure that the goods delivered will comply with those restrictions.

Price Indicate the price per unit or other measure, such as per pound or ton, and the extended price.

Packaging arrangements

Set forth packaging specifications, especially for goods that can be damaged in transit. At a minimum, this provision should require the seller to package the goods in such a way as to withstand transportation. If special packaging requirements are necessary to meet consumer and product liability standards in the end market, you should specify them also.

Transportation arrangements

Carrier Name a preferred carrier for transporting the goods. You should designate a particular carrier if, for example, a carrier offers you special pricing or is better able than others to transport the product.

Storage Specify any particular requirements for storage of the goods before or during shipment, such as security arrangements, special climate demands, and weather protection needs.

Notice provisions Require the seller to notify the buyer when the goods are ready for delivery or pickup, particularly if the goods are perishable or fluctuate in value. If your transaction is time-sensitive, you could even provide for several notices to allow the buyer to track the goods and take steps to minimize damages if delivery is delayed.

Shipping time State the exact date for shipping or provide for shipment within a reasonable time from the contract date. If this clause is included and the seller fails to ship on time, the buyer may claim a right to cancel the contract, even if the goods have been shipped, provided that the buyer has not yet accepted delivery.

Costs and charges

Specify which party is to pay the additional costs and charges related to the sale.

International Sales Contract Provisions (cont'd.)

Duties and taxes Designate the party that will be responsible for import, export, and other fees and taxes and for obtaining all required licenses. For example, a party may be made responsible for paying the duties, taxes, and charges imposed by that party's own country, since that party is best situated to know the legal requirements of that country.

Insurance costs Identify the party that will pay costs of insuring the goods in transit. This is a critical provision because the party responsible bears the risk if the goods are lost during transit. A seller is typically responsible for insurance until title to the goods passes to the buyer, at which time the buyer becomes responsible for insurance or becomes the named beneficiary under the seller's insurance policy.

Handling and transport Specify the party that will pay shipping, handling, packaging, security, and any other costs related to transportation, which should be specified.

Terms defined Explain the meaning of all abbreviations—for example, FAS (free alongside ship), FOB (free on board), CIF (cost, insurance, and freight)—used in your contract to assign responsibility and costs for goods, transportation, and insurance. If you define your own terms, you can make the definitions specific to your own circumstances and needs. As an alternative, you may agree to adopt a particular standard, such as the Revised American Foreign Trade Definitions or Incoterms 1990. In either case, this clause should be clear enough that both parties understand when each is responsible for insuring the goods.

Insurance or risk of loss protection

Specify the insurance required, the beneficiary of the policy, the party who will obtain the insurance, and the date by which it will have been obtained.

Payment provisions

Provisions for payment vary with such factors as the length of the relationship between the contracting parties, the extent of trust between them, and the availability of certain forms of payment within a particular country. A seller will typically seek the most secure form of payment before committing to shipment, while a buyer wants the goods cleared through customs and delivered in satisfactory condition before remitting full payment.

Method of payment State the means by which payment will be tendered—for example, prepayment in cash, traveler's checks, or bank check; delivery of a documentary letter of credit or documents against payment; credit card, credit on open account, or credit for a specified number of days.

Medium of exchange Designate the currency to be used—for example, US currency, currency of the country of origin, or currency of a third country.

Exchange rate Specify a fixed exchange rate for the price stated in the contract. You may use this clause to lock in a specific price and ensure against fluctuating currency values.

Import documentation

Require that the seller be responsible for presenting to customs all required documentation for the shipment.

Inspection rights

Provide that the buyer has a right to inspect goods before taking delivery to determine whether the goods meet the contract specifications. This clause should specify the person who will do the inspection—for example, the buyer, a third party, a licensed inspector; the location where the inspection will occur—for example at the seller's plant, the buyer's warehouse, a receiving dock; the time at which the inspection will occur; the need for a certified document of inspection; and any requirements related to the return of nonconforming goods, such as payment of return freight by the seller.

Warranty provisions

Limit or extend any implied warranties, and define any express warranties on property fitness and quality. The contract may, for example, state that the seller warrants that the goods are of merchantable quality, are fit for any purpose for which they would ordinarily be used, or are fit for a particular purpose requested by the buyer. The seller may also warrant that the goods will be of the same quality as any sample or model that the seller has furnished as representative of the goods. Finally, the seller may warrant that the goods will be packaged in a specific way or in a way that will adequately preserve and protect the goods.

Indemnity

Agree that one party will hold the other harmless from damages that arise from specific causes, such as the design or manufacture of a product.

Enforcement and Remedies

Time is of the essence Specify that timely performance of the contract is essential. The inclusion of this clause allows a party to claim breach merely because the other party fails to perform within the time prescribed in the contract. Common in United States contracts, a clause of this type is considered less important in other countries.

Modification Require the parties to make all changes to the contract in advance and in a signed written modification.

Cancellation State the reasons for which either party may cancel the contract and the notice required for cancellation.

Contingencies Specify any events that must occur before a party is obligated to perform the contract. For example, you may agree that the seller has no duty to ship goods until the buyer forwards documents that secure the payment for the goods.

Governing law Choose the law of a specific jurisdiction to control any interpretation of the contract terms. The law that you choose will usually affect where you can sue or enforce a judgment and what rules and procedures will be applied.

Choice of forum Identify the place where a dispute may be settled—for example, the country of origin of the goods, the country of destination, a third country that is convenient to both parties.

Arbitration provisions Agree to arbitration as an alternative to litigation for the resolution of any disputes that arise. You should agree to arbitrate only if you seriously intend to settle disputes in this way. If you agree to arbitrate but later file suit, the court is likely to uphold the arbitration clause and force you to settle your dispute as you agreed under the contract.

An arbitration clause should specify whether arbitration is binding or nonbinding on the parties; the place where arbitration will be conducted (which should be a country that has adopted a convention for enforcing arbitration awards, such as the United Nations Convention on Recognition and Enforcement of Foreign Awards); the procedure by which an arbitration award may be enforced; the rules governing the arbitration, such as the United Nations Commission on International Trade Law Model Rules; the institute that will administer the arbitration, such as the International Chamber of Commerce (Paris), the American Arbitration Association (New York), the Japan Commercial Arbitration Association, the United Nations Economic and Social Commission for Asia and the Pacific, the London Court of Arbitration, or the United Nations Commission International Trade Law; the law that will govern procedural issues or the merits of the dispute; any limitations on the selection of arbitrators (for example, a national of a disputing party may be excluded from being an arbitrator); the qualifications or expertise of the arbitrators; the language in which the arbitration will be conducted; and the availability of translations and translators if needed.

Severability Provide that individual clauses can be removed from the contract without affecting the validity of the contract as a whole. This clause is important because it provides that, if one clause is declared invalid and unenforceable for any reason, the rest of the contract remains in force.

Increased Opportunity for Foreign Ownership of Land

The Korean government is introducing changes that liberalize foreigners' access to land. This is a significant departure from the current regulation of foreign acquisition and ownership of real property. These legislative changes are due for passage at the regular session of the National Assembly in September, 1993 and should be effective from 1994.

Under the current regulations introduced in 1968, the only foreigners permitted to purchase land were those engaged in a few select industries, such as high-technology or manufacturing industries, and only then with the approval of the appropriate Ministries. In contrast, the proposed regulations will permit all types of foreign businesses or foreign invested businesses to purchase land. Furthermore, the foreign firm's domestic operation terms and size of domestic capital assets will no longer be determining factors in the acquisition of land by foreigners.

The aim of this new policy is two-fold. First, by adopting an Alien Land Law that is less ambiguous and more in line with such laws in developed nations, the Korean government hopes to attract foreign investment and thus improve the technical expertise and competitiveness of domestic industries. Secondly, the changes are expected to relieve trade frictions between Korea and its foreign trading partners, particularly the United States.

Ownership changes

Under the proposed revision of the law, foreign individuals and corporations will be allowed to have ownership and leasehold interests in real estate. Only the Korean branches of foreign corporations in the banking and insurance industries, however, will be permitted to acquire real estate as security.

Foreign individuals will be allowed to own land not exceeding 660 square meters in area. Such land must only be used as a place of personal residence. Each foreign household is limited to one such residence.

Foreign corporations will be allowed to acquire real property to the extent needed to carry out normal business activities. This includes:

- land directly utilized by manufacturing or service industries in their business operations;
- employee housing; and
- sites for auxiliary facilities deemed indispensable by the Presidential Decree of the Alien Land Law.

Procedural changes

The approval procedure for foreign acquisitions has also been simplified. Currently, foreign individuals and companies seeking to obtain rights to real estate must receive the approval of the Minister of Home Affairs. However, under the new law, notifying the Minister will be sufficient.

Restrictions

The proposed plan also attempts to prevent foreigners from purchasing real estate for non-business or speculative purposes. For example, if a foreigner sells land without good cause or loses property rights in the land, the foreigner will be forced to sell the property to the government at either the original purchase price or a price announced by the government, whichever is lower. In addition, if the land is not utilized for the approved purpose within two years, then the government can recommend that the foreign purchaser proceed according to the original plan. Failure to do so will result in the government cancelling the land acquisition permit and ordering the sale of the property.

Foreigners who acquire real estate without a proper permit or who sell their property without good cause will be subject to a jail sentence not exceeding two years, or a maximum fine of 20 million won (about US$25,000).

Reprinted from Asia Pacific Legal Developments Bulletin, vol. 8, no. 3, Baker & McKenzie, Sept. 1993, with permission of the authors, Sai Ree Yun and David T. Han, Seoul, the law firm of Yoon & Partners, Seoul, and the law firm of Baker & McKenzie.

Increased Opportunity for Foreign Investment and Technology

The Korean government intends to improve the procedures for foreigners investing in businesses and introducing new technology. These changes are expected to be effective next year.

The government's new foreign investment policy was announced on July 1, 1993, by Mr. Chang Yul Park, the Second Assistant Secretary of the Ministry of Finance, at a joint conference of the American Chamber of Commerce and the European Community Chamber of Commerce. Mr. Park also disclosed that, in furtherance of the new foreign investment policy, the government plans to revise the Foreign Capital Inducement law later this year.

Reduced approval time

By revising the current procedures, the Ministry of Finance plans to shorten the processing time for foreign businesses and investment applications to 10 days. This is a significant reduction from the current 20 days for foreign investment ratios of less than 50% and 30 days for ratios of more than 50%. If the investment processing of an application has not been completed within the 10 day period it will be deemed to be accepted by the Ministry of Finance or the Bank of Korea.

The Ministry of Finance will simplify the process by which foreign invested enterprises can increase capital or apply for tax reductions or exemptions. Currently, foreign investors in foreign invested enterprises must pass through the same procedures as new investors, such as consulting with and receiving the approval of the relevant authorities. In contrast, under the revised regulations, the consultation will be omitted in cases involving simple increases of capital or the introduction of identical technology. The processing period for capital increases and tax reductions or exemptions is expected to be reduced from the current 30 or 60 days to 10 days.

In cases involving the introduction of foreign technology, a technology introduction report must be submitted to the relevant ministry, and processing time for this procedure is expected to be reduced to 10 days from the current 20 day period.

Possible future reductions

To further simplify these procedures, the Ministry of Finance is considering a plan that would abolish the Foreign Capital Inducement Commission which is empowered to deliberate and decide major foreign capital inducement policies, including public loan agreements, foreign equity investment, and tax reduction and exemption for foreign invested enterprises.

The Ministry is also exploring the possibility of repealing measures that were designed to ascertain whether the investment funds or foreign businesses were used for their approved purposes. These current measures, which apply only to investments exceeding one billion won (about US$1.25 million), include the obligatory submission of a written plan for the use and withdrawal of the investment funds and a system of designated bank accounts.

Conclusion

In the wake of these and other measures, including the three-phase plan for internationalization of the financial market and the plan to open Korea to foreign investment, the domestic investment conditions for foreigners will be improved significantly.

Reprinted from Asia Pacific Legal Developments Bulletin, vol. 8, no. 3, Baker & McKenzie, Sept. 1993, with permission of the authors, Sai Ree Yun and David T. Han, Seoul, the law firm of Yoon & Partners, Seoul, and the law firm of Baker & McKenzie.

LAW DIGEST

(Abbreviations used are: A.L. for Arbitration Law; B.N.A. for Bills and Notes Act; C.C. for Civil Code; C.C.P. for Code of Civil Procedure; C.L.A. for Conflict of Laws Act; B.L. for Bankruptcy Law; Com. C. for Commercial Code; C.R.L. for Company Reorganization Law; L.D.A.L. for Labor Disputes Adjustment Law; L.M.C.L. for Labor Management Council Law; L.S.L. for Labor Standards Law; L.U.L. for Labor Union Law; S.E.L. for Security Exchange Law; F.E.C.A. for Foreign Exchange Control Act; F.C.I.L. for Foreign Capital Inducement Law; C.A. for Copyright Act; T.A. for Trademark Act; E.E.C.A. for Exit and Entry Control Act; M.R.F.T.A. for Monopoly Regulation and Fair Trade Act; U.C.P.L. for Unfair Competition Prevention Law; C.P.A. for Consumer Protection Act; P.A. for Patent Act).

ACKNOWLEDGMENTS

Formal acknowledgment is not usually necessary to validate instrument. Acknowledgment of notary does, however, authenticate identity of parties, verify required performance of party and creates presumption of genuineness to private instruments similar to official documents. Acknowledgment of articles of incorporation of stock and limited corporations is mandatory. (Com. C. 292, 543[3]). In civil actions, some papers submitted to court require acknowledgments. (C.C.P. 81[2], 326[1]). Recorded instruments are usually written and certified by notaries. *See* Notaries Public.

Acknowledgments for use in other countries usually may be taken by diplomatic representatives of those countries who are accredited to Korean government.

Authentication Private documents must be authenticated unless acknowledged by opposite party. (C.C.P. 328). In civil procedure practice, however, documents submitted to court need to be authenticated irrespective of whether they are private or not. (C.C.P. 330). Documents prepared by public officials, including foreign public officials in exercise of their duties evidenced by form and purport thereof, or private documents bearing signature or seal of principal or representative, shall be presumed to be authentic. (C.C.P. 327, 329). Authenticity of document may be proven by comparison of handwriting or seal impressions or, more generally in civil procedure, by witness. (C.C.P. 330).

Seals Most transactions in Korea are consummated by use of seals rather than signatures. Some seals may be registered with municipal office of owner (registry office in case of commercial transactions). Certificate of seals may be issued as to such seals. For foreigners, signatures may substitute seals although some kind of consular verification is required. (Foreigner's Signature and Seal Act).

ALIENS

Aliens are persons not of Korean nationality or of no nationality. Aliens are now afforded virtually all rights of Korean nationals with certain restricted exceptions. In general, aliens are permitted to own property and to contract without governmental approval but cannot practice professions of quasi-public character (e.g., law and public accounting). Alien may not own mines or register aircraft or vessel in Korea. Acquisition of land or rights related thereto require government approval. (Alien Land Acquisition Act). Fishery business license requires consent from National Assembly. Alien having no residence in Korea may not enjoy patent rights, with certain exceptions.

Aliens must report at municipal offices having jurisdiction over their residence within 90 days from entry and register within 14 days after reporting. Entrance into country is subject to governmental approval except for members of US Armed Forces, UN's agencies, diplomats, consuls and their dependents, and public officials of foreign governments and international organizations recognized by Korea. Aliens have equal access to courts in bankruptcy, compulsory composition proceedings and certain tort actions against Korean government; they are equally treated only if country of their nationality provides same treatment to Korean nationals.

Corporations owned by or controlled by aliens are regarded as "foreign investors" for purpose of inward direct investments including acquisition of shares, restrictions on acquisition and registration of mines, land, aircraft, vessels, fishery business licenses and patent rights. *See also* Corporations.

ARBITRATION AND AWARD

Written agreement to submit any controversy thereafter arising between parties or any existing controversy to arbitration is enforceable. Furthermore, dispute under arbitration agreement is not allowed to be litigated. (A.L. 3). There is only one institutional arbitration body, Korean Commercial Arbitration Board. Arbitration award has same legal effect as that given to judgment but may be enforced only after enforcement judgment is made by court. Enforcement judgment will he entered unless any of following prescribed grounds for canceling or vacating award are found: (1) When selection of arbitrators or arbitration proceeding was contrary to provisions of Arbitration Act or arbitration agreement; (2) when either party was legally incapable of selecting arbitrators or following course of arbitration proceedings or when parties were not lawfully represented in proceedings; (3) when award directs actions that are prohibited by law; (4) when parties were, without justification, not heard or no reasons for award were given; or (5) when causes for bringing retrial as prescribed in Code of Civil Procedure exist.

Korea, party to UN Convention on Recognition and Enforcement of Foreign Arbitral Awards of June 10, 1958, will enforce arbitration award rendered in another party country.

ASSIGNMENTS

Assignment of property may be made by agreement between assignor and assignee and, for real property, registration of transfer of title, and for personal (tangible) property, delivery of possession. Assignment of credits will be effective upon agreement between assignor and assignee; however to be effective against obligor, assignor must give notice of assignment to such obligor or have his consent. (C.C. 450 [I]). Notice of assignment or consent must bear officially confirmed date in order to assert assignment against third parties other than obligor. (C.C. 450 [II]).

ATTACHMENT

Attachment of chattels, real estate, or accounts receivable is effected upon judgment or enforcement judgment of arbitral award as first step of execution of judgments. Where it is shown to satisfaction of court that without provisional attachment execution of future money judgment might be frustrated or rendered difficult, provisional attachment may be granted prior to judgment. Security deposit for protection of respondent is usually required to be paid before court issues order. Amount of deposit is within court's discretion and ranges between one third and one eighth of amount sought to be protected by provisional attachment.

BANKRUPTCY

Insolvency in bankruptcy means inability to make debt payments. (B.L. 116). Stock company's inability to pay debts but continue in business are grounds for reorganization.

Petition Bankruptcy process is begun by submitting petition to district court having jurisdiction. (B.L.

96). Petitions may be made by debtor or creditors. (B.L. 122). Petition of juridical person may be submitted by its director or liquidator. (B.L. 123). Debtor's failure to make debt payments is prima facie evidence of his inability to make payments and grounds for adjudication of bankruptcy. (B.L. 116). Juridical persons may be bankrupt when liabilities exceed assets. (B.L. 117).

Administration After judgment of bankruptcy, court appoints receiver, orders listing of claims, and sets up meeting of creditors. (B.L. 132). Creditors may appoint advisers, grant allowances, decide whether to continue operating business and consent to important acts of liquidation of estate. (B.L. 170, 184, 187, 188). Consequently, bankrupt is immediately deprived of control over his property involved in bankruptcy proceedings. (B.L. 6, 7).

Outstanding Obligations Debtor's obligations to third parties become due and owing as of adjudication of bankruptcy. (B.L. 16). If debtor and another party to contract have not completed performance, receiver may complete debtor's performance and demand other party to fulfill its obligation or may cancel contract. (B. L. 50). Other party may demand election by receiver of performance or rescission. Failure to answer within reasonable period creates presumption of rescission. (B.L. 50).

Power of Receiver Receiver has exclusive power to administer and dispose of bankrupt estate. (B.L. 7). Receiver is bankrupt estate representative for litigation. (B.L. 152). Restoration of third person's properties and payments of preferential claims are accomplished by application to receiver. Receiver may also institute actions to avoid and annul acts of debtor intentionally prejudicial to creditors taken before adjudication of bankruptcy. (B.L. 64).

Preferential Payment Lien holders, pledgees or mortgagees of specific property in bankrupt estate may receive satisfaction from property independently of bankruptcy proceeding and may be involved in bankruptcy proceedings only to make up deficiencies. (B.L. 84 through 88). Person whose property has not come under receivership as part of bankrupt estate can get it back. (B.L. 79 through 83). Receiver can pay certain taxes independent of bankruptcy proceedings. (B.L. 38, 40). Lien holders on general property have next level of priority to receive distributions before ordinary creditors. (B.L. 32). Receiver declares payments made to creditors by bankrupt within certain period prior to, or after insolvency or filing of application for bankruptcy, and restores them to estate; also any payments made in bad faith purposely to adversely affect other creditors. (B.L. 64 et seq.).

Termination Distribution of assets to creditors terminates bankruptcy proceedings. Creditors may unanimously consent to dissolution of bankruptcy proceeding. (B.L. 319 et seq.). Bankruptcy proceedings may also be terminated if costs of liquidation are greater than value of bankrupt estate. (B.L. 135, 325). Petty bankruptcy may be used for estates less than 5,000,000 Won in which court makes decisions usually made by assembly of creditors and is generally simplified. (B.L. 330 through 338).

Disabilities of Bankrupt Person against whom adjudication of bankruptcy is pending loses certain rights. Full payment of indebtedness, discharge, or lapse of ten years absent fraud will allow court to remove all disabilities. (B.L. 358, 359).

Composition Debtors may present to court plans for continuing of business and stop bankruptcy proceeding. (B.L. 262 et seq.). Majority of creditors holding three-fourth of total obligations of debtor can decide on compulsory composition and all other creditors must comply. (B.L. 278, also see 304).

Foreigners of countries that allow reciprocity for Koreans in bankruptcy procedures are treated in same manner as Koreans. Bankruptcy adjudications affect only property found in Korea, to both Koreans and foreigners. (B.L. 2, 3).

BILLS AND NOTES

Korea is in conformity with Geneva International Conventions on Uniform Law of 1930 and 1931.

Bills of Exchange Bill of exchange must contain: (1) Term "bill of exchange," (2) unconditional order for payment of specified sum of money, (3) name of drawee, (4) maturity (payment is deemed to be at sight when no maturity is stated), (5) designation of place for payment (unless otherwise stated, place of payment is deemed residence of drawee), (6) name of payee, (7) date and place drawn if absent deemed address of drawer, and (8) signature and seal of drawer. Bill of exchange may be payable to drawer, his order, or for account of third person. (B.N.A. 1 through 3).

Indorsements must be unconditional but may have designations or be in blank. All bills of exchange may be transferred by indorsement. (B.N.A. 11 through 13, 15).

Bills payable at specified period after sight must be presented for acceptance within one year after date of issue at residence of drawee. Drawer or endorsers prescribe time of presentment. (B.N.A. 21 through 23).

Name and seal of drawee on face of instrument is deemed as acceptance. Bills payable at specified period after sight must have dated acceptance. Acceptance must be unconditional but may be only for part of total sum payable. Third parties may guarantee bills or notes by signing and sealing on their face or tag. (B.N.A. 25, 26, 30, 31).

Bills of exchange may be paid: (1) At sight, (2) at specified period after sight, (3) at specified period after date of issue, and (4) at specified date. (B. A. 33). Sight bills of exchange are payable on presentment within one year of issue date. (B.N.A. 34). Bill of exchange payable on specified date or period after issue or sight must be presented for payment on due date or within two business days after due date. (B.N.A. 38). There is no grace period. (B.N.A. 74). Bills of exchange payable in currency other than currency of place of payment, may be paid in currency of place of payment. Exchange rate will be that on day of maturity or payment. (B.N.A. 41). Words prevail over figures, and smallest amount is amount payable. (B.N.A. 6).

Indorsers, drawer and guarantors are liable on bill of exchange if payment is not made at maturity or before maturity in events of: Total or partial refusal of acceptance; drawee becoming bankrupt or insolvent; or drawer of bill of exchange prohibited from presentment for acceptance becoming bankrupt. (B.N.A. 43). Instrument to prove default must be officially authenticated. When bill becomes payable nonpayment must be protested within two business days from due date, except for sight bills. (B.N.A. 44). Notice of refusal of acceptance or payment must be given to drawer and indorser within four business days. Indorser must notify party from whom he received instrument within two business days of indorser's receipt of notice. (B.N.A. 45).

Invalid signatures on instrument do not remove liability of persons who actually signed bill. (B.N.A. 7). Agent signing bill is personally liable if he had no authority to do so. (B.N.A. 8). Drawer guarantees acceptance and payment, but may disclaim guarantee of acceptance. (B.N.A. 9).

Drawers, acceptors, indorsers and guarantors have joint and several liability. Holder may sue each individual without regard to order of liability or join all in one action. (B.N.A. 47). Holder may recover any amount unpaid on bill, 6% per annum interest from date of maturity, plus expenses. (B.N.A. 48, 49). If time limit for presentment for protest or payment passes, holder has no recourse against any party except acceptor. (B.N.A. 53). Presentment prevented by vis major or any other legal prohibition may be made after cause for delay has terminated. (B.N.A. 54).

Capacity is determined according to law of party's nationality, but he may still be bound if he signed in country wherein he had capacity. (C.L.A. 34). Formal acts required for bill of exchange, promissory note or check are governed by law of place where it is signed. Checks may follow requirements of law of place of payment. (C.L.A. 36). Obligations of acceptor of bills of exchange and issuer of promissory notes will be governed by law of place of payment. Obligations on checks will be governed by law of place of signing. (C.L.A. 37).

Holder's claims on bill of exchange against acceptors lapse three years from date of maturity, and against endorsers and drawers are actionable only one year from date of protest. Claims of indorser against other indorsers and drawer are actionable six months from date of payment or commencement of action by indorsee. (B.N.A. 70).

Promissory notes must, with certain exceptions, contain: (1) Term "promissory note," (2) unconditional promise to pay specified sum of money, (3) maturity date, (4) place of payment, (5) name of payee, (6) date and place issued, (7) signature and seal of maker. (B.N.A. 75). Rules governing bills of exchange apply mutatis mutandis to promissory notes. (B.N.A. 77).

Bills of Lading Shipowner must, upon demand by charterer or shipper, furnish him with bill of lading in one or more parts after receipt of goods carried. Shipowner must, upon demand by charterer or shipper, furnish him with shipped bill of lading in one or more parts after loading of goods, or shall show effect of such loading on bill of lading mentioned in preceding sentence. (Com. C. 813 [I] [II]). Shipowner may authorize master or any other employee to furnish bills of lading or show above effect mentioned in preceding sentence. (Com. C. 813 [III]).

Bill of lading must contain following particulars and be signed and sealed by issuer: (1) Name, nationality and tonnage of ship, (2) full name of master; (3) description and weight or quantity of goods, and description, number and marks of their packages; (4) full name or trade name of charterer or shipper; (5) full name or trade name of consignee; (6) port of loading, (7) port of unloading; (8) freight; (9) place and date on which bill of lading was made; and (10) if bill of lading has been made in two or more parts, their number. (Com. C. 814).

At designated port of unloading, master may not refuse to deliver goods carried, even though holder of only one of two or more parts of bill of lading demands such delivery. If holder of only one of two or more parts of bill of lading has taken delivery of goods carried, other part or parts shall lose their effect. (Com. C. 816). At places other than designated port of unloading, master may not deliver goods carried except upon receipt of all parts of bill of lading. (Com. C. 817). If two or more holders of bill of lading have demanded delivery of goods carried, master must without delay deposit goods with competent authority and dispatch notice thereof to each holder who has demanded such delivery. (Com. C. 818).

As to goods deposited with competent authority, holder of bill of lading to whom bill of lading was handed over earliest from assignor of bills of lading common to all holders, may exercise his right in preference to other holders of bill of lading. In regard to bill of lading delivered to absentee, time when bill of lading has been dispatched will be deemed as time when it has been handed over. (Com. C. 819).

Checks must contain: (1) Term "check," (2) unconditional order to pay specified sum of money, (3) name of drawee, (4) place of payment, (5) date and place where check is drawn, and (6) signature and seal of drawer. (Checks Act 1). Absence of any element invalidates check with certain exceptions as in bills of exchange. (Checks Act 2). Check must be drawn on bank with funds controlled by drawer. (Checks Act 3). Check must be payable at sight and presented for payment within ten days after issued. (Checks Act 28, 29). If presented for payment outside country but on same continent of place issued it must be within 20 days, 70 days if on different continents. (Checks Act 29). Crossed check may be paid by drawee only to banker or to customer of drawee. (Checks Act 38).

Holder's claims against indorsers, drawer and guarantors lapse six months from last day when presentment must be made. Claims of other parties lapse six months from date of payment or commencement of proceedings. (Checks Act 51). Checks are not accepted. (Checks Act 4). All other rules governing checks coincide with those governing bills of exchange.

Person who may become drawee of check shall be governed by law of place of payment. Even if check is invalid because person who may not become drawee according to law of place of payment has become drawee, obligation arising from signature which was affixed in another country in which there is no such law shall not be affected. (C.L.A. 35).

Days of grace, whether legal or judicial, are not permitted. (Checks Act 62).

Warehouse Receipts Warehouseman must, upon demand by bailor, furnish him with warehouse receipt. (Com. C. 156[1]). Warehouse receipt shall contain following particulars, and be signed and sealed by warehouseman: (1) Description, quality, quantity of goods bailed, and description, number and marks of packages; (2) full name or trade name, place of business or domicile of bailor; (3) place of storage, (4) storage fee; (5) period for storage, if such has been fixed; (6) amount insured, period of insurance, full name or trade name, and place of business or domicile of insurer, in case goods bailed have been insured; and (7) place where and date on which warehouse receipt has been made. (Com. C. 156[2]). Holder of warehouse receipt may return such instrument and may demand warehouseman to divide goods bailed and furnish him with warehouse receipt in respect of each portion of goods thus divided. (Com. C. 158).

If, even in cases where goods bailed have been pledged by means of warehouse receipt, pledgee has given his consent, bailor may demand return of part of goods bailed even prior to maturity of debt. In such case warehouseman shall enter on warehouse receipt description, quality and quantity of goods thus returned. (Com. C. 159).

COMMERCIAL REGISTER

Commercial matters to be registered shall be entered in Commercial Register maintained by court having jurisdiction over locality of place of business. (Com. C. 34). Business names, seals, business activities by minors, managerial positions, and details relating to corporate matters must be registered (Commercial Registration Regulations). If foreign company intends to engage in commercial transactions in Korea, it shall effect same registration as that of branch office of company incorporated in Korea either of same nature or of kind which it most closely resembles, and also register full name and permanent residence of representative and governing law under which it had been incorporated. (Com. C. 614). Foreign company may not engage in commercial transactions on continuing business until it has affected above registration. (Com. C. 616). Valid registration may provide defense as against third parties. (Com. C. 37).

CONTRACTS

Contracts create legal obligations by agreement between two or more parties. Legal entities as well as natural persons have power to contract. Civil Code Provisions govern many standard contract forms: Gift, sale, exchange, loan for consumption, loan for use, lease, employment, contract for specific performance, mandate, bailment, partnership, life annuity, and compromise. Many standard commercial transactions are governed by special Commercial Code provisions: Sales, current accounts, undisclosed associations, brokers, agency commissions, forwarding agencies, carriers, deposits, and insurance. Parties may modify these forms.

Formation Contract exists when offer is accepted. Offer specifying period for acceptance shall expire unless offeror receives notice of acceptance within such period. (C.C. 528). Offer which does not specify period for acceptance shall expire within reasonable period. (C.C. 529). Contract arises when acceptance is sent. Any act which can be deemed declaration of intent to accept will also give rise to contract. (C.C. 532). There is no conditional acceptance, only refusal with counter-offer. (C.C. 534).

Effect Obligation to perform in either party to bilateral contract arises when opposite party tenders performance, unless such obligation has not yet accrued. (C.C. 536). Original, contracting parties cannot take away vested rights of third parties. (C.C.

541). In contract to create or transfer real rights in identified property if that property is lost or damaged or performance becomes impossible due to intervening causes not attributable to assignor, assignee absorbs loss. (C.C. 537).

Rescission Right of rescission may be included in contract, or be implied by law. Formal demand for performance is usually required before rescission. (C.C. 544). Rescission restores parties to same condition they were in prior to contract. (C.C. 548). Declaration of intention to rescind is made to opposite party, though not always required. (C.C. 543). Rescission does not extinguish right to damages. (C.C. 551). Each individual of group of persons who make up single party to contract must either send or receive notice of rescission. (C.C. 547).

Excuse for Nonperformance Nonperformance, except for payment of money, may be excused if causes are not attributable to or responsibility of obligor. (C.C. 390, 397). Parties may limit liability for nonperformance except where specifically prohibited by law.

Conflict of Laws According to provisions of Law of Conflicts, issue of execution and enforceability of contract is to be decided by law expressly or implicitly chosen by parties. In absence of such laws, those prevailing in place where act creating contractual relationship will apply; rights to chattels or real estate are governed by law prevailing over place where subject asset is located; legal effect on assignment of credit is to be decided by law prevailing over debtor's residence; and most admiralty issues including ownership of vessel are to be decided by law of country where vessels concerned are registered. (International Private Law 9, 12, 14, 44).

Set-off If two persons have obligations to each other of same subject matter, both of which have become due, each obligor may set-off amount corresponding to extent of his obligation, unless nature of obligation does not so permit. (C.C. 492). Set-off is effected by manifestation of intent to opposite party; such manifestation may not be conditional nor limited in time. Obligations are presumed to be extinguished, by manifestation of intent, to extent of set-off. (C.C. 493). However, if obligation has arisen from tort or attachment, set-off may not constitute defense against obligee. Obligor under garnishment order may not set off claim subsequently acquired by him against his obligee as defense against garnishor. (C.C. 496 through 498).

Government contracts contain certain statutory requirements for competitive bidding, use of written contracts with specifically required provisions, and performance bonds. (National Accounting Law 70 through 70-18. Enforcement Decree thereunder 74 through 118).

COPYRIGHT

New Copyright Act (C.A.) was enacted by National Assembly in Dec. 1986 and took effect on July 1, 1987. Following information is based upon new C.A.

Upon creation of works, as that term is defined in C.A., copyright is established. (C.A. 4-10).

Protection of Foreign Works Copyright protection will be granted to foreigner under following conditions: (1) If foreign work is entitled to protection under any treaties which Korea has entered into or signed; and (2) if work is authored by one who resides in Korea or incorporated entity which has main office in Korea; and (3) if foreign work is first published in Korea or is published within 30 days after works were first published in foreign country. (C.A. 3).

Copyright Treaties Korea acceded to Universal Copyright Convention on July 1, 1987, effective on Oct. 1, 1987.

Duration In principle, author's property right shall subsist for term of 50 years after his death. (C.A. 36). Author's property right in anonymous or pseudonymous works, if pseudonym is not widely known, shall subsist for term of 50 years after its release. (C.A. 37).

Limitation of Author's Property Rights Author's property rights are limited to some extent in certain circumstances as provided in C.A. 22-35, e.g., where works are reproduced in judicial proceedings (C.A. 22), where works are used for purpose of school education (C.A. 23), etc.

Compulsory Licensing Anyone may use another's work with approval from Minister of Culture and Information in certain circumstances as provided in C.A. 47-50, e.g., where consent to use of work is not obtainable because property right owner of published works is unknown or his abode is unknown, in spite of reasonable efforts to determine them (C.A. 47), where broadcaster who intends to broadcast released work for public interest has negotiated property right owner, but no agreement has been reached (C.A. 48), etc.

Neighboring Rights Stage performance, phonograph records, and broadcasts are entitled to protection for 20 years under C.A. as neighboring rights. (C.A. 61-73).

Infringement Copyright holder may make claim for cessation of infringement, may demand destruction of infringing articles (C.A. 91), and may claim damage compensation (C.A. 93) against infringer. Author may make claim for any action necessary to restore his reputation against anyone who has infringed author's personal rights. (C.A. 95).

Penal Provisions Certain types of acts which are deemed to be in violation of C.A. are subject to criminal punishment. (C.A. 98-103).

Protection of Computer Program Works C.A. provides that provisions necessary to protect computer program works shall be provided in special law. (C.A. 4). Thus, special law entitled "The Computer Program Protection Act" was enacted by National Assembly in Dec. 1986. Right equivalent to copyright is granted to author of computer program for 50 years from time when it was created.

CORPORATIONS

Legal persons must come into existence in accordance with provisions of Civil Code, Commercial Code, special acts of legislation, or special legislative charter. (C.C. 31). Although classified as private and public, or for profit and for nonprofit, etc., they are grouped together for convenience under title "Corporations."

Legal Persons Under Civil Code Civil Code has two kinds of legal entities or juridical persons, associations and foundations. Natural persons may form association through articles of association and managed by directors elected by general assembly. (C.C. 40, 58). Foundation is created by endowment of property for particular purpose and managed by self-perpetuating or court appointed directorate. (C.C. 43). Both may be incorporated as legal persons subject to permission of competent authorities dealing with science, religion, charity, art, social intercourse or other nonprofit enterprises. (C.C. 32). Both act only through authorized representatives, and are liable for acts done by them if within scope of their duties. (C.C. 35, 59). Damages incurred as result of ultra vires act are joint and several liability of those members, directors and other representatives who have acted or supported resolutions for such ultra vires acts. (C.C. 35). Both associations and foundations may be dissolved upon expiration of period of duration, fulfillment of objectives or impossibility thereof, occurrence of any cause of dissolution specified in articles of incorporation, bankruptcy, or annulment of permission for incorporation. Associations may also be dissolved if no member remains, or by resolution of general assembly. (C.C. 77).

Companies, and legal persons organized under Commercial Code, are associations incorporated for purpose of engaging in commercial transactions and acquisition of gains. (Com. C. 169). Four kinds of companies are provided for by Commercial Code: Partnership Companies (hapmyong-hoesa), Limited Partnership Companies (hapcha-hoesa), Stock Companies (chusik-hoesa), and Limited Companies (yuhan-hoesa). If organized in compliance with all legal preconditions and properly registered no government approval is necessary.

Partnership companies create new and independent legal entities. (Com. C. 170, 171). Partnership companies are created by articles of incorporation with signature of each member stating value of respective contribution. (Com. C. 179). Managers are appointed by majority vote. Additionally members must see to administration of company's business; however, articles may remove this duty. (Com. C. 200). Consent must he unanimous for changes in articles of incorporation or transfer of any individual member's share. (Com. C. 197, 204). Members may not conduct or assume official position in competing business without consent. (Com. C. 198). Members have joint and several liability for obligations in excess of company's assets. (Com. C. 212). Members subsequently admitted to company incur liability for all prior obligations. (Com. C. 213). Members may, with six months notice, withdraw from partnership at end of any fiscal year if company was established for indefinite period or for life of partner. Also members may withdraw at any time should unavoidable circumstances exist. (Com. C. 217). Membership may be terminated upon occurrence of any causes specified in articles of incorporation, unanimous consent, death, adjudication of incompetency, bankruptcy, and expulsion. (Com. C. 218). Failure to make contribution is cause for expulsion which requires court order. (Com. C. 220). Withdrawing members must be paid for services rendered and reimbursed for contributions. (Com. C. 222). Partnership company may be dissolved upon expiration of prescribed term or occurrence of any cause of dissolution specified in articles of incorporation, unanimous consent, loss of all except one member, merger, bankruptcy or by court. (Com. C. 227). Court supervises liquidation. (Com. C. 245 et seq.).

Limited partnership companies resemble partnership companies but differ in liabilities each member has for company obligations. (Com. C. 268). Liability of each member must be provided in articles of incorporation, and those with limited liability may not make their contribution in form of personal services or credit. (Com. C. 270, 272). Members with unlimited liability have responsibilities as in partnership company. Members with limited liability may not represent company, but may inspect and supervise its operations. (Com. C. 273, 277). Loss of all members of either class requires dissolution. (Com. C. 285).

Stock companies are most common in business circles. Incorporation through articles of incorporation must be drawn by seven or more promoters. Articles must state business objective, trade name, total number of shares authorized, amount of each share, total number of shares to be issued at time of incorporation (at least 25% of shares authorized), address of principal office, manner of giving company's public notices, and full name and domicile of each promoter. (Com. C. 288, 289). Following must be in articles to have legal effect: Company's duration, special promoter benefits, contributions in kind, property to be acquired upon incorporation.

(Com. C. 227, 290, 344). Articles of incorporation must be acknowledged by notary public. (Com. C. 292). Company comes into existence after court approval upon registration or upon registration after first meeting of shareholders when there are shareholders other than promoters. (Com. C. 299, 300, 308, 309, 311 through 314, 316, 317). Incorporation does not limit liability of promoters from acts in course of incorporation. (Com. C. 322). At time of incorporation, only promoters may receive stock for property contribution. Court must confirm property's value and delivery. (Com. C. 294, 299).

Capital of stock company must be 50,000,000 Won or greater, and divided into shares. Only par value shares may be issued and each share should be of equal value of at least 5,000 Won. (Com. C. 329). Shares are usually nonbearer but articles may provide for bearer certificates. (Com. C. 357). Those holding nonbearer shares and not wanting certificates may request that certificates not be issued and return any certificates already issued. (Com. C. 358-2). Company may issue two or more classes of shares which differ in respect to distribution of profits, interest, or surplus assets. Such particulars and numbers of each class of shares must be determined by articles of incorporation. (Com. C. 344). Transfer of shares may not be prohibited or restricted even by articles of incorporation. (Com. C. 335). Transfer before issuance of share certificates is not effective against company (this does not apply more than six months after incorporation or payment for new shares). (Com. C. 335). Company cannot purchase its own shares nor hold them as pledgee. Company more than 40% of whose shares are held by another company (parent company) cannot acquire shares of such parent company, except in special circumstances as where company must dispose of shares immediately. (Com. C. 341, 341-2, 342, 342-2). Transfer of shares becomes effective upon delivery of certificates. However, nonbearer shares must be registered in stockholders' registry to be treated as transferred by company. (Com. C. 336, 337).

Authorized shares may be issued at any time by resolution of board of directors unless articles of incorporation require resolution of stockholders. (Com. C. 416). Each stockholder has preemptive rights to new shares according to number of shares he owns, and such rights may be made transferable by resolution of board of directors or, if articles of incorporation so provide, by stockholders. (Com. C. 416, 418). Transfer of preemptive rights to new shares must be done by delivery of subscription warrant. (Com. C. 420-3).

Stockholder's Liability After subscription price is paid, stockholder has no other personal liability for obligations of company. (Com. C. 331).

Organs of stock company are general meeting of

stockholders, directors, and auditors. General meeting of stockholders may resolve only matters provided for in Commercial Code or articles of incorporation. (Com. C. 361). Ordinary general meeting must be convened at least once each fiscal term and extraordinary general meeting may be convened whenever necessary. (Com. C. 365). Each stockholder has one vote for each share. However, company is not entitled to vote its own shares. Company more than 10% of whose issued shares are held by another company or by both parent and subsidiary company or subsidiary company is not entitled to vote its shares in such other company or parent company. (Com. C. 369, 434). Split votes may be cast with prior notice. (Com. C. 368-2).

Quorum for resolutions is more that one-half total number of issued shares unless otherwise provided by law or in articles and are adopted by simple majority of shares present. (Com. C. 368). Major resolutions require two-thirds majority of shares present (e.g., amendment of articles of incorporation, capital decrease, merger, transfer of whole or important part of company's business, taking over business of another company, dissolution, or removal of directors or auditors [Com. C. 374, 384, 385, 415, 434, 438, 518, 522]). (Com. C. 368).

Proxies Shareholder may vote by proxy. Proxy statements must be filed with general meeting to establish power of representation. (Com. C. 368). Proxy holders may be limited to shareholders by articles of incorporation but representing others' voting rights shall not be prohibited or compelled.

Board of directors' duties include execution of business, appointment or removal of managers, establishing, moving or closing branch offices, and supervision of performance of individual directors. (Com. C. 393). Resolutions of board of directors are adopted by majority vote if more than one-half of all directors are present unless articles of incorporation have stricter requirements. (Com. C. 391).

There must be three or more directors, elected at general meeting by stockholders, and may each hold office for term usually not to exceed three years. (Com. C. 383, 384). One or more directors with authority to represent company must be appointed from among directors by resolution of board or, if articles so provide, by stockholders. (Com. C. 389). Company has liability for any acts of director who has used any title such as president, vice-president, chief director or managing director though not authorized representative if third party acted in good faith. (Com. C. 395). No director may, without consent of general meeting of stockholders, effect transaction for himself or third persons or become partner (other than limited) or director of another company in same kind of business. (Com. C. 397).

There must be at least one auditor, appointed at general meeting of stockholders. In selecting auditors, individual stockholder although owning, may not vote more that 3% of total number of issued voting shares. (Com. C. 409). Auditors serve until adjournment of ordinary general meeting of stockholders for final settlement of accounts held within two years from assuming office. (Com. C. 410). Auditors may not concurrently assume office of director, manager or other employee. (Com. C. 411). Auditors may attend board of directors' meetings, can supervise directors' performance of duties, may at any time require directors to file business report, and may examine business and financial condition of company. (Com. C. 391-2, 412). Auditors have duty to report on and examine financial statements and business reports prepared by directors issued to general meeting. (Com. C. 413).

Amending articles of incorporation requires two-thirds majority vote of more than one-half of total number of issued shares who are present at general meeting of stockholders. (Com. C. 434). If company has issued two or more classes of shares, and certain class of stockholders is prejudiced by proposed amendment, resolution of meeting of such class of stockholders is required in addition to that of general meeting of stockholders. (Com. C. 435).

Statutory reserves are capital and earned surplus reserves. Capital surplus reserve is amount applied to stated capital and is limited to excess of issue price over par. (Com. C. 459). Ten% of cash dividends paid out of profits each fiscal period must be credited to statutory earned surplus account until such account is one-half value of stated capital. (Com. C. 458). Statutory reserve funds can be transferred to stated capital to raise it or remove deficiencies. (Com. C. 460, 461).

Dividends to extent net assets exceed stated capital, statutory reserves (capital surplus reserve and earned surplus reserve), and required amount of retained earned surplus reserve may be declared each fiscal period. (Com. C. 462). Company can pay dividends with new shares by resolution of general meeting of stockholders. Stock dividends cannot exceed one-half of total sum of dividends. (Com. C. 462-2).

Bonds may be issued by resolution of board of directors. (Com. C. 469). Value of bonds may not be greater than twice stated capital and statutory reserves or net assets set forth on latest balance sheet whichever is smaller. (Com. C. 470). Company may issue convertible bonds and bonds with warrants to subscribe for new shares. (Com. C. 513, 516-2). Bondholders may call assembly to adopt resolutions with court approval if their interests are being prejudiced unless provided otherwise in Commercial Code. (Com. C. 490).

Company may be dissolved by expiration of term in articles of incorporation, merger, bankruptcy, court order and resolution of general meeting of stockholders. (Com. C. 517). Except in merger court supervised liquidation follows dissolution. (Com. C. 531 et seq.).

Limited companies are created by two or more members not exceeding 50 who jointly execute articles of incorporation which provide business object, trade name, name and residence of each member, capitalization, value of each unit of contribution, number of units of contribution made by each member, and principal office. (Com. C. 543, 545). Capitalization of 10,000,000 Won or greater and at least 5,000 Won per unit of contribution are required. (Com. C. 546). Transfer of units to nonmember must be approved by general meeting. (Com. C. 556). Directors, elected by general meeting, are company's business representatives. Directors may not compete against business of company. (Com. C. 397, 547, 562, 567). Limited company is otherwise similar to stock company.

Other Legal Persons Certain acts of special legislation distinct from Civil or Commercial Codes may create associations and other legal entities such as trade associations and labor unions. Municipalities are also legal entities. Special charters for corporations such as The Bank of Korea have been passed by National Assembly.

Foreign corporations are those which have addresses abroad or are incorporated in compliance with foreign laws. There are no provisions in Civil Code about foreign corporations but generally they enjoy same rights and powers as similar domestic corporations under Korean law, absent treaty or provisions to contrary; for example, foreign corporations cannot enjoy mining rights (Mining Law 6), and cannot acquire real property rights (excluding mortgage) without permission of Minister of Home Affairs (Alien Land Acquisition Act 5).

Commercial Code provides for foreign companies in detail. Foreign company which intends to engage in commercial transactions must appoint representative in Korea, establish business office and, in respect to establishment of its office of business, register office in same manner of registration as that of branch office of same or similar kind of company incorporated in Korea. Company which establishes its principal office in Korea or whose chief objective is to carry on business in Korea must, even though incorporated in foreign country, comply with same provisions as company incorporated in Korea. (Com. C. 617). Foreign company must also register law under which it had been incorporated, as well as full name and permanent residence of its representative in Korea. (Com. C. 614). Until registered, foreign company cannot engage in commercial transactions and persons doing so are jointly and severally liable along with company. (Com. C. 616).

Failure to commence business within one year after registration, engaging in illegal business, and acting in contravention of law, decree, good moral or other social orders by representative or any other person administering affairs of company are grounds for issuance of court order for termination and liquidation of business office. (Com. C. 619, 620).

Except as otherwise provided, foreign company is deemed to be company formed in Korea either of same nature or kind which it most closely resembles, insofar as other laws apply. (Com. C. 621).

EXECUTIONS

Execution or realization of secured interests held by mortgagees, lien holders, pledgees, or Chonse-Kwon holders (special type of statutory lease involving key money for lease) are made generally through auctioning chattels or real estate secured. Such auction procedure is conducted by court according to Code of Civil Procedure upon application from secured creditors.

Code of Civil Procedure provides various means of execution of judgments. In order to execute judgment or other enforceable instruments, judgment creditors in general must obtain certification of enforceability on face of certified copy of judgment. Movable assets of judgment debtor are seized and auctioned off by court bailiff. Credits owned by judgment debtor are attached, and collected by or transferred to judgment creditors by court decrees. Execution on real estate or immovable properties of judgment debtor is effected by attachment and public sale by court decree.

Arbitration awards or foreign judgment may be executed after local court permits execution by issuing enforcement judgment. Settlements made and recorded in court or special types of payment orders by court are enforceable and executable. Based on special legislation, settlements between parties to pay sum of money, securities or fungibles, and promissory notes or checks notarized and confirmed that immediate execution is possible by notary public, are enforceable upon acquiring certification of enforceability from notary public without requiring judgment.

Judgment requiring specific performance by debtor may be enforced by employing others to do required performance in place of debtor and holding judgment debtor responsible for costs. Specific performance which by nature may not be performed by anyone other than judgment debtor himself may not be specifically enforced. If judgment debtor fails to do as ordered, judgment creditor can apply to court to fix appropriate period to make performance and to order, in case judgment debtor defaults performance within period, to make reparation of certain amount in proportion to period of delay or in lump sum immediately.

Fieri facias shall be granted when judgment has

become final and conclusive or when provisional execution order has been given. (C.C.P. 480).

FOREIGN EXCHANGE

Foreign Exchange Control Act ("F.E.C.A.") is most comprehensive act controlling contractual relationship, settlement method, payment and receipt, etc. between "residents" and "nonresidents." ("Residents" means all natural persons who have their domicile or residence in Korea and also juridical persons having their main office in Korea. [F.E.C.A. 4-12]. Branches, local offices and other offices in Korea of nonresidents are considered to be residents irrespective of whether or not they have legal authority to represent "nonresidents" and even if their main office is located abroad. "Nonresidents" means all persons, natural or juridical, other than "residents." [F.E.C.A. 4-13].)

As general rule, foreign exchange approvals are required, in effect, on two separate occasions under F.E.C.A. First, initial approval is required for proposed underlying transaction itself (e.g., establishment of monetary credit between resident and nonresident). (F.E.C.A. 23). Second, payment authorization is required at time of actual conversion of Won into foreign currency for purpose of effecting payment. (F.E.C.A. 21). Different foreign exchange authorities such as Minister of Finance, Bank of Korea or foreign exchange banks may issue approvals and payment authorization depending on contents of transaction. Failure to obtain foreign exchange approval does not affect validity of agreement as between parties. However, without such approvals, remittance of foreign exchange will not be permitted. Failure to obtain requisite foreign exchange approval is also criminal violation under F.E.C.A. and subject to substantial fines and/or imprisonment. (F.E.C.A. 35 through 37).

FOREIGN INVESTMENT

All foreign investment in Korea must obtain governmental approval. (F.C.I.L. 7). Investment is permitted in all except following fields: (1) Business which undermines national security or maintenance of public order; (2) business having a negative effect on national economy; (3) business administration of which results in infringement of laws of Korea (F.C.I.L. 3). Minister of Finance should approve, investment by foreigners without delay, provided, however, that he discuss approval with minister concerned with type of business in following cases: (1) When foreign investment ratio exceeds 50%; (2) when amount of foreign investment exceeds certain amount specified by Presidential Decree; (3) when foreign investor wishes to receive tax exemptions; (4) when foreign investment is made in prescribed

business lines for which foreign investment is restricted. (F.C.I.L. 7). When foreign investors acquire additional shares through merger of company, amalgamation or partition of shares, change of reserves to capital, etc., they must report to Minister of Finance. (F.C.I.L. 8). Upon completion of investment procedures foreign investors must register with Minister of Finance. (F.C.I.L. 12). Business is subject to regulation by Korean government. Certain tax benefits are granted for five years to foreign investors and companies invested in by foreigners if certain criteria are met. However, such tax benefits have been and will be gradually reduced pursuant to Korean government policy.

Technology Inducement Agreement Korean or juridical person who wants to enter into any technology inducement agreement, as defined in FCIL, with foreigners or change contents of previously concluded agreement must report to relevant ministry. Agreement becomes enforceable when report is received by relevant ministry. Royalties received by foreign party are exempt from income and corporation taxes for five years if technology meets high technology criteria. (F.C.I.L. 23, 24).

Repatriation Right All dividends of foreign investors, proceeds from sale of shares, or royalties from technology introduction agreements may be repatriated. (F.C.I.L. 4). Other rights of foreign investors related to investment in Korean industry are same as Koreans. (F.C.I.L. 5, 6).

FOREIGN TRADE REGULATIONS

Foreign trade in Korea is basically regulated by Foreign Trade Law (F.T.L.) and Enforcement Decree and regulations thereof. With certain exceptions, international trading business is required to be licensed in Korea under F.T.L. (F.T.L. 7). Only licensed trading company can apply for export license or import license for actual export of Korean goods or import of foreign goods. Consequently, if non-licensed manufacturer or end-user wishes to export Korean goods or import foreign goods, actual exportation or importation must be done through existing licensed trading company which charges, in general, commission for such services. Amendment of 1986 permits some instances, as will be determined by Enforcement Decree, where no export or import license will be required. (F.T.L. 19).

Exportability and importability of item is regulated by Export and Import Notice and Consolidated Notice issued by Ministry of Trade and Industry under F.T.L. (F.T.L. 19). Export and Import Notice generally classifies three levels of export and import status: (1) Automatic approval items, meaning that product in question may be freely exported or imported subject to normal export or import licensing requirement; (2) restricted approval items, meaning that product may be exported or imported subject to recommendation, confirmation or approval from designated ministry or industry association; and (3) banned items. (F.T.L. 18). Notices adopt Harmonized System for classification of items.

Amendment of 1986 establishes import damage relief system whereby imports can be restricted if damage to any domestic industry concerned occurs. (F.T.L. 32-36).

FRAUDS, STATUTE OF

Korea has no statute of frauds, however certain items, such as articles of incorporation, must be in writing or executed before notaries according to specific statutes. (C.C. 1068, 1069; Com. C. 292).

GARNISHMENT

As means of execution of money judgment, outstanding credit of judgment debtor may be attached by judgment creditor through court order of garnishment, which prohibits garnishee from discharging debts to original debtor and also forbids judgment debtor from disposing of or accepting payment for credit. Payment made in violation of garnishment order will not have legal effects against garnishor.

INSOLVENCY

See Bankruptcy.

INTEREST

Agreement on payment of interest and interest rate is valid and enforceable unless it violates usury law. Absent agreement on interest rate, rate of 5% per annum is applicable to normal private transactions (C.C. 379) and of 6% per annum to commercial transactions (Com. C. 54). Statutory interest at rate of 25% per annum is payable from time when court judgment is given ordering payment of money. (Special Law on Expedition of Court Proceedings, Etc. 3).

Usury applies only to obligations to pay money. Contract for interest rate over 25% per annum is null and void. (Interest Limitation Law 1).

LABOR RELATIONS

Labor Standards Law (L.S.L.) provides legal minimum labor standards in Korea. L.S.L. applies to all employers regardless of number of employees, however, employers having less than five employees are subject to only certain provisions of L.S.L.

Hours of labor are limited to eight hours per day and 44 hours per week (46 hours as interim period until Sept. 30, 1991) for enterprises or workplaces with less than 300 employees or those appointed by Ministry of Labor (L.S.L. 42) with certain exceptions. At least one day off per week is required. (L.S.L. 45).

Wages and Salaries Amount of wage is determined by individual employment agreement or collective bargaining agreement. Attachment of right to receive wage is limited to protect livelihood of laborers. (C.C.P. 579). In accordance with L.S.L. employer cannot set off wage by debt which employee owes to him. (L.S.L. 25). Wages and salaries are preferred claims having priority over other creditors of employers except for claims secured by mortgages or pledges. (L.S.L. 30-2). Wages must be paid directly to employees, in full, in legal tender. (L.S.L. 36). With certain exceptions, wages must be paid once per month or more frequently on fixed day. (L.S.L. 36[2]).

Leave One-day monthly leave with pay and annual leave with pay (period thereof varies depending on attendance and period of service) are required. (L.S.L. 47, 48). One day menstruation leave per month with pay must be granted to female employees. (L.S.L. 59). Maternity leave of 60 days must be given to pregnant employees. (L.S.L. 60).

Child Labor With certain exceptions, minors under 13 years of age may not be employed. (L.S.L. 50). Females or minors under 18 years of age may not be employed in occupations detrimental to their morality or health. (L.S.L. 51).

Severance allowances must be paid to employees having worked for not less than one year in amount of not less than 30 days' average wage per each year of consecutive years employed. (L.S.L. 28).

Discharge Employers may not discharge employees without just reasons. (L.S.L. 27). With certain exceptions, at least 30-days notice, or pay in lieu thereof, is necessary for discharge. (L.S.L. 27-2).

Rules of employment in compliance with minimum standards of law must be established by every employer of ten or more workers. (L.S.L. 94). Establishment of such rules requires presentation of rules to representative employees and then filing with Ministry of Labor. Such rules must deal with wage programs and scales, working hours, time off, holidays, paid vacations, discharge, retirement allowances, safety, sanitation, accident compensation, and other matters applicable to all employees. (L.S.L. 94).

Occupational Injuries and Diseases Employers must, at their expense, provide medical care for employees suffering from occupational injury or illness. (L.S.L. 78). Employers must pay compensation in amount provided for in L.S.L. for loss of wages, physical impairments, or death due to occupational illnesses. Employers having five or more employees must subscribe to industrial accident compensation insurance with certain exceptions.

Insurance Object of Industrial Injury Compensation Insurance Act (I.I.C.I.A.) is to protect employees by compensating for damages caused by occupational disasters and establishing or administrating insurance facilities necessary for such compensation. (I.I.C.I.A. 1).

Proprietor of enterprise shall automatically become insurer. (I.I.C.I.A. 6). Insurance allowances shall be as follows: Allowances for treatment and recovery, leaves, inconvenience, permanent physical impairment, mental anguish suffered by family members, and funeral expenses. (I.I.C.I.A. 9). Premiums to be paid by employers are product of total compensation multiplied by factor set by Ministry of Labor for applicable industry.

Labor Unions Employees have right of self organization, to form, join or assist labor unions, to bargain collectively through their own representatives. Rights of governmental officials and employees working at state-run enterprises, defense industries and public utilities which have serious impact on national economy may be restricted or denied with respect to labor unions.

Collective bargaining agreements are made between employer or employer's organization and lawfully organized union. When collective bargaining agreements become applicable to at least one-half of regular workers of plant, their terms then become applicable to all regular workers of that plant. (L.U.L. 37). Those parts of rules of employment or employment agreement in violation of terms provided in collective bargaining agreements are null and void. (L.U.L. 36). Collective bargaining agreements may be for two years or less (collective bargaining agreements concerning wages may be for one year or less). (L.U.L. 35).

Unfair Labor Practice It is unfair practice for employer to: (1) Discharge or discriminate against employee because employee became member of labor organization or is about to organize labor union; (2) require employees or potential employees not to join company union or to join company union which represents not more than two thirds of total employees; (3) refuse to bargain collectively and discuss grievances with employees' representatives; (4) interfere with or dominate employee organization; (5) pay administrative expense of labor organization; and (6) discharge or disadvantage employee because he has participated in collective action or has notified governmental agency of fact that employer committed above violations. (L.U.L. 39). Commission of unfair labor practices by employers may be punished by imprisonment or fines. (L.U.L. 46-2).

Labor Disputes Labor Disputes Adjustment Law (L.D.A.L.) provides matters necessary to settle disputes between employer and employees. (L.D.A.L. 1). Employees who are employed in national or local government or national defense industry cannot initiate labor disputes. (L.D.A.L. 12). It is unlawful for employees who are engaged in labor disputes to resort to violence to influence resolution of dispute. (L.D.A.L. 13). Occurrence of labor disputes must be reported to labor authorities who shall conduct conciliation and mediation. (L.D.A.L. 16 and 18-29). Act of dispute may not be commenced during cooling-off period of ten days after dispute was reported (15 days in case of business deemed vital to public interest). (L.D.A.L. 14). If labor disputes are not resolved, Labor Committee shall arbitrate them if: (1) Both parties jointly apply for arbitration, (2) either party applies for arbitration pursuant to collective bargaining agreement, or (3) administrative agency demands arbitration or Labor Committee itself determines that dispute, which involves business which is vital to public interest, must be arbitrated. (L.D.A.L. 30).

Labor Management Council is organized within each business in accordance with Labor Management Council Law (L.M.C.L.) for purpose of improving welfare of employees and to help sound development of business. (L.M.C.L. 3, 4). Council consists of three to ten representatives of employer and employees. Council may debate on following affairs: (a) Improvement of productivity and welfare of employees, (b) prevention of disputes between employer and employees, (c) educational training of employees, (d) disposal of grievances of employees, (e) security, health care, and other affairs regarding improvement of labor conditions, and (f) other affairs regarding cooperation between employer and employees. (L.M.C.L. 20). Agreement of two-thirds of members present is necessary to pass resolution. (L.M.C.L. 13). Central Council is established under guidance of Minister of Labor which consists of representatives of employer, employees, and public interests. (L.M.C.L. 28).

Unemployment compensation does not exist in Korea. Under National Welfare Pension Law, company which has ten or more employees must join government administered national pension program. Currently, employee and employer each contribute 1.5% of employee's monthly salary. From 1993, such figures will increase to 2.0%, and employer will additionally contribute 2.0% to be transferred from mandatory severance pay reserves. Figure will ultimately be 3.0% respectively from 1998. Amount transferred to national pension fund will be deducted from final amount of severance payment mandatorily payable to employees.

Minimum Wage Law provides minimum wage system. Currently, employers with ten or more employees must pay at least 820 Won per hour in manufacturing, mining, and construction industries. Minimum wage system may possibly apply to all enterprises and workplaces in future.

Equal Employment Treatment for Males and Females Law provides plan for enhancing welfare of female employees and establishment of Female Employees Committee. It also prohibits discrimination against women in regard to employment, training opportunity, assignments, wages, promotions, retirement, and dismissal with punishment of fine and imprisonment in case of violations.

Handicapped Persons Employment Promotion Act provides that employer shall perform several statutory obligations in order to enhance welfare of handicapped persons, including employing certain ratio of handicapped persons where employer maintains 300 or more employees.

LIENS

Liens Lien is statutory right to retain possession of movable until certain credit owed is paid. There are two different types of liens created under Civil and Commercial Code; in former credit secured by lien should be related to object; in latter object must be owned by debtor but not necessarily related to debt owed. There are no other types of liens such as supplier's lien or equity liens. Certain statutory right of receiving payment from proceeds of certain objects in priority over general creditors must be differentiated from liens.

Lien affords holder right to deprive owner of possession and maintain possession until payment obligation is performed and affords holder right to apply for auction sale of concerned property for collection of debt owed. Retention of possession is essential for most types of liens.

MONOPOLIES AND RESTRAINT OF TRADE

Unfair Trade Practices No entrepreneur shall engage in any of following or any act Fair Trade Commission ("FTC") deems detrimental to fair trade and publicly announces such as constituting unfair trade practice: (1) Unreasonably refusing to transact with opposite parties or discriminating against opposite parties to transactions; (2) unreasonably engaging in activities designed to eliminate competitors; (3) unreasonably inducing or coercing competitor's customers to deal with oneself; (4) dealing with opposite party by taking unreasonable use of one's bargaining position; (5) dealing with opposite party on terms and conditions which unreasonably restrict business activity thereof; and (6) false or exaggerated marking or advertising of enterprise, its commodities or services. (M.R.F.T.A. 23). Entrepreneur who has committed unfair trade practices is subject to civil, administrative or criminal sanctions. (U.C.P.L. 24, 56, 67).

Market Abuse Entrepreneurs who meet criteria provided for by Presidential Decree for "market-dominating" entrepreneurs shall not engage in any of following acts of abuse: (1) Unreasonably determining, maintaining, or altering price of commodity or services; (2) unreasonably controlling sales of commodities or services; (3) unreasonably interfering with business activities of others; (4) unreasonably interfering with entry off new competitors; and (5) substantially restricting competition or damaging interest of consumers. (M.R.F.T.A. 3).

Regulation of Acquisitions Firm must report acquiring or holding 20% or more outstanding shares or equity investment of another firm to FTC within 30 days of date of acquisition. Those intending to merge, take over, lease all or substantial part of another firm, or to establish new firm leading to substantial restraint of competition must report to Fair Trade Committee and must wait 30 days before acting. (M.R.F.T.A. 7, 12). Cross capital investment among affiliates of designated conglomerates is prohibited. (M.R.F.T.A. 9). Capital investment in other companies by company belonging to designated conglomerate is limited to 40% or less of net assets of company in question. (M.R.F.T.A. 10).

Collaborative activities designed to undertake any of following are, in principle, prohibited: (1) Fixing, maintaining, or altering prices; (2) determining terms and conditions for sale of commodities or services, or terms and conditions for payment; (3) restricting production, delivery, transportation, or sales of commodities or services; (4) restricting sales territory or trade of customers; (5) restricting new establishment, expansion of facilities, or installation of equipment for production of commodities or services; (6) restricting kinds or sizes of commodities at time of production or sale; (7) establishing new companies in order to manage or control major parts of business collaboratively; and (8) interfering with business activities of others. (M.R.F.T.A. 19).

Restrictions on International Agreements No entrepreneur or trade association (with some exceptions) shall enter into international agreement or international contract which comes within any one of following sub-paragraphs which constitute undue collaborative activities, resale price fixing or unfair trade practices, as defined by relevant guidelines: (1) Foreign loan agreement, joint-venture agreements, or technology inducement agreements made pursuant to Foreign Capital Inducement Act; (2) copyright license agreement (where Korean party is licensee) with term of not less than three years; (3) import agent agreements (excluding offer agent business) or long-term import contracts with regard to continuous import of commodities or supply of services for period not less than one year; excluding import agreements for raw materials (raw materials or semi-finished materials) and capital goods; and (4) technology and service inducement agreement with royalty amount of one million US dollars or more pursuant to Technology and Service Support Law.

When entrepreneur or trade association has entered into international agreement as specified above, it shall report to FTC. FTC may, when international agreement violates or is likely to violate provisions, order report of contract execution, cancellation, amendment or alteration of agreement, or other necessary corrective measures. (M.R.F.T.A. 32, 33, 34).

NOTARIES PUBLIC

Notaries public are appointed by Minister of Justice and they are public officials of district public prosecutor's office. Notaries public, upon commission of party or other persons, prepare and authenticate instruments, deeds signed by private citizens, or articles of incorporation of company.

Notaries may act in localities where they are licensed to act and are liable, for damages which result from their intentional or negligent acts performed in course of discharging their duties. Documents prepared or authenticated by notaries carry strong presumption of authenticity. When purport of instrument is claim for delivery of fungible or payment of sum certain or transfer of negotiable instruments, instrument itself is sufficient to obtain immediate execution against obligor if statement is made therein that obligor, at time of preparation of instrument, agrees to execution in event of default.

Under special legislation, practicing attorneys practicing in group may obtain license to act as notaries public. Lawyer's professional corporation is entitled to act as notary public.

PARTNERSHIP

Partnership becomes effective when two or more persons agree to carry on joint undertaking by making mutual contribution thereto. Money, property, or services may be made object of contribution. (C.C. 703).

Affairs of partnership are conducted by majority of partners or, if several managers have been designated, by such managers. But ordinary affairs may be conducted by any partner or any manager acting alone, unless objections are raised by other partners or managers. (C.C. 706). One or more managers may be designated by partnership contracts or be elected with affirmative votes of more than two-thirds of all partners, and thereafter, managers who are also partners may not resign without due reason or be removed without unanimous consent of other partners. (C.C. 708).

Value of profit and loss to be shared is proportional to each partner's contribution in absence of specific agreement between partners. But creditor who was not aware of proportion of liability among partners at time when his claim arose may exercise his right against each partner in equal shares. (C.C. 711, 712). Debtor of partnership may not set off his claim against partner from his obligation to partnership. (C.C. 715).

When duration of partnership is not fixed, or is fixed at lifetime of partner, each partner, may retire at any time. However, such partner may not, in absence of any unavoidable reason, retire at time which would be unfavorable to partnership. Even when duration of partnership is fixed, each partner may retire, if any unavoidable reason exists for doing so. (C.C. 716). Partner is deemed to have retired also in event of death, bankruptcy, adjudication of incompetency, or expulsion. (C.C. 717). Accounts between retired partner and other partners are based on status of property of partnership at time he retires, but accounting of matters not yet completed at that time may be made when completed. (C.C. 719).

Causes for dissolution of partnerships are fulfillment of object of creation, impossibility of such fulfillment, or expiration of duration set by partnership contract. Upon dissolution, affairs of partnership are liquidated and assets distributed. (C.C. 721 through 724).

PATENTS

Korea is member country of Paris Convention for Protection of Industrial Properties ("Paris Convention") and Patent Cooperation Treaty. Patent rights become effective when patent application is granted by and registered with Korea Industrial Property Office ("KIPO"). Foreigners residing or doing business in Korea may also apply for patent with KIPO. Nonresident foreigners may also apply for patents based on Paris Convention or if foreign country allows grant of patents to Korean nationals. (PA 25). Foreign applicants may claim priority on basis of foreign filing by making filing in Korea within one year from first foreign application date and satisfying procedural requirements. Nonresidents taking action involving patent rights are required to be represented by local patent attorney.

Patentable inventions must be ones which are "highly creative results of a technical idea utilizing the laws of nature" (PA 29), and be novel and inventive. However, following types of inventions are unpatentable: (i) inventions relating to substances which can be manufactured by transforming atomic nuclei; and (ii) inventions which are likely to injure public order, morality or health. (PA 32). With certain exceptions, inventions publicly used or known in Korea, or disclosed in publications distributed anywhere in world prior to filing date of patent application therefore, are unpatentable for lack of novelty and/or inventiveness. (PA 29).

Inventions concerning articles which involve lower degree of ingenuity may be protected as utility models, which have duration of ten years being five years less than that of patent (see infra). Patent application may be changed into utility model application or design patent application and vice versa.

When several applications are made for identical inventions, first application is entitled to patent regardless of which applicant first conceived or completed invention. (PA 36). If multiple applications are made for identical invention on same date, applicant chosen by agreement among competing applicants will be entitled to patent, and, in absence of such agreement, none of the applicants will be entitled to patent. KIPO under direction of Minister of Trade and Industry, is responsible for receiving and processing patent applications, granting patents, conducting trials for canceling, invalidating or confirming scope of claim of patent and reviewing appeals from rejection of applications. Korea adopts so-called "domestic priority claim system" wherein benefit of earlier filing date of co-pending national application can be claimed in subsequent application if such subsequent application is made by same inventor(s). (PA 55).

Applications obviously relating to national security or falling within fields indicated by defense agencies cannot be filed in foreign countries without government approval. (PA 41).

Patent application is subject to substantive examination by examiners only when request for examination thereof is filed. Such request may be filed by its applicant or interested party and must be made within five years after filing. In absence of request for examination during such period, application lapses. (PA 57, 59).

Unless sooner published or rejected, every patent application will be subject to early publication in Official Gazette of Early Patent Publication 18 months after filing date (or priority date, if convention priority is claimed) for purposes of inviting comments from public. Applicant for patent is entitled to claim damages from infringers irrespective of giving written warning to them after application is disclosed through publication. This claim is based on early publication and can only be exercised when application is published for granting of patent. (PA 64 and 65).

Appeal from final rejection of patent application may be filed within 30 days from date or which final rejection is served. (PA 167 and 168). If such appeal is brought and amendment/correction to specification, claims and/or drawings of application are made within 30 days from date appeal was filed, Appellate Board of KIPO must return application file to examiner who rejected application so that he can reconsider or reexamine application based on amendment/

correction. If examiner decides to allow application, he must withdraw his rejection. If he does not find reason to withdraw his rejection, then Appellate Board will consider application. (PA 173-175).

Once any grounds for rejection are overcome, patent application will be published for public inspection and opposition purposes in Official Gazette of Patent Publication for two months. After publication, patent applicant is given rights equal to patentee, with certain limitations. (PA 68).

Term of patent is 15 years from date of publication, but cannot exceed 20 years from date it is filed in Korea. Patent rights, being property rights, may be transferred, inherited or pledged, etc., but all such acts except inheritance take legal effect only upon registration. (PA 101). Patent term may be restored up to five years from expiration of original term, depending on nature of invention involved, pretesting and other variables. (PA 89-92 and 95). Patents may be subject to invalidation for various causes, such as wrongful patenting or nonworking by means of trial initiated by interested party and/or by examiners.

Employees are granted certain right in "in service" inventions. (PA 39 and 40).

Patent may be licensed exclusively or nonexclusively. Exclusive license gives licensee exclusive rights for patent (even excluding patentee). Nonexclusive license may contain limitation on time and territory.

Patentee or its exclusive or nonexclusive licensee may not work his patented invention if such working would require use of another's prior patent, registered utility model or registered design unless consent of prior patentee, etc. is obtained or unless nonexclusive license is granted as result of trial therefore. (PA 98). In order to obtain nonexclusive license by means of such trial, owner of later patent must prove that later invention represents significant technical progress over prior invention. (PA 138[2]).

If patented invention has not been worked for more than three consecutive years in Korea without justifiable reason, person who wishes to work patented invention may require patentee or its exclusive licensee to negotiate for grant of nonexclusive license. If no agreement is reached or no consultation is possible, person who wishes to work invention may petition Commissioner of KIPO to render mediation decision granting nonexclusive license. Upon filing of such petition, Commissioner must serve duplicate copy of petition on patent holder, giving him opportunity to reply. Official decision on petition must specify: (i) Scope of nonexclusive license to be granted, if any, and (ii) royalty to be paid by licensee and manner and time for payment thereof. Decision must take into account comments and views of Industrial Property Council of KIPO. Failure to pay royalties as required can result in cancellation of decision. If nonexclusive licensee fails to work patented invention within scope of nonexclusive license, Commissioner may, on motion by interested party or on his own motion, cancel decision, resulting in termination of nonexclusive license. (PA 107-116).

Applicant for international patent under PCT may submit its application translated into Korean to KIPO up to 30 months from earliest priority date in order to enter national phase in Korea.

PLEDGES

Pledge is real right created by contract and delivery. Creditor obtains possession as security for indebtedness and gains preference to proceeds from sale by auction over general creditors. (C.C. 329 through 355). Any item of personal property or property right may be pledged with some statutory prohibitions. Except for pawn shops, pledgor may not agree before obligation becomes due and owing for any disposition of pledged property other than that provided by law. (C.C. 339). Pledges of movables require continuous possession and pledgor may not hold item on behalf of pledgee. (C.C. 332). When claim is being pledged obligor must be notified or his consent obtained to make pledge valid against such obligor or third party. Pledgee may collect pledged claim. (C.C. 353). Negotiable instrument must be endorsed upon delivery to establish pledge. (C.C. 350). Pledge may be satisfied by sale by auction or upon appropriation with reason upon application to court. (C.C. 338).

PRINCIPAL AND AGENT

Agent acting within scope of his authority for his principal, binds such principal by any valid manifestation of intent. (C.C. 114). Unless other party knows or should have known of agent's status he binds only himself personally. In commercial transaction, principal is nevertheless still bound and performance by agent may additionally be demanded. (C.C. 115, Com. C. 48).

Individual with no legal capacity may be agent. (C.C. 117). Unless otherwise provided, agent may only perform acts of preservation or improvement of object of agency but may not alter it. (C.C. 118). Agent may not appoint subagent without consent of principal unless unavoidable reason exists. (C.C. 120). One may not be agent for both sides of legal act without consent, or if required to perform obligations. (C.C. 124). Person who holds himself out as authorizing agent to third parties is responsible for acts done by apparent agent within his apparent authority. (C.C. 125). If agent is outside scope of his authority but third party reasonably believes agent

has authority, principal is bound by acts of agent. (C.C. 126). Death of principal (other than in case of commercial transactions) or agent, bankruptcy, or adjudication of agent's incompetency, completion of terms of contract all terminate agency relationship. (C.C. 127, Com. C. 50).

Commission merchant is person who effects sales or purchases of goods or of valuable instruments in his own name for account of another person. By sale or purchase effected for his principal, commission merchant directly acquires rights and incurs obligations with regard to other party to transaction. (Com. C. 102). Goods or negotiable instruments which have been received by commission merchant from his principal, or acquired through sales and purchases, shall be deemed to belong to principal insofar as relationship between principal and commission merchant, and creditors of commission merchant are concerned. (Com. C. 103). As relationship between principal and commission merchant is mandate, commercial merchant owes general duty to properly manage affairs entrusted to him with due care. Also he is under special obligations stipulated in Commercial Code. (Com. C. 104, 105, 106, 108). Commission merchant has right to demand remuneration, right of retention, right for deposit and auction of subject matter, and right to intervene. (Com. C. 61, 67, 91, 107).

RECORDS

Registration offices are established under courts to maintain records relating to property including ships and commercial transactions and are located throughout Korea. Patent Office in Seoul maintains registers of patents, trademarks, designs, and utility models.

Real rights in immovables requiring registration include ownership, superficies, deposit lease (Chonse-gwon) and mortgage. Real rights in immovables may be created by registration of such rights with relevant record office. In Korea, separation of ownership of buildings and land upon which it is erected and maintenance of separate records thereof is possible. Provisional registration system affords protection against subsequent transfers of property to third parties through recording of contractual arrangements or incomplete assignments.

Records are required of injunctions prohibiting disposition of registered right, attachments of registered property, adjudications of bankruptcy, and commencement of reorganization procedures.

See also Commercial Register.

SALES

Nature Sale is contract for transfer of property rights in exchange for purchase price. (C.C. 563). Unless otherwise dictated by agreement or custom, transfer and payment must be made simultaneously. (C.C. 568). When neither party has begun to perform contract of sale in which earnest money has been paid, purchaser may rescind contract of sale by waiving that sum and vendor may rescind by refunding double that amount. This bars further claims for damage. (C.C. 565).

Warranties Following warranties are made in sales, and even express disclaimers will not release vendor if he had knowledge of defects but did not reveal them to purchaser or if breach results from rights given to third persons by vendor (C.C. 584): (1) Vendor must acquire from third persons and transfer to purchaser all rights that are subject of sale (C.C. 569). If vendor fails to perform, purchaser may rescind contract, and receive damages if at time of contracting he did not know that right did not belong to vendor. Vendor may also rescind, if he did not know that he did not possess such right, but must pay damages (C.C. 570, 571); (2) purchaser may request lower price if goods are not up to stipulated quantity, or if vendor cannot transfer all rights. He may rescind contract if (in good faith) he would not have entered into contract if he had such knowledge. However, vendor is still liable for damages if purchaser acted in good faith (C.C. 572, 574). All these rights must be exercised within one year of purchaser's knowledge of fact, if he acted in good faith or one year from day of contract if not (C.C. 573); (3) if object of sale is subject to superficies, servitude, registered lease right (chunse-kwon), pledge or lien, or contains defect of which purchaser had no knowledge at time of contract, purchaser may rescind contract if it thwarts purpose for which contract was made; otherwise purchaser may only seek damages. Damages and rescission are barred one year after discovery (C.C. 575, 580); (4) if purchaser loses ownership of immovable as result of exercise of preferential right or mortgage or registered lease right (chunse-kwon) covering property, he may rescind contract and claim damages as well (C.C. 576).

Price Expenses of sale are divided equally between parties. (C.C. 566). Fruits of thing are vendor's even after purchase but before delivery. Absent credit arrangement purchaser must pay interest on purchase price after delivery. (C.C. 587). If third party asserts right to goods purchaser may refuse or withhold payment until vendor provides suitable security. (C.C. 588).

Repurchase Vendor may, by special provision in sale contract have right to repurchase goods through repayment of purchase price plus expenses or other agreed amount. Unless otherwise agreed, upon re-

purchase, fruits of immovable and interest on purchase price are deemed to offset one another. (C.C. 590). Right to repurchase cannot exceed five years for immovables and three years for movables, and in absence of specifically provided term, repurchase must be within such corresponding periods. (C.C. 591). When creditor of vendor seeks to exercise vendor's right of repurchase, purchaser may retain ownership of property by paying to vendor value of property which exceeds purchase price plus expenses. (C.C. 593). If one co-owner has sold his share in property with provision for repurchase, which is later partitioned, former co-owner (vendor) may repurchase that part of property received by purchaser in division. (C.C. 595). If purchaser receives payment upon auction of co-owned property, former co-owner (vendor) may assert claim against proceeds. (C.C. 595).

Resale Between merchants, if purchaser refuses or is unable to accept delivery, vendor may deposit goods or sell goods at public auction after notifying purchaser if purchaser does not accept within reasonable time. Perishable goods may be sold without notification. Vendor must deposit proceeds of sale after deduction of expenses with government deposit office but has right to proceeds of sale for satisfaction of purchase price. (Com. C. 67). If purpose for which contract was entered into cannot be fulfilled unless performed at specified time or period, and it has lapsed without performance of one party, other party is deemed to have rescinded contract unless he immediately demands performance. (Com. C. 68).

Inspection and Rescission Between merchants, purchaser must examine goods upon delivery, and give notice of all defects or shortages if he later wishes to rescind, claim damages, or price reductions. Vendor must be notified immediately of hidden defects found within six months, if purchaser also wishes to preserve those rights. There is no requirement of immediate notification, if vendor has acted in bad faith. (Com. C. 69). When purchaser rescinds, goods are to be kept or deposited at expense of vendor. If goods may lose value or deteriorate after rescission, purchaser must obtain court order and sell goods at auction; proceeds must be deposited or kept by purchaser in his custody under approval of court. Vendor must be notified immediately of auction sale, if he does not reside or do business in same area as purchaser. (Com. C. 70). Similar rules apply to goods differing from or more than those ordered. (Com. C. 71).

Notices Required In general, no written notice is required for claim of nonconformity against vendor after delivery (however, see subhead Inspection and Rescission, supra).

Applicable Law Conflicts of Laws Act rules follow rules of contracts in general (*See* Contracts) but with regard to transfer of title, law where property is located governs. (C.L.A. 12).

Consumer Protection Consumer Protection Act ("C.P.A.") provides administrative power to protect consumers and provides for mediation of disputes by Consumer Protection Board. Civil remedies must be pursued through general principles of existing civil law. Manufacturers, importers, or packagers are required to mark goods with any necessary information. (C.P.A. 16). Competent government agency may order or implement collection, destruction or other measures with respect to goods which may cause harm to consumers. (C.P.A. 6).

Credit sale is ipso jure permitted since "sale" does not necessarily mean cash sale. Credit sale is simply payment method to be agreed on between parties. Usually seller who extends credit requires promissory note evidencing his right to payment. Recently, retailers have begun to use credit cards to facilitate credit sales.

Installment Sales Any sale in which payments are made in installments, usually monthly, is installment sale. Subject goods may be delivered upon final payment of total purchase price. However, they are usually delivered prior to payment of initial installment or upon payment thereof.

Seller may take certain steps to assure full payment by purchaser. Seller usually retains title to subject goods until payment of purchase price is made in full and then he transfers it to purchaser upon receipt thereof. If payment of installments is delayed seller can terminate purchase agreement and demand return of subject goods. Also, if any installment payment is missed seller can accelerate remaining installment payments and demand lump sum payment of remaining purchase price. Seller must try to avoid actions against public order or abuse of rights. (C.C. 103, 2).

Fraudulent Sales If obligor willfully prejudices property rights of obligee by transferring rights to goods to subsequent purchaser who is aware that such transfer is prejudicial, obligee may apply to court to have such sale rescinded. Sale for purpose of defrauding creditors (e.g. sale at price substantially undervalued) may be declared void by court and property returned.

SECURITIES

Regulation and Registration Securities and Exchange Law ("S.E.L."), Enforcement Decree and various regulations thereunder regulate securities business in Korea. Administrative functions are given to Ministry of Finance ("MOF"), Securities and Exchange Commission ("SEC") and Securities Supervisory Board ("SSB"). MOF is given powers to approve establishment of securities companies (S.E.L. 28),

branches of foreign securities companies (S.E.L. 28-2), to supervise businesses of, and to receive reports from SEC, SSB and Korea Stock Exchange ("KSE") (S.E.L. 126, 141, 142, 116 and 117, etc.). SEC is given wide power of registration of securities and securities issuers; it may issue necessary regulations and order investigations into violations of SEC regulations and orders and review and resolve various matters. (S.E.L. 118 et seq.). Under instruction and supervision of SEC, SSB enforces resolutions of SEC, supervises and inspects securities companies and other security related institutions. (S.E.L. 130, et seq.). Securities are defined as government bonds, municipal bonds, bonds issued by statutory juridical entities, corporate debentures, certificates of capital contribution issued by statutory juridical entities, stock certificates, instruments representing preemptive rights, certificates or instruments issued by foreign government or foreign companies having same nature as foregoing certificates or instruments and being designated by MOF, beneficial certificates issued by trust companies or investment trust companies. (S.E.L. 2[I], E.D. of S.E.L. 2-2).

Companies wishing to list securities other than exempt securities on exchanges, companies which have not listed securities on KSE ("non-listed companies") and intend to make public offering of securities other than exempt securities, non-listed companies wishing to merge with listed companies, non-listed companies wishing to have their securities other than exempt securities, traded at over-the-counter market and companies designated by SEC which meet certain criteria as is prescribed by Enforcement Decree must be registered with SEC in advance. (S.E.L. 3). With certain exceptions issuers of securities, before publicly offering or selling securities issued or to be issued, and listed companies, before issuing new shares, must file registration statement with SEC in advance. (S.E.L. 8). This is not applicable to government bonds, municipal bonds, bonds and share certificates issued by statutory juridical entities and beneficial certificates.

Tender Offers With certain exceptions, offerors of tender offers outside exchanges to unspecified persons for stock certificates, instruments representing preemptive rights and convertible bonds issued by listed companies and companies registered with SEC ("registered companies"), which would result in offeror (including his family and other people having special relationship with offeror) beneficially owning 10% or more of total shares issued and outstanding must file tender offer disclosure statement with SEC prior to tender offer, send copy of such statement to issuer of subject securities, and make public notice in two or more daily newspapers. (S.E.L. 21 and 22, Enforcement Regulation of S.E.L. 6). SEC may order offeror to follow terms, conditions and method of purchase determined by SEC. (S.E.L. 23 [III]).

Proxy Solicitation Solicitor of proxies with respect to listed stock certificates must, on or prior to solicitation, provide solicitees with reference documents prepared as provided by SEC and at same time file copies of reference documents and form of proxy with SSB. (S.E.L. 199, E.D. of S.E.L. 85, Paras. 1 and 3). Form of proxy must include box-type ballot to permit stockholders to choose between approving and disapproving each item to be discussed in shareholders' meeting. (E.D. of S.E.L. 85 [II]). *See also* Corporations.

Shareholding Restrictions With certain exceptions, one may not hold beneficial ownership of shares issued by listed company in excess of: (i) Number of shares held, at time of listing if more than 10% of total shares issued and outstanding or (ii) 10% of total shares issued and outstanding. (S.E.L. 200, Paras. 1 and 2). Anyone holding shares in excess of above limitation may not exercise voting rights of excess shares. (S.E.L. 200[III]). SEC may order such shareholders to rectify shareholding position. (S.E.L. 200[III]).

SEC may set restrictions on foreigners' acquisition of securities issued by listed corporations or registered corporations. (E.D. of S.E.L. 87-2 [I] and [II]). Unless otherwise approved by SEC, foreigners wishing to buy or sell listed securities must do so through exchanges. (E.D. of S.E.L. 87-2[III]).

Secured Bonds Secured bond is bond which has security. Because it is impracticable to provide specific security for each bond holder, Secured Bonds Trust Act enacted Jan. 10, 1962 enables company to provide collective security. Bond issuing company acting as trustor, and trust company acting as trustee, execute trust agreement. Trust agreement obligates trustee to acquire security, to maintain same on behalf of all bond holders, to enforce security, and to distribute foreclosure price to bond holders pari passu according to their credit amount. (Secured Bonds Trust Act 60, et seq.).

SHIPPING

Primary features of shipping and maritime law are contained in Part V of Commercial Code and other laws (e.g., Ship Act, Ship Registration Act, Seaman's Act, Marine Transportation Business Act, Maritime Transportation Industry Fostering Act).

Ships are of Korean nationality if they belong to: (1) Korean government, (2) Korean national, (3) corporation incorporated under Law of Korea where more than half of equity capital and more than three fifths of directors (including representative directors) of company are Korean nationals (representative director shall also be Korean national), and (4) company whose principal office is in Korea and whose legal representatives are Korean. Register of Ships at Korean Maritime and Port Administration contains information concerning type, name, port of registry, ownership, and tonnage.

Records relating to ownership and rights in vessels of gross tonnage of more than 20 tons can be found at registration office of home port of ship. (Ship Registration Law 2, 3, 4). *See also* Records.

Liability of consignee for freight and other expenses arises upon receipt of cargo. If consignee fails to accept cargo, shipowner becomes entitled to deposit cargo with competent authority. (Com. C. 803). Shipowner may, in case of failure to pay for freight etc. with approval of court, sell cargo at auction within 30 days after date of delivery, in order to receive freight and other incidental expenses, so long as third party has not acquired possession thereof.

Charterer of entire ship may rescind contract at any time before commencement of voyage if he pays one-half of freight. Part charterer may rescind before commencement of voyage but must pay entire amount of freight. Damages and expenses resulting from disposition by master to save vessel or cargo from common danger are shared among interested persons in accordance with rules of general average contribution. General average contribution and loss shall be determined based upon remaining value of ship and cargo at time and place of ship's arrival and unloading of cargo. (Com. C. 836).

Regarding limitation of shipowner's liability, Commercial Code adopts basic features of International Convention for Unification of Certain Rules of Law in Regard to Collisions (Brussels, Sept. 23, 1910); International Convention for Unification of Certain Rules of Law Relating to Assistance and Salvage (Brussels, 1910); International Convention Relating to Limitation of Liabilities of Owners of Seagoing Ships; and International Convention for Unification of Certain Rules of Law Relating to Bills of Lading, although Korea is not signatory thereto. Korea is signatory to International Convention on Civil Liability for Oil Pollution Damage of 1969.

Maritime lien extends to ships, appurtenances thereof, and unpaid freight for: (1) Legal expenses incurred in interest of creditors, expenses incurred in respect to auction sale of ships and their appurtenances, taxes levied on ships in respect to voyage, pilotage and towing fees, and cost of maintenance and survey of ship and its appurtenances at last port; (2) claims arising from contract of employment of mariners and other employees of ship; (3) salvage remuneration and general average contributions; (4) indemnities for damages caused to navigational institutions and or navigable ways by collision between ships or any other accident, for loss of lives or for personal injuries to mariners or passengers. and for damages caused to cargo and luggage; (5) claims arising from contracts entered into or performance thereof by master acting within scope of his authority and away from ship's home port, where such contracts or performance thereof are necessary for preservation of ship or continuation of its voyage; and (6) claims in respect to equipment, food, and fuel of ship required for preparation of its last voyage.

TRADEMARKS AND TRADENAMES

Trademarks Newly revised Trademark Act was promulgated on Jan. 13, 1990. Enforcement to commence on Sept. 1, 1990. Following explanation is based on newly revised Trademark Act. Trademark rights are obtained only when trademark is registered. (T.A. 41). Anyone who wishes to register trademark may file registration application with Korea Industrial Property Office regardless of whether trademark has actually been used. Materials which substantiate use of trademark thus need not be submitted when new application is filed. However, proof of use must be submitted when renewal application is filed. (T.A. 42 [II][ii]). Further, trademark registration is subject to cancellation through trial brought by interested party if owner or its registered licensee has not used trademark on any of designated goods for any three consecutive years before cancellation hearings (trials) are brought. (T.A. 73 [I][iii]).

Further, Korea has adopted national classification system regarding goods and services. This classification system includes 53 classes for goods and 12 classes for services. Applicant must classify goods or services to be covered by mark in appropriate class using national classification system and must also describe goods or services in detail on item by item basis. (T.A. 10).

Term of trademark right is ten years and may be renewed for subsequent ten year period. (T.A. 42). Trademarks may be transferred together with related business. (T.A. 54).

If owner of registered trademark permits another to use their trademark for six months or longer without registering this party as exclusive or non-exclusive licensee, interested party can bring cancellation action against registration. (T.A. 73[I][i]). Registration of exclusive or non-exclusive licensee is accomplished by submitting trademark license agreement executed by parties to Korea Industrial Property Office. Further, if trademark license agreement does not provide for royalty payments, no government approval is required. Only royalty-bearing trademark licenses must be approved by government authorities in accordance with Foreign Exchange Control Law and Foreign Capital Inducement Law.

Trade Names Individual may use business name or not, but business organization must use trade name to conduct its trade. (Com. C. 179[II], 270, 289[I][ii]). Trade name need not include name of proprietor or refer to type of business involved. However, trade names of business organizations must include descriptor as prescribed in Commercial Code, such as joint stock company, etc., and such descriptors may only be used when actually applicable. (Com. C. 19, 20). Company can do business only under single trade name. (Com. C. 21). None may use trade name which is likely to cause confusion, with trade name of another for improper purposes. Civil liability may arise from such activity. (Com. C. 23).

Trade names may be registered with civil district court having jurisdiction over main and/or branch offices of business. Registration in one judicial district cannot be used to attack or prevent registration of similar trade name in different district. (Com. C. 22, 23). Transfer of trade name must be registered in commercial register to be enforceable against third parties (Com. C. 25).

TREATIES

International Conventions Treaties duly concluded and promulgated in accordance with Constitution and generally recognized rules of international law have same effect as domestic laws of Korea. (Const. 6[1]).

Agriculture and Food Constitution of the United Nations Food and Agriculture Organization (16/10/45), International Agreement for the Creation of International Office of Epizootics in Paris (25/1/24), International Plant Protection Convention (6/12/51), Constitution of International Rice Commission (13/3/48), International Cotton Advisory Committee (9/9/39), Wheat Trade Convention (20/2/71), Constitution of Afro-Asian Rural Reconstruction Organization (31/3/62), Agreement establishing Food and Fertilizer Technology Center for Asian and Pacific Region (11/6/69), Charter of Asian Vegetables Research and Development Center (22/5/71), International Sugar Agreement (7/10/77), Convention Placing International Poplar Commission within framework of Food and Agriculture Organization of United Nations (19/11/59), Agreement Establishing International Fund for Agricultural Development (13/6/76), International Sugar Agreement, 1977 (7/10/77), Convention on the Conservation on the Living Resources of the South East Atlantic (23/10/69), Plant Protection Agreement for the South East Asia and Pacific Region (27/2/56), International Sugar Agreement, 1984 (5/7/84), International Tropical Timber Agreement, 1983 (18/11/83), Wheat Trade Convention, 1986 (14/3/86).

Customs Customs Convention on Temporary Importation of Packings (6/10/60), Customs Convention Concerning Facilities for Importation of Goods for Display or Use at Exhibitions, Fairs, Meetings or

Similar Events (8/6/61), Customs Convention Concerning Welfare Materials for Seafarers (1/12/64), Customs Convention on A.T.A. Carnet for Temporary Admission of Goods (6/12/61), Customs Convention on Temporary Importation of Professional Equipments (8/6/61), Convention Establishing Customs Cooperation Council (15/12/50), Convention on Valuation of Goods for Customs Purposes (15/12/50), Convention on Nomenclature for Classification of Goods in Customs Tariffs (15/12/50), Convention Concerning Formation of an International Union for Publication of Customs Tariffs, Regulations of Execution, and Final Declarations (5/6/1890), Customs Convention on the Temporary Importation of Professional Equipment (8/6/61), International Convention to Facilitate the Importation of Commercial Samples and Advertising Material (7/11/52), Customs Convention on the International Transport of Goods under cover of TIR Carnets (14/11/75), Customs Convention on the Temporary Importation of Scientific Equipment (11/6/68), Customs Convention on the Temporary Importation of Pedagogic Material (8/6/70), International Convention of the Simplification and Harmonization of Customs Procedures (18/5/73), Annex concerning the Temporary Storage of Goods (Annex A2) (18/5/73), Annex concerning the Customs Warehouses to the International Convention on the Simplification and Harmonization of Customs Procedures (18/5/73), Customs Convention on Containers, 1972 (2/12/72), Annex A1 (Annex concerning Customs Formalities prior to the Lodgement of the Goods Declaration) to the International Convention on the Simplification and Harmonization of Customs Procedures (18/5/73), Annex E1 (Annex concerning Customs Transit) to the International Convention on the Simplification and Harmonization of Customs Procedures (18/5/73).

Disputes Settlement Convention on Settlement of Investment Disputes between States and Nationals of Other States (18/3/65), U.N. Convention on Recognition and Enforcement of Foreign Arbitratal Awards (10/6/58).

Finance Articles of Agreement of International Monetary Fund (22/7/44), Articles of Agreement of International Bank of Reconstruction and Development (22/7/44), Articles of Agreement of International Finance Corporation (11/4/55), Agreement Establishing Asian Development Bank (4/12/65), Agreement Establishing Asian Reinsurance Corporation (11/12/76), Agreement Establishing the African Development Fund (29/11/72), Agreement Establishing the African Development Bank (4/8/63).

Fisheries Agreement for Establishment of Indo-Pacific Fisheries Council (26/2/48), International Convention for Conservation of Atlantic Tunas (14/5/66), International Convention for Regulation of Whaling (2/12/46), Protocol to International Convention for Regulation of Whaling (19/12/56).

Health and Tourism Constitution of World Health Organization (22/7/46), Statute of World Tourism Organization (27/9/70).

Maritime Matters International Convention on Load Lines (5/4/66), International Convention for Safety of Life at Sea (17/6/60), Convention on Inter-Governmental Maritime Consultative Organization (6/3/48), Convention on International Hydrographic Organization (3/5/67), Convention on International Regulations for Preventing Collisions at Sea (20/10/72), International Convention on Civil Liability for Oil Pollution Damage (29/11/69), International Convention for Prevention of Pollution of Sea by Oil (12/5/54), International Convention for Safe Containers (2/12/72), Convention on Code of Conduct for Liner Conveyances (6/4/74), Protocol to the Treaty concerning the Permanent Neutrality and Operation of the Panama Canal (7/9/77), International Convention for the Safety of Life at Sea, 1974 (1/11/74), Protocol of the 1978 Relating to the International Convention for the Safety of Life at Sea, 1974 (17/2/78), International Convention on Tonnage Measurement of Ships, 1969 (23/6/69), United Nations Convention on the Law of the Sea (30/4/82), International Convention for the Prevention of Pollution from Ships, 1973 and Protocol of 1978 relating to the International Convention for the Prevention of Pollution from Ships, 1973 (2/11/73, 17/2/78), International Convention on Standards of Training, Certification and Watchkeeping for Seafarers, 1979 (7/7/78), Convention on the International Maritime Satellite organization (INMARSAT) (3/9/76).

Nationality Convention Relating to Status of Stateless Persons (28/9/54).

Patents *See* Patents.

Trade and Commerce Long-term Arrangement Regarding International Trade in Cotton Textiles (9/2/62), Protocol for Accession of Republic of Korea to General Agreement on Tariffs and Trade (2/3/67), Geneva Protocol to General Agreement on Tariffs and Trade (30/6/67), First Agreement on Trade Negotiation Among Developing Member Countries of Economic and Social Commissions for Asia and Pacific (31/7/75), International Convention to Facilitate Importation of Commercial Samples (7/11/52), Protocol Relating to Trade Negotiations with Developing Countries (8/12/71), Arrangements Regarding International Trade in Textiles (20/12/73), International Tin Agreement (1/3/54), Agreement on Interpretation and Application of Articles XVI and XXIII of the General Agreement on Tariffs and Trade (12/4/79), Agreement on Technical Barriers to Trade (12/4/79), Protocol Supplementary to the Geneva Protocol (1979) to the General Agreement on Tariffs and Trade (22/11/79), Agreement on Implementation of Article VII of the General Agreement on Tariffs and Trade and the Protocol thereto (12/4/79, 1/11/79), Arrangement Establishing the International Textiles and Clothing Bureau (13/12/83), Agreement on Implementation of Article VI of the General Agreement on Tariffs and Trade (GATT Anti-Dumping Code) (12/4/79), Protocol Extending the Arrangement Regarding International Trade in Textiles (31/7/86), Agreement on the Global System of Trade Preferences among Developing Countries (21/6/89).

Weights and Measures Meter Convention (20/5/1875), Convention Concerning Creation of an International Office of Weights and Measures, Regulations and Transient Provisions (20/5/1875), Convention Establishing International Legal Meteorology (12/10/55).

Bilateral treaties number more than 640.

Financial Institutions

South Korean financial institutions are relatively undeveloped for several reasons. Pervasive government intervention has prevented the development of a market-driven financial sector. Bureaucracy and lack of experience with international standards have further hindered the development of independent service-oriented financial professionals. And, as in every other area of Korean business, corruption and graft have been widespread.

The recently instituted crackdown on corruption by the government of President Kim Young Sam offers some strong indications that Korean officialdom is making a serious attempt to root out the worst practices. However, the government continues to manipulate the financial sector in a heavy-handed manner, using it as a policy tool and temporizing on reforms that would open it up to transparent, market-based operations. Foreign banks offer a ray of hope. Their presence eases the way for foreign investors and provides the germ of competition needed to prod domestic commercial banks into upgrading their own level of sophistication and service.

Financial markets such as the stock market are still somewhat rudimentary and nontransparent in their operation. Current reform efforts should speed their development and allow increased foreign participation. In general, observers expect the 1990s to be a time of adjustment and experimentation as Korea's financial sector matures.

Reform The Republic of Korea's (ROK) financial sector is the target of a major five-year reform effort. Traditionally, the sector has functioned as a tool of government policy rather than as an independent part of the economy. Recently, through a combination of international pressure coming mainly from the United States and a major shift in the domestic political situation, banks and other financial institutions began taking steps toward autonomous operations. Korean leaders hope to bring the financial system up to international standards by 1997 in an attempt to garner some of the financial business that they expect Hong Kong to lose when it is taken over by China. Some of their main goals include deregulation of deposit and lending rates, an end to government-directed preferential lending, limits on ownership of financial institutions and control by conglomerates known as *chaebol,* reduced restrictions on foreign bank operations, increased foreign participation in the securities market, and an end to blatant corruption as standard operating procedure.

At present the financial sector remains even more restricted than other areas of the nation's economy. Banks are strictly controlled by the ROK government's Ministry of Finance (MOF) and the Bank of Korea (BOK). Government officials set interest rates and directly allocate scarce funds by designating the areas, and on occasion the firms, into which such resources are to be channeled. Until recently, the government even appointed senior officers of private banks.

THE BANKING SYSTEM

South Korea has a central bank, 14 national banks, 10 local banks, 72 foreign bank branches, and seven specialized banks. Banks are divided into commercial banks, which offer short-term financing, and specialized banks, which offer sector-specific long-term loans. The banking system was effectively nationalized in 1961 by the military government, which appropriated a large portion of the ownership of the private banks in order to obtain greater control over the financial system. The government has since gradually reprivatized the financial system so that the vast majority of ownership is again in private hands, although the government continues to keep a tight rein over Korean financial institutions. (Refer to "Important Addresses" chapter for contact information for major Korean financial institutions.)

The Bank of Korea

Established in 1950, the Bank of Korea (BOK) functions as the nation's central bank. It ultimately regulates all financial activity in the country, issues currency, manages government debt issues, manages the money supply through open-market operations, manages foreign exchange, operates the discount window, sets reserve requirements, manages interest rates, and generally controls money and credit flows. The bank's operations are administered by the Monetary Board (MB), which is presided over by the Ministry of Finance. The board formulates Korea's monetary, credit, and foreign exchange policies and exercises broad powers over all aspects of the banking system. Only the Korea Development Bank is exempt from direct MB control.

Commercial Banks

Twenty-four domestic commercial banks operate in South Korea. Fourteen of them, known as city banks, operate nationwide. Branch facilities throughout the country number about 1,275. Under the General Banking Act, banks are limited to lending for terms that usually do not exceed one year and cannot exceed three years. Most lending is based on a promissory note issued by the borrower, and banks customarily require appraised collateral of up to 125 percent of the loan amount. These short-term loans are usually allowed to roll over at maturity, albeit often at a higher interest rate. Compounding the problem of a scarcity of funds available for lending, domestic commercial banks have been hampered by government rules requiring them to make about half of their loans to targeted sectors and firms, usually at below-market rates. This practice has contributed substantially to the remarkable rise of Korean industry but has retarded the development of the Korean financial sector.

Commercial banks can also handle investment in securities, trade financing such as guarantees and acceptances, remittances and collections, foreign exchange transactions, and government payments, acting as agents of the BOK. Product areas have expanded to include credit card issue and processing, the sale of private bills and public debt repurchase agreements, factoring, and the trust business. Banks are authorized to handle international business through overseas branches and correspondent relationships. However, domestic commercial bank services remain unsophisticated because of government restrictions and intervention, a lack of expertise, and limited automation and infrastructure. Korean commercial banks raise capital through domestic deposit taking, international loans, and borrowing at the discount window of the BOK.

The five largest private commercial banks—Hanil Bank, Commercial Bank of Korea, Cho-Heung Bank, Korea First Bank, and the Bank of Seoul and Trust Co.—dominate the domestic banking market. However, in the late 1980s two new city banks were formed as joint ventures, the Shinhan Bank with Japa-nese investors and the Kor-Am Bank with American bank partners. Most firms in Korea have a primary or house bank with which they do business exclusively. Each of the largest banks is closely allied to one or more of the nation's *chaebol*, or major conglomerates, giving the banks added importance in the national economy. Although the *chaebol* are technically prohibited from even partial ownership of financial institutions, the tight and often exclusive links between major city banks and the conglomerates enhance the power of the *chaebol* and their companion banks. Firms doing business with a *chaebol* unit will usually be expected to channel all their financial dealings through its official bank.

The 14 nationwide banks fared well financially in 1992. Total assets rose more than 20 percent over 1991, to W123.1 trillion (about US$156 billion), and before-tax profits soared 35.6 percent, to W2.2 trillion (about US$2.75 billion). This rise was spurred by an increase in the average interest rate spread between deposits and loans. Due to a drop in interest rates early in the year, profits were expected to be significantly lower in 1993, and domestic banks could see profits drop by 60 percent, according to some estimates. Moreover, the BOK has had to inject substantial funds into the system to enable banks to meet reserve requirements, which are far below those established for international banks by the Bank for International Settlements (BIS). Bad debt ratios are officially listed at 2 percent; however, observers consider this figure to be meaningless because it strategically ignores some major credit problems. Some sources estimate the real figure at closer to 10 percent.

The 10 local banks maintain offices in Seoul, but operate primarily in specific provinces. Their operations, which focus on wholesale or business banking, are generally more limited and smaller in scale than those of city banks, and the local banks usually do not operate in foreign exchange markets. None of these local banks makes a specialty of retail consumer service. All were established between 1967 and 1971 to promote regional development and decentralize banking services. Although they are prominent locally, they play a relatively minor role in overall financial activity.

Overseas Expansion

South Korean banks have been hampered in their efforts to do business overseas by their relatively meager resources and by intense domestic competition. Foreign banks have upstaged them to some extent at home, but their main competition has come from specialized bank and nonbank domestic financial institutions that have stolen market share from them right and left. Although Korean banks have a substantial presence in Japan, where they compete to serve Japan's large resident Korean population,

Recent Developments in the Financial Sector

Kim Young Sam, the new president of South Korea, based his campaign on the promise to crack down on Korea's endemic corruption. The financial sector has been hit hard as he has begun to make good on his promise since taking office in February 1993. By June 1993 the presidents of the Bank of Seoul, Korea First Bank, and Boram Bank had all resigned under suspicion of irregular practices, primarily the taking of kickbacks to approve loans. The president of Donghwa Bank was arrested on charges of paying bribes to government officials, and a senior economic planner for former President Roh Tae Woo was charged with accepting such bribes. Most shocking to the financial community was the flight to avoid arrest on similar charges of former Minister of Finance Rhee Yong Man, perhaps the most powerful individual in Korea's financial system, and of politically connected banker Lee Won-Jo.

These and other high-level arrests may signal that the era of rampant official corruption in Korea is actually on the wane. Reports indicate that as many as 200 officials of the nationwide commercial banks are under investigation for corrupt practices. However, many observers feel that the root of the problem will not be addressed unless the new five-year financial reform package insulates the banks from political interference and allows lending to be based on economic rather than political considerations.

In early 1992 President Kim's administration initiated a new financial policy designed to jump-start Korea's sluggish economy. The program includes a price freeze for major commodities and a reduction of officially set interest rates to a 10-year low. The goal is to provide more affordable financing for businesses, especially cash-starved small- and medium-sized companies, and to stifle inflation.

As a result of this program, the BOK's rediscount rate fell from 6 percent to 5 percent, and interest rates on loans at domestic commercial banks dropped by about 2 percentage points to close to 9 percent overnight, making them more competitive with foreign banks, which generally provide better service but charge rates in the 13 to 14 percent range. As foreign banks see their already slim share of the lending business fall, they could begin to concentrate on providing more specialized services, such as handling foreign exchange transactions, securities services, and venture capital placements.

Korea is dealing with its worst economy in ten years. More than 10,000 Korean firms declared bankruptcy in 1992, and many of them defaulted on substantial bank loans. In 1992 nonperforming loans rose 22.9 percent to about W10 trillion (about US$13 billion), almost 10 percent of total commercial bank assets, further exacerbating Korea's shortage of available investment funds.

Against the backdrop of this worsening situation, the government fired central bank governor Cho Soon over disagreements on how the BOK should be run. Cho had been a champion of reforms that would insulate the BOK from political interference and allow it to operate independently based on economic and market considerations. He advocated rapid deregulation of the banking industry, especially in the area of interest rates, which are currently dictated by the government. Although reform-minded administration policymakers agreed in theory with Cho's free-market stance, they succumbed to the temptation to continue manipulating the financial sector to serve near-term political needs. Cho's successor, Kim Myung Ho, is expected to operate the BOK according to orders, and financial reform, which has suffered from a lack of specific targets and timetables, is expected to proceed very slowly and cautiously.

Nevertheless, reforms continue to inch their way through the system. In May 1993 the government announced that the MOF would no longer directly appoint senior bank officers, who had often come from among the ranks of senior MOF officials. In the future such appointments will be made by a committee composed of shareholders, customers, and

Recent Developments (cont'd.)

former bank presidents, with the largest *chaebol* prohibited from serving on such committees. In the first exercise of this newfound freedom, two city banks have chosen to promote internal candidates who under the previous system would have had little chance of further advancement. The opening of such opportunities could serve to promote institutional loyalty, which has been weak, and break the cartel-like behavior of domestic banks.

Foreign exchange regulations, which have been highly restrictive, are also being liberalized, with the latest revision consisting of a change from a positive to a negative system. Under the prevailing positive system, everything is prohibited unless expressly permitted by the regulations. Under the proposed negative system, all activities are permitted unless expressly forbidden by law. This shift is designed to ease regulations in this critical area, although the general approach is likely to remain restrictive in nature.

The issue of the deregulation of interest rates is also a touchy one. As noted, the government has traditionally used the manipulation of interest rates to achieve policy goals and is loath to give up this tool. Nevertheless, the government has begun easing into such deregulation by lifting or easing limits in ancillary areas. In 1991 it relaxed limits on rates charged on overdrafts—one way firms have of obtaining short-term financing—on mutual savings and finance companies, life insurance activities, overdue payment charges, and a range of money market instruments and transactions. Rates were further eased on large deposits and long-term instruments, including corporate bonds with maturities of greater than two years. In a recent round of announcements, the government promised to deregulate 90 percent of all lending rates and 30 percent of all deposit rates by the end of 1993.

they have a minimal branch presence in Hong Kong, Singapore, and the Philippines and only operate representative offices in such important developing markets as Russia, China, and Thailand. Internally generated resources needed to fund a major overseas presence are unlikely to be forthcoming, and the government is not expected to be of much help. Rather than giving in an effort to strengthen its national financial institutions, the government has traditionally taken from the banks by requiring them to underwrite industrial and other development.

Foreign Banks

Foreign banks cannot open subsidiaries organized as separate corporate entities in Korea, but they are allowed to operate branches and representative offices. Branches of foreign banks are classed as commercial banks, although foreign banks can also operate in areas of merchant banking. Since the operation of such financial institutions was first authorized in 1967, their presence has grown in line with Korea's increased trade with other nations. Few foreign banks bothered to operate in Korea before the late 1970s. As of mid-1993 there were 51 foreign banks in South Korea. However, Korea has been a difficult market for these banks and while newcomers are constantly seeking entry, some major players, such as Mellon Bank, Wells Fargo, and Morgan Guaranty (all from the United States) have left the country since 1986. Australia's Westpac Banking Corporation was set to pull out by the end of 1993. Over half belonged to US or Japanese banks, reflecting the dominant role of those two countries in trade and investment in the ROK. In addition, more than 20 other foreign banks maintain representative offices, and many of these are expected to open Korean branches in the future.

The original reason for allowing foreign banks into the country was to facilitate foreign trade and investment and to gain access to foreign currency. Since 1967 the ROK has accrued substantial foreign reserves, and its need for such bank-facilitated access to foreign currency is not as great as it once was. Foreign banks still play a major role in merchant banking due to their international ties and access to foreign investment capital, and many are now being allowed to move into previously restricted areas of domestic specialized services and project financing. Foreign banks also have taken over nearly 50 percent of the growing market in foreign exchange transactions.

Foreign banks are allowed certain operating privileges not granted to domestic banks. They have been allowed to buy won with foreign currency, with government forward repurchase contracts on the local currency guaranteeing a positive spread. However, the BOK has been steadily reducing foreign bank access to this swap market as well as narrowing the spread as it finds other sources of foreign exchange. Foreign banks can also make loans in either local or foreign currency subject to strict limitations and prior approval from the MOF, and they can hold independent foreign currency reserves for financing joint ventures and foreign businesses.

Although restrictions on foreign bank operations have steadily eased, reform has been gradual. Despite their somewhat privileged position in some areas of operation, foreign banks are still barred from competing freely on a par with domestic banks. Foreign banks have been limited to only one or two branch office locations, although this restriction is expected to be eased under new reforms. With the exception of Citibank, which operates under a special arrangement, foreign banks are not allowed to engage in traditional retail banking services such as the taking of individual savings deposits. They are allowed to accept deposits from domestic individuals and firms in both won and foreign currency accounts, although such deposits remain at low levels, providing less than 10 percent of funding. About 50 percent of funding comes from interoffice borrowing from parent organizations. The remaining major source of funding is foreign currency swap transactions with the BOK, although the BOK has begun reducing access to and terms on such swaps. Since 1988 foreign branches have been allowed to borrow funds at the BOK's discount window, a major source of funding for domestic banks, if only to finance shortages in their required reserve positions.

Foreign bank branches were allowed to join the Korean Federation of Banks in 1984 for the purpose of trading information with domestic banks, and since 1986 a very few large foreign banks have been granted special status in the national clearing house association. The MB permitted foreign bank branches to use the rediscount services at the BOK for export financing in 1985 and for commercial bills in 1986. In 1985 the MB also granted foreign banks the right to handle money trusts and negotiable certificates of deposit. Since 1990 Korea has raised the ceiling on the amount of certificates of deposit that foreign banks can issue and eliminated restrictive limits on capital. However, other restrictions continue to hamper the ability of foreign banks to offer many services to clients.

Since 1985 the MB has required foreign banks to make so-called policy loans. Such loans, which have long been required of domestic commercial banks, are directed to specific sectors in pursuit of official development goals. Domestic banks have had to lend as much as half their funds to targeted sectors and firms, usually at below-market rates. According to MB stipulations, foreign banks must lend at least 25 percent of their funds held in Korean won to small- and medium-sized firms. This requirement is increased to 35 percent for banks using BOK rediscount services.

The government's stated goal is to deregulate both foreign and domestic banks, relieving them of the requirement to earmark any amount of their lending for specified sectors or projects by 1998. However, the only alternative to such lending would be a government credit facility, which would be politically difficult to set up and fund, and the current rules are expected to remain in place for the foreseeable future.

The presence of reputable foreign banks in Korea offers a lifeline to foreign firms doing business there. Without these banks, foreign firms in Korea would be at the mercy of domestic commercial banks, which are not skilled service providers, have few funds to lend, and are subject to government directives and political considerations that are often contrary to the business interests of individual firms. And even when they must work with Korean banks, particularly in dealings with *chaebol* that require the use of a house bank, foreign firms can obtain tactical advice from established foreign banks.

Specialized Banks

Unlike the commercial banks which are chartered under the General Banking Law and focus on short-term lending, Korea's seven specialized banks have been created under specific laws and are designed primarily to provide long-term financing or special operational capabilities for particular sectors of the economy or areas of business. They are funded by deposits, the sale of debt, and government borrowings. Many of these specialized banks have developed substantial networks and have taken significant amounts of business away from traditional commercial banks.

The Korea Exchange Bank (KEB) was established in 1967 to operate in the area of foreign exchange. It has taken over the management of most of the foreign exchange functions previously performed by the BOK, which, however, continues to set policy in this area. The KEB operates as a regular commercial bank while serving as a clearing house for foreign exchange transactions, in which it claims a 15 percent share of the market. It operates six wholly owned subsidiaries, 19 overseas branch offices, and 14 overseas representative offices. The bank is jointly owned by the BOK and the government.

The National Agricultural Cooperative Federation emphasizes lending for agricultural and forestry development projects. It extends loans to farmers and provides commercial banking services to rural as well as to urban customers. Similar specialized functions are performed by the National Livestock Cooperatives Federation and the Central Federation of Fisheries Cooperatives for their respective industries.

The Small and Medium Industry Bank (SMIB), Citizens National Bank (CNB), and Korea Housing Bank

(KHB) are government-controlled banks designed to meet the needs of certain sectors of the economy. The SMIB finances small- and medium-sized businesses and is engaged in short-term working capital financing and long-term capital projects lending. The CNB specializes in retail consumer and small business banking services, extending loans and accepting contractual and regular deposits. To avoid direct competition with the commercial banks, it grants loans only to those persons having accounts with the bank. The KHB was founded to make building loans to middle-income families.

NONBANK FINANCIAL INSTITUTIONS

Nonbank financial institutions include development, investment, merchant, and savings banks and insurance and leasing companies. These institutions are regulated by the MOF. They usually charge interest rates that are higher than those of commercial and specialized banks, but they often have more funds available to lend in their specific areas of operation. Most concentrate on serving domestic borrowers and are not available to foreign entities as a significant source of financing. However, nonbank financial institutions are gaining increased freedom of operation and a greater share of total financing in the Korean economy. This shift could serve to free up funds for foreign operators from more traditional banking sources that are losing market share to these entities.

Development Institutions

Development institutions have played an important role in Korea's economic miracle primarily because they are the key financial intermediaries for government-sponsored projects. These institutions offer medium- and long-term financing and credit facilities for the development of targeted key economic sectors. The government is the main source of their funding, but they can also borrow abroad and issue debt. The three main development institutions are the Export-Import Bank of Korea, the Korea Long-Term Credit Bank, and the Korea Development Bank.

The Export-Import Bank opened in 1976 to provide support for Korean export industries. Modeled on the United States Export-Import Bank, it functions primarily to make medium- and long-term loans for international trade, overseas investment, and large overseas natural resource development projects. It extends credit to foreign governments, banks, and corporations and also underwrites export insurance. The bank's capital comes from the National Investment Fund and domestic and foreign banks.

The Korea Long-Term Credit Bank, incorporated in 1967, is a private institution that makes loans in both foreign and local currencies to private manufacturers and joint ventures. Its capital is based on stock subscriptions from the International Finance Corporation (IFC), foreign and domestic banks, insurance companies, and private investors. The Long-Term Credit Bank is Korea's first and so far only nongovernmental source of long-term industrial loans and equity financing.

The Korea Development Bank (KDB) acts as an intermediary for channeling government funds and foreign loans to domestic industry. The loans extended by the KDB are heavily concentrated in the manufacturing and electric power-generation sectors. It lends mostly to large established firms for medium to long terms. The KDB is the only national financial institution that does not fall under the jurisdiction of the MB, giving it some limited freedom of operation outside the straitjacket of regular state controls.

Investment Companies, Merchant Banks, and Leasing Companies

Investment companies were established in 1972 to develop short-term money market operations. They engage in short-term financing by issuing three- to six-month commercial paper themselves, dealing in the commercial paper issued by other companies, accepting and guaranteeing commercial paper, and handling cash management accounts (money market mutual funds designed to serve individuals). They are allowed to issue long-term debt to fund their operations. Such investment companies are also allowed to operate in the securities markets as underwriters and broker-dealers. Despite the development of an active and growing money market, most of the firms involved in this business are expected to move on into commercial banking, merchant banking, or securities brokerage, leaving money market operations to a small core of about eight Seoul-based firms.

Merchant banks assist companies in finding foreign investment capital and extend medium- and long-term loans themselves. All are joint ventures with foreign investors, having been set up specifically to fund domestic projects with foreign capital available in the international capital markets accessible to their foreign partners. To provide additional incentives to such foreign operators, merchant banks are allowed to engage in virtually all areas of commercial banking except deposit taking and can also operate leasing companies and securities dealers. The government authorized the spin-off of separate leasing companies in 1989.

Insurance Companies

The insurance industry is relatively undeveloped in Korea. It has been open to foreign firms only since 1988, and few foreign insurers operate in Korean markets. The industry is split between life insurance and property and casualty insurance business lines, and no company may engage in both areas. Establishing an insurance company requires approval by the MOF, which directly controls premium rates for life insurance. The insurance industry is regulated by the Insurance Supervisory Board. The Post Office also issues life insurance.

Insurance companies have been conservative in the placement of their funds. Usually they limit their investments to government paper or placement with official or quasi-official agencies. They have generally avoided private placements or direct securities and money market investments and are not considered a current source of funding for foreign businesses.

Savings Companies

Separate savings entities in Korea include the trust operations of commercial banks, mutual savings and finance companies, credit unions, mutual credit facilities, community finance associations, and the postal savings system. These institutions were introduced primarily to bring into the official sector the small-scale individual and small business financial activity that had found its way into unofficial channels when traditional institutions failed to serve the needs of these consumers. Some of these institutions represent official recognition of existing unofficial operations. There are more than 6,500 such institutions nationwide, most of them quite small and serving narrow clienteles in specific localities and niches. By definition, most serve only members, individuals, or small local businesses. These institutions do not provide financing for foreign investors, nor are foreigners allowed to invest in such businesses with the narrow exception of foreign banks, which are allowed to carry on limited trust operations.

Most domestic and foreign commercial banks operate trust companies. Trust accounts are the equivalent of long-term deposits, and the interest rates paid on such accounts are slightly higher than on regular time and savings deposits.

Credit unions also function as savings companies. They are usually set up by the members of private groups such as churches to take deposits and provide small loans for members. They set their own interest rates, within the parameters established by the MOF.

Mutual savings and finance companies that operate on an installment basis, mutual credit facilities, and the newly organized community finance associations (saemaul) are all designed to draw informal activity into officially approved channels by accepting deposits and extending loans locally within an officially sanctioned framework.

The Post Office also runs a large and ubiquitous savings operation. Deposits and withdrawals can be made at most post office branches nationwide, and accounts earn somewhat higher than market interest rates because the post office system is not subject to bank reserve requirements.

Unofficial Financing

Because of the scarcity of available funding and its essentially short-term nature, onerous conditions including high collateral requirements, and heavy government involvement in most financial arrangements, large sectors of the Korean economy have traditionally gone unserved by official, mainstream financial institutions. To fill the needs of these individuals and small- and medium-sized businesses, an informal so-called curb market has sprung up. Some observers estimate that the curb market accounts for as much as 50 percent of total lending in the Korean economy. Despite interest rates as high as 25 percent and usually 5 to 10 percentage points above those on already high conventional loans, the curb market attracts many borrowers who have been frozen out of an official system that allocates scarce credit largely according to policy rather than market factors. Such informal operations are not strictly illegal, operating in a gray area without controls or legal recourse.

As noted, the government has tried to use the carrot of official recognition rather than the stick of an official crackdown to bring some of these unofficial operations into the fold as savings companies. Some observers suggest that such unofficial financial operations have been left relatively undisturbed not only because without them the financial system would collapse, but also because they make hefty payoffs and provide sources of political slush funds.

However, in August 1993 the administration of Kim Young Sam decreed the closure of so-called false name accounts, which provided much of the funding for under-the-table, speculative, and outright illegal operations. These accounts, held by nominees or under fictitious names to conceal true ownership—and often to conceal the source of the funds—are estimated to represent at least 4 percent of the Korean financial system's total deposit base. The administration stated that its move was designed to eliminate the reserves of so-called black money used to operate outside the review of regulatory agencies, and that it would investigate all such accounts valued at over W50 million (about US$62,000).

However, despite such strong and unaccustomed attempts at housecleaning, it is unlikely that such operations or the need for them will disappear until the overall financial system is deregulated and modernized. Some foreign firms have reportedly used the curb market for short-term operating funds. However, because of the questionable status of such transactions and the tight controls on foreign exchange, which require that foreign businesses establish the pedigree of any funds that they wish to be eligible for repatriation, foreign entities are generally advised to avoid curb market dealings.

KOREAN FINANCIAL MARKETS

Money Markets

Investment companies were established in 1972 for the express purpose of developing a short-term money market. They engage in short-term financing by issuing three- to six-month commercial paper themselves, dealing in commercial paper issued by other companies, accepting and guaranteeing commercial paper, and handling cash management accounts which are money market mutual funds designed for individuals. They are allowed to issue longer-term debt to fund their operations. As an added incentive, such investment companies are also allowed to operate in the securities markets as underwriters and broker-dealers.

Since the early 1970s money market instruments have proliferated, and the market has become more efficient and sophisticated. In addition to plain vanilla commercial paper and treasury bills, the South Korean money market deals in monetary stabilization bonds, issued by the government to regulate the money supply, negotiable certificates of deposit, broker call loan paper, and repurchase agreements on both public and private paper. Foreign firms still find it difficult to impossible to raise funds by issuing securities in or by investing in this market, but the market is expected to open further to them as part of general deregulation.

Despite the rapid development of the money markets, most of the firms involved are expected to move on into commercial banking, merchant banking, or securities brokerage, leaving the money markets to a small core of Seoul-based firms. This could serve either to increase expertise and professionalism, or to reinforce cartel-like behavior among the few participants.

The Securities Industry

The Korean Stock Exchange In mid-1993 the Korean Stock Exchange (KSE) was the fourth largest in Asia after Japan, Hong Kong, and Taiwan, although the KSE and the Taiwanese and Malaysian exchanges are all about the same size. With 692 companies listed and a total capitalization about US$118.8 billion, the KSE represents roughly 1 percent of global stock value. Between 1985 and mid-1993, the KSE delivered total returns of 327 percent in US dollar terms and 319 percent in local currency terms. During the same period the New York Stock Exchange rose 198 percent. The KSE index peaked at 1,007 in 1988, and hit a five-year low of 459 in August 1992. The KSE has

fared better in 1993, reaching 768 points in May on a daily trading volume of more than three million shares. Optimists hope the market will end 1993 above 800 points.

The KSE opened in 1956 but was not regularized until the passage of the Stock Exchange Act in 1962. The exchange became a member of the Federation Internationale des Bourses des Valeurs in 1979, gaining international standing and recognition. Foreigners were allowed to invest indirectly through trust funds operated in Korea beginning in 1981. The Korea Fund was opened in 1984, allowing foreigners to invest in Korean equity proxies abroad; the success of this closed-end fund has led to other similar vehicles being set up overseas. In 1985 domestic firms were allowed to issue convertible bonds, depository receipts, and bonds with warrants, all proxies for equity securities, to foreigners in overseas markets. Korean securities firms have been allowed to operate directly in foreign markets since 1987, although this practice does not enable foreign investors to gain access to Korean markets. Until 1992, when direct foreign participation was finally allowed, resident foreigners could trade directly on the KSE, but nonresident foreigners could not.

Foreigners still operate at a disadvantage. The government has made it difficult for foreign securities firms to gain permission to set up in Korea and has limited the types of products that they can offer. Operating rules such as those requiring foreign buyers to register trading orders are said to give local brokers advance notice of foreign buy and sell plans, and the government has retained broad rights to block repatriation of capital gains on securities trades for vaguely defined reasons of national interest.

The KSE has not proved to be as popular with either foreign or domestic investors as other Asian exchanges. For one thing, until the late 1980s interest rates on bank deposits outpaced dividend yields on stocks, and the short-term orientation of Korean investors has discounted the long-term appreciation opportunities of equities markets. For a long time securities in which to invest were lacking. The government has pressured foreign and domestic firms to list a minimum of 30 percent of their stock on the exchange, although relatively few firms have done so. This policy comes with a threat to restrict access to financing if eligible firms fail to list shares. This threat has not been explicitly carried out because one of the acknowledged causes of the poor recent performance of the KSE is an oversupply of securities relative to the size and characteristics of the market.

The KSE is dominated by largely unsophisticated individual investors, who hold 85 percent of stocks on the exchange and who generally trade based on themes or trends rather than on fundamental analy-

Banking and Financing for Foreign Businesses

Foreign businesspeople operating in Korea must use caution when dealing with domestic commercial banks. An air of uncertainty persists in the midst of reform, and questionable banking practices that have been standard operating procedure may now be quite dangerous. Foreigners operating in South Korea report that in the past virtually any loan received from a domestic commercial bank included a 2 to 3 percent interest rate surcharge to pay a kickback to the chief loan officer or bank president. With the new crackdown on corruption, such practices are under attack and should be avoided.

In addition to outright bribery and graft, domestic commercial banks have used coercive methods such as demanding that a company channel all its other financial business through them or maintain high compensating balances as preconditions for receiving loans. Such practices are known as *koggi*. When all the add-ons are taken into account, all but the top credits can end up paying as much as 20 percent in effective costs, nearly double the nominal cost. In general, foreigners should avoid borrowing from domestic commercial banks if at all possible.

Because foreign banks provide merchant bank services and loans, they can often be used for business banking needs. They do charge substantially higher interest rates than domestic banks; however, their level of service, international connections, and relatively unbiased advice can make the investment worthwhile.

Foreign businesses dealing with *chaebol* or other established Korean entities may be forced into dealing with domestic banks for foreign exchange, trade financing, or international payments. In this situation, it is best to establish a separate business account with a major international bank operating in Korea, as this institution can provide experienced advice on how to deal with Korean banks.

Financing is limited and expensive. The government maintains tight controls over fiscal policy to achieve its economic and political goals, driving up the price of such limited credit as is available. Korean banks tend to limit credit to one- to three-year loans that may be rolled over, often at higher interest rates.

Longer-term financing, such as that required for capital investment, is not generally available. The BOK requires commercial operations to report all imported equity and further restricts them from borrowing from offshore creditors or shareholders, forcing them into the limited and manipulated local credit market.

Foreign businesses can borrow from commercial or specialized banks using overdraft privileges, discounted notes, or regular secured business loans. The BOK can also approve direct offshore borrowing if the proceeds are used to buy Korean goods. Qualified businesses are allowed to issue stocks and bonds to raise funds, although doing so is complicated and heavily hedged with restrictions.

Foreign companies seeking lines of credit can expect to use a creative mix of commercial bank loans and even multiple loans in small amounts from various sources; access to credit through joint-venture partners; appeals to the Ministry of Finance to approve or raise already approved offshore financing arrangements; private sources such as the unregulated, expensive, and largely illegal curb market; commercial paper; and straight or convertible bonds. In principle, Korean government regulations do not allow financing with personal checks or credit cards. However, the BOK usually allows their use when foreign exchange is withdrawn from resident accounts to pay for import transactions authorized under standard settlement methods.

With strict government control of interest rates and restraints on the growth of the money supply, the Korean financial system is perennially hard-pressed to meet the demand for won. Foreign companies in a start-up operation with a Korean partner often provide the capital for the venture while the Korean partner makes an investment in kind, such as land or facilities, as its share of equity because of a lack of access to local currency financing. Joint-venture companies and foreign firms usually work with branches of foreign banks that have special limited funds designated for local currency financing of such enterprises. Other sources of potential financing include the BOK, the Korea Exchange Bank, the Korea Development Bank, and the National Agricultural Cooperative Federation.

sis. Institutional investors remain a minor factor. Much of what happens on the KSE remains in the hands of a relatively small number of local large-scale private buyers known as the "big hands" of the market. The market capitalization of the 10 largest stocks listed on the exchange accounts for just over 30 percent of its total value, making the market relatively easy to manipulate. Because the market has been open to foreign investors only since 1992, and foreign holdings remain low, the big hands can work together to drive particular stocks up or down, depending on their needs. Even local brokers admit that the market is overbought and that perhaps only 50 percent of listed issues are investment-grade securities.

Government interference in the market is also fairly extensive, with periodic campaigns to force banks and securities firms to commit funds to buying programs in attempts to jump-start the lagging market. Regulators impose a daily limit on price movements based on the previous day's trading. Operations generally lack sophistication (although an automated trading system exists) and there are few products other than straight buy-sell securities deals. The MOF regulates stock market activity through the Securities Exchange Commission (SEC) and its executive council, the Securities Supervisory Board (SSB). These bodies establish stock exchange policy and oversee daily operations. In addition to these government bodies, KSE member firms participate in a self-regulating organization, the Korean Securities Dealers Association. There are 31 domestic securities firms operating in the market. Disclosure and adequate accounting standards are lacking, confidentiality is poor, and regulators are relatively ineffective in preventing abuses.

The MOF sets limits on how much brokers can charge their clients for services. The current maximum brokerage commission is 0.6 percent; however, securities firms generally set a maximum limit of 0.5 percent. When stock is bought or sold, a 0.2 percent transfer tax is tacked on. The ROK collects a withholding tax of 10.75 percent of the amount sold from foreign investors unless a bilateral tax treaty exists between South Korea and the country of origin of the investor.

Insider trading and other questionable activities are rampant, and efforts to increase regulation and develop a level playing field have met stiff resistance. President Kim Young Sam promised during his campaign to get rid of the common practice among big investors of hiding their identities through several false names when registering their stock transactions and bank accounts. Observers estimate that although only 2 percent of securities accounts are held in fictitious names, 20 percent of the activity on the KSE is funneled through such accounts. With several different accounts covertly controlled by a single investor, stock prices can easily be manipulated.

President Kim's August 1993 decree abolishing false name accounts sent shock waves through the financial world, and banks and financial institutions were closed the day after the announcement to prevent mass redemptions of these accounts. Kim allowed a two-month grace period to transfer assets under false names into real-name accounts. Investors failing to comply were threatened with forfeiture of up to 60 percent of the value of their false name accounts. Kim's move drove stock prices down in the near term but is expected to control market manipulations over the longer term and attract more overseas investors.

Foreign Participation Some 34 branches and representative offices of foreign securities firms operate in Korea. Ironically, the authorities delayed allowing direct foreign participation because they feared that foreign speculators would add volatility to the markets. In reality, international institutional investors have provided a much needed element of professionalism and stability. To mollify local investors' fears of the savvy foreign hordes, the government placed tight restrictions on the degree of foreign investment allowed.

Foreign individuals or firms can hold no more than 10 percent cumulatively or 3 percent per entity of shares of a listed stock; foreigners can own no more than 8 percent cumulatively of shares of certain listed utilities; and controls on foreign ownership in certain so-called strategic industries are even more restrictive. Foreigners must put down a 40 percent deposit and use a registration number when buying stocks, allowing local authorities and investors to easily track foreign stock purchases. Foreigners cannot sell shares short, and the bond market remains closed to them.

The start of foreign participation on the KSE at the beginning of 1992 was greeted with much fanfare and high expectations. However, the actual results were disappointing to all parties involved. In 1991 local securities houses were overburdened with too much undervalued stock, much of which they had acquired at government behest to shore up the market. They held an estimated US$6.6 billion worth of stocks previously purchased at levels far above their market value at the end of the year. When the KSE opened to foreign investors, stock prices shot up on the expectations that foreign purchases would boost values across the board. A few days later, the local securities houses dumped their excess inventory, sending prices tumbling across the board. Foreigners caught unawares lost 30 percent of their investment almost immediately and felt they had been duped into providing the liquidity for Korean brokers to dump their losing positions.

Despite these early disappointments, confidence

in the KSE appears to have returned. Total foreign inflows into the market in the first five months of 1993 totaled W378.2 billion (about US$475 million), with 1,952 foreign investors participating. Many of these purchases were in issues linked to companies in the large *chaebol* conglomerates, with Samsung, Hyundai, and Lucky-Goldstar leading the way. However, largely because of a lingering mistrust among foreign investors, foreign ownership in stocks remains low, with foreigners owning fewer than 5 percent of all KSE-listed shares.

The biggest problem facing foreign investors on the KSE is their limit on percentage of ownership. This problem is compounded because foreign ownership has already reached its maximum allowable level among the most attractive stocks. Despite international pressure to raise the allowable levels, the government recently announced that foreign participation would not be increased in 1993. Anxious foreign investors hope to see limits raised to between 15 and 20 percent in 1994. However, as of early 1994 the BOK was holding firm on its limits on foreign investments in listed shares, presenting its position as an anti-inflation measure.

Bond Markets The total size of the Korean bond market is estimated to be around US$110 billion. The major instrument traded on the bond market is the government monetary stabilization bond (MSB), which is used to regulate the money supply and interest rates. During 1992 W10.9 billion (about US$13.5 million) of corporate debt was issued on the bond market.

Only primary issues are traded on the KSE; secondary trading occurs in the over-the-counter (OTC) market, which is relatively competitive in terms of spreads. Even so, the government frequently intervenes for macroeconomic policy purposes, calling on bond houses not to trade at prices that are out of line with government expectations. Although it privately places most of its MSBs at set rates, the government began auctioning 20 to 30 percent of the instruments issued in mid-1993. However, the government's idea of an auction is one with a reserve price: all bids under the price are accepted. If there are no acceptable bids, the government simply cancels the auction.

The authorities are working on upgrading operations in this market ostensibly in preparation for allowing foreign participation, although actual approval for foreign participation is not scheduled anytime soon. The upgrades envisioned include the establishing of an index futures market, dealer licensing and training programs, and the standardization of trading procedures, systems, and mechanisms. The authorities are considering allowing domestic investment firms to package bonds into funds that can be sold as depository receipts to foreign inves-

tors without allowing them to participate directly, but no action is expected before 1995. Other ideas include placing limits, such as those on foreign participants in the stock market, on percentage holdings and foreign bond-trading activity.

Two moves are considered likely. Foreigners may be allowed to buy government paper perhaps as early as sometime in 1994, but only with a lower coupon than is available to domestic investors. And, foreigners, who can already invest in higher-rated convertibles, may also be allowed to buy the convertible bonds of smaller, lower-rated firms.

One reason for the caution in allowing foreigners into the bond market is that Korea's high interest rates are expected to attract a flood of foreign investment, which could help drive down high domestic interest rates, but could also boost inflation.

Other Securities Markets Korea's small over-the-counter (OTC) market deals primarily in odd lots of listed shares as well as in bonds. There are no authorized or functioning markets in commodities, futures, options, or other derivative instruments. The KSE has held talks with the Chicago Board of Trade concerning the requirements of options markets, but the volume and level of sophistication needed to operate such a venture appears to be lacking.

One standard complaint about Korean securities markets is the lack of products and the difficulty in gaining approval to develop new products. Despite its stated goal of becoming an international financial market, Korea, which is seen as being roughly 20 years behind Japan in its level of development and sophistication, is likely to continue to lag behind more developed countries in its financial operations for the foreseeable future.

Currency & Foreign Exchange

INTERNATIONAL PAYMENT INSTRUMENTS

The three principal mechanisms used for international payments in Korea are letters of credit (L/Cs), documents against acceptance (D/As), and documents against payment (D/Ps). The most common method is an irrevocable letter of credit at sight. The use of these instruments follows generally established international practice.

Transactions are considered to be standard if they are completed within 360 days, are handled through a bill of exchange under an irrevocable L/C or D/A (revocable L/Cs are considered nonstandard), are completed under a D/P within 60 days, are prepaid within 120 days of shipment, or are completed within 60 days on COD terms. Any other arrangements are considered nonstandard and require prior approval by a foreign exchange bank or the Bank of Korea (BOK), unless the amounts are less than US$10,000 and the transaction is to be completed within 360 days.

Imports on deferred payment terms (D/As and usance L/Cs) are allowed only for commodities that are not subject to specific commercial duties with a tariff rate of 10 percent or less, commodities imported for incorporation into export products, and petroleum imports. Deferred payment terms are valid only up to a maximum term of 60 days. The only exceptions to this limit are lower 30 day limits for imports from nearby sources requiring sailing time of not more than 10 days, such as Japan, Hong Kong, Taiwan, and the Philippines, and higher 90 day limits for some petroleum products, primarily from the Middle East. All imports except those by official government agencies are subject to a deposit requirement of 10 percent for small- and medium-sized firms and 15 percent for large firms. (Refer to "International Payments" chapter.)

CURRENCY

South Korea's currency is the won (W). Coins are issued in denominations of W1, W5, W10, W50, W100, and W500. Smaller-denomination coins are rare and not in general use because of their lack of purchasing power. Notes are issued in denominations of W1,000, W5,000, and W10,000. At the end of 1993 the exchange rate was 1US$ = W808.1. The W10,000 bill is worth about US$12.40.

REMITTANCE AND EXCHANGE CONTROLS

All foreign exchange transactions are subject to control under the terms of Korea's Foreign Exchange Control Act (FECA), which is administered by the Ministry of Finance (MOF), BOK, and the banks authorized to deal in foreign exchange. Because of the stringency of foreign exchange controls, the won is not considered a freely convertible currency and is not used outside the country. Korean has stated its goal of making the won an international currency; however, its unwillingness to deregulate foreign exchange transactions continues to militate against this aim.

All foreign exchange transactions must be carried out in one of 66 designated currencies, the main ones being the US dollar and the Japanese yen. Inward remittances have generally been freely allowed. However, in recent years inward remittances have been more strictly monitored to prevent the importation of funds to be used in speculation. Foreign firms may be required to demonstrate that the funds imported are necessary for current operations.

Residents and nonresidents are allowed to maintain foreign currency accounts at home and abroad, although controls on transfers between foreign and domestic currency accounts attempt to prevent money laundering, speculation, and evasion of foreign exchange controls. Nonresident won accounts are closely monitored, with payments allowed only for a narrow range of acceptable expenses, again to restrain speculation and avoidance of currency controls. With very few exceptions, all foreign exchange proceeds of more than US$5,000 owned by Korean residents must be either surrendered to the Korea Exchange Bank or to one of the designated foreign exchange banks within 20 days (within 10 days for foreign bank notes) for payment in won or deposited in a resident's registered foreign exchange account. The exceptions are limited to large general trading companies, which may hold up to US$10 million, and to nonresident foreigners.

Prior BOK approval is required for a foreign branch or liaison office to bring amounts greater than US$1 million into the country. No approval is required for lesser amounts, however all flows of funds must be reported quarterly to the BOK. Approved and registered foreign entities are guaranteed remittance of earnings from approved activities. Prior approval is required from the BOK or a foreign exchange bank to obtain foreign exchange for specific outward remittances of royalties, earnings, interest, loan repayments, and capital, and the source of the funds must be documented. Approval may be denied for proceeds derived from activities outside those authorized in the foreign firm's charter.

Foreigners and Koreans may carry South Korean currency into or out of the country, as long as the amount does not exceed W2 million (about US$2,475). Foreigners may bring any amount of foreign currency in any form into Korea. However, amounts equivalent to US$5,000 or more must be declared to customs. A foreigner may take out of Korea any foreign currency that was declared to customs at the time it was brought into the country. Prior to departure, visitors also may convert won back to foreign currency at any authorized foreign exchange bank. However, they can only convert a maximum value of US$500 into foreign currency unless they can provide receipts showing that they legally converted into won at least as much as they wish to exchange during their stay.

Most banks can exchange foreign currency or traveler's checks. Rates are better for traveler's checks than for cash, but the commission charged on the checks usually cancels out the differential. An active, illicit street market in foreign exchange runs primarily out of electronics shops around the post office in Seoul, although this unofficial market usually handles relatively small transactions. Rates are usually 6 to 8 percent better than bank exchange rates.

FOREIGN EXCHANGE OPERATIONS

Only entities authorized by the BOK to deal in foreign exchange can conduct transactions. However, this authority is fairly widely delegated, with most major foreign and domestic national banks being authorized as foreign exchange banks. Basic consumer foreign exchange transactions can be handled at most banks and in larger hotels.

There is a small, thin, and not very active forward foreign exchange market, run primarily by foreign exchange banks as an accommodation for clients interested in purchasing hedge contracts for their trading operations. Foreign banks can also buy swap contracts, essentially forward hedging contracts, from the BOK.

As part of ongoing foreign exchange deregulation, the MOF has eased controls on fees that can be charged on foreign exchange transactions, allowing more room for price competition among providers of foreign exchange services. The MOF has also raised

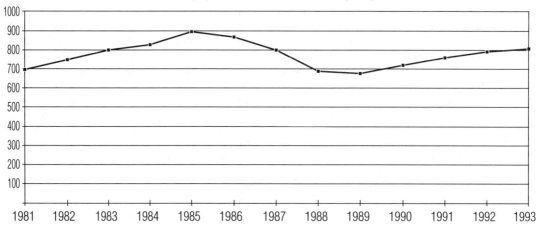

Korea's Foreign Exchange Rates - Year End Actual
Won (W) to United States Dollar (US$)

January 1, 1994 US$1 = W808.10

Exchange Rates—W/US$

	Jan	Feb	Mar	Apr	May	Jun	Jul	Aug	Sep	Oct	Nov	Dec
1982	705.2	710.1	714.7	721.0	724.3	738.3	743.1	744.4	743.6	743.6	745.6	746.4
1983	749.8	752.2	757.9	765.3	768.0	755.8	779.9	787.2	790.8	791.4	796.3	799.2
1984	800.3	799.1	794.5	796.4	801.5	802.2	810.9	811.4	815.8	820.0	818.9	825.7
1985	832.2	839.2	850.7	861.2	871.1	875.0	876.4	885.1	894.0	894.5	893.3	893.1
1986	892.7	888.6	886.7	887.9	889.1	890.7	888.6	886.4	883.1	879.2	873.5	868.4
1987	862.9	857.4	856.1	844.7	832.5	818.4	811.4	811.9	810.1	808.5	802.3	798.3
1988	757.4	776.8	757.4	745.3	739.4	732.9	728.7	725.7	723.0	712.7	696.1	687.9
1989	685.3	680.3	675.7	672.1	669.2	669.4	669.8	671.1	672.7	673.8	674.9	677.6
1990	686.2	692.5	700.5	708.8	711.8	718.1	718.7	718.3	717.9	717.8	717.0	718.6
1991	720.8	724.0	727.7	728.4	728.0	728.0	731.8	733.9	744.2	753.5	757.4	759.9
1992	767.1	769.9	775.7	782.5	786.8	793.6	789.9	792.6	788.8	786.8	787.1	790.8
1993	794.9	799.2	796.4	798.6	801.2	805.9	809.6	811.9	811.8	814.4	808.8	808.1

Source: US Federal Reserve System

the ceiling on foreign currency loans that can be made to foreign borrowers by local banks from US$10 million to US$20 million and allowed foreign branches of Korean banks to participate in international loan syndications. State-run, local, and merchant banks are also being allowed to raise their holdings of foreign exchange to an amount equal to that allowed for city banks or equal to 200 percent of the amount they bought during the previous month, giving them more leeway to conduct transactions.

RATES OF EXCHANGE

Between 1981 and 1993 the won traded as high as 669.2 to the US dollar in May 1989 and as low as 894.5 in October 1985. The won appreciated 25.1 percent against the US dollar from 1985 to 1990. However, it has depreciated by 14.3 percent against the dollar since the market average rate exchange system was instituted in March 1990. As of the end of December 1993 the won was trading at 808.1 to US$1. This development makes Korean goods cheaper for foreign buyers and will help the nation's export competitiveness.

Since 1990 foreign exchange rates have been set through the so-called market average rate exchange system. Under this system, exchange rates are set in principle according to the previous day's weighted average interbank rates on W-US$ spot transactions, with rates for the won and other currencies being set with reference to international cross-rates between those currencies and the US dollar. The primary W-US$ exchange rate is allowed to fluctuate by as much as 0.6 percent daily, up from an earlier 0.4 percent limit.

This system represents a significant advance over the previous one in which the MOF and the BOK more or less arbitrarily set exchange rates based on current policy goals more than on supply and demand and relative purchasing power. However, observers suspect that the government continues to manage the exchange rate to a large extent, and the thicket of regulations surrounding all foreign exchange dealings continues to make foreign exchange operations difficult. The government has stated that it wishes to substantially deregulate foreign exchange, but, even by its own reckoning, it won't come close to realizing its goal before 1996 at the earliest.

FOREIGN RESERVES AND FOREIGN DEBT

South Korea's foreign currency reserves were US$18.9 billion in June 1993, up nearly 30 percent from a year earlier despite a worsening trade deficit. International reserves have fluctuated around the

US$15 billion level since the late 1980s. After falling since 1986, Korea's foreign debt began growing again in 1990 as the country's assets abroad shrank and public and private short-term debt increased to fund domestic development projects.

FURTHER READING

The preceding discussion is provided as a basic guide to money, finances, financial institutions, and financial markets in South Korea. Those interested in current developments may wish to consult the *Far Eastern Economic Review, Business Korea,* and *Asia Money,* all of which frequently cover economic and financial developments in South Korea.

International Payments

International transactions add an additional layer of risk for buyers and sellers that are familiar only with doing business domestically. Currency regulations, foreign exchange risk, political, economic, or social upheaval in the buyer's or seller's country, and different business customs may all contribute to uncertainty. Ultimately, however, the seller wants to make sure he gets paid and the buyer wants to get what he pays for. Choosing the right payment method can be the key to the transaction's feasibility and profitability.

There are four common methods of international payment, each providing the buyer and the seller with varying degrees of protection for getting paid and for guaranteeing shipment. Ranked in order of most security for the supplier to most security for the buyer, they are: Cash in Advance, Documentary Letters of Credit (L/C), Documentary Collections (D/P and D/A Terms), and Open Account (O/A).

Cash in Advance

In cash in advance terms the buyer simply prepays the supplier prior to shipment of goods. Cash in advance terms are generally used in new relationships where transactions are small and the buyer has no choice but to pre-pay. These terms give maximum security to the seller but leave the buyer at great risk. Since the buyer has no guarantee that the goods will be shipped, he must have a high degree of trust in the seller's ability and willingness to follow through. The buyer must also consider the economic, political and social stability of the seller's country, as these conditions may make it impossible for the seller to ship as promised.

Documentary Letters of Credit

A letter of credit is a bank's promise to pay a supplier on behalf of the buyer so long as the supplier meets the terms and conditions stated in the credit. Documents are the key issue in letter of credit transactions. Banks act as intermediaries, and have nothing to do with the goods themselves.

Letters of credit are the most common form of international payment because they provide a high degree of protection for both the seller and the buyer. The buyer specifies the documentation that he requires from the seller before the bank is to make payment, and the seller is given assurance that he will receive payment after shipping his goods so long as the documentation is in order.

Documentary Collections

A documentary collection is like an international cash on delivery (COD), but with a few twists. The exporter ships goods to the importer, but forwards shipping documents (including title document) to his bank for transmission to the buyer's bank. The buyer's bank is instructed not to transfer the documents to the buyer until payment is made (Documents against Payment, D/P) or upon guarantee that payment will be made within a specified period of time (Documents against Acceptance, D/A). Once the buyer has the documentation for the shipment he is able to take possession of the goods.

D/P and D/A terms are commonly used in ongoing business relationships and provide a measure of protection for both parties. The buyer and seller, however, both assume risk in the transaction, ranging from refusal on the part of the buyer to pay for the documents, to the seller's shipping of unacceptable goods.

Open Account

This is an agreement by the buyer to pay for goods within a designated time after their shipment, usually in 30, 60, or 90 days. Open account terms give maximum security to the buyer and greatest risk to the seller. This form of payment is used only when the seller has significant trust and faith in the buyer's ability and willingness to pay once the goods have been shipped. The seller must also consider the economic, political and social stability of the buyer's country as these conditions may make it impossible for the buyer to pay as promised.

DOCUMENTARY COLLECTIONS (D/P, D/A)

Documentary collections focus on the transfer of documents such as bills of lading for the transfer of ownership of goods rather than on the goods themselves. They are easier to use than letters of credit and bank service charges are generally lower.

This form of payment is excellent for buyers who wish to purchase goods without risking prepayment and without having to go through the more cumbersome letter of credit process.

Documentary collection procedures, however, entail risk for the supplier, because payment is not made until after goods are shipped. In addition, the supplier assumes the risk while the goods are in transit and storage until payment/acceptance take place. Banks involved in the transaction do not guarantee payments. A supplier should therefore only agree to a documentary collection procedure if the transaction includes the following characteristics:

- The supplier does not doubt the buyer's ability and willingness to pay for the goods;
- The buyer's country is politically, economically, and legally stable;
- There are no foreign exchange restrictions in the buyer's home country, or unless all necessary licenses for foreign exchange have already been obtained;
- The goods to be shipped are easily marketable.

Types of Collections

The three types of documentary collections are:
1. Documents against Payment (D/P)
2. Documents against Acceptance (D/A)
3. Collection with Acceptance (Acceptance D/P)

All of these collection procedures follow the same general step-by-step process of exchanging documents proving title to goods for either cash or a contracted promise to pay at a later time. The documents are transferred from the supplier (called the remitter) to the buyer (called the drawee) via intermediary banks. When the supplier ships goods, he presents documents such as the bill of lading, invoices, and certificate of origin to his representative bank (the remitting bank), which then forwards them to the buyer's bank (the collecting bank). According to the type of documentary collection, the buyer may then do one of the following:

- With Documents against Payment (D/P), the buyer may only receive the title and other documents after paying for the goods;
- With Documents against Acceptance (D/A), the buyer may receive the title and other documents after signing a time draft promising to pay at a later date;

- With Acceptance Documents against Payment, the buyer signs a time draft for payment at a latter date. However, he may only obtain the documents after the time draft reaches maturity. In essence, the goods remain in escrow until payment has been made.

In all cases the buyer may take possession of the goods only by presenting the bill of lading to customs or shipping authorities.

In the event that the prospective buyer cannot or will not pay for the goods shipped, they remain in legal possession of the supplier, but he may be stuck with them in an unfavorable situation. Also, the supplier has no legal basis to file claim against the prospective buyer. At this point the supplier may:

- Have the goods returned and sell them on his domestic market; or
- Sell the goods to another buyer near where the goods are currently held.

If the supplier takes no action the goods will be auctioned or otherwise disposed of by customs.

Documentary Collection Procedure

The documentary collection process has been standardized by a set of rules published by the International Chamber of Commerce (ICC). These rules are called the Uniform Rules for Collections (URC) and are contained in ICC Publication No. 322. (See the last page of this section for ICC addresses and list of available publications.)

The following is the basic set of steps used in a documentary collection. Refer to the illustration on the following page for a graphic representation of the procedure.

(1) The seller (remitter, exporter) ships the goods.
(2) and (3) The seller forwards the agreed upon documents to his bank, the remitting bank, which in turn forwards them to the collecting bank (buyer's bank).
(4) The collecting bank notifies the buyer (drawee, importer) and informs him of the conditions under which he can take possession of the documents.
(5) To take possession of the documents, the buyer makes payment or signs a time deposit.
(6) and (7) If the buyer draws the documents against payment, the collecting bank transfers payment to the remitting bank for credit to the supplier's account. If the buyer draws the documents against acceptance, the collecting bank sends the acceptance to the remitting bank or retains it up to maturity. On maturity, the collecting bank collects the bill and transfers it to the remitting bank for payment to the supplier.

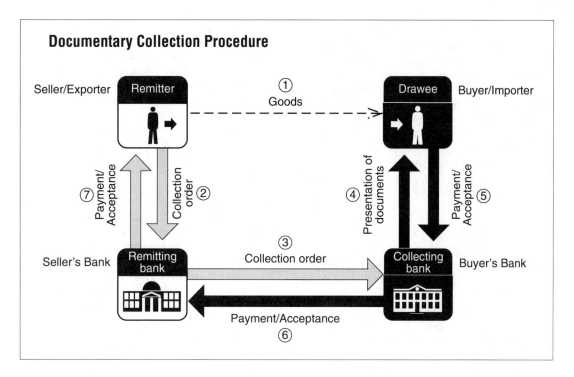

Documentary Collection Procedure

TIPS FOR BUYERS

1. The buyer is generally in a secure position because he does not assume ownership or responsibility for goods until he has paid for the documents or signed a time draft.
2. The buyer may not sample or inspect the goods before accepting and paying for the documents without authorization from the seller. However, the buyer may in advance specify a certificate of inspection as part of the required documentation package.
3. As a special favor, the collecting bank can allow the buyer to inspect the documents before payment. The collecting bank assumes responsibility for the documents until their redemption.
4. In the above case, the buyer should immediately return the entire set of documents to the collecting bank if he cannot meet the agreed payment procedure.
5. The buyer assumes no liability for goods if he refuses to take possession of the documents.
6. Partial payment in exchange for the documents is not allowed unless authorized in the collection order.
7. With documents against acceptance, the buyer may receive the goods and resell them for profit before the time draft matures, thereby using the proceeds of the sale to pay for the goods. The buyer remains responsible for payment, however, even if he cannot sell the goods.

TIPS FOR SUPPLIERS

1. The supplier assumes risk because he ships goods before receiving payment. The buyer is under no legal obligation to pay for or to accept the goods.
2. Before agreeing to a documentary collection, the supplier should check on the buyer's creditworthiness and business reputation.
3. The supplier should make sure the buyer's country is politically and financially stable.
4. The supplier should find out what documents are required for customs clearance in the buyer's country. Consulates may be of help.
5. The supplier should assemble the documents carefully and make sure they are in the required form and endorsed as necessary.
6. As a rule, the remitting bank will not review the documents before forwarding them to the collecting bank. This is the responsibility of the seller.
7. The goods travel and are stored at the risk of the supplier until payment or acceptance.
8. If the buyer refuses acceptance or payment for the documents, the supplier retains ownership. The supplier may have the goods shipped back or try to sell them to another buyer in the region.
9. If the buyer takes no action, customs authorities may seize the goods and auction them off or otherwise dispose of them.
10. Because goods may be refused, the supplier should only ship goods which are readily marketable to other sources.

LETTERS OF CREDIT (L/C)

A letter of credit is a document issued by a bank stating its commitment to pay someone (supplier/exporter/seller) a stated amount of money on behalf of a buyer (importer) so long as the seller meets very specific terms and conditions. Letters of credit are often called documentary letters of credit because the banks handling the transaction deal in documents as opposed to goods. Letters of credit are the most common method of making international payments, because the risks of the transaction are shared by both the buyer and the supplier.

STEPS IN USING AN L/C

The letter of credit process has been standardized by a set of rules published by the International Chamber of Commerce (ICC). These rules are called the Uniform Customs and Practice for Documentary Credits (UCP) and are contained in ICC Publication No. 400. (See the last page of this section for ICC addresses and list of available publications.) The following is the basic set of steps used in a letter of credit transaction. Specific letter of credit transactions follow somewhat different procedures.

- After the buyer and supplier agree on the terms of a sale, the buyer arranges for his bank to open a letter of credit in favor of the supplier.
- The buyer's bank (the issuing bank), prepares the letter of credit, including all of the buyer's instructions to the seller concerning shipment and required documentation.
- The buyer's bank sends the letter of credit to a correspondent bank (the advising bank), in the seller's country. The seller may request that a particular bank be the advising bank, or the domestic bank may select one of its correspondent banks in the seller's country.
- The advising bank forwards the letter of credit to the supplier.
- The supplier carefully reviews all conditions the buyer has stipulated in the letter of credit. If the supplier cannot comply with one or more of the provisions he immediately notifies the buyer and asks that an amendment be made to the letter of credit.
- After final terms are agreed upon, the supplier prepares the goods and arranges for their shipment to the appropriate port.
- The supplier ships the goods, and obtains a bill of lading and other documents as required by the buyer in the letter of credit. Some of these documents may need to be obtained prior to shipment.
- The supplier presents the required documents to the advising bank, indicating full compliance with the terms of the letter of credit. Required documents usually include a bill of lading, commercial invoice, certificate of origin, and possibly an inspection certificate if required by the buyer.
- The advising bank reviews the documents. If they are in order, the documents are forwarded to the issuing bank. If it is an irrevocable, confirmed letter of credit the supplier is guaranteed payment and may be paid immediately by the advising bank.
- Once the issuing bank receives the documents it notifies the buyer who then reviews the documents himself. If the documents are in order the buyer signs off, taking possession of the documents, including the bill of lading, which he uses to take possession of the shipment.
- The issuing bank initiates payment to the advising bank, which pays the supplier.

The transfer of funds from the buyer to his bank, from the buyer's bank to the supplier's bank, and from the supplier's bank to the supplier may be handled at the same time as the exchange of documents, or under terms agreed upon in advance.

Parties to a Letter of Credit Transaction

Buyer/Importer   Buyer's bank

Seller/Supplier/Exporter   Seller's bank

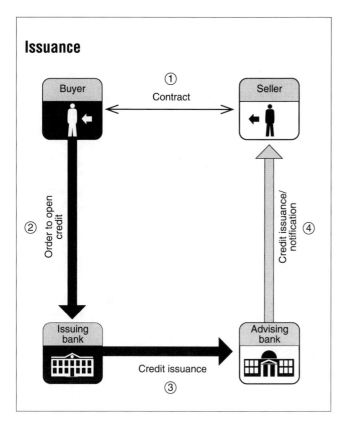

Issuance of a Letter of Credit

① Buyer and seller agree on purchase contract.

② Buyer applies for and opens a letter of credit with issuing ("buyer's") bank.

③ Issuing bank issues the letter of credit, forwarding it to advising ("seller's") bank.

④ Advising bank notifies seller of letter of credit.

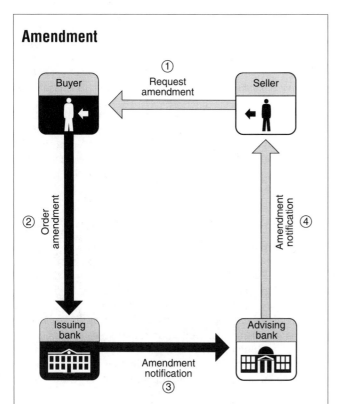

Amendment of a Letter of Credit

① Seller requests (of the buyer) a modification (amendment) of the terms of the letter of credit. Once the terms are agreed upon:

② Buyer issues order to issuing ("buyer's") bank to make an amendment to the terms of the letter of credit.

③ Issuing bank notifies advising ("seller's") bank of amendment.

④ Advising bank notifies seller of amendment.

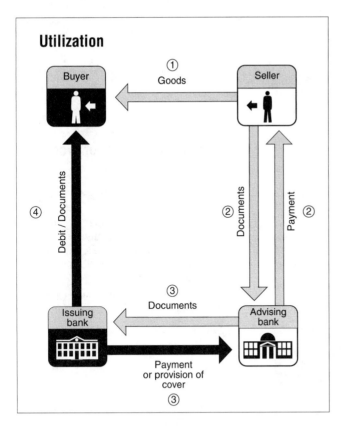

Utilization

Utilization of a Letter of Credit

(irrevocable, confirmed credit)

① Seller ships goods to buyer.
② Seller forwards all documents (as stipulated in the letter of credit) to advising bank. Once documents are reviewed and accepted, advising bank pays seller for the goods.
③ Advising bank forwards documents to issuing bank. Once documents are reviewed and accepted, issuing bank pays advising bank.
④ Issuing bank forwards documents to buyer. Seller's letter of credit, or account, is debited.

COMMON PROBLEMS IN LETTER OF CREDIT TRANSACTIONS

Most problems with letter of credit transactions have to do with the ability of the supplier to fulfill obligations the buyer establishes in the original letter of credit. The supplier may find the terms of the credit difficult or impossible to fulfill and either tries to do so and fails, or asks the buyer for an amendment to the letter of credit. Observers note that over half of all letters of credit involving parties in East Asia are amended or renegotiated entirely. Since most letters of credit are irrevocable, amendments to the original letter of credit can only be made after further negotiations and agreements between the buyer and the supplier. Suppliers may have one or more of the following problems:

- Shipment schedule stipulated in the letter of credit cannot be met.
- Stipulations concerning freight cost are deemed unacceptable.
- Price is insufficient due to changes in exchange rates.
- Quantity of product ordered is not the expected amount.
- Description of product to be shipped is either insufficient or too detailed.
- Documents stipulated in the letter of credit are difficult or impossible to obtain.

Even when suppliers accept the terms of a letter of credit, problems often arise at the stage where banks review, or negotiate, the documents provided by the supplier against the requirements specified in the letter of credit. If the documents are found not to be in accord with those specified in the letter of credit, the bank's commitment to pay is invalidated. In some cases the supplier can correct the documents and present them within the time specified in the letter of credit. Or, the advising bank may ask the issuing bank for authorization to accept the documents despite the discrepancies found.

Limits on Legal Obligations of Banks

It is important to note once again that banks *deal in documents and not in goods*. Only the wording of the credit is binding on the bank. Banks are not responsible for verifying the authenticity of the documents, nor for the quality or quantity of the goods being shipped. As long as the *documents* comply with the specified terms of the letter of credit, banks may accept them and initiate the payment process as stipulated in the letter of credit. Banks are free from liability for delays in sending messages caused by another party, consequences of Acts of God, or the acts of third parties whom they have instructed to carry out transactions.

TYPES OF LETTERS OF CREDIT

Basic Letters of Credit

There are two basic forms of letters of credit: the Revocable Credit and the Irrevocable Credit. There are also two types of irrevocable credit: the Irrevocable Credit not Confirmed, and the Irrevocable Confirmed Credit. Each type of credit has advantages and disadvantages for the buyer and for the seller. Also note that the more the banks assume risk by guaranteeing payment, the more they will charge for providing the service.

1. Revocable credit This credit can be changed or canceled by the buyer without prior notice to the supplier. Because it offers little security to the seller revocable credits are generally unacceptable to the seller and are rarely used.

2. Irrevocable credit The irrevocable credit is one which the issuing bank commits itself irrevocably to honor, provided the beneficiary complies with all stipulated conditions. This credit cannot be changed or canceled without the consent of both the buyer and the seller. As a result, this type of credit is the most widely used in international trade. Irrevocable credits are more expensive because of the issuing bank's added liability in guaranteeing the credit. There are two types of irrevocable credits:

a. The Irrevocable Credit not Confirmed by the Advising Bank (Unconfirmed Credit) This means that the buyer's bank which issues the credit is the only party responsible for payment to the supplier, and the supplier's bank is obliged to pay the supplier only after receiving payment from the buyer's bank. The supplier's bank merely acts on behalf of the issuing bank and therefore incurs no risk.

b. The Irrevocable, Confirmed Credit In a confirmed credit, the advising bank adds its guarantee to pay the supplier to that of the issuing bank. If the issuing bank fails to make payment the advising bank will pay. If a supplier is unfamiliar with the buyer's bank which issues the letter of credit, he may insist on an irrevocable confirmed credit. These credits may be used when trade is conducted in a high risk area where there are fears of outbreak of war or social, political, or financial instability. Confirmed credits may also be used by the supplier to enlist the aid of a local bank to extend financing to enable him to fill the order. A confirmed credit costs more because the bank has added liability.

Special Letters of Credit

There are numerous special letters of credit designed to meet specific needs of buyers, suppliers, and intermediaries. Special letters of credit usually involve increased participation by banks, so financing and service charges are higher than those for basic letters of credit. The following is a brief description of some special letters of credit.

1. Standby Letter of Credit This credit is primarily a payment or performance guarantee. It is used primarily in the United States because US banks are prevented by law from giving certain guarantees. Standby credits are often called non-performing letters of credit because they are only used as a backup payment method if the collection on a primary payment method is past due.

Standby letters of credit can be used, for example, to guarantee the following types of payment and performance:

- repayment of loans;
- fulfillment by subcontractors;
- securing the payment for goods delivered by third parties.

The beneficiary to a standby letter of credit can draw from it on demand, so the buyer assumes added risk.

2. Revolving Letter of Credit This credit is a commitment on the part of the issuing bank to restore the credit to the original amount after it has been used or drawn down. The number of times it can be utilized and the period of validity is stated in the credit. The credit can be cumulative or noncumulative. Cumulative means that unutilized sums can be added to the next installment whereas noncumulative means that partial amounts not utilized in time expire.

3. Deferred Payment Letter of Credit In this credit the buyer takes delivery of the shipped goods by accepting the documents and agreeing to pay his bank after a fixed period of time. This credit gives the buyer a grace period, and ensures that the seller gets payment on the due date.

4. Red Clause Letter of Credit This is used to provide the supplier with some funds prior to shipment to finance production of the goods. The credit may be advanced in part or in full, and the buyer's bank finances the advance payment. The buyer, in essence, extends financing to the seller and incurs ultimate risk for all advanced credits.

5. Transferable Letter of Credit This allows the supplier to transfer all or part of the proceeds of the letter of credit to a second beneficiary, usually the ultimate producer of the goods. This is a common financing tactic for middlemen and is used extensively in the Far East.

6. Back-to-Back Letter of Credit This is a new credit opened on the basis of an already existing, nontransferable credit. It is used by traders to make payment to the ultimate supplier. A trader receives a letter of credit from the buyer and then opens another letter of credit in favor of the supplier. The first letter of credit is used as collateral for the second credit. The second credit makes price adjustments from which come the trader's profit.

OPENING A LETTER OF CREDIT

The wording in a letter of credit should be simple but specific. The more detailed an L/C is, the more likely the supplier will reject it as too difficult to fulfill. At the same time, the buyer will wish to define in detail what he is paying for.

Although the L/C process is designed to ensure the satisfaction of all parties to the transaction, it cannot be considered a substitute for face-to-face agreements on doing business in good faith. It should therefore contain only those stipulations required from the banks involved in the documentary process.

L/Cs used in trade with East Asia are usually either irrevocable unconfirmed credits or irrevocable confirmed credits. In choosing the type of L/C to open in favor of the supplier, the buyer should take into consideration generally accepted payment processes in the supplier's country, the value and demand for the goods to be shipped, and the reputation of the supplier.

In specifying documents necessary from the supplier, it is very important to demand documents that are required for customs clearance and those that reflect the agreement reached between the buyer and the supplier. Required documents usually include the bill of lading, a commercial and/or consular invoice, the bill of exchange, the certificate of origin, and the insurance document. Other documents required may be copies of a cable sent to the buyer with shipping information, a confirmation from the shipping company of the state of its ship, and a confirmation from the forwarder that the goods are accompanied by a certificate of origin. Prices should be stated in the currency of the L/C, and documents should be supplied in the language of the L/C.

THE APPLICATION

The following information should be included on an application form for opening an L/C.

(1) **Beneficiary** The seller's company name and address should be written completely and correctly. Incomplete or incorrect information results in delays and unnecessary additional cost.

(2) **Amount** Is the figure a maximum amount or an approximate amount? If words like "circa," "ca.," "about," etc., are used in connection with the amount of the credit, it means that a difference as high as 10 percent upwards or downwards is permitted. In such a case, the same word should also be used in connection with the quantity.

(3) **Validity Period** The validity and period for presentation of the documents following shipment of the goods should be sufficiently long to allow the exporter time to prepare his documents and ship them to the bank. Under place of validity, state the domicile of either the advising bank or the issuing bank.

(4) **Beneficiary's Bank** If no bank is named, the issuing bank is free to select the correspondent bank.

(5) **Type of Payment Availability** Sight drafts, time drafts, or deferred payment may be used, as previously agreed to by the supplier and buyer.

(6) **Desired Documents** Here the buyer specifies precisely which documents he requires. To obtain effective protection against the supply of poor quality goods, for instance, he can demand the submission of analysis or quality certificates. These are generally issued by specialized inspection companies or laboratories.

(7) **Notify Address** An address is given for notification of the imminent arrival of goods at the port or airport of destination. Damage of goods in shipment is also cause for notification. An agent representing the buyer may be used.

(8) **Description of Goods** Here a short, precise description of the goods is given, along with quantity. If the credit amount carries the notation "ca.," the same notation should appear with the quantity.

(9) **Confirmation Order** It may happen that the foreign beneficiary insists on having the credit confirmed by the bank in his country.

Sample Letter of Credit Application

Sender American Import-Export Co., Inc. 123 Main Street San Francisco, CA ——— Our reference AB/02	**Instructions** **to open a Documentary Credit** San Francisco, 30th September 19.. Place / Date

Please open the following [X] irrevocable [ ] revocable documentary credit	**Domestic Bank Corporation** Documentary Credits P.O. Box 1040 San Francisco, California

Beneficiary ① Korea Trading Corporation 75, Sejong-no, Chongno-ku Seoul / KOREA	Beneficiary's bank (if known) ④ Korean Commercial Bank Seoul Main Branch Seoul / KOREA

(vertical text, left margin:) This credit is subject to the »Uniform customs and practice for documentary credits« fixed by the International Chamber of Commerce. It is understood that you do not assume any responsibility neither for the correctness, validity or genuineness of the documents which will be remitted to you nor for the description, quality, quantity and weight of the goods thereby represented.

Amount ② US$ 70,200.--	Please advise this bank [ ] by letter [X] by letter, cabling main details in advance [ ] by telex / telegram with full text of credit
Date and place of expiry ③ 25th November 19.. in San Francisco	

Partial shipments	Transhipment	Terms of shipment (FOB, C & F, CIF)
[X] allowed [ ] not allowed	[ ] allowed [X] not allowed	CIF Oakland

Despatch from / Taking in charge at	For transportation to	Latest date of shipment	Documents must be presented not later than
Korea	Oakland	10th Nov. 19..	③ 15 days after date of despatch

Beneficiary may dispose of the credit amount as follows [X] at sight upon presentation of documents ⑤ [ ] after ....days, calculated from date of	[ ] by a draft due .... drawn on [ ] you [ ] your correspondents which you / your correspondents will please accept

against surrender of the following documents ⑥
 	
[X] invoice   (....3...copies)
 	
Shipping document
[X] sea: bill of lading, to order, endorsed in blank
[ ] rail: dublicate waybill
[ ] air: air consignment note
[ ]
	[X] insurance policy, certificte (............... copies)
	covering the following risks:
	"all risks" including war up to
	[ ] Additional documents final destination in
	                    the United States
	[X] Confirmation of the carrier that the
	    ship is not more than 15 years old
	
	[X] packing list (3 copies)

Notify address in bill of lading / goods addressed to American Import-Export Co., Inc. ⑦ 123 Main Street San Francisco, California	Goods insured by [ ] us [X] seller

Goods ⑧
 	
1,000 "Record players ANC 83 as per proforma invoice
      no. 74/1853 dd 10th September 19.."
 	
    at US$ 70.20 per item

Your correspondents to advise beneficiary [ ] adding their confirmation [X] without adding their confirmation ⑨ Payments to be debited to our US Dollars........................account no 10-32657910

NB. The applicable text is marked by [X]

American Import-Export Co., Inc.

E 6801 N 1/2 3.81 5000

Signature _

For mailing please see overleaf

TIPS FOR PARTIES TO A LETTER OF CREDIT

Buyer

1. Before opening a letter of credit, the buyer should reach agreement with the supplier on all particulars of payment procedures, schedules of shipment, type of goods to be sent, and documents to be supplied by the supplier.
2. When choosing the type of L/C to be used, the buyer should take into account standard payment methods in the country with which he is doing business.
3. When opening a letter of credit, the buyer should keep the details of the purchase short and concise.
4. The buyer should be prepared to amend or renegotiate terms of the L/C with the supplier. This is a common procedure in international trade. On irrevocable L/Cs, the most common type, amendments may be made only if all parties involved in the L/C agree.
5. The buyer can eliminate exchange risk involved with import credits in foreign currencies by purchasing foreign exchange on the forward markets.
6. The buyer should use a bank experienced in foreign trade as the L/C issuing bank.
7. The validation time stated on the L/C should give the supplier ample time to produce the goods or to pull them out of stock.
8. The buyer should be aware that an L/C is not failsafe. Banks are only responsible for the documents exchanged and not the goods shipped. Documents in conformity with L/C specifications cannot be rejected on grounds that the goods were not delivered as specified in the contract. The goods shipped may not in fact be the goods ordered and paid for.
9. Purchase contracts and other agreements pertaining to the sale between the buyer and supplier are not the concern of the issuing bank. Only the terms of the L/C are binding on the bank.
10. Documents specified in the L/C should include those the buyer requires for customs clearance.

Supplier

1. Before signing a contract, the supplier should make inquiries about the buyer's creditworthiness and business practices. The supplier's bank will generally assist in this investigation.
2. The supplier should confirm the good standing of the buyer's bank if the credit is unconfirmed.
3. For confirmed credit, the supplier should determine that his local bank is willing to confirm credits from the buyer and his bank.
4. The supplier should carefully review the L/C to make sure he can meet the specified schedules of shipment, type of goods to be sent, packaging, and documentation. All aspects of the L/C must be in conformance with the terms agreed upon, including the supplier's address, the amount to be paid, and the prescribed transport route.
5. The supplier must comply with every detail of the L/C specifications, otherwise the security given by the credit is lost.
6. The supplier should ensure that the L/C is irrevocable.
7. If conditions of the credit have to be modified, the supplier should contact the buyer immediately so that he can instruct the issuing bank to make the necessary amendments.
8. The supplier should confirm with his insurance company that it can provide the coverage specified in the credit, and that insurance charges in the L/C are correct. Insurance coverage often is for CIF (cost, insurance, freight) value of the goods plus 10 percent.
9. The supplier must ensure that the details of goods being sent comply with the description in the L/C, and that the description on the invoice matches that on the L/C.
10. The supplier should be familiar with foreign exchange limitations in the buyer's country which may hinder payment procedures.

GLOSSARY OF DOCUMENTS IN INTERNATIONAL TRADE

The following is a list and description of some of the more common documents importers and exporters encounter in the course of international trade. For the importer/buyer this serves as a checklist of documents he may require of the seller/exporter in a letter of credit or documents against payment method.

Bill of Lading A document issued by a transportation company (such as a shipping line) to the shipper which serves as a receipt for goods shipped, a contract for delivery, and may serve as a title document. The major types are:

Straight (non-negotiable) Bill of Lading Indicates that the shipper will deliver the goods to the consignee. The document itself does not give title to the goods. The consignee need only identify himself to claim the goods. A straight bill of lading is often used when the goods have been paid for in advance.

Order (negotiable or "shippers order") Bill of Lading This is a title document which must be in the possession of the consignee (buyer/importer) in order for him to take possession of the shipped goods. Because this bill of lading is negotiable, it is usually made out "to the order of" the consignor (seller/exporter).

Air Waybill A bill of lading issued for air shipment of goods, which is always made out in straight non-negotiable form. It serves as a receipt for the shipper and needs to be made out to someone who can take possession of the goods upon arrival—without waiting for other documents to arrive.

Overland/Inland Bill of Lading Similar to an Air Waybill, except that it covers ground or water transport.

Certificate of Origin A document which certifies the country of origin of the goods. Because a certificate of origin is often required by customs for entry, a buyer will often stipulate in his letter of credit that a certificate of origin is a required document.

Insurance Document A document certifying that goods are insured for shipment.

Invoice/Commercial Invoice A document identifying the seller and buyer of goods or services, identifying numbers such as invoice number, date, shipping date, mode of transport, delivery and payment terms, and a complete listing and description of the goods or services being sold including prices, discounts, and quantities. The commercial invoice is usually used by customs to determine the true cost of goods when assessing duty.

Certificate of manufacture A document in which the producer of goods certifies that production has been completed and that the goods are at the disposal of the buyer.

Consular Invoice An invoice prepared on a special form supplied by the consul of an importing country, in the language of the importing country, and certified by a consular official of the foreign country.

Dock Receipt A document/receipt issued by an ocean carrier when the seller/exporter is not responsible for moving the goods to their final destination, but only to a dock in the exporting country. The document/receipt indicates that the goods were, in fact, delivered and received at the specified dock.

Export License A document, issued by a government agency, giving authorization to export certain commodities to specified countries.

Import License A document, issued by a government agency, giving authorization to import certain commodities.

Inspection Certificate An affidavit signed by the seller/exporter or an independent inspection firm (as required by the buyer/importer), confirming that merchandise meets certain specifications.

Packing List A document listing the merchandise contained in a particular box, crate, or container, plus type, dimensions, and weight of the container.

Phytosanitary (plant health) Inspection Certificate A document certifying that an export shipment has been inspected and is free from pests and plant diseases considered harmful by the importing country.

Shipper's Export Declaration A form prepared by a shipper/exporter indicating the value, weight, destination, and other information about an export shipment.

GLOSSARY OF TERMS OF SALE

The following is a basic glossary of common terms of sale in international trade. Note that issues regarding responsibility for loss and insurance are complex and beyond the scope of this publication. The international standard of trade terms of sale are "Incoterms," published by the International Chamber of Commerce (ICC), 38, Cours Albert Ier, F-75008 Paris, France. Other offices of the ICC are British National Committee of the ICC, Centre Point, 103 New Oxford Street, London WC1A 1QB, England and US Council of the ICC, 1212 Avenue of the Americas, New York, NY 10010 USA.

C&F (Cost and Freight) Named Point of Destination The seller's price includes the cost of the goods and transportation up to a named port of destination, but does not cover insurance. Under these terms insurance is the responsibility of the buyer/importer.

CIF (Cost, Insurance, and Freight) Named Point of Destination The seller's price includes the cost of the goods, insurance, and transportation up to a named port of destination.

Ex Point of Origin ("Ex Works" "Ex Warehouse" etc.) The seller's price includes the cost of the goods and packing, but without any transport. The seller agrees to place the goods at the disposal of the buyer at a specified point of origin, on a specified date, and within a fixed period of time. The buyer is under obligation to take delivery of the goods at the agreed place and bear all costs of freight, transport and insurance.

FAS (Free Alongside Ship) The seller's price includes the cost of the goods and transportation up to the port of shipment alongside the vessel or on a designated dock. Insurance under these terms is usually the responsibility of the buyer.

FOB (Free On Board) The seller's price includes the cost of the goods , transportation to the port of shipment, and loading charges on a vessel. This might be on a ship, railway car, or truck at an inland point of departure. Loss or damage to the shipment is borne by the seller until loaded at the point named and by the buyer after loading at that point.

Ex Dock—Named Port of Importation The seller's price includes the cost of the goods, and all additional charges necessary to put them on the dock at the named port of importation with import duty paid. The seller is obligated to pay for insurance and freight charges.

GLOSSARY OF INTERNATIONAL PAYMENT TERMS

Advice The forwarding of a letter of credit or an amendment to a letter of credit to the seller, or beneficiary of the letter of credit, by the advising bank (seller's bank).

Advising bank The bank (usually the seller's bank) which receives a letter of credit from the issuing bank (the buyer's bank) and handles the transaction from the seller's side. This includes: validating the letter of credit, reviewing it for internal consistency, forwarding it to the seller, forwarding seller's documentation back to the issuing bank, and, in the case of a confirmed letter of credit, guaranteeing payment to the seller if his documents are in order and the terms of the credit are met.

Amendment A change in the terms and conditions of a letter of credit, usually to meet the needs of the seller. The seller requests an amendment of the buyer who, if he agrees, instructs his bank (the issuing bank) to issue the amendment. The issuing bank informs the seller's bank (the advising bank) who then notifies the seller of the amendment. In the case of irrevocable letters of credit, amendments may only be made with the agreement of all parties to the transaction.

Back-to-Back Letter of Credit A new letter of credit opened in favor of another beneficiary on the basis of an already existing, nontransferable letter of credit.

Beneficiary The entity to whom credits and payments are made, usually the seller/supplier of goods.

Bill of Exchange A written order from one person to another to pay a specified sum of money to a designated person. The following two versions are the most common:

Draft A financial/legal document where one individual (the drawer) instructs another individual (the drawee) to pay a certain amount of money to a named person, usually in payment for the transfer of goods or services. Sight Drafts are payable when presented. Time Drafts (also called usance drafts) are payable at a future fixed (specific) date or determinable (30, 60, 90 days etc.) date. Time drafts are used as a financing tool (as with Documents against Acceptance D/P terms) to give the buyer time to pay for his purchase.

Promissory Note A financial/legal document wherein one individual (the issuer) promises to pay another individual a certain amount.

Collecting Bank (also called the presenting bank) In a Documentary Collection, the bank (usually the buyer's bank) that collects payment or a time draft from the buyer to be forwarded to the remitting bank (usually the seller's bank) in exchange for shipping and other documents which enable the buyer to take possession of the goods.

Confirmed Letter of Credit A letter of credit which contains a guarantee on the part of both the issuing and advising bank of payment to the seller so long as the seller's documentation is in order and terms of the credit are met.

Deferred Payment Letter of Credit A letter of credit where the buyer takes possession of the title documents and the goods by agreeing to pay the issuing bank at a fixed time in the future.

Discrepancy The noncompliance with the terms and conditions of a letter of credit. A discrepancy may be as small as a misspelling, an inconsistency in dates or amounts, or a missing document. Some discrepancies can easily be fixed; others may lead to the eventual invalidation of the letter of credit.

D/A Abbreviation for "Documents against Acceptance."

D/P Abbreviation for "Documents against Payment."

Documents against Acceptance (D/A) *See* Documentary Collection

Documents against Payment (D/P) *See* Documentary Collection

Documentary Collection A method of effecting payment for goods whereby the seller/exporter instructs his bank to collect a certain sum from the buyer/importer in exchange for the transfer of shipping and other documentation enabling the buyer/importer to take possession of the goods. The two main types of Documentary Collection are:

Documents against Payment (D/P) Where the bank releases the documents to the buyer/importer only against a cash payment in a prescribed currency; and

Documents against Acceptance (D/A) Where the bank releases the documents to the buyer/importer against acceptance of a bill of exchange guaranteeing payment at a later date.

Draft *See* Bill of exchange.

Drawee The buyer in a documentary collection.

Forward Foreign Exchange An agreement to purchase foreign exchange (currency) at a future date at a predetermined rate of exchange. Forward foreign exchange contracts are often purchased by buyers of merchandise who wish to hedge against foreign exchange fluctuations between the time the contract is negotiated and the time payment is made.

Irrevocable Credit A letter of credit which cannot be revoked or amended without prior mutual consent of the supplier, the buyer, and all intermediaries.

Issuance The act of the issuing bank (buyer's bank) establishing a letter of credit based on the buyer's application.

Issuing Bank The buyer's bank which establishes a letter of credit in favor of the supplier, or beneficiary.

Letter of Credit A document stating commitment on the part of a bank to place an agreed upon sum of money at the disposal of a seller on behalf of a buyer under precisely defined conditions.

Negotiation In a letter of credit transaction, the examination of seller's documentation by the (negotiating) bank to determine if they comply with the terms and conditions of the letter of credit.

Open Account The shipping of goods by the supplier to the buyer prior to payment for the goods. The supplier will usually specify expected payment terms of 30, 60, or 90 days from date of shipment.

Red Clause Letter of Credit A letter of credit which makes funds available to the seller prior to shipment in order to provide him with funds for production of the goods.

Remitter In a documentary collection, an alternate name given to the seller who forwards documents to the buyer through banks.

Remitting Bank In a documentary collection, a bank which acts as an intermediary, forwarding the remitter's documents to, and payments from the collecting bank.

Sight Draft *See* Bill of Exchange.

Standby Letter of Credit A letter of credit used as a secondary payment method in the event that the primary payment method cannot be fulfilled.

Time Draft *See* Bill of Exchange.

Validity The time period for which a letter of credit is valid. After receiving notice of a letter of credit opened on his behalf, the seller/exporter must meet all the requirements of the letter of credit within the period of validity.

Revocable Letter of Credit A letter of credit which may be revoked or amended by the issuer (buyer) without prior notice to other parties in the letter of credit process. It is rarely used.

Revolving Letter of Credit A letter of credit which is automatically restored to its full amount after the completion of each documentary exchange. It is used when there are several shipments to be made over a specified period of time.

FURTHER READING

For more detailed information on international trade payments, refer to the following publications of the International Chamber of Commerce (ICC), Paris, France.

Uniform Rules for Collections This publication describes the conditions governing collections, including those for presentation, payment and acceptance terms. The Articles also specify the responsibility of the bank regarding protest, case of need and actions to protect the merchandise. An indispensable aid to everyday banking operations. (A revised, updated edition will be published in 1995.) ICC Publication No. 322.

Documentary Credits: UCP 500 and 400 Compared This publication was developed to train managers, supervisors, and practitioners of international trade in critical areas of the new UCP 500 Rules. It pays particular attention to those Articles that have been the source of litigation. ICC Publication No. 511.

The New ICC Standard Documentary Credit Forms Standard Documentary Credit Forms are a series of forms designed for bankers, attorneys, importers/exporters, and anyone involved in documentary credit transactions around the world. This comprehensive new edition, prepared by Charles del Busto, Chairman of the ICC Banking Commission, reflects the major changes instituted by the new "UCP 500." ICC Publication No. 516.

The New ICC Guide to Documentary Credit Operations This new Guide is a fully revised and expanded edition of the "Guide to Documentary Credits" (ICC publication No. 415, published in conjunction with the UCP No. 400). The new Guide uses a unique combination of graphs, charts, and sample documents to illustrate the Documentary Credit process. An indispensable tool for import/export traders, bankers, training services, and anyone involved in day-to-day Credit operations. ICC Publication No. 515.

Guide to Incoterms 1990 A companion to "Incoterms," the ICC "Guide to Incoterms 1990" gives detailed comments on the changes to the 1980 edition and indicates why it may be in the interest of a buyer or seller to use one or another trade term. This guide is indispensable for exporters/importers, bankers, insurers, and transporters. ICC Publication No. 461/90.

These and other relevant ICC publications may be obtained from the following sources:

ICC Publishing S.A.
International Chamber of Commerce
38, Cours Albert Ier
75008 Paris, France
Tel: [33] (1) 49-53-28-28 Fax: [33] (1) 49-53-28-62
Telex: 650770

International Chamber of Commerce
Borsenstrasse 26
P.O. Box 4138
8022 Zurich, Switzerland

British National Committee of the ICC
Centre Point, New Oxford Street
London WC1A QB, UK

ICC Publishing, Inc.
US Council of the ICC
156 Fifth Avenue, Suite 820
New York, NY 10010, USA
Tel: [1] (212) 206-1150 Fax: [1] (212) 633-6025

Corporate Taxation

AT A GLANCE

Corporate Income Tax Rate (%)	34 (a)
Capital Gains Tax Rate (%)	25 (a)
Branch Tax Rate (%)	34 (a)
Withholding Tax (%)	
Dividends	0 (b)
Interest	20 (a)(b)
Royalties from Patents, Know-how, etc.	0 (b)
Branch Remittance Tax	0
Net Operating Losses (Years)	
Carryback	0
Carryforward	5

(a) A 7.5 percent surtax is also levied (See Other Significant Taxes).
(b) For payments to domestic corporations and foreign corporations with a place of business in South Korea. For withholding rates applicable to payments to foreign corporations that do not have a place of business in South Korea, see Taxes on Corporate Income and Gains.

TAXES ON CORPORATE INCOME AND GAINS

Corporate Income Tax

South Korean domestic corporations are taxed on their worldwide income, including income earned by foreign branches. A domestic corporation is one that has its head office in South Korea. Foreign corporations are taxed on Korean-source income.

Rates of Corporate Tax

The rates for 1993 are indicated below.

Domestic Corporations Taxable income up to W100 million is taxed at 20%. Taxable income exceeding W100 million is generally taxed at 34%.

For the two fiscal years beginning after January 1, 1992, a temporary tax reduction applies to small and medium-size manufacturing corporations. In general, such corporations are those with less than 300 full-time employees (but in certain exceptional cases, companies with up to 1,000 employees are in this category). Certain types of businesses must also have total assets between W8 billion and W30 billion. A 40 percent tax reduction applies to the annual taxable income of such companies up to W100 million. A 20 percent tax reduction applies to their annual taxable income exceeding that amount.

Foreign Corporations with a Domestic Business Operation The same tax rates as those for domestic corporations apply. The temporary tax reduction for small and medium-size manufacturing corporations discussed above also applies.

Foreign Corporations without a Domestic Business Operation A foreign corporation which does not have a domestic business place in South Korea is subject to the following withholding tax rates on its Korean-source income (unless other rates apply under a tax treaty):

Lease income from vessels, aircraft, heavy equipment, etc., and business income	2%
Personal service income	20%
Interest, dividends, royalties, and other income	25%
Gain from transfer of security or shares	Lesser of 10% of gross and 25% of net gain

Domestic Place of Business A foreign corporation that has any of the following fixed operations in South Korea is deemed to have a domestic place of business:

- a branch, office, or any other business office;
- a store or any other fixed sales place;

- a workshop, factory, or warehouse;
- a construction site or place of installation or assembly; or
- a mine or quarry.

A fixed place of business does not include:

- a purchasing office;
- a storage or custody area of nonsalable property; or
- an office involved in advertising, public relations, collection and furnishing of information, market survey, and other preparatory or auxiliary activities.

Even though a foreign corporation does not have a fixed place of business in South Korea, it may be considered to have a domestic place of business if it operates a business by having a person in South Korea authorized to conclude contracts or perform similar activities on its behalf.

Foreign Capital Inducement Act If tax exemption is approved by the Ministry of Finance under the Foreign Capital Inducement Act, the following tax privileges are granted to foreign investors:

- The foreign-owned corporation (the foreign investor) may benefit from a 100 percent tax exemption for the first year of the business and the following 36 months and a 50 percent tax reduction for the two years following the fully exempt years.
- Withholding tax on dividends paid on the stock of the foreign investor is reduced up to 50 percent during the period the business is exempt from tax.
- Properties acquired and held by a foreign-owned corporation are exempt from 50 percent of acquisition and property tax for the period the business is exempt from tax.

Royalty fees received in accordance with contracts classified as high-technology and accepted by the Ministry of Finance under the Foreign Capital Inducement Act are exempt from income tax for five years.

Capital Gains

Capital gains are included in ordinary taxable income for corporate tax purposes. In addition, a special surtax is levied for income from transfers of property. The rate is 25%, increased to 40 percent if ownership of the property is not registered. When property is expropriated by the government under circumstances prescribed by law, no taxable capital gains result.

Administration

A corporation must file a tax return within 30 days from the date of finalization of settlement of accounts.

This time limit is 15 days if a tax return is filed without a tax reconciliation prepared by a certified public accountant or a tax accountant. Tax due must be paid at the time of submitting the tax return.

Dividends

Dividends received from a corporation are included in taxable income of an individual corporation.

Foreign Tax Relief

A tax credit is allowed for corporate tax paid to a foreign government. The relief cannot exceed the lesser of the tax paid abroad and the tax amount equivalent to the ratio of the income from foreign sources to the total taxable income.

DETERMINATION OF TRADING INCOME

General

The tax law defines the specific adjustments which are required in computing taxable income. If not specified by law, the accrual basis is applied.

Inventories

A corporation must select and notify the tax office of its basis for the valuation of inventories: market value; the lower of cost or market value; and the cost method according to FIFO, LIFO, moving average, total average, latest purchase price or retail. In the absence of such notification, the corporation must use the latest purchase price method.

Reserves

Reserves for Employee Retirement Allowance Under the Korean Labor Standard Law, employees with more than one year of service are entitled to a retirement allowance equivalent to one month's pay for each year of service upon termination of employment. Reserves for retirement allowances are permitted, up to 10 percent of the total amount of wages paid to employees who have been in service for one year or more. However, the accumulated amount of the reserves is limited to not more than 50 percent of the estimated retirement allowances payable to all employees if they retire on the closing date of the business year.

A company may claim a tax deduction for the remainder of the estimated retirement allowances by funding the portion of the reserve in excess of the tax deductible limit. The only funding method permitted under the tax law is to deposit an amount equal to the excess portion in an interest-bearing account with an insurance company.

Bad Debt Reserve A corporation is allowed to set up a reserve for bad debts of 1 percent (2 percent for financial institutions) of receivables at the end of the accounting period.

Other Reserves A corporation may set up reserves for export losses, overseas market development costs, and overseas investment losses within the limit prescribed in the Corporate Income Tax Law.

Deduction for Capital Increases

When a domestic corporation (other than a nonprofit corporation) increases its capital by receiving cash investments and registers that change in capital, 10 percent (12 percent for listed or small and medium-size companies) of the increased capital must be deducted from the taxable income of each business year for the 36 month period following the initial registration.

Depreciation and Amortization

A corporation may deduct depreciation or amortization determined by the following methods:

- Tangible fixed assets: either straight-line method or the declining-balance method.
- Intangible fixed assets: straight-line method.

Statutory useful lives are established by the government. Special depreciation is allowable for certain assets in accordance with the Corporate Income Tax Law as well as the Tax Exemption and Reduction Control Law.

Relief for Losses

Tax losses can be carried forward for five years. No carryback is allowed

Groups of Companies

No form of consolidated income reporting for groups of companies applies in South Korea.

OTHER SIGNIFICANT TAXES

The table below summarizes other significant taxes.

Nature of Tax	Rate (%)
Resident tax, levied as a surtax on corporate income tax	7.5
Value-added tax	
Standard rate	10
Acquisition tax, on land, buildings, ships, automobiles. and heavy equipment	
Normal Rate	2
Acquired for business purposes in a major city	10
Payroll taxes, on salaries and wages; paid by employer	5 to 50

TREATY WITHHOLDING TAX RATES

	Dividends A %	Dividends B %	Interest %	Royalties C %	Royalties D %		Dividends A %	Dividends B %	Interest %	Royalties C %	Royalties D %
Australia	15	15	15	15	15	Poland	10	10	10	10	10
Austria	10	15	10	10	10	Singapore	10	15	10	15	15
Bangladesh	10	15	10	10	10	Sri Lanka	10	15	10	10	10
Belgium	15	15	15	10	15	Sweden	10	15	15 (c)	10	15
Brazil	15	15	15 (c)	15	15 (d)	Switzerland	10	15	10	10	10
Canada (b)	15	15	15	15	15	Thailand (b)	20	15	10	15	15
Denmark	15	15	15	10	15	Tunisia	15	15	12	15	15
Finland	10	15	10	10	10	Turkey	15	20	15 (a)	10	10
France	10	15	10	10	10	UK	10	15	15 (a)	10	15
Germany	10	15	15 (c)	10	15	US (b)	10	15	12	10	15
Hungary	5	10	0	0	0	Nontreaty					
India	15	20	15	15	15	countries (e)	25	25	25	25	25
Indonesia	10	15	10	15	15						
Ireland	10	15	0	0	0						
Italy	10	15	10	10	10						
Japan	12	12	12	12	12						
Luxembourg	10	15	10	10	15						
Malaysia	10	15	15	10	15						
Netherlands	10	15	15 (c)	10	15						
New Zealand	15	15	10	10	10						
Norway	15	15	15	10	15						
Pakistan	10	12.5	12.5	10	10						
Philippines	10	15	15	15	15						

A Controlling Parent
B Other Shareholders
C Industrial Royalties
D Other Royalties
(a) Reduced to 10 percent if repayment period is over two years.
(b) Resident tax of 7.5 percent of the corporate income tax will be assessed in addition.
(c) Reduced to 10 percent if repayment period is over seven years.
(d) For royalties for trademarks, the rate is increased to 25%.
(e) Applicable to foreign corporations that do not have a place of business in South Korea.

Personal Taxation

AT A GLANCE—MAXIMUM RATES

Income Tax Rate (%)	50
Capital Gains Tax Rate (%)	75
Net Worth Tax Rate (%)	0
Inheritance Tax Rate (%)	55
Gift Tax Rate (%)	60

INCOME TAXES—EMPLOYMENT

Who Is Liable

Residents are subject to income tax on worldwide income. A nonresident is liable for income tax only on South Korean-source income.

A resident is a person who has a domicile or residence in South Korea for more than one year.

Taxable Income

Personal income is classified into four separate categories:

- global income (includes wages, interest, dividends, royalties, real estate, business income, and other income on a worldwide basis);
- severance pay;
- forestry income; and
- capital gains.

Salary and wage income includes the following in addition to basic monthly payroll:

- reimbursement for personal expenses, entertainment expenses, and other allowances not considered proper business expenses;
- various allowances for family, position, housing, health, overtime, and so forth; and
- insurance premiums paid by the company, except medical insurance premiums.

The following is excluded from earned income:

- overseas allowances for living cost differentials, housing, home leave, education, and so forth for resident aliens (total deduction for living cost differentials and housing allowance not to exceed 20 percent of basic monthly fixed pay or one-sixth of total compensation, whichever is greater); and
- reimbursements for automobile operating expenses up to W200,000 a month to employees using their own car for company business.

Salary and wage income is classified into either Class A income or Class B income.

Class A income is earned income received in South Korean currency (won). It is subject to the withholding of taxes by the payer on a monthly basis. Class B income is earned income received in foreign currency, on which the payer is not obliged to withhold South Korean taxes at the time of payment. Instead, the individual recipient is responsible for declaring income through a taxpayer association and is entitled to a tax credit in the amount of 20 percent of tax liabilities.

Income Tax Rates

Tax rates applied to global income, severance pay and forestry income in 1993 are set forth in the following table.

Taxable Income Exceeding W	Taxable Income Not Exceeding W	Tax on Lower Amount W	Rate on Excess %
0	4,000,000	0	5
4,000,000	8,000,000	200,000	10
8,000,000	16,000,000	600,000	20
16,000,000	32,000,000	2,200,000	30
32,000,000	64,000,000	7,000,000	40
64,000,000	—	19,800,000	50

In addition, resident taxes are imposed as a surtax on income tax at the rate of 7.5%.

Deductible Expenses

A maximum earned income deduction of W6 million a year is permitted.

Premiums paid for life, casualty, and other insurance are deductible up to W240,000 a year. However, medical insurance premiums are deductible without limit.

Medical expenses in excess of 3 percent of total compensation are deductible up to a maximum annual amount of W1 million. In addition, all medical expenses paid on behalf of elderly parents residing with the taxpayer are deductible.

Education expenses of the taxpayer-employee (excluding graduate school) and of two children and two brothers or sisters of the taxpayer are deductible.

Contributions made to the government are deductible in full as well as other designated donations up to a limit of 5 percent of total income.

Personal Allowances and Deductions

The following personal allowances and deductions are permitted for 1993.

Basic exemption	W600,000
Spouse	W540,000
Additional deduction if spouse also works	W540,000
Dependent (each)	W480,000
Disabled person (each)	W480,000
Elderly dependent	W480,000

Tax Exemption for Aliens

The following resident aliens are exempt from personal income taxes.

- Aliens assigned to Korea under a bilateral agreement between governments are exempt. Compensation received from either government is fully exempt from Korean income taxes without limitation.
- Aliens employed under a technology inducement contract in the Foreign Capital Inducement Act are exempt from taxes for five years from the date when the technological inducement contract is approved. The technology should be high technology.
- Foreign technicians who offer their services to domestic companies or persons are exempt from personal income taxes on earned income if they have had five years' work experience in one of the following industries (three years if they hold a degree higher than the bachelor's degree) and if the employment contract was concluded with a domestic corporation or with persons running a domestic corporation:

- manufacturing;
- mining;
- construction;
- technical services rendered in accordance with the Technical Service Promotion Law;
- development and operation of electronic data processing systems; or
- research, manufacture, assembling, or maintenance of military supplies and equipment in accordance with the special government military supply measures.

INCOME TAXES— SELF-EMPLOYMENT/ BUSINESS INCOME

Who Is Liable

Residents are liable on worldwide income. Nonresidents are liable only on South Korean-source income.

Taxable Income

Business income includes all income from businesses and personal services, such as those provided by

- entertainers;
- athletes;
- lawyers, accountants, architects, and other professionals; and
- persons having expert knowledge or skills in science and technology, business management, or other fields.

Business income is added to an individual's other income and is taxed accordingly.

Deductible Expenses

Most normal business-related expenses are deductible, including depreciation and bad debts.

Individual manufacturers are temporarily eligible for a 40 percent tax reduction on annual taxable manufacturing income up to W50 million and a 20 percent tax reduction on taxable manufacturing income exceeding W50 million. The tax reduction is available only for the 1992 and 1993 income years.

DIRECTORS' FEES

Directors' fees are taxed as business income (*See* Income Taxes—Self-Employment/Business Income).

INVESTMENT INCOME

Dividends, interest, royalties, and rental income are categorized as global income (*see* Taxable Income in Income Taxes—Employment) and are taxed at the rates set forth in Income Tax Rates in Income Taxes—Employment.

RELIEF FOR LOSSES

Business losses of a self-employed person may be carried forward for five years.

CAPITAL GAINS AND LOSSES

Capital gains are taxed separately from global income. Capital losses may not be carried forward. Tax rates on capital gains are as follows:

	Rate (%)
Listed securities	0
Unlisted securities	20
First house and related land registered in the seller's name that is smaller than national set size and held for more than five years or used as a residence for more than three years	0
Houses and related land registered in the seller's name that is smaller than national set size and held for two years or more	30
Real property registered in the seller's name held for less than two years	60
Real property not registered in the seller's name	75

The capital gains rates for real property, other than a house, registered in the seller's name and held for two years or more are as follows.

Taxable Income		Tax on Lower	Rate on
Exceeding	Not Exceeding	Amount	Excess
W	W	W	%
0	30,000,000	0	40
30,000,000	60,000,000	12,000,000	45
60,000,000	100,000,000	25,500,000	50
100,000,000	500,000,000	45,500,000	55
500,000,000	—	265,500,000	60

Special deductions are generally available to reduce the amount of capital gains. These deductions are designed to eliminate the effects of inflation and to encourage long-term possession.

Exemptions are available for the following property:

- land and buildings transferred for the purpose of moving a factory that has operated for two or more years;
- land and buildings transferred for the purpose of moving a ranch that has operated for five or more years; and
- land reclaimed by December 31, 1976, and transferred by December 31,1991, to farmers who had rented and cultivated the land for more than 20 years as of December 31, 1988,

or to the Agriculture and Fishery Development Corporation.

INHERITANCE AND GIFT TAXES

Each heir or legatee who acquires property pays inheritance tax at the following rates, provided the taxable amount exceeds W200,000 after deduction of exempt amounts:

Taxable Income		Tax on Lower	Rate on
Exceeding	Not Exceeding	Amount	Excess
W	W	W	%
0	20,000,000	0	10
20,000,000	200,000,000	2,000,000	20
200,000,000	500,000,000	38,000,000	30
500,000,000	1,000,000,000	128,000,000	40
1,000,000,000	—	328,000,000	55

The following amounts are exempt:

Basic deduction	W60,000,000
Personal deductions:	
Spouse allowance	W100,000,000 + 6,000,000 x the number of years after marriage
Allowance for children (20 years old or younger)	W3,000,000 x the number of years up to the age of 20
Old age allowance (60 years old or older)	W30,000,000
Allowance for the handicapped	W3,000,000 x the number of years up to the age of 75
Allowance for children	W20,000,000 x number of children (maximum two)
Special deductions:	
Insurance deductions	W7,000,000
Retirement allowance deduction	W1,000,000

Donees who acquire property pay gift tax at the following rates, provided the taxable amount exceeds W100,000 after deduction of exempt amounts:

Amount of Taxable Gift		Tax on Lower	Rate on
Exceeding	Not Exceeding	Amount	Excess
W	W	W	%
0	10,000,000	0	15
10,000,000	90,000,000	1,500,000	25
90,000,000	250,000,000	21,500,000	35
250,000,000	500,000,000	77,500,000	45
500,000,000	—	190,000,000	60

The following gifts are exempt:

- gifts contributed to the government or a public authority;
- gifts contributed to public organizations for the promotion of religion, charity, academic research, or public welfare; and
- other properties prescribed by law and Presidential Decree.

SOCIAL SECURITY TAXES

There are no social security taxes in South Korea.

ADMINISTRATION

The income year is the calendar year.

Taxes on Class A income (employment income in South Korean currency) are withheld by the employer.

Residents must file an annual income tax return between May 1 and May 31 each year if they receive income other than Class A income. Tax due must be paid with the return.

Taxpayers who receive other types of income, such as interest, dividends, or rents, must file a return on their combined worldwide income. Taxpayers reporting Class B income (earned income received or accrued in foreign currency outside South Korea for services rendered in South Korea) have the option of:

- Making an interim payment by November 30 of the income year based on half of the tax paid the previous year and filing an annual return.
- Joining an authorized taxpayer's association, through which monthly tax payments must be made. In return for payments to an authorized association, taxpayers receive a 20 percent credit on income tax liability if the Class B income is not recorded in the books of a South Korean permanent establishment of the paying company. Estimated payments must also be made for capital gains. Aliens must file a return prior to departing from South Korea.

Self-employed persons must make interim payments during the tax year.

NONRESIDENTS

Nonresident aliens are taxable only on income derived from Korea.

A nonresident with a place of business or employment income is taxed similarly to a resident.

The South Korean-source income of a nonresident without a place of business in South Korea is subject to final withholding tax at the rates indicated in the following list.

Rate

Business income and income from leasing ships, airplanes, registered vehicles, and similar items 2%

Income from professional or technical services 20%

Interest, dividend, royalty, and other income 25%

Capital gains derived from the transfer of securities .... 10% of sales price or 25% of capital gain, whichever is less

DOUBLE TAX TREATIES/ DOUBLE TAX RELIEF

A credit for foreign income taxes paid is available in the ratio of foreign-source income to total taxable income.

As of January 1993 South Korea had concluded treaties with the following countries to avoid double taxation:

Australia	Ireland	Philippines
Austria	India	Poland
Bangladesh	Indonesia	Singapore
Belgium	Italy	Sri Lanka
Brazil	Japan	Sweden
Canada	Luxembourg	Switzerland
Denmark	Malaysia	Thailand
Finland	Netherlands	Tunisia
France	New Zealand	Turkey
Germany	Norway	United Kingdom
Hungary	Pakistan	United States

For the withholding of income tax on dividends and interest, tax treaty rates, will apply if there is a tax treaty between South Korea and the relevant country.

Ports & Airports

The late 1980s and early 1990s have seen a major increase in the amount of air and shipping traffic passing through East Asia. Planners saw this coming some years back, and have been scrambling to expand and improve facilities at ports and airports throughout the region; many are currently at or over capacity. Air cargo traffic has been growing faster in Asia than anywhere else in the world, and passenger traffic has increased by leaps and bounds. With all the new facilities opening in the near future, there are estimates that by 1997 airport capacity will actually exceed demand even at current growth rates. This may mean that airlines and cargo carriers will be able to schedule more frequent service with smaller aircraft, something which is not currently possible given the small number of landing slots available at terminals and the many airports operating with only one runway and the consequent need to use the largest aircraft possible to maximize throughput.

Long a major center for shipping, Asia is fast becoming the leader in container port traffic. The largest increases in container traffic worldwide have been at the Asian hub ports. Four of the world's five leading countries in container traffic—Japan, Singapore, Hong Kong, and Taiwan, ranked respectively two through five—are located on the western edge of the Pacific Rim, while the number one ranked United States services the traffic from the other side of the Pacific. South Korea is ranked ninth in the world, and its port of Pusan is the fifth busiest individual container port worldwide.

AIRPORTS

Korea has three international airports, Kimpo (near Seoul), Kimhae (near Pusan), and Cheju, on the resort island of the same name, plus nine domestic airports. Kimpo, located 25 km (16 miles) west of downtown Seoul, is by far the most important airport to international trade, handling 95 percent of international cargo and 85 percent of the international passenger traffic as well as 37 percent of do-

mestic traffic. Compared to many other airports in Asia, Kimpo is relatively uncongested, and has the best record of on-time flights, with 92 percent of flights taking off at their appointed time. However, Kimpo is fast approaching its capacity of 18 million passengers a year, and it is expected that the Seoul airport will need to accommodate 60 million passengers by 2010.

Kimpo has also become an important air cargo facility, handling 743,000 metric tons of cargo in 1992, a 6 percent increase over the previous year. This makes Kimpo the tenth busiest cargo airport in the world and the third busiest in Asia.

Because of anticipated continued growth and Korea's eagerness to remain at the forefront of the competitive Asian air transport market, the Ministry of Transportation has put together a plan for what it claims will be the largest airport in the world, capable of handling 100 million passengers and 7 million tons of cargo annually. Korean officials hope to make Seoul's new airport the hub of northeast Asia, in much the same way that Hong Kong and Singapore have become hubs for southeast Asia. Work has already begun on this New Seoul Metropolitan Airport. It is expected to be operational in 1997, but final completion is not scheduled until 2035. The first phase involves land reclamation and the construction of two runways, one terminal, an international business center, and cargo-handling facilities. Tariffs at Kimpo, low by international standards, are being raised by approximately 10 percent annually to pay for the new airport.

The existing Kimpo Airport is only 25 km (16 miles) west of downtown Seoul, while the New Seoul Metropolitan Airport will be twice as far from the city—56 km (35 miles). The increased distance is not necessarily a negative feature for several reasons. The new airport is being built on reclaimed land about three miles offshore, so it will not be subject to the strict curfew laws that close Kimpo from 11 pm to 6 am every night. It will also be very close to the port of Inchon, making coordination of air and

National Transportation

North Korea

Sokcho

Chunchon

Kangnung

Seoul

Yoyang-ni

Samchok

Ferry to China

Inchon

Suwon

Wonju

Ansong

Chechon

Chonan

Yongju

Chongju

Taejon

Taechon

Kimchon

Pohang

Changhang

Kunsan

Iri

Chonju

Yongchon

Kyongju

Taegu

Ulsan

Changwon

Kwangju

Chinju

Yosu

Sunchon

Samchonpo

Pusan

Mokpo

Masan

Chungmu

Koje-do

Ferry to Japan

Chin-do

Tsushima

South Korea

✪	**National Capital**
◉	**Administrative Capital**
●	**Secondary City**
—	**Primary Road**
⎓	**Railroad**
- - -	**Demarcation Line**
▓	**Demilitarized Zone**
⚓	**Major Ports**
✈	**Major Airports**

Iki

Japan

Cheju

Cheju-do

0 25 50 75 km
0 25 50 mi

sea freight shipments much easier. Korean officials are planning to build an international business center at the airport and are encouraging companies to locate offices there, so that many employees and clients may not have to travel into Seoul at all. For those making the trip into the capital, there will be a major expressway and railway routed past Kimpo, which will remain a domestic airport.

Kimpo is currently served by 30 air cargo carriers, including national carriers Korean Airlines and Asiana Airlines, North American carriers Canadian Airlines, Continental, Delta, Northwest, and United, European lines Air France, Alitalia, British Airways, KLM, and Swissair as well as several Asian carriers, plus all-cargo carriers Federal Express, United Parcel Service, and Nippon Cargo. (For address and telephone information, refer to the Transportation section of the "Important Addresses" chapter.)

Kimpo International Airport and the New Seoul International Airport are administered by:

Korean Airport Authority
274, Gwahae-dong, Gangseo-ku
Seoul 157-701, Rep. of Korea
Tel: [82] (2) 660-2200 Fax: [82] (2) 663-8833

PORTS

Korea now has 26 operating ports, but Pusan and Inchon handle the vast majority of Korea's shipping. They are administered by:

Korea Maritime and Port Authority
112-2, Inui-dong, Chongno-ku
Seoul 110, Rep. of Korea
Tel: [82] (2) 744-4030

Pusan

The Port of Pusan is by far the largest port in Korea. Nearly all of Korea's international container traffic goes through Pusan, as well as half of its domestic shipping. There is a natural harbor at Pusan which makes accommodation of ships up to 50,000 dead weight tonnage (dwt) relatively easy. Specialized facilities exist for handling bulk grain, coal, scrap iron, and ore shipments. Construction and expansion at Pusan is ongoing as Korea's import and export traffic expands dramatically. During the 1970s and 1980s, Korean import-export cargo volume increased 12-fold, the bulk of it passing through Pusan. The port is administered by:

Pusan District Maritime and Port Authority
1116-1, Chachun-dong, Dong-ku
Pusan, Rep. of Korea
Tel: [82] (51) 633-5950 Fax: [82] (51) 633-2620

Port facilities:
Transportation Service —Truck, rail, and barge.
Cargo Storage—Covered, 44,622 square meters. Open, 64,957 square meters.
Special Cranes—Heavy lift capacity is 360 metric tons. Container, 9 to 35 metric ton capacity.
Air Cargo—Kimhae Airport, located 17 km (10.5 miles) from port.
Cargo Handling—Containerized, bulk, and general cargo can all be handled at Pusan, the major port of South Korea. Tanker, ore, and bulk, and container and Ro-Ro berths are available for specialized commodities.
Weather—Temperatures range from -13°C to 33°C with annual rainfall of 50 cms. Typhoons can occur from June to September.
Construction—A new bulk complex to handle grain, sugar, cement, scrap iron, and chemicals has recently been completed.

Inchon

The Port of Inchon, located about 40 km (25 miles) west of Seoul, is Korea's second major port. Although it is near the country's capital and main trade and business center, Inchon is far smaller than Pusan. The Inner Harbor, where six of the eight piers are used for international cargo, are accessible only through locks. The larger of the two locks accommodates a 50,000 dwt ship, while the smaller accommodates a 10,000 dwt ship. The port is administered by:

Inchon Port Authority
1-7, 7-ga, Hang-dong, Jung-gu
Inchon 160, Rep. of Korea
Tel: [82] (32) 883-4061 Fax: [82] (32) 885-0024

Port facilities:
Transportation Service—Truck, rail, and barge
Cargo Storage—Covered 59,428 square meters. Open 120,000 square meters. Refrigerated 8,910 square meters.
Special Cranes—Heavy lift capacity is 225 metric tons. Container, 7 to 35 metric ton capacity.
Air Cargo—Kimpo International Airport is located 32 km (20 miles) from seaport.
Cargo Handling—Containerized, bulk, and general cargo can all be adequately handled by existing port equipment. Ore, bulk, tanker, liquefied gas, specialized goods, and Ro-Ro terminals are available.
Weather—Typhoons can be expected during the late July to September rainy season. Temperatures range from -14°C to 35°C.

Business Dictionary

PRONUNCIATION GUIDE

Because Korean has a number of sounds that do not exist in English and cannot be represented by a single letter, we have adopted a number of conventions in the Guide below.

Vowels

Hangul	Romanization	English Sound
아	a	f**a**ther
어	eo	**ea**rth, ott**er**
오	o	f**o**r
우	u	f**oo**d
으	eu	thick**e**n
이	i	s**ea**
애	ae	**a**rrow
에	e	**e**pisode
애	ae	**a**rrow
외	way	**wa**y
왜	way	**wa**y
웨	way	**wa**y
위	wi	**we**

Hangul	Romanization	English Sound
야	ya	*yah*
여	yeo	*yea*rn, *yea*r
요	yo	*yo*del, *yo*ke
유	yu	*you*
예	ye	*ye*sterday
의	eui	thick*en* + m*eat*
와	wa	Ha*wa*ii
워	weo	*wo*rld, sho*wer*

Consonants

Hangul	Romanization	English Sound
ㄱ	g	*g*rass
ㄴ	n	*n*oon
ㄷ	d	*d*iamond
ㄹ	r, l	*r*oom, *l*arge
ㅁ	m	*m*oon
ㅂ	b	*b*uy, hum*b*le
ㅅ	s, sh	*s*mall, wa*sh*
ㅇ	silent*	
ㅇ	ng	you*ng*
ㅈ	j	*j*oke
ㅊ	ch	*ch*ur*ch*
ㅋ	k	*k*een
ㅌ	t	*t*iime
ㅍ	p	*p*eople
ㅎ	h	*h*ire
ㄲ	g	*g*ossip
ㄸ	d	*d*ot
ㅃ	b	*b*utt
ㅆ	ss	*sc*ent
ㅉ	j	*j*ack

*   when used as initial sound

English	*Korean*	*Phonetic Representation*

GREETINGS AND POLITE EXPRESSIONS

Hello (Honorific Expression)

(morning)	안녕하세요?	an-nyeong-ha-se-yo?
	(안녕하십니까?)	(an-nyeong ha-shim-ni-ka?)
	안녕히 주무셨습니까?	an-nyeong-hi ju-mu-ssyeo-sseum-ni-ka?
		(Did you have a good sleep?)
(daytime)	안녕하세요?	an-nyeong ha-se-yo?
	(안녕하십니까?)	(an-nyeong ha-shim-ni-ka?)
(evening)	안녕하세요?	an-nyeong ha-se-yo?
	(안녕하십니까?)	(an-nyeong ha-shim-ni-ka?)
(on the telephone)	여보세요.	yeo-bo-se-yo

Good-bye.

(to one who is leaving)	안녕히 가세요.	an-nyeong-hi ga-se-yo.
	(안녕히 가십시요.)	(an-nyeong-hi ga-ship-shi-yo)
(to one who is staying)	안녕히 계세요.	an-nyeong-hi gye-se-yo.
	(안녕히 계십시요.)	(an-nyeong-hi gye-ship-shi-yo.)
How do you do?	처음 뵙겠습니다.	cheo-eum bwayb-ge-sseum-ni-da.
Please	어서, 좀	eo-seo, jom
Pleased to meet you.	만나서 반갑습니다.	man-na-seo bang-gap-seum-ni-da.
Please excuse me.	실례합니다.	shil-lye ham-ni-da.
Excuse me for a moment.	잠깐 실례하겠습니다.	jam-kan shil-lye ha-ge-sseum-ni-da.
(when leaving a meeting)		
Congratulations.	축하합니다.	chuk-ha ham-ni-da.
Thank you.	감사합니다.	gam-sa ham-ni-da.
Thank you very much.	대단히 감사합니다.	dae-dan-hi gam-sa ham-ni-da.
Thank you for the gift.	선물을 주셔서 감사합니다.	seon-mu-reul ju-syeo-seo
		gam-sa ham-ni-da.
I am sorry, I don't	죄송합니다만 (한국말)을	jway-song-ham-ni-da-man
understand (Korean).	모릅니다.	(hang-gung-ma)-reul mo-reum-ni-da.
Do you speak English?	영어를 하십니까?	yeong-eo-reul ha-shim-ni-ka?
My name is (John Smith).	제 이름은 (쫀 스미스)	je i-reum-eun (jyon sseu-mi-sseu)
	입니다.	im-ni-da.
I am (John Smith).	저는 (쫀 스미스) 입니다.	jeo-neun (jyon sseu-mi-sseu) im-ni-da.
Is Mr/Ms. (Smith) there?	(스미스)씨 좀 바꿔	(sseu-mi-sseu)-ssi jom ba-kweo
(on the telephone)	주시겠습니까?	ju-shi-ge-sseum-ni-ka?
Can we meet (tomorrow)?	(내일) 만나뵐 수 있을까요?	(nae-il) man-na bwayl su i-sseul-ka-yo?

English	*Korean*	*Phonetic Representation*
Would you like to have dinner together?	저녁을 함께 하시겠습니까?	jeo-nyeo-geul ham-ke ha-shi-ge-sseum-ni-ka?
Yes	네.	ne.
No	아니오.	a-ni-yo.

DAY/TIME OF DAY

morning	아침	a-chim
noon	정오	jeong-o
afternoon	오후	o-hu
evening	저녁	jeo-nyeog
night	밤	bam
today	오늘	o-neul
yesterday	어제	eo-je
tomorrow	내일	nae-il
Monday	월요일	weo-ryo-il
Tuesday	화요일	hwa-yo-il
Wednesday	수요일	su-yo-il
Thursday	목요일	mo-gyo-il
Friday	금요일	geum-yo-il
Saturday	토요일	to-yo-il
Sunday	일요일	i-ryo-il
holiday	공휴일	gong-hyu-il
New Year's Day	새해	sae-hae
time	시간	shi-gan

NUMBERS

Korean numerals are generally used in counting hours, times, ages, and months, and with specific classifiers; Chinese numerals are used with specific classifiers in dealing with money matters, the metric system, and counting floors of buildings, minutes, days, and years. Up to 99, both numerals are used; for 100 and up, Chinese numerals are used

	Korean Origin	Pronunciation	Chinese Origin	Pronunciation
one	하나	ha-na	일	il
two	둘	dul	이	i
three	셋	set	삼	sam
four	넷	net	사	sa
five	다섯	da-seot	오	o

Korean Origin		Pronunciation	Chinese Origin	Pronunciation
six	여섯	yeo-seot	육	yuk
seven	일곱	il-gop	칠	chil
eight	여덟	yeo-deol	팔	pal
nine	아홉	a-hop	구	gu
ten	열	yeol	십	ship
eleven	열 하나	yeol ha-na	십일	ship il
fifteen	열 다섯	yeol da-seot	십오	ship o
twenty	스물	seu-mul	이십	i-ship
twenty-one	스물 하나	seu-mul ha-na	이십 일	i-ship il
thirty	서른	seo-reun	삼십	sam-ship
thirty-one	서른 하나	seo-reun ha-na	삼십 일	sam-ship il
fifty	쉰	shuin	오십	o-ship

for 100 and up, Chinese numerals are used.

English	*Korean*	*Phonetic Representation*
one hundred	일백	il-baek
one hundred one	백 일	baek il
one thousand	일천	il-cheon
one million	일백만	il-baek-man
first	첫째	cheot-jae
second	둘째	dul-jae
third	셋째	set-jae

English	*Korean*	*Phonetic Representation*

GETTING AROUND TOWN

English	Korean	Phonetic Representation
Where is (the railway station)?	(기차역)이 어디에 있습니까?	(gi-cha yeok)-i eo-di-e i-sseum-ni-ka?
Does this train go to (Washington)?	이 기차가 (워싱턴)으로 갑니까?	i gi-cha-ga (weo-shing-teon)-euro gam-ni-ka?
Please take me to (Washington).	(워싱턴)으로 좀 데려다 주십시요.	(weo-shing-teon)-euro jom de-ryeo-da ju-ship-shi-yo
Where am I?	여기가 어디입니까?	yeo-gi-ga eo-di im-ni-ka?
airplane	비행기	bi-haeng-gi
airport	비행장	bi-haeng-jang
bus (public)	일반 버스	il-ban beo-seu

English	Korean	Phonetic Representation
taxi	택시	taek-shi
train	기차	gi-cha
train station	기차 역	gi-cha yeok
ticket	표	pyo
one-way (single) ticket	편도표	pyon-do-pyo
round trip (return) ticket	왕복표	wang-bok-pyo

PLACES

airport	비행장	bi-haeng-jang
bank	은행	eun-haeng
barber shop	이발소	i-bal-so
beauty parlor	미장원	mi-jang-weon
business district	상가	sang-ga
business district	상공 회의소	sang-gong hway-eui-so
clothes store	옷 가게	ot ga-ge
exhibition	전시회	jeon-shi-hway
factory	공장	gong-jang
hotel	호텔	ho-tel
hospital	병원	byeong-weon
market	시장	shi-jang
post office	우체국	u-che-guk
restaurant	식당	shik-dang
rest room/toilet (W.C.)	화장실 (더블류 씨)	hwa-jang-shil (deo-beul-lyu ssi)
sea port	항구	hang-gu
train station	기차 역	gi-cha yeok

At the bank

What is the exchange rate?	환시세가 어떻게 됩니까?	hwan-shi-se-ga eo-teo-ke dwaym-ni-ka?
I want to exchange (dollars).	(달러)로 바꿔 주십시요.	(dal-leo)-ro ba-kweo ju-ship-shi-yo.
Australian dollar	호주 달러	ho-ju dal-leo
British pound	영국 파운드	yeong-guk pa-un-deu
Chinese yuan (PRC)	중공 유안 (중화 인민 공화국)	jung-gong yuan (jung-hwa in-min gong-hwa-guk)
French franc	불란서 프랑	bul-lan-seo feu-rang
German mark	독일 마르크	do-gil ma-reu-keu
Hong Kong dollar	홍콩 달러	hong kong dal-leo

English	Korean	Phonetic Representation
Indonesia rupiah	인도네시아 루피아	in-do-ne-shi-a ru-pi-a
Japanese yen	일본 엔	il-bon en
Korean won	한국 원	hang-guk weon
Malaysia ringgit	말레이시아 링깃	mal-lei-shi-a ring-git
Philippines peso	필리핀 페소	pil-li-pin pe-so
Singapore dollar	싱가포르 달러	shing-ga-po-reu dal-leo
New Taiwan dollar (ROC)	대만 달러 (자유 중국)	dae-man dal-leo (ja-yu jung-guk)
Thailand baht	태국 바트	tae-guk ba-teu
U.S. dollar	미국 달러	mi-guk dal-leo
Can you cash a personal check?	개인 수표를 현찰로 바꿀 수 있습니까?	gae-in su-pyo-reul hyeon-chal-lo ba-kul su i-sseum-ni-ka?
Where should I sign?	어디에 서명을 해야 합니까?	eo-di-e seo-myeong-eul hae-ya ham-ni-ka?
traveler's check	여행자 수표	yeo-haeng-ja su-pyo
bank draft	은행 환어음	eun-haeng hwan-eo-eum

At the hotel

I have a reservation.	저는 예약을 했습니다.	jeo-neun ye-yak-eul hae-sseum-ni-da.
Could you give me a single (double) room?	독실 (2인용) 방이 있습니까?	dok-shil (i-in-yong) bang-i i-sseum-ni-ka?
Is there...?	...있습니까?	...i-sseum-ni-ka?
air-conditioning	환기 장치가 있습니까?	hwan-gi jang-chi-ga i-sseum-ni-ka?
heating	난방 장치가 있습니까?	nan-bang jang-chi-ga i-sseum-ni-ka?
private toilet	전용 화장실이 있습니까?	jeon-yong hwa-jang-shi-ri i-sseum-ni-ka?
hot water	온수가 있습니까?	on-su-ga i-sseum-ni-ka?
May I see the room?	방을 볼 수 있습니까?	bang-eul bol su i-sseum-ni-ka?
Would you mail this for me please?	편지 좀 부쳐 주시겠습니까?	pyeon-ji jom bu-chyeo ju-shi-ge-sseum-ni-ka?
Do you have any stamps?	우표가 있습니까?	u-pyo-ga i-sseum-ni-ka?
May I have my bill?	계산서 좀 주시겠습니까?	gye-san-seo jom ju-shi-ge-sseum-ni-ka?

At the store

Do you sell (books)?	(책)을 팝니까?	(chaek)-eul pam-ni-ka?
Do you have anything less expensive?	더 싼 것이 있습니까?	deoh ssan-geo-shi i-sseum-ni-ka?

English	*Korean*	*Phonetic Representation*
I would like (three books).	(책 세권)을 사고 싶습니다.	(chaek se-gweon)-eul sa-go ship-sseum-ni-da.
I'll take it.	그것을 사겠습니다.	geu-geo-seul sa-ge-sseum-ni-da.
I want this one.	이것을 사고 싶습니다.	i-geo-seul sa-go ship-sseum-ni-da.
When does it open?	언제 문을 엽니까?	eon-je mun-eul yeom-ni-ka?
When does it close?	언제 문을 닫습니까?	eon-je mun-eul da-sseum-ni-ka?

COUNTRIES

America (USA)	미국 (미 합중국)	Mi-guk (mi hap-jung-guk)
Australia	호주	Ho-ju
China (PRC)	중공 (중화 인민 공화국)	Jung-gong (Jung-hwa in-min gong-hwa-guk)
France	불란서	Bul-lan-seo
Germany	독일	Do-gil
Hong Kong	홍콩	Hong-kong
Indonesia	인도네시아	In-do-ne-shi-a
Japan	일본	Il-bon
Korea	한국	Hang-guk
Malaysia	말레이시아	Mal-lei-shi-a
Philippines	필리핀	Pil-li-pin
Singapore	싱가포르	Shing-ga-po-reu
Taiwan	대만	Dae-man
Thailand	태국	Tae-guk
United Kingdom	영국	Yeong-guk

EXPRESSIONS IN BUSINESS

* *(n)= noun;   (v)= verb*

1) General business-related terms

accounting	회계	hway-gye
additional charge	추가료	chu-ga-ryo
advertise	광고, 광고하다	gwang-go (n), gwang-go ha-da (v)
bankrupt	파산	pa-san (n)
brand name	상표	sang-pyo
business	사업	sa-eop
buyer	구매자	gu-mae-ja

English	Korean	Phonetic Representation
capital	자본	ja-bon
cash	현금	hyeon-geum
charge	요금	yo-geum
check	수표	su-pyo
claim	청구	cheong-gu
collect	징수, 수금	jing-su, su-geum
commission	수수료, 중개료	su-su-ryo, jung-gae-ryo
company	회사	hway-sa
copyright	판권	pan-kweon,
corporation	법인 회사	beob-in hway-sa
cost	경비	gyeong-bi
currency	통화, 화폐	tong-hwa, hwa-pye
customer	고객	go-gaek
D/A (documents against acceptance)	영수 증서	yeong-su jeung-seo
D/P (documents against payment)	지불 증서	ji-bul jeung-seo
deferred payment	유예 지불, 거치 지불	yu-ye ji-bul, geo-chi ji-bul
deposit (n)	예금	ye-geum
design	계획, 설계	gye-hwayk (plan or arrangement), seol-gye (specifications or draft)
discount	할인	ha-rin
distribution	판매, 배급	pan-mae (sell), bae-geup (distribution)
dividends	배당, 배당금, 배당율	bae-dang, bae-dang-geum, bae-dang-yul
documents	서류	seo-ryu
due date	지급 기일	ji-geup gi-il
exhibit	전시	jeon-shi
ex works	현장 인도, 공장도	hyeon-jang in-do, gong-jang-do
facsimile (fax)	팩스	paek-seu
finance	재정	jae-jeong
foreign businessman	외국인 사업가	way-gug-in sa-eop-ga
foreign capital	외국 자본	way-gug ja-bon
foreign currency	외국 화폐	way-gug hwa-pye
foreign trade	외국 무역	way-gug mu-yeok
government	정부	jeong-bu

English	Korean	Phonetic Representation
industry	산업	san- eop
inspection	검사	geom-sa
insurance	보험	bo-heom
interest	이자	i-ja
international	국제적	guk-je-jeok
joint venture	공동 사업체	gong-dong sa-eop-che
label	상표	sang-pyo
letter of credit	신용장	shin-yong-jang
license	면허	myeon-heo
loan	대부	dae-bu
model (of a product)	모형	mo-hyeong
monopoly	독점, 전매	dok-jeom, jeon-mae
office	사무실	sa-mu-shil
patent	특허권	teuk-heo-kweon
pay (v)	지불하다	ji-bul ha-da
payment for goods	물품에 대한 지불	mul-pum-e dae-han ji-bul
payment by installment	분할 지불	bun-hal ji-bul
permit	허가, 인가	heo-ga, in-ga
principal	원금	weon-geum
private (not government)	개인	gae-in
product	생산품, 제품	saeng-san-pum, je-pum
profit margin	이윤 폭	i-yun pok
registration	등록	deung-nok
report	보고 , 보도	bo-go, bo-do
research and development (R&D)	연구 개발	yeon-gu gae-bal
return (on investment)	수익	su-ik
sample	견본	gyeon-bon
seller	판매자	pan-mae-ja
settle accounts	액수를 결정하다, 계산을 치르다	aek-su-reul gyeol-jeong ha-da, gye-sa-neul chi-reu-da
service charge	봉사료	bong-sa-ryo
sight draft	일람불 어음	il-lam-bul eo-eum
tax	세금	se-geum
telephone	전화	jeon-hwa
telex	텔렉스	tel-lek-seu

English	Korean	Phonetic Representation
trademark	상표 , 상호	sang-pyo (logo), sang-ho (brand name)
visa	비자	bi-ja

2)   Labor

compensation	급료	geub-nyo
employee	고용인	go-yong-in
employer	고용주	go-yong-ju
fire, dismiss (v)	해고하다	hae-go ha-da
foreign worker	외국인 고용인	way-gug-in go-yong-in
hire (v)	임대하다, 고용하다	im-dae ha-da (things), go-yong ha-da (person)
immigration	이민	i-min
interview	면담, 회견	myeon-dam (between individuals), hway-gyeon (public audience)
laborer:	노동자	no-dong-ja
skilled	숙련	sung-nyeon
unskilled	미숙련	mi-sung-nyeon
labor force	노동력	no-dong-nyeok
labor shortage	노동력 부족	no-dong-nyeok bu-jok
labor stoppage	작업 중단	ja-geop jung-dan
labor surplus	잉여 노동력	ing-yeo no-dong-nyeok
minimum wage	최저 임금	choe-jeo im-geum
profession/occupation	직업	ji-geop
salary	봉급	bong-geup
strike	동맹 파업	dong-maeng pa-eop
training	훈련	hul-lyeon
union	조합	jo-hap
wage	임금	im-geum

3) Negotiations (Buying/Selling)

agreement	계약, 동의	gye-yak (contract), dong-eui (consent)
arbitrate	중재	jung-jae
brochure, pamphlet	소책자, 팜플렛	so-chaek-ja, pam-peul-let
buy (v)	구매하다	gu-mae ha-da
confirm (v)	확인하다	hwa-gin ha-da
contract	계약	gye-yak

English	Korean	Phonetic Representation
cooperate(v)	협조하다	hyeob-jo ha-da
cost	원가	weon-ka
counteroffer	수정 제의	su-jeong je-eui
countersign	암호	am-ho
deadline	한계선	han-gye-seon
demand (n)	청구, 요구	cheong-gu, yo-gu
(v)	청구하다, 요구하다	cheong-gu ha-da, yo-gu ha-da
estimate (v)	평가하다	pyeong-ka ha-da
guarantee (v)	보증하다	bo-jeung ha-da
label	상표	sang-pyo
license	면허	myeon-heo
market	시장	shi-jang
market price	시가, 시세	shi-ka, shi-se
minimum quantity	최저 양	choe-jeo yang
negotiate (v)	협상하다	hyeop-sang ha-da
negotiate payment	협상 지불 가격	hyeop-sang ji-bul ga-gyeok
order	주문	ju-mun
packaging	포장	po-jang
place an order	주문을 하다	ju-mun-eul ha-da
price	가격	ga-gyeok
price list	가격표	ga-gyeok-pyo
product features	제품 외형, 제품 특징	je-pum way-hyeong (shape), je-pum teuk-jing (characteristics)
product line	제품 종목	je-pum jong-mok
quality	품질	pum-jil
quantity	양, 분량	yang, bul-lyang
quota	몫, 할당액	mok, hal-tang-aek
quote (offer)	가격을 내다, 견적을 내다	ga-gyeok-eul nae-da (offer the price), gyeon-jyeok-eul nae-da (quote the specifications)
sale	판매	pan-mae
sales confirmation	판매 확인	pan-mae hwa-gin
sell	팔다, 판매하다	pal-da, pan-mae ha-da
sign	서명하다	seo-myeong ha-da
specifications	내역, 명세서	nae-yeok, myeong-se-seo
standard (quality)	표준품	pyo-jun-pum

English	Korean	Phonetic Representation
superior (quality)	우량품	u-ryang-pum
trade (n)	무역, 거래	mu-yeok (trade), geo-rae (deal)
(v)	무역하다, 거래하다	mu-yeok ha-da (trade), geo-rae ha-da (deal)
unit price	단가	dan-ka
value	가치	ga-chi
value added	부가 가치	bu-ga ga-chi
warranty (and services)	보증 (및 아프터 서비스)	bo-jeung (mit a-peu-teo sseo-bi-seu)
The price is too high.	가격이 너무 비쌉니다.	ga-gyeo-gi neo-mu bi-ssam-ni-da.
We need a faster delivery.	더 신속한 배달을 원합니다.	deoh shin-sok-han bae-da-reul weon-ham-ni-da.
We need it by (tomorrow).	(내일) 까지 필요합니다.	(nae-il)-ka-ji pi-ryo ham-ni-da.
We need a better quality.	품질이 더 좋은 것을 원합니다.	pum-ji-ri deoh jo-eun-geo-seul weon-ham-ni-da.
We need it to these specifications.	이러한 내역으로 해주십시요.	i-reo-han nae-yeo-geu-ro hae-chu-ship-shi-yo.
I want to pay less.	가격을 좀 할인 해주십시요.	ga-gyeo-geul jom ha-rin hae-ju-ship-shi-yo.
I want the price to include ( ).	( )이 가격 속에 포함 되기를 원합니다.	( )-i ga-gyeok so-ge po-ham dway-gi-reul weon-ham-ni-da.
Can you guarantee delivery?	배달을 보증할 수 있습니까?	bae-da-reul bo-jeung-hal su i-sseum-ni-ka?

4) Products/Industries

English	Korean	Phonetic Representation
aluminum	알루미늄	al-lu-mi-nyum
automobile	자동차	ja-dong-cha
automotive accessories	자동차 부속물	ja-dong-cha bu-song-mul
biotechnology	생물공학	saeng-mul-gong-hak
camera	카메라	ka-me-ra
carpets	융단	yung-dan
cement	시멘트	shi-men-teu
ceramics	도자기	do-ja-gi
chemicals	화학약품	hwa-hak yak-pum
clothing:	옷	ot
for women	여성용	yeo-seong yong
for men	남성용	nam-seong yong
for children	어린이용	eo-ri-ni yong

English	Korean	Phonetic Representation
coal	석탄	seok-tan
computer	컴퓨터	keom-pyu-teo
computer hardware	컴퓨터 기계	keom-pyu-teo gi-gye
computer software	컴퓨터 소프트웨어	keom-pyu-teo so-peu-teu way-eo
construction	건축	geon-chuk
electrical equipment	전기 장치	jeon-gi jang-chi
minerals	광물	gwang-mul
musical instruments	악기	ak-gi
paper	종이	jong-i
petroleum	석유	seo-gyu
pharmaceuticals	조제품	jo-je-pum
plastics	플라스틱	(like English 'plastic')
pottery	도기	do-gi
rubber	고무	go-mu
silk	비단	bi-dan
silver	은	eun
spare parts	여분	yeo-bun
sporting goods	운동구	un-dong-gu
steel	강철	gang-cheol
telecommunication equipment	원격 통신 장치, 텔레콤 장치	won-gyeok tong-shin jang-chi, te-le-com (like English ' Telecom') jang-chi
television	텔레비젼	te-le-bi-jyeon
textiles	직물	jing-mul
tobacco	담배	dam-bae
tools:	도구	doh-gu
hand-tool	손 도구	son doh-gu
power-tool	전기 도구	jeon-gi doh-gu
tourism	관광 사업	gwan-gwang sa-eop
toys	장난감	jang-nan-kam
watches/clocks	시계	shi-gye
wood	나무	na-mu

5) Services

accounting service	회계 업무	hway-gye eom-mu
advertising agency	광고 대리점	gwang-go dae-ri-jeom

English	Korean	Phonetic Representation
agent	대리인, 대리점	dae-ri-in, dae-ri-jeom
customs broker	세관 화물 취급인, 통관사	se-gwan hwa-mul chwi-geup-in, tong-gwan-sa
distributor	판매인, 배급업자	pan-mae-in (seller), bae-geup-eop-ja (one who distributes)
employment agency	직업 소개소	ji-geop so-gae-so
exporter	수출업자	su-chul-eop-ja
freight forwarder	운송업자	un-song-eop-ja
importer	수입업자	su-ip-eop-ja
manufacturer	제조업자, 제조업체	je-jo-eop-ja, je-jo-eop-che
packing service	포장 업무	po-jang eom-mu
printing company	인쇄소	in-sway-so
retailer	소매업자	so-mae-eop-ja
service(s)	봉사	bong-sa
supplier	공급자	gong-geup-ja
translation services	번역 업무	beon-yeok eom-mu
wholesaler	도매업자	do-mae-eop-ja

6) Shipping/Transportation

English	Korean	Phonetic Representation
bill of lading	선하 증권	seon-ha jeung-kweon
cost, insurance, freight (CIF)	운임 보험료 포함 (씨이 아이 에프)	un-im bo-heom-nyo po-ham (ssi a-i e-peu)
customs	세관	se-gwan
customs duty	관세 제도	gwan-se je-do
date of delivery	수도 일자	su-do il-ja
deliver (delivery)	배달하다 (배달)	bae-dal ha-da (bae-dal)
export (n)	수출	su-chul
(v)	수출하다	su-chul ha-da
first class mail	제 1종 우편	je il-jong u-pyeon
free on board (F.O.B.)	본선도	bon-seon-do
freight	화물 운송	hwa-mul un-song
import	수입	su-ip
in bulk	대량으로, 포장 않은 채로	dae-ryang-euro (in a big quantity), po-jang a-neun-chae-ro (without packing)
mail (post)	우편	u-pyeon

English	*Korean*	*Phonetic Representation*
country of origin	원산지, 원산국	weon-san-ji (place of origin), weon-san-guk (country of origin)
packing	포장	po-jang
packing list	포장 명세서	po-jang myeong-se-seo
port	항구	hang-gu
ship (to send):	싣다, 선적하다	shi-ta (v.: by all transportation), seon-jeok ha-da (by ship only)
by air:	항공편	hang-gong pyeon
by sea:	선편	seon pyeon
by train:	기차편	gi-cha pyeon
by truck:	화물차편, 트럭편	hwa-mul-cha pyeon, teu-reok pyeon

WEIGHTS, MEASURES, AMOUNTS

barrel	통	tong
bushel	부셸	bu-shel
centimeter	센티미터	sen-ti-mi-teo
dozen	다스	da-seu
foot	푸트	put-teu
gallon	갈론	gal-lon
gram	그램	geu-raem
gross (144 pieces)	그로스	geu-ro-seu
gross weight	총 중량	chong jung-nyang
hectare	헥타르	hek-ta-reu
hundred (100)	백	baek
inch	인치	in-chi
kilogram	킬로그램	kilo-geu-raem
meter	미터	mi-teo
net weight	정미 중량	jeong-mi jung-nyang
mile (English)	마일	ma-il
liter	리터	li-teo
ounce	온스	on-seu
pint	파인트	pa-in-teu
pound (weight measure avoirdupois)	파운드	pa-un-deu
quart (avoirdupois)	쿼트	kweo-teu
square meter	평방 미터	pyeong-bang mi-teo

English	Korean	Phonetic Representation
square yard	평방 야드	pyeong-bang ya-deu
size	크기,	keu-gi (general magnitude),
	치수	chi-su (units)
ton	톤	ton
yard	야드	ya-deu

KOREA-SPECIFIC ORGANIZATIONAL TITLES

board of directors	이사회, 중역회	i-sa-hway, jung-yeok-hway
chairman	의장	eui-jang
manager	지배인, 간사	ji-bae-in, gan-sa
(assistant manager)	부지배인, 보조 간사	bu-ji-bae-in, bo-jo gan-sa
president	사장	sa-jang
(vice president)	부사장	bu-sa-jang

COMMON SIGNS

Entrance	입구	ip-gu
Exit	출구	chul-gu
Man	남성	nam-seong
Woman	여성	yeo-seong
Up	위	wi
Down	아래	a-rae

KOREAN-SPECIFIC EXPRESSIONS AND TERMS

Greetings

Hello (on the phone)	여보세요.	yeo-bo-se-yo.
How do you do?	처음 뵙겠습니다.	cheo-eum bwayb-ge-sseum-ni-da.
See you later.	나중에 뵙겠습니다.	na-jung-e bwayb-ge-sseum-ni-da.
Are you ill?	편찮으십니까?	pyeon-cha-neu-shim-ni-ka?
How are you doing?	어떻게 지내십니까?	eo-teo-ke ji-nae-shim-ni-ka?
How is your business going?	사업이 잘 되십니까?	sa-eo-bi jal dway-shim-ni-ka?
The weather is good.	날씨가 좋습니다.	nal-ssi-ga jo-sseum-ni-da.
The weather is bad.	날씨가 나쁩니다.	nal-ssi-ga nab-beum-ni-da.
I like your dress.	옷이 잘 어울립니다.	o-shi a-ju jal eo-ul-lim-ni-da.
You look very handsome (pretty).	아주 멋있게 보입니다.	a-ju meo-shik-ke bo-im-ni-da.

English	Korean	Phonetic Representation

Asking for favors

English	Korean	Phonetic Representation
(Form used when asking for a favor.)	부탁합니다.	bu-tak ham-ni-da.
Excuse me (when interrupting or seeking attention.)	잠깐만요.	jam-kan-man-yo.
I am sorry.	미안합니다.	mi-an ham-ni-da.

Forms of thanks

English	Korean	Phonetic Representation
Thanks (general)	감사합니다.	gam-sa ham-ni-da.
- before a meal:		
(said by person who was invited for a meal)	잘 먹겠습니다.	jal meok-ge-sseum-ni-da.
(person who gave the invitation)	많이 드십시요.	ma-ni deu-ship-shi-yo.
- after a meal:		
(said by person who was invited for a meal)	잘 먹었습니다.	jal meo-geo-sseum-ni-da.
Ginseng tea	인삼차	in-sam cha
European tea	홍차	hong-cha
Radio	라디오	ra-di-o
Meal	식사	shik-sa
Food	음식	eum-shik
Soccer	축구	chuk-gu
American football	미식 축구	mi-shik chuk-gu
Baseball	야구	ya-gu
Stars and Stripes (American Flag)	성조기	seong-jo-gi

Important Addresses

GOVERNMENT

GOVERNMENT AGENCIES

Customs Administration
71, Nonhyun-dong, Kangnam-gu
Seoul 135-00
Tel: (2) 542-7141 Tlx: 24346, 24716

Economic Planning Board
1, Jungang-dong
Gwachon City, Kyonggi Province
Tel: (2) 503-9020 Fax: (2) 503-9033
Tlx: 23202

Fisheries Administration
541, 5-ga Namdaemun-no, Chung-ku
Seoul
Tel: (2) 777-8271 Tlx: 24719

Forestry Administration
207, Chongyangni 2-dong, Tongdaemun-ku
Seoul
Tel: (2) 961-2114

Inchon Maritime & Port Authority
1-17, 7-ga, Hang-dong, Chung-ku
Inchon 160
Tel: (32) 883-4061

Industrial Advancement Administration (IAA)
2, Jungang-dong
Gwachon City, Kyonggi Province
Tel: (2) 503-7950/9
Bureau of Standards
Tel: (2) 503-7928

Industrial Property Administration
58-3 Socho-dong, Kangnam-ku
Seoul
Tel: (2) 568-5830/2, 568-8151

Korea Maritime & Port Authority
112-2, Inui-dong, Chongno-ku
Seoul 110
Tel: (2) 744-4030

Korean Overseas Information Services
82-1, Sejong-no, Chongno-ku
Seoul
Tel: (2) 720-4817, 739-4481, 739-4483 Tlx: 23203

All addresses and telephone numbers are in South Korea unless otherwise noted. The country code for South Korea is [82].

Ministry of Agriculture, Forestry and Fisheries
1, Jungang-dong
Gwachon City, Kyonggi Province
Tel: (2) 503-7209, 503-7208 Tlx: 24759

Ministry of Communications
100, Sejong-no, Chongno-ku
Seoul 110-777
Tel: (2) 750-2811, 750-2800 Tlx: 24819

Ministry of Construction
1, Jungang-dong
Gwachon City, Kyonggi Province
Tel: (2) 503-7312 Fax: (2) 503-7409 Tlx: 24755

Ministry of Culture
82-1, Sejong-no, Chongno-ku
Seoul 100-050
Tel: (2) 736-7946 Fax: (2) 736-8513 Tlx: 23203

Ministry of Education
77, Sejong-no, Chongno-ku
Seoul 110-760
Tel: (2) 720-3053, 720-3570 Fax: (2) 736-3402
Tlx: 24758

Ministry of Energy and Resources
1, Jungang-dong
Gwachon City, Kyonggi Province
Tel: (2) 503-9611, 503-9605 Tlx: 23472

Ministry of Finance
1, Jungang-dong
Gwachon City, Kyonggi Province
Tel: (2) 503-9211, 503-9206 Fax: (2) 503-9324
Tlx: 23243
Foreign Investment Advice Office
Tel: (2) 503-7171
Foreign Investment Information Center
Tel: (2) 503-9259
Foreign Investment Promotion Division I
Tel: (2) 503-9276
One-Stop Service Office
Tel: (2) 503-9258

Ministry of Foreign Affairs
77, Sejong-no, Chongno-ku
Seoul
Tel: (2) 720-2687, 738-9601 Tlx: 24651

Ministry of Government Administration
77-6, Sejong-no, Chongno-ku
Seoul
Tel: (2) 720-4351 Tlx: 24803

Ministry of Health & Social Affairs
1, Jungang-dong
Gwachon City, Kyonggi Province
Tel: (2) 503-7524, 503-7504 Fax: (2) 503-7505
Tlx: 23230

Ministry of Home Affairs
77, Sejong-no, Chongno-ku
Seoul
Tel: (2) 731-2121 Tlx: 24756

Ministry of Justice
1, Jungang-dong
Gwachon City, Kyonggi Province
Tel: (2) 503-7012 Fax: (2) 504-3337 Tlx: 24757

Ministry of Labor
1, Jungang-dong
Gwachon City, Kyonggi Province
Tel: (2) 503-9700 Fax: (2) 503-9771 Tlx: 24718

Ministry of National Defense
101, Huam-dong, Yongsan-ku
Seoul
Tel: (2) 754-3843

Ministry of Public Information
82-1, Sejong-no, Chongno-ku
Seoul 110-050
Tel: (2) 720-4728, 720-1456 Tlx: 23203

Ministry of Science and Technology
1, Jungang-dong
Gwachon City, Kyonggi Province
Tel: (2) 503-7609 Fax: (2) 503-7673 Tlx: 24230

Ministry of Sports and Youth
77, Sejong-no, Chongno-ku
Seoul
Tel: (2) 734-5283, 720-2181 Tlx: 22926

Ministry of the Environment
7-16, Sincheon-dong, Songpa-ku
Seoul
Tel: (2) 421-0217, 422-0282, 423-0282
Fax: (2) 421-0280

Ministry of Trade and Industry
1, Jungang-dong
Gwachon City, Kyonggi Province
Tel: (2) 503-9405 Fax: (2) 503-9496 Tlx: 24478

Ministry of Trade and Industry
Consultation Office for Overseas Companies
Rm. 524, Bldg. 3, Govt. Complex II
Gwachon City, Kyonggi Province
Tel: (2) 500-2539, 507-2152 Fax: (2) 503-9655

Ministry of Transportation
168, 2-ka, Bongnae-dong, Chung-ku
Seoul
Tel: (2) 392-9801, 392-7606 Fax: (2) 392-9809
Tlx: 24778

Ministry of Transportation
Maritime and Port Administration
112-2, Inui-dong, Chongno-ku
Seoul
Tel: (2) 774-4030 Tlx: 26528 HANGMAN

Ministry of Transportation
National Railroad Administration
168 2-ga, Pongnai-dong, Chung-ku
Seoul
Tel: (2) 392-0078 Tlx: 24802 KHRAIL

National Tax Administration
108-4, Susong-dong, Chongno-ku
Seoul
Tel: (2) 739-6768 Tlx: 24717 ONATAX

Office of Supply of the ROK
520-3, Bangpo-dong, Kangnam-gu
Seoul, Rep. of Korea
Tel: (2) 533-9656 Tlx: OSROK K23244, 23703

Pusan Maritime & Port Authority
1116-1, Jwachun-dong, Dong-ku
Pusan
Tel: (51) 633-2620 Tlx: 3371

Taedok Science Town Administration Office
386-3, Toryong-dong, Yusung-gu
Taejon 305-340
Tel: (42) 861-5005/6 Fax: (42) 861-1276

OVERSEAS DIPLOMATIC MISSIONS
OF THE REPUBLIC OF KOREA

Argentina
Embassy
Av. Libertador 2257
1425 Buenos Aires, Argentina
Tel: [54] (1) 802-8865, 805-9665

Australia
Embassy
113 Empire Circuit
Yarralumla, ACT 2600, Australia
Tel: [61] (62) 273-3044

Consulate General (Sydney)
Level 8, Challenge Bank
32-26, Martin Place
Sydney, NSW 2000, Australia
Tel: [61] (2) 221-3866, 221-3697

Austria
Embassy
Prater Str. 31
1020 Wein, Austria
Tel: [43] (1) 2163441/5, 2163438

Belgium
Embassy
Avenue Hamoir 3
1180 Brussels, Belgium
Tel: [32] (2) 375-3980

Brazil
Embassy
Sen-Av. Das Nocoes, Lote 14
70436 Brasilia DF, Brazil
Tel: [55] (61) 223-3466, 223-3977, 223-3807

Canada
Embassy
151 Slater St., 5/F.
Ottawa, ON K1P 5H3, Canada
Tel: [1] (613) 232-1715/7

Consulate General (Montreal)
1000 Sherbrooke St. West, Suite 1710
Montreal, PQ H3A 3G4, Canada
Tel: [1] (514) 845-3243/4

Consulate General (Toronto)
555 Avenue Rd.
Toronto, ON M4V 2J7, Canada
Tel: [1] (416) 920-3809

Consulate General (Vancouver)
830-1066 West Hastings St.
Vancouver, BC V6E 3X1, Canada
Tel: [1] (604) 681-9581/2

Chile
Embassy
Av. Alcantara 74
Las Condes, Santiago, Chile
Tel: [56] (2) 2284214, 2284997

China
Embassy
3-4/F., China World Trade Center
1 Jian Guo Men Wai Ave.
Beijing, PRC
Tel: [86] (1) 505-3171, 505-2586, 505-2573
Fax: [86] (1) 505-3067

Consulate General (Shanghai)
4/F., Shanghai International Trade Center
2200 Yan An Rd. (W)
Shanghai, PRC
Tel: [86] (21) 2196917, 2196921

Colombia
Embassy
Calle 94 No. 9-39
Bogóta DC, Colombia
Tel: [57] (1) 236-1616, 236-2028, 236-9299

Costa Rica
Embassy
Calle 28, Avenida 2, Apdo 3150
Barrio San Bosco, paseo Colon
San José, Costa Rica
Tel: [506] 203160, 212398

Denmark
Embassy
Svanemøllevej 104
2900 Hellerup, Denmark
Tel: [45] 39-40-12-33 Fax: [45] 39-40-18-18

Dominican Republic
Embassy
Avenida Sarasota No. 98
Santo Domingo DN, Republica Dominicana
Tel: [1] (809) 532-4314/5, 533-8365 Tlx: 4368

Ecuador
Embassy
Calle Reina Victoria 1539 y Av. Colon
Edif. Banco de Guayaquil 11 Piso
Quito, Ecuador
Tel: [593] (2) 528-553, 524-991, 560-573 Tlx: 2868

Egypt
Consulate General
3 & 5 Boulos Hannastreet, Dokki
Cairo, Arab Republic of Egypt
Tel: [20] (2) 3611234

Finland
Embassy
Annankatu 32A
00100 Helsinki, Finland
Tel: [358] (0) 6940966

France
Embassy
125 rue de Grenelle
75007 Paris, France
Tel: [33] (1) 47-53-01-01

All addresses and telephone numbers are in South Korea unless otherwise noted. The country code for South Korea is [82].

Germany
Embassy
Adenauerallee 124
5300 Bonn 1, Germany
Tel: [49] (228) 267960

Consulate General (Berlin)
Kurfuers Tendamm 180
10707 Berlin 33, Germany
Tel: [49] (30) 8859550

Consulate General (Frankfurt)
Escherscheimer-Landstr. 327
6000 Frankfurt am Main 1, Germany
Tel: [49] (69) 563051/3

Consulate General (Hamburg)
Hagedom Str. 53
2 Hamburg 13, Germany
Tel: [49] (40) 4102031/2

Greece
Embassy
Odos Eratosthenous 1, 6/F.
GR-11635 Athens, Greece
Tel: [30] (1) 7012122, 7514382, 7016997

Guatemala
Embassy
Avenida Reforma 1-15, Zona 9
Edif. el Reformador 7 Nivel
Guatemala City, Guatemala
Tel: [502] 321578, 347045

Hong Kong
Consulate General
5-6/F., Far East Finance Center
16 Harcourt Rd.
Central, Hong Kong
Tel: [852] 5294141

Hungary
Embassy
Andrassy Ut. 109
1063 Budapest, Hungary
Tel: [36] (1) 268-0456/8

India
Embassy
9 Chandragupta Marg. Chanakyapuri Ext.
New Delhi 110 021, India
Tel: [91] (11) 6885374/6, 6885412, 6885419

Indonesia
Embassy
57, Jalan Gatot Subroto
Jakarta Selatan, Indonesia
Tel: [62] (21) 5201915 Tlx: 62204

Ireland
Embassy
20 Clyde Rd., Ballsbridge
Dublin 4, Ireland
Tel: [353] (1) 6608800 Tlx: 91776

Italy
Embassy
Via Barnaba Oriani 3
00197 Rome, Italy
Tel: [39] (6) 808-8769, 808-8820/1

Jamaica
Embassy
2/F., Pan-Jamaican Bldg.
60 Knutsford Boulevard
Kingston 5, Jamaica, West Indies
Tel: [1] (809) 9293035, 9278395 Tlx: 2491

Japan
Embassy
2-5, Minami-Azabu, 1-chome, Minato-ku
Tokyo, Japan
Tel: [81] (3) 3452-7611/9

Consulate General (Fukuoka)
29-7, 1-chome, Jigyohama, Chuo-ku
Fukuoka, Japan
Tel: [81] (92) 751-7034

Consulate General (Kobe)
2-21-5 Nakayamate-Dori, Chuo-ku
Kobe, Japan
Tel: [81] (78) 221-4853/5

Consulate General (Nagoya)
9-25, Higashi Ozone-cho, Higashi-ku
Nagoya, Japan
Tel: [81] (52) 935-9221

Consulate General (Osaka)
2-3-4, Nishi-Shinsaibashi, Chuo-ku
Osaka, Japan
Tel: [81] (6) 213-1401, 213-1410

Consulate General (Sapporo)
Kita 3-cho, Nisi 21-chome, Chuo-ku
Sapporo, Japan
Tel: [81] (11) 621-0288/9

Consulate General (Sendai)
5-22, Kamisugi, 5-chome
Sendai, Japan
Tel: [81] (22) 221-2751/4, 265-7820

Malaysia
Embassy
Wisma MCA, 22/F.
163 Jalan Ampang
50400 Kuala Lumpur, Malaysia
Tel: [60] (3) 262-2377, 262-1385

Mexico
Embassy
Lope de Armendáriz Nom. 110
Col. Lomas de Chapultepec
11000 México City, D.F., Mexico
Tel: [52] (5) 202-9866, 596-7131

Morocco
Embassy
41 Avenue Bani Iznassen, Souissi
Rabat, Morocco
Tel: [212] (7) 7151767, 7151966

Netherlands
Embassy
Verlengde Tolweg 8
2517 JV The Hague, Netherlands
Tel: [31] (70) 3520621

New Zealand
Embassy
86-96 Victoria St., 6/F.
Wellington, New Zealand
Tel: [64] (4) 473-9073/4, 473-9376

Nigeria
Embassy
Plot 934, Idejo St., Victoria Island
Lagos, Nigeria
Tel: [234] (1) 615353, 617262

Norway
Embassy
Inkognitogaten 3
0224 Oslo 2, Norway
Tel: [47] (2) 2552018/9, 2436385

Pakistan
Embassy
72 Main Margallah Rd. F-6/2
Islamabad, Pakistan
Tel: [92] (51) 824926/9, 924920 Tlx: 5720

Panama
Embassy
Calle Ricardo Arias 51E, Compo Alegre
Edifico Plaza, Planta Baja
Apartado 8096
Zona 7 Panama City, Republic of Panama
Tel: [507] 64-8203, 64-8360

Paraguay
Embassy
Mcal. Lopez 486
C/Peru, Asunción, Paraguay
Tel: [595] (21) 26-256, 27-556,

Peru
Embassy
Av. Principal 190, Piso 7, La Victoria
Lima 13, Peru
Tel: [51] (14) 70-4201/7 Tlx: 25539

Philippines
Embassy
ALPAP 1 Bldg., 140 Alfaro St.
Salcedo Village, Makati
Metro Manila, Phillipines
Tel: [63] (2) 817-5703/5/8 Tlx: 22426

Poland
Embassy
ul. Ignacego Krasickiego 25
02-611 Warsaw, Poland
Tel: [48] (2) 4833337 Tlx: 817069

Portugal
Embassy
Av. Miguel Bombarda, Piso 36-7
1000 Lisbon, Portugal
Tel: [351] (1) 793-7200/3

Romania
Embassy
Mircea Eliadeno Blvd. No. 14
Bucharest, Romania
Tel: [40] (1) 6146294

Russia
Embassy
ul. Alexeya Tolstova 14
Moscow, Russian Federation
Tel: [7] (95) 203-3850, 203-8018
Fax: [7] (95) 202-7466

Saudi Arabia
Embassy
PO Box 94399
Riyadh 11693, Saudi Arabia
Tel: [966] (1) 4882211

Singapore
Embassy
101 Thomson Rd. #10-02/04 & 13-05
United Sq.
Singapore 1130
Tel: [65] 2561188

South Africa
Embassy
PO Box 11056
Brooklyn 0011, Rep. of South Africa
Tel: [27] (11) 342-3401/2

Spain
Embassy
Miguel Angel 23
28010 Madrid, Spain
Tel: [34] (1) 4100053, 4100349

Consulate General (Barcelona)
Paseo de Gracia 85, 9°
08008 Barcelona, Spain
Tel: [34] (3) 215-2063, 215-2180

Sweden
Embassy
Sveavägen 90
PO Box 45-220
104-30 Stockholm, Sweden
Tel: [46] (8) 16-04-80/4

Switzerland
Embassy
Kalcheggweg 38
3006 Bern, Switzerland
Tel: [41] (31) 431081/2

Taiwan
Trade Representative Office
Rm. 1506, Trade Bldg.
333, Keelung Rd.
Sec. 1, Taipei, Taiwan
Tel: [886] (2) 758-8320

Thailand
Embassy
23 Thirmruammit Rd.
Ratchadapisek Huay-Kwang
Bangkok 10310, Thailand
Tel: [66] (2) 247-7537, 247-7549

Turkey
Embassy
Cinnah Caddesi Alacam Sokak
No. 5 Cancaya
06690 Ankara, Turkey
Tel: [90] (4) 4684822

All addresses and telephone numbers are in South Korea unless otherwise noted. The country code for South Korea is [82].

United Arab Emirates
Embassy
PO Box 3270
Abu Dhabi, UAE
Tel: [971] (2) 338337 Fax: [971] (2) 345348

United Kingdom
Embassy
4 Palace Gate
London W8 5NF, UK
Tel: [44] (71) 581-0247/9

United States of America
Embassy
2370 Massachusetts Ave. NW
Washington, DC 20008, USA
Tel: [1] (202) 939-5600

Consulate General (Anchorage)
101 Benson Blvd., Suite 304
Anchorage, AK 99503, USA
Tel: [1] (907) 561-5488, 561-4111

Consulate General (Atlanta)
229 Peachtree St., Cain Tower, Suite 500
Atlanta, GA 30303, USA
Tel: [1] (404) 522-1611/3

Consulate General (Boston)
1 Financial Center, 15/F.
Boston, MA 02111, USA
Tel: [1] (617) 348-3660

Consulate General (Chicago)
455 North Cityfront Plaza Drive
NBC Tower, 27/F.
Chicago, IL 60611, USA
Tel: [1] (312) 822-9485/8

Consulate General (Honolulu)
2756 Pali Highway
Honolulu, HI 96817, USA
Tel: [1] (808) 595-6109, 595-6274

Consulate General (Houston)
1990 Post Oak Blvd., Suite 1250
Houston, TX 77056
Tel: [1] (713) 961-0186, 961-0798

Consulate General (Los Angeles)
3243 Wilshire Blvd.
Los Angeles, CA 90010, USA
Tel: [1] (213) 385-9300

Consulate General (Miami)
Suite 800, Miami Center 201
South Biscayne Blvd.
Miami, FL 33131, USA
Tel: [1] (305) 372-1555

Consulate General (New York)
460 Park Avenue, 5/F.
New York, NY 10022, USA
Tel: [1] (212) 752-1700

Consulate General (San Francisco)
3500 Clay St.
San Francisco, CA 94118, USA
Tel: [1] (415) 921-2251/3

Consulate General (Seattle)
Suite 1125, United Airline Bldg.
2033 Sixth Avenue
Seattle, WA 98121, USA
Tel: [1] (206) 441-1011/4 Tlx: 240020

Uruguay
Embassy
Jaime Zudáñez 2836, Apdo 1001
Montevideo, Uruguay
Tel: [598] (2) 70-99-96, 70-95-34 Tlx: 22343

Venezuela
Embassy
Edificio Atrium, Piso 3 Av.
Sorocaima Con Av.
El Rosal Caracas, Venezuela
Tel: [58] (2) 952-3456, 952-5505, 952-5121

FOREIGN DIPLOMATIC MISSIONS IN THE REPUBLIC OF KOREA

Argentina
Embassy
135-53 Itaewon-dong, Yongsan-ku
Seoul
Tel: (2) 793-4062 Fax: (2) 792-5820 Tlx: 24329

Australia
Kyobo Bldg., 11/F.
1-1, Chongno 1-ka, Chongno-ku
Seoul
Tel: (2) 730-6490/1 Fax: (2) 734-5085 Tlx: 23663

Austria
Embassy
Kyobo Bldg., 19/F.
Chongno, Chongno-ku
Seoul 110-714
Tel: (2) 732-9071 Fax: (2) 732-9486 Tlx: 23663

Consulate
Ssangyong Bldg., 15/F.
24-1, Juhdong 2-ka, Choong-ku
Seoul
Tel: (2) 266-6550 Tlx: 27233

Belgium
Embassy
1-65, Dongbinggo-dong, Yongsan-ku
Seoul 140-230
Tel: (2) 797-7517 Fax: (2) 797-1688 Tlx: 27551

Brazil
Embassy
Kum Jung Bldg. 301-6
192-11, 1-ka, Ulchiro, Chung-ku
Seoul
Tel: (2) 776-4717 Fax: (2) 752-2180 Tlx: 27349

Canada
Embassy
Kolon Bldg., 10/F.
45 Mugyo-dong, Jung-ku
Seoul 100-170
Tel: (2) 735-2605 Fax: (2) 755-0686 Tlx: 27425

Chile
Embassy
Youngpoong Bldg., 9/F.
142 Nonhyun-dong, Kangnam-ku
Seoul
Tel: (2) 549-1654 Fax: (2) 549-1656 Tlx: 28495

Colombia
Embassy
House 125, Namsan Village
Itaewon-dong, Yongsan-ku
Seoul
Tel: (2) 793-1369 Tlx: 34447

Costa Rica
Embassy
House 133, Namsan Village
Itaewon-dong, Yongsan-ku
Seoul
Tel: (2) 793-0652

Denmark
Embassy
Namsong Bldg., Suite 701
260-199 Namsan Kwankwang Rd.
Itaewon-dong, Yongsan-ku
Seoul
Tel: (2) 795-4187/9 Fax: (2) 796-0986 Tlx: 23497

Consulate (Pusan)
306-2, Amnam-dong, Seo-ku
Pusan 600-606
Tel: (51) 244-4849 Fax: (51) 244-2691 Tlx: 53115

Dominican Republic
Embassy
1803 Garden Tower Bldg.
98-78 Wooni-dong, Chongro-ku
Seoul 110-350
Tel: (2) 744-1803

Ecuador
Embassy
133-20 Itaewon-dong, Yongsan-ku
Seoul
Tel: (2) 795-1278

Finland
Embassy
Kyobo Bldg., Suite 1602
1-1, 1-ka Chongro, Chongro-ku
Seoul
Postal add: PO Box 1518, Seoul 110-615
Tel: (2) 732-6223 Fax: (2) 737-3107 Tlx: 24343

Consulate
c/o Kyungbang Ltd.
Seoul 100-607
Tel: (2) 678-5241 Tlx: 24273

Consulate
c/o Jindo Industries Co. Ltd.
Jindo Bldg., 3/F.
37 Dohwa-dong, Mapo-ku
Seoul 121-040
Tel: (2) 719-2045 Fax: (2) 701-0254 Tlx: 26541

France
Embassy
30 Hap-dong, Seodaemun-ku
Seoul
Tel: (2) 312-3272 Tlx: 27368

Germany
Embassy
Daehan Fire and Marine Insurance Bldg., 4/F.
51-1 Namchang-dong, Chung-ku
Seoul 100-060
Postal add: PO Box 1289, Seoul
Tel: (2) 726-7114 Fax: (2) 726-7141 Tlx: 23620

Consulate (Pusan)
U-I-dong, 956-45, Haeundae-ku
Pusan 612-021
Postal add: PO Box 44, Pusan 612-600
Tel: (51) 742-5929 Fax: (52) 741-5920

Guatemala
Embassy
B-1116, Namsan Village
Itaewon-dong, Yongsan-ku
Seoul
Tel: (2) 793-1319

Hungary
Embassy
1-103 Dongbinggo-dong, Yongsan-ku
Seoul 140-230
Tel: (2) 792-2105 Fax: (2) 792-2109 Tlx: 24968

Commercial Office
9/F., Chang Wha Bldg.
1-1, 5-ka, Namdaemunro, Chung-ku
Seoul
Tel: (2) 752-1626 Fax: (2) 797-2110 Tlx: 24794

India
Embassy
37-3 Hannam-dong, Yongsan-ku
Seoul
Tel: (2) 798-4257 Tlx: 24641

Indonesia
Embassy
55 Yoido-dong, Youngdeungpo-ku
Seoul
Tel: (2) 783-5372 Tlx: 23374

Ireland
Embassy
Daehan Fire and Marine Insurance Bldg.
51-1, Namchang-dong, Chung-ku
Seoul 100-060
Tel: (2) 774-6455 Fax: (2) 774-6458 Tlx: 32611

Italy
Embassy
1-398, Hannam-dong, Yongsan-ku
Seoul 140-210
Tel: (2) 796-0491 Fax: (2) 797-5560 Tlx: 24619

Japan
Embassy
18-11, Chunghak-dong, Chongro-ku
Seoul
Tel: (2) 733-5626 Fax: (2) 734-4528 Tlx: 23687

All addresses and telephone numbers are in South Korea unless otherwise noted. The country code for South Korea is [82].

Consulate-General (Pusan)
1147-11 Choryang-dong, Dong-ku
Pusan
Tel: (51) 465-5101 Fax: (51) 464-1630 Tlx: 53338

Malaysia
Embassy
4-1, Hannam-dong, Yongsan-ku
Seoul 140-210
Tel: (2) 795-9203 Fax: (2) 794-5488 Tlx: 27382

Mexico
Embassy
Hwan-Kyung Bldg., 3/F.
118 Changchung-dong, 1-ka, Chung-ku
Seoul 100-391
Tel: (2) 269-4011 Fax: (2) 742-2682 Tlx: 23553

Commercial Office
642 KCCI Bldg.
45 Namdaemunno 4-ka
Seoul 100-743
Tel: (2) 755-5613

Morocco
Embassy
S-15, UN Village
270-3, Hannam-dong, Yongsan-ku
Seoul
Tel: (2) 793-6249 Fax: (2) 792-8178 Tlx: 22948

Netherlands
Embassy
Kyobo Bldg., 14/F.
1-1, 1-ka, Chongro, Chongro-ku
Seoul
Tel: (2) 737-9514 Fax: (2) 735-1321 Tlx: 23624

New Zealand
Embassy
Rms. 1802-1805, Kyobo Bldg.
1 Chongro 1-ka, Chongro-ku
Seoul
Tel: (2) 730-7794 Fax: (2) 737-4861 Tlx: 27367

Consulate (Pusan)
84-10 Chungang-dong, 4-ka, Chung-ku
Pusan
Tel: (51) 462-5055 Fax: (51) 462-3222

Nigeria
Embassy
158, Hannam-dong, Yongsan-ku
Seoul
Postal add: CPO Box 3754, Seoul
Tel: (2) 797-2370 Fax: (2) 796-1848 Tlx: 24695

Norway
Embassy
124-12, Itaewon-dong, Yongsan-ku
Seoul
Postal add: CPO Box 355, Seoul
Tel: (2) 795-6850 Fax: (2) 798-6072 Tlx: 25155

Pakistan
Embassy
58-1, Shinmun-no, 1-ka, Chongro-ku
Seoul
Tel: (2) 739-4422 Fax: (2) 739-0428 Tlx: 29346

Panama
Embassy
1101 Garden Tower Bldg.
98-78, Wooni-dong, Chongro-ku
Seoul
Tel: (2) 765-0363 Fax: (2) 742-5874

Paraguay
Embassy
B-902, Namsan Village
San 1-139, Itaewon-dong, Yongsan-ku
Seoul
Tel: (2) 794-5553 Fax: (2) 793-8582 Tlx: 22289

Peru
Embassy
House 129, Namsan Village
Itaewon-dong, Yongsan-ku
Seoul 140-202
Tel: (2) 795-2235 Fax: (2) 797-3736 Tlx: 28612

Philippines
Embassy
559-510, Yeoksam-dong, Kangnam-ku
Seoul
Tel: (2) 568-9131

Portugal
Embassy
Citicorp Center Bldg.
89-29, Shinmunno 2-ka, Chongro-ku
Seoul 110-062
Tel: (2) 738-2078 Fax: (2) 738-2077

Russia
Embassy
1001-3, Daechi-dong, Kangnam-gu
Seoul
Tel: (2) 552-7094/5 Fax: (2) 563-3589 Tlx: 29500

Consular Section
c/o Russian Chamber of Commerce & Industry
159 Samsung-dong, Kangnam-ku
Seoul 601
Tel: (2) 554-9674

Saudi Arabia
Embassy
1-112, 2-ka, Shinmun-no, Chongro-ku
Seoul
Tel: (2) 739-0631 Fax: (2) 732-3110 Tlx: 26216

Singapore
Citicorp Center Bldg.
89-29, Shinmun-no 2-ka, Chongno-ku
Seoul 110-062
Tel: (2) 722-0442 Fax: (2) 722-5930

Spain
Embassy
726-52, Hannam-dong, Yongsan-ku
Seoul 140-212
Tel: (2) 794-3581 Fax: (2) 796-8207 Tlx: 25067

Sweden
Embassy
8th Floor, Boyung Bldg.
108-2, Pyung-dong, Chongro-ku
Seoul
Tel: (2) 738-0846 Fax: (2) 733-1317 Tlx: 27231

Switzerland
Embassy
32-10, Songwol-dong, Chongro-ku
Seoul 110
Tel: (2) 739-9511 Fax: (2) 737-9392 Tlx: 27201

Taiwan
Embassy
83, 2-ka, Myung-dong, Chung-ku
Seoul
Tel: (2) 776-2721 Tlx: 27529

Thailand
Embassy
653-7, Hannam-dong, Yongsan-ku
Seoul
Tel: (2) 795-3098 Fax: (2) 798-3448 Tlx: 27906

Turkey
Embassy
726-116, Hannam-dong, Yongsan-ku
Seoul
Tel: (2) 794-0255 Tlx: 26538

United Arab Emirates
Embassy
66, Nonhyun-dong, Kangnam-ku
Seoul
Tel: (2) 540-4032

United Kingdom
Embassy
4, Chung-Dong, Chung-ku
Seoul
Tel: (2) 735-7341 Fax: (2) 733-8368 Tlx: 27320

Consulate (Pusan)
Chairman's Room, 12/F., Yoochang Bldg.
25-2, 4-ka, Chungang-Dong, Chung-ku
Pusan
Postal add: PO Box 75, Pusan
Tel: (51) 463-0041 Tlx: 53323

Uruguay
Embassy
Rm. 1802, Daewoo Center Bldg.
541, Namdaemoon 5-ga, Chung-ku
Seoul
Postal add: PO Box 3155, Seoul
Tel: (2) 753-7893 Fax: (2) 777-4129 Tlx: 28242

United States of America
Embassy
82, Sejong-ro, Chongro-ku
Seoul
Tel. (2) 732-2601 Fax: (2) 738-8845

Consulate (Pusan)
24, 2-ga, Daechung-dong, Chung-ku
Pusan
Tel: (51) 23-7791

Venezuela
Embassy
Garden Tower Bldg., 18/F.
98-78, Wooni-dong, Chongro-ku
Seoul
Postal add: PO Box 10043, Seoul
Tel: (2) 741-0036 Fax: (2) 741-0046 Tlx: 28889

All addresses and telephone numbers are in South Korea unless otherwise noted. The country code for South Korea is [82].

TRADE PROMOTION ORGANIZATIONS

WORLD TRADE CENTER

Korea World Trade Center
159-1, Samsung-dong, Kangnam-ku
Seoul
Tel: (2) 551-5251/2 Fax: (2) 551-5181 Tlx: 24265

GENERAL TRADE ASSOCIATIONS & LOCAL CHAMBERS OF COMMERCE IN KOREA

Andong Chamber of Commerce
139-5, Wunheung-dong, Kyung-buk
Andong
Tel: (571) 2-2643 Fax: (571) 2-6519

Association of Foreign Trading Agents of Korea
(AFTAK)
Dongjin Bldg.
218, Hangangno 2-ga, Yongsan-gu
Seoul
Tel: (2) 792-1581/4 Fax: (2) 785-4373

Customs Friendship Association
62-13, Nonhyon-dong, Kangnam-gu
Seoul
Tel: (2) 544-3032 Fax: (2) 549-8711

Federation of Korean Industries
28-1, Yoido-dong, Yungdungpo-ku
Seoul
Tel: (2) 780-0821 Fax: (2) 784-1640

Federation of Korean Trade Unions (FKTU)
35 Youido-dong, Yongdeungpo-ku
Seoul
Tel: (2) 782-3884 Fax: (2) 784-6396

Korea Chamber of Commerce & Industry
45, 4-ka, Namdaemun-ro, Chung-ku
Seoul
Tel: (2) 316-3114 Fax: (2) 757-9475 Tlx: 25728

Korea Employers' Federation
538, Tohwa-dong, Mapo-gu
Seoul 121-743
Tel: (2) 706-0618 Fax: (2) 706-1059

Korea Export Buying Offices Association
Rm. 3102, KWTC Bldg.
159, Samsung-dong, Kangnam-gu
Seoul
Tel: (2) 551-3195/8

Korean Federation of Small Business
16-2, Youido-dong, Yongdungpo-gu
Seoul
Tel: (2) 785-0010 Fax: (2) 782-0247

Korea Foreign Trade Association
159-1, Samsung-dong, Kangnam-gu
Seoul
Tel: (2) 551-5114 Fax: (2) 551-5100

Korea Institute for Economics & Trade
206-9, Chongnyangi-dong, Tongdaemun-gu
Seoul
Tel: (2) 962-6211/8 Fax: (2) 963-8540

Korea Marketing Association
45, Namdaemunno 4-ga, Chung-gu
Seoul
Tel: (2) 753-5011 Fax: (2) 752-8074

Korea Overseas Development Corporation
128, Yongon-dong, Chongno-gu
Seoul
Tel: (2) 764-0161/6 Fax: (2) 744-1092

Korea Productivity Center
122-1, Chockson-dong, Chongno-gu
Seoul
Tel: (2) 739-5868 Fax: (2) 736-0322

Pusan Chamber of Commerce & Industry
853-1, Pomchon 1-dong, Pusanjin-gu
Pusan
Tel: (51) 654-7771 Fax: (51) 645-3003

Seoul Chamber of Commerce
45, 4-ka, Namdaemun-ro, Chung-ku
Seoul
Tel: (2) 757-0757 Fax: (2) 776-8213

Small & Medium Industry Promotion Corporation
24-3, Youido-dong, Yongdungpo-gu
Seoul
Tel: (2) 783-9611/8 Fax: (2) 784-9230

Sunchon Chamber of Commerce & Industry
58-2, Changchon-dong
Sunchon, Kyoonggi
Tel: (661) 741-5511 Fax: (661) 741-2398

FOREIGN CHAMBERS OF COMMERCE & BUSINESS ORGANIZATIONS

American Chamber of Commerce in Korea
Rm. 307, Westin Chosun Hotel
87, Sogong-dong, Chung-gu
Seoul
Tel: (2) 753-6471, 752-3061 Fax: (2) 755-6577

British Chamber of Commerce in Korea
13/F., Naewoi Bldg.
9-1, Ulchiro 2-ga, Chung-gu
Seoul
Tel: (2) 757-5143 Fax: (2) 757-7444

French Chamber of Commerce & Industry in Korea
6/F., 22, Chong-dong, Chung-gu
Seoul
Tel: (2) 584-8813

International Executive Service Corporation
Rm. 601, Leema Bldg.
146-1, Susong-dong, Chongno-gu
Seoul
Tel: (2) 733-1021 Fax: (2) 733-1028

Italian Trade Commission
Rm. 311, KCCI Bldg.
45, Namdaemunno 4-ga, Chung-gu
Seoul
Tel: (2) 779-0811/3 Fax: (2) 757-2927

Japan Chamber of Commerce & Industry
6/F., KCCI Bldg.
45, Namdaemunno 4-ga, Chung-gu
Seoul
Tel: (2) 755-6672 Fax: (2) 755-2415

Japan External Trade Organization (JETRO)
7/F., The Korea Press Center Bldg.
25, 1-ka, Taepyung-ro, Chung-ku
Seoul
Postal add: CPO Box 8499, Seoul
Tel: (2) 739-8657, 739-4503 Fax: (2) 739-4658

Korea-US Economic Council, Inc.
Rm. 4304, KWTC Bldg.
159, Samsung-dong, Kangnam-gu
Seoul
Tel: (2) 551-3366 Fax: (2) 551-3365

Korean-German Chamber of Commerce & Industry
10/F., KCCI Bldg.
45, Namdaemunno 4-ga, Chung-gu
Seoul
Tel: (2) 776-1546/9 Fax: (2) 756-7828

KOREA TRADE PROMOTION CORPORATION (KOTRA) OFFICES IN THE ROK

Seoul (Head office)
KWTC Bldg.
159-1, Samsung-dong, Kangnam-gu
Seoul, Korea
Postal add: Trade Center POB 123, Seoul
Tel: (2) 551-4181 Fax: (2) 551-4477
Tlx: KOTRA K23659, K27326

Inchon
7/F., Chamber of Commerce and Industry
Incheon 9-1, Sa-dong, Choong-ku
Inchon
Tel: (32) 764-8325/6 Fax: (32) 764-8327

Kimhae Airport
Rm. 112, Kimhae International Airport
2347 Daejeo 2-dong, Kangseo-ku
Pusan
Tel: (51) 971-6665 Fax: (51) 971-7070

Kimpo Airport
Rm. 162, Kimpo International Airport
272 Gwahae-dong, Kangsu-ku
Seoul
Tel: (2) 663-3026 Fax: (2) 665-1060

Pusan
6/F., Trade Center Bldg.
87-7, Choongang-dong 4-ka, Choong-ku
Pusan
Tel: (51) 463-3691/2 Fax: (51) 463-3690

KOTRA OFFICES OVERSEAS

Argentina
Av. Cordoba 456-19B
1054 Buenos Aires, Argentina
Tel: [54] (1) 312-2203/6 Fax: [54] (1) 312-5218
Tlx: 17230 KOTRA AR

Australia
PO Box 275, World Trade Center
Melbourne, Vic. 3005, Australia
Tel: [61] (3) 614-1733 Fax: [61] (3) 629-6746
Tlx: AA 34085

Suite 1811, Tower Bldg.
264 George St.
Sydney, NSW 2000, Australia
Tel: [61] (2) 247-3369 Fax: [61] (2) 251-5826
Tlx: 25517 KOTRA AA

Austria
1/3 Gerneralli Center, 3/F.
Mariahifferstrasse 77-79
A-1060 Wien, Austria
Tel: [43] (222) 5863876/7 Fax: [43] (222) 5863879
Tlx: 134945 KOTRA A

Belgium
World Trade Center 2ème étage
blvd. Emile Jacqmain 162
1210 Brussels, Belgium
Tel: [32] (2) 218-5132, 218-5499
Fax: [32] (2) 218-7511 Tlx: 26256 KOTRA B

Brazil
av. Paulista 1439, Conj. 132, Bela Vista
São Paulo SP, CEP 01311, Brazil
Tel: [55] (11) 289-4200, 284-5984
Fax: [55] (11) 289-4684 Tlx: 1134181

Canada
Suite 600, The Thomson Bldg.
65 Queen St.
W. Toronto, ON M5H 2M5, Canada
Tel: [1] (416) 368-3899 Fax: [1] (416) 368-2893
Tlx: 0623426

Suite 1710, One Bentall Center
505 Burrard St.
Vancouver, BC V7X 1M6, Canada
Tel: [1] (604) 683-1820, 687-7322
Fax: [1] (604) 687-6289 Tlx: 0454276

Chile
Av. 11 de Septiembre 1901, of 52
Providencia, Santiago, Chile
Tel: [56] (2) 204-9833, 251-2227
Fax: [56] (2) 204-9833 Tlx: 645207

China
Rm. 2317, China World Tower
1 Jian Guo Men Wai Ave.
Beijing 100004, PRC
Tel: [86] (1) 505-2324/7 Fax: [86] (1) 505-2310
Tlx: 210681 PKKTC CN

Rm. 1305/6, Shanghai International Trade Center
2200 Yan An Rd. (W)
Shanghai, PRC
Tel: [86] (21) 219-7592/3 Fax: [86] (21) 268-9470

Colombia
Calle 72, No. 10-03, of.
201, Bogotá, Colombia
Tel: [57] (1) 217-1393, 248-5696
Fax: [57] (1) 217-2191 Tlx: 43189 KOTRA CO

All addresses and telephone numbers are in South Korea unless otherwise noted. The country code for South Korea is [82].

Costa Rica
Apartado 929-1007, Centro Colon
San José, Costa Rica
Tel: [506] 334207, 331836 Fax: [506] 554018
Tlx: 3141 KOTRA CR

Denmark
Hobergsgade 14, PO Box 1520
DK-1020 Copenhagen K., Denmark
Tel: [45] 33-12-66-58, 128039 Fax: [45] 33-32-66-54
Tlx: 15291 KTC DK

Dominican Republic
Edif. Santanita
1 av. San Martin No. 253
Calle 43, Local 302
Santo Domingo, Dominican Republic
Tel: [1] (809) 567-3391/3 Fax: [1] (809) 567-3393
Tlx: 0720 KOTRA DR

Egypt
PO Box 358 Dokkt
Cairo, Arab Republic of Egypt
Tel: [20] (2) 302-1279, 302-1280
Fax: [20] (2) 302-1281 Tlx: 92317 KOTRA UN

Finland
Hallituskatu 15
SF-00100 Helsinki, Finland
Tel: [358] (0) 638122 Fax: [358] (0) 638611
Tlx: 122863 KOTRA SF

France
25/27 rue d'Astorg
75008 Paris, France
Tel: [33] (1) 47-42-00-17 Fax: [33] (1) 47-42-02-70
Tlx: 281186

Germany
Im Internationalen Handelszenrum, 4/F.
Friedrichstrasse 95
D-10117 Berlin, Germany
Tel: [49] (30) 2643-2637 Fax: [49] (30) 305-2363

Mainzer Landstr, 27-31
6000 Frankfurt am Main-1, Germany
Tel: [49] (69) 236895/7, 253589
Tlx: 416357 KOTARA D

Heidenkampsweg 66
20097 Hamburg, Germany
Tel: [49] (40) 232235 Fax: [49] (40) 233998

Greece
43, Academias St.
Athens 106 72, Greece
Tel: [30] (1) 362-6540, 364-4839
Fax: [30] (1) 364-1567 Tlx: 216569 KTCA GR

Guatemala
Edificio Geminis 10
Oficina 513 12 Calle, 1-25
Zona 10, Guatemala City, Guatemala
Tel: [502] (2) 353435, 353422 Fax: [502] (2) 352944
Tlx: 5026 COREA GU

Hong Kong
GPO Box 5573
Central, Hong Kong
Tel: [852] 5459500, 5459509 Fax: [852] 8150487
Tlx: 73497 KOTRA HX

Hungary
PO Box 571
Budapest H-1373, Hungary
Tel: [36] (1) 117-2183, 2082 Fax: [36] (1) 117-2358
Tlx: 223308 KOTRA H

India
c/o Embassy of the Republic of Korea
703, Int'l Trade Tower, Nehru Place
New Delhi 110 119, India
Tel: [91] (11) 646-1312, 1331 Fax: [91] (11) 646-1482
Tlx: 0095 KTRA IN

Indonesia
PO Box 1362
Jakarta, Indonesia
Tel: [62] (21) 511408 Fax: [62] (21) 521514
Tlx: 62814 MUGONG IA

Italy
Via Larga 31-20122
Milan, Italy
Tel: [39] (2) 5830-3967, 5830-3934
Fax: [39] (2) 5830-3643 Tlx: 302522 KOTRA I

Japan
7/F., Daiichi Seimei Bldg.
4-1, 1-chome Hakataekimae, Hakata-ku
Fukuoka, Japan
Tel: [81] (92) 473-2005/6 Fax: [81] (92) 473-2007
Tlx: 811201 HOTBTVT

9/F., Nagoya International Center Bldg.
47-1, Nagono 1-chome, Nakamura-ku
Nagoya, Japan
Tel: [81] (52) 561-3936, 3946 Fax: [81] (52) 561-3945
Tlx: J59860

10/F., Honmachi Meidai Bldg.
5-5, 2-chome Azuchimachi, Chuo-ku
Osaka, Japan
Tel: [81] (6) 262-3831 Fax: [81] (6) 262-4607
Tlx: 64880 KOTRAJ

5/F., Taiyo Twin Bldg. 2
13-22, Honcho 1-chome, Aoba-ku
Sendai 980, Japan
Tel: [81] (22) 268-9720 Fax: [81] (22) 268-9470

Yurakucho Bldg.
10-1, 1-chome, Yurakucho, Chiyoda-ku
Tokyo, Japan
Tel: [81] (3) 3214-6951/4 Fax: [81] (3) 3214-6950
Tlx: J24393

Jordan
PO Box 4371
Amman, Jordan
Tel: [962] (6) 684253 Fax: [962] (6) 684254
Tlx: 21993 KOTRA MJO

Kenya
PO Box 40569
Nairobi, Kenya
Tel: [254] (2) 220458, 228928 Fax: [254] (2) 332850
Tlx: 22360 MOOGONG

Kuwait
PO Box 20771
Safat 10368 Kuwait
Tel: [965] 255-4206 Fax: [965] 257-0894
Tlx: DOTRA 22606KT

Malaysia
10/F., Mui Plaza Jln P Ramlee
50250 Kuala Lumpur, Malaysia
Tel: [60] (3) 242-0756, 242-9939, 248-3944
Fax: [60] (3) 242-2107 Tlx: 31191 KORTRA MA

Mexico
Paseo de la Reforma, 250-207 Col. Juarez
06600 Mexico City D.F., Mexico
Tel: [52] (5) 514-5457, 208-5197
Fax: [52] (5) 511-9299 Tlx: 01774465 KTC ME

Morocco
Tour Habous 8ème étage
Avenue des F.A.R.
Casablanca, Morocco
Tel: [212] 2314280, 2314232 Fax: [212] 2319780
Tlx: LOTRA 27636M

Netherlands
Strawinskylaan 767
1077 Amsterdam, Netherlands
Tel: [31] (20) 6730555/6 Fax: [31] (20) 6736918
Tlx: 16368 KOTRA NL

New Zealand
CPO Box 4007
Auckland, New Zealand
Tel: [64] (9) 373-5792/3 Fax: [64] (9) 373-2952
 Tlx: 2818

Nigeria
Plot 1388A, Olosa St., Victoria Island
Lagos, Nigeria
Tel: [234] (1) 914294 Fax: [234] (1) 611519
Tlx: 22370 KECA NG

Norway
PO Box 191, Kern 0510
Oslo 5, Norway
Tel: [47] (2) 72-1155/6 Fax: [47] (2) 72-1151
Tlx: 77334 KOTRA N

Pakistan
Bahria Complex Ground Fl.
24, Moulvi Tamizuddin Khan Rd.
Karachi 74000, Pakistan
Tel: [92] (21) 551659, 552219 Fax: [92] (21) 552190
Tlx: 23687 KTC PK

Panama
Apartado Postal 87-2082
Panama 7, Rep. de Panama
Tel: [507] 648105, 647970 Fax: [507] 640928
Tlx: 2199 MOOGONG

Peru
PO Box 18-0337
Lima, Peru
Tel: [51] (14) 42-2834 Fax: [51] (14) 42-0841
Tlx: 21182 PE KOREA LM

Philippines
PO Box 1881, MCC, Makkati
Metro Manila, Philippines
Tel: [63] (2) 873244, 871183 Fax: [63] (2) 8173369
Tlx: 22512 KTM PH

Poland
ul. Mokotowska 4/6
00-641 Warsaw, Poland
Tel: [48] (22) 25-3536, 25-3547
Fax: [48] (22) 25-2935 Tlx: 813488 KOTRA PL

Portugal
Av. Eng, Duarte Pacheco, Torre 2
10 Andar Sala 2
1000 Lisbon, Portugal
Tel: [351] (1) 690816 Fax: [351] (1) 690814
Tlx: 62158 KOTRA P

Russia
Krasnoper-Snenskaya, NAB.12
Hotel Mexhdunarodnaya-2, Rm. 747
123610 Moscow, Russia
Tel: [7] (95) 253-1569, 253-1571/4
Fax: [7] (95) 253-1698

Saudi Arabia
PO Box 4323
Jeddah 21491, Saudi Arabia
Tel: [966] (2) 6690031, 6690073
Fax: [966] (2) 6608918 Tlx: 600066 KOTRA SJ

Singapore
Robinson Rd. PO Box 421
Singapore 9008
Tel: [65] 221-3055/6, Fax: [65] 223-5850

South Africa
PO Box 1086
Johannesburg 2000, South Africa
Tel: [27] (11) 331-1076/7 Fax: [27] (11) 331-2111
Tlx: 420343

Spain
Paseo de Castellana, 140 (Edif., Lima) 6C
28046 Madrid, Spain
Tel: [34] (1) 564-6668/9 Fax: [34] (1) 564-7302
Tlx: 44093 KTPCE

Sweden
Tegnergaten 34, 4tr Box 45188
10430 Stockholm, Sweden
Tel: [46] (8) 308090 Fax: [46] (8) 306190
Tlx: 12384 MOOGONG S

Switzerland
Biberlin str. 6
8032 Zurich, Switzerland
Tel: [41] (1) 422-1232, 422-1581
Fax: [41] (1) 422-4318 Tlx: 816415 KTCZ

Taiwan
PO Box 1555
Taipei, Taiwan
Tel: [886] (2) 7252324, 7252343
Fax: [886] (2) 7577240 Tlx: 21053 MOOGONG

All addresses and telephone numbers are in South Korea unless otherwise noted. The country code for South Korea is [82].

Thailand
GPO Box 1896
Bangkok, Thailand
Tel: [66] (2) 233-1322/3, 233-9397
Fax: [66] (2) 237-1956 Tlx: 82335 MOOGONG TH

Turkey
Taksim, Mete Cad. Mete Apt. 25, D-7
Istanbul, Turkey
Tel: [90] (1) 243-5075, 249-8223
Fax: [90] (1) 249-8571 Tlx: 24490 KOTCTR

United Arab Emirates
PO Box 12859
Dubai, U.A.E
Tel: [971] (4) 220643, 223285 Fax: [971] (4) 216330
Tlx: 46294 KOTRA EM

United Kingdom
Ground Floor, Vincent House
Vincent Square
London SW1P 2NB, UK
Tel: [44] (71) 834-5082, 828-4275
Fax: [44] (71) 630-5233 Tlx: 22375 KOTRA G

United States of America
111 East Wacker Dr., Suite 519
Chicago, IL 60601, USA
Tel: [1] (312) 644-4323/4 Fax: [1] (312) 644-4879
Tlx: 253005

1000 Tower Lane, Suite 110
Bensenville, IL 60106, USA
Tel: [1] (708) 350-0102 Fax: [1] (708) 350-0747
Tlx: 200426

12720 Hillcrest Rd., Suite 390
Dallas, TX 75230, USA
Tel: [1] (214) 934-8644 Fax: [1] (214) 934-4191
Tlx: 732343

4801 Wilshire Blvd., Suite 104
Los Angeles, CA 90010, USA
Tel: [1] (213) 954-9500 Fax: [1] (213) 954-1707
Tlx: 674639 LSA

One Biscayne Tower, Suite 1620
Miami, FL 33131, USA
Tel: [1] (305) 826-0900 Fax: [1] (305) 888-4930

1 California St., Suite 1905
San Francisco, CA 94111, USA
Tel: [1] (415) 434-8400 Fax: [1] (415) 434-8450

1129 20th St. NW, Suite 410
Washington, DC 20036, USA
Tel: [1] (202) 857-7919, 857-7921
Fax: [1] (202) 857-7923 Tlx: 289608 KTCW UR

Venezuela
PO Box 5368, Carmelitas
Caracas 1010, Venezuela
Tel: [58] (2) 62-2130, 62-6013 Fax:[58] (2) 762-0659
Tlx: 21531 KOTRA VC

KOREA FOREIGN TRADE ASSOCIATION (KFTA) OFFICES IN KOREA

Seoul (Head office)
159-1, Samsung-dong, Kangnam-gu
Seoul
Postal Add: Trade Center PO Box 100, Seoul
Tel: (2) 551-5114, 551-5267/9
Fax: (2) 551-5100, 551-5200, 551-5161
Tlx: KOTRASO K24265

Changwon
97-6, Shinwol-dong
Changwon, Kyongnam
Tel: (551) 82-4115/6 Fax: (551) 82-2010

Chunchon
179/7, Woonkyo-dong
Chunchon, Kangwon-do
Tel: (361) 56-3067/8 Fax: (361) 56-3069

Chungju
1571, Wooncheon-dong
Chuingju, Chungbuk
Tel: (431) 271-1647/8 Fax: (431) 271-1649

Daejeon
226, Sunwha-dong, Chung-ku
Daejeon
Tel: (42) 253-4737/8 Fax: (42) 252-1021

Inchon
989-1, Juan-dong, Nam-gu
Inchon
Tel: (32) 420-0011/5 Fax: (32) 420-0016

Jeonju
658-17, Seonosong-dong
Jeonju, Jeonbuk
Tel: (652) 77-6861/2 Fax: (652) 77-6864

Kwangju
24-2, 2-ka, Kumnam-ro, Dong-ku
Kwangju
Tel: (62) 232-1228/9 Fax: (62) 232-0765

Pusan
Pusan Trade Center
87-7, 4-ka, Chungang-dong, Chung-ku
Pusan
Tel: (51) 462-5166/9 Fax: (51) 463-4402
Tlx: KTABSN K53728

Taegu
299-2, Shinchun 4-dong, Dong-gu
Taegu, Korea
Tel: (53) 753-7531/3 Fax: (53) 753-7530

KFTA OFFICES OVERSEAS

Belgium
Avenue Louise 165
1050 Brussels, Belgium
Tel: [32] (2) 646-2180 Fax: [32] (2) 646-7006
Tlx: 6566 KTAB

China
Rm. 1201, China World Tower
1, Jian Guo Men Wai Dai Jie
Beijing 100004, China
Tel: [86] (1) 505-2671/3 Fax: [86] (1) 505-2670

Germany
Immermannstrasse 65A
4000 Düsseldorf 1, Germany
Tel: [49] (211) 36-2044/5
Fax: [49] (211) 36-5614 Tlx: 8584754 KTA D

Hong Kong
Rm. 301/2, Korea Centre Bldg.
119-121 Connaught Rd. C
Hong Kong
Tel: [852] 5422234/6 Fax: [852] 8540006
Tlx: 74386 KOCEK HX

Japan
No. 15, 8F., Mori Bldg.
2-8-10, Toranomon, Minato-ku
Tokyo, Japan
Tel: [81] (3) 3592-2601, 3592-2626/7
Fax: [81](3) 3592-2610

United States of America
Rm. 600, Hahn Kook Center
460 Park Ave.
New York, NY 10022, USA
Tel: [1] (212) 421-8804/6
Fax: [1] (212) 223-3827 Tlx: 425572 KTANY

1800 K St. NW, #700
Washington, DC 20006, USA
Tel: [1] (202) 828-4400/3
Fax: [1] (202) 828-4404 Tlx: 757427 KTA WSH

INDUSTRY-SPECIFIC TRADE ORGANIZATIONS

Abrasives Industry Cooperative [Korea]
7, Pongnae-dong 1-ga, Chung-gu
Seoul
Tel: (2) 752-6545 Fax: (2) 754-6057

Agriculture & Fisheries Food Trade Association
[Korea]
Rm. 1905, KWTC Bldg.
159, Samsung-dong, Kangnam-gu
Seoul
Tel: (2) 551-1936/9 Fax: (2) 551-1940

Agriculture & Fishery Marketing Cooperation
191, Hangangno 2-ga, Yongsan-gu
Seoul
Tel: (2) 795-8201/5 Fax: (2) 790-5265, 798-7513

Alcohol & Liquor Industry Association [Korea]
10, Youido-dong, Yongdungpo-gu
Seoul
Tel: (2) 780-6411/5, 780-6661/4 Fax: (2) 783-8787

Apparel Sub-Material Association [Korea]
2A-1, KOEX Bldg.
159, Samsung-dong, Kangnam-gu
Seoul
Tel: (2) 551-6000/2 Fax: (2) 551-6006

As-Con (Asphalt-Concrete) Industry Cooperative
[Korea]
1599-11, Socho-dong, Socho-gu
Seoul
Tel: (2) 583-5241/3 Fax: (2) 583-5244

Assorted Feed Industry Cooperative [Korea]
1581-13, Socho-dong, Socho-gu
Seoul
Tel: (2) 586-8720 Fax: (2) 521-5508

Auto Industries Cooperative Association [Korea]
1683-3, Socho-dong, Socho-gu
Seoul
Tel: (2) 587-3416 Fax: (2) 583-7340

Automobile Manufacturers Association [Korea]
8/F., 63 Bldg.
Youido-dong, Yongdungpo-gu
Seoul
Tel: (2) 782-1360/1 Fax: (2) 782-0464

Bag & Luggage Industry Cooperative [Korea]
44-35, Youido-dong, Yongdungpo-gu
Seoul
Tel: (2) 782-2159, 782-2161

Bakers Association [Korean]
120-3, Chungmuro 4-ga, Chung-gu
Seoul 100-014
Tel: (2) 273-1830 Fax: (2) 271-1822

Banks [Korea Federation of]
33, Sorin-dong, Chung-gu
Seoul
Tel: (2) 399-5811 Fax: (2) 399-5810

Battery Industry Cooperative [Korea]
1304-4, Socho-dong, Socho-gu
Seoul
Tel: (2) 553-2401/3 Fax: (2) 556-1290

Bedding Goods Industry Cooperative [Korea]
159-1, Samsung-dong, Kangnam-gu
Seoul
Tel: (2) 551-1919 Fax: (2) 551-1918

Bicycle Industry Association [Korea]
Rm. 604, Sanjung Bldg.
15-16, Youido-dong, Yongdungpo-gu
Seoul
Tel: (2) 784-2582/3 Fax: (2) 785-7270

Boiler Industry Cooperative [Korea]
288-1, Dohwa-dong, Mapo-gu
Seoul
Tel: (2) 719-4151/3 Fax: (2) 719-4154

Book Binding Industry Cooperative [Korea]
614-7, Ahyon-dong, Mapo-gu
Seoul
Tel: (2) 362-7182

Can Industry Cooperative [Korea]
7-15, Nonhyon-dong, Kangnam-gu
Seoul
Tel: (2) 543-0140 Fax: (2) 548-0640

Canning Fisheries Cooperative [Korea]
Rm. 502, Sungi Bldg.
538, Tohwa 2-dong, Mapo-gu
Seoul
Tel: (2) 715-1057, 715-1060 Fax: (2) 702-0408

Canvas Products Industry Cooperative [Korea]
19-1, Namdaemunno 5-ga, Chung-gu
Seoul
Tel: (2) 755-9033/6

Cement Industrial Association [Korea]
539-11, Shinsa-dong, Kangnam-gu
Seoul
Tel: (2) 546-3861 Fax: (2) 546-7398

Ceramic Industry Association [Korea]
53-20, Taehyon-dong, Sodaemun-gu
Seoul
Tel: (2) 363-0361/3 Fax: (2) 392-8149

Chaff Charcoal Industry Cooperative [Korea]
Rm. 304, Chungyou Bldg.
910-14, Pangbae-dong, Socho-gu
Seoul
Tel: (2) 522-9802 Fax: (2) 522-9803

Chemical Fibers Association [Korea]
80, Chokson-dong, Chongno-gu
Seoul
Tel: (2) 734-1191/4 Fax: (2) 738-0111

Coal Association [Korea]
80-6, Susong-dong, Chongno-gu
Seoul
Tel: (2) 734-8891/4 Fax: (2) 734-7959

Coal Mining Industry Cooperative [Korea]
10-2, Youido-dong, Yongdungpo-gu
Seoul
Tel: (2) 784-7821/7

Construction Association of Korea
8/F., Construction Bldg.
71-2, Nonhyon-dong, Kangnam-gu
Seoul
Tel: (2) 547-6101/7 Fax: (2) 542-6264

Construction Equipment Association [Korea]
44-1, Youido-dong, Yongdungpo-gu
Seoul
Tel: (2) 783-4001/3 Fax: (2) 734-7959

Consumer Goods Exporters Association [Korea]
Rm. 1802, KWTC Bldg.
159, Samsung-dong, Kangnam-gu
Seoul
Tel: (2) 551-1858, 551-1869 Fax: (2) 551-1870

Cooks Association [Korean Center]
Union Bldg.
69-75, Kalwol-dong, Yongsan-gu
Seoul 140-150
Tel: (2) 712-2183 Fax: (2) 713-7148

Corrugated Paper Board Packaging Industry
Cooperative [Korea]
45, Mugyo-dong, Chung-gu
Seoul
Tel: (2) 756-7781/3 Fax: (2) 774-8605

Cosmetic Industry Association [Korea]
17-1, Youido-dong, Yongdungpo-gu
Seoul
Tel: (2) 782-0948, 785-7984/5 Fax: (2) 784-7639

Customs Association [Korea]
Hangang Grand Officetel
16-91, Hanganno 3-ga, Yongsan-gu
Seoul
Tel: (2) 701-1457 Fax: (2) 701-1459

Customs Brokers Association [Korea]
209-9, Nonhyon-dong, Kangnam-gu
Seoul
Tel: (2) 547-9714/6 Fax: (2) 549-7813

Dairy & Beef Farmers Association [Korea]
4/F., Livestock Center Bldg.
1516/5, Socho-dong, Socho-gu
Seoul
Tel: (2) 588-7055/6, 584-5143 Fax: (2) 584-5144

Data Processing Cooperative [Korea]
14-8, Youido-dong, Yongdungpo-gu
Seoul
Tel: (2) 780-0511/3

Deep Sea Fisheries Association [Korea]
6/F., Samhomulsan Bldg.
Yangjae-dong, Socho-gu
Seoul
Tel: (2) 589-1621/4 Fax: (2) 589-1030/1

Department Stores Association [Korea]
Rm. 643, KCCI Bldg.
45, Namdaemunno 4-ga, Chung-gu
Seoul
Tel: (2) 754-6054 Fax: (2) 776-9528

Die & Mold Industry Cooperative [Korea]
KOAMI Bldg.
13-31, Youido-dong, Yongdungpo-gu
Seoul 150-010
Tel: (2) 783-1711/3 Fax: (2) 784-5937

Dyestuff & Pigment Industry Cooperative [Korea]
17-1, Youido-dong, Yongdungpo-gu
Seoul
Tel: (2) 783-0721 Fax: (2) 786-1888

Earthenware Industry Cooperative [Korea]
1423, Sung-in-dong, Chongno-gu
Seoul
Tel: (2) 252-0663 Fax: (2) 235-8327

Electric Power Corporation [Korea]
167, Samsung-dong, Kangnam-gu
Seoul
Tel: (2) 550-3114 Fax: (2) 550-5982

Electrical Manufacturer's Cooperative [Korea]
103-10, Shingil 2-dong, Yongdungpo-gu
Seoul
Tel: (2) 849-2811/9 Fax: (2) 848-8337

Electronic Industries Association of Korea
5/F., Danwoo Bdlg.
850-22, Pangbae-dong, Sochu-gu
Seoul
Tel: (2) 553-0941/7, 553-8725 Fax: (2) 555-6195

Electronic Industries Cooperative [Korea]
813-5, Pangbae-dong, Sochu-gu
Seoul
Tel: (2) 533-2309 Fax: (2) 553-0949

Energy Management Corp.[Korea]
1467-3, Socho 3-dong, Socho-gu
Seoul 137-073
Tel: (2) 520-0095 Fax: (2) 582-5057

Farm Machinery & Tool Industry Cooperative
[Korea]
11-11, Tongja-dong, Yongsan-gu
Seoul
Tel: (2) 757-1451/6 Fax: (2) 757-1430

Fastener Industry Cooperative [Korea]
221, Hyoje-dong, Chongno-gu
Seoul
Tel: (2) 743-1219, 763-7442 Fax: (2) 743-1219

Fire-Fighting Equipment Industry Cooperative
[Korea]
16-2, Yoido-dong, Yongdungpo-gu
Seoul
Tel: (2) 785-4121/4 Fax: (2) 785-4125

Fishery Exporters Association [Korea]
Rm. 1904, KWTC Bldg.
159, Samsung-dong, Kangnam-gu
Seoul
Tel: (2) 551-1925 Fax: (2) 551-1931

Foods Industry Association [Korea]
1002-6, Pangbae-dong, Socho-gu
Seoul
Tel: (2) 585-7062 Fax: (2) 586-4906

Footwear Exporters Association [Korean]
Rm. 1001, KWTC Bldg.
159, Samsung-dong, Kangnam-gu
Seoul
Tel: (2) 551-1411/29 Fax: (2) 551-1430

Forestry Association [National Federation of]
111-5, Samjon-dong, Songpa-gu
Seoul
Tel: (2) 416-9416 Fax: (2) 416-7381

Freight Forwarders Association [Korea
International]
80, Chockson-dong, Chongno-gu
Seoul
Tel: (2) 783-8000 Fax: (2) 733-7249

Furniture Industry Cooperatives
[Korea Federation of]
374-2, Changan-dong, Tongdaemun-gu
Seoul
Tel: (2) 215-8838/9 Fax: (2) 215-9729

Garment Industry Cooperative [Korea]
105-238, Kongdok-dong, Mapo-gu
Seoul
Tel: (2) 717-3191, 715-8998 Fax: (2) 718-3192

Garments & Knitwear Export Association [Korea]
Rm. 801, KWTC Bldg.
159, Samsung-dong, Kangnam-gu
Seoul
Tel: (2) 551-1456 Fax: (2) 551-1519

Gauge & Meter Industry Cooperative [Korea]
13-31, Youido-dong, Yongdungpo-gu
Seoul
Tel: (2) 783-5686

Ginseng Products Manufacturers Association
[Korean]
30-6, Chamwon-dong, Socho-gu
Seoul
Tel: (2) 549-4330 Fax: (2) 511-4533

Glass Industry Cooperative [Korea]
53-20, Taehyon-dong, Sodaemun-gu
Seoul
Tel: (2) 364-7799 Fax: (2) 312-8838

Handicrafts Cooperatives [Korea Federation of]
Rm. 202, Bosung Bldg.
163-3, Ulchiro 2-ga, Chung-gu
Seoul 100-192
Tel: (2) 757-1678 Fax: (2) 757-8582

Illuminating Industry Cooperative [Korea]
94-357, Yongdungpo-dong, Yongdungpo-gu
Seoul
Tel: (2) 676-9391/3, 633-4590 Fax: (2) 675-2482

Industrial Safety Corp. [Korea]
Kookje Bldg.
191, Han-gangno 1-ga, Yongsan-gu
Seoul 140-702
Tel: (2) 797-5996 Fax: (2) 795-4872

Industrial Technology [Korea Academy of]
790-2, Yoksam-dong, Kangnam-gu
Seoul
Tel: (2) 563-6891 Fax: (2) 554-8016/8

Invention and Patent Association [The Korea]
143-19, Samsung-dong, Kangnam-gu
Seoul
Tel: (2) 557-1077/8 Fax: (2) 554-1532

Iron and Steel Association [Korea]
51-8, Susong-dong, Chongno-gu
Seoul
Tel: (2) 732-9231/5 Fax: (2) 739-1090

Jewelry Industry Cooperative [Iri]
215-2, Yongdung-dong
Iri City, Chonbuk
Tel: (653) 855-0363/4 Fax: (653) 856-7275

Kitchen Furniture Cooperative [Korea]
910-14, Pangbae-dong, Socho-gu
Seoul
Tel: (2) 586-2451/3 Fax: (2) 586-2454

Knitting Industry Cooperatives
[Korea Federation of]
48, Shinmunno 1-ga, Chongno-gu
Seoul
Tel: (2) 735-5951/3 Fax: (2) 735-1447

Lighting Fixtures Industry Cooperative [Korea]
Rm. 308, KFS Bldg.
16-2, Youido-dong, Yongdungpo-gu
Seoul
Tel: (2) 786-9876 Fax: (2) 701-0944

Lumber Industry Cooperative [Korea]
44-35, Youido-dong, Yongdungpo-gu
Seoul
Tel: (2) 783-0657/9 Fax: (2) 782-5738

Machinery & Metals [Korea Institute of]
66, Sangnam-dong
Changwon-shi, Kyongnam
Tel: (551) 80-3000 Fax: (551) 80-3333

Machinery Industry Cooperative [Korea
Federation of]
172-11, Yomni-dong, Mapo-gu
Seoul
Tel: (2) 715-7172 Fax: (2) 702-6974

Machinery Industry [Korea Association of]
(KOAMI)
13-31, Youido-dong, Yongdungpo-gu
Seoul
Tel: (2) 780-3611/4 Fax: (2) 784-6749, 784-1032

Machine Tool Manufacturers' Association [Korea]
35-4, Youido-dong, Yongdungpo-gu
Seoul
Tel: (2) 780-3521 Fax: (2) 784-8023

Marine Equipment Association [Korea]
12-5, Youido-dong, Yongdungpo-gu
Seoul
Tel: (2) 783-6952/4 Fax: (2) 785-7647

Medical Instrument Industry Cooperative [Korea]
284-6, Nagwon-dong, Chongno-gu
Seoul
Tel: (2) 764-3815, 762-3814 Fax: (2) 744-6567

Mining Association of Korea
35-24, Tongui-dong, Chongno-gu
Seoul
Tel: (2) 736-2501 Fax: (2) 720-5592

Musical Instrument Industry Association [Korea]
51-1, Tohwa-dong, Mapo-gu
Seoul
Tel: (2) 719-5037/8 Fax: (2) 718-0493

Non-Ferrous Metal Industry Cooperatives [Korea
Federation of]
Rm. 715, Backsang Bldg.
35-2, Youido-dong, Yongdungpo-gu
Seoul
Tel: (2) 780-8551/4 Fax: (2) 784-9473

Nonwoven Industry Cooperative [Korea]
Rm. 1513, Yoowon Office
164-11, Chungjongno 2-ga, Sodaemun-gu
Seoul
Tel: (2) 365-2332 Fax: (2) 393-5098

Optical Industrial Cooperative [Korea]
708-27, Yoksam-dong, Kangnam-gu
Seoul
Tel: (2) 563-6532 Fax: (2) 563-6533

Overseas Construction Association of Korea
Rm. 1108, Kukdong Bldg.
60-1, Chungmuro 3-ga, Chung-gu
Seoul
Tel: (2) 274-1611/9 Fax: (2) 274-0743

Paper Industry Cooperative [Korea]
831, Yoksam-dong, Kangnam-gu
Seoul
Tel: (2) 567-5912/3 Fax: (2) 567-6984

Paper Manufacturers' Association [Korea]
Rm. 302, Songpa Bldg.
505, Singsa-dong, Kangnam-gu
Seoul
Tel: (2) 549-0981 Fax: (2) 549-0980

Petrochemical Industry Association [Korea]
1-1, Yonji-dong, Chongno-gu
Seoul
Tel: (2) 744-0116 Fax: (2) 743-1887

Pharmaceutical Manufacturers Association
[Korea]
990-2, Pangbae-dong, Socho-gu
Seoul
Tel: (2) 581-2101 Fax: (2) 581-2106

Pharmaceutical Traders Association [Korea]
Rm. 1801, KWTC Bldg.
159, Samsung-dong, Kangnam-gu
Seoul
Tel: (2) 551-1841 Fax: (2) 551-1850

Plastic Industry Cooperative [Korea]
146-2, Ssangnim-dong, Chung-gu
Seoul
Tel: (2) 275-7991/4 Fax: (2) 277-5150

Plating Industry Cooperative [Korea]
KOAMI Bldg.
13-31, Youido-dong, Yongdungpo-gu
Seoul 150-010
Tel: (2) 784-0721/2 Fax: (2) 784-0723

Plywood Industries Association [Korea]
Rm. 203, Wonchang Bldg.
26-3, Youido-dong, Yongdungpo-gu
Seoul
Tel: (2) 780-3631 Fax: (2) 780-3634

Poultry Association [Korea]
1516-5, Socho 3-dong, Socho-gu
Seoul 137-073
Tel: (2) 588-7651 Fax: (2) 588-7655

Printing Industry Cooperatives
[Korea Federation of]
352-26, Sogyo-dong, Mapo-gu
Seoul
Tel: (2) 335-6161/3 Fax: (2) 716-2995

Publishers Cooperative [Korea]
448-6, Shinsu-dong, Mapo-gu
Seoul
Tel: (2) 716-5621 Fax: (2) 716-2995

Raw Medicine Trader Association [Korea]
124, Chongno 6-ga, Chongno-gu
Seoul
Tel: (2) 762-8255 Fax: (2) 742-5662

Raw Silk Exporters Association [Korea]
17-9, Youido-dong, Yongdungpo-gu
Seoul
Tel: (2) 785-5911/4 Fax: (2) 785-5915

Refrigeration and Air-Conditioning Industries
Association [Korea]
13-31, Youido-dong, Yongdungpo-gu
Seoul
Tel: (2) 780-9038 Fax: (2) 785-1195

Register of Shipping [Korean]
1465-10, Socho 3-dong, Socho-gu
Seoul
Tel: (2) 582-6601

Rubber Industry Cooperative [Korea]
7, Shinmunno 1-ga, Chongno-gu
Seoul
Tel: (2) 733-8584/6 Fax: (2) 730-3355

Science & Technology
[Korea Advanced Institute of]
373-1, Kusong-dong, Yusong-gu
Taejon
Tel: (42) 869-2114 Fax: (42) 869-2210

Science & Technology [Korea Institute of]
39-1, Hawolgok-dong, Songbuk-gu
Seoul
Tel: (2) 982-8801 Fax: (2) 963-4013

Scientific Instruments Industry Cooperative
[Korea]
60, Myo-dong, Chongno-gu
Seoul
Tel: (2) 742-6083 Fax: (2) 744-4934

Securities Dealers Association [Korea]
34, Youido-dong, Yongdungpo-gu
Seoul
Tel: (2) 783-5391/5 Fax: (2) 785-1513

Seed Association [Korea]
1358-6, Socho-dong, Socho-gu
Seoul
Tel: (2) 568-2034 Fax: (2) 563-6711

Shipbuilders Association [Korea]
65-1, Unni-dong, Chongno-gu
Seoul
Tel: (2) 766-4631/5 Fax: (2) 766-4307, 739-4306

Shipbuilding Industry Cooperative [Korea]
915-14, Pangbae-dong, Socho-gu
Seoul
Tel: (2) 587-3121/3 Fax: (2) 583-2922

Shipowners' Association [Korea]
10/F., Sejong Bldg.
100, Tangju-dong, Chongno-gu
Seoul
Tel: (2) 739-1551/7 Fax: (2) 739-1558

Shippers Council [Korean]
Rm. 4404, KWTC Bldg.
159, Samsung-dong, Kangnam-gu
Seoul
Tel: (2) 551-5383/5 Fax: (2) 551-5231

Shipping Agency Association [Korea]
Rm. 901, Hyundae Bldg.
80, Chockson-dong, Chongno-gu
Seoul
Tel: (2) 734-1531/3 Fax: (2) 738-3760

Shipping Association [Korea]
3, Yangpyong 2-dong 6-ga, Yongdungpo-gu
Seoul
Tel: (2) 675-2711 Fax: (2) 675-2714

Soy Sauce Industry Cooperative [Korea]
3/F., Paint Bldg.
204-6, Nonhyon-dong, Kangnam-gu
Seoul
Tel: (2) 549-1186/7 Fax: (2) 547-6893

Spinners & Weavers Association of Korea
43-8, Kwanchol-dong, Chongno-gu
Seoul
Tel: (2) 735-5741/8 Fax: (2) 735-5749

Sporting Goods Industry Cooperative [Korea]
Rm. 814, Life Officetel
61-3, Youido-dong, Yongdungpo-gu
Seoul
Tel: (2) 786-7761 Fax: (2) 786-7764

Stainless Steel Pipe Industry Cooperative [Korea]
4/F., Cheil Bldg.
58-85, Mullae-dong 3-ga, Yongdungpo-gu
Seoul
Tel: (2) 679-1932 Fax: (2) 633-0379

Stationery Industry Cooperative [Korea]
36-3, Chungmuro 5-ga, Chung-gu
Seoul
Tel: (2) 278-7891 Fax: (2) 275-1065

Stationery Wholesaler Cooperative [Korea]
355, Chungnim-dong, Chung-gu
Seoul
Tel: (2) 393-1344/6 Fax: (2) 393-4650

Steel Industry Cooperative [Korea]
16-2, Youido-dong, Yongdungpo-gu
Seoul
Tel: (2) 785-4127/9

Steel Pipe Association [Korea]
35-6, Youido-dong, Yongdungpo-gu
Seoul
Tel: (2) 782-8211/3 Fax: (2) 784-0971

Stone Products Industry Cooperative [Korea]
741-11, Yoksam-dong, Kangnam-gu
Seoul
Tel: (2) 565-0631 Fax: (2) 558-3430

Sugar Manufacturers Association [Korea]
Rm. 501, Choyang Bldg.
49-17, Chungmuro 2-ga, Chung-gu
Seoul
Tel: (2) 275-6071/3 Fax: (2) 277-5858

Tanners Association [Korea]
Rm. 805, Samhwa Bldg.
204-4, Nonhyon-dong, Kangnam-gu
Seoul
Tel: (2) 549-5432/3 Fax: (2) 549-6733

Tele-Communication Industry Cooperative [Korea]
KCE Bldg.
16-6, Hangango 3-ga, Yongsan-gu
Seoul
Tel: (2) 711-2266 Fax: (2) 711-2272

Textile Industrial Cooperative [Korea PP]
1-1, Yonji-dong, Chongno-gu
Seoul
Tel: (2) 741-7801/5 Fax: (2) 741-7851

Textile Industries [Korea Federation of]
944-31 Daechi-dong, Kangnam-gu
Seoul
Tel: (2) 528-4005 Fax: (2) 528-4069

Textile Inspection & Testing Institute [Korea]
819-5, Yoksam-dong, Kangnam-gu
Seoul
Tel: (2) 567-7591 Fax: (2) 557-3739

Textiles [Korea Export Association of]
Rm. 1803/4, KWTC Bldg.
159, Samsung-dong, Kangnam-gu
Seoul
Tel: (2) 551-1876, 551-1895 Fax: (2) 551-1896

Tire Manufacturers Association [Korea]
Rm. 1910, KWTC Bldg.
159, Samsung-dong, Kangnam-gu
Seoul
Tel: (2) 551-1903/7 Fax: (2) 551-1910

Tools Industry Cooperative [Korea]
Rm. 401, Bohun Bldg.
12-5, Youido-dong, Yongdungpo-gu
Seoul 150-010
Tel: (2) 780-0731 Fax: (2) 785-2457

Towel Industry Cooperative [Korea]
20-20, Chungmuro 5-ga, Chung-gu
Seoul
Tel: (2) 275-7288/9 Fax: (2) 277-0896

Toy Industry Cooperative [Korea]
361-1, Hangangno 2-ga, Yongsan-gu
Seoul
Tel: (2) 795-9505, 795-9818 Fax: (2) 795-0401

Umbrella & Parasol Industry Cooperative [Korea]
134, Kosong 3-ga, Puk-gu
Taegu
Tel: (53) 352-9119

Valve Industry Cooperative [Korea]
16-2, Youido-dong, Yongdungpo-gu
Seoul
Tel: (2) 783-5611/2 Fax: (2) 783-5613

Wadding Industry Cooperative [Korea]
51-1, Tohwa-dong, Mapo-gu
Seoul
Tel: (2) 702-6678/9 Fax: (2) 702-6612

Weaving Industry Cooperatives
 [Korea Federation of]
169-2, Namchang-dong, Chung-gu
Seoul
Tel: (2) 778-4295, 752-8098 Fax: (2) 755-6994

Woolen Spinners & Weavers Industry Cooperative
[Korea]
120-3, Chungmuro 4-ga, Chung-gu
Seoul
Tel: (2) 273-0677/9 Fax: (2) 277-9789

FINANCIAL INSTITUTIONS

BANKS

Korea Federation of Banks
33, Sorin-dong, Chung-gu
Seoul
Tel: (2) 399-5811 Fax: (2) 399-5810

Central Bank

Bank of Korea
110, 3-ka, Namdaemun-no, Chung-ku
Seoul 100-794
Tel: (2) 759-4114 Fax: (2) 752-7389 Tlx: 24711

Domestic Banks

Bank of Seoul
10-1, 2-ka, Namdaemun-no, Chung-ku
Seoul 100-746
Tel: (2) 771-6000 Fax: (2) 775-4983 Tlx: 23311

Cho Hung Bank
14, 1-ka, Namdaemun-no, Chung-ku
Seoul 100
Tel: (2) 733-2000 Fax: (2) 732-0835 Tlx: 23321

Citizen's National Bank
9-1, 2-ka, Namdaemun-no, Chung-ku,
Seoul 100
Postal add: CPO Box 815, Seoul
Tel: (2) 754-1211, 771-4000
Fax: (2) 777-4239, 757-3679 Tlx: 23481

Commercial Bank of Korea Ltd.
111-1, 2-ka, Namdaemun-no, Chung-ku
Seoul 100-792
Tel: (2) 754-3920, 775-0050
Fax: (2) 754-9203, 753-5264 Tlx: 24611

Daegu Bank
118, 2-ka, Suseung-dong, Suseung-ku
Daegu
Tel: (53) 756-2001

Export-Import Bank of Korea
16-1, Yoido-dong, Yongdeungpo-ku
Seoul 150-010
Tel: (2) 784-1021 Fax: (2) 784-1030 Tlx: 26595

Hanil Bank
130, 2-ka, Namdaemun-no, Chung-ku
Seoul
Tel: (2) 771-2000 Fax: (2) 754-0479 Tlx: 23823

Industrial Bank of Korea
50, 2-ka, Ulchiro, Chung-ku
Seoul
Tel: (2) 729-6114 Fax: (2) 777-2982 Tlx: 23932

KorAm Bank
(Joint venture with Bank of America)
Hanmi Bldg.
1, Kongpyung-dong, Chongno-ku
Seoul 110-160
Tel: (2) 731-8114 Fax: (2) 731-8115 Tlx: 27814

Korea Development Bank
10-2, Kwanchul-dong, Chongno-ku
Seoul 110-111
Tel: (2) 733-2121, 733-4141 Fax: (2) 733-4768
Tlx: 27463

Korea Exchange Bank
181, 2-ka, Ulchiro, Chung-ku
Seoul 100-192
Tel: (2) 729-0114 Fax: (2) 734-5976 Tlx: 24244

Korea First Bank
100, Kongpyung-dong, Chungno-ku
Seoul 100-160
Tel: (2) 733-0070 Fax: (2) 734-5976 Tlx: 23685

Korea Long Term Credit Bank
15-22, Yoido-dong, Yongdeungpo-ku
Seoul 150-010
Tel: (2) 782-0111 Fax: (2) 784-7310 Tlx: 26342

Kyungki Bank
9-1, Sadong, Chung-ku
Inchon 400-600
Postal add: PO Box 6, Inchon
Tel: (32) 72-5151 Fax: (32) 764-0196

Pusan Bank
830-38, Pomil-dong, Dong-ku
Pusan
Tel: (51) 670-3151 Fax: (51) 642-1446 Tlx: 53392

Shinhan Bank
120, 2-ka, Taepyong-no, Chung-ku
Seoul 100
Tel: (2) 756-0505 Fax: (2) 757-1024

Foreign Banks

Bank of America NT & SA (USA)
8/F., Sunghwa Bldg.
192-18, Kwanhoon-dong, Chongno-ku
Seoul 110-300
Tel: (2) 733-2455 Fax: (2) 738-0624 Tlx: 23294

Bank of Tokyo Ltd. (Japan)
12/F., Doosan Bldg.
101, 1-ka, Ulchiro, Chung-ku
Seoul
Tel: (2) 752-5041, 752-0111 Fax: (2) 752-5040
Tlx: 23286

Bankers Trust Company (US)
91-1, Songog-dong, Chung-ku
Seoul
Tel: (2) 752-6781 Fax: (2) 756-2648

Banque Nationale de Paris (France)
50, Sogong-dong, Chung-ku
Seoul
Tel: (2) 753-2594 Fax: (2) 757-2530

Barclays Bank PLC (UK)
Samdo Bldg., 2/F.
1-6, Soonhwa-dong, Chung-ku,
Seoul 100-130
Postal add: CPO Box 3010, Seoul
Tel: (2) 754-3680 Fax: (2) 752-9690 Tlx: 24480

All addresses and telephone numbers are in South Korea unless otherwise noted. The country code for South Korea is [82].

Chase Manhattan Bank (USA)
Chase Plaza, 34-35, Jung-dong, Chung-ku
Seoul
Tel: (2) 758-5211 Fax: (2) 758-5423

Citibank N.A. (USA)
Citicorp Center Bldg.
89-29, Shinmum-no 2-ka, Chongno-ku
Seoul 110-062
Tel: (2) 731-1114 Fax: (2) 733-8473 Tlx: 23293

Deutsche Bank AG (Germany)
51-1, Namchang-dong, Chung-ku
Seoul 100-689
Postal add: CPO Box 8904, Seoul
Tel: (2) 754-3071 Fax: (2) 755-2364 Tlx: 26353

First National Bank of Chicago (USA)
15/F., Oriental Chemical Bldg.
50, Sokong-dong, Chung-ku
Seoul 100-070
Tel: (2) 757-9870 Fax: (2) 753-7917 Tlx: 27534

Hongkong and Shanghai Banking Corporation
(Hong Kong)
6/F., Kyobo Bldg.
1, 1-ka, Chongno, Chongno-ku
Seoul 110-714
Tel: (2) 739-4211 Fax: (2) 739-1387 Tlx: 22022

International Bank of Singapore Ltd.
Suite 806, Kyobo Bldg.
1, 1-ka, Chongno, Chongno-ku
Seoul 110-714
Tel: (2) 739-3441 Fax: (2) 732-9004 Tlx: 26485

Kyowa Saitama Bank (Japan)
1, 1-ka, Chongno, Chongno-ku
Seoul
Tel: (2) 738-5183 Fax: (2) 736-1242

National Australia Bank Ltd.
14/F., Kyobo Bldg.
1, 1-ka, Chongno, Chongno-ku
Seoul 110-714
Tel: (2) 739-2220 Fax: (2) 733-0738 Tlx: 28844

National Bank of Canada
6/F., Leema Bldg.
146-1, Soosong-dong, Chongno-ku
Seoul 110-140
Tel: (2) 733-5012 Fax: (2) 736-1508 Tlx: 25043

Sakura Bank (Japan)
87, 1-ka, Ulchi-ro, Chung-ku
Seoul
Tel: (2) 777-7092 Fax: (2) 756-9675

Swiss Bank Corporation
1704, Kyobo Bldg.
1, 1-ka, Chongno, Chongno-ku
Seoul 110-714
Tel: (2) 730-9161 Fax: (2) 730-9162 Tlx: 32290

INSURANCE COMPANIES

Korea Non-Life Insurance Association
KRIC Bldg., 6/F.
80, Susong-dong, Chongno-ku
Seoul
Tel: (2) 739-4161 Fax: (2) 739-3769 Tlx: 27947

Ankuk Fire and Marine Insurance Co., Ltd.
87, 1-ga, Ulchi-ro, Chung-gu
Seoul 100-191
Tel: (2) 758-7114 Fax: (2) 752-4875

Daehan Fire and Marine Insurance Co., Ltd.
51-1, Namchang-dong, Chung-gu
Seoul
Tel: (2) 754-6234 Fax: (2) 757-5737

First Fire and Marine Insurance Co., Ltd.
12-1, Sosomun-dong, Chung-gu
Seoul 100-110
Tel: (2) 771-7300 Fax: (2) 756-6602

Haedong Fire and Marine Insurance Co., Ltd.
185-10, 2-ga, Chungjong-ro, Sodaemun-gu
Seoul 120
Tel: (2) 363-3411 Fax: (2) 392-2933

Hyundai Marine and Fire Insurance Co., Ltd.
178, Sejong-ro, Chongno-gu
Seoul 100-050
Tel: (2) 732-1133 Tlx: EASTERN K27270

International Fire and Marine Insurance Co., Ltd.
120, 5-ga, Namdaemun-ro, Chung-gu
Seoul 100-704
Tel: (2) 753-1101 Fax: (2) 753-0745

Korea Fidelity and Surety Co., Ltd.
136-74, Yonji-dong, Chongno-gu
Seoul
Tel: (2) 744-0021 Fax: (2) 743-0016

Koryo Fire and Marine Insurance Co., Ltd.
60, Toryom-dong, Chongno-gu
Seoul
Tel: (2) 735-4254 Fax: (2) 739-4251

Lucky Insurance Co., Ltd.
85, Ta-dong, Chung-gu
Seoul 100-180
Tel: (2) 310-2114 Fax: (2) 753-1002

Oriental Fire and Marine Insurance Co., Ltd.
25-1, Youido-dong, Yongdungpo-gu
Seoul 150-010
Tel: (2) 785-7711 Fax: (2) 784-9264

Shindong-A Fire and Marine Insurance Co., Ltd.
166, 5-ga, Namdaemun-ro, Chung-gu
Seoul 100-095
Tel: (2) 771-6900 Fax: (2) 755-8006

STOCK EXCHANGE

Korean Securities Dealers Association
34, Youido-dong, Yongdungpo-gu
Seoul
Tel: (2) 783-5391/5 Fax: (2) 785-1513

Korean Stock Exchange
33, Yoido-dong, Youngdeungpo-gu
Seoul 150-010
Tel: (2) 783-3371

SERVICES

ACCOUNTING FIRMS

Ahn Kwon & Co.
(Deloitte Touche Tohmatsu International)
International Insurance Bldg.
120, Namdaemoon-ro 5-ka, Chung-ku
Seoul 100-095
Postal add: CPO 5928, Seoul 100-095
Tel: (2) 753-0215 Fax: (2) 753-3486

Arthur Andersen & Co.
Anjin Accounting Corporation
5/F., Samwhan Camus Bldg.
17-3, Yoido-dong, Youngdeungpo-ku
Seoul 150-604
Tel: (2) 7679114 Fax: (2) 7854753

Ernst & Young Consulting Co., Ltd.
Citicorp Center, 6/F.
39-29, Shinmunro 2-ka, Chongno-ku
Seoul
Tel: (2) 734-9571 Fax: (2) 739-4530

KMPG San Tong & Co.
7/F., Koreana Bldg.
61-1, 1-ka Taipyung-ro, Chung-ku
Seoul 100-101
Postal add: CPO Box 7144, Seoul 100-671
Tel: (2) 733-2345 Fax: (2) 733-5317
Tlx: 26432 PEATCO

KMPG San Tong & Co.
9/F., Pusan Daily News Bldg.
1-10, Sujeong-dong, Dong-ku
Pusan 601-738
Postal add: CPO Box 7144, Pusan 601-738
Tel: (51) 463-7221/2 Fax: (51) 436-6229

Price Waterhouse
Korea International Business Center
Royal Bldg., 8/F.
5 Dangju-dong, Chongno-ku
Seoul 110-071
Tel: (2) 723-3015/6 Fax: (2) 723-3017

PW Associates, Inc.
Samwhan Bldg., 9/F.
98-5 Unni-dong, Chongno-ku
Seoul 110-350
Tel: (2) 745-8500 Fax: (2) 738-0447, 745-3484
Tlx: K24908 PRICEHS

Samil Accounting Corporation
(Coopers & Lybrand)
Kukje Center Bldg., Suite 2100
191, 2-ka Hankang-ro, Yongsan-ku
Seoul 140-702
Postal add: CPO Box 2170, Seoul 100-621
Tel: (2) 709-0800, 792-7000 Fax: (2) 796-7027/8
Tlx: 27549

Samil Accounting Corporation
(Coopers & Lybrand)
Hanil Officetel, Suite 602
815, Moon-Hyun-dong, Nam-ku
Pusan 608-040
Tel: (51) 631-5500/4 Fax: (51) 631-5505

Seihwa Accounting Corporation
(Corespondent firm of Price Waterhouse)
International Accounting & Tax Division
Samwhan Bldg., 9/F.
98-5 Unni-dong, Chongno-ku
Seoul 110-350
Tel: (2) 745-8500 Fax: (2) 738-0447, 745-3484
Tlx: K24908 PRICEHS

Young Wha Accounting Corporation
(Ernst & Young International)
Dae Yu Bldg., 11-14/F.
25-15 Yeoido-dong, Youngdeungpo-ku
Seoul
Postal add: CPO Box 338, Seoul
Tel: (2) 783-1100, 784-6991/5 Fax: (2) 783-5890
Tlx: K24263

Young Wha Accounting Corporation
(Ernst & Young International)
Rm. 1104, Korean Teachers Bldg.
1205-1, Choryang-1 dong, Dong-ku
Pusan
Tel: (51) 462-7308/9 Fax: (51) 462-4436

Young Wha Consultants, Inc.
(Ernst & Young)
6/F., Press Center Bldg.
25, 1-ka, Taepyung-ro, Chung-ku
Seoul
Tel: (2) 739-2531 Fax: (2) 738-2538

ADVERTISING AGENCIES

International Public Relation Association
42/F., 63 Bldg.
60, Yoido-dong, Youngdeungpo-ku
Seoul 150-010
Tel: (2) 782-7151 Fax: (2) 756-3635

Korea Advertisers Association
11/F., 28-1 Youido-dong, Youngdeungpo-ku
Seoul 150-010
Tel: (2) 782-8390 Fax: (2) 780-2391

Korea Advertising Society
Rm. 802, Maeil Kyungje Shinmun
51-9, Pil-dong 1-ka, Chung-gu
Seoul 100-271
Tel: (2) 269-1755 Fax: (2) 780-2249

Korea Broadcasting Advertising Corporation
(KOBACO)
16-18/F., Press Center
25, Taepyung-ro 2-ka, Chung-ku
Seoul 100-102
Tel: (2) 731-7200 Fax: (2) 731-7100
KOBACO controls the broadcasting advertising market.

Korea Federation of Advertising Associations
Rm. 410, Hyundai Bldg.
80, Jeoksun-dong, Chongro-ku
Seoul 110-062
Tel: (2) 733-1201 Fax: (2) 738-7824

All addresses and telephone numbers are in South Korea unless otherwise noted. The country code for South Korea is [82].

Korea Newspapers Advertising Association
13/F., Press Center
25, Taepyung-ro 2-ka, Chung-ku
Seoul 100-101
Tel: (2) 733-5518 Fax: (2) 720-3291

Korea Outdoor Advertising Association
381-21, Hapjung-dong, Mapo-gu
Seoul 121-220
Tel: (2) 333-3654 Fax: (2) 333-3656

Korea Public Relation Association
Wonchang Bldg.
25-4, Yoido-dong, Youngdeungpo-ku
Seoul 150-010
Tel: (2) 784-8717 Fax: (2) 780-2249

Adworld International
1031-28, Sadang 1-dong, Tongjak-gu
Seoul
Tel: (2) 585-5744 Fax: (2) 581-6626

Cheil Bozell, Inc.
5/F., Jung-Dong Bldg.
15-5, Jung-Dong, Choong-gu
Seoul 100-120
Tel: (2) 773-5321 Fax: (2) 773-7990

Cheil Communications, Inc.
Samsung Bldg.
501, 1-ga, Euiji-ro, Chongno-gu
Seoul
Tel: (2) 724-0317 Fax: (2) 724-0193
Tlx: 28694 KFACO K

Dae Hong Advertising Inc.
(Affil. with DDB Needham Worldwide)
1, Kongpyong-dong, Chongno-gu
Seoul
Tel: (2) 724-8114 Fax: (2) 735-7112

Dentsu, Young & Rubicam
5-6/F., Woomi Bldg.
98-6, Nonhyun-dong
Seoul
Tel: (2) 548-7150 Fax: (2) 548-8639

Diamond Ad Ltd.
Sunyeong Bldg.
1554-3, Seocho-dong, Seocho
PO Box 303
Seoul 137-070
Tel: (2) 525-2411 Fax: (2) 525-3011

Dong Bang Advertising Co., Ltd.
(Affil. with Leo Burnett)
114, Nonhyon-dong, Kangnam-gu
Seoul
Tel: (2) 541-2171 Fax: (2) 549-5380

Eastern Advertising Co., Ltd.
151-11, Ssanglim-dong, Chung-gu
Seoul
Tel: (2) 272-5889 Fax: (2) 272-7632

Geoson Advertising Inc.
(Affil. with FCB International)
60, Youido-dong, Yongdungpo-gu
Seoul
Tel: (2) 785-1341

J. Walter Thompson Korea Ltd.
Dongwon Bldg.
41-4, 2-ka, Myungryun-dong
Chongro-ku
Seoul 110-522
Tel: (2) 745-8663 Fax: (2) 745-8662

Jin Advertising Co., Ltd.
50-10, 2-ga, Chungmu-ro, Chung-gu
Seoul
Tel: (2) 275-7001 Fax: (2) 277-0040

Korad, Ogilvy & Mather
Samtan Bldg.
947-7, Daechi-dong, Kangnam-ku
Seoul
Tel: (2) 564-0066 Fax: (2) 565-2676/77

Korea First Advertising Co., Ltd.
108-2, Ryong-dong, Chongno-gu
Seoul
Tel: (2) 730-9711 Fax: (2) 739-5672

Leo Burnett Sonyon Inc.
9/F., Youone Bldg.
75-95 Seosomun-dong, Chung-ku
Seoul 100-110
Tel: (2) 7448222 Fax: (2) 7742226

LG Ad, Inc.
(Affil. with BBDO)
Lucky-Goldstar Mapo Bldg.
275, Kongdok-dong, Mapo-gu
Seoul
Tel: (2) 701-1114 Fax: (2) 701-1610

Lintas Korea
112-2 Itaewon-dong, Yong San-ku
Seoul
Tel: (2) 798-9162 Fax: (2) 798-9437

McCann-Erickson, Inc.
Yonkang Bldg.
13 Changro 4-ka, Chongro-ku
Seoul
Tel: (2) 745-6151 Fax: (2) 743-3649

Medicus Intercon Korea
Rm. 1403, Daejong Bldg.
143-148 Samsung-dong, Kangnam-ku
Seoul 135-090
Tel: (2) 554-7971 Fax: (2) 554-7972

Nara Advertising Inc.
28-1, Chamwon-dong, Socho-gu
Seoul
Tel: (2) 549-0691 Fax: (2) 549-0690

Oricom Inc.
105-7, Nonhyon-dong, Kangnam-gu
Seoul
Tel: (2) 510-3114 Fax: (2) 542-3966

Saatchi & Saatchi/Ye-Eum
7/F., Iljin Bldg.
50-1, Dohwa-dong, Mapo-ku
Seoul
Tel: (2) 707-9700 Fax: (2) 707-9800, 707-9840

Samhee Communications Inc.
(Affil. with Lintas Worldwide)
34, Sosomun-dong, Chung-gu
Seoul
Tel: (2) 774-3232 Fax: (2) 756-6675

Seoul Advertising Co., Ltd.
(Affil. with Chiat/Day/Mojo)
58-7, Sosomun-dong, Chung-gu
Seoul
Tel: (2) 752-7888 Fax: (2) 757-2088

Seoul DMB&B, Inc.
15/F. Dong-Hwa Bldg.
58-7 Seosomoon-dong, Jung-gu
Seoul
Tel: (2) 752-7888 Fax: (2) 757-2088

Union Advertising Inc.
(Affil. with Grey Pacific)
22, Chong-dong, Chung-gu
Seoul
Tel: (2) 739-2951 Fax: (2) 736-4218

LAW FIRMS

Korean Commercial Arbitration Board
159, Samsung-dong, Kangnam-ku
Seoul
Tel: (2) 551-2000 Fax: (2) 551-2020

Consultation Office for Overseas Companies,
Ministry of Trade and Industry
1/F., KOEX Main Bldg.
159 Samsung-dong, Kangnam-ku
Seoul 135-731
Tel: (2) 551-6781 Fax: (2) 551-6784

Bae, Kim & Lee, P.C.
5-6/F., Shin-A Bldg.
39-1 Seosomun-Dong, Chung-ku
Seoul 100-752
Postal add: CPO Box 4576, Seoul
Tel: (2) 755-1177 Fax: (2) 757-2267
Tlx: LAWBKL K24960

Central International Law Firm
5/F., Korea Reinsurance Bldg.
80, Soosong-dong, Chongro-ku, Kwangwhamoon
Seoul
Postal add: PO Box 356, Seoul
Tel: (2) 735-5621/6, 735-5072/4 Fax: (2) 733-5206/7
Tlx: CENTPAT 23250

CJ International Law Offices
1714 Kyobo Bldg.
Chong-ro 1-ka
Seoul
Tel: (2) 736-0145 Fax: (2) 736-2232
Tlx: K33766 CJKIM

Kim & Associates
Salvation Army Office Bldg.
1-58, Shinmun-ro, Chongro-ku
Seoul 110-061
Tel: (2) 732-5656/8 Fax: (2) 733-0949
Tlx: KIMLAW K24534

Kim & Chang
Seyang Bldg.
223, Naeja-dong, Chongro-ku
Seoul
Tel: (2) 737-4455 Fax: (2) 737-9091
Tlx: LAWKIM K28588

Kim & Kim Law Offices
Kyobo Bldg.
Suite 1611, 1-1, Chongro 1-ka, Chongro-ku
Seoul
Postal add: CPO Box 6869, Seoul
Tel: (2) 735-2980 Fax: (2) 732-3370
Tlx: K23653

Kim, Shin & Yu
12/F., Leema Bldg.
146-1, Susong-dong, Chongro-ku
Seoul
Postal add: CPO Box 3238, Seoul
Tel: (2) 735-5822/4, 735-3782 Fax: (2) 739-6606
Tlx: K23168 ATTKSY

Lee & Ko
17/F., Marine Center, Main Bldg.
118, 2-ka, Namdaemun-ro, Chung-ku
Seoul
Postal add: CPO Box 8735, Seoul
Tel: (2) 753-2151 Fax: (2) 753-0375

Shin & Kim
Kyunghee Bldg.
1-122, Shinmoonno, 2-ga, Jongno-gu,
Seoul 110
Tel: (2) 732-5120/9 Fax: (2) 739-4949
Tlx: Justice K22375

Yoon & Partners
Suite 831, KCCI Bldg.
45, Namdaemoon-ro, 4-ka, Chung-ku
Seoul
Postal add: CPO Box 4160, Seoul
Tel: (2) 773-0161 Fax: (2) 773-4947

TRANSLATORS & INTERPRETERS

Inlingua
CPO Box 50951
Seoul 100-650
Tel: (2) 733-3804 Fax: (2) 732-7570

International Convention Services
#612, Hanam Bldg.
44-27, Youido-dong, Youngdungpo-ku
Seoul
Tel: (2) 780-1981/3 Fax: (2) 780-1257

International Translation Company, Ltd.
69-3, 2-ga, Taepyung-ro, Chung-gu
Seoul
Mailing Address: CPO Box 3070, Seoul
Tel: [82] (2) 779-2222, 752-2244, 778-3344
Fax: [82] (2) 755-2757 Tlx: K25806

Interpretation & Translation Center
Hankuk University of Foreign Studies
270, Imun-dong, Dongdaemun-gu
Seoul
Tel: (2) 963-5356 Fax: (2) 963-8780

All addresses and telephone numbers are in South Korea unless otherwise noted. The country code for South Korea is [82].

Korea Institute of Simultaneous Translation
#505 Won-il Bldg.
78-3, Samsung-dong, Kangnam-gu
Seoul 135-082
Tel: (2) 540-0770 Fax: (2) 515-1634

Korea International Corporation
Rm. 306, Keunwon Bldg.
361-1, 2-ka, Taepyung-ro, Choong-ku
Seoul
Tel: (2) 756-1355 Fax: (2) 756-1279

Korea Translation-Interpretation Service
Hyundai Department 7F, Korea World Trade Center
159-2 Samsung-dong, Kangnam-gu
Seoul 135-090
Mailing Address: CPO Box 6699, Seoul
Tel: [82] (2) 555-5373/4, 555-5594/5, 535-2000
Fax: [82] (2)557-5533
Tlx: K29165 SSTARS; CABLE: KOTICORP.

Star Communications, Inc.
#306, Westin Chosun Hotel
87, Sokong-dong, Chung-gu
Seoul
Mailing Address: CPO Box 8541
Tel: [82] (2) 756-0761/3, 753-0760, 752-5948
Fax: [82] (2) 756-0755
Tlx: K23256, K23745; CABLE: BUMARST AR

TRANSPORTATION

AIRLINES

Aeroflot
Rm. 404, Konghang Terminal Bldg.
159-1, Samsung-dong, Kangnam-gu
Seoul
Tel: (2) 665-8672, 551-0321 Fax: (2) 569-3276

Air France
6/F., Samhwa Bldg.
21, Sogong-dong, Chung-gu
Seoul
Tel: (2) 773-3151, 773-5171 Fax: (2) 774-4533

Alitalia
Rm. 1907, Marine Center Bldg.
118, Namdaemunno 2-ga, Chung-gu
Seoul
Postal add: PO Box 1094, Seoul
Tel: (2) 779-1675, 757-8340 Fax: (2) 771-5259

All Nippon
Rm. 1501, Seoul Center Bldg.
91-1, Sogong-dong, Chung-gu
Seoul
Tel: (2) 752-5500, 752-1160 Fax: (2) 753-3942

Asiana Airlines
10-1, Hoehyon-dong, 2-ga, Chung-gu
Seoul
Tel: (2) 774-4000, 758-8114 Fax: (2) 758-8090
Pusan Tel: (51) 4654000

British Airways
2/F., Chosun Hotel
87, Sogong-dong, Chung-gu
Seoul
Tel: (2) 774-5511 Fax: (2) 757-5427

Cathay Pacific
5/F., Chase Bldg.
34-35, Chong-dong, Chung-gu
Seoul
Tel: (2) 773-0321, 773-0331
Fax: (2) 756-1070, 664-6707

China Airlines
Rm. 705, Baeknam Bldg.
188-3, Ulchiro 1-ga, Chung-gu
Seoul
Tel: (2) 775-1525, 774-1010 Fax: (2) 774-1017

Continental
4/F., Dangil Bldg.
55, Shinmunno 2-ga, Chongno-gu
Seoul
Tel: (2) 773-0100, 755-1500 Fax: (2) 739-8153

Delta
Rm. 1402, Samsung Life Bldg.
150, Taepyongno 2-ga, Chung-gu
Seoul
Tel: (2) 754-1921, 754-3693 Fax: (2) 755-6961

EVA Airways
2/F., Royal Bldg.
5, Tangju-dong, Chongno-gu
Seoul
Tel: (2) 723-2131 Fax: (2) 723-2144

Garuda Indonesia
7/F., Youone Bldg.
75-95, Sosomun-dong, Chun-gu
Seoul
Tel: (2) 773-2092, 319-0098 Fax: (2) 319-0096

Japan Airlines
Rm. 202, Baiknam Bldg.
188-3, Ulchiro 1-ga, Chung-gu
Seoul
Tel: (2) 757-1720, 757-1714 Fax: (2) 757-5127
Pusan Tel: (51) 4691215

Japan Air System
Rm. 503, Poeknam Bldg.
188-3, Ulchiro 1-ga, Chung-gu
Seoul
Tel: (2) 752-8081, 752-9090 Fax: (2) 752-8081

KLM
9/F., Samhwa Bldg.
21, Sogong-dong, Chung-gu
Seoul
Tel: (2) 755-7040, 753-1093 Fax: (2) 774-4677

Korean Airlines (KAL)
41-3, Sosomun-dong, Chung-gu
Seoul
Tel: (2) 756-2000, 751-7114 Fax: (2) 773-2475
Pusan Tel: (51) 4632000

Lauda Air
Tel: (2) 776-9607

Lufthansa
Rm. 601, Center Bldg.
91-1, Sogong-dong, Chung-gu
Seoul
Tel: (2) 756-4332, 777-9655 Fax: (2) 756-8244

Malaysia Airlines
14/F., Samsung Life Bldg.
150, Taepyongno 2-ga, Chung-gu
Seoul
Tel: (2) 777-7761, 753-6241 Fax: (2) 753-0978

Northwest
9/F., Inju Bldg.
111-1, Sorin-dong, Chongno-ku
Seoul
Tel: (2) 734-7800, 735-8500, 734-7100
Fax: (2) 734-7108

Philippine Airlines
Rm. 7005, Baeknam Bldg.
188-3, Ulchiro 1-ga, Chung-gu
Seoul
Tel: (2) 774-3581~5, Fax: (2) 774-3847

All addresses and telephone numbers are in South Korea unless otherwise noted. The country code for South Korea is [82].

Qantas
8/F., Dongmin Bldg.
95, Mugyo-dong, Chung-gu
Seoul
Tel: (2) 777-6871 Fax: (2) 774-8514

Singapore Airlines
Rm. 202, Chosun Hotel
87, Sogong-dong, Chung-gu
Seoul
Tel: (2) 755-1226~9 Fax: (2) 774-1266

Swissair
3/F., Oriental Chemical Bldg.
50, Sogong-dong, Chung-gu
Seoul
Tel: (2) 757-8901 Fax: (2) 753-2644

Thai Airways
Rm. 214, Chosun Hotel
87, Sogong-dong, Chung-gu
Seoul
Tel: (2) 754-9960, 755-7231 Fax: (2) 755-5251

United
Rm. 1505, Ankuk Insurance Bldg.
87, Ulchiro 1-ga, Chung-gu
Seoul
Tel: (2) 757-1691, 778-4965 Fax: (2) 752-2970

VASP
Tel: (2) 7795651

TRANSPORTATION & CUSTOMS BROKERAGE FIRMS

Companies may offer more services in addition to those listed here. Service information is provided as a guideline and is not intended to be comprehensive.

Korea Customs Brokers Association
209-9, Nonhyon-dong, Kangnam-gu
Seoul
Tel: (2) 547-9714/6 Fax: (2) 549-7813

Korea International Freight Forwarders Association
80, Chockson-dong, Chongno-gu
Seoul
Tel: (2) 783-8000 Fax: (2) 733-7249

Korean Register of Shipping
1465-10, Socho 3-dong, Socho-gu
Seoul
Tel: (2) 582-6601

Korean Shippers Council
Rm. 4404, KWTC Bldg.
159, Samsung-dong, Kangnam-gu
Seoul
Tel: (2) 551-5383/5 Fax: (2) 551-5231

Korea Shipping Agency Association
Rm. 901, Hyundae Bldg.
80, Chockson-dong, Chongno-gu
Seoul
Tel: (2) 734-1531/3 Fax: (2) 738-3760

Korea Shipping Association
3, Yangpyong 2-dong 6-ga, Yongdungpo-gu
Seoul
Tel: (2) 675-2711 Fax: (2) 675-2714

Air Cargo International Korea, Ltd.
378-1, Hapjong-dong, Mapo-gu
Seoul
Tel: (2) 325-2010/9 Fax: (2) 325-1101/2 Tlx: 22378
Air cargo

American President Lines Ltd.
14/F., Daehan Fire Ins. Bldg.
51-1, Namchang-dong, Chung-gu
Seoul
Tel: (2) 772-0701 Fax: (2) 756-9688/9
Tlx: 53820
Shipping agency

Choyang Shipping Co., Ltd.
Chongam Bldg.
85-3 Sosomun-dong, Chung-gu
Seoul
Postal add: CPO Box 1163, Seoul
Tel: (2) 771-4300 Fax: (2) 756-8245, 774-2216
Tlx: 24281
Shipping service

Dongbu Express Co., Ltd.
106-9, Cho-dong, Chung-gu
Seoul
Postal add: CPO Box 7735, Seoul
Tel: (2) 279-4161/9 Fax: (2) 272-4515 Tlx: 24366
Pusan Tel: (51) 469-0051/6
Shipping agency, transportation, container yard, stevedoring operation, freight forwarder

Dongwoo Express International Co., Ltd.
9/F., Sejong Bldg.
100, Tanglu-dong, Chongno-gu
Seoul
Tel: (2) 739-9801 Fax: (2) 737-7254 Tlx: 26791
Shipping agency and freight forwarder

Dongwoo Express International Co., Ltd.
Sejong Bldg.
100, Tanglu-dong, Chongno-gu
Seoul
Tel: (2) 739-9801 Fax: (2) 737-7254
Tlx: 26791
Freight forwarder

Dongwoo Marine Co., Ltd.
8/F., Sejong Bldg.
100, Tanglu-dong, Chongno-gu
Seoul
Tel: (2) 739-1121/9 Fax: (2) 739-9805, 739-3540
Tlx: 26554
Shipping agency

Dooyang Line Co., Ltd.
Dooyang Bldg.
170-7, Samsung-dong, Kangnam-gu
Seoul
Tel: (2) 565-6100 Fax: (2) 564-9301
Tlx: 24691
Shipping agency, marine transportation, vessel chartering, ship management.

Federal Express
7/F., Ankuk Fire Insurance Bldg.
87, Ulchiro 1-ga, Chung-gu
Seoul
Tel: (2) 754-5011/8 Fax: (2) 774-0696
Air cargo, courier

Global Enterprises
2-118, Nam Dae Moon Ro, Jung Gu
Seoul
Tel: (2) 728-5633 Fax: (2) 779-1785
Shipping agency, freight forwarder

Hanjin Shipping Co., Ltd.
7/F., Marine Center Bldg.
Shinkwan, 51, Sogong-dong, Chung-gu
Seoul
Tel: (2) 757-0161 Fax: (2) 753-2442, 756-1431
Tlx: 24220
*Full container liner service, bulk-cargo ship (liner &
tramper service), freight forwarders, custom brokers*

Ho-Sung (Ent) Air Cargo, Ltd.
75, Sosomun-dong, Chung-gu
Seoul
Tel: (2) 756-7161/6, 9531 Fax: (2) 756-0112
Tlx: 22346
Air cargo, freight forwarder

Hyundae Express Co., Ltd.
6/F., Dongsong Bldg.
17-7, Namdaemunno 4-ga, Chung-gu
Seoul
Postal add: CPO Box 2731, Seoul
Tel: (2) 753-0311/5 Fax: (2) 755-9997 Tlx: 24797
*Chartering agent, cargo, shipping agent, freight
forwarder*

Hyundai Merchant Marine Co., Ltd.
92, Mugyo-dong, Chung-gu
Seoul
Postal add: CPO Box 742
Tel: (2) 775-1700 Fax: (2) 775-8788 ,Tlx: 24402
World-wide marine transportation service

IHWA Aircargo Service, Ltd.
Duksan Bldg.
204-57, Tonggyo-dong, Mapo-gu,
Seoul
Tel: (2) 335-5007, 312-2077 Fax: (2) 335-5055
Air cargo

Korea Air Cargo Service, Ltd.
3, Yangpyong-dong, 6-ga, Yongdungpo-gu
Seoul
Tel: (2) 679-0088 Fax: (2) 676-7426 Tlx: 22527
Air cargo, freight forwarder

Korea Air Freight Limited (UPS)
111-1, Whakok-dong, Kangseo-ku
Seoul
Postal add: CPO Box 4225, Seoul
Tel: (2) 601-3300/5500 Fax: (2) 690-2489
Tlx: 26374 KAFAIRS K
Air cargo, courier

Korea Container Terminal Co.
2-118 Nam Dae Moon-ro, Jung-gu
Seoul
Tel: (2) 752-4381 Fax: (2) 752-4404
Shipping

Korea Line Corporation
7/F., Hanmi Bldg.
1, Kongpyong-dong, Chongno-gu
Seoul
Postal add: CPO Box 6451, Seoul
Tel: (2) 735-0371/5 Fax: (2) 739-1610 Tlx: 24205
Marine transportation

Korean Airlines (KAL)
41-3, Sosomun-dong, Chung-gu
Seoul
Tel: (2) 756-2000, 751-7114 Fax: (2) 773-2475
Air cargo

Korea Express Co.
58-12 Seoso Moon-dong, Jung-gu
Seoul
Tel: (2) 753-2141 Fax: (2) 752-8135
Shipping, freight forwarder

Maersk Korea Ltd.
4-5/F., Citicorp. Bldg.
2-ga, Sinmun-ro, Jongro-gu
Seoul
Tel: (2) 721-4114 Fax: (2) 720-1179 Tlx: 32962
Shipping

Nippon Cargo Airlines
Rm. 1902, Marine Center Bldg.
118, Namdaemunno 2-ga, Chung-gu
Seoul
Tel: (2) 775-3921/4 Fax: (2) 775-3925
Air cargo

Orient Shipping Co., Ltd.
21, Sogong-dong, Chung-gu
Seoul
Tel: (2) 757-3100 Fax: (2) 756-8947 Tlx: K23519
Pusan Tel: (51) 469-0906
*Forwarding, air freight, shipping agent, marine
transportation.*

Overseas Aircargo Service, Inc.
93-62, Pukchang-dong, Chung-gu
Seoul
Tel: (2) 779-0741, (2) 778-0271/5
Fax: (2) 756-9400, 774-6261 Tlx: 26366
Air cargo

Pan Ocean Shipping Co., Ltd.
51-1, Namchang-dong, Chung-gu
Seoul
Postal add: Central POB 3051
Tel: (2) 316-5530 Fax: (2) 754-8492 Tlx: 23511
Shipping service.

PRI-EX Inc. (Federal Express)
1154-1, Choryang 3-dong, Dong-ku
Pusan
Tel: (51) 464-8881 Fax: (51) 464-8788
Air cargo, courier

PRI-EX Inc. (Federal Express)
Samok Bldg.
93-3, Bukchang-dong, Chung-gu
Seoul
Tel: (2) 319-1526, 754-8726 Fax: (2) 319-1527
Air cargo, courier

PRI-EX Inc. (Federal Express)
Jinsung Bldg.
58-6, Samsung-dong, Kangnam-ku
Koex, Seoul
Tel: (2) 514-8800, 514-0471/2 Fax: (2) 514-0470
Air cargo, courier

PRI-EX Inc. (Federal Express)
Air Cargo Terminal, 2/F.
Kimpo International Airport
281, Konghang-dong, Kangseo-ku
Seoul
Tel: (2) 661-8000/8800 Fax: (2) 664-6303/4
Air cargo, courier

Sea-Land Service, Inc.
10/F., Dusan Bldg.
10-1, 1-ga, Eulji-ro, Chung-gu,
Seoul
Tel: (2) 775-7210/30 Fax: (2) 775-7231 Tlx: 53362
Shipping, custom broker, freight forwarder

Ssangyong Shipping Co., Ltd.
6/F., Kukdong Bldg.
60-1, Chungmuro 3-ga, Chung-gu
Seoul
Tel: (2) 275-1728 Fax: (2) 274-8466 Tlx: 28446
Shipping line and freight forwarder

TNT
687-8, Konghand-dong, Kangseo-ku
Seoul
Tel: (2) 666-6600, 666-4865 Fax: (2) 666-9001
Tlx: K23977 TNTSEL
Air cargo, courier

TNT
1194-11, Choryang 3 Dong, Dong-ku
Pusan
Tel: (51) 465-6677 Fax: (51) 465-0198
Tlx: K23977 TNTSEL
Air cargo, courier

Trans World Airlines, Inc.
Rm. 301, Daeyoung Bldg.
48-2, Sosomun-dong, Chung-gu
Seoul
Tel: (2) 777-4864/5 Fax: (2) 774-7970
Air cargo

United Parcel Service
Rm. 301, Jinyoung Bldg.
209-5, Songsan-dong, Mapo-gu
Seoul
Tel: (2) 323-0011/6 Fax: (2) 703-5677
Air cargo, courier

Woosung Shipping Co., Ltd.
11/F., Daeil Bldg.
18, Namdaemunno 1-ga, Chung-gu
Seoul
Postal add: CPO Box 3074, Seoul
Tel: (2) 735-2451/7 Fax: (2) 732-7184
Tlx: 28409
Shipping agency, international freight forwarder.

PUBLICATIONS, MEDIA & INFORMATION SOURCES

All publications are in English unless otherwise noted.

DIRECTORIES & YEARBOOKS

Annual Report, The Export-Import Bank of Korea
(Annual)
Export-Import Bank of Korea
16-1, Yoido-dong, Yongdeungpo-ku
Seoul 150-010
Tel: (2) 784-1021 Fax: (2) 784-1030
Tlx: 26595

Asia Pacific Leather Directory
(Annual)
Asia Pacific Leather Yearbook
(Annual)
Asia Pacific Directories, Ltd.
6/F. Wah Hen Commercial Centre
381 Hennessy Rd.
Hong Kong
Tel: [852] 8936377 Fax: [852] 8935752

Asian Computer Directory
(Monthly)
Washington Plaza
1/F., 230 Wanchai Rd.
Wanchai, Hong Kong
Tel: [852] 8327123 Fax: [852] 8329208

Asian Printing Directory
(English/Chinese, Annual)
Travel & Trade Publishing (Asia)
16/F., Capitol Centre
5-19 Jardines Bazaar
Causeway Bay, Hong Kong
Tel: [852] 8903067 Fax: [852] 8952378

Bankers Handbook For Asia
(Annual)
Dataline Asia Pacific Inc.
3rd Fl., Hollywood Center
233 Hollywood Road
Hong Kong
Tel: [852] 8155221 Fax: [852] 8542794

Business Korea Yearbook
(Annual)
Business Korea Co., Ltd.
Yoido PO Box 273
Seoul
Economic overview, analysis of industrial performance, detailed facts on 600 leading companies.

Compact Directory of Korean Exporters
Buyers Guide Ltd.
CPO Box 4922
Seoul

Computer-Asia Software Guide
(Annual)
Syme Media Enterprises
6-12 Wing Kut St.
Central, Hong Kong

Directory of Korean Electronics Exporters
(English and Korean)
Korea World Trade Center
159-1, Samsung-dong, Kangnam-ku
Seoul
Tel: (2) 551-5251/2 Fax: (2) 551-5181 Tlx: 24265

Directory of Korean Small Business
(Annual)
Federation of Korean Industries
28-1, Yoido-dong, Yungdungpo-ku
Seoul
Tel: (2) 780-0821 Fax: (2) 784-1640

Directory of Korean Trading Agents
(Annual)
Association Of Foreign Trading Agents Of Korea
(AFTAK)
Dongjin Bldg.
218, Hangangno 2-ga, Yongsan-gu
Seoul
Tel: (2) 792-1581/4 Fax: (2) 785-4373
Import-export agents and items by firm, commodity, supplier.

Economic Statistics Yearbook
(Annual)
Bank of Korea
110, 3-ka, Namdaemun-no, Chung-ku
Seoul 100-794
Tel: (2) 759-4114 Fax: (2) 752-7389 Tlx: 24711

Electric Power in Korea
(Annual)
Korea Electric Power Corporation
167, Samsung-dong, Kangnam-gu
Seoul
Tel: (2) 550-3114 Fax: (2) 550-5982

Fact Book
(Annual)
Korean Stock Exchange
33, Yoido-dong, Youngdeungpo-gu
Seoul 150-010
Tel: (2) 783-3371

International Tax and Duty Free Buyers Index
(Annual)
Pearl & Dean Publishing, Ltd.
9/F. Chung Nam Bldg.
1 Lockhart Rd.
Hong Kong
Tel: [852] 8660395 Fax: [852] 2999810
Aimed at duty-free shop managers and concessionaires worldwide.

Korea Annual
(Annual)
Yonhap News Agency
PO Box Kwanghwamun 1039
Seoul

Korea Apparel Sub-Material Directory
(Biennial)
Apparel Sub-Material Association [Korea]
2A-1, KOEX Bldg.
159, Samsung-dong, Kangnam-gu
Seoul
Tel: (2) 551-6000/2 Fax: (2) 551-6006

Korea Automobile & Auto Parts Catalogue
(Biennial)
Korea Auto Industries Cooperative Association
1683-3, Socho-dong, Socho-gu
Seoul
Tel: (2) 587-3416 Fax: (2) 583-7340

Korea Banking & Finance Yearbook
(Annual)
Doory International, Inc.
Yoido PO Box 1167
Seoul

Korea Directory
(Annual)
The Korea Directory Company
CPO Box 3955
Seoul 100-639
Tel: (2) 237-9451 Fax: (2) 738-4357
Airlines, hotels, traders, agents, manufacturers, economic organizations, support services. .

Korea Electronics Buyer's Guide
(Biennial)
Korea Electronic Industries Cooperative
813-5 Pangbae-dong, Sochu-gu
Seoul
Tel: (2) 533-2309 Fax: (2) 553-0949

Korea Electronics Directory and Catalog
(Annual)
Electronic Industries Association of Korea
5/F., Danwoo Bldg..
850-22, Pangbae-dong, Sochu-gu
Seoul
Tel: (2) 553-0941/7, 553-8725 Fax: (2) 555-6195

Korea Export
(Annual)
Korea Foreign Trade Association
159-1, Samsung-dong, Kangnam-gu
Seoul
Tel: (2) 551-5114 Fax: (2) 551-5100
Catalogues featuring Korean export goods.

Korea Export Buying Offices Directory
(Annual)
Korea Export Buying Offices Association
Rm. 3102, KWTC Bldg.
159, Samsung-dong, Kangnam-gu
Seoul
Tel: (2) 551-3195/8

Korea Medical Instrument Directory
(Annual)
Korea Medical Instrument Industry Cooperative
284-6, Nagwon-dong, Chongno-gu
Seoul
Tel: (2) 764-3815, 762-3814 Fax: (2) 744-6567

Korean Business Directory
(Annual)
Korea Chamber of Commerce & Industry
45, 4-ka, Namdaemun-ro, Chung-ku
Seoul
Tel: (2) 316-3114 Fax: (2) 757-9475 Tlx: 25728
Manufacturers, exporters, importers, buying offices; finance, service and economic organizations.

Korean Journal of Comparative Law
(Annual)
Suite 17, 105 Hangang Mansion Apt.
Yongsan-ku
Seoul

Korean Machinery
(Annual)
Korea Association of Machinery Industry
13-31, Youido-dong, Yongdungpo-gu
Seoul
Tel: (2) 780-3611/4 Fax: (2) 784-6749, 784-1032
Catalogue of Korean machinery.

Korean Trade Directory
(Annual)
Korea Foreign Trade Association
159-1, Samsung-dong, Kangnam-gu
Seoul
Tel: (2) 551-5268/9 Fax: (2) 551-5100
Exporters, manufacturers and trade associations.

Korea Statistical Handbook
(Annual)
Economic Planning Board
1, Jungang-dong
Gwachon City, Kyonggi Province
Tel: (2) 503-9020 Fax: (2) 503-9033 Tlx: 23202

Korea Yellow Pages
(Annual)
Korea Yellow Pages, Ltd.
384-43, Hapjong-dong, Mapo-ku
Seoul

Major Statistics of Korea Economy
(Annual)
Bank of Korea
110, 3-ka, Namdaemun-no, Chung-ku
Seoul 100-794
Tel: (2) 759-4114 Fax: (2) 752-7389 Tlx: 24711

Statistical Yearbook of Foreign Trade
(Annual)
Office of Customs Administration
71, Nonhyun-dong, Kangram-gu
Seoul
Tel: (2) 542-7141 Tlx: 24346, 24716 DOCAROK
Export and import statistics by year and month, exports by type, imports by source of funds, H.S. heading number and country.

Textile Asia Index
(Annual)
Business Press Ltd.
30-32 d'Aguilar St.
11/F., Tak Yan Commercial Bldg.
Central, Hong Kong
Tel: [852] 5247441 Tlx: 60275

The Status of Korean Small Business
(Annual)
Korean Federation of Small Business
16-2, Youido-dong, Yongdungpo-gu
Seoul
Tel: (2) 785-0010 Fax: (2) 782-0247

Trade Today of Korea
(Annual)
Overseas Media Corporation
CPO Box 6494
Seoul
List of associations' members, general trading
companies, government offices, and the top 100
companies in Korea.

World Jewelogue
(Annual)
Headway International Publications Co.
907 Great Eagle Center
23 Harbour Rd.
Hong Kong
Tel: [852] 8275121 Fax: [852] 8277064

DAILY NEWSPAPERS

Asian Wall Street Journal
Dow Jones Publishing Co. (Asia)
2/F. AIA Bldg.
1 Stubbs Rd.
GPO Box 9825
Hong Kong
Tel: [852] 5737121 Fax: [852] 8345291
Wall Street Journal Seoul office:
7, Sunhwa-dong, Chongno-gu
Seoul
Tel: (2) 774-3802

Chosun Ilbo
(Korean)
61, 1-ga, Taepyong-ro, Chung-gu
Seoul
Tel: (2) 724-5114

Dong-A Ilbo
(Korean)
139, Sejong-ro, Chongno-gu
Seoul
Tel: (2) 721-7114

Han Kook Ilbo
(Korean)
14, Chunghak-dong, Chongno-gu
Seoul
Tel: (2) 724-2114

International Herald Tribune
7/F. Malaysia Bldg.
50 Gloucester Rd.
Wanchai, Hong Kong
Tel: [852] 8610616 Fax: [852] 8613073

Joong-ang Ilbo
(Korean)
7, Sunhwa-dong, Chung-gu
Seoul
Tel: (2) 751-5114

Korea Herald
1-12, 3-ga, Hoehyon-dong, Chung-gu
Seoul
Tel: (2) 756-7711 Fax: (2) 755-4894

Korea Times
14, Chunghak-dong, Chongno-gu
Seoul
Tel: (2) 724-2114

GENERAL BUSINESS & TRADE PERIODICALS

Asia Labour Monitor
(Bimonthly)
Asia Monitor Resource Center
444-446 Nathan Rd., 8/F. Flat B
Kowloon, Hong Kong
Tel: [852] 3321346

Asian Business
(Monthly)
Far East Trade Press, Ltd.
2/F Kai Tak Commercial Bldg.
317 Des Voeux Rd.
Central, Hong Kong
Tel: [852] 5457200 Fax: [852] 5446979

Asian Finance
(Monthly)
3rd Fl., Hollywood Center
233 Hollywood Road
Hong Kong
Tel: [852] 8155221 Fax: [852] 8504437

Asian Monetary Monitor
(Bimonthly)
Asian Monetary Monitor
GPO Box 12964
Hong Kong
Tel: [852] 8427200

Asiaweek
(Weekly)
Asiaweek Ltd.
199 Des Voeux Road
Central, Hong Kong
Tel: [852] 8155662 Fax: [852] 8155903

Business Week, Asia Edition
(Weekly)
2405 Dominion Centre
43-59 Queens Rd. East
Hong Kong
Tel: [852] 3361160 Fax: [852] 5294046

Economic Bulletin
(Monthly)
Economic Planning Board
1, Jungang-dong
Gwachon City, Kyonggi Province
Tel: (2) 503-9020 Fax: (2) 503-9033 Tlx: 23202

The Economist, Asia Edition
(Weekly)
The Economist Newspaper, Ltd.
1329 Chater Rd.
Hong Kong
Tel: [852] 8681425

Far Eastern Economic Review
(Weekly)
Review Publishing Company Ltd.
6-7/F., 181-185 Gloucester Rd.
GPO Box 160
Hong Kong
Tel: [852] 8328381 Fax: [852] 8345571

KCCI Quarterly Review
(Quarterly)
Korea Chamber of Commerce & Industry
45, 4-ka, Namdaemun-ro, Chung-ku
Seoul
Tel: (2) 316-3114 Fax: (2) 757-9475 Tlx: 25728

KDB Report
(Monthly)
Korea Development Bank
10-2, Kwanchul-dong, Chongno-ku
Seoul 110-111
Tel: (2) 733-2121, 733-4141 Fax: (2) 733-4768
Tlx: 27463

Korea Business World
(Monthly)
Korea Business World Ltd.
Suite 303, Shinsong Bldg.
25-4, Yoido-dong, Yongdungpo-gu
Seoul
Postal add: Yoido PO Box 720, Seoul 150-607

Korea Buyers Guide
(Monthly)
Buyers Guide Corp.
Korea World Trade Center
PO Box 8
Seoul

Korea Trade
(6 per year)
KOTRA
KWTC Bldg.
159-1, Samsung-dong, Kangnam-gu
Seoul
Tel: (2) 551-4181 Fax: (2) 551-4477
Product catalogs.

Korea Trade & Business
(Monthly)
KOTRA
KWTC Bldg.
159-1, Samsung-dong, Kangnam-gu
Seoul
Tel: (2) 551-4181 Fax: (2) 551-4477

Korea Trading Post
(Bimonthly)
Korea Foreign Trade Association
159-1, Samsung-dong, Kangnam-gu
Seoul
Tel: (2) 551-5114 Fax: (2) 551-5100
Newsletter covering specific Korean industries and their products.

Korean Business Review
(Monthly)
Federation of Korean Industries
28-1, Yoido-dong, Yungdungpo-ku
Seoul
Tel: (2) 780-0821 Fax: (2) 784-1640

Korean Source
(Biannual)
The Korea Directory Company
CPO Box 3955
Seoul 100-639
Tel: (2) 237-9451 Fax: (2) 738-4357
Export catalogue of Korean products.

MOF Bulletin
(Monthly)
Ministry of Finance
1, Jungang-dong
Gwachon City, Kyonggi Province
Tel: (2) 503-9211, 503-9206 Fax: (2) 503-9324
Tlx: 23243

Monthly Foreign Trade Statistics
(Monthly)
Office of Customs Administration
71, Nonhyun-dong, Kangram-gu
Seoul
Tel: (2) 542-7141 Tlx: 24346, 24716 DOCAROK

Monthly Review
(Monthly)
Korea Exchange Bank
181, 2-ka, Ulchiro, Chung-ku
Seoul 100-192
Tel: (2) 729-0114 Fax: (2) 734-5976 Tlx: 24244

Monthly Statistical Bulletin
(Monthly)
Bank of Korea
110, 3-ka, Namdaemun-no, Chung-ku
Seoul 100-794
Tel: (2) 759-4114 Fax: (2) 752-7389 Tlx: 24711

Monthly Statistics of Korea
(Monthly)
Economic Planning Board
1, Jungang-dong
Gwachon City, Kyonggi Province
Tel: (2) 503-9020 Fax: (2) 503-9033 Tlx: 23202

Newsweek International, Asia Edition
(Weekly)
Newsweek, Inc.
47/F., Bank of China Tower
1 Garden Rd.
Central, Hong Kong
Tel: [852] 8104555

Time, Asia Edition
(Weekly)
Time, Inc.
31/F., East Tower, Bond Centre
89 Queensway
Hong Kong
Tel: [852] 8446660 Fax: [852] 5108799

All publications are in English unless otherwise noted.

Weekly Import Journal
Association Of Foreign Trading Agents Of Korea
(AFTAK)
Dongjin Bldg.
218, Hangangno 2-ga, Yongsan-gu
Seoul
Tel: (2) 792-1581/4 Fax: (2) 785-4373

World Executives Digest
(Monthly)
3/F. Garden Square Bldg.
Greenbelt Drive Cor.
Legaspi Makati
Metro Manila, Phillipines
Tel: [63] (2) 8179126

INDUSTRY-SPECIFIC PERIODICALS

Asian Computer Monthly
(Monthly)
Computer Publications Ltd.
Washington Plaza, 1st Fl.
230 Wanchai Road
Wanchai, Hong Kong
Tel: [852] 9327123 Fax: [852] 8329208

Asia Computer Weekly
(Bimonthly)
Asian Business Press Pte., Ltd.
100 Beach Rd., #26-00 Shaw Towers
Singapore 0718
Tel: [65] 2943366 Fax: [65] 2985534

Asiamac Journal: The Machine-Building and Metal
Working Journal for the Asia Pacific Region
(Quarterly; English, Chinese)
Adsale Publishing Company
21/F., Tung Wai Commercial Bdlg.
109-111 Gloucester Rd.
Hong Kong
Tel: [852] 8920511 Fax: [852] 8384119, 8345014

Asian Architect and Contractor
Monthly
Thompson Press Hong Kong Ltd.
Tai Sang Commercial Bldg., 19/F.
24-34 Hennessy Rd.
Hong Kong

Asian Aviation
(Monthly)
Asian Aviation Publications
2 Leng Kee Rd., #04-01 Thye Hong Centre
Singapore 0315
Tel: [65] 4747088 Fax: [65] 4796668

Asian Defence Journal
(Monthly)
Syed Hussain Publications (Sdn)
61 A&B Jelan Dato, Haji Eusoff
Damai Complex
PO Box 10836
50726 Kuala Lumpur, Malaysia
Tel: [60] (3) 4420852 Fax: [60] (3) 4427840

Asian Electricity
(11 per year)
Reed Business Publishing Ltd.
5001 Beach Rd., #06-12 Golden Mile Complex
Singapore 0719
Tel: [65] 2913188 Fax: [65] 2913180

Asian Electronics Engineer
(English/Chinese/Korean, Monthly)
Trade Media Ltd.
29 Wong Chuck Hang Rd.
Hong Kong
Tel: [852] 5554777 Fax: [852] 8700816

Asian Hospital
(Quarterly)
Techni-Press Asia Ltd.
PO Box 20494, Hennessy Rd.
Hong Kong
Tel: [852] 5278682 Fax: [852] 5278399

Asian Hotel & Catering Times
(Bimonthly)
Thomson Press (HK)
19/F Tai Sang Commercial Bldg.
23-34 Hennessy Rd.
Hong Kong
Tel: [852] 5283351 Fax: [852] 8650825

Asian Manufacturing
Far East Trade Press Ltd.
2/F., Kai Tak Commercial Building
317 Des Voeux Rd.
Central, Hong Kong
Tel: [852] 5453028 Fax: [852] 5446979

Asian Medical News
(Bimonthly)
MediMedia Pacific Ltd.
Unit 1216, Seaview Estate
2-8 Watson Rd.
North Point, Hong Kong
Tel: [852] 5700708 Fax: [852] 5705076

Asian Meetings & Incentives
(Monthly)
Travel & Trade Publishing (Asia)
16/F, Capitol Centre
5-19 Jardines Bazaar
Causeway Bay, Hong Kong
Tel: [852] 8903067 Fax: [852] 8952378

Asian Oil & Gas
(Monthly)
Intercontinental Marketing Corp.
PO Box 5056
Tokyo 100-31, Japan
Fax: [81] (3) 3667-9646

Asian Plastic News
(Quarterly)
Reed Asian Publishing Pte., Ltd.
5001 Beach Rd.
#06-12 Golden Mile Complex
Singapore 0719
Tel: [65] 2913188 Fax: [65] 2913180

Asian Printing: The Magazine for the Graphic Arts
Industry
(Monthly)
Travel & Trade Publishing (Asia)
16/F, Capitol Centre
5-19 Jardines Bazaar
Causeway Bay, Hong Kong
Tel: [852] 8903067 Fax: [852] 8952378

Asian Security & Safety Journal
(Bimonthly)
Elgin Consultants, Ltd.
Tungnam Bldg.
Suite 5D, 475 Hennessy Rd.
Causeway Bay, Hong Kong
Tel: [852] 5724427 Fax: [852] 5725731

Asian Shipping
(Monthly)
Asia Trade Journals Ltd.
7/F., Sincere Insurance Bldg.
4 Hennessy Rd.
Wanchai, Hong Kong
Tel: [852] 5278532 Fax: [852] 5278753

Asian Sources: Computer Products
Asian Sources: Electronic Components
Asian Sources: Gifts & Home Products
Asian Sources: Hardware
Asian Sources: Timepieces
(Monthly)
Asian Sources Media Group
22/F., Vita Tower
29 Wong Chuk Hang Rd.
Wong Chuk Hang, Hong Kong
Tel: [852] 5554777 Fax: [852] 8730488

Asian Water & Sewage
(Quarterly)
Techni-Press Asia, Ltd.
PO Box 20494, Hennessy Rd.
Hong Kong
Fax: [852] 5278399

Asia Pacific Broadcasting & Telecommunications
(Monthly)
Asian Business Press Pte., Ltd.
100 Beach Rd.
#26-00 Shaw Towers
Singapore 0718
Tel: [65] 2943366 Fax: [65] 2985534

Asia Pacific Dental News
(Quarterly)
Adrienne Yo Publishing Ltd.
4/F., Vogue Building
67 Wyndham St.
Central, Hong Kong
Tel: [852] 5253133 Fax: [852] 8106512

Asia Pacific Food Industry
(Monthly)
Asia Pacific Food Industry Publications
24 Peck Sea St., #03-00 Nehsons Bldg.
Singapore 0207
Tel: [65] 2223422 Fax: [65] 2225587

Asia Pacific Food Industry Business Report
(Monthly)
Asia Pacific Food Industry Publications
24 Peck Sea St., #03-00 Nehsons Bldg.
Singapore 0207
Tel: [65] 2223422 Fax: [65] 2225587

Asiatechnology
(Monthly)
Review Publishing Company Ltd.
6-7/F., 181-185 Gloucester Rd.
GPO Box 160
Hong Kong
Tel: [852] 8328381 Fax: [852] 8345571

Asia Travel Guide
(Monthly)
Interasia Publications, Ltd.
190 Middle Rd., #11-01 Fortune Center
Singapore 0718
Tel: [65] 3397622 Fax: [65] 3398521

ATA Journal: Journal for Asia on Textile & Apparel
(Bimonthly)
Adsale Publishing Company
21/F., Tung Wai Commercial Bldg.
109-111 Gloucester Rd.
Wanchai, Hong Kong
Subscriptions: PO Box 20032, Hennessy Rd., Hong
Kong
Tel: [852] 8920511 Fax: [852] 8384119

Building & Construction News
(Weekly)
Al Hilal Publishing (FE) Ltd.
50 Jalan Sultan, #20-06, Jalan Sultan Centre
Singapore 0719
Tel: [65] 2939233 Fax: [65] 2970862

Business Traveller Asia-Pacific
(Monthly)
Interasia Publications
200 Lockhart Rd., 13/F.
Wanchai, Hong Kong
Tel: [852] 5749317 Fax: [852] 5726846

Cargo Clan
(Quarterly)
Emphais (HK), Ltd.
10/F. Wilson House
19-27 Wyndam St.
Central, Hong Kong
Tel: [852] 5215392 Fax: [852] 8106738

Cargonews Asia
(Bimonthly)
Far East Trade Press, Ltd.
2/F Kai Tak Commercial Bldg.
317 Des Voeux Rd.
Central, Hong Kong
Tel: [852] 5453028 Fax: [852] 5446979

Catering & Hotel News, International
(Biweekly)
Al Hilal Publishing (FE) Ltd.
50 Jalan Sultan, #20-26, Jalan Sultan Centre
Singapore 0719
Tel: [852] 2939233 Fax: [852] 2970862

Computer Journal
(Monthly)
Miraesidae Corp.
12-20, Daeheung-dong, Mapo-ku
Seoul
Tel. (2) 716-7291

Computer World
(Monthly)
Computer Engineering Co., Ltd.
63-1, 3-ka, Choongjung-ro,
Seoul
Tel: (2) 587-0211

Electronic Business Asia
(Monthly)
Cahners Publishing Company
249 West 17th St.
New York, NY 10011-5301, USA

Electronic Times
(Daily)
14-11, Yoido-dong, Yungdungpo-ku
Seoul
Tel. (2) 784-3091/7

Energy Asia
(Monthly)
Petroleum News Southeast Asia, Ltd.
6/F., 146 Prince Edward Rd. West
Kowloon, Hong Kong
Tel: 3805294 Fax: 3970959

Far East Health
(10 per year)
Update-Siebert Publications
Reed Asian Publishing Pte
5001 Beach Rd.
#06-12 Golden Mile Complex
Singapore 0719
Tel: [65] 2913188 Fax: [65] 2913180

Fashion Accessories
(Monthly)
Asian Sources Media Group
22nd Fl., Vita Tower
29 Wong Chuk Hang Road
Wong Chuk Hang, Hong Kong
Tel: [852] 5554777 Fax: [852] 8730488

Information Age
(Monthly)
Information Age Co.
1575-8, Suhcho-dong, Suhcho-ku
Seoul
Tel: (2) 587-7291

International Construction
(Monthly)
Reed Business Publishing, Ltd.
Reed Asian Publishing Pte
5001 Beach Rd.
#06-12 Golden Mile Complex
Singapore 0719
Tel: [65] 2913188 Fax: [65] 2913180

Jewellery News Asia
(Monthly)
Jewellery News Asia Ltd.
Rooms 601-603, Guardian House
32 Oi Kwan Rd.
Wanchai, Hong Kong
Tel: [852] 8322011 Fax: [852] 8329208

Journal of Korean Electronics
(Annual)
Electronic Industries Association of Korea
5/F., Danwoo Bldg.
850-22, Pangbae-dong, Sochu-gu
Seoul
Tel: (2) 553-0941/7, 553-8725 Fax: (2) 555-6195

Journal of the Korean Institute of Surface
Engineering
(Quarterly)
Korean Institute of Surface Engineering
Korean Fed. of Science and Technology Bldg
Rm. 308, 635-4 Yeoksam-dong Kangnam-ku
Seoul 135-703
Tel: (02) 563-0935, 558-2230

Korea Buyers Guide Electronics
(Monthly)
Buyers Guide Corp.
Korea World Trade Center
PO Box 8
Seoul

Korea Non-Life Insurance Industry
(Semiannual)
Korea Non-Life Insurance Association
KRIC Bldg., 6/F.
80, Susong-dong, Chongno-ku
Seoul
Tel: (2) 739-4161 Fax: (2) 739-3769 Tlx: 27947

Korea Shippers News
(Quarterly)
Korea Foreign Trade Association
159-1, Samsung-dong, Kangnam-gu
Seoul
Tel: (2) 551-5114 Fax: (2) 551-5100

Korea Tools Magazine
Korea Tools Industry Cooperative
Rm. 401, Bohun Bldg.
12-5, Youido-dong, Yongdungpo-gu
Seoul 150-010
Tel: (2) 780-0731 Fax: (2) 785-2457

Lloyd's Maritime Asia
(Monthly)
Lloyd's of London Press (FE)
Rm. 1101 Hollywood Centre
233 Hollywood Rd.
Hong Kong
Tel: [852] 8543222 Fax: [852] 8541538

Management & Computer
(Monthly)
Mincom Ltd.
393-4, Seokyo-dong, Mapo-ku
Seoul
Tel: (2) 333-4101

All addresses and telephone numbers are in South Korea unless otherwise noted. The country code for South Korea is [82].

Media: Asia's Media and Marketing Newspaper
(Biweekly)
Media & Marketing Ltd.
1002 McDonald's Bldg.
46-54 Yee Wo St.
Causeway Bay, Hong Kong
Tel: [852] 5772628 Fax: [852] 5769171

Medicine Digest Asia
(Monthly)
Rm. 1903, Tung Sun Commercial Centre
194-200 Lockhart Rd.
Wanchai, Hong Kong
Tel: [852] 8939303 Fax: [852] 8912591

Oil & Gas News
(Weekly)
Al Hilal Publishing (FE) Ltd.
50 Jalan Sultan, #20-06, Jalan Sultan Centre
Singapore 0719
Tel: [65] 2939233 Fax: [65] 2970862

Petroleum News, Asia's Energy Journal
(Monthly)
Petroleum News Southeast Asia, Ltd.
6/F., 146 Prince Edward Rd. West
Kowloon, Hong Kong
Tel: [852] 3805294 Fax: [852] 3970959

Shipping & Transport News
(Monthly)
Al Hilal Publishing (FE) Ltd.
50 Jalan Sultan, #20-06, Jalan Sultan Centre
Singapore 0719
Tel: [65] 2939233 Fax: [65] 2970862

Telecom Asia
(Bimonthly)
CCI Asia-Pacific (HK)
Suite 905, Guardian House
32 Oi Kwan Rd.
Wanchai, Hong Kong
Tel: [852] 8332181 Fax: [852] 8345620

Textile Asia: The Asian Textile and Apparel
Monthly
(Monthly)
Business Press Ltd.
11/F., California Tower
30-32 d'Aguilar St.
Central, Hong Kong
Tel: [852] 5247467 Fax: [852] 8106966

Travel News Asia
(Bimonthly)
Far East Trade Press, Ltd.
2/F Kai Tak Commercial Bldg.
317 Des Voeux Rd.
Central, Hong Kong
Tel: [852] 5453028 Fax: [852] 5446979

Travel Trade Gazette Asia
(Weekly)
Asian Business Press Pte., Ltd.
100 Beach Rd., #26-00 Shaw Towers
Singapore 0718
Tel: [65] 2943366 Fax: [65] 2985534

What's New in Computing
(Monthly)
Asian Business Press Pte., Ltd.
100 Beach Rd., #26-00 Shaw Towers
Singapore 0718
Tel: [65] 2943366 Fax: [65] 2985534

RADIO & TELEVISION STATIONS

Korea Broadcasting Commission (KBC)
14-15/F., Press Center
25, Taepyung-ro 2-ka, Chung-ku
Seoul
Tel: (2) 735-2640 Fax: (2) 722-5296
*Government body which oversees television
programming and advertising.*

Korean Broadcasting System (KBS)
18 Youido-dong, Yongdungpo-gu
Seoul 150-010
Tel: (2) 781-1000
*Operates a national network of radio stations and
two national television networks.*

Munhwa TV-Radio Broadcasting Corp. (MBC)
31, Youido-dong, Yongdungpo-gu
Seoul 150-728
Tel: (2) 780-0114

Seoul Broadcasting System (SBS)
10-2, Youido-dong, Yongdungpo-gu
Seoul
Tel: (2) 320-0114

LIBRARIES

Central National Library of Korea
60-1, Panpo-dong Seocho-gu
Seoul
Tel: (2) 535-4142 Fax: (2) 599-6942

Seoul National University Library
56-1, Shinlim-dong Gwankak-gu
Seoul
Tel: (2) 886-0101

Korea Institute for Industrial Economics &
Technology (KIET)
Dept. of Information Resources
Cheong Ryang PO Box 205
Seoul 131
Tel: (2) 965-6211 Tlx5850

Index